In the Name of Liberty

For years now, unionization has been under vigorous attack. Union membership has been steadily declining, and as a result, unions have lost much of their bargaining power and a great deal of their significance as a political force. If these trends continue – and at this point we have no reason to believe that they will not – it may not be long before unions lose whatever remains of their ability to protect working people from economic and personal abuse. *In the Name of Liberty* responds to this worrying state of affairs by presenting a new argument for unionization, one that does not depend on disputed claims that unionization has good effects, but instead derives a right to universal unionization in both the private and the public sector from concepts of liberty that we already accept. In short, *In the Name of Liberty* reclaims the argument from liberty from the political right and shows how liberty not only requires the unionization of every workplace but also how it supports a wide variety of other progressive policies that are also now the subject of frequent attack.

Mark R. Reiff is the author of four previous books: *On Unemployment*, Volumes I and II (Palgrave Macmillan, 2015); *Exploitation and Economic Justice in the Liberal Capitalist State* (Oxford University Press, 2013); and *Punishment, Compensation, and Law* (Cambridge, 2005).

In the Name of Liberty

The Argument for Universal Unionization

MARK R. REIFF
University of California, Davis

CAMBRIDGE
UNIVERSITY PRESS

University Printing House, Cambridge CB2 8BS, United Kingdom

One Liberty Plaza, 20th Floor, New York, NY 10006, USA

477 Williamstown Road, Port Melbourne, VIC 3207, Australia

314-321, 3rd Floor, Plot 3, Splendor Forum, Jasola District Centre, New Delhi - 110025, India

103 Penang Road, #05-06/07, Visioncrest Commercial, Singapore 238467

Cambridge University Press is part of the University of Cambridge.

It furthers the University's mission by disseminating knowledge in the pursuit of education, learning and research at the highest international levels of excellence.

www.cambridge.org
Information on this title: www.cambridge.org/9781108818599
DOI: 10.1017/9781108849784

© Mark R. Reiff 2020

This publication is in copyright. Subject to statutory exception and to the provisions of relevant collective licensing agreements, no reproduction of any part may take place without the written permission of Cambridge University Press.

First published 2020
First paperback edition 2022

A catalogue record for this publication is available from the British Library

ISBN 978-1-108-49540-0 Hardback
ISBN 978-1-108-81859-9 Paperback

Cambridge University Press has no responsibility for the persistence or accuracy of URLs for external or third-party internet websites referred to in this publication, and does not guarantee that any content on such websites is, or will remain, accurate or appropriate.

To all those who have helped advance the union movement

with wisdom, skill, and determination

and

grace, too

Contents

Acknowledgments	*page* xi
Introduction	1

FIRST ESSAY

1 The Libertarian Argument for Unions	21
1.1 The Landscape of Utopia	25
1.2 The Rise of Unions	29
1.3 The Public Sector	42
1.4 The Problem of Independents	45
1.5 Libertarians and Liberty	55

SECOND ESSAY

2 The Union as a Basic Institution of Society	63
2.1 Three Levels of Moral Evaluation	67
2.2 Moral Evaluation and the Basic Structure	69
2.3 The Moral Evaluation of Basic Institutions	72
2.4 How to Determine Whether the Union Is a Basic Institution	82
2.4.1 The Context of the Inquiry	82
2.4.2 The Primary Importance of Pre-institutional Rights	83
2.4.3 What We Talk about When We Talk about Liberty	86
2.4.4 The Firm as a Threat to Liberty	95
2.4.5 The Basic Institution as a Check on Threats to Liberty	102
2.5 Unionization in Context	111
2.5.1 The Basic Effects of Unionization	111
2.5.2 Some Preliminary Points about These Effects	118
2.5.3 The Relationship between Voice and Republican Liberty	120
2.5.4 Voice, Liberty, and Workplace Democracy	122

	2.5.5	Liberty and Profitability	124
	2.5.6	Unions, Corruption, and the Use of Force and Violence	128
	2.5.7	Unions and Unemployment	131
	2.5.8	Unions and Inflation	134
	2.5.9	Unions as a Check on Managerial Incompetence	137
	2.5.10	Unions as a Check on the Antisocial Inclinations of Management	139
	2.5.11	Unions as a Check on the Authoritarian Inclinations of the Working Class	145
2.6	How Recognizing Unions as a Basic Institution Protects Liberty		148
2.7	Limitations and Qualifications		153
	2.7.1	Union Shops Are Not Closed Shops	153
	2.7.2	While We Are Working toward Universal Unionization: The Perfect Is Not the Enemy of the Good	154
	2.7.3	Some Comments about Universal Unionization in the Public Sector	156
	2.7.4	Feasibility Constraints on Universal Unionization in the Private Sector	158
	2.7.5	Questions Remaining for Post-institutional Regulation	163
	2.7.6	Application of the "Basic Institution" Test to Other Kinds of Institutions	164

THIRD ESSAY

3	In Defense of Public Sector Unionization	169
3.1	The Difference between the Private and the Public Sector	173
3.2	Public Sector Unionization and the Proper Size of Government	177
	3.2.1 Is Government Really Getting Bigger?	178
	3.2.2 Is There a Relationship between Public Sector Unionization and the Size of Government?	179
	3.2.3 Is Big Government a Threat to Liberty?	180
	3.2.4 How Can We Tell How Big Government Should Be? Problems with the Functional Test	185
	3.2.5 Problems with the Efficiency Test	190
	3.2.6 Can "Govern Locally" Serve as a Small Government Principle?	195
	3.2.7 Do We Simply Have More Government Than We Can Afford?	196
	3.2.8 If Preserving Liberty Is the Real Concern, Why Ignore the Threat to Liberty Posed by Private Parties?	197
3.3	The Essential Services Argument	200
3.4	The Argument against Collective Bargaining	203
3.5	Are Public Sector Unions Undermining Our Democracy?	209

	3.5.1 The Historical Roots of the Claim	210
	3.5.2 The Argument from Disproportionate Influence	212
	3.5.3 The Argument from Interadministration Bindingness	218
	3.5.4 Public Sector Unions and the "Deep State"	221
3.6	Are They Bankrupting Us?	222
3.7	Freedom of Speech, Agency Fees, and the Compelled Extension of Right-to-Work Laws to the Public Sector	230

Notes 239
Bibliography 341
Index 407

Acknowledgments

Many people have helped me to clarify my thoughts about liberty and unionization over the years and have provided me with valuable feedback and helpful comments and criticisms on the work that eventually become this book. I would especially like to thank Chris Bailey, Ian Carter, Karen Challe, Rutger Classen, Harriet Davidson, Simon Deakin, Peter Dietsch, Joseph J. Fahey, Benjamin Ferguson, Lisa Herzog, Ruxandra Ivanescu, Gregory Jackson, Matthew Kramer, Chandran Kukathas, Christian Neuhäuser, Marin O'Neill, James Pattison, David Rosner, N. E. Simmonds, Abe Singer, Daniel Statman, Hillel Steiner, Robert S. Taylor, Christian Schemmel, Liam Shields, Alan Thomas, Sebastian Voigt, Jaron Wilde, and Stefan Wurster. My thanks also to two anonymous referees for Cambridge University Press, whose insightful comments and suggestions led to significant improvements in the manuscript.

During a critical point in the writing of this book, Lisa Herzog arranged a visiting professorship for me at the Technical University of Munich, as well as numerous meetings with German academics working on unionization and various German union officials, all of which I found most helpful and for which I am most grateful.

Early versions of one or more of the essays in this volume were presented at the University of California, Davis, the Technical University of Munich, the University of Manchester Political Theory Workshops, and the annual meeting of the Philosophy, Politics, and Economics Society in New Orleans. My thanks to all those in attendance for their comments and suggestions.

My thanks also to Robert Dreesen and the people at Cambridge University Press for all their guidance and assistance in bringing the manuscript to publication.

Introduction

For some time now, union membership has been steadily declining. After reaching a peak of 33 percent in the United States in 1953, unionization hit 10.7 percent in 2016, its lowest level in one hundred years, and it shows no sign of rising.[1] In the United Kingdom, union membership is now half of what it was in 1979, or about the level it was just after World War II.[2] In many other liberal capitalist democracies, unionization rates have been falling steadily as well.[3] In part this decline is due to the success that unions have had in establishing a more just baseline for the treatment of all workers, for this makes joining a union seem less necessary for current employees. In part the decline is due to shifts in the nature of the relevant economies, in which large numbers of union jobs in heavy manufacturing have been shifted to less-unionized countries and replaced by jobs in industries that are more difficult to unionize. In part it is due to local outsourcing of what were high-paying unionized jobs to smaller, exploitive, currently nonunionized contractors who are also more difficult to organize. And in part this decline results from technological advances that have allowed many previously unionized jobs to be performed by robots.[4] But especially in the United States, this decline is also in large part the result of continuous attacks made against the very idea of unionization over the last thirty-plus years,[5] attacks that have been increasing in both frequency and vigor for some time now[6] and which are increasing even further under the administration of President Trump.[7] In any event, regardless of the cause of this decline, union membership is now becoming sufficiently small that unions may soon lose their ability to adequately protect workers from economic and personal abuse (if they haven't already) and may even lose their significance as a political force.[8]

Not surprisingly, this decline in unionization has been accompanied by a dramatic rise in the share of income going to the top one percent, a lengthy stagnation in real wages for everybody else, a steep rise in unemployment followed by the replacement of high-paying permanent jobs providing good benefits with low-paying temporary ones providing no benefits as the unemployment rate has come down, and various other negative turns in the economic situation of masses of Americans, as well as the citizens of many other liberal capitalist democracies.[9] Of course, this sorry state of economic affairs is the product of many causes, not just one, and identifying all the contributing causes much less the precise contribution of each is a difficult exercise – indeed, the exact causal story behind this negative turn in so many measures of economic well-being may never be entirely clear. But as we shall see, there is strong evidence that many of our current economic problems here in the United States and, by contagion, in other parts of the liberal capitalist world have at least been partially caused by the decline in unionization.[10]

In two previous books, I have discussed these rising economic problems (and particularly the economic problems of inequality and unemployment) and proposed new ways of assessing and implementing our moral obligation to address them.[11] In this book, I turn to the problem of unionization. But the idea is not simply to propose reversing the decline in unionization as an (additional) remedy to the economic problems of inequality and unemployment. Indeed, because it makes wages higher than they would otherwise be, unionization is sometimes claimed to be a cause of unemployment, for employers will hire fewer workers if they are more expensive. Unionization is also sometimes claimed to be a cause of inequality, for if fewer workers have jobs, more people will be poorer, even if the income gap between those who are working and the rich is somewhat smaller.[12] There is a great deal of empirical evidence showing that neither of these consequentialist claims are true (more on this later), but whether they are true is irrelevant to the argument I will be making here. In this book, I will be arguing for unionization in its own right – that is, I will be presenting a moral argument for unionization that does not depend on the effects of unionization on inequality or unemployment, although I shall do my best to outline these effects whenever possible. Instead, I shall be arguing that unionization is required not because it is good, but because it is right. This, after all, is exactly what those who have been arguing against unionization have been doing all these years – defusing the argument that unions raise wages and benefits, create job security, and improve working conditions by claiming that unionization, and especially what they derogatively refer to as "compulsory" unionization, is an infringement of liberty; therefore, the effects of unionization on the good of workers, or even the common good, are morally irrelevant because liberty cannot be justifiably infringed for any of these reasons.

Of course, the anti-union argument from liberty can take a variety of forms. Sometimes it is expressed as a straightforward argument derived from a supposed general right to liberty.[13] As we shall see, however, the concept of liberty is not at all as straightforward as those who make this argument pretend, and those who raise this objection to unionization rarely acknowledge

Introduction

that various versions of liberty might be involved here or clarify which version they are referring to when they refer to liberty. Sometimes the argument from liberty is expressed as a more particularized argument regarding freedom of association. Here the claim is that even if voluntary unionization may accord with freedom of association (the liberty to associate with whomever we wish), compulsory unionization is contrary to it, and therefore workers cannot be compelled to join a union or pay dues even if they benefit from the activities of the union.[14] In the public sector, the argument from liberty is also sometimes expressed as an argument for free speech (the liberty to speak our mind), the claim being that under the First Amendment, public sector workers cannot be compelled to pay union dues if this compels them to pay for speech with which they do not agree or, even more nefariously, if such a payment would actually *constitute* speech with which they disagree.[15] And finally, in the public sector once again, the argument from liberty is sometimes expressed as a claim that unionization is leading to the runaway growth of government, bankrupting us, and otherwise undermining our democracy, which is said to be the ultimate assurance of our liberty. I shall say much more about each of these arguments from liberty in the pages that follow. But for now, I simply want to point out what all these arguments have in common: because liberty, either in general or in one or more of its constituent parts, is a right, the argument goes, it renders consequentialist arguments for the common good irrelevant, for rights cannot be overridden by consequentialist concerns.

Indeed, this latter argument – the argument that rights cannot be infringed even if the consequences of doing so would be better in some sense than not doing so – enjoys wide support on both sides of the political spectrum. For example, Robert Nozick, one of the leading libertarian theorists of the twentieth century, describes rights as "side-constraints," meaning they may not be justifiably infringed for consequentialist reasons even if this would make rights violations in general or violations of the specific right in question less common.[16] And on the other side of the political spectrum, John Rawls, one of the leading liberal egalitarians of the twentieth century, and one of the most influential liberal voices on equality and distributive justice ever, criticizes utilitarianism extensively for putting the good before the right and argues that the right must instead be put before the good.[17] So the anti-union argument from liberty, if sound, presents a formidable rebuttal to any consequentialist arguments presented by the union movement.

Note that the anti-union argument from liberty, while not usually denying that workers have a moral right to join unions and that unions therefore have a right to exist, effectively makes these rights largely worthless by blocking compulsory unionization and eliminating mandatory dues and, in the public sector, by barring unions from bargaining collectively. The latter prevents unions from delivering one of the primary benefits that unionization is designed to provide, therefore dramatically reducing the attraction of becoming a member of the union, and the former does the same in both the public and the private sector by depriving unions of the financial resources necessary to organize workers and effectively advance their interests with employers and with the government more generally.[18] The idea behind limiting what unions can do is to "corral the beast"; the idea behind depriving unions of the ability to collect dues from all those who benefit from union services even if they are not members is to "starve the beast," a tactic that has already been used by those on the right for some time with much success in an attempt to cut government programs that they don't like but which are too popular to be attacked directly.[19] Both tactics are designed to ensure that the rate of unionization will drop and remain low in both the private and the public sector and that union influence will become and remain politically inconsequential.[20]

One of the reasons why this anti-union strategy has been so successful is that while there has of course been much pro-union material generated over the years by those in the union movement and those who are sympathetic to it, the overwhelming majority of the positive arguments for unionization have almost all been presented in purely consequentialist terms. In other words, the argument for unionization typically proceeds by making empirical claims about the positive effects of unionization in both the private and the public sector and then by making the moral claim that these empirical effects promote the good of workers and in turn the common good.[21] Sometimes, of course, the typical argument for unionization also relies in part on an argument from right and not just an argument from consequences, these rights being the right to freedom of association and the right to equality. Freedom of association, however, does not turn out to do much work, for despite the fact that it is widely acknowledged to give workers the right to voluntarily form associations if they want to, it does not give these associations the right to *do* anything, such as bargain collectively, strike, or even collect dues. In any event, the dramatic decline in unionization demonstrates that the minimal protection provided by the right of free association alone is not having much of an effect. The right to equality, in turn, is more of a concept than a right – it is difficult to show how the right to equality should be cashed out. At best, it merely provides a connection between the equalizing effects of unionization on economic inequality and the non-consequentialist moral claim that economic inequality is a moral bad. So while the argument from equality is an argument from right, it is an argument from right that is nevertheless dependent on controversial consequentialist claims.

More importantly, perhaps, those who claim that economic inequality is a moral bad are rarely strict egalitarians – that is, few people claim that economic inequality is *always* a moral bad. Most people are liberal egalitarians – that is, they claim that economic inequality is sometimes a moral bad and sometimes not, and they offer "sorting principles" designed to help us tell the difference. Rawls's difference principle is one such principle, the various principles offered by those who are collectively described as "luck egalitarians" are another, and there are others still.[22] Under the difference principle, in order to determine whether a particular form of economic inequality is unjust, we must determine whether it works to the advantage of the worst-off members of society.[23] Under luck egalitarianism, we must determine whether the economic inequality at issue is a product of luck or choice.[24] Whether we are trying to predict the effect on an inequality on the worst off, or trying to determine whether an inequality is caused by luck or choice, however, the relevant borderlines are subject to a great deal of indeterminacy; there is a lot to argue about before we can come to any firm conclusion under either theory about the injustice of any particular inequality. This makes both theories amenable to being hijacked by the anti-egalitarian right through restrictive interpretations of the key working concepts that these theories each employ.[25] Modestly and highly egalitarian interpretations of these theories are, of course, also possible, but the arguments for any particular interpretation is controversial given the indeterminacy inherent in each principle. Even if unionization does reduce economic inequality, this does not by itself establish that the economic inequality that would otherwise prevail is an injustice under either of these theories – this has to be argued for separately. And under either of these theories, the road from the general concept of equality to the applied conclusion that anti-union legislation is unjust because it supports inequality is lengthy and complex.[26]

There is yet another problem with the argument from equality. The argument from equality is not an argument from right in the same way as the argument from liberty, at least when the inequality at issue is economic inequality. Unlike violations of equality such as those that result from various kinds of invidious discrimination based on race, ethnicity, age, religion, or the like, restrictions on unionization would be a *distributive* injustice and not a *commutative* injustice even if they do produce or exacerbate unjust economic inequality. In other words, the injustice here would be a social problem that we as a society have a moral duty to remedy in some broad sense but not one that necessarily imposed a duty on some individual or entity to cease engaging in the conduct that contributed to this problem and remedy past violations. Individuals have a duty to cease committing an injustice and to remedy injustices they significantly contributed to creating only when they commit commutative violations of individual rights. This makes the argument from equality, at least in its economic form, a potentially weaker argument than the argument from liberty, for the latter purports to be an argument from *individual* right – that is, from commutative injustice.[27] It is usually very clear what could be done to prevent a commutative injustice from arising; what could be done to prevent a distributive injustice from arising is much more open to debate. There are probably a variety of possible remedies here, and it is probably the case that no one of these is unquestionably better than the others, leaving the possibility that even if restrictions on unionization contribute to distributive injustice, they may still be able to remain intact because the resulting injustice can be dealt with in some other way.

The argument from liberty, in contrast, is much more simple, direct, and quick. Whereas the argument from equality arguably takes the utilitarian conception of the common good and puts a controversial conception of equality in its place, the argument from liberty seems to depend on empirical claims (to the extent it depends on empirical claims at all) that are far easier to understand and not controversial at all. That is, while the argument from equality is an argument from right, the right here depends on a conception of what equality is with inherently controversial empirical contentions built into it. The argument from liberty, in contrast, is far less controversial, for it seems to be relatively clear what liberty is and is not, and in any event, the assertion that liberty is infringed does not seem to depend on disputed empirical claims to the same extent. Many people no doubt find this appealing, which is why the argument from liberty is so often used to attack progressive proposals based on the argument from equality, no matter what the subject matter of those proposals may be.[28] But for present purposes, the most important feature of the argument from liberty is that it constitutes a direct argument against unionization in general and against the mandatory payment of the dues even if some form of unionization is allowed. None of the arguments for unionization that I have mentioned so far – not the argument from consequences nor the argument from freedom of association nor the argument from equality – constitute an argument for the contrary position.

I should note, however, that my own theory of exploitation does present a more determinate conception economic inequality and defines exploitation as both a distributive and commutative injustice, so not all conceptions of economic inequality suffer from the disadvantages I have outlined above.[29] But my point here is not that the argument from equality is inherently disadvantageous, merely that the currently most used arguments from equality have problems that are difficult to uncontroversially overcome. And while I could derive an argument for unionization and even for the mandatory payment of dues from my theory of exploitation, perhaps one that is even more direct than the usual arguments from equality, I will not attempt to do so here because, even if I did so, all the only thing this would establish in the eyes of most of those who are anti-union is that, in this instance, equality and liberty happen to conflict.

Establishing such a conflict has long been a tactic of the right,[30] and it has been a mistake by those on the left to cede the argument from liberty to those on the other side. For if equality and liberty do conflict, it is difficult to explain why equality and not liberty should be given priority in our moral deliberations. Even Rawls concedes that liberty – or at least certain "basic" kinds of liberty – has priority over equality.[31] In fact, Rawls goes even further than this, for he contends that protecting basic liberty from infringement has *lexical* priority over addressing economic inequality, meaning that *no* amount of basic liberty, no matter how small, may be traded off for an improvement in economic inequality, no matter how large.[32] Moreover, even if we were to reject the Rawlsian position and claim that all forms of equality and all forms of liberty are to be given equal weight, it would still be difficult to explain why the argument from equality should be treated as decisive in determining what we should do. At most, relying on the argument from equality and the consequentialist claims on which it is effectively, although not expressly, based to counteract an argument from liberty produces a moral standoff. Such a lack of moral clarity is simply not sufficient if we are going to convince anyone whose mind may still be open that supporting unionization is a moral imperative in the circumstances in which we now find ourselves.

Accordingly, my objective in this book is to reclaim the argument from liberty from the anti-union movement. This means that my main focus in this book is the right to liberty and the various subsidiary rights that the right to liberty is said to generate. I will, of course, be talking about the right to equality too, as well as exploring the usual consequentialist claims about the effects of unionization and the relationship between these effects and the good of workers and the common good. But the primary focus of each of the essays in this book is the right to liberty and how we might derive a right to unionization from it. And when I speak of a right to unioniziation, I mean a right to *universal* unionization, not merely a right to unionization when certain contingencies are met. That is, I will be arguing that justice, and especially that component of justice that protects liberty, requires all private and all public sector workers to be unionized – this is not something that is open to resolution by majority vote of either workers or the electorate at large and does not depend on whether the employer has agreed to this as part of the collective bargaining process once a workplace has been unionized.

Given my objectives, it is important to understand that this book is a work of political theory. Although there is an enormous amount of literature available on unionization, and there is obviously a very strong connection between unionization and political activism and various aspects of public policy, very little of the literature available on unionization consist of works of political theory, at least among liberal political theorists (and by "liberal" here I mean all political theorists who draw their inspiration from the Enlightenment, including those on the moderate right as well as the moderate left).[33] Instead, liberal political theorists mostly treat unionization as a specialty reserved for those in other disciplines, such as industrial relations or labor economics. There is certainly much about unionization that these specialties can explore and help us to explain, and I will rely on a great deal of this literature in making my argument in this book. But given the direct relevance of both equality and liberty (two of the principal concerns of political theory) to unionization and vice versa, we have reason to be concerned that there is relevant expertise here that has not been sufficiently brought to bear, especially because the specialties of industrial relations and labor economics are each driven primarily by empirical questions and not by questions of justice, equality, and liberty. These latter questions have empirical elements too, of course, but they also require a sophisticated understanding of how to reason about political morality and how questions about these various aspects of political morality should be understood. Much confusion has been generated and continues to persist as a result of the general neglect of the issue of unionization by liberal political theorists. As I will attempt to show in this book, there is much that the approach and techniques of political theory can contribute to an understanding of unionization on both the theoretical and the practical level, and without such contributions, it is unlikely that any society will ever have enough information and understanding to get the issue correct.

Given my approach, it may be helpful to say a little more at this point about the role that empirical arguments will play in the essays in this book. I have said that I will primarily be making an argument from right – the right to liberty – rather than an argument from consequences, when arguing for universal unionization. But I am not suggesting that we can distinguish between acts and omissions that are morally right and those that are morally wrong completely independent of their actual, expected, or possible effects. Consequences always matter. As Rawls noted in the course of articulating his own argument from right, "All ethical doctrines worth our consideration take consequences into account in judging rightness. One which did not would simply be irrational, crazy."[34] Indeed, it is difficult to imagine how one could even think, much less derive an ethical position, without some consideration of how the available courses of action might affect the existing state of affairs, and to consider this, it requires not only an understanding of human nature and circumstances but also an understanding of the principles of causation and how those principles might operate in the particular case at hand. The difference between an argument from right and an argument from consequences is therefore not that one considers consequences and the other doesn't – it is simply that, in an argument from right, the expected consequences are not the *only* factor to be considered. Certain pre-existing principles matter too. An argument from right will therefore sometimes recommend we do or refrain from doing something even though we are fairly certain some other course of action would, in some sense, produce "better" consequences.

Nevertheless, it is also important to realize that rights are not *a priori* conceptions that exist independently of facts about the world. If we are to determine whether a right has been infringed, for example, we must take into account various facts about causation, about human nature, and about the state of the world. But one of the most important benefits of employing an argument from right is that even when questions about these various empirical matters are vigorously disputed and these disputes are not likely to be resolved to a reasonable degree of certainty anytime soon, an argument from right can still provide categorical recommendations on what to do. In other words, arguments from right can give us recommendations on what to do under what game theorists call "conditions of risk and uncertainty," whereas arguments from consequences can only do this when the relevant probabilities of the various possible outcomes – that is, the consequences – are not themselves reasonably disputed.[35] When these are reasonably disputed, basing a recommendation for action or belief on an argument from right may make it seem like consequences do not matter, but they do matter. They are still taken into consideration, they are simply not treated as determinative. Whatever argumentative power they may have or would have if they could be resolved one way or the other is accordingly supplemented and, in certain cases, overcome by an argument derived through some other method.[36]

One such other method (there might be others still) involves beginning with something we embrace as what we might call a fundamental presupposition – something that establishes the framework for moral reasoning to take place rather than something that is derived by using that framework once it is in place.[37] All moral argument has to begin somewhere, but this starting point cannot be argued for morally, it can merely be accepted, for at this point there are no moral arguments to make. Liberty is such a fundamental presupposition, one that is accepted by both the pro-union left and the anti-union right. The argument from liberty therefore provides a basis on which each side can meaningfully engage the other. Of course, fundamental presuppositions are general concepts, not detailed conceptions,[38] and therefore need to be given further specificity to be operationalized; that is, they need to be further refined before they will generate recommendations as to what we should actually do about the problems that confront us in the real world. This can often if not always and perhaps even almost always be done in various ways. We therefore need to know more about what the concept means and what our understanding of its demands entails before we apply it. And this, in turn, means we often have to make judgments about the effect of certain kinds of acts and omissions on certain aspects of our lives. This is another sense, then, in which even an argument from right, like the argument from liberty, must contain elements of an argument from consequences. But once again, this does not make the two forms of argument equivalent. In an argument from consequences, we have to assemble our conception of the common good from a great many components of that good. What to include in this assemblage and how to prioritize different elements of it when they happen to conflict is often highly controversial. In an argument from right, we have only one particular aspect of individual life in mind. We call this an individual right because we judge it important enough to pursue regardless of the effect of this on the common good. While empirical matters may be relevant when deciding whether this right is being infringed or whether something further must be done to protect it, this does not make the underlying grounds of the argument consequentialist. Accordingly, saying that I am making an argument from right does not mean that I have strayed from this approach whenever I consider empirical matters, especially those that are not reasonably disputable, in constructing that argument or defending it from attack. Facts of this nature are indeed commonly included in arguments from right of all sorts.

I also want to say something about the distinction between what is called "ideal" and "non-ideal" theory, for this also has an effect on the extent to which empirical matters are relevant to my argument. All moral theories, whether they are arguments from right or arguments from consequences, have to consider basic facts about human nature, circumstances, and the methods of human reasoning. These include a scarcity of resources, the fact that we tend to care more about ourselves than other people (usually referred to as "limited altruism"), our tendency to rely on certain irrational heuristics and to harbor certain biases when evaluating our reasons for action or belief, and the resulting difficulty this all presents for successfully organizing collective action and producing public goods. These basic facts about human nature, circumstances, and reasoning are in some sense contingent; that is, they could be different if humans were to transform their basic nature or circumstances or methods of reasoning. Sometimes such a transformation might be possible, at least in small ways, without making us into different kinds of beings living in a different kind of world altogether. Because of this, philosophers often do what they call "ideal theory," that is, they assume some kind of transformation has or at least could take place. Sometimes this kind of theory is entirely unrealistic given where we are now and therefore provides no real guidance as to how we should behave in or what we should believe about the world in which we currently live. But sometimes we can derive important insights into our world from considering what would happen if we or our world were more ideal in certain ways.[39] In these cases, the ideal does not have to be attainable; it is simply used to clarify our thinking on certain problems that present themselves to us in the real world. The first essay in this volume is an attempt to derive such insights from a hypothetical thought experiment about a world that does not exist and is not likely to exist anytime soon, which makes it, I suppose, an exercise in ideal theory. The other two, in contrast, are exercises in "non-ideal" theory; that is, they take the world as we find it. Describing how the world operates is accordingly more important in these later essays, but that does not make the arguments presented in them any less arguments from right – the unfortunate judgmental overtones of the label "non-ideal" notwithstanding. Each of these essays looks at fundamental principles to which we claim to be committed and derives what I believe are feasible and practical recommendations as to how we should think about universal unionization. Consequences matter in these essays, and it is important to get our understanding of these correct, but this is not the only thing that matters. Therefore, the arguments presented in these latter essays are still arguments from right that are meant to have real purchase even if some of the connections between the right to liberty and various kinds of conduct raise empirical questions. In cases where the answers to these empirical questions are not reasonably disputable, however, there is nothing about taking these facts as given that transforms an argument otherwise based on right into something else. What I avoid in these essays is relying on consequentialist factual assertions that remain highly controversial and unresolved, the kind of factual assertions that typically make up a great part of an argument about the common good.

Also note that my argument proceeds on what we might call the institutional level. By this I mean that it is about whether unions are a kind of association essential to ensure background justice in our society. I shall say much more about this later, but briefly the idea is that unionization and therefore the core functions that an association must perform to be a union are not open for prohibition the way noncore functions are. Of course, both core and noncore functions may be regulated, but I will make no attempt here to develop a fine-tuned set of regulations dictating what unions should and should not be allowed to do or even discuss how their core functions might be regulated once universal unionization is recognized as an essential principle of justice in a particular liberal capitalist democracy. I shall stop once the institutional argument is complete. Details such as the nature and extent of appropriate post-institutional regulation are simply to be decided according to the political preferences of the electorate once the basic elements of unionization are established and protected from direct or indirect attack.[40] What I argue for in this book is the right for unions to exist, in both the private and the public sector, to bargain collectively for their members, to represent their members in disputes with management, to lobby government for legislation in their members' interests, and to negotiate for and fully enforce what are commonly called union shop agreements – agreements that require all employees to join the union upon being hired and pay dues designed to cover the costs of the various services that the union ultimately provides.

But beyond this, and subject to certain feasibility constraints, I also argue that every firm *must* have a union, and every government employer too, and that such unions are to be treated as a basic institution that we all bear an obligation to provide rather than something that employees bear the initial burden of organizing before it may come into existence. After all, even the "Powell Memo," the 1971 document that is frequently characterized as setting forth the blueprint for the conservative right's subsequent attack on a wide variety of economic regulations and progressive policies and institutions in the name of freedom (then a Richmond, Virginia corporate lawyer, Lewis F. Powell, Jr. would later ascend to the Supreme Court following nomination by President Nixon), describes labor unions and collective bargaining as among our "essential freedoms."[41] Extending Powell's argument only a little bit, I simply contend that in order to ensure that these essential freedoms (which are themselves necessary guarantors of other essential freedoms) are not as a practical matter rendered illusory or toothless, unionization must be universal – that is, all employees, private and public, must be represented by a union, whether they would prefer to act exclusively on their own or not – for universal unionization is a necessary element of the background circumstances that every liberal capitalist society must provide in order for it to be just.

Obviously, the argument for universal unionization takes us quite a ways beyond the current status quo in which unions are permitted in the workplace (if at all) only after a certain percentage of the workforce votes for them and, in right-to-work states, collectively negotiated agreements that require all employees to join the relevant union are impermissible even so. Indeed, even some of those who are sympathetic to my objectives may worry that I am arguing for changes that are politically unachievable under current conditions. But if this is what morality requires, then saying that achieving this will be difficult is not a counter to my argument. Although the ultimate claim I present in this book is that universal unionization is morally required, this does not mean that my argument is irrelevant to beginning that journey by struggling first toward less ambitious short-term goals such as the elimination of right-to-work laws and restrictions on what can be the subject of collective bargaining agreements. On the contrary, my argument should provide a more effective basis for challenging these union-suppressing laws. The long-term goal of requiring all firms of at least a certain size to have a unionized workforce is also not as unachievable as some may think, for as we shall see, something very close to this is already in place in many liberal capitalist European states.

To make my argument, I proceed by presenting three separate essays, each of which is conceived of as being able to stand on its own, but each of which also establishes an essential part of my overall claim. The essays can be read in any order, although the order they are offered here seems to me to be the most effective when viewed from the perspective of the whole. In any event, taken together these essays provide a comprehensive defense of my principle of universal unionization of both the private and the public sector. In the first essay, I deal with the question of whether universal unionization violates what are commonly thought of as libertarian rights. This argument is primarily directed at those who think of themselves as political libertarians or economic neoliberals or, as is most commonly the case, both. The idea is to show that even in a libertarian utopia, where liberty is given priority over everything else, unions would arise in both the private and the public sector and would eventually negotiate agreements with the relevant employers requiring all new hires to join the union and pay dues as a condition of their continued employment. This essay is designed to establish that unionization – even when it leads to such agreements – is not a violation of anyone's right to liberty, and that such agreements would naturally arise out of free market transactions in any society that ensured that this market was indeed free.

In the second essay, which is longer and more complex, I move beyond the argument that unions would only arise naturally in a free market society and should be able to negotiate union shop agreements if they wish. Here, I argue that at least in the private sector, the union is a basic institution in a liberal capitalist democracy. That is, in a society in which the basic form of business organization is the firm, unionization in the private sector is not simply optional – it is one of the background circumstances necessary for a liberal capitalist society to be just. Here, I am using the term "liberal" in its broadest, children-of-the-Enlightenment sense, not just as a shorthand way of referring again to libertarianism, as the term "liberal" is sometimes used in continental Europe. By liberal I mean to include not only liberal egalitarians, prioritarians, sufficientarians, left-libertarians, and others on the moderate left, but also right-libertarians, traditional conservatives, and others on the moderate right, who are nevertheless liberals in the broad, history-of-political-philosophy sense rather than the man-on-the-street sense of the term. In other words, the purpose of this essay is to address all those who find the anti-union argument from liberty persuasive no matter what liberal political theory they happen to embrace. In any event, to make this argument, I discuss what the idea of a basic institution means, how we tell whether a particular institution is basic, and what flows from this determination once it is made with regard to unions. I also show that this argument is not as radical as it may seem, for something very much like universal unionization has already been recognized in a number of highly successful liberal capitalist democracies. Finally, I discuss how the idea of the union as a basic institution might be implemented and what kinds of issues would remain to be decided by post-institutional regulation.

In the third essay, I turn my attention to public sector unions and address the argument that, regardless of whether we think that unions in the private sector are a basic institution, the background circumstances in the public sector are different and therefore a similar conclusion should not apply. I address the various arguments raised in support of this claim and show that while the circumstances are indeed different in the private and the public sector, they are not *materially* different – meaning that the differences do not suggest that our conclusion about the necessity of universal unionization in the private sector does not apply. I then go on to address various other supposedly liberty-based arguments against public sector unionization, including that it inappropriately promotes the growth of government, that it puts essential services at risk, that collective bargaining by public employees is unfair to the public, that public sector unionization is undemocratic, that it is bankrupting us, and that it somehow constitutes a violation of free speech. What we end up with then, after the completion of the third essay, is an argument for a modern, liberal capitalist society in which unionization is not merely optional but required in both the private and public sector, where collective bargaining, being one of the core functions of unions, cannot be restricted or eliminated in either sector, and where union shop arrangements must be honored should the parties collectively agree to them. Beyond this, the details of what unions can and cannot do and how they must be organized are up for post-institutional regulation, just as is the case with firms and agencies of government.

In the course of presenting the arguments that I make in these essays, I will, of course, talk a great deal about liberty. It may be helpful at the outset to note that the term "liberty" is surprisingly general and vague – it can and often is used to refer to what are actually some very different aspects of our life in the world. In one of the most famous essays of the twentieth century, the political philosopher and historian of ideas Isaiah Berlin argued that the various ways in which people have spoken about liberty over the centuries could be broken down into two general categories or concepts: negative liberty and positive liberty.[42] By using these terms, however, Berlin was not trying to suggest that negative liberty is "bad" and that positive liberty is "good." Negative liberty is negative only in the sense that it protects people from interference – it focuses on whether people are restrained in some way from doing what they would otherwise have the capacity to do. Positive liberty is positive, in contrast, only in the sense that it "posits," or proposes, that certain kinds of actions must be done rather than simply may be done if one is to be truly free. Berlin's essay and especially his use of these terms has shaped the discussion of liberty ever since, but now a third concept, called republican liberty, has joined the two concepts Berlin identified.[43] Republican liberty is freedom from the arbitrary will of another, a form of domination that is argued to be demeaning, dehumanizing, and dispiriting and, if wide-ranging enough, tantamount to slavery. Republican liberty is republican, however, not because it is the kind of liberty that members of the GOP embrace (they may or may not), but because it is derived from what are thought by some to be the principles of the republics of ancient Greece and Rome. In any event, each of these concepts of liberty is very different from the others and is best used to perform very different functions in any philosophical analysis. I shall go into all this in great depth in the course of these essays. But for now, all that is necessary to keep in mind is that liberty is a complex notion, and whenever the word "liberty" is used, one must be careful to note which of these very different concepts of liberty is being employed.

It will also be important to keep in mind the difference between a concept of liberty and a conception.[44] A concept is a more general principle, such as the idea that people should be free to self-actualize or be the best that they can be, which is what positive liberty claims. But a concept is usually expressed in such general terms that it may not be specific enough to tell us what we should do in concrete situations. Concepts often need to be further refined, or cashed out, before they can give us specific advice about what to do in the real world. There are usually many ways any particular concept can be cashed out, and how it is cashed out can have a dramatic effect on its real-world implications. Each of the various concepts of liberty that I have mentioned can be cashed out in a variety of ways and distinguishing between these differing conceptions of each concept of liberty is important. It will be especially important to keep in mind that my conception of republican liberty is very different than the conception of republican liberty that is currently attracting a great deal of attention in academic circles. This latter conception of republican liberty is very thick – that is, it has been and is being used by many theorists as a comprehensive principle of justice that can be applied to a wide variety of specific situations. In contrast, I will be using a very thin conception of republican liberty – one that does not attempt to do the work of a comprehensive principle of justice but remains a conception of liberty alone. In the present context, this is an advantage not a failing, for it means that embracing my conception of republican liberty does not require commitments that are unlikely to draw agreement from people holding a variety of comprehensive moral views. It can therefore be used to do things in our moral reasoning that a thick conception of republican liberty would be too controversial to do. I will talk about this more at the end of essay one, "The Libertarian Argument for Unions," but I will go into it at even greater length in essay two, "The Union as a Basic Institution of Society." To get the full picture of my conception of republican liberty, one must accordingly read the relevant sections in both essays.

I also want to say something about language, and especially about how I will refer to certain policies, practices, and forms of agreement in these essays and what terms I shall use to refer to them. In the debate about unionization, each side often uses different terms to refer to the same thing. I refer to "universal" unionization, but those on the right would refer to this as "compulsory" unionization, for "compulsory" tends to carry a negative connotation, while "universal," I admit, tends to carry a positive one. Those on the right attack "closed shop" agreements, for most people have a positive emotional response to the idea of something being open and a negative one to anything being closed. However, a closed shop is one in which the employer has agreed to hire only those who are already members of the union and such agreements have been illegal in the United States since 1947. What many union critics actually have in mind when they refer to a closed shop agreement is a union shop agreement, which as I have already mentioned allows the employer to hire union or nonunion workers but requires all new currently nonunion employees to join the union and begin paying union dues shortly after being hired. Even these agreements, however, are not enforceable to the extent they require actual union membership, although many agreements still purport to require this. Employees covered by such agreements can therefore refuse to join the union, although they still must pay an "agency fee" that covers the cost of collective bargaining and certain other activities that directly involve the employment relationship but not the cost of lobbying, union organizing, or other more generalized activities. Union shop agreements are therefore, in effect, currently no different than what are expressly called "agency agreements," which do not require employees to join the union and pay union dues but do require them to pay agency fees – often called "fair share fees" by those on the left – if they don't join.[45] Despite the fact that no one is being denied a job because of their union status under either a union shop or agency shop agreement, however, those on the right often decry these agreements as denying people the right to work. To maintain the rhetorical pretense that these agreements do deny people jobs, some states have in turn banned union and agency shop agreements using what are expressly, though misleadingly, labeled "right-to-work" laws, providing that workers cannot be compelled to join a union nor pay union dues or even an agency fee.[46] Those on the left, in turn, combat this rhetoric with rhetoric of their own, referring to these laws as "free-rider" laws, for they allow employees who benefit from unionization to refuse to pay for it. Because this argument proved convincing in a healthy minority of states, those which expressly rejected attempts to pass right-to-work/free-rider laws, the political right then opened up a second front in response, recasting the practice of insisting on the mandatory payment of union or agency fees as "compelled speech" and arguing that, under the First Amendment, public sector workers should not be forced to pay for speech with which they may disagree. While initially unsuccessful, this argument has now been accepted by the Supreme Court, effectively making all states right-to-work states with regard to public sector workers, even those whose elected representatives have rejected right-to-work proposals.[47]

What all this means is that whatever choices one makes as to how to describe the various arrangements that are at issue between workers and employers, one is going to have to use a term that is, to some degree, loaded with either negative or positive connotations and therefore open oneself up to the charge of trying to subliminally influence how people react to a discussion of these issues by associating some emotional baggage with one view or the other. But by and large, throughout these essays, I will use the terms favored by the right, although I shall use the terms "closed shop" and "union shop" in their correct sense, despite the use of the term "closed shop" to refer to both kinds of practices by some of those on the right. I will otherwise use the terms favored by the right because these are the terms that are now in common use among the general public, despite the efforts of the left to introduce more neutral or even favorable versions of them. I will even use the term "compulsory unionization" in some places instead of "universal unionization," despite the fact that given the arguments I present in these essays I believe that the term "universal" more accurately captures the feeling that should be associated with this practice. I will use the terms favored by the right because my argument is strong, and I am not afraid of having to overcome the rhetorical power of the more negative versions of these terms in the process of asserting my argument. Nevertheless, it is important to keep in mind the subtle influence these terms may be having on one's thought processes and be especially alive to and resist the idea that the negative or positive connotations associated with these terms are justified.

I should also point out that while everything I say in these essays should be equally applicable to any liberal capitalist democracy, the book is primarily oriented toward the situation in the United States of America. The same problems that have beset unions there have also arisen in many other liberal capitalist democracies, of course, but nowhere else are they as severe. Indeed, some of the proposals I make in these essays have effectively already been accepted and instantiated in some liberal capitalist democracies because these approaches seem intuitively more plausible and appealing given the different cultural and historical traditions in place. Nevertheless, even though this book is primarily about the United States, its arguments can also be applied to other liberal capitalist democracies. Take, for example, the United Kingdom, where unionization has also been dramatically declining for many years and for many of the same reasons that apply in the United States. While I do not discuss the UK situation in anywhere near the detail that I discuss the situation in the United States, the application of my arguments to what is happening in the United Kingdom should be obvious. Moreover, even those residing in the countries of Northern Europe, where unionization is already close to being institutionalized, should be able to draw something from my discussion. Unionization is under attack even in these countries, and understanding how unionization can be supported by the argument from liberty should accordingly be helpful in resisting attempts to roll back the clock in Northern Europe too.

Finally, it may also be helpful to mention that just because my argument focuses on the application of the argument from liberty to unionization, this does not mean that it will not generalize and apply to other issues of contemporary import. The argument from liberty is currently being used by those on the right to push back against all sorts of achievements of the liberal state that have been driven mostly by the argument from equality. Indeed, the argument from liberty is being used against almost every progressive proposal currently in play, from prohibiting discrimination against LGBT people, to the mandatory purchase of health insurance, to almost every attempt at government regulation to protect our health and safety as well as the environment, to attempts to regulate the financial industry, to what kinds of limits may be placed on campaign contributions, and so on.[48] But as Emile Durkheim pointed out more than 100 years ago

Nothing is more false than the antimony that people have too often wished to establish between the authority of rules and the freedom of the individual. On the contrary, liberty (by which we mean a just liberty, one for which society is duty bound to enforce respect) is itself the product of a set of rules. I can be free only in so far as the other person is prevented from turning to his own benefit that superiority, whether physical, economic or of any other kind, which he possesses, in order to fetter my liberty. Only a social rule can serve as a barrier against such abuses of power.[49]

Without such rules, complex as they may need to be, whatever liberty remains "is purely nominal," Durkheim then went on to say.[50] Gaining a deeper understanding of how complex the idea of liberty is, what kinds of liberty a liberal democracy is designed to promote and protect, and how the promotion and protection of certain kinds of liberty may actually undermine the kinds of liberty that most of us hold dear is therefore critical if we are to meaningfully engage with one of the key arguments currently being used in a wide variety of public policy debates. By reclaiming the argument of liberty from the right with regard to unionization in this work, those who are so inclined should be able to draw arguments to defend a wide variety of progressive policies that currently rely exclusively on the argument from equality and may be foundering as a result.

With these points in mind, our journey toward universal unionization is now ready to begin.

FIRST ESSAY

I

The Libertarian Argument for Unions

Assume that we are living in a libertarian utopia, a utopia very much like the one described in Robert Nozick's most famous work, *Anarchy, State, and Utopia (1974)*, now generally considered one of the most influential works of libertarian thought in the modern era.[1] What Nozick calls "dominant protective associations" – that is, organizations that specialize in the enforcement of libertarian rights and the adjudication of disputes between those who subscribe to the association's services – have naturally arisen in each geographic area because these are specialized services, and many individuals lack the skill, time, or inclination to perform such services for themselves. It is therefore more efficient for most of those living in this utopia to subscribe to these services rather than to develop the requisite skills and take the time to enforce their rights on their own. For reasons that I will discuss in detail later, these associations have by now also compelled all "independents" within their respective areas – those who initially refused to sign up for the association's services on their own – to join the association and are providing protective services to them in return. These protective services include the enforcement of contracts, the recognition and protection of private property, the prohibition of fraud, theft, and anticompetitive behavior, the provision of adjudicative services aimed at settling disputes between members, the issuance of authoritative decisions on the scope of member's respective rights, and the design and enforcement of coordination solutions to collective action problems. In other words, life within the jurisdiction of each dominant protective association looks a lot like life within what Nozick calls "the minimal state."[2] And while I have argued elsewhere that this would also look a lot like life in almost every existing fully developed liberal capitalist state,[3] nothing in any of the arguments I am about to make depends on this being true. As far as these arguments are concerned, those who are uncomfortable with the notion that a great deal of modern regulation and other government activity is totally consistent with the idea of a minimal state can assume we are dealing with something that looks more like a very pared-down modern capitalist nation. For what I want to explore in this essay is how business would be conducted in a libertarian utopia – not because we are likely to be living in a such a utopia anytime soon but because libertarian arguments, or rather arguments that purport to be libertarian arguments, are often trotted out in opposition to various proposals to regulate the market or otherwise counter the power of the firm. Of course, I cannot take on all these arguments against government regulation in a single essay. But I can address one common argument that seems to be gaining strength of late – the argument that unionization, or at least compulsory unionization, is a violation of libertarian values and that union activity should accordingly be severely limited by government and in some cases entirely prohibited.

It is ironic, of course, that while libertarian values are often used to argue *against* government regulation of business activity, libertarian values in this case are being used to argue *for* government regulation of the business activity of workers. Indeed, given that the libertarians who oppose unions also tend to be economic neoliberals who believe that economic activity is likely to be most efficient and productive when the market is left to its own devices and not subjected to government interference, they should be doubly opposed to any attempt to regulate the marketplace, regardless of whether the target of that regulation is the firm or the workers the firm employs.[4] Other than noting that there appears to be an inconsistency here, however, I will not use this as a basis for any of the arguments I present in this essay.[5] Instead, I shall simply go straight to the substance of the arguments that some self-proclaimed libertarians make against union activity and explore whether unions would exist in a libertarian utopia, and if so, what limits, if any, we could expect to be placed on their formation and their activity.

Note, however, I am not suggesting that libertarianism is a monolithic view and that all libertarians take exactly the same position on everything, or even on unionization. There are as many varieties of libertarianism as there are of any other family of political theories. Right-libertarians, for example, think that the redistribution of wealth is never permissible in a libertarian society, while left-libertarians think that it is often required. There are other differences both between and within these two very broad forms of libertarianism as well.[6] But while many libertarians on both the left and the right would not object to unionization to the extent that it is an uncoerced product of free market forces, some would. And many would object to barring provisions in employment contracts that prohibit the employee from agreeing to join a union or engage in union organizing activities, provisions that were once a common part of most employment agreements. Finally, even more libertarians would object to enforcing provisions in collective bargaining agreements that require all persons hired as employees of the firm to join the union and pay dues, an issue that forms a key front in the battle over unionization today. For example, Friedrich Hayek – one of the most prominent libertarians of the twentieth century and someone who still exerts enormous influence on many people who consider themselves libertarians – saw unionization (and especially but not only compulsory unionization) as a serious threat to a free society even when agreed to by an employer.[7] Republican Senator and one-time presidential candidate Rand Paul, a self-professed libertarian, was the primary sponsor of a 2013 bill that attempted to enact a federal right-to-work law,[8] and he introduced a similar bill in 2017.[9] The billionaires Charles and David Koch, who are among the primary funders of many libertarian organizations and claim to be libertarians themselves (David Koch actually ran for vice president on the Libertarian Party ticket in 1980), are vociferous critics of unionization and the workers' rights that unions have established and continue to promote.[10] James Buchanan, the libertarian economist and an intellectual hero for many on the libertarian right, was extremely hostile to unions, referring to them as "the labor monopoly movement."[11] Many other individuals and organizations that purport to be and generally are recognized as libertarian, especially on the right, are critics of unionization too.[12] And while the precise objections to unionization raised by these critics may differ somewhat, all these people present some conception of liberty as an impediment to important aspects of the practice of unionization.[13] Obviously, many members of the general public, both those who consider themselves libertarians and those who are merely open to some libertarian ideas, find these arguments persuasive or unionization would not currently be suffering such a dramatic decline. My focus on libertarianism in this essay is therefore not an attempt to construct a straw man and knock it down, as some shockingly out-of-touch academics to whom I have presented the arguments in this essay have surprisingly claimed. Libertarian thinking, or what often passes today for libertarian thinking, is very much a driving force behind some of the most vehement and effective arguments currently being used to undermine the union movement. In light of what I will argue are the inconsistencies and errors in their views, these supposedly libertarian critics of unionization, although almost exclusively on the right, may be more accurately described as *faux* libertarians, since I will be arguing that the libertarian values they claim to embrace actually do not support the anti-union positions that they take.[14] But those who think like this consider themselves and are commonly thought of as real libertarians nonetheless.

In any event, to address this libertarian critique of unionization and show that it is both misguided and inconsistent with the fundamental presuppositions that all libertarians claim to embrace, I intend to explore the following questions. First, I will consider what private enterprise might look like in a libertarian utopia and specifically whether something similar to what we call "the firm" in the real world would arise. Next, I will consider how large such firms might be expected to grow and what factors might impose limits, if any, on such growth. I will then consider how large firms are likely to be managed and, given the likelihood of certain kinds of management structures being adopted, how employees and potential employees of such firms are likely to react. And this will bring me to the heart of the essay: determining whether unions could be expected to arise in our libertarian utopia, whether we could expect them to arise in both the private and the public sector, and what limits, if any, could we expect to be imposed on union organizing and behavior. Indeed, the primary question of interest here is whether rules making the workplace a union shop – that is, a place where all nonmanagerial employees are required to join the union and contribute to the cost of collective bargaining after being hired, something we would expect to find in our libertarian utopia? Or are so-called right-to-work rules, which prohibit union shops, and rules that prohibit the collection of agency fees, which cover the costs of collective bargaining for nonunion employees, and rules that authorize yellow dog contracts, which expressly prohibit union membership and activity (let's think of these together as the anti-union regulatory package) more consistent with the demands of libertarianism?

Before I set off in search of answers to these questions, however, there are two more introductory points I want to make. The first is about the relationship between libertarianism and neoliberalism, and how that relationship is implicated by the arguments in this essay. Libertarianism is predominantly a political view, neoliberalism is predominantly an economic one, or at least that is how I believe these views can best be understood. Many libertarians, however, consider themselves neoliberals – indeed, they view their economic neoliberalism as entailed by their libertarianism. While I do not think this view is correct, and have so argued elsewhere,[15] it is nevertheless true as a contingent matter that people who embrace one often embrace both views. This sometimes makes it difficult to tell whether the anti-union views expressed by such people are driven by their libertarianism or their neoliberalism.[16] But this unfortunate conflation of what should be treated as separate and independent viewpoints – one political and one economic – does not matter for the purposes of any of the arguments I will be making in this essay. In the course of addressing the anti-union argument from liberty, I will be addressing both the argument from political liberty and the argument from economic liberty. I will accordingly show that libertarianism does not support the suppression of unions whether it entails neoliberalism or not.

The final introductory point I want to make is about the conception of the person to be applied in our thought experiment. G. A. Cohen repeatedly pressed the following argument against Rawls: if people really internalized the values that Rawls said his principles of justice as fairness were designed to express, then they would not need financial incentives to engage in socially productive behavior. The Rawlsian difference principle, which was designed to justify at least some economic inequalities by the need for such incentives, is accordingly self-contradictory, according to Cohen, for it assumes that members of a Rawlsian society possess the very qualities that the embrace of the difference principle should eventually eliminate.[17] Could a version of this argument have some application here? In other words, if we assume that we are living in a libertarian utopia, does this mean we could no longer take the history of the real world and our understanding of the kinds of people living in it as instructive about what would happen in our hypothetical society? Could we still assume that labor markets are neither completely open nor perfectly competitive and that workers cannot always find jobs doing what they want to do for better pay and better terms whenever they might want to? Could we still assume that workers would, as they do in the real world, generally feel that their interests were in conflict with those of their employers? By beginning this essay with "assume we are living in a libertarian utopia," however, I do not mean that we are to assume that the people living in such a society are any different than they are out in the real world. Such an assumption would only make sense if we were trying to explore what the world would look like if people were different. But that is not the purpose of our thought experiment. Our thought experiment is designed to explore what the world would look like if people were as they are in the real world but governments were run on strict libertarian principles. This is what allows us to test the anti-union argument from liberty, and that is what makes our thought experiment, even though it is an exercise in ideal theory, potentially instructive about the relationship between unionization and liberty. So it is perfectly proper for us, in the course of conducting this thought experiment, to rely on our actual knowledge of labor history, real events, and our current understanding of human nature and circumstances and assume that workers in our hypothetical world have the same attitudes and preferences as workers in the real world, as varied as they actually are. The conception of the person to be used in our thought experiment is, as it should be, no different than the conception of the person we use to try to understand human behavior in society as it actually exists.

1.1 THE LANDSCAPE OF UTOPIA

The first question I want to explore is what form the typical business enterprise might take in our libertarian utopia. I hope, however, that it will not be controversial to assert that the kinds of business entities we typically call "firms" are very likely to arise. And by "firms," I mean business organizations with a hierarchical structure that contain numerous employees with a variety of specialized skills who are performing different but complimentary tasks directed from above and who thereby act together as a single integrated unit. For in a modern, economically developed industrialized society it is simply not feasible for business organizations to perform complex tasks of production if they are composed of a loose association of a large number of individuals functioning as independent contractors who are constantly having to negotiate their relations. Also the libertarian argument, at least as most of its contemporary advocates describe it, is not a plea for a return to a simpler, mostly agrarian form of life. If it were, libertarianism would not have become the seemingly irrepressible alternative model for running a modern industrialized society that it has turned out to be, and it would not be worthy of being taken seriously by those who otherwise oppose it. For what the firm does is provide a mechanism for taking full advantage of the division of labor, one of the great technological innovations of all time. Within the structure provided by the firm, some people can specialize in predicting wants, in deciding what is to be produced, and in acquiring and allocating the necessary factors of production; some people can specialize in familiarizing themselves with the logistical demands of managing labor and developing the interpersonal skills necessary to do so effectively; some people can specialize in providing the various kinds of substantive labor required to produce whatever it is that the firm is aiming to produce; and so on. The cooperation of each of these groups within the firm is what enables a business enterprise to be maximally productive, and maximal productivity is beneficial to everyone as long as each group's share of any increase in productivity exceeds what they could obtain without the cooperation of the other groups, as it usually will. Indeed, the dominant protective association is itself such a firm, an example of the concentration of specialized expertise that the division of labor allows, for it is the dominant protective association's special expertise in adjudicating disputes and enforcing rights that makes its existence attractive to the initial subscribers and thereby gets the whole "protective association" enterprise off the ground. But if those in our libertarian utopia want to take full advantage of the efficiencies generated by the division of labor, then protective associations are not the only specialized organizations that would arise; other kinds of associations with different kinds of special expertise, much like modern business firms, would naturally arise as well.

The question, then, is whether the dominant protective association would allow these firms to arise or attempt to suppress them. To do the latter, however, the existence of firms would have to violate the rights of the some of the dominant protective association's members, and it is difficult to see how this could be the case. Firms are examples of two rights in motion: the right of freedom of association, which suggests (at the very least) that people should be able to form business associations, and the right of freedom of contract, which suggests (again at the very least) that people should be able to contract to work for one another. Both of these are rights that the dominant protective association is committed to protect. I will get to whether these two rights are each "rights" in the same sense for the libertarian later in this essay, but for now, this issue is not apposite because in this instance both rights support the existence of firms. Thus, regardless of whether this is something the dominant protective association has an obligation to encourage, it should be uncontroversial to suggest that the formation of firms is something the dominant protective association has no right to suppress. Of course, these firms would be subservient to the dominant protective association in the sense that they would have to be members of it, and they would have to submit to the same rules and regulations that applied to all members. But firms would otherwise be free to conduct business just as individuals do, so there would be a multiplicity of firms in our libertarian utopia nonetheless.

How big would these firms get? Firms in certain industries, like the gas company, the electric company, the water company, and so on, would be natural monopolies, of course, even in our libertarian utopia, so these firms would be rather large, just as they are in the real world. But if our thought experiment is to be instructive, at least some of the firms in industries that are more competitive would have to be expected to grow to the size that we actually find in most modern industrialized societies too. For guidance on whether we could expect this, it is useful to turn to Ronald Coase. According to Coase, the primary factor influencing firm size is transaction costs. In a capitalist economic system, economic resources are allocated by the market's price mechanism rather than by command, which is how they are allocated in a socialist economic system. But the existence of firms in a capitalist economy means that the capitalist method of resource allocation is not in fact in use "all the way down," especially, although not exclusively, with regard to labor, for workers are required to do what they are told rather than allowed to bargain over the terms on which they will perform each individual task asked of them. As Coase notes, "the distinguishing mark of the firm is the suppression of the price mechanism."[18] So while capitalists reject central planning by the government as a method of allocating the available factors of production, they do not reject central planning by firms. This kind of planning requires a special kind of expertise, of course, but this kind of planning is okay, the argument goes, because it still leaves enough of the economy subject to the price mechanism to generate sufficient information for those in command of the firm to make the required allocation decisions.[19] Under socialism, in contrast, the price mechanism is completely suspended, meaning that those charged with making allocation decisions lack the information required for them to do their jobs.[20] But having economic resources allocated by command within firms that are participants in an overall capitalist structure, instead of through a continuous series of individually negotiated exchange transactions, saves a great deal of transaction costs. By reducing the number of exchange transactions, the firm also reduces the number of transactions that are subject to tax, which provides yet another form of cost savings. The abandonment of the price mechanism as a method of allocation and the reliance on firms with a hierarchical structure to internally allocate resources by command is therefore justified within an overall capitalist economy, Coase argues, by the efficiencies that this creates.[21]

Moreover, Coase says (relying on insights from Alfred Marshall and the marginalists), as long as there are further cost savings to be had from growing bigger and therefore eliminating the need for further external individual transactions, these firms will and indeed should tend to increase in size. Only when a firm gets so big that it actually costs more to allocate a required or desired resource by internal command, rather than by engaging in an external market transaction, will the firm stop growing.[22] This should be true, Coase argues, even though greater size may allow a firm to generate monopoly profits and thereby prosper despite being intentionally inefficient.[23] Because we are imagining this taking place in a libertarian utopia, however, and further assuming anticompetitive behavior is a violation of libertarian rights, we can expect that the incentive provided by monopoly power will not be allowed to operate unchecked. But even if we assume vigorous enforcement of the antitrust laws, the limit encountered when marginal costs begin to exceed marginal profits will still not kick in for quite some time. Most business enterprises do enjoy economies of scale, and while these may slow as the firm grows, they will still remain significant until the firm becomes very large indeed.[24] Given the modesty of this limit, we can accordingly expect that firms in our libertarian utopia will naturally grow until they are relatively big by any reasonable definition of the word. And remember, if prohibiting anticompetitive behavior is *not* a violation of libertarian rights, then my argument here actually gets stronger, not weaker, for firms will tend to grow even bigger than they otherwise would.

But there is another factor that affects the size of the firm, one that Coase does not discuss directly. This is what we might call "friction." Friction refers to the fact that in real life everything is more complicated than it seems – things show up late, are not where they are supposed to be, break down unexpectedly, and so on. And it is not just the movement of things that can cause friction. People can too – in any cooperative enterprise, people will have their own personal agendas and may therefore have interests that conflict to some extent with the goals of the overall enterprise. Even with the best of intentions, people who are nominally part of a joint enterprise will sometimes fail to follow instructions. They may even subvert the goals of the collective intentionally on some number of occasions, or they may divert time and resources that could be spent pursuing the goals of the collective by jockeying for position within the collective, thereby weakening its ability to pursue its goals efficiently and perhaps even making it impossible to pursue those goals at all. While all organizations experience friction, and a hierarchical structure can do more to limit its incidence than a collective one because that latter structure requires even more cooperation, friction is nevertheless impossible to eliminate entirely and gets more difficult to manage as an organization grows in size. Indeed, it is well-known that the bigger a firm gets, the more likely its size will serve to stifle innovation. At some point, friction will reduce and eventually eliminate the benefit of having specialist advice on the allocation of resources available in-house, and those providing such advice will have to form a new firm in order to pursue their vision, especially when it comes to implementing controversial new ideas or distinctive changes in direction.

Even though this limit is likely to kick in before the limit imposed by marginal economic efficiency, it is not going to kick in that often or that quickly. There are both psychological and practical barriers that are likely to be encountered first. For one, most people are risk averse.[25] They will accordingly be reluctant to leave the shelter of the firm, no matter how frustrating it might be to slog toward their particular entrepreneurial vision inside it, until they feel forced to do so. Indeed, this is why it is often said that people start businesses only as a last resort. And even those who are not so risk averse or who are nevertheless capable of overcoming this psychological barrier will still have to raise the capital required to launch the enterprise, and capital is often very difficult to access. So while we can expect some entrepreneurs to break off and start their own firms in our libertarian utopia, even when it would still be more efficient to start these business ventures in-house, this is not going to mean that the business landscape we find there is going to be significantly different than what we find out in the real world. And this means that we would still expect firms with hierarchical organizational structures to arise naturally in our libertarian utopia and to grow in size in much the way this happens in the world in which we find ourselves.

1.2 THE RISE OF UNIONS

What would the reaction be of those who become employees of these firms? Given the dynamics of the situation, many employees would recognize that on an individual basis they lack bargaining power and even expertise, for they only negotiate for themselves once in a while, but the management of the firm negotiates all the time. So these employees would soon realize that (1) they could benefit by hiring specialist negotiators to negotiate for them; (2) incurring the cost of doing this would only be feasible and economically efficient if it were done by large groups of employees rather than by individuals; and (3) if they were able to negotiate collectively rather than individually, they would not only be able to better distribute the cost of doing so, they would also have more bargaining power and therefore be more likely to obtain a greater share of whatever surplus value their labor happened to create.[26] The bigger the firm, the stronger this incentive would be.[27] Indeed, "the whole of history suggests the powerful psychological need for workers with common concerns to get together in the formation of associations to represent their common interests."[28] Even if some workers in some firms in some situations might have a different attitude, preferring to individually negotiate their own contracts or to seek representation through something other than a union,[29] we could accordingly expect a significant number of workers to find the idea of unionization attractive, and some of these to become activists and actually attempt to form unions and convince others to join.[30] But this does not mean there will be unions. To determine that, we first have to consider whether the formation of unions is something the dominant protective association would be obligated to allow or to suppress.

In answering this question, it is important to remember what kinds of arguments are eligible to be raised here. A great many of the arguments for and against unionization in the real world are consequentialist arguments.[31] In other words, these are arguments about whether the effect of the existence of unions will be good or bad, and how one determines whether an effect is good or bad depends on what are often controversial predictions of the economic effects of not only actual but also counterfactual choices, as well as on what philosophers' call "the conception of the good" one applies; that is, the individual's view as to what outcomes should be thought of as better than others. Determining what conception of the good to apply will be controversial too: some people might want to consider only the effect of the various options available on the economic efficiency of the firm; some might also or only want to consider the effect on the wages, working conditions, and lives of the individual worker; and some might also or only want to consider the effect on the economy as a whole. Even those who want to consider all these things may disagree as to the relative priority to be assigned to each. But arguments over these various issues are not available in our libertarian utopia, for the following two reasons.

First, to the extent these arguments depend on which particular conception of the good one adopts – and they almost always will – they are not available because the dominant protective association must remain neutral between competing controversial conceptions of the good. These conceptions vary way too much from person to person for a protective association to become dominant if it is to embrace anything other than a very thin theory of the good – a conception of the good that is useful in the pursuit of a wide range of thicker, more comprehensive conceptions.[32] And while some people do think, against the overwhelming weight of the evidence, that the bad effects of unionization outweigh the good effects, even these people should be willing to concede that their view is not so uncontroversial as to no longer be subject to reasonable challenge and therefore something that can be assumed to fall within a thin theory of the good. If anything, the view that the good effects of unionization overwhelmingly outweigh the bad is the far less controversial position. Rather than rely on this to make my argument here, however, I will simply assume that whether the good effects of unionization outweigh the bad or the other way around, neither argument is uncontroversial enough to be made part of our thin theory of the good. This means that neither consequentialist argument can be the basis of a decision by the dominant protective association to justify either its support for or suppression of unionization. The dominant protective association's attitude toward unionization is going to have to be determined on some other basis.

Second, consequentialist arguments are not available because in a libertarian utopia (if not also out in the real world), rights always take precedence over consequentialist considerations, at least until these consequentialist considerations

1.2 The Rise of Unions

become overwhelming.[33] Once again, the rights most libertarians recognize as being involved here are the right to freedom of association and the right to freedom of contract, and it seems unlikely that the formation of unions could be a violation of either of these rights. Unions are associations, so it seems hard to see how the formation of such an association, at least if membership is noncompulsory, could be a violation of the right to freedom of association, and few people today try to argue that it could.[34] And the only way the right to freedom of contract could be implicated is if each worker's contract of employment prohibited the employee from joining a union.

Of course, this is a possibility. It may seem fanciful to suggest that employers might insist on contracts prohibiting their employees from forming a union, when in fact, there is a long history of the use of such contracts. Called "yellow dog contracts," these were upheld by the Supreme Court in *Hitchman Coal & Coke Company v. Mitchell*, 245 U.S. 229 (1917) and were extremely common in the United States until they were made unlawful in the private sector in 1932 by Section 3 of the Norris–LaGuardia Act.[35] They remained common in the public sector, however, until the 1960s.[36] So clearly such clauses will be "on the table" in our libertarian utopia and what to do about them (if anything) up for evaluation by the dominant protective association. The question, then, is whether *banning* yellow dog contracts or *enforcing* them is more consistent with libertarian values.

The conflict here, of course, is a classic one within libertarianism: does libertarianism, a view committed to protecting the liberty of all members of society, permit members from signing their liberty away? Clearly, it must in some cases, for there are lots of things people agree not to do once they sign a contract to do something else, or in a certain way, and nobody has a problem enforcing these kinds of contracts. And while contracts for slavery are a clear exception for many (but not all) libertarians,[37] one could distinguish contracts for slavery from yellow dog contracts on the grounds that whatever libertarianism allows, it does not allow someone to alienate their freedom in its entirety on an ongoing and permanent basis, for this kind of "suicide of the autonomous self" removes the whole basis for the existence of libertarianism. But many libertarians who object to slavery object not only to slavery but also to anything that is "tantamount" to slavery, into which category they may place any number of things, including, most prominently, taxation, for taxation effectively means you spend part of your time laboring against your will for someone else. For these libertarians, little argument should be required to convince them that yellow dog contracts should also be prohibited on this basis. But I do not wish to rely on such an extreme position. Rather, if my argument here is going to generalize, it would be best to assume that yellow dog contracts are not even close to contracts for slavery, and in this case, it is unlikely that the antislavery argument could do much work here, even if it were a more consistent position among libertarians.

The first issue we must consider is whether yellow dog contracts are voluntary enough, or voluntary in the right way, such that these contracts cannot be overturned on the grounds they are the product of coercion, which is always impermissible in a libertarian utopia (except as a punishment for rights violations). Of course, they might be held coercive in particular cases based on the individual circumstances presented. What we are looking for here is not a test we can apply to particular cases, but whether we can say that yellow dog contracts are coercive either intrinsically or as a practical matter on so many occasions that they should be banned outright without the need for an investigation into the particular circumstances of each one. For example, one of the arguments against contracts for slavery is that slavery is such an imposition on the basic nature of freedom – something that everyone in a libertarian society is irrefutably presumed to value – that it could only be agreed to by someone who is not acting rationally or who is under the kind of pressure that we should never allow to fall within the confines of what we consider to be a voluntary agreement.[38] Similarly, we could assume that employers would not seek yellow dog provisions in their offers of employment unless they thought that employees would otherwise seek to unionize, which would reduce the amount of surplus value that the employer could appropriate and otherwise be disadvantageous for the firm's management and owners. If employers do seek yellow dog contracts in our libertarian utopia, then we can also safely assume that many employees would want to unionize in our libertarian utopia, as the history of the real world suggests they would. In such circumstances, as is the case with supposedly "voluntary" contracts for enslavement, one could argue that a worker's willingness to sign away the right to join a union by entering into a yellow dog contract is likely to be the product of irrationality or coercion. Irrationality because no one would ever voluntarily agree to something which they believed would lessen their wages and benefits, and coercive because one must have work to survive, and survival has priority over association for most people. Therefore, we could reasonably conclude that the combination of the need to work and the lack of work that did not prohibit unionization makes the agreement to a yellow dog provision inherently coercive.

While this may be true for many people, however, it would clearly not be true for everybody. It is undeniable that some people would rather not be members of a union, regardless of the benefits, simply because they do not want to be required to join something. Or they may see unionization as carrying certain detriments as well as benefits, and find avoiding the detriments more motivating. Or finally, they may object to some other policy that the union is inclined to favor, other than increased wages and benefits, and be willing to sacrifice some economic benefits to avoid being a party to this. So it seems that while the argument that "yellow dog contracts are either inherently coercive or necessarily irrational from the employee's perspective" has some persuasive power, it is ultimately not sufficiently compelling.

But perhaps we can do better by turning the argument around. Just as it is true that some people will not want to join unions no matter what, many people would want to join if given the opportunity to do so. If only some employers demand yellow dog contracts, workers who want to be a member of a union could simply find work elsewhere. They would have a reasonable alternative to working for a firm where they could not join a union, so their right to association would not be totally frustrated. And the availability of reasonable alternatives is considered a key factor in determining whether something is improperly coercive in a wide variety of other circumstances.[39] Something very much like this test is even endorsed by Nozick himself.[40] Applying this qualification to the present situation, then, there might be an argument that were union and nonunion work both readily available, yellow dog contracts should be permitted, for those who want to join a union could still find work. But if *all* employers require employees to sign yellow dog contracts, then there would be no reasonable alternative available for those who wish to work but also want to exercise their right of free association and join a union. Their right to freely associate with other employees in this way would be totally frustrated, and this would accordingly constitute the kind of coercion that the dominant protective association would be required to prohibit. The issue, then, is whether we could expect some employers to require such agreements but not all, leaving enough opportunities for employees who wanted to join a union to find a firm that allowed them to do so, rather than leaving them with no option but to take nonunion work.

The problem is it does not seem possible to ensure this happy medium. If left to their own devices, the vast majority of employers in our libertarian utopia would demand yellow dog contracts, and all employers in certain industries (for example, large manufacturing operations) that are easier to unionize would certainly do so – the history of the labor movement makes this abundantly clear (that's why legislative action was required to outlaw such contracts). Indeed, despite the ban on yellow dog contracts out in the real world, some nonunionized companies seem to be trying to accomplish the same thing today by calling these contracts "confidentiality agreements," prohibiting employees from speaking out "about wages or working conditions," not mentioning unionizing activities expressly, and hoping that these agreements will at least have an *in terrorem* effect (and they do).[41] The natural attractiveness to employers of yellow dog contracts and their equivalents is clear – some intervention on the part of the dominant protective association will be required to ensure that a mix of employment opportunities with and without what are in effect yellow dog provisions exist in each industry.

But how are employers to be allocated to one category or the other? Employers have a right to be treated equally even in libertarian society, and it seems unlikely that substantive criteria could be found that would produce the necessary allocation without treating similarly situated employers differently. Even if a lottery were used to ensure that similarly situated employers all would have an equal chance of bearing the burden of allowing unionization, and this was held to satisfy the demands of equality,[42] those who won the lottery and could then prohibit unionization would enjoy a competitive advantage and eventually drive those who could not out of business, so only those employers who could demand such contracts would remain. In other words, there is no way to ensure that only some employers prohibit unionization, while others do not. Which means that there is a strong argument that banning such contracts in their entirety is the only way to protect the libertarian value of free association.

But what about those employees who did not want to join the union? Is not their right to freedom of association being violated now? Later, I shall argue in some detail that the right to free association does not imply a right to remain unassociated as well, but for now, I need only point out that banning yellow dog contracts does not require anyone to join a union. It just makes that option available for those employees who want to do so. And of course, even if some particular set of employees are required to join a particular union because there is a union shop agreement in place, employees who are so inclined are still free to form or join an association that lobbies against the existence of unions, collective bargaining, or any of the other policies and practices that unions promote. Employees' freedom of association is therefore unaffected in this way. Of course, banning yellow dog contracts does prevent employers from contracting on terms they would prefer. But they have no right to use economic coercion to obtain these terms when no reasonable alternatives are available to those who both want to work and join a union, so banning yellow dog contracts does not interfere with an employer's freedom to contract either. And an employer's freedom to associate does not give that employer the right to interfere with the freedom to associate of anyone else. Banning rather than enforcing such contracts is accordingly the position that is most consistent with the values that are supposed to be protected in our libertarian utopia. Banning them infringes no one's rights, and it protects the rights of everyone else.

Nevertheless, despite concluding that the dominant protective association could and must ban yellow dog contracts for the above reasons, let us assume for purposes of argument that employers could legitimately require their employees to waive their right to join a union as a condition of employment. What would happen then? Well, we have a hundred years of labor history that suggests that some employees would attempt to join unions anyway given the benefits that unionization provides. Also, even if the dominant protective association did try to punish these people and otherwise enforce yellow dog contracts and suppress the formation of unions, as non-libertarian governments did for many, many years, these attempts at suppression would ultimately fail. Eventually, unions would form despite the contractual prohibitions contained in yellow dog contracts, and enough employees would violate their contracts and join these unions that the unions would have sufficient bargaining power to force employers to waive their right to enforce the anti-union provisions of existing labor contracts and leave these out of future ones. Joining a union would then cease to be a contractual violation, and unions would then thereafter be able to openly recruit members and thrive.

Some people to whom I have made this argument, however, feel there is something morally troubling about allowing one party to a contract to use subsequently gained economic bargaining power to force a modification to an existing contract. But remember, this happens in the real world every day. One party to a contract often seeks *and obtains* a modification of a contract by impliedly or even expressly threatening not to perform their preexisting contractual obligations – and those modifications are nevertheless routinely recognized as valid. The only exception is when the modification is obtained by unlawful coercion, which requires the threat or use of physical violence – economic coercion is usually not enough.[43] At least there is no case on record where the subsequent unionization of a workforce, despite the existence of yellow dog contracts with existing employees, was found to constitute the kind of economic coercion sufficient to deny enforcement of the improved terms subsequently negotiated by the union. It would be odd indeed if employees could legitimately be economically coerced to initially waive their right to join a union in our libertarian utopia, as they largely would be in a world where yellow dog contracts were common, and there would be nothing wrong with *that*, yet there would be something wrong with employers being subsequently economically coerced to waive *their* right to enforce these waivers. The degree of economic coercion on display here is no greater or lesser in either direction, and so there should be nothing to be troubled about, at least as long as the terms negotiated by the union were not substantively unreasonable.[44] And the chances of this are slim – indeed, it is much more likely that the *original* terms of employment were the unreasonable ones, and fairly dramatically so, for only then would the workforce have been willing to form a union, despite the provisions of their yellow dog contracts, and risk being fired. Which means that notwithstanding the initial widespread use of yellow dog contracts, employers would eventually agree to waive their right to enforce these contracts, and the dominant protective association would have no right or reason to try to restrict union activity any further as long as there were not some other grounds for arguing that the dominant protective association was still obligated to do so.

The only grounds for such an argument in our libertarian utopia would be that unionization is an anticompetitive practice and anticompetitive practices are something the association is committed to suppress, even if these practices would otherwise be legitimate exercises of freedom of association or freedom of contract. Before I discuss this particular argument, however, I should mention that not all libertarians agree that the suppression of anticompetitive behavior is one of the jobs the dominant protective association should undertake. Nozick, for example, does not specifically mention suppressing anticompetitive behavior as one of the jobs of the minimal state. He makes it clear elsewhere, however, that he thinks anticompetitive behavior is a form of improper coercion, and that wherever such coercion exists the dominant protective association should police it.[45] And it is hard to see how one can believe that government should leave most things to the workings of the free market without believing that one of the jobs of government is to ensure that the market remains free, which means uncorrupted by anticompetitive behavior as well as fraud, theft, and violence. In any event, many prominent libertarians do expressly make the suppression of anticompetitive behavior one of the jobs of the minimal state.[46] True, some of these libertarians have been criticized for being "hybrid" or "consequentialist" libertarians rather than "pure" or "deontological" libertarians because they connect competition to liberty via a consequentialist argument. While some of the latter still argue that preventing anticompetitive behavior is a legitimate job of the minimal state, others argue that this cannot be squared with a pure deontological libertarian outlook.[47] Elsewhere, I have argued that there is indeed a deontological as well as a consequentialist connection between liberty and free market competition.[48] But I will not repeat this argument here, primarily because nothing in this essay turns on a resolution of this issue. If the suppression of anticompetitive behavior is *not* a proper occupation for the minimal state in our libertarian utopia, no matter what the reason, then this would merely make my argument in this essay stronger, not weaker, because it would remove one more possible objection to unionization – that it is an act of monopolization – not provide one. I therefore do not need to prove that the dominant protective association can suppress anticompetitive behavior for my argument to move forward; I merely need to prove that if it can, this does not justify the suppression of unionization.

Assuming then that one of the jobs of the minimal state is to suppress anticompetitive behavior, price-fixing cartels composed of all the firms in a particular industry, to cite just one example, would be something the dominant protective association would be committed to suppress, even though they may be voluntary associations formed by agreement. And the view that unionization is a similarly anticompetitive practice in some or even all of its manifestations has been an irrepressible one out in the real world, notwithstanding the fact that the legislature and the courts have repeatedly made it clear that the antitrust laws are not to be used to suppress union activity.[49] While the presence of these repeated legislative and judicial exemptions of union activity from the reach of the antitrust laws has rendered continuing real-world objections to unionization on the grounds that it is an anticompetitive practice largely pointless (even though those on the anti-union right keep hoping), there would be no such exemptions in our libertarian utopia. For the purposes of the exercise that we are conducting here, it is accordingly important for us to consider whether the anticompetitive aspects of unionization are such as to render associations of individual laborers a violation of the rights of the consumers of that labor and something that the dominant protective association would therefore be required to suppress.

1.2 The Rise of Unions

The view that unionization is an anticompetitive practice is easy to understand. Just as an agreement between various suppliers of a product to not sell that product below a certain price would be anticompetitive and constitute an unlawful restraint on trade, an agreement among individual suppliers of labor to sell their labor only at a certain price would seem to be so as well.[50] Even the authors of one of the leading pro-union works of the twentieth century accept that unions are monopolistic, although they argue that the positive effects of unionization outweigh the negative effect of their monopoly power.[51] Libertarians, however, would not tolerate such consequentialist balancing, and so libertarians who considered unions to be monopolistic would have to see them as something that should be banned.[52] But not all libertarians would agree that unions are properly viewed as monopolistic. Both Ludwig von Mises and Murray Rothbard, for example, argue that unionization is *not* an act of monopolization and that union wages are not monopoly wages because while they increase the price of labor, they do not result in the potential supply of labor being reduced.[53] Accordingly, at least some libertarians would see no violation of the right not to be subjected to anticompetitive actions in unionization.

But there is a further response to those that do because the claim that unions are monopolistic has other serious defects as well. The two cases (fixing the prices of a product and fixing the prices of the labor used to produce that product) are not as similar as they superficially seem. Economists have long distinguished between the labor market and the product market (for these purposes, the product market includes both finished goods and services but not the labor utilized to produce those finished goods or services), and it is not at all clear that the idea of a "free market" in labor is coherent. The reason that there can be no such thing as a perfectly competitive labor market, however, is not because in real life all markets are imperfect, but because in the ideal circumstances imagined in the description of a perfectly competitive market (an infinite number of agents, no barriers to entry or exit, perfect factor mobility, perfect information, and no transactions costs), multi-person firms would not exist. Proprietors would simply hire labor as needed on an independent contractor basis, for there would be no transaction costs to save by doing otherwise. There would still be a product market in such ideal circumstances, but there would be no employment relationships or firms and therefore no need for unions.[54] And if there cannot be such a thing as a perfectly competitive labor market, then it is hard to see what those who are trying to prevent workers from joining unions are trying to accomplish. Preventing workers from joining unions in the less than ideal circumstances of the real world does not make the market more competitive. This simply makes the imperfect conditions that are already present work to the advantage of only one party – the employer, thereby reducing overall freedom rather than increasing it.

Selling a thing in even an imperfectly competitive market is also not the same as selling labor. A thing has no right to liberty – indeed it has no rights at all – and the fundamental presupposition of libertarianism and indeed any political viewpoint that values liberty is that a human being is entitled to be treated differently than a thing. Things can be owned by other people, but no one can own another human being. Humans are self-owners, and ever since Locke, most libertarians believe that self-ownership implies ownership of one's labor; one person therefore cannot be the owner of the labor of anybody else.[55] Things, in contrast, are not connected to particular people in this way. They can simultaneously have many owners or be transferred from one owner to another over and over again, and sometimes they may even have no owner at all. Things can accordingly be property, while labor cannot be property, for if it could, it could be owned by someone else. Indeed, this is the whole point of the concept of property – it can be transferred from one person to another, and this attribute of property is what gives the market a reason to exist. When one talks about the free market and ensuring that the market is not corrupted by anticompetitive behavior, it is the product market that one should have in mind. To establish a free market in labor would mean we would have to disconnect labor from the person, for the idea of there being a connection is an anticompetitive limitation on free transferability too. Also, there would be no intellectually consistent way to prohibit this disconnection but otherwise treat labor as if it were simply another form of property, for people have the freedom to associate and things do not. While the sellers of products have the freedom to associate, and this freedom can still be restrained if it violates the rights of others, say by creating an anticompetitive cartel, workers are not merely the sellers of labor but are the sellers of their own labor in a way that sellers of their own products are not. There is an equivocation here in the idea of something being one's "own": the seller of one's own labor is the embodiment of that labor as well, something the seller of a product is not. So the analogy of the labor market to the product market is weak – it provides no good reason why we should treat the former like the latter for purposes of determining what constitutes anticompetitive behavior.

The two markets are also different in another important way. The product market is almost never monopsonistic, but the labor market often is, or at least oligopsonistic.[56] That is, there are typically many potential buyers in the product market. In the labor market, however, there is sometimes only one and often only a few, at least for particular kinds of labor in particular geographic areas, especially the kinds of labor provided by those most likely to want to organize themselves into unions. Labor is also not as mobile as products are. Products can be manufactured in one place and sold in another relatively easily, but people can usually only sell their labor where they are based. Relocation is expensive, and housing is often (not surprisingly) more expensive and less plentiful where jobs pay more and are more plentiful.[57] But more importantly, people, unlike products, have roots. They have emotional,

1.2 *The Rise of Unions*   39

familial, and cultural ties to their communities and corresponding moral and legal duties to others in their community that are entitled to be treated with respect. Accordingly, people cannot reasonably be expected to and therefore should not be penalized for being unable or unwilling to move themselves and their families to some other geographic area where jobs may be more plentiful or pay more or provide better working conditions, especially if this means abandoning a profession out of which one has created an identity and adopting a profession that requires transforming what one identifies as into something else.[58] "The idea that people should be endlessly malleable and ready to recreate themselves to accommodate every change in the job market is probably not realistic and certainly not respectful of existing skills."[59]

In contrast, there are no such concerns that would apply when there are changes in the product market. Products can be shipped to wherever there are buyers. If consumers are dissatisfied with some aspect of a particular product, producers can simply change it, or can switch to producing a different kind of product altogether. There may be transaction costs to such adaptation, of course, but usually not the deep social and personal costs of adapting to changes in employment. And every instantiation of a product does not usually have to be sold for its producer to survive. Labor, however, often does, for most people cannot afford to be without a full-time job, at least for long, and therefore have far more limited bargaining power than their employer in a market where alternative suppliers of that labor are plentiful. The monopsonistic/oligopsonistic nature of the labor market gives employers the ability to exploit labor in the sense that it enables them to purchase labor for less than these employers would have to pay if these conditions imposing limits on the free movement of labor did not exist. Rather than being anticompetitive entities that raise the price of labor above the perfectly competitive price, unions act as a way of counteracting the anticompetitive power that monopsony and oligopsony provides to the employer. Unions indeed raise the price of labor; in this case, though, the increased price is not an anticompetitive effect that needs to be prohibited but a cure for an anticompetitive effect that would otherwise occur.[60]

I should note, I suppose, that for a long time many economists simply dismissed the idea that there might be monopsony or oligopsony in the labor market, claiming that such a possibility was unworthy of being taken seriously (clearly a great many economists never had to work blue-collar jobs and simply cannot get their heads around the fact that in the real world there are limitations on the mobility of human labor that should not be treated as market defects).[61] This has been changing recently, however, and the problem of monopsony power in the labor market is now being more widely discussed and even beginning to be accepted.[62] And this was before more and more employers began formalizing their monopsonistic power by requiring more and more employees to sign "noncompete agreements"; that is, agreements that purport to prevent the employee from taking up a similar kind of work for some significant period of time (often five years) in a specified and sometimes very large geographic area.[63] Indeed, "once reserved for a corporations most treasured rainmakers, noncompetes are now routinely applied to low-wage workers like warehouse employees, fast-food workers and even dog sitters."[64] These agreements not only make it more difficult and sometimes impossible for workers to change jobs, they also suppress wages for everybody.[65]

As a result, there is substantial reason to question whether such agreements would be permitted in our libertarian utopia given their anticompetitive effect. But they might be. The argument for enforcement of such agreements is that they prevent employees who leave or are dismissed from subsequently using allegedly "proprietary" knowledge gained through their employment to "unfairly" compete against their former employer. This argument has so far prevailed in many states out in the real world where the same standards supposedly apply for determining whether an agreement is an impermissible restraint on trade.[66] If enforceable, these agreements would clearly exacerbate the monopsony power of employers in our libertarian utopia.[67] The same effect can also be created or exacerbated by the growing trend of including provisions in employment contracts that require the employee to make a substantial cash payment to the employer if the employee leaves before the contract term ends.[68] But even if these agreements were not enforceable, there is still reason to believe employers in our libertarian utopia would hold a troubling amount of monopsony power. After all, noncompete agreements and early termination penalties are a relatively new phenomena out in the real world. Even though the precise extent of employers' monopsonistic power has always been difficult to measure, a wide range of phenomena in the labor market from before the use of these agreements became more common can be explained only if significant monopsonistic power among employers is assumed.[69]

Nevertheless, some economists counter that unions have no incentive to limit their demands to what is necessary to offset the anticompetitive advantage that employers would otherwise enjoy, and because they cannot be counted on not to abuse the power that collective bargaining delivers to them, unionization can still be monopolistic.[70] But unions do indeed have an incentive not to make abusive demands. While there is no downside for a rational employer to try to depress his unorganized workers' wages as low as they will go, there is a limit on what organized workers can rationally demand. If wages become so high that the employer cannot afford to stay in business, they will lose their jobs. And if the union's wage demands put one particular employer at a competitive disadvantage with another, those who work for the first employer will eventually lose their jobs too. So a well-run union has a great deal of incentive to be reasonable, and at least it has more incentive to be reasonable than an employer does when dealing with unorganized workers. Indeed, arguing that the threat of irrational unions is greater than the threat of rational employers is itself irrational. There is accordingly no reason to believe that anyone's rights against anticompetitive behavior would be violated by the rise of unions. And this means the dominant protective association has no reason to intervene to prevent the formation of unions. On the contrary, the formation of unions is something that the dominant protective association should be committed to protect.[71]

Finally, even if unions are in some way anticompetitive, they are no more anticompetitive than firms. Indeed, if we are to take advantage of the technological innovation of the division of labor, and the whole idea of our libertarian utopia is that even in such a utopia we can – the very existence of the dominant protective association is built upon this idea – there are going to have to be firms and therefore employment relationships. Also, if there are going to be firms and the employment relationships that come with them, workers are going to want to form unions. If the existence of firms is not anticompetitive and therefore something the dominant protective association would be required to suppress – that is, if the dominant protective association is not to be required to suppress itself – then the existence of unions cannot be considered anticompetitive either, or at least not anticompetitive in a way that makes the suppression of unions something the dominant protective association would be required to do in order to protect the rights of others. As far as suppressing anticompetitive behavior goes, firms and unions rise and fall together. Both are the products of agreements to band together to conduct certain business activities collectively in search of greater profits, both result in the withdrawal of certain resources from allocation by the price mechanism, and both result in an increase in prices of the factors of production under each particular association's control. Either they both exist, or neither do.[72] In other words, both may be a restraint on trade, but neither is an *unreasonable* restraint on trade, and the latter not the former is the appropriate test.[73] And since we have already concluded that the dominant protective association is not going to find the formation of firms an unreasonable restraint on trade, accepting the existence of firms entails accepting the existence of unions too.

This is not to say that unions are incapable of violating the antitrust laws or engaging in unreasonably anticompetitive behavior. Some kinds of agreements negotiated between a union and an employer might amount to a secondary boycott, for example, or other forms of anticompetitive collusion that should indeed be banned by the dominant protective association.[74] It may also be prudent to insist that no single union represent all workers in any industry – competition between unions here is useful for the same reasons as competition among firms useful, and union concentration (the number of workers represented by each union in a particular industry) should not be permitted to become so high that workers in a particular industry have no meaningful choice as to whom they choose to represent them, for then the union would lose some of its incentive to provide high-quality services to its members.[75] But this does not mean that the union as an organization or the general idea of collective bargaining is anticompetitive in the sense that it is something the dominant protective association must prohibit. If a union does violate the rights of others by engaging in anticompetitive collusion with an employer in some way that has a direct impact on third parties, then this is something the dominant protective association can prohibit. But the formation of the union or the normal results of its collective bargaining efforts to set prices, benefits, and working conditions for those who work for a particular employer are not something that is within the dominant protective association's remit to prohibit.

1.3 THE PUBLIC SECTOR

What about unions in the public sector? These are unions formed within the dominant protective association itself, for that is the equivalent of the public sector in our libertarian utopia. The incentives to form unions here would be the same as in the private sector, and history tells us that just like their private sector brothers and sisters, public sector workers would indeed attempt to form unions.[76] Unions would therefore tend to arise in our libertarian utopia even in the public sector, unless there was some reason why this would constitute a violation of someone's rights or otherwise constitute something the dominant protective association was committed or at least entitled to prohibit, even though it was not entitled to interfere with the formation of unions in the private sector. In considering this question, then, we once again have to recognize almost all of the arguments both contemporary and historical about the legitimacy of public sector unions are about whether the existence of such unions has good or bad effects. But once again, these arguments are all welfarist arguments – they are highly contentious consequentialist arguments about what most furthers the common good, in whatever way the common good happens to be defined. These arguments are accordingly ruled out as too controversial to be a basis for government action by libertarianism itself, for otherwise a dominant protective association could not arise and we could never have a libertarian state that formed without violating anybody's rights. Public sector workers must be allowed to organize, and such organizing activity must be affirmatively protected by the dominant protective association, even in our libertarian utopia, regardless of whether public sector unions are good for people generally or whether unions are good for public sector workers themselves or not. The only issue is whether such activity might infringe on someone else's rights.

I have several arguments to deploy here in support of the idea that public sector unions *are* something workers have a right to form and that this right must be protected even in our libertarian utopian state. The first relates to the argument about the scope of the bounds of permissible government activity within the libertarian utopian state. I believe these bounds are very big, but let's assume for the moment that they are very small, as many people who consider themselves libertarians contend. To the extent those bounds are broken – meaning the dominant protective association starts engaging in functions

1.3 The Public Sector

in which it should not be engaged because these functions are not properly within the remit of the minimal state – then unions in these areas are just like private sector unions and therefore have the same rights to form and exist as private sector unions. In other words, those who argue that certain functions currently performed by contemporary government in the liberal capitalist state should be performed only by the private sector cannot oppose the formation of unions in these areas because if these functions were performed by the private sector, then the relevant workers would indeed be allowed to unionize. In any event, we need not worry that government is exceeding the bounds of its legitimate authority in our libertarian utopia because for purposes of our hypothetical thought experiment, we can simply stipulate that government is appropriately sized whatever size this happens to be. In other words, we can assume there are no functions that the dominant protective association performs in our libertarian utopia that should be performed by the private sector instead. The issue in our hypothetical is whether workers may form unions within the dominant protective association itself with regard to functions that are entirely appropriate for the dominant protective association to perform.

Well, the default libertarian response would seem to be "why not?" Indeed, because controversial consequentialist arguments cannot be made here, it is hard to see how the suppression of unionization could be thought consistent with the dominant protective association's obligation to protect the rights of its members, even if consequentialist arguments could otherwise be used to overcome people's rights. I know of no one who suggests that people automatically lose their right to freedom of association simply by becoming public employees. But perhaps the thought here is that while the dominant protective association would permit the formation of unions by private employees, it would not want to allow unions to form when it comes to its own employees and therefore would request that all hires waive their right to unionize as a condition of their offer of employment. It would effectively insist on making all its employees sign yellow dog contracts. Because those who do not want to sign these yellow dog contracts could find employment in the private sector, where we have already concluded that such contracts would be banned, these contracts would at least arguably be permissible in the public sector. Nevertheless, to come to the view that it should insist on yellow dog provisions in its employees' contracts, the dominant protective association would have to conclude that it would be better off if its own employees are not represented by unions – it would have to *desire* to prohibit unionization within its ranks. But how is the dominant protective association to come to this conclusion? Where is this desire supposed to come from? Once again, to arrive at such a view, it would have to apply a controversial conception of the good, and this is ruled out for reasons I have already stated. Indeed, it would not only have to adopt a controversial conception of the good, it would also have to make some controversial factual assumptions in order to conclude that the existence of unions within its ranks violates that conception of the good, making such action doubly controversial.[77]

And remember, "controversial" does not just mean contrary to the wishes of the majority – the dominant protective association wouldn't be entitled to demand that its employees waive their right to unionize even if the majority of its members would approve of such action. The dominant protective association simply does not have the power to remove people's rights, only to enforce the ones they do have by nature or create by contract. If anything, requiring its employees to waive of their right to unionize as a condition of employment would seem to be a violation of its employees' rights to freedom of association itself, something that the dominant protective association is committed to prevent.

But once again, let's assume that it would not be a violation of anyone's rights to require them to waive their right to unionize as a condition of employment and therefore the dominant protective association could demand such waivers if it wanted to. Let's further assume that it did want to because it wanted to minimize taxes, and preventing its own employees from unionizing would keep salaries lower and therefore reduce the cost of its services and lower taxes (in our libertarian utopia, the dues that subscribers are required to pay to the dominant protective association). Indeed, one recent study suggests that public and private employees earn equivalent amounts of total compensation (wages plus benefits) when public employees are unionized, but when they are not represented by unions, public employees earn 10 percent less on average than their private sector counterparts.[78] Minimizing expenses seems to be something that might be within a thin theory of the good, so it might not be too controversial a motivation for the dominant protective association to embrace. Of course, once a particular protective association becomes dominant, this incentive would be fairly weak, for the association would not have to worry about competitors arising and trying to challenge its role as the dominant association, but such a motivation might still exist in any case. So let us assume that the dominant protective association could permissibly ask its employees to waive their right to unionize as a condition of employment and that a legitimate motivation was available that might lead it to decide to do so.

How could it enforce this decision? While the dominant protective association might be able to eliminate the right of its employees to unionize by requiring its employees to sign yellow dog contracts, just as employers in the private sector would do, this would not change the fact that its employees would still have an *incentive* to unionize. Just as unions would arise in the private sector, there is accordingly every reason to believe that employees would attempt to form unions in the public sector too.[79] Like their privately employed brethren before them, public employees might initially have to engage in union activity in secret, but once these efforts were successful, they could present the dominant protective association with a demand that the association agree to modify their existing employment agreements and recognize their union as a *fait accompli* under threat of strike, just as would be the case in the private sector in firms that initially required their employees to sign yellow dog contracts.

1.4 The Problem of Independents

And even if the dominant protective association were to make strikes by public sector workers illegal, at some point, when employees become desperate enough due to financial deprivation, strikes would still occur, as the recent strike by West Virginia teachers helpfully illustrates.[80] The threat of strike is therefore something the dominant protective association in its capacity as an employer would have to take seriously, for a strike that included enough of the dominant protective association's existing employees would threaten the continued existence of the dominant protective association itself, or at least its continued dominance. We have more than a hundred years of labor history that supports the idea that this is exactly what public employees would do in the face of a ban on unionization and that they would eventually be successful. The association would then have to decide whether to enforce the ban on union activity in the contracts their employees had already signed or renegotiate this term. And while the association could attempt to fire those employees who had violated the ban and formed a union, the whole idea of forming a union is to give the employees greater bargaining power, enough bargaining power to get the employer to agree to things to which it would not otherwise agree. Regardless of the existence of any prior waiver of a right to unionize in its employees' contracts, once enough employees were prepared to join the union anyway, the dominant protective association would – just like any other employer – eventually have to agree to waive enforcement of this ban and recognize the union or face a potentially crippling loss of employees. And just as in the private sector, if the economic coercion that forced employees to agree to waive their right to unionize in the first place were not a violation of libertarian rights, then the economic coercion that leads the dominant protective association to waive enforcement of these waivers would not be either. Which means that even if the dominant protective association were entitled to require its employees to waive their right to unionize as a condition of employment and this waiver were enforceable, unions formed by employees within its ranks would still arise and once large enough to wield sufficient bargaining power would have to be recognized by the dominant protective association.[81]

1.4 THE PROBLEM OF INDEPENDENTS

The next question is how are we to deal with independents? Some employees would no doubt recognize that they could free ride on the union's efforts once the union reached sufficient size to have real influence in negotiations and therefore would be tempted not to join out of sheer self-interest. Why pay unions dues and subject oneself to union discipline, if one can get all the benefits of union membership without joining? And even if an employer were not legally required to provide the same salary and benefits to both union and nonunion employees in our libertarian utopia, something they *are* required to do by nondiscrimination rules out in the real world, employers would have incentives to be sure this was the case to keep the number of union members down. Some employees might also refuse to join because they had a prior bad experience with a union, which would no doubt be the case for some people if union membership were large enough. After all, sometimes unions will fail to stand up when they should, or even worse, get people all riled up and then fail to the deliver the goods, thereby alienating a portion of their members and leading some to no longer want anything to do with that union or any other. And some people of course would refuse to join out of sheer bloody-mindedness. Would the union nevertheless be able to compel those who preferred to remain independents to join and pay dues, compensating them by providing them with union services, or would this be a violation of their rights? In other words, are right-to-work laws consistent with libertarianism, as they are often argued to be? Or are union shop rules, the kind of rules that right-to-work laws are designed to overcome, the ones that we might expect to find in our libertarian utopia?

The way the right-to-work versus union shop issue is typically argued is as an instantiation of the right of freedom of association.[82] This right implies not only a right to associate when one wants to, it is claimed, but the right to *not* associate when one does not want to. Therefore, union shop rules are said to be improper because they violate the right of third parties (those who are not yet employees or members of the union at the time the agreement is made and therefore have not effectively consented to it through the collective bargaining process) to choose to not become union members if they are hired.[83] But I do not think this is the appropriate way to analyze this issue. Remember, in justifying the rise of the dominant protective association itself, Nozick deals with the problem of independents. He argues that the dominant protective association could compel independents to join because the association has the right to prevent risky behavior, and being an independent is risky behavior, for it exposes those who are members of the association to the possibility of rogue acts of enforcement or retaliation by independents who might erroneously perceive themselves as victims of violations of their rights and do not recognize the dominant protective association's ruling on the scope of everyone's rights as authoritative. Of course, merely because being an independent is risky behavior does not mean that any particular independent would have actually committed a violation or caused any damage. To compensate independents who are compelled to join for the possibility that they would not actually have violated the dominant protective association's monopoly on the enforcement of rights, Nozick argues, these independents have to be provided with protective services by the association just like those who joined voluntarily.[84]

Note importantly that Nozick did *not* argue that the mere fact that independents could be free riders on the efforts of the dominant protective association would justify compelling them to join and pay dues. On the contrary, he vigorously denied that the mere conferral of a benefit on those who did not ask for it, but cannot be excluded from receiving it, is grounds for forcing them to pay for it.[85] And while one might argue that Nozick was wrong about preventing

1.4 *The Problem of Independents*

free riding not being a sufficient justification to compel independents to join and pay dues in a libertarian utopia, I don't think he was, so I do not want to argue otherwise. If I am wrong about this, of course, it only makes my argument stronger, but the argument on which I want to rely is the one Nozick articulates that "not joining" is risky behavior, not that it amounts to free riding. It is on that basis that he concludes that independents could be compelled to join and pay dues without violating their rights, resulting in everybody in our libertarian utopia being both a member of the dominant protective association and protected by it.

I should note at this point, however, that some theorists (Eric Mack, in particular, but perhaps others as well) suggest that according to Nozick, independents must be provided protective services free of charge.[86] Nozick's discussion of this point is not a model of clarity, but I nevertheless think this is a misinterpretation of Nozick's view. What would being compelled to "join" the protective association (and thereby by analogy the minimal state) mean if one were not required to pay dues (or taxes, in the case of the minimal state)? True, one could be prohibited from taking "private justice," but one hardly needs to be a member of the protective association to be prohibited from doing that. Being a "member," whether this is the result of some sort of compulsion or not, means being able to take advantage of the services that the association provides to all members and having to render onto the association the same dues that other members have rendered on to it, and not just being prohibited from engaging in rogue behavior. True, Nozick also argues that providing services to independents who are compelled to join is required because this is how independents are compensated for the possibility that they might not have engaged in rogue behavior. But being provided services is not compensation if the independent has to pay for them. This, I suppose, is where Mack and those similarly inclined get the notion that protective services must be provided for free. Nozick, however, also states that independents must indeed pay for the costs of the services provided. The only exception he notes is that this payment may be subsidized by higher charges to other members of the association for particular independents who are unable to afford to pay their dues themselves.[87] But this is not equivalent to saying that services must be provided free of charge. In these cases, services are subsidized or provided free because the independent is unable to pay, not because services must be provided for free to all independents. Presumably, the same benefit would also be provided to those who voluntarily joined but found themselves at some point unable to pay. In any case, Nozick reasons that people cannot be left disadvantaged by being compelled to join (or not allowed to resign), and if they were not provided services when they could not pay but were still not allowed to engage in self-help, they would be disadvantaged. But those who can afford to pay are not being disadvantaged. After all, they would incur *greater* costs if they were to engage in enforcement activity on their own, for if this were not true no one would join the association in the first place. The cost savings (including both monetary and nonmonetary costs) available from the division of labor here is what drives the protective association to form. No one would join or remain in the association willingly if this were not true, for there is no reason to pay for something you can get at less cost (broadly defined to include time and effort and not merely monetary expense) by doing it for yourself, and the whole operation would fall apart.[88]

Whether I have correctly stated Nozick's argument – and if I have, whether this argument actually works – is irrelevant, however, for as I shall explain in a moment, I am not going to rely on this argument one way or the other to explain why independents have to pay for the services provided. For Nozick's arguments about this and various other associated claims have been highly criticized on several points, and with good reason. If engaging in risky behavior is a rights violation, then why is compensation from the dominant protective association required when the association suppresses that rights violation?[89] Normally, compensation is required only when a right is violated, and it is paid to the victim of the violation not the violator. Furthermore, rights in the Nozickian sense cannot conflict.[90] Risky behavior therefore cannot be a rights violation, and suppression of it be a rights violation too. And if suppression of risky behavior is not a rights violation, then where is the requirement supposed to come from that says independents who are forced to join the association must be compensated? And this is important, because unless we can explain why independents who are forced to join must be provided services, we cannot explain why those who refuse to voluntarily join the union can be forced to do so (meaning, forced to pay dues and submit to union discipline) in our libertarian utopia *and be provided services too*.

One way to approach this problem is to recognize that Nozick's argument is only partially correct. He is correct about being an independent constituting risky behavior and that risky behavior is a rights violation that can be prohibited and punished just like reckless driving, even if the reckless driver does not cause an accident or otherwise cause any injury or damage.[91] He is incorrect, however, that the mere fact a rights violation and resulting injury might not have occurred triggers a simultaneous need for compensation. For even if compensation is not required for the possibility that the risky behavior would have produced no actual injury, we can still justify providing protective services to independents who are forced to join the protective association in other ways. First, by submitting to the protective association and paying dues, even under threat, independents confer positive benefits on other members of the association and, for that matter, on the association itself. Because these benefits are being conferred involuntarily, they must be paid for by the association. And payment here is most naturally made in the form of protective services, just as it is for those who have voluntarily bargained for these services. In other words, the fact that independents are free riding is not being used to compel them to join and pay dues; they are being compelled to join and pay dues because "not joining" and not paying dues is risky behavior. But if they are compelled to join, free riding on their membership by *other*

1.4 The Problem of Independents

members of the association is not permissible; independents accordingly have to be provided protective services if they are compelled to join, otherwise they would be conferring benefits and paying for services they are not receiving. And while Nozick argues that one is not required to pay for benefits one did not ask to receive, he says nothing to suggest that one should not be compelled to pay for benefits one *did* ask to receive, which is effectively what the association has done in this case.[92] To deny the independents protective services would accordingly violate their rights. That is what justifies the provision of protective services to them, not the claim that their failure to join is both a rights violation and not a rights violation at the same time. If they could be compelled to join without conferring any benefits on others, then they would not be entitled to compensation in the form of protective services, but they cannot. So the former independents can be compelled to join, and once they do join, they are entitled to receive protective services too.[93]

There is another argument for providing independents protective services as well. If independents were not provided protective services, this would encourage voluntary members of the protective association to engage in acts or predation against them, for in this case, independents would be prohibited from retaliating and would not be able to enlist the protective association to vindicate their right or otherwise protect them. This kind of rights-violating behavior, even though committed against nonmembers, would nevertheless be destabilizing with regard to rights-respecting behavior within the dominant protective association's territory as a whole, for it would encourage the development of antisocial dispositions among members and create the risk of collateral injury to members on those occasions when independents' rights are violated. In other words, this would be another form of risky behavior that the association was entitled to prevent, and the most efficient way of preventing this would be to simply provide independents with protective services as well as preventing rogue behavior on their part, thereby removing the incentive for voluntary members to engage in predatory behavior against them at the start.

With regard to the case for compulsory union shops, the same reasoning would apply. Indeed, if not joining the dominant protective association is risky behavior, it is hard to see why not joining the union would not constitute risky behavior as well. If independents were protected by the union, then the employer would be free to engage in predatory acts of exploitation or discrimination against them. This would create a risk of collateral damage to union members and encourage the development of dispositions on the part of the employer that are antithetical to smooth labor-management relations between the employer and the union and its members. And if there were enough independents who refused to join and pay dues, the union will not only be deprived of necessary financial resources, it will also no longer wield sufficient bargaining power to accomplish its aims, for independents have not agreed to strike when the union strikes or work when the union says go back, and they might even demand that special arrangements be negotiated with them on an individual basis regardless of the terms to which the union agrees, thereby removing the benefits for both union members and the employer of bargaining with the union collectively. In this case, it is easy to see that the whole union association might come crashing down, frustrating completely the aims of its members.[94] And without a union, workers are at much greater risk of rights violations. It is true that individual employees could still seek the help of the dominant protective association's itself to enforce their rights, but the dominant protective association could not punish all rights violations: it simply would not have sufficient resources to do so. Anyone who doubts this need simply look back at the history of the treatment of labor in any country to see that this is correct – in the absence of unions, many violations of workers' rights go uninvestigated and unpunished, despite the technical availability of the elaborate enforcement mechanism of the state. Indeed, reducing the number of effectively irremediable rights violations is one of the primary reasons that unions exist. And even when individual workers do manage to defend their rights, they are often subject to retaliation, which is itself a rights violation but often very difficult and costly to prove.[95] The fear of such retaliation alone is often sufficient to deter many workers who are not protected by unions from attempting to enforce their rights.[96] Just as the existence of independents is risky behavior with regard to other members of the dominant protective association, the existence of independents is risky behavior with regard to the other members of the union. Ronald Dworkin, in fact, makes a similar argument in the course of explaining why people can be compelled to buy underemployment insurance through the hypothetical insurance market in the thought experiment he uses to explain why people can be taxed by the state to provide for a social minimum for those who would otherwise have insufficient funds to provide for their own subsistence.[97] There is a significantly and unacceptable increased risk of rights violations if people are not compelled to join in either case. Meaning that unions may indeed negotiate union shop agreements and compel all new hires and existing independents to join and pay the usual dues. And once they do, these independents must be provided services in return, just as the dominant protective association can and must do so with regard to those residing in its geographical area of dominance, the only difference being that "dominance" here is defined by employment status rather than by geographic residence.

Instead of analogizing unions to the dominant protective association, we can also defend the union shop rule by analogizing the structure of unions to the structure of firms themselves. Firms are just like union shops in the sense that one cannot be an employee of the firm without joining it. One can provide services to the firm as an outsider of course, what we would call an independent contractor. If you are an independent contractor, you need not submit to the direction of the firm as to how the task you are contracted to complete is performed (indeed, this is how being an independent contractor is in part defined). But if you do not submit, you cannot be an employee; therefore,

1.4 The Problem of Independents

you cannot get the benefits that those who do submit receive, benefits that most workers find desirable (otherwise no one would submit, and the firm would fall apart). In other words, one cannot be an independent *within* the firm. Either you join the firm and submit to its commands in return for payment and other benefits or you don't. You cannot obtain the benefits of being an insider without paying the price, which in this case is submission. If you do join the firm, you must be paid and receive the same benefits everyone else receives. So once again, if firms (which are simply groups of people organized for a particular economic purpose with an internal hierarchical structure) can be "firm shops" in our libertarian utopia, then unions (also groups of people organized for a particular economic purpose with an internal hierarchical structure) can be firm shops as well – that is, union shops. And if such unions negotiate union shop agreements with employers, there would be no reason why the dominant protective association in our libertarian utopia should not enforce them.

But there is yet another way to justify the compelling/compensation combination. This is to analogize it to Joel Feinberg's well-known mountain cabin hypothetical. In this hypothetical, a hiker who is trapped by an unexpected turn in the weather breaks into an empty mountain cabin to shelter from the storm and prevent his otherwise almost certain death. The prevailing view seems to be that the break-in itself is not a rights violation in these circumstances (the circumstances of necessity). Nevertheless, the hiker must pay compensation for any damage he causes and for the fair value of the shelter he temporarily obtains. Why he should have to pay compensation when there has been no rights violation is a matter of some dispute, but the most popular answer seems to arise out of a distinction first articulated by Judith Thomson between *violating* a right and *infringing* a right. Thomson argues that both infringements and violations are wrongful, but only violations could be enjoined and punished. Infringements merely give rise to a right to compensation. Feinberg himself adopts this distinction to explain why the hiker is justified in breaking into the mountain cabin but still owes compensation,[98] and many people since have accepted this distinction too.[99]

Nevertheless, I am reluctant to rely on the infringing/violating distinction for the proposition that those compelled to join the union must be provided services, for as I have argued extensively elsewhere, I do not believe the argument based on the infringing/violating distinction is sound. In my view, the distinction is meant to solve a problem that does not exist: the worry that a violation of right can always be enjoined. But rights violations cannot always be enjoined – in fact, they rarely can, for the standards for obtaining such relief are very strict. This means that creating a distinction between violations and infringements to ensure that injunctive relief is not available in certain circumstances is completely unnecessary. I have set forth this point in greater detail elsewhere,[100] and those who find it difficult to grasp can go further into it if they wish. But it is unnecessary to do so here because even if the infringing/violating distinction is sound, the argument based on this distinction is not an argument available to the libertarian. This is because it entails the proposition that rights are not absolute, and this is a proposition that Nozick and other libertarians expressly reject.[101] Of course, I myself have argued that while rights may indeed be absolute "side-constraints" and therefore cannot conflict in the formal sense, they must still end up getting balanced against one another in the course of resolving what become definitional disputes of the proper scope of the apparently conflicting rights involved.[102] But that argument is not available to me here given my assumption that we are living in a libertarian utopia. Keep in mind, however, that even if I am wrong about the infringing/violating distinction being unsound and wrong about it not being available to libertarians, this does not weaken my argument. On the contrary, it merely gives us yet another reason for thinking that independents must be compensated for being compelled to join and thereby makes my argument stronger.

In any event, there is a much more satisfying answer to the question of why compensation might be due in the mountain cabin example (and therefore by extension to independents who are compelled to join not only by the dominant protective association but also by the relevant union if they are employed), even though breaking into the cabin in the particular circumstances specified in that example is not a rights violation. This answer is that the right to private property does not include the right to exclude everyone, no matter what the circumstances. Note that this is not an argument that there are two conflicting rights and the hiker's right to obtain shelter prevails; rather, it is an argument that once properly and more carefully defined, the rights of the various parties here complement each other and do not conflict. The cabin-owner's property right is indeed *absolute*, it simply is not *comprehensive* in the sense that it does not include the right to exclude the hiker in these circumstances, although it does include the right to demand compensation from the hiker for what is effectively the forced rental of the cabin.[103] And once the scope of the private property right here is properly defined, we can see why a payment is due even though there has initially been no rights violation. Only if payment is *not* made would a rights violation arise. Applying this same reasoning to the situation of independents, we can see that independents may not have a right to refuse to join the protective association, but if they are compelled to join and pay dues, they may nevertheless have a right to compensation in the form of the provision of services. This is simply what the right of free association means when we make the effort to see that it is carefully defined.

For those who are still not convinced, however, I have one final argument. It is commonly believed (not only by many libertarians but by many non-libertarians as well) that the right to freely associate when one wants includes the right to refuse to associate when one objects.[104] But as others have pointed out before me, the "right to free association" is a general description of a particular kind of Hohfeldian relationship. If we describe that relationship in more precise terms, we can see that a right to associate when one wants to does *not* imply a right to refuse to associate as well. For example, the American legal theorist Wesley Newcomb Hohfeld argued many years ago that when we use the term "right" in common or even legal speech, there are a variety of things we could mean, and we often mean one thing in one situation and another in another.[105] A more precise vocabulary is accordingly required if we want to eliminate any ambiguity here. When we speak of the right to freely associate, for example, we can just as easily be speaking of what Hohfeld calls a "liberty" rather than a "claim-right." While a claim-right implies a duty on someone else not to interfere, a liberty does not. Thus, there is nothing about the right to free association, which we all agree entails the liberty to associate when one wants, that necessarily implies a claim-right not to associate when one doesn't.[106] In short, there is a difference between permissibility and inviolability,[107] and we have no reason to assume that the right to freely associate is a right in the latter sense and not merely the former. If we think it does entail a claim-right not to associate as well as a liberty to associate, then we have to independently establish this.

Indeed, if we think that what we mean by a right to freely associate is that we have a right to associate with all those *and only those* we want to, we can quickly see that this would be completely unworkable. How could any association exist if each association must include all those, and only those, each member wants in the association? If A wants to associate with B and C, and B wants to associate with A but not C, and C wants to associate with A and D, whom nobody else likes and who does not want to associate with anybody, then how can an association form that does not violate someone's preferences? It cannot. One cannot insist that an association include all those and only those *each* member wants, for the preferences of any association larger than a few people would invariably be at least partially inconsistent as to who should be a member. This means that for the idea of a right to free association to be capable of being operationalized, it must be limited to a liberty to associate when one wants and include neither the right to veto who else gets to join the association nor the right to refuse to join a particular preexisting association if one does not want to do so. One might have such a right; for example, one could not compel all Jews to become Catholics – but this is because such an action would violate the right to freedom of religion, but not because it would violate the right to freedom of association. Indeed, rights that confer inviolability refer to individual actions, whereas "association" by its very nature cannot be accomplished by individual action alone. Therefore, it cannot be inviolable in the sense of including both a right to associate with whom you want and a right not to associate with whom you don't.[108] The contention that the right to free association includes the right to refuse to join a union accordingly renders the whole idea of a right to free association incoherent. While preventing someone from joining an association they want to join and that wants them *is* a violation of the right to freedom of association, compelling someone to join an association they do not want to join is not, even if all firms are union shops and there remain no options for employment that do not require joining a union (although those steadfastly opposed to joining a union could always opt for the self-employment option and join neither a union nor a firm). Similarly, an association may decide whom they permit to join (at least within certain a nondiscriminatory limits), but their decision to admit certain individuals is not a violation of existing or other potential members' individual right to free association, even if those individuals object to this decision (for example, because they do not want to be members of an association that admits nonwhites or women). Which means that when agreed by both the relevant union and the relevant employer, union shop rules that require independents to join even over their principled objections are not a violation of the right to free association, for this is not something that the right to free association could possibly entail.

This also explains why it is not inconsistent to ban yellow dog contracts yet enforce union shop agreements, despite the claims of some to the contrary.[109] Yellow dog contracts infringe the right of free association by not allowing employees to join unions if they want to. Union shop agreements do not infringe the right to free association because that right does *not* include the right to refuse to join a union, even if one would prefer not to. While it would be inconsistent to accept yellow dog contracts and reject union shop agreements, this is not true in reverse. In a libertarian utopia, the dominant protective association would be required to ban the first and enforce the latter. When the scope of the right of free association is properly understood, we can see that this is what the embrace of libertarianism actually requires.

In any event, if the dominant protective association can legitimately compel independents to join and provide them services, and firms can legitimately condition the receipt of certain benefits on being a member of the firm, then why cannot unions legitimately compel workers to join as well and, after they do, provide them services? Treating the first two instances of compulsion as justified means that the third must be justified as well, and if we did not treat the first two as justified, nothing like the modern industrial state could exist in a libertarian utopia. In that case, the whole libertarian project would fail, for if we accept that the right of freedom of association entails a right to refuse to join, the whole idea of libertarianism as being something distinct from anarchism falls apart. And remember, the whole point of Nozick's argument for the minimal state presents an argument that libertarianism and anarchism are indeed different, and that something very much like the modern state could arise and continue to exist in a libertarian utopia, even if that state had to be shorn of some of its more intrusive aspects.[110] Given that most libertarians are not prepared to abandon the distinction that Nozick attempts to make between anarchism and libertarianism,[111] the argument that there is a libertarian justification for right-to-work laws and against union shop agreements necessarily fails.

1.5 LIBERTARIANS AND LIBERTY

There is one more question we need to consider before I can bring this argument to a close. Libertarians are not simply about protecting rights, whatever these may be, or so the general public seems to believe. On the contrary, libertarians are perceived to be most concerned with one very special kind of right – the right to liberty. That is, after all, why they are called libertarians, or at least this is what the man on the street typically thinks whether he considers himself a libertarian or not. And what most people think libertarians mean by liberty, whether they are a libertarian or not, is what Isaiah Berlin called "negative liberty" – that is, freedom from constraint.[112] If being compelled to join a union as a condition of employment, public or private, is an interference with negative liberty, then perhaps the previous argument has moved too fast. Surely, maximizing individual negative liberty has got to be of the utmost importance in a libertarian utopia. If union shop rules interfere with this, isn't that a reason for such rules to be rejected?

I think not. As I have argued elsewhere, the popular belief that libertarians do (or should) believe in maximizing individual negative liberty is not correct.[113] Negative liberty is an analytical concept, not a political theory. By that I mean the concept of negative liberty is designed to identify when one human agent has interfered in some way with an act another human agent has the capacity to do. Nothing in the concept of negative liberty claims that such interference is a violation of right, therefore always wrongful. Unfettered individual negative liberty would equate to anarchy, and as I have already noted, most libertarians deny that they are anarchists in disguise. It is accordingly a mistake to think that libertarianism could be accurately described more fully as "negative libertarianism" or, perhaps more pithily, as "negatarianism" – an obsessive focus on freedom from restraint, and that's all. Indeed, all libertarians worthy of being taken seriously recognize that social life would be impossible if the rules of society did not inflict massive interference with each individual's negative liberty every day. There are a host of things you cannot do to me, and that I cannot do to you, such as murder, theft, fraud, trespass, assault, and so on, even though we would each have greater individual negative liberty if we could do any of these things. And some of us would also have more if we could do these things while others could not.[114] All the concept of negative liberty suggests is that when there is such an interference, it must be justified.[115] The concept of negative liberty itself does not include a theory about what counts as a justification, or how strong that justification must be. Some other theory – an independent, political as opposed to merely analytical theory – must be applied before we can determine that. Negative liberty is only political in the sense that it sets noninterference as the preferred default position. Otherwise, with regard to whether any particular act of interference with negative liberty is justified, it tells us nothing.

The fact that almost everyone accepts that some kinds of interference with negative liberty can be justified also establishes that there is no general right to negative liberty, even in a libertarian utopia. Remember, while there can be boundary disputes over the borders between one right and another, once properly defined, rights for libertarians are absolute – no interference with a right can be permissible. So contrary to popular belief, there can be no general right to negative liberty because this would mean that conflicts between this and almost every other right would be arising all the time. And this would be contrary to the whole concept of what constitutes a right in a libertarian utopia. True, many libertarians (and many non-libertarians as well, of course) believe there is a general right to *equal* negative liberty – that is, an amount of individual negative liberty consistent with an equal amount of negative liberty being available for everyone else. But this is not because it is entailed by the concept of negative liberty. Rather it is because this is entailed by the concept of equality. Equality, which *is* a political rather than a mere analytical theory, provides a justification for a certain kind of interference with everyone's individual negative liberty or, more precisely, it provides that an interference with negative liberty is *not* justified unless the same interference is applied to everyone else.[116] Even this, however, does not tell us everything we want to know, for such an equality constraint could be satisfied at either very low or very high levels of individual negative liberty and anything in between. Some further political theory is still required to tell us how much individual negative liberty we each should have.

So what is that theory? In my view (and in Nozick's as well), the fundamental notion from which all other rights are derived under libertarianism is not negative liberty, as many self-professed libertarians and even some of their critics mistakenly believe, but self-ownership.[117] From self-ownership we get equality of negative liberty because someone cannot be a self-owner if they have less negative liberty than somebody else. Which is not to say that we can derive a comprehensive theory of equality from the concept of self-ownership. Many theorists have argued that such a comprehensive theory would require the redistribution of holdings and that this would be inconsistent with self-ownership.[118] While I have argued that such redistribution would *not* be inconsistent with self-ownership,[119] and others have too,[120] I need not engage in this debate to make the much narrower point I am making here. In this essay, I am not arguing that one can derive a general theory of distributive justice from self-ownership, merely that one can use it to derive a theory of equality of negative liberty.

More importantly, there is another constraint we can derive from self-ownership with which our otherwise equal negative liberty also must comply. This is the constraint that explains why a very minimal amount of negative liberty would not be sufficient, even if everyone were subject to the same constraints. We do not get this constraint, however, because it is derived from the (merely analytical) theory of negative liberty that self-ownership implies. We get this constraint because libertarianism *does* embrace a political theory of liberty, one directly implied by self-ownership, and this is the political theory now commonly called "republican liberty," or the right to be free from interference by the arbitrary will of another. I will say much more about republican liberty in the next essay, but for now, I will merely note that under my conception of republican liberty (and I am not alone in this), subjecting another to your arbitrary will is an act of domination, and an act of domination, and not just an act of enslavement, is inconsistent with self-ownership.[121] To have a free society, no one must be subject to such domination, and this is how we would describe the ultimate objective of the social order in our libertarian utopia. The amount of equal negative liberty that is enjoyed by people in a libertarian utopia would tend toward the upper end of the scale because only if an interference with negative liberty is not an act of domination is it permissible, and a great many potential acts of interference would fall afoul of this constraint. Which does not mean it will always be clear whether a particular constraint is or is not an act of domination within the meaning of republican liberty. I will say much more about how we might do this in the following essay, but for now, I will be content with pointing out that coming to a decision on this is what determines the scope of equal negative liberty that people would enjoy in our libertarian utopia.

Applying this to the current issue, then, the issue is whether union shop rules are an act of domination, the imposition of the arbitrary will of another, and therefore an impermissible interference with liberty as defined as self-ownership. But there is nothing arbitrary about this. As we have already seen, there are good reasons for requiring all employees of any particular employer to be members of the union representing their fellow employees. In states that do not have right-to-work laws and therefore allow union shops, wages and benefits are consistently higher, terminations for reasons of race, gender, age, religion, sexual preference, and other arbitrary reasons are fewer, applicable standards regarding working conditions are less often violated and when they are violated they are more often enforced, and so on.[122] So requiring those compelled to join to pay the same dues that all members pay is not arbitrary as long as the dues reflect the cost of collective bargaining and enforcement of the collective bargaining agreement and the other services the union provides, as they would in our libertarian utopia. At the very least, requiring all employees to be members of the relevant union can be no more an act of domination than requiring all those who want the benefits available to employees of the firm to be an employee rather than an independent contractor. If the latter is not an imposition of the arbitrary will of another, and we have already decided it is not, then the former cannot be either. There is accordingly nothing about union shop rules that is contrary to libertarian values.

This is not to say that in an occasional individual case a union cannot be a source of domination itself with regard to its relations with an individual member. But the question is not whether a union can violate a member's right to republican liberty on occasion with regard to some particular issue – this is true of every organization that exchanges benefits for membership. The question is whether compulsory union membership is in and of itself an inherently arbitrary act, even if both union and the employer agree to it, and for the reasons I have set forth, it is not. When a union does violate a member's right, or the member simply believes this may have been the case, the member has recourse to the dominant protective association's enforcement services like anybody else, just as he does when the firm violates his rights and the union is unable to rectify this. Of course, with regard to a violation by the dominant protective association itself, it seems unlikely that the association would be much help if the union isn't. But this merely means that unionization cannot fully solve every preexisting problem, not that it creates new ones. In any event, this actually makes the case for unionization in the public sector even stronger, for the public sector worker has fewer realistic remedies available than the private sector worker. In either case, however, there is nothing inherent in compulsory membership that would make such a requirement arbitrary and therefore a violation of republican liberty.

I should also note that in making this argument, I am not relying on a controversial conception of the good; that is, the kind of conception I have argued is not open for consideration. First, what I have argued is that in a libertarian utopia, one has a *right* to republican liberty, as I have defined it. This is accordingly a deontological constraint, not a consequentialist one that is subject to being balanced against countervailing considerations. Second, because the whole point of libertarianism, properly understood, is to protect republican liberty, or liberty as self-ownership, this would necessarily be part of the thin theory of the good embraced by the dominant protective association in our libertarian utopia. Because it is part of our thin theory of the good, it can indeed be the basis for determining whether union shop rules are consistent with libertarian values or contrary to them, even if we do not treat republican liberty as a right.

I will stop here, for this shows that union shop rules would be permissible in our libertarian utopia (and therefore by extension in the real world for those who embrace libertarian values) and that there is no cause to interfere with them should the parties (the employer and the union) choose to agree to them, which real-world history tells us they regularly would. But I will suggest that things might actually go even further in our libertarian utopia. Few relationships are as ripe with opportunities for domination as the employer-employee relationship.[123] The absence of union shop rules in a particular jurisdiction makes *all* employees in that jurisdiction – union and nonunion – more susceptible to domination by their employers. This means there is an argument that union shop rules would not only be *permissible* in our libertarian utopia, they should be *required*, for external government regulation of management's republican liberty-interfering conduct toward employees in our hypothetical libertarian utopia is likely to be far less extensive than it is in the

1.5 Libertarians and Liberty

real world. For now, however, all that it is important to take from our hypothetical thought experiment is that the argument that union shop rules are a violation of libertarian values is unsound and cannot stand.

But of course, it is also important to remind ourselves that we do not live in a libertarian utopia. We live in a liberal capitalist democracy. While the thought experiment I have just completed is informative with regard to the liberty objection to unionization in both the private and the public sector, even outside of a libertarian utopia, given that supposedly libertarian objections to unionization are so frequently made in the real world, it is not likely to be recognized as determinative given that we actually live in a different kind of society altogether. If we are to convincingly resolve how the argument from liberty would play out with regard to unionization in the society in which we actually live, an argument that is more tailored to the fundamental values of and the priorities assigned to these values in a liberal capitalist democracy is also necessary. I present just such an argument in the next essay. There, I argue that universal or compulsory unionization is necessary if we are to adequately protect workers' right to republican liberty, *even in the presence of extensive government regulation aimed at doing the same thing*. To that argument I now turn.

SECOND ESSAY

2

The Union as a Basic Institution of Society

Determining whether workers may form a union, what these unions may and may not do, and most importantly, whether workers can be compelled to join over their objection and required to pay dues for the services the union provides, is usually treated a question of post-institutional regulation. By this I mean that the very question of whether unions are to be permitted to form, and if so, what they are to be permitted to do, is treated as a question that is to be decided against a given and presumably largely immutable background of the basic structure and constitution of a particular society. Everything about unionization is accordingly seen as up for grabs – whether unions may or should exist and what they may, must, or cannot do is matter to be determined by the just operation of these existing institutions; unions are not to be treated as a basic institution in themselves. Even the principles that go into deciding whether some aspect of a society is a basic institution, and whether these basic institutions, taken together, are just are not considered applicable to the question of unionization. Indeed, Rawls himself, in one of the few instances in which he mentions labor unions expressly, suggests that like the family, unions are not subject to regulation by his principles of justice as fairness:

> The primary subject of political justice is the basic structure of society understood as the arrangement of society's main institutions into a unified system of social cooperation over time. The principles of political justice are to apply directly to this structure, but are not to apply directly to the internal life of the many associations within it, the family among them... The same question arises in regard to all associations, whether they be churches or universities, professional or scientific associations, business firms or labor unions. The family is not peculiar in this respect.[1]

In other words, according to Rawls, when it comes to deciding what role if any unions should play in our society, the question is to be resolved either by the application of post-institutional principles derived from our constitution and designed to regulate our basic institutions, or by the application of principles generated by these basic institutions themselves and designed to regulate the internal operation of other, nonbasic institutions and their outputs, and not his pre-institutional principle of justice as fairness or the pre-institutional concepts of liberty and equality it instantiates. In any case, what is not at issue is the development or application of more general normative principles designed to govern institutional design. Instead of some general concept of liberty, we must apply instantiations of liberty that are already enshrined in the constitution like freedom of association, freedom of contract, and freedom of speech. Instead of the difference principle, or luck egalitarianism, or some other general principle of liberal egalitarianism or of equality more generally, we must apply the various constitutional and postconstitutional rules generated by one or more of those ideas.

But in this essay, I intend to argue that this way of thinking about unionization is a mistake. The issue of unionization is not to be decided by application of the individual rights of free speech or free association or by principles designed to instantiate some particular conception of equality, but by more senior principles of political morality – principles of liberty and equality that must be in place before these more derivative expressions of equality and liberty can have meaning. Under these more senior principles, I will argue, unions are a basic institution of society, for they not only protect workers from exploitation and other exercises of arbitrary power by their employers and their government, they also play an important role in protecting all of us from the corruption, incompetence, and antisocial inclinations of those managing the bulk of the economic resources of our society. They accordingly help ensure that firms, especially large ones that hold large amounts of economic and therefore political power, do not use this power to put private benefit or the satisfaction of the personal discriminatory external preferences of the few above the common good.[2] In other words, in a liberal capitalist society, unionization is not simply to be treated as an option, to be permitted or not according to the preferences of workers. Rather, unionization is to be affirmatively encouraged, and in larger business organizations formally required, for unionization is the only reliable way most workers in a capitalist society can ensure adequate protection of their liberty and other rights. Unionization, like other basic institutions, simply must be universal if we are to ensure background justice, and not contingent on the outcome of some post-institutional procedure.

To make this argument, I shall begin by discussing what a basic institution is and what role this concept should play in determining how a just society should be organized. Because there is no currently accepted definition of what makes an institution basic or even what role the concept of a basic institution should play in structuring a just society, our understanding of these issues remains murky and incomplete (more on this is in a moment). My discussion of these issues may strike some as both somewhat abstract and rather lengthy, leaving them to wonder when I will get to discussing unionization itself. But developing a more complete and determinate working understanding of how the concept of a basic institution should be understood, and how this concept can help instantiate our ideas about what makes a society just, is absolutely essential before we can apply these insights to the issue of unionization itself. Indeed, striving to get our understanding of our fundamental principles set before embarking on an investigation of more applied questions the approach that underlies all analytical political philosophy.[3] I accordingly encourage readers who are unfamiliar with the analytical method to not become impatient. Rest assured that the conceptual discussion that begins this essay is both necessary and instructive with regard to developing and applying the arguments about unionization that follow suit. Indeed, this initial, and unfortunately somewhat lengthy, conceptual and theoretical discussion about the nature of institutions is what makes my argument an argument about political theory and not merely about industrial relations and labor economics, and further, it is what differentiates my argument from those that simply depend on claims about whether unionization promotes or impedes the pursuit of the common good.[4] While my argument is never fact-free, it does not depend on how deeply contested factual claims are resolved. And while I do refer to various facts that are *not* reasonably contested, this does not make my argument any less an argument from right or otherwise transform it into an argument from consequences, for these facts are only ever a part of the picture and never determinative of it.

Before I move on, there are two more points I want to emphasize about the scope of what I am arguing here. The first is that the argument I develop in this essay with regard to universal unionization is designed to apply to the private sector. I believe this argument supports universal unionization in the public sector too, but it is not decisive. There are different forces in play in the public sector: some aspects of my argument would not apply, there are some additional points that would, and plus there are different objections to be considered and addressed.[5] One of these – indeed, one of the most significant – is the contention that allowing unions to charge nonmembers agency fees to cover the cost of collective bargaining on their behalf (unions are required by law to represent both members and nonmembers in collective bargaining) is a violation of the First Amendment's guarantee of freedom of speech, a contention that the Supreme Court recently accepted in *Janus* v. *AFSCME*,[6] effectively making all states right-to-work states with regard to public sector workers.[7] But I will not elaborate on the differences between the public and private sector or address any of the special objections that have been raised to public sector unionization here. Instead, while I will say a few things about public sector unionization at the end of this essay, I will leave the question of whether my principle of universal unionization applies to the public sector or just the private sector open until the third essay in this volume, in which I address the question of unionization in the public sector directly.

The second point I want to emphasize at the outset is that when I am talking about unionization, and especially what functions I have in mind when addressing the question of whether unions should be treated as a basic institution, I am talking about the core functions that unions typically provide: bargaining collectively on behalf of the workers they represent over wages, benefits, and working conditions; representing employees in disputes with management over work-related issues; lobbying government for legislation or executive action that will benefit their members; and monitoring management for incompetence and corruption and compliance with applicable legislation, regulations, and the provisions of the collective bargaining agreement. Unions can and do perform other functions, of course, but I shall treat these other functions as being outside the core. Whether and to what extent these noncore functions are to be limited or permitted is therefore a post-institutional issue not bearing on whether and if so to what extent unions should be treated as a basic institution as far as their core functions are concerned. Note, however, that the fact that the core function of a union is to represent its members before management and the government necessarily implies that unions must be democratic in some meaningful sense of the word – that is, union members must have a voice in selecting their leaders, although how this is to be cashed out is a matter for post-institutional regulation. For even core functions can be regulated. Being a core function does not make something immune to oversight or, in some cases, regulation or limitation. It merely means that problems with core functions are to be dealt with post-institutionally and not by expressly or effectively eliminating the institution in its entirety. Exactly what I mean by this will become clear as we move on.

With that said, my argument proceeds as follows. In the first section of this essay, I identify the various levels at which moral evaluation can occur. In the second section, I explore the nature of the first of these levels, that of the basic structure, and discuss what choices regarding the basic structure might imply, if anything, regarding the design and composition of the basic institutions of society. I also examine what kind of moral evaluation might be appropriate with regard to choices made at the basic structure level itself. In the third section, I explore the second of these potential levels of moral evaluation, that of the basic institutions of society, and focus on what makes an institution "basic," examine whether such institutions may be evaluated independently of their outputs, and explore what kind of moral evaluation might be appropriate at this level. It is the fourth section, however, that contains the theoretical heart of my argument. In this section, I first explore the various ways in which the concept of liberty can be cashed out and examine the relationship between negative liberty, positive liberty, economic liberty, republican liberty, voluntariness, neutrality, and equality. I then go deeper into my conception of republican liberty, explain how it differs from conceptions now frequently employed, and show why the institution of the firm poses a real threat to republican liberty so conceived. I also discuss how negative liberty and economic liberty figure into the determination of whether unions should be recognized as a basic institution. This discussion accordingly provides the framework for everything that follows: specifically, the argument that the union is indeed a basic institution. Section five contains the empirical elements of this argument, for remember, even an argument from right considers consequences, although the only empirical claims I rely on here are ones that cannot be reasonably disputed. The consequences at issue here accordingly include the effects of unionization on wages, benefits, inequality, productivity, profitability, management incompetence and antisocial behavior, the voice of workers, unemployment, inflation, and so on. In section six, I discuss how these effects might promote and protect the kinds of liberty that are relevant considerations at the basic institution level. Finally, in section seven, I show how certain other liberal capitalist democracies have already effectively recognized the union as a basic institution. I also discuss various practical problems that might arise in treating the union as a basic institution and how we might resolve them.

2.1 THREE LEVELS OF MORAL EVALUATION

Rawls famously makes several distinctions that are relevant to the argument I am making here. First, as I have already mentioned, he notes that certain principles of justice apply only to the "basic structure" of society. Indeed, he states, "*the primary subject of justice is the basic structure of society.*"[8] By basic structure, he means "the way in which the major social institutions distribute fundamental rights and duties and determine the distribution of advantages from social cooperation."[9] "Now admittedly," Rawls says, "the concept of the basic structure is somewhat vague."[10] According to Sam Freeman, however, Rawls meant for it to be understood like this:

> The *basic structure of society* consists of the arrangements of the political, social and economic institutions that make social cooperation possible and productive. These institutions have a profound influence on individuals' everyday lives, their characters and desires, as well as their future prospects. The *basic institutions* that are part of the basic structure include, first, the political constitution and the resulting form of government and the legal system it supports, including the system of trials and other legal procedures; second the system of property, whether public or private, that must exist in any society to specify who has exclusive rights to and responsibilities for the use of goods and resources... third, the system of markets and other means of transfer and disposal of economic goods, and more generally the structure and norms of the economic system of production, transfer, and distribution of goods and resources among individuals; and fourth, the family in some form, which from a political perspective is the primary mechanism any society must have for the raising and education of children, and thus the reproduction of society over time.[11]

In other words, as Arnold Toynbee points out, "without institutions, societies could not exist."[12] A society cannot have a basic structure without basic institutions. But it is still useful to distinguish between the basic structure of society and the basic institutions that make up that structure, for the basic structure may be instantiated in many different ways with many different sets of institutions.

While I am not sure that this is indeed what Rawls meant (that is, I am not sure if Rawls intended to distinguish between the moral evaluation of the basic structure and the moral evaluation of the basic institutions that make it up), I think this is a helpful gloss on Rawls's view. If we do not distinguish between the basic structure and the institutions that instantiate that structure, it is more difficult to see that different types of analyses may be appropriate at each level. Indeed, it is helpful to think of society as actually having *three* levels at which an analysis of its justness could occur. First, there is the basic structure of society. Second, there are the basic institutions that make up and instantiate the basic structure. And third, there are the outputs of these basic institutions. These, in turn, include both *direct* outputs in the form of decisions or actions, and *indirect* outputs in the form of the creation of subsidiary nonbasic institutions and the subsequent outputs of these institutions.

There is of course one other potential level of evaluation I should mention. Beneath the evaluation of institutions and their outputs, there is the conduct of individuals. Rawls suggests that different rules apply to institutions and individuals. For example, even if institutions must comply with the difference principle, individuals do not.[13] In other words, he claimed his principles apply only to institutions (or only to the basic structure, which is the phrasing he often used) and were not designed to be part of an individual's theory of personal morality, which is the kind of theory that individuals need to advise them about what they should do – what other theorists often call a personal theory of the good. And many theorists have supported Rawls's idea that different rules apply to the conduct of institutions and individuals.[14] A number of theorists, however, have argued to the contrary – that is, that Rawls's principles cannot (or at least should not) be limited in this way.[15] But I will not be engaging in this debate here. Instead, with one exception, I will be focusing on what is to be taken into account in evaluating justice at the first three levels of inquiry, and not on whether the principles that I develop can and should also be used by individuals to guide their personal conduct. The exception, of course, is that I will argue that in a democratic society, where individual views have an effect on the design and regulation of institutions, justice requires that individuals generally endorse the principles we develop with regard to the design and operation of our basic institutions; otherwise there would be no way to put such principles into effect.[16] Given the nature of these principles, I do not think they could be used to guide other kinds of individual actions or decisions, even if one wanted them to, but whether there would be room for individuals to apply or reject these principles in other parts of their lives, and if so, whether they should do so, is not something that I am going to address.

2.2 MORAL EVALUATION AND THE BASIC STRUCTURE

Obviously, no society can exist without a basic structure; the basic structure is what makes social cooperation possible. A society must have an economic system (a system for trading goods and services and a method for making production and pricing decisions), a legal system (a system for deciding what rights people have and how these rights will be enforced), a system of governance (a system for deciding how to manage social cooperation beyond simply assigning rights and duties to everyone, or to put it another way, a system for determining and then instantiating social choice within the limits of the rights and duties assigned), and a system for facilitating the reproduction, education, and maturation of its members.[17] A group of people that lacks any of these fundamental pieces of the basic structure cannot be a society – that is, a group of individuals that are in some sense willing to coordinate their activities for the benefit of all and can continue to exist despite the death or departure of its founding members. The basic structure requires what it requires not because of the demands of justice, however, but because of contingent facts about human nature and circumstances. Without a basic structure, we have a state of nature, and instead of social cooperation, we have anarchy. And when those in such a relationship are also in competition with one other, we have the situation that Thomas Hobbes famously warned would quickly degenerate into a "war of all against all," as neighbor preemptively attacks neighbor out of fear his neighbor would be planning acts of predation against him.[18]

It is possible, of course, that there might not be a sharp borderline between a group of individuals who have formed an imperfect society and those who live together in something closer to anarchy. Most groups will be in one state of affairs or the other, but there may be some groups that manage to straddle this divide, functioning in the grey area, which in another context, H. L. A. Hart called the "penumbra" of uncertainty.[19] But we are concerned here only with what we might call the central case of what constitutes a society: a group that has functional mechanisms in place for all four main aspects of social organization. Whether all groups have a basic structure or not and therefore either clearly qualify as a society or not, or whether some groups can be a society to some extent or for some purposes but not for others, I leave to others to decide, for it seems uncontroversial that the state of affairs in which we live in the liberal capitalist world is smack dab in the middle of the central case.

The point I wish to make, then, is this: despite what often seem to be Rawls's remarks to the contrary and the fact that many scholars have followed him on this, the content of the basic structure is *not* subject to moral evaluation. The basic structure is the thing stuff social cooperation is made on; it separates anarchy from order. And while I recognize that some people think that order is always morally superior to anarchy, at least when we are talking about social order,[20] this is doubtful. A society of psychopathic killers who work together to destroy those who are not members of their group is morally inferior to a group of psychopathic killers who function not as a society but as like-minded individuals who do not coordinate their activities or only coordinate them when it appears to be in their individual interests at that particular moment, something that could change at any time. Order can make evil more efficient, just as it can good.[21] The answer to the question of whether a basic structure is morally good or bad in that sense will depend on the ambitions that a particular social organization embraces and the nature of the acts it undertakes. The criterion for the analysis of the basic structure itself, however, is accordingly purely or at least primarily functional: what we want to know is whether a group of individuals has sufficient mechanisms in place to function more or less as a society; that is, as a coordinated ongoing organism that replaces and even improves its working parts over time, can select and pursue objectives, and determine how it will pursue these objectives in a way that is generally recognized as binding on all members.[22] Whether such mechanisms are in place is purely a question of fact, determined by observation as to what members of the (at this point merely putative) group believe and how they behave.

While *some* mechanism must exist in each of these areas, however, there are many possible candidates from which to choose. In the United States, for example, the political system is democracy, the economic system is capitalism, the legal system is that of the common law, under which the legislature and the judiciary meaningfully share responsibility for the enactment and development of legal rights and duties, and the system of social reproduction is the family in which children are generally raised privately by those that gave them life as long as certain minimum standards can be met and (subject to some exceptions) parents allow their children to be enrolled in education services provided or at least approved by the state. But these choices are contingent. Instead of capitalism, a society could employ socialism as its economic system. Instead of a common law system, a society could employ a civil law system in which the only legitimate originator of the law is the legislature and judges are reduced to the status of mere bureaucrats. Instead of democracy, a society could employ some form of autocracy as its political system. And instead of reproduction *via* the family with supplemental education provided by the state, a society could employ something like the method of creating and raising children set forth in Aldous Huxley's novel *Brave New World* with its human hatcheries and programmatic indoctrination of children who are conceived as homogenized products rather than as autonomous living, breathing, individualized human beings.

Are the choices between different types of basic structure subject to moral evaluation? Marxists, of course, insist that the choices necessary to create the basic structure are "beyond justice," and therefore beyond morality; that is, made before we have decided what morality is and therefore made before choices as to the content of morality can be made.[23] Non-Marxists, in contrast, mostly believe that moral criticism can be leveled at these choices. In this case, if such criticism were sufficiently severe with regard to most of the

2.2 Moral Evaluation and the Basic Structure

forms the basic structure might take, it would be possible that a moral argument could exist for preferring one possible basic structure over all others. Rawls, after all, claims something like this when he argues that a society (that is, a group of individuals who have embraced a basic structure for their group) can be "well-ordered" or not, a well-ordered society being one that embraces a public conception of justice, which is in place and in practice and not just in theory, and society is effectively regulated according to its precepts.[24] But not only are there a lot of candidates from which to choose when assembling a basic structure, a great many versions of the basic structure can be well-ordered. So even if Rawls is right, it is most likely that all we can do here is make some very broad generalizations. One might not even know whether capitalism or socialism is the better choice until we knew fairly precisely how these competing economic systems would be cashed out. Which means there is not a lot of work for morality to do, if there is any work for it to do at all, with regard to choices made concerning the basic structure.

More importantly, perhaps, even if some type of moral evaluation might be appropriate at the basic structure level, it is not the kind of moral evaluation that most of us have in mind when we are talking about political morality. We already live in a society in which choices have been made as to the basic structure, and these choices are not likely to be open for significant adjustment any time soon.[25] The questions that are open to us for closer moral examination and adjustment are those that arise only when we start asking how the basic institutions that make up the basic structure are to be designed. Indeed, what Rawls had in mind when he spoke of "the primary subject of justice" was *not* a moral evaluation of the basic structure, despite his frequent use of language to the contrary, but rather a moral evaluation of some of the choices that can be made once we have settled on a certain form of basic structure, and in particular, what morality had to say about how we might implement the economic system of capitalism when it is conjoined with the political system of liberal democracy. Admittedly, Rawls does say a few things about socialism,[26] but his argument is not designed to promote capitalism over socialism.[27] It is designed to tell us what kind of capitalism a liberal democracy should support.[28] At least, this is his approach in *A Theory of Justice*. In his later writings, he does rule out both *laissez faire* capitalism and welfare state capitalism because he sees them as unable to fully instantiate his two principles of justice. He also says that the only forms of regime that could fully instantiate his two principles would be a property-owning democracy and liberal democratic socialism, both of which he claims are not forms of capitalism.[29] But the former is pretty close – while individual ownership of assets is widely dispersed in a property-owning democracy, the economic system remains fully capitalistic in the sense that the means of production are generally privately owned and prices and outputs are determined by the market rather than by central command.[30] Even democratic socialism, often called market socialism, is a lot closer to capitalism than it is to state socialism, for it also relies on the market to make price and output decisions.[31]

The main difference between each of these systems and welfare state capitalism, according to Rawls, it that both systems tend to prevent large inequalities from arising and therefore dramatically reduce the need for *ex post facto* redistribution and the tensions such redistribution can create.[32] While Rawls thinks this amounts to a rejection of capitalism, it is perhaps more accurate to think of this as merely a rejection of a cowboy capitalism, where anything goes, and welfare state capitalism, where almost anything goes and then an effort is made to repair the damage, and neither a rejection of an appropriately adjusted form of political liberalism mixed with economic capitalism nor an endorsement of some form of economic socialism. In other words, how society should go about designing the basic institutions of the liberal capitalist state (broadly conceived) is the topic on which Rawls has had a lot to say, and this is how his theories have been widely understood.[33] It is only because he came to view the political ramifications of the economic system of capitalism as insufficiently mutable in his later writings that he seemed to become disheartened about the possibility of it being compatible with political liberalism. But capitalism comes in many varieties, and if one does not conflate a particular basic structure with the composition and design of the basic institutions that instantiate it, one need not be so discouraged. Making the liberal capitalist state better was the focus of the bulk of Rawls's work, and this is exactly what I am aiming at as well.[34]

In a sense, then, I am carrying forward the ideas and approach of the early institutionalists in economics – Thorstein Veblen, Wesley Mitchell, Walter Hamilton, Walter Stewart, John M. Clark, and John R. Commons – and applying them to political theory. While the institutionalists disagreed about many things, most of them wanted labor unions to be stronger and government to play a more active role in regulating the predatory practices of business.[35] What they lacked is a coherent normative theory that provided something other than a mere consequentialist argument for their position.[36] The same problem is said to have undermined the version of "corporatism" that was a dominant part of social democracy movements in Europe in the 1960s and 1970s (especially in Germany) and argued for tripartite negotiations between business, labor, and the state with regard to developing economic policy.[37] But while I will draw on the thinking of both these movements,[38] what I will be proposing in this essay is neither a form of neo-institutionalism nor a more principled form of neo-corporatism. My purpose is not to help revive either *ism*, even if this may be one effect. Rather, it is to provide a moral theory for understanding the role that unions should play in the contemporary liberal capitalist state we already have, given what we, as liberal capitalists, already claim to believe.

2.3 THE MORAL EVALUATION OF BASIC INSTITUTIONS

Once we decide it is the design of the basic institutions that make up the basic structure which is the primary subject of justice, however, and not the basic structure itself, more needs to be said about exactly what this means.

2.3 *The Moral Evaluation of Basic Institutions*

First of all, it is worth noting that while the word "basic" connotes functionality when it is applied to the basic structure, it connotes much more than this when applied to particular institutions: it connotes a moral claim about the importance of the institution and its role in determining the overall justness of society. It might accordingly be better to use some word other than "basic" when we are talking about the moral evaluation of basic institutions. Because the word "basic" has already become an accepted part of the taxonomy of institutions, however, replacing it with something else at this point might end up being more confusing than helpful, so I will continue to use it. In any event, what is most important to note here is that once we move from focusing on the basic structure to focusing on the design of the basic institutions that make up this structure, we have moved from a primarily functional analysis to one that is heavily influenced by moral considerations, and there are many different ways in which these moral considerations could enter into our analysis.

Here is where another Rawlsian distinction – that between substantive and procedural justice – comes in. The design of the basic structure's basic institutions could be required to comply with both procedural and substantive justice; in other words, both their procedures and their outputs could be subjected to moral evaluation. But Rawls famously argues that establishing procedural justice is a way of ensuring a high degree of substantive justice without actually having to test every individual output of that procedure for compliance with the applicable substantive rules.[39] Once we have decided that the procedures employed by these basic intuitions are just, the output of those institutions should be just too, at least in most instances. Or so Rawls contends.[40]

But this is clearly wrong. Take the example Rawls uses – that of dividing a cake between a group of men (why Rawls specifies men is not clear – the example works best if we think of the potential claimants here as children of either sex). Rawls argues that the best way to ensure a just result here is "obviously" to have the child who divides the cake receive the last slice.[41] He calls this a case of "perfect" procedural justice, by which he means that the method of distribution guarantees that whatever independent criteria for just division there are, these will always be met.[42] He also specifies that, in this case, a just division of the cake would be an equal division. But if the divider has a trembling hand or is otherwise not capable of dividing the cake evenly or something close to this,[43] or if the divider does not understand that he will get the smallest piece if the cake ends up divided unevenly, or happens to be masochistic or altruistic rather than egoistic (that is, more concerned about maximizing the outcome for others rather than for himself),[44] or if there are good reasons why the cake should *not* be divided evenly but should be divided according to some other formula, the result will not be just. I should note that Rawls recognizes these limitations too, but he claims that, for the purposes of the argument he is making, "we can ignore these details."[45] Why he thinks we can do this, however, is never made clear. Having the child who divides the cake choose last may be a way of maximizing the chances that the cake is divided evenly (but not necessarily justly) when no fully informed nonpartisan third party "expert" cake-cutter is available to attempt to divide the cake according to criteria that take all the morally relevant considerations into account, but the method of division in either case does not free the output of this process from moral evaluation. Uneven as well as even but unjust divisions of the cake here are possible and perhaps even likely, notwithstanding the procedure used.

As applied to the design of the basic structure's basic institutions, however, Rawls makes an even stronger claim. Rawls recognizes that cases of perfect procedural justice "are rare, if not impossible, in cases of much practical interest."[46] But he argues that the design of the basic structure's basic institutions is a matter of "pure" procedural justice; that is, instead of it being the case that the procedure used guarantees that the outcome will be substantively just, as in perfect procedural justice, in this case, "there is no independent criterion for the right result."[47] Outputs are not just because the procedure used has ensured that the relevant criteria for a just substantive result has necessarily been met; they are just because the only criteria for determining whether the output is just is whether the requisite procedure has been used. Now Rawls adds an important qualification to this: he postulates that pure procedural justice applies only "against the background of a just basic structure, including a just political constitution and a just arrangement of economic and social institutions."[48] This qualification, however, takes all the power out of the concept of pure procedural justice, for all the relevant work is now actually being done offstage according to some set of specified or perhaps even unspecified substantive criteria. It is like saying "there are no independent criteria for the correct result except for the independent criteria that there are." In any event, the only example that Rawls gives here of pure procedural justice is gambling. The idea being that if the rules of the game are fair, and are actually followed, the distribution of chips at the end must be just, and no independent criteria need be applied to establish this.[49] But this is a rather baffling example, for Rawls himself recognizes elsewhere that real people have vastly different skills, knowledge, risk preferences, and starting positions. Since these factors clearly have an effect on the ultimate distribution of chips when gambling, even if the rules are fair and are scrupulously followed, it is hard to see how the resulting distribution can be necessarily just unless we assume that even though these differences between players result in different chip distributions, this is morally irrelevant, an approach Rawls elsewhere expressly rejects. Of course, he might be suggesting that these differences in skill, knowledge, and so on *are* morally irrelevant when applied to gambling. But it is hard then to see how this example is instructive about anything else, or at least about anything that relates to how we should design our basic institutions. Rawls's whole approach to distributive justice is based on the idea that our basic institutions should be designed to regulate, if not prohibit, differences in distribution resulting from differences in natural talents and abilities and, in some cases, from acquired talents and abilities too.

2.3 The Moral Evaluation of Basic Institutions

Later, however, Rawls uses a different example to illustrate what he means by pure procedural justice, and that example is also worth examining.[50] He suggests that if the basic structure and the institutions which instantiate that basic structure were just, wages would necessarily be just as matter of pure procedural justice as long as the economy was perfectly competitive. Indeed, he says that even if the economy were only "reasonably competitive and open, the notion of pure procedural justice is a feasible one to follow."[51] His thought seems to be that in this case, wages would necessarily reflect the marginal net product of labor, which would make them automatically just. This is the view articulated and defended most extensively by A. C. Pigou in 1920 in *The Economics of Welfare*,[52] but it is based on the work of John Bates Clark (to whom Rawls attributes it) and Alfred Marshall. Then, after Pigou, it was taken up and defended by Joan Robinson, among others, although it has not been taken seriously by any economist of significance since.[53] This is because there are huge problems with Pigou's view. I have discussed these in depth in *Exploitation and Economic Justice in the Liberal Capitalist State*, and so will mention them only briefly here. First, calculating marginal net productivity turns out to be a rather difficult and controversial task. The concept is actually so indeterminate that depending on how one gives it further content, almost any wage can be viewed as either too low or too high. In either case, however, further independent criteria are necessary in order to determine whether any particular wage is indeed just. Second, ensuring that labor is paid its marginal net product would ensure that economic resources are allocated efficiently, but why assume that this is necessarily just? Rawls actually raises this objection himself, noting that the principle of efficiency is subordinate to his principles of justice of fairness.[54] He even goes on to list various reasons why an efficient outcome with regard to wages might not be just.[55] He then seems to suggest, however, that if the basic structure is just, these problems would not arise. But it is not obvious why this would be so, which means that at least some further argument and perhaps the application of independent criteria on this point would also be required. Third, except in the unusual case where there are constant returns to scale, the sum of the marginal net product of each factor of production will not equal the total productivity of all factors taken as a whole. This is known among economists as "adding up problem," and it seems fatal to pure procedural justice here, for compensating each factor of production according to its marginal net product cannot be just if we end up with a remainder or a shortfall. Which means that we are once again left without a real example of pure procedural justice in motion.

In fairness, I should note that Rawls is fairly critical of Pigou's view himself, even though Rawls nevertheless suggests that if background justice were otherwise established, the setting of wages in a reasonably competitive economy could constitute an example of pure procedural justice. So I am not entirely sure what we should make of Rawls's discussion here. But let's put these points aside for now. If it were the case that the design of basic institutions presented a question of pure procedural justice, this would seem to allow us to make a neat division between the kinds of moral inquiries appropriate at each level: at the basic institution level, we would be concerned only with issues of procedural justice, whereas issues of substantive justice would only concern us at the applied level, where we are evaluating the justness of the particular outputs of a social institution. But this is not what Rawls's view actually implies. If pure procedural justice could be implemented at the basic institution level, whether this were the case because we had already established that the basic structure was just (and remember, I deny that we can even evaluate the justness of the basic structure – moral evaluation does not become possible until we reach the basic institution level), or because our basic institutions themselves adopted fair procedures and enforced strict compliance (another way of looking at what Rawls is suggesting, one that I argue more accurately captures what he is really suggesting), there would *never* be any need to evaluate the outputs of just basic institutions for compliance with principles of substantive justice. As Rawls says, the outputs of these institutions would be necessarily just; independent criteria for determining whether they were just would not even exist.[56] So we would not be applying procedural and substantive principles at different levels of inquiry. There would simply be no call for substantive principles of justice to be applied at any time at all except at the uppermost level of moral evaluation, what Rawls calls the basic structure level, and I call the basic institution level.

Of course, this cannot be what Rawls actually meant either, for yet another example Rawls cites – that of the criminal trial system – shows that Rawls does indeed think that there is a role for principles of substantive justice to play at all levels. Rawls describes the criminal trial system as a case of "imperfect" procedural justice where, unlike pure procedural justice, there are independent criteria for a correct result, and unlike perfect procedural justice, it is impossible to design a procedure that ensures such criteria will always be met. But the fact of the matter is that all cases of procedural justice are imperfect unless the sole relevant standard of evaluation is efficiency – the speed and cost of achieving ends, no matter what these ends might be – and I know of no putative basic institution for which this could plausibly be the case.[57] And this includes the economy, for if it were otherwise, there would be no such thing as economic justice or injustice and Rawls's entire project would be unnecessary. Indeed, Rawls implicitly, if not explicitly, recognizes that we cannot evaluate the justness of any putative basic institution without considering both the procedures it employs in generating outputs and the substantive justness of the outputs themselves, for the whole system of justice as fairness that Rawls develops is designed to provide exactly the criteria necessary for conducting such a multilevel inquiry.

Now one person to whom I have made the above argument has tried to parry my attack on pure procedural justice by using Robert Nozick's Wilt Chamberlain example. Without going into too much detail, the argument embodied in this example is that if an initial distribution is just, and everyone

2.3 The Moral Evaluation of Basic Institutions

thereafter transfers their wealth purely through a series of voluntary transactions, the resulting distribution cannot be anything other than just.[58] The justness of this outcome would be a matter of pure procedural justice, or so the parry goes. But this is not correct. For one thing, this depends on first deciding that voluntariness is the only relevant criterion for justness in transfer, and this is vigorously denied by many theorists who contend that even voluntary transactions can produce injustice in a variety of ways.[59] Indeed, I myself deny this in *Exploitation and Economic Justice in the Liberal Capitalist State*, in which I argue that exchange transactions must meet the requirements of reciprocity and not merely voluntariness in order to be just.[60] For another thing, even if voluntariness were the only relevant criterion, one would still have to have substantive criteria for determining what voluntariness means in the relevant circumstances, for anything from a very thin to a very thick conception of voluntariness would be possible. And when these more detailed criteria for voluntariness are not met, the resulting distribution would still be unjust. One would accordingly always have to check to see that these detailed criteria are met; one couldn't simply rely on the procedure here to establish the justness of outcomes. Indeed, the law of contracts is full of procedures designed to ensure some degree of moral voluntariness, yet no one thinks compliance with those procedures means moral (or for that matter, legal) voluntariness is guaranteed. Which means that in the real world, the criteria of voluntariness cannot even work to generate perfect procedural justice, much less pure procedural justice. And finally, even if comprehensive and completely determinate criteria for voluntariness could be specified, and we could be categorically assured that the criteria would always be complied with, voluntariness is itself still an "independent [substantive] criterion." Even if voluntariness were the test, we would accordingly still need to decide on a set of procedures that would ensure this test is met in connection with any transfer. It would therefore still not be the case that voluntary transfer would be an example of pure procedural justice. Independent criteria always exist and always matter, and the justness of outcomes of any institution we might plausibly consider basic must always be judged according to them.

There is one way to reconcile the seemingly conflicting statements that Rawls makes about what is to be done here, of course, and this is to conclude that what we should be doing is conducting a kind of rule utilitarian analysis – that is, trying to determine if there is a particular institutional design that is significantly more likely to produce substantively just outputs than any other institutional design. While this approach would allow us to eliminate certain possible institutional designs, it is very unlikely that it would enable us to settle on one particular design, for each possible design would have different advantages and disadvantages and presumably have similar net chances of success. Using a rule utilitarian approach would also be inconsistent with the entire thrust of Rawls's argument, which is primarily designed as an attack on utilitarianism. And even so, it would still not eliminate the need for the evaluation of an institution's outputs, for the same reason that rule utilitarianism is often claimed to collapse into act utilitarianism – there are always moral arguments to make when the applicable rule seems to direct us to do something that is contrary to the overall utilitarian ideal.[61] True, some choices are political – that is, there are a range of just designs for any institution, and the choice among these remains a matter of preference, not justice. There is also a feasibility limit: to draw on H. L. A. Hart again, there is a limit to the amount of justice that any society can afford, a limit that by definition expands and contracts according to the resources currently available to the particular society in question.[62] A rich society may accordingly be justly required to have more redundancies built into its institutional designs than a poor one. But to ensure that all outputs of basic institutions would be just in every instance would require that we build redundancy after redundancy into the system to the point where the mere operation of the institution would eat up all the resources that were available to distribute. This kind of obsession with institutional justice would obviously be self-defeating. So even if the institutions we design are basically just, we must accept that even these institutions can produce outputs that are unjust. Outputs always matter if we are to assure ourselves that justice has been done. It is accordingly not clear what Rawls's suggestion that we distinguish between substantive and procedural criteria is capable of doing for us.

On the contrary, what should be clear is that the idea of pure procedural justice is incoherent, at least as applied to the basic institution level of analysis. It is impossible to determine the justness of a procedure unless we have first decided what the relevant criteria are for determining the justness of the outcomes of that procedure, and this requires a full-fledged inquiry into what substantive criteria should apply to evaluate those outcomes. Independent criteria for evaluating the justness of a basic institution must always exist, and no matter what procedure is used, it can always produce outcomes that are unjust; that is, that deviate from the substantive criteria that are used to design the procedure that suggests what we should do in a particular case. Indeed, even a fair lottery can be unjust, as Rawls specifically notes when he describes the natural lottery for talents and abilities as "arbitrary from a moral perspective."[63] We are accordingly never free to ignore the relevant substantive criteria when it comes to evaluating the justness of outcomes, no matter what procedures were used in generating those outcomes, and no matter how fair general background justice may otherwise be. We are not even free to ignore substantive criteria that were not considered when we designed the basic institution, for the apparent injustice of an outcome may lead us to realize that we left some important substantive criteria out when we were designing the basic institution and the procedures it was to follow. For example, if people always agree to be exploited rather than starve, we would have to rethink our conclusion about what voluntariness is and whether voluntariness is all that mattered. Each output necessarily reflects back upon the method, informing us how just that method is and what factors might influence this output toward or away

2.3 The Moral Evaluation of Basic Institutions

from a just result, whether that be equal division or some other kind of distribution. Indeed, outcomes are actually important in two ways: *expected* outcomes are important in that they help guide us toward the institutional design that would seem to be most just; and *actual* outcomes are important for they tell us whether our *ex ante* assumptions regarding institutional design were correct. Thus, to the extent that Rawls has been taken to suggest that just procedures can relieve us of the need to conduct a substantive evaluation of the justness of outcomes, either in whole or in part, this is incorrect. The procedural/substantive distinction does not give us a basis for differentiating the kind of moral evaluation that takes place at the basic institution as opposed to outcome level.

Even the idea of what constitutes a basic institution is somewhat vague, despite the fact that it is an improvement in terms of specificity on the idea of the basic structure. Are all institutions basic, or are there some institutions that are subject to some lesser form of moral evaluation? What is the relationship between our evaluation of the design of the institution and our evaluation of its outputs? Do the same rules or at least the same kind of rules apply to both institutions and their outputs? The idea that some institutions might be basic and therefore subject to a more stringent kind of moral evaluation than nonbasic institutions is hard to justify. It is even harder to explain exactly what this more stringent kind of moral evaluation might look like. What is at issue here? The burden of proof? The standard of proof? Something else? Even distinguishing between basic institutions and institutions within the same basic category can be difficult to do. For example, it is easy to see that the choice between capitalism and socialism implies different kinds of basic institutions – a free market of some kind if we select capitalism, and a vast government agency charged with making pricing and production decisions if we don't. But once that choice is made, is a central bank a basic institution too? A basic "sub-institution?" A nonbasic institution? How are we to decide this? Basic institutions not only have many moving parts (are each of these moving parts basic institutions in themselves or sub-institutions or something else?), basic institutions are also often codependent and the lines between them blurry. Therefore, it may be hard to tell whether some aspect of our social system represents two basic institutions or one larger integrated basic institution. Even explaining what is meant to be included in the concept of an institution itself, basic or not, is difficult to answer. It could refer to an organization, a pattern of behavior, a set of rules for a certain practice, that practice itself, some combination of these, or all of the above, to name just a few possibilities.[64] If the category of "basic institutional analysis" is to be at all analytically useful, it must be much clearer that the distinctions on which it is based tell us something about how moral evaluation should proceed. In other words, there must be a way to differentiate between the moral analysis that takes place at the basic institution level and the analysis that takes place at the nonbasic institution and outcome level, even if we use a very inclusive definition for the term "institution" itself.

And there is. An institution is basic, whether it is considered a freestanding institution or a sub-institution of some larger, even more basic institution, if and only if it's existence, given all other currently existing institutions and sub-institutions, is necessary to make the basic structure as a whole more likely to be just, that is, reasonably calculated to maximize the chances that its outputs will be just given the limits of the feasible set. If the absence of a certain institution would make the outputs of the basic structure more likely to be unjust within the context of an existing basic structure, then its absence is unjust even though it might not be if the basic structure were instantiated in some other way. In other words, to evaluate whether a particular institution is basic and therefore necessary, we hold all other existing institutions constant, basic or not, and assume that regardless of their justness or lack thereof they are not subject to alteration, even if they are less than ideal. We then ask whether the particular institutional candidate we have before us is necessary in the context that this question happens to arise. If that context happens to change, we can ask that question again, but the question only has meaning if we assume for the moment that the parameters within which our evaluation will occur happen to be fixed. The same kind of moral evaluation applies to both basic and nonbasic institutions: the difference is that the creation or continued existence of a nonbasic institution is simply a matter of preference; the creation and continued existence of a basic institution on the other hand, is matter of justice.

But what happens when one of these existing institutions is manifestly unjust? For example, slavery was an institution in the United States for a very long time – not a basic institution, for its existence was never necessary to make society more just, but an institution nonetheless. Is it appropriate to determine whether some other institution is or is not required by justice in a society where slavery is included in the moral baseline? But this is not what we are doing. To apply the test that I have articulated, we do not need to assume that all existing institutions are just. The test I have articulated simply asks whether, given the existing standard of justice in a particular society, adding a particular institution will make the outputs of that society more likely to be just. The test is designed to let us know when a proposed new institution is basic – that is, required to make a society more just. The test does not claim that the sum total of society will be best characterized as just after the addition of that institution, and it does not tell us whether eliminating some existing unjust institution will render the institutional addition we are contemplating unnecessary. The test is therefore not designed to tell us how to get the most "bang" for our justice "buck." It is simply designed to tell us whether a particular institution must be considered basic given the current state of affairs in a particular society. It is not an overall measure of the justness of a particular society but merely a way of determining when institutional adjustments may be required.

2.3 The Moral Evaluation of Basic Institutions

There is a possible proviso here, however, that I want to consider. Even if a certain institution *is* necessary to make the outputs of society more likely to be just under existing conditions, we might still not want to instantiate the institution if this would make it less likely that an already existing manifestly unjust institution will be significantly reformed. For example, if we are considering instituting a new Ministry of Slavery that would promulgate and vigorously enforce rules requiring the humane treatment of slaves and thereby ensure that all slaves are well-treated, we might worry that, while this will make society that allows slavery more just, it might also retard efforts to eliminate slavery entirely. The problem here, however, is that a proviso such as this could swallow the rule. Indeed, Marxists often object to *any* change that would make capitalist societies more just because they believe that this only delays the inevitable coming of the socialist revolution. Better to allow capitalism to make life as solitary, poor, nasty, brutish, and short as it can get, for the sooner it does, the sooner we will be rid of it – the reasoning might go. Any change, therefore, that might make society more just could be rejected on the grounds that it makes what is a fundamentally unjust society less likely to fall. Insisting that things must be allowed to get worse so one system can be replaced by another system that is more just, however, effectively requires that we sacrifice those suffering now for the benefit of individuals who may not even be born yet. Things can always get worse until they become so bad that revolution actually seems like the least risky alternative, and the kind of sacrifice this requires violates the idea of the distinctness of persons because it allows some and perhaps many current people to be used as mere means to better the lives of other current and even future people. Moreover, doing so can be even more morally perverse than this, for it is often hard to tell whether one change now will make another more or less likely in the future. People often may and obviously do differ on how clear the answer to that question is. As long as it could be argued that some change now would make a more significant change later less likely, we could end up stuck in the mud of a terrible situation that might last longer even if some improvement were made now. In that case, we have not merely sacrificed some for the benefit of others, we have done so for no benefit at all. Best not to take this risk, even if we are to reject the categorical imperative. As the song by the famed early twentieth-century labor activist Joe Hill goes, it is far better to gain some ground now than to give that up for "pie in the sky when you die."[65] Therefore, the proposed proviso on our test is neither necessary nor helpful. Our test privileges improvements now over greater improvements later, even if it could be determined with relative certainty that this would be the effect.

Note that this means that whether any particular institution is necessary is contingent on both the nature and the content of whatever other institutions have been selected. If one is going to have a system for regulating various aspects of social cooperation, for example, one must have a system for enforcing those regulations if those regulations are to be meaningful. The existence of the former implies the need for the latter. Both are accordingly basic institutional parts of any legal system, even if the regulations at issue are themselves not required by justice but are enacted simply as matter of preference, for regulations that are not enforceable are not *bona fide* regulations but rather some kind of joke.[66] This test, I hope, should ensure that we avoid what are largely semantic arguments about whether an institution is basic or not. An institution is basic if its existence is necessary, given all the other institutions that exist whether they are basic or not, to make society most likely to be just within the feasible set.

2.4 HOW TO DETERMINE WHETHER THE UNION IS A BASIC INSTITUTION

2.4.1 The Context of the Inquiry

What does this tell us about unions? First, it tells us that for purposes of determining whether, and if so when, unions are a basic institution, we need to evaluate them in the context in which they actually arise; that is, as existing (or not) in the midst of a liberal capitalist society and not in some idealist vacuum. In other words, we are not interested in whether unions would be a necessary (and therefore basic) institution within some society that is designed from scratch according to some particular libertarian, liberal egalitarian, or perfectionist ideal, but whether they are a necessary institution in order for it to be more likely that there will be greater background justice in the society in which we actually live.[67] The economic system that provides the preselected context for our inquiry is accordingly capitalism, meaning the basic method used for allocating economic resources in our society is the free market, the distinguishing feature of which is the use of the price mechanism to reveal and prioritize the fulfillment of preferences. The primary method of organizing economic resources in such a society, in turn, is through the collection of these resources into entities known as firms, whose actions are subject to moderation by various principles drawn from among the family of theories known as political liberalism. The question we are faced with is accordingly whether unions should be treated as a basic institution given the attributes that already exist in our actual liberal capitalist economic system.[68]

Of course, even within the liberal capitalist economies, there are a variety of approaches being taken toward unionization.[69] Given that the test I have proposed for determining the normative status of any particular putative or existing institution requires us to otherwise take things as they are, it is accordingly possible that different answers may be generated for different liberal capitalist democracies. Unions have a different history, have played a different role in the development of different national economies, and have different cultural significance and affinities in different capitalist societies.

Thus, it is not necessarily true that if unions are a basic institution in the United States they must also be in the United Kingdom or France or Germany or Italy or Japan. Or, even more importantly, they may *already* be treated as a basic institution in some of these countries, either formally or informally, but not in others. Despite globalization, there has been little convergence on our approach to unionization within the liberal capitalist world, so differences in our approach to unionization remain live on a national level, and the ramifications of these differences are important. Accordingly, while I will draw on what is happening with regard to unionization in other countries when appropriate, my argument is directed primarily at the United States and secondarily at the United Kingdom, although there are important differences even here. For example, unlike the United States, the United Kingdom has a political party that is at least ostensibly formally associated with the labor movement, and this difference must be taken into consideration.[70] But the advantage of my approach is that it allows us to consider these varieties of capitalism and use them as a resource rather than as a homogenizing hammer.

2.4.2 The Primary Importance of Pre-institutional Rights

The other important lesson to be drawn from our theoretical discussion is that when determining whether unions should be treated as a basic institution, we should not be focusing on whether unions infringe or support certain individual rights such as freedom of speech or freedom of association. These are post-institutional rights – that is, posited rights that are designed primarily as limits on the power of institutions to restrain or compel the activities of individuals rather than rights that tell us which particular combination of basic institutions a just society should have. What we should be focusing on are pre-institutional rights – that is, more general rights like liberty and equality from which more particularized rights to types of liberty and equality are derived.[71] Freedom of speech and freedom of association can only have meaning in the context of a society that has a basic structure and accompanying basic institutions. Liberty and equality, in contrast, have meaning even before any basic institutions are designed. This does not mean that the various post-institutional expressions of these rights are to be ignored. It merely means that these post-institutional expressions are not the only or even the first conception of these rights to be considered. Rather, when we are determining whether something is a basic institution, it is pre-institutional conceptions of our rights that are naturally our primary focus. Post-institutional conceptions are only to be considered to the extent they throw light on the nature and content of what we determine our pre-institutional rights to be.

The idea that we have rights even before there are institutions has a long history and comes up in variety of contexts. John Locke, for example, famously argued that everyone has a right to enforce their rights in the state of nature, before government of any kind exists.[72] Today, however, the *pre* versus *post* distinction comes up most often in the context of discussing what *natural* or *human* rights we might have.[73] Of course, the view that there are such things as natural or human rights is controversial – Jeremy Bentham called this view "nonsense on stilts."[74] But many, many theorists, on both the left and the right, accept that such rights do exist in one form or another.[75] Some modern theorists have even argued that unionization, and perhaps certain other aspects of workers' cooperative activity as well, and not just free association, are human rights.[76] I do not necessarily disagree with those who advance such a position, but the argument I am about to make is both broader and narrower than the arguments made by those who argue that worker rights are human rights. It is broader in the sense that in arguing that unions are a basic institution, I am not simply arguing that workers have an individual human right to unionize if they wish, but that all workplaces *must* be unionized as mater of background justice; the matter is not up for majority vote and cannot be waived like other individual rights. It is narrower in the sense that my argument only applies if we determine that justice does indeed require that we recognize unions as a basic institution, a question that depends on the existing attributes of a particular society and not on some conception of human rights that applies at all times and all places and in all conditions, as recognized by some international institution or declaration. In other words, my argument will be derived in a very different manner than arguments about the nature and content of human rights. Those are derived primarily from presuppositions about the nature of human attributes and circumstances and from the supposed authority of international institutions to override national attempts to disregard them. My argument, in contrast, is derived from philosophical presuppositions about what counts in determining whether the basic institutions of society are just, given our actual observations about not only human nature and circumstances but also social cooperation and the social and economic circumstances found in the particular society under examination. In any event, while the precise number and contours of other forms of pre-institutional rights, whether they be human or natural or something else, can be controversial, there is widespread agreement that these rights include some kind of liberty and some kind of equality.[77] Indeed, when it comes to discussing issues about justice, the existence of these pre-institutional rights is pretty much assumed.[78] In any event, given the fact that the anti-union argument, and indeed a great many of the other arguments against what are viewed as progressive policies, rely on the idea of there being pre-institutional rights of liberty and equality, and that Rawls himself embraces this in the context of delineating between the basic structure, basic institutions, and the outputs of these institutions, I will take the idea that rights do exist in both a pre-institutional and a post-institutional form to be given.[79]

Of course, the pre-institutional rights of liberty and equality are concepts not conceptions and therefore need to be further cashed out before we can derive specific guidance from them,[80] but I shall get to this in a moment. And as I have already noted, the justness of the outputs of a basic institution reflects back on the justness of its design. When an institution threatens individual rights, however, the first solution is to prevent such individual violations through regulation of the institution. Elimination of the institution would only be the just solution to misconduct by an otherwise liberty or equality promoting institution when all attempts at post-institutional regulation are bound to fail. The fact that government may attempt to ban certain associations or suppress certain kinds of speech is accordingly a reason to regulate government, not to eliminate it, for there is nothing about such attempts to suggest that properly regulated government power would still be inherently antithetical to either of these rights. We also do not want to give protecting mere aspects of these rights moral priority over protecting the more general rights from whence they came. Which means at the basic institution level of analysis, we are more interested in the impact of institutions on liberty and equality *per se* rather than on mere aspects of liberty and equality. The impact (or potential impact) of an institution on more particularized versions of these rights is paramount only when we are focusing on evaluating the outputs of an institution that has already been established as a necessary element of a just society.

But as I said, the concepts of liberty and equality can each be cashed out in various ways. I will take equality to require something like Rawls's first two principles of justice as fairness (equal basic liberties and fair equality of opportunity) plus either the difference principle or luck egalitarianism or my own theory of exploitation or something along these lines. For our purposes, the precise principle to be used for regulating social and economic inequalities is not important because all of them suggest that the current state of affairs, in which economic inequality is higher than it has been at any time since the Great Depression, is morally unacceptable.[81] Because there is a strong correlation between decreasing levels of unionization and increasing economic inequality, we therefore already have some reason to think there may be a causal relationship between these two factors and not just a correlation. I will say more about this possibility later, but I do not need to do so now because the argument against unionization is usually phrased as an argument from liberty – that is, as an argument that unions impermissibly interfere with individual liberty and therefore are to be suppressed or even banned but, at the very least, not encouraged because regardless of their effect on inequality, protecting liberty trumps suppressing inequality, or at least economic inequality, or so the argument goes. Indeed, this approach to arguing against unionization goes back a long time. For example, one of the primary opponents of the National Labor Relations Act of 1935, which is still the foundational instrument governing labor-management relations in the United States today, was a collection of corporate executives and conservative lawyers calling themselves "The Liberty League."[82] I will therefore treat the argument from liberty as providing the primary framework for deciding whether unions are a basic institution, with the argument from equality playing only a secondary and subsidiary role.

2.4.3 What We Talk about When We Talk about Liberty

Curiously, those who make the liberty argument against unions are never very clear about what they exactly have in mind, and there are in fact several ways the concept of liberty can be cashed out. First, there is negative liberty, or freedom from interference by other human agents.[83] Second, there is positive liberty, or the ability to self-actualize, to live the kind of life one would voluntarily choose if one were fully informed and free to choose what form of life one might wish.[84] And finally, there is republican liberty, or freedom from the arbitrary will of another, a form of domination that threatens the even more fundamental concept of self-ownership from which many theorists (including me) think that all theories of liberty and even equality can be derived. I will explain these concepts further and develop my own particular conceptions of them in a moment,[85] but for now, I want to simply make one particularly important point. Despite what their names suggest, negative and positive liberty are not opposing poles on some single liberty scale. They are actually different types of theories altogether. Negative liberty is analytical theory, not a political one. By this I mean the concept of negative liberty does not claim that all interference with negative liberty is morally objectionable – indeed, social order would be impossible if government did not massively interfere with negative liberty in a myriad of ways every day. All negative liberty does is tell us when there is some interference and claim that such interference has to be justified. It does not purport to say what reasons might justify such interference or how strong such reasons would have to be. That information must be provided by some other theory, a political theory, one that actually embraces moral ends and gives us some guidance as to what priority competing ends might have.[86] Negative liberty is only political in the sense that it sets noninterference as the preferred default position. Otherwise, in terms of whether, and if so when, any particular act of interference can be justified, it tells us nothing.

But does not negative liberty tell us something? Does it not tell us that interferences with negative liberty are to be *minimized*? Indeed, negative liberty theorists are often accused of arguing exactly this. Or at least they are accused of having to endorse this view, even if they deny having to do so. And a quantitative theory of negative liberty – in other words, a version of the theory that claims the fewer interferences with negative liberty a society imposes, the freer it is – is intuitively highly implausible. Charles Taylor made this precise point very effectively many years ago. He pointed out that under quantitative theory, Albania before the fall of communism might be considered more free than England was at the time because there were far fewer traffic lights in Albania,

2.4 How to Determine Whether the Union Is a Basic Institution

and on a sheer numbers basis, people were much more likely to encounter traffic lights than restrictions on how they could practice their religion or what they could say in public, restrictions that apply in Albania but not in England. But these latter restrictions, Taylor argued, are far more important. It is therefore ludicrous to say that people in Albania are more free than people in England.[87] And if we reject the quantitative version of negative liberty, as on this basis Taylor says we should, we then still need some other theory such as a qualitative theory (what I am calling a political theory) to tell us when an interference with negative liberty is justified and when it is not.

Equality, of course, is one such theory.[88] At the very least, equality tells us that an interference with negative liberty is *not* justified unless all members of society are subject to the same kind and degree of interference themselves. In other words, under liberalism, everyone must enjoy an equal degree of negative liberty. The problem here is that this constraint can be satisfied at either a very high or a very low level of negative liberty and everything in between. If this is all that equality tells us, it does not tell us when an infringement of negative liberty is justified and when it is not. It merely tells us that the same kind and degree of infringement must apply to everyone if anyone is to be subject to it. But it is possible that equality can tell us more than this. If certain kinds of negative liberty make people unequal in certain ways (for example, economically) even when negative liberty is distributed equally to everyone, then we may be able to derive not only a requirement of equal negative liberty from the principle of equality but also a rule directing us to reject certain kinds of negative liberty and embrace others. I shall argue exactly this in a moment, but for now, I will assume that this is not true, for as I said, I do not want to rest my claim that unions are a basic institution on the argument from equality. And if we do not rely on the argument from equality, some other political theory is required before we can know whether, and if so when, certain kinds of negative liberty can be justly regulated and therefore infringed as long as these regulations are equally applied.

For this, then, we need to look at positive and republican liberty, for unlike negative liberty, these concepts of liberty *are* political theories. To see why, remember that for most theorists, negative liberty is an opportunity concept, one that looks at what you have the capacity to do, regardless of whether you take advantage of these opportunities or not. Positive liberty, in contrast, is an exercise concept – that is, it purports to tell you what you must actually do to be free (this is why it is called "positive liberty").[89] If someone prevents you from doing what the theory tells you to do, then this is unjust, theories of positive liberty claim – no other theory need be referred to in order to establish this. (Theories of positive liberty are also violated if you simply fail to take advantage of the opportunities open to you, but for our purposes, this is irrelevant because the issue we are looking at is how to tell when an interference with negative liberty is unjustified.) Republican liberty, on the other hand, is political in another way. It describes what others cannot do to you – at least under the conception I will articulate here – and therefore it is structured like an opportunity concept. People cannot interfere with you in certain ways if this deprives you of the opportunity to make certain choices that would otherwise be available to you. But unlike general conceptions of negative liberty, republican liberty does contain criteria for determining when infringements of negative liberty are not justified, so both positive and republican liberty are potential candidates for explaining when infringements of negative liberty are justified and when they are not.

Conceptions of positive liberty, however, tend to be very comprehensive – while limited conceptions of positive liberty are possible, if the idea is to describe how to become your fully realized self, to be all that you can be, a conception is going to have to prescribe a great many things you must do, not just one or two. Moreover, because they are so detailed, people will disagree about these details, and there will accordingly be an enormous number of possible conceptions of positive liberty one could embrace. Some of these would permit unionization; some of these would require it; and some would prohibit it. And in any case, this would be only one tiny part of the many comprehensive conceptions of positive liberty one could embrace, and many, many aspects of these views would be controversial, not just the attitude it expressed toward unionization. Indeed, because these comprehensive views are so controversial, enforcing one view or another of positive liberty is generally (although not universally) thought to be inconsistent with the role of government under liberalism, for embracing one conception over another would violate the idea that government should be neutral between reasonable but inconsistent competing comprehensive conceptions of the good – an idea that enjoys wide acceptance on both the left and the right.[90] Enforcing or even promoting some particular conception of positive liberty is accordingly not going to be available as a justification for interfering with negative liberty in a liberal capitalist state.[91]

Republican liberty, in contrast, is different. It does not have as many versions as positive liberty has, and the versions it does have tend to employ far fewer moving parts.[92] There may sometimes be disagreements as to exactly when the will of another is being imposed in a "arbitrary" manner, but the idea that being subjected to the arbitrary will of another is an interference with an important kind of liberty is not seriously disputed. Of course, we do need specify what we mean by arbitrariness in greater detail if we are to use this as an important factor in determining whether an institution is basic or not, for republican liberty theorists can differ on this. Consider, for example, the work of Philip Pettit and Quentin Skinner, the two modern theorists who are primarily responsible for bringing the concept of republican liberty back from the dustbin of history and into the contemporary philosophical debate. Each of their theories of republican liberty started out as rather narrow and limited. But as they developed their respective conceptions, they each began to assign republican liberty more and more content, using republican liberty to address more and more problems.[93] Following Pettit's and Skinner's lead, other theorists also began developing very comprehensive conceptions of republican liberty as well and then applying those conceptions to resolve a wide variety of political, social, and economic problems.[94] Indeed, some conceptions of republican liberty have now become so thick that they purport to be complete theories of justice rather than mere theories of republican liberty.

But the conception of republican liberty on which I am going to rely is much thinner than this. Not because I necessarily disagree with the conceptions articulated by Pettit or Skinner or any of their followers. Nothing I am about to say turns on whether any of these thicker conceptions can be persuasively defended or attacked. And I am certainly not suggesting that anyone's theory of republican liberty is wrong merely because it is comprehensive. We simply do not need to use a thick conception here to address the question of whether unionization infringes or supports liberty in the relevant sense. Indeed, we couldn't use one of these thick conceptions here even if we wanted to, for the thicker a conception becomes, the more comprehensive it is, and the more comprehensive it becomes, the more controversial it is, for there is more to disagree with. For reasons that I have already mentioned when explaining why theories of positive liberty are ineligible for determining whether a particular institution is basic or not, a comprehensive, controversial conception of republican liberty would be ineligible too because of the restrictions imposed by our embrace of liberalism and its corresponding principle of neutrality. So the conception of republican liberty that I am going to employ here is very thin. Thin enough, in fact, to be thought of as part of what Rawls famously called "a thin theory of the good" — that is, a good that is compatible with and even essential for a wide range of reasonable comprehensive conceptions of the good and plans of life.[95] As such, its use will not violate the principle of neutrality. While it is still political, it is political in the right way, and therefore we can use it to determine which institutions are to be considered basic and which are not.

What, then is my conception? Under my conception, a decision is arbitrary only when it is based on no criteria, is made without relevant criteria being adequately considered, is based in whole or in part on criteria that are unrelated to the performance of the task or role under consideration, or is based on performance-related criteria but does not treat similarly situated people the same. In other words, under my conception of republican liberty, arbitrariness can be the result of either a defect in the procedure that produced a particular outcome or a defect in the nature of what has been considered, and/or the weight assigned to various factors. And that's it.

As an example of the kind of arbitrariness that arises from treating similarly situated people differently, consider a black employee fired for being late to work on three occasions. Being late to work is performance related, of course, but if white employees who have been late to work three times are never fired, then the decision here is still arbitrary and an interference with the republican liberty of the black employee. Indeed, one of the principal methods of discriminating against certain categories of people in employment is not terminating or otherwise disciplining them even though they have *not* violated the rules (most employers are sophisticated enough to know they cannot usually get away with *that*), but terminating or otherwise disciplining minority employees when they *have* violated the rules even though a nonminority employee would not have been terminated or treated equally harshly under the same circumstances. In this case, the problem is not that criteria unrelated to job performance has been considered, but that the weight assigned to an infraction of performance-related criteria for one employee is very different than the weight assigned to the that same infraction when committed by others who are similarly situated. What is arbitrary here is that factors are given different and indeed decisive weights according to the identity of the employ, when identity is not itself a relevant factor.[96]

Of course, arbitrary treatment can arise in a myriad of other ways, and I am not suggesting that it will always be easy to tell whether a decision is arbitrary or not. There may, for example, be disagreements about whether people are similarly situated or not, about what factors are performance related, and about what it means for a factor to be adequately considered. Indeed, there is a range of weightings of relevant reasons that are perfectly acceptable – the range that Rawls describes as within the burdens of judgment, which are the reasons why reasonable people might reasonably disagree.[97] It is not arbitrary when one decision maker uses different weights within this range than another, unless that decision maker is using different weights than he would for others similarly situated. But while there is a full basket of jurisprudence in the legal systems of most liberal capitalist democracies that has arisen to guide us toward a resolution of any dispute about the precise borders of arbitrariness,[98] we actually need not have such a fine-grained conception of arbitrariness at the basic institution level of analysis. All we need it to do at this level of analysis is to alert us to general threats, tendencies, and reasons for concern. Fine-tuning the conception we apply and pruning any rough edges that may arise can be done after we have decided whether something is a basic institution. And for those purposes, the fact that determining whether a decision is arbitrary or not has been a standard of legality for thousands of years suggests that the standard provides a workable principle of review, even if there might be many details to work out about how the concept is to apply in particular situations, once the necessary basic institutions are established.

Note that there are several factors I have *not* included as part of my definition of arbitrariness. This is why my conception of republican liberty is thinner than most. One of the factors that I have not included, for example, is intent – under my conception of republican liberty, intent to interfere with another's liberty is neither necessary nor sufficient.[99] One must intend to do what one does, of course; that is, whatever one does must be a voluntary act in the philosophy of action sense and not the product of some uncontrollable reflex action. But otherwise, for purposes of my conception, arbitrariness is conceived of as a strict liability offense. Now this may seem odd in the sense that the "arbitrary will of another" is imposed through a decision, and it seems like a "decision" must be an intentional act. But one can also be subjected to the arbitrary will of another by a lack of decision, and a failure to decide need not be an intentional act. And even though a decision is an intentional act, one need not intend that this decision interfere with someone else's liberty for it to have that effect. In determining whether republican liberty has been violated, what matters is whether, and if so, what kind of reasons were behind a particular decision and whether they are the same kinds of reasons weighted in the same way as when the same decision maker has made a similar decision with regard to someone else in similar circumstances. A lack of intent to interfere with someone else's liberty does not change the nature of the reasons considered by the decision maker or the decision weight assigned to each, nor does it change whether a restriction on another's liberty was the decision's effect. On the other hand, an intent to interfere with the liberty of another does not amount to an act of arbitrariness, no matter what the reasons behind it, just as an intent to commit murder does not constitute murder if the act is not successfully carried out. At most, what we have is an attempt and perhaps merely a threat. There may be reasons why we want to punish or protect against attempts and/or threats, and attempts or even threats may constitute a violation of republican liberty in some cases given their actual effects. But under my conception of republican liberty an intent to interfere is not required, and intent by itself, when this produces none of the effects that we are concerned about, is not enough.[100]

Another element I have not included in my definition of arbitrariness is that a decision is not arbitrary under my conception merely because it fails to consider the interests or opinions of those affected by it. Some republican liberty theorists do include these factors in their test for arbitrariness,[101] but in my view, this is a mistake. Criteria that are relevant to the decision at issue may or may not need to include consideration of the interests or opinions of those affected by it – this depends on what it at issue. For example, the determination of which soldier should be sent on a dangerous mission should be made by considering which of the available soldiers are most likely to complete the mission successfully. Because the mission is dangerous, however, and anyone who is sent is likely to be killed, it may be in no one's individual interest to go on the mission, and each of the available soldiers may believe (in good faith or otherwise) that someone else among their group would be better suited to undertake it. It is therefore not arbitrary for the commander to rely exclusively on his own judgment regarding which soldier is most likely to successfully accomplish the mission when deciding whom he should send.[102]

Here is another example: despite now having the right to drive, some women in Saudi Arabia, and perhaps even a majority, continue to think that women should not to be allowed to drive.[103] Because everyone has an "interest" in having their opinions considered, it accordingly might be considered arbitrary to have lifted the ban on women driving because the decision to do this did not include consideration of their interests and opinions. Additionally, it might even have been considered arbitrary not to take into account the interests and opinions of most men. Determining what criteria are relevant to a decision, however, must depend on the relation between that criteria and performance of the task at issue and not on what we might perceive as the interest and opinions of the affected group, for we otherwise would have to decide what is in someone's interest (often a controversial issue), whether someone's opinions should be respected or actually represent adaptive preferences that are entitled to no moral weight (again very controversial),[104] and what to do when the interests and opinions of the members of the affected group happen to conflict (does majority rule with regard to a group?). What do we do, moreover, when a particular individual's interests and opinions happen to conflict? Under the test I have proposed, these problems are avoided: we would characterize the ban on women driving as arbitrary given that there is no reason to believe that women cannot drive as competently as men, regardless of what we decide is in the relevant affected group's interest and what their opinions on the matter might be.

There are other problems with considering interests and opinions as well. If a decision is necessarily arbitrary if it does not consider the interests and opinions of those affected (and note this would seem to mean we would have to consider preferences too, as these are opinions about what one desires and possibly even about what is good for one), we have a problem with circularity – one has an interest in having republican liberty, and most people would prefer more republican liberty over less of it. But if republican liberty is itself defined by what is in one's interest and consistent with one's preferences, where is one supposed to start? The process of defining what republican liberty requires becomes hopelessly trapped in a logical loop. Therefore, even if the interest and opinion test might be useful in some other context, it is not part of what we would want to consider here.

Finally, there is one other factor I have not included in my list of what does and does not make a decision arbitrary. I have not specified that a decision is to be considered arbitrary if it is based on criteria that is unrelated to any *legitimate* (that is, substantively just) objective of the decision maker, even if that criteria might be considered relevant to the performance of the task. It is true, of course, that principles which tell us that something is not a substantively just criterion for decision are sometimes claimed to be derived from the principle of arbitrariness. In US constitutional law, for example, cases that use this approach as the grounds for decision are often thought of as vindicating a right to "substantive" (as opposed to "procedural") due process. For example, property rights were for a time thought of something that could not be interfered with without violating the right to liberty protected by the due process clause, and the relationship between a parent and a child still generally is, as are certain aspects of privacy.[105] Some of these decisions may be proper interpretations of the due process clause, but whether they are is irrelevant for our purposes. When these decisions really do reflect concerns about arbitrariness in the sense I have identified, we do not need to expand our conception of arbitrariness to include a list of concerns that are otherwise nonarbitrary but are substantively objectionable; we simply need to do a better job explaining why our concern really is driven by one of the aspects of arbitrariness I have identified above. And if our concern is actually driven by some substantive objection, other than the arbitrariness as I have identified it, then it is best that we base our objection on that substantive concern expressly and not try to expand our conception of arbitrariness in order to accommodate what is bound to be a controversial conception of what ends are legitimate, for that moves us beyond our thin conception of republican liberty and into a more comprehensive conception of positive liberty and therefore is really a concern derived from some post-institutional conception of substantive justice and not a pre-institutional conception of arbitrariness. In other words, including what is really a concern about ends as part of our test for arbitrariness would require that we have a preexisting moral baseline of what is just and unjust. While such a baseline could be fully specified post-institutionally, it could not be fully specified pre-institutionally without reference to some other, controversial political theory, and controversial elements cannot be included in our thin theory of the good and therefore cannot supply criteria for pre-institutional justice. And if the particular criterion were sufficiently noncontroversial that it could be included in a thin theory of the good, then it would not need to be incorporated into our conception of arbitrariness because it could simply be used pre-institutionally on its own account.

Moving on from my definition of arbitrariness, there are a couple of other nuances in the literature about republican liberty that I also want to address so that they do not become distractions here. First, on some accounts, republican liberty is violated whenever one is in a state of dependence on the arbitrary will of another, regardless of whether one is actually subjected to arbitrary interference.[106] For my purposes, I am treating the former state of affairs as simply being exposed to a threat to republican liberty; a violation of republican liberty occurs only when there is actual interference. Treating mere dependence as a violation renders republican liberty useless as a concept, for if broadly construed, this could mean we are all without republican liberty all the time. If we want the concept do some meaningful work, the narrower view is far more helpful.[107] Second, but related to the first, some theorists suggest that republican liberty requires that one be allowed to play a participatory part in the local polity.[108] The idea here, I suppose, is that if one does not have a voice in the formation and application of the rules that govern one's behavior, those rules are in some sense arbitrary. But even requiring participation would, at least in an extremely large number of instances, be highly controversial, for there are literally millions of regulations that affect our lives, and we have participated in devising them only in the most indirect and inconsequential way. For our purposes, participation is neither necessary nor sufficient to prevent a violation of republican liberty. Our thin conception of republican liberty, which avoids all these controversial elements of these various comprehensive conceptions, will suffice.

But there is one other type of liberty that I should mention before we move onto examining the relationship between unionization, negative liberty, and republican liberty. In a capitalist society, many people embrace some conception of economic liberty – that is, the idea that an economy does best (in the sense of being most efficient and most productive) when it utilizes the free market system for allocating goods and services, and that any interference with the free market system threatens economic performance. This conception of liberty, of course, is just a narrow version of negative liberty: it is a claim for complete negative liberty within the economic realm, a claim that is often expressed as a right to "freedom of contract" and not merely to economic liberty. But as I have said elsewhere, there is no such thing as freedom of contract, only freedom. No specific kind of freedom exists independently of the concept of freedom from which it was born. It is therefore a mistake to treat freedom from interference with X as something necessarily different in kind than negative freedom full stop. Indeed, doing this would suggest we may sacrifice certain kinds of freedom for freedom of other kinds, and one cannot derive any grounds for this from a general conception of negative liberty. In other words, economic liberty is merely a liberty, not a right, or at least if it is a right, the argument for this cannot be based on a conception of negative liberty.[109]

Another point to keep in mind is that even though economic liberty makes a bigger claim than negative liberty – it does not merely claim that interference has to be justified, it claims that all such interference is improper – it is still an economic theory, not a political one. In other words, the end it embraces – economic efficiency – is a prudential not a moral one. And of course, as an absolutist claim about the effects of all government regulation, it is patently untrue. Government regulation can also spur economic growth, advance technological innovation, create new markets, attract new customers, and so on.[110] But the argument from economic liberty has not stayed within its economic bounds – primarily because certain theorists worry that any government that has the tools to interfere with the free market also has the tools to interfere with political liberty. Infringements of economic liberty, whether they be good or bad for the economy, are accordingly often seen as the first step down a slippery slope toward totalitarianism, for in order to interfere effectively in a market economy, the government would have to develop tools that would enable it, and probably also encourage it, to interfere in all aspects of our lives.[111] For those that hold this view, economic liberty effectively morphs from an economic theory into a political one, and this is indeed what explains how classical economic liberalism became what we now call neoliberalism.[112] While I believe the slippery-slope argument and therefore the key assumption underlying the modern political version of neoliberalism to be mistaken,[113] I will not argue this position here. Instead, I will take this position seriously and attempt to show that even if it is correct, unionization does not represent a threat to either the economic or the politicized version of economic liberty, but actually supports it.

While not actually claimed to be a form of liberty by any theorist worth being taken seriously, I should mention one other concept that is sometimes trotted out by the "man on the street" as an explanation of when an interference with negative liberty is not unjust. This is the concept of voluntariness. The idea behind this popular intuition, which I have already mentioned in other contexts, is that an infringement of negative liberty cannot be unjust if the person subject to this infringement voluntarily consents to it and, conversely, cannot be just if that infringement is imposed involuntarily. The problem with this idea, of course, is that voluntariness is hopelessly indeterminate as a concept. There are lots of reasons why consent to the infringement of negative liberty could be treated as involuntary, and many of these reasons have to do with background conditions that exist only after we have decided what basic institutions should exist. Indeed, voluntariness only has meaning after we have decided what rights we have and therefore what kinds of coercion we may justly impose on others. In some sense, the traveler who chooses to give the highwayman his money after the highwayman threatens him with "your money or life" is acting voluntarily. The problem with using voluntariness as a useful test here is that it requires a moral baseline for what we can and cannot do to have already been set, and the content of this baseline is the very issue we are trying to address.[114] Therefore, voluntariness is not a political theory that can tell us when an interference with negative liberty is just and when it is not.

2.4.4 The Firm as a Threat to Liberty

The first thing to note as we begin our particularized examination of the effects of unionization on liberty – and this is something people often forget – is that the private firm – the very association that is at the center of capitalism – is not itself an expression of free market principles. Within the firm, resources such as human capital (but not only human capital) are allocated centrally by command, just as they would be for the economy as a whole under socialism, and not by the price mechanism. In other words, in a capitalist system, the free market mechanism of allocating goods and services is not in place all the way down.[115] Because resources are allocated within the firm by command rather than by the price mechanism, those in command have the opportunity to exercise domination over others, by which I mean the opportunity to subject those under their command to their arbitrary will. This is a threat to liberty, but not because (or rather not merely because) it is a threat to *negative* liberty. As I have said, many things infringe on negative liberty, but this by itself is not a reason to reject them, for many such acts of interference are justified. It is a threat to liberty because it is a threat to *republican* liberty, which tells us that some threats to negative liberty are acceptable (those that do not represent acts of domination) and some are not (those that do), or at least, that is how my conception of republican liberty can best be understood.[116] And threats to republican liberty are threats to be taken seriously, for where the opportunity for domination exists, it is very likely that people will take it up. Indeed, as Adam Smith himself recognized: "The love of domination and authority over others...is I am afraid natural to mankind."[117] Some theorists even argue that instead of being an unavoidable side effect of the hierarchical structure of the firm, the firm has actually become the central means of economic production precisely *because* it offers opportunities for domination, opportunities that many people find irresistibly attractive.[118] In any event, given the power that those in management of the firm have to determine the quality of one of the most important relationships in the lives of workers, and the natural attraction of opportunities for domination, we can rightly worry that those within the firm who have the authority to command will use that power to infringe their employees republican liberty. Indeed, Pettit himself expressly warns us about this: "In the absence of other employment opportunities and appropriate controls—say, those that a vigilant union might guarantee—employers and managers will enjoy subjugating power over their workers."[119] Yet this threat is exactly the kind of threat that the free market system was supposed to allow us avoid.

What, then justifies the existence of the firm, despite the infringement of negative liberty and the threat to republican liberty it represents? Despite being what may be the most superficially appealing answer, it is *not* actual consent. With regard to these questions, it is irrelevant that workers have in some sense expressly agreed to subject themselves to the authority of their employers, and the supervisors those employers put over them, when they agree to take employment with the firm. As Rawls and many others since have made abundantly clear, actual consent in these circumstances has little moral force. When people have unequal bargaining power, unequal bargaining skill, unequal information, and start from unequal positions, as they often do out in the real world, they can easily end up agreeing to things that are seriously unjust.[120] While there are no doubt a few employees who are not handicapped by bargaining inequalities, the fact that this may be true on an exceptional basis does not make actual consent a sufficient guarantor of just outcomes. Even LeBron James, for example, who may have more bargaining power and start from at least as strong an initial bargaining position as his potential employers, still needs high-priced representatives to equalize deficiencies in his personal contractual bargaining skills and his access to relevant information. In any event, actual consent to an infringement of republican liberty, even when not the product of bargaining inequalities, is tantamount to consent to being treated as a slave, and consensual slavery is something that almost all versions of liberalism reject. But most importantly, post-institutional consent simply cannot justify the existence of an institution, so the fact that workers agree to subject themselves to the authority of their employers for certain purposes in the post-institutional world does not justify the interference with liberty that the firm as an institution represents. Only pre-institutional hypothetical consent – the kind of consent that would be given by free and equal persons considering whether to instantiate the particular institution – can justify an institution that represents a threat to republican liberty and an act of interference with negative liberty as well.

Note that this pre-institutional decision situation is similar to what Rawls famously called "the original position" but is not identical to it. First, because the Rawlsian original position has a thicker veil of ignorance than is necessary to give consent moral weight in these circumstances (the only thing these decision makers need not know in this hypothetical decision situation is who they are and therefore how their decision would affect them directly). And second, because the decisions that Rawls places in the original position occur before the applicable principles of justice have been articulated and the relevant institutions of the basic structure governed by these principles have been cashed out. The hypothetical decision situation that I am constructing, in contrast, takes place when all these questions have been decided, *except* the one at issue in this particular case.[121] Even so, hypothetical consent has moral force in these circumstances because the possibility of the exercise of personal bias by or the application of coercion upon the relevant decision makers is eliminated. The question we need to ask here is do we have reason to believe that free and equal people in this situation would indeed consent to subject themselves to the threat to republican liberty and interference with negative liberty that institutionalization of the firm creates?

The accepted view seems to be yes, based on the efficiency gains the firm provides.[122] As I noted in the first essay in this volume, it is very costly, both in terms of time and money, for the resources of a society to be allocated through free market exchange all the way down. By eliminating the need for constant negotiation between every individual every time something is to be done, the firm and the hierarchical method of allocating economic resources that it entails offers cost savings that can be quite substantial. A more efficient application of resources, in turn, means that an economy can produce more of what it needs and less of it what it doesn't. There is accordingly more of what people actually need and want to go around, and so there is at least the potential for everyone to enjoy a higher standard of living. In other words, the efficiency gains here outweigh and loss of negative liberty and any threat to republican liberty combined. Making this trade is accordingly most likely to be in furtherance of the common good. While those in the original position cannot know whether they will be one of those who benefit from this arrangement or suffer under it, the odds are that they will benefit and therefore would agree to it if asked to choose behind the relevant veil of ignorance.

One might query, of course, whether a concern for efficiency, which is not a moral notion, can justify an interference with negative liberty, much less allow us to disregard the threat to republican liberty that the firm represents. Remember, though, negative liberty is itself a moral notion in only a very weak sense. It merely says that interferences with negative liberty have to be justified and leaves the question of what might count as a sufficient justification to some other theory. It does not require that such a justification be moral. We have already noted that justice is also subject to a feasibility constraint. This is why efficiency can be relevant to our determination of when an interference with negative liberty might be justified (I will get to whether, and if so, this can also be a justification for infringements of republican liberty in a moment). For there is no point to insisting on justice to the point where the gains from social cooperation that we are trying to protect will be eliminated or dramatically reduced.

The attraction of efficiency gains, however, means that the threat to liberty posed by the firm can be quite substantial. As long as there are cost savings to be had from acquiring resources for internal allocation rather than contracting for their temporary use externally, the firm will be the preferred form of business organization. As I discussed in the first essay in this volume, once a firm is formed, it can be expected to increase in size as long as there are further cost savings to be had.[123] And the larger it gets, the greater the infringement of negative liberty involved and greater the threat that those in the upper reaches of management of the firm pose to the republican liberty of those below them. But while efficiency may justify the infringement of negative liberty that the firm represents, and may even justify putting republican liberty *at risk*, it does not justify any actual *infringement* of republican liberty that may result.[124] Because republican liberty, unlike negative liberty, *is* a strongly moral notion, no amount of efficiency gains could justify its infringement, at least as long as it is feasible to have these efficiency gains (or most of them) yet avoid or at least compensate for the violations of republican liberty that the firm may inflict. And to do that, post-institutional regulation is not enough because it is often too costly and cumbersome to do the job all by itself (I shall say much more about this later). What this means is that, with regard to unionization, the institutional threats created by the firm require institutional countermeasures if justice is to be assured, even if post-institutional regulation is still required or even merely helpful. Only if the threat to republican liberty that the institution of the firm represents can be largely countered on an institutional level can the institution of the firm can possibly be considered just.

Note also that this threat to republican liberty is not merely a danger to the employees of the firm – it is also a threat to the economic efficiency of the firm itself, the very justification used for putting the republican liberty of its employees at risk. Indeed, it has long been recognized that the more autocratic the management style in a firm – the more management discourages input and criticism from below – the more likely inefficiencies in production and marketing and even product selection and design are likely to arise.[125] In other words, the very argument used to justify the infringement of negative liberty and the threat to republican liberty the firm represents can begin to evaporate whenever this threat is actually carried out. Without sufficient checks on this threat to republican liberty, the very efficiency gains used to justify the actual infringement of negative liberty the firm represents can be undermined as well.

It is also important to recognize that the scope of the threat to liberty here goes beyond the threat of domination of the individual employee by his or her line manager, or some higher-ranking supervisor. Given that they represent concentrations of economic and therefore also political power, firms also pose a more general threat to the liberty of the population at large. Neoliberals, of course, focus exclusively on the threat to liberty represented by government, but their ordoliberal cousins eschew such tunnel vision. Instead, ordoliberals – who are just as committed to the idea that economic freedom and political freedom are inextricably intertwined as neoliberals are – recognize that public power and private power each represent a threat to liberty and that the use of public power is sometimes necessary to reign in the tendencies toward excess and domination commonly associated with private power.[126] They recognize this, of course, because it was the failure to reign in the economic power of large trusts and corporations in Germany in the 1930s that contributed significantly to the rise of Hitler, the consequences of which many prominent ordoliberals experienced firsthand.[127] And the Nazis were not the only ones to benefit from the support of large private concentrations of economic power. In Italy, industrialists and large landholders seeking to avoid investigations into their financial dealings and the imposition of limitations on their economic activity gave Mussolini and his Fascist Party critical support in his rise to power.[128] In Russia, the same process seems to have been involved in Putin's rise and in the consolidation of his grip on power.[129] Time and again, it has been demonstrated that unregulated private economic activity leads to oligarchy, and if this were not enough of a threat to the republican liberty of those who are not members of this elite class, a threat that grows ever larger as one moves down the economic ladder, oligarchs tend to become plutocrats and kleptocrats, if not outright fascists, and not only institutionalize their assault on the republican liberty of everyone else but actually celebrate it. Indeed, a similar concern is now officially part of the doctrine of the Catholic Church:

Market operators must be effectively free to compare, evaluate and choose from among various options. Freedom in the economic sphere, however, must be regulated by appropriate legal norms so that it will be placed at the service of integral human freedom. "Economic Freedom is only one element of human freedom. When it becomes autonomous, when man is seen more as a producer or consumer of goods than as a subject who produces and consumes in order to live, then economic freedom loses its necessary relationship to the human person and ends up by alienating and oppressing him."[130]

And this is exactly what we are seeing going on in the United States today.[131] A phenomenon that began in the 1980s, but has reached new heights with the rise of Trump and Trumpism, has resulted in the step-by-step dismantling of years of carefully calibrated economic regulation.[132] Administration after administration (especially, although unfortunately not exclusively, those headed by Republican presidents) have seen public power over economic activity as a threat to liberty but ignored the dangers posed by concentrations of private economic power and have effectively raged ahead toward unleashing the oppressive power of the unregulated market with blinders on. Economic regulation enacted by liberal democratic governments may indeed represent a threat to liberty under some conditions. But allowing economic power to concentrate in too few private firms and the even smaller number of super-wealthy individuals who control them can represent such a threat too, even within a liberal capitalist democracy. When this is the case, government intervention is necessary to address it. Only a fool would focus on one threat to the exclusion of the other.[133]

Interestingly, while neoliberals claim that government regulation is what sends us barreling down the road to serfdom, they seem more than willing to make one exception: they recognize the threat to liberty that nongovernmental organizations may present when these organizations are unions. Hayek was especially vigorous in his opposition to unionization, claiming at one point that "the whole basis of a free society is gravely threatened by the powers arrogated to the unions."[134] Similar statements can be found in the work of neoliberals such as Machlup, Hutt, Petro, and Mises.[135] Why these self-proclaimed defenders of liberty were not able to recognize the threat to liberty posed by firms is difficult to understand. Unless we assume that given the historical context in which they labored, they simply reflexively associated unions with socialism, and even more nefariously with communism, while they simply associated private firms with anti-communism without thinking the matter through more carefully.[136] In any event, the fact that even the most vehement neoliberals were able to recognize that private economic organizations, and not just the government, can be a threat to liberty, whether they had the right private organizations in mind or not, proves my point and the point long recognized by their ordoliberal cousins: private organization such as firms can pose not only a threat to economic liberty but a threat to political liberty too.

Firms also pose a threat to liberty because of the importance of employment itself. In a capitalist system, employment is the primary method not only of production but also of distribution of the means of subsistence and the bases of self-respect.[137] The loss of employment, even if the worker finds employment again later on, can be a devastating event in anyone's life. And with the economy struggling as it is now and has been for some time despite the continued drop in the rate of unemployment, which in this context provides a misleading insight into the true employment situation, any loss of employment could become permanent or at least lead to permanent underemployment.[138] Even when an employer is not inclined to subject his workers to arbitrary interference with their lives, sheer incompetence or corruption can lead to the loss of employment through contraction or dissolution of the business. While incompetence and corruption is inefficient, and the market will eventually punish firms that are inefficient in this way, at least as long as such incompetence and corruption is not typical of the market at large (something the 2008 financial crisis has given us reason to doubt, if we did not have sufficient reason before), the market can only do so *ex post* after this incompetence and corruption has put all those who depend on the particular firm involved at risk and already ruined the lives of many. Workers accordingly have a liberty interest, and not just an economic interest, in taking *ex ante* measures to ensure the efficient running of the firm. Firms that are managed poorly or corruptly not only put their shareholders at risk but they put their employees at risk as well. And what is at risk is not merely money, it is the very basis of self-respect that employment represents.

Finally, the concentration of economic and political power that firms represent pose a threat to liberty in yet another way. It is often in the private interests of the firm to reduce costs by externalizing them, or to otherwise engage in antisocial behavior in order to capture a private benefit at the expense of the public at large. Causing pollution, sending defective or otherwise unreasonably dangerous products into the marketplace, providing unsafe working conditions, exploiting workers, evading taxes, and so on are all examples of antisocial behavior in which firms frequently engage.[139] These efforts not only make the firm seem more efficient than it is, thereby causing a misallocation of economic resources, they are also behaviors that we want to discourage because they put the liberty of all at risk. In some cases, they do this by causing physical injury or even death; in all cases, they force others to pay some of the costs of the productive activities of the firm, a form of theft. To counter these threats to liberty, it is accordingly essential that there be checks and balances on those in control of the firm and its activities.

Under political liberalism, of course, post-institutional external checks on the activities of the firm are numerous. They are provided by rules preventing fraud, theft, and anticompetitive behavior, rules prohibiting the production of unreasonably dangerous products and imposing liability for compensation on those that do, rules imposing various occupational health and safety protections, rules attempting to prohibit the evasion of taxes, and so on. And note that these checks not only promote political liberty, they promote economic liberty too, for anticompetitive behavior creates economic inefficiency, as does the failure to internalize all actual costs of production, including social costs.[140] While these external checks are helpful in preventing widespread and systematic violation of these rules, however, the expensive machinery provided by external methods of control for enforcing these regulations are more symbolic than real unless the amount of money at stake for an individual violation is unusually large.[141] If compliance is going to be encouraged on an individual basis, this is going to have to be accomplished in some other way. Some internal counterweight to the firm's natural inclination to threaten liberty in all these ways must be in place. Some internalized check is required if the basic institution of capitalism and its sub-institutions the free market and the firm are to be as just as they can feasibly be. And that check is the union.

2.4.5 The Basic Institution as a Check on Threats to Liberty

Before I explain why unionization protects liberty rather than infringes it, as is so often claimed, let me address one preliminary issue that is often raised in an attempt to disguise the threat to liberty that the firm represents. This is the claim that any attempt to include internal as well as external checks on this type of threat to liberty is itself an infringement of liberty; that is, the negative liberty of the owners and managers of the firm. Merely because an internal check on firm corruption, incompetence, and antisocial behavior would be an interference with the negative liberty of those in control of the firm to behave as they might wish, however, does not render such an internal check unjust. After all, the firm itself represents an interference with negative liberty, and this is justified merely by the economic efficiencies the firm creates. If unionization reduces the externalities of the firm's activities, it has an efficiency justification too. And if unionization also acts as a countermeasure to the threat to republican liberty that the firm represents, this creates an even stronger justification for unionization than the efficiency justification that supports creation of the firm. In either case, it is no objection to point to the infringements of negative liberty that unionization might entail. I will say much more about each of these justifications in the course of determining whether the union is basic institution, so I won't say more now. I will simply move on to that ultimate question: whether the union is indeed a basic institution. In other words, in a world where large amounts of economic resources are controlled by firms and allocated by command, do unions act as a check on the threat to liberty that these firms represent? Or, to put in another way, in the context of a liberal capitalist society where the primary unit of economic organization is the firm, do unions make the background circumstances more likely to produce just outcomes within the feasible set?

To answer this question, I will not attempt to develop a set of necessary and sufficient criteria for determining whether any particular institution should be deemed basic in a liberal capitalist society. Instead, I will proceed as Rawls suggests we do when evaluating principles of justice: by pairwise comparison.[142] We compare our particular society, given its actual institutions and not idealized versions of them, with a hypothetical society that is exactly identical to our own in every respect, except that it embraces universal unionization. In other words, we compare the society in which we actually live, where unions are post-institutional voluntary associations that have been declining in membership over the years to their actual current levels, to one that has the same institutions, forms of government, economic and social practices, and culture and in which people have the same knowledge, beliefs, values, and desires. The only difference here is that in this counterfactual world all firms are unionized. We then ask: Which society is likely to be more just?

Let me make a few preliminary comments before I begin this counterfactual comparison. First, in making this comparison, we assume that the empirical knowledge we have gained from the existing world still holds; that is, that the mere presence of universal unionization would not render our existing empirical knowledge with regard to the state of the world and to the nature and limits of what causes what invalid. I recognize that this assumption might be subject to challenge, in the sense that one counterfactual change might have all sorts of unforeseeable and therefore unintended indirect causal consequences (the so-called butterfly effect).[143] But this is a risk we accept whenever we employ hypothetical counterfactuals in our moral reasoning. Given that we seem to be comfortable doing this in our moral reasoning with regard to all sorts of other moral questions, and indeed have been comfortable doing this for thousands of years, I do not think such an assumption is an unreasonable one to use in our comparison.

Second, in deciding which world is more just, we use our pre-institutional conceptions of equality and liberty as our benchmark. By this I mean that we recognize that our need for post-institutional regulation and the nature and scope of that regulation – including the nature and scope of our post-institutional rights – is to some extent dependent on our selection of basic institutions. If, for example, we were to assume the validity of state "right-to-work" laws – that is, laws that prohibit compulsory unionization or the compulsory payment of union dues,[144] our comparison would never get off the ground. Post-institutional rights and regulations are to be used to trim and shape our institutions, not to dictate the selection of our institutions through some sort of backwards induction.[145] Accordingly, despite our commitment to otherwise hold everything constant, post-institutional rights and regulations are not to be considered fixed points in our comparison. Instead, they are to be considered adjustable if institutional arrangements are changed as long as those adjustments do not themselves infringe on our pre-institutional conception of our rights.

This also means that an assessment of the effectiveness of our current post-institutional regulation is built into our comparison. The more effective existing post-institutional regulation is, the less likely it will be that treating universal unionization as a basic institution will make society more just. In making our comparison, we can accordingly consider whether strengthening existing post-institutional regulation and/or enforcement would render the institutionalization of unions unnecessary. As long as such increased regulation and/or enforcement would be feasible, this would be one of the post-institutional adjustments to which I was referring. In this way, we consider the possibility of post-institutional adjustments when this might affect our determination of the institutionalization question in either direction.

Finally, while our pre-institutional rights include both liberty and equality, for reasons that I have already explained, I will not focus on the argument from equality here. Not because the argument from equality is unconvincing – on the contrary, for reasons that should be apparent in just a moment, it seems that whatever pre-institutional conception of equality we were to adopt it would uncontroversially support universal unionization.[146] I shall nevertheless focus my attention primarily on the argument from liberty, for as I have already pointed out, the argument from liberty is currently where the action is. Because the enforcement of any particular conception of positive liberty is ruled out by our commitment to neutrality, however, what I shall focus on in my discussion is negative, economic, and republican liberty.

With regard to negative and economic liberty, which remember is merely a subset of negative liberty, what we are looking for is whether unionization, on balance and overall, represents an interference with such liberty or an expression of it. Of course, if Hillel Steiner's "strong" version of the law of conservation of liberty is correct, negative liberty cannot be increased or decreased, it can only be redistributed.[147] If this were the case, there could be no net loss of negative liberty resulting from unionization (or anything else for that matter) no matter what, and therefore there would be no issue to resolve. But since the strong version of Steiner's claim is highly controversial,[148] I will not rely on it here. Instead, I shall assume that there can be a net increase or decrease in total negative liberty (that is, the combined negative liberty of both employers and employees) as a result on any action that infringes on the negative liberty of employers. And if this is true, then what we are looking for when determining whether unionization enhances total negative liberty is a Kaldor-Hicks improvement. We do this rather than look for a Pareto improvement because even if there can be an increase or decrease in total negative liberty and therefore a *net* gain or loss, there cannot be a gain in negative liberty for one without some loss for someone else. In other words, even though these gains and losses may not cancel each other out, there is always some gain for one and some loss for someone else. This, indeed, is what is referred to by Steiner as the "weak" version of the law of the conservation of liberty.[149] And as long as there are always both gains and losses, no change in the status quo could ever be a Pareto improvement, so using Pareto to test for whether something is a basic institution would effectively make our whole inquiry pointless. And while even the weak version of Steiner's view is controversial – his critics argue there can be situations in which there are *only* losses or *only* gains – the weak version holds in a great many cases, at least in the set of cases that we are talking about here; that is, questions about government intervention in the world, and specifically about whether government should be structured in a way that includes unions as a basic institution, for what we are looking at is what impact government interference with negative liberty has on negative liberty overall.

2.4 How to Determine Whether the Union Is a Basic Institution

To help distinguish this version of the law of the conservation of liberty from the weak version that Steiner defends, let us call this the *ultra*-weak version. While the breadth of the claim made by this version is very limited, it is broad enough to do all of the work we need it to do here, for it tells us that in deciding whether the government should interfere with someone's capacity to interfere with the negative liberty of someone else, there will always be winners and losers in terms of negative liberty. If government intercedes, it is necessarily infringing on potential interferers' ability to do something they have the capacity to do and taking some steps toward ensuring that the potential objects of this interference will not have their negative liberty infringed in this particular way. If government does not intercede, then these people are free to interfere with the negative liberty of others in whatever way we would have regulated, and those subject to this interference continue to be lawfully subject to having their negative liberty infringed. Someone's negative liberty is reduced, and someone's is increased, no matter what we do. The point being that even in these cases, all we need find is a Kaldor-Hicks improvement to determine that there has been an increase in negative liberty. And as long as there is no diminishment of negative liberty in the Kaldor-Hicks sense, there is no "reduction of negative liberty" objection to treating unions as part of the basic structure.

This inquiry is not, however, as straightforward as it seems. To determine the extent to which something constitutes a "gain" or "loss," we must consider both quantitative and qualitative factors. If we proceeded strictly on a quantitative basis, gains in some trivial aspect of negative liberty (such as the ability to drive around free of any traffic regulations) might overwhelm losses in some much more important aspect (the ability to drive without being exposed to an unreasonable chance of death or serious injury). I recognize that this requires we apply a conception of the good to develop an operator for our Kaldor-Hicks calculation, but this conception of the good need not be controversial. To the contrary, for purposes of conducting this inquiry, a thin conception of the good – one that represents the noncontroversial core of a great many comprehensive conceptions of the good – will do. Fine qualitative differences are not to be considered here. All we are looking for is whether there is a clear net gain, a clear net loss or no clear change whatsoever. Which is not to say that there must be a clear gain in negative liberty for any particular infringement to be acceptable. Whether there is a net gain in negative liberty is not the only factor to consider when determining whether an infringement of a particular kind of negative liberty is justified. Even if there is a net loss, an infringement of negative liberty can still be justified for other reasons. All I am suggesting is that if there is a net gain, then this alone is sufficient to justify the infringement.

Note also that this this holds even if I am wrong and the ultra-weak version of the law of the conservation of liberty is not correct – in other words, even if there are cases where government intervention *only* increases or decreases negative liberty. This merely shows that some cases may be appropriately evaluated under the more stringent Pareto test for determining whether there has been an improvement or a diminishment of negative liberty. But in all these cases – that is, in all cases whether there are *only* gains or *only* losses – the Pareto test does not lead us to do anything differently than the Kaldor-Hicks test would. In either case, there is either an increase in negative liberty or there is not. And as long as there is an increase in negative liberty under Kaldor-Hicks if there are both losses and gains, and an increase under both tests otherwise, we have a positive reason for treating unions as part of the basic structure.

When we move from negative liberty to republican liberty, however, things first get a little less and then a little more complicated. They get less complicated in the sense that it is hard to imagine how freedom from arbitrary domination for one could be purchased only by the arbitrary domination of someone else. There is no law of conservation of liberty with regard to republican liberty under my conception of it – that is, it is not true that gains in republican liberty for one are always or even mostly accompanied by losses in republican liberty for someone else. Of course, gains in republican liberty for one may be accompanied by losses in *negative* liberty for someone else, for prohibiting domination is an interference with the negative liberty of the prospective dominator. The opposite is also true – increases in negative liberty may be accompanied by losses in republican liberty. But this is irrelevant. Losses in republican liberty cannot be offset by gains in negative liberty, economic of otherwise. One has a right to republican liberty, whereas no one has a general right to negative liberty, whatever its form. With regard to republican liberty, then, only Pareto improvements are acceptable.

But a number of people have queried whether Pareto improvements in republican liberty really can be guaranteed when it comes to unionization. They offer a variety of counterexamples in which it seems possible that the creation or activities of a union might threaten the republican liberty of someone in a different way or to a greater extent than was the case before. The most obvious example is that of domination within the union, even though it has a democratic structure – by individual union officers over individual members, by one ethnic or racial group of members over another, or by the leadership in general over the membership in general.[150] And of course there is also the possibility of domination by the union over the employer. Indeed, the claim that unions are constantly trying to dominate employers and often succeeding is one that those on the anti-union right are very fond of making, and it is pointless to deny that such acts of domination are indeed possible. Someone who is not subject to domination is more free to dominate someone else – free people may always exercise their freedom in inappropriate ways.[151] But such acts of domination are not *entailed* by unionization – they are simply *risks* created by unionization. And when it comes to republican liberty, a risk of interference is not the same as an act of interference, at least under my conception of it. The relevant test for determining whether there has been a Pareto improvement in terms of republican liberty is accordingly whether freedom from domination for one is being purchased by the actual domination of someone else. And while such a price is always or at least often extracted with regard to the protection of negative liberty, republican liberty is different. In none of the supposed counterexamples cited by these Pareto skeptics does the protection of the republican liberty of one group or individual come only at the price of an actual reduction in republican liberty of another. Protecting the republican liberty of some from interference by others may put the republican liberty of others more at risk, but it does not amount to an infringement of that liberty in itself.[152]

Note that I am not denying that "risky behavior" can sometimes amount to a rights violation in and of itself. As we saw in the previous essay, preventing risky behavior is the justification for compelling independents to join the dominant protective association in our libertarian utopia and would also serve as a justification for compelling independent workers to join the union at their particular place of work. And in the real world, preventing or minimizing risk is often a reason for government action. Indeed, this provides the justification for a massive amount of real-world regulation every day. But even though risky behavior may sometimes be so risky it does constitute a rights violation, this does not mean that all behavior that creates a risk of a rights violation is a rights violation itself. Obviously, every action and inaction creates *some* risk of a rights violation. No theory that contends that this alone makes something a rights violation would be worthy of consideration, for this would drain the very idea of a rights violation of any meaning. Only behavior that creates an *unreasonable* risk of a rights violation would constitute a rights violation it itself. And determining whether a particular kind of behavior constitutes an unreasonable risk is an all-things-considered inquiry that takes into account a myriad of factors.

Which brings us back to the issue of whether we can use the Pareto test to determine if there is "an improvement" in the risk environment as a result of a particular action or inaction. Because every action or inaction presents some risk of going wrong, the Pareto test cannot be the appropriate measure of whether there has been "an improvement" in the risk environment, for in terms of risk, one state of affairs can never be Pareto superior or Pareto inferior to another. But we cannot apply Kaldor-Hicks either. To conduct a Kaldor-Hicks analysis, we must be able to net gains against losses. Risks, however, do not net out in the same way as outcomes. For example, while it is easy to compare a slight risk of a small setback with a big risk of disaster, how do we compare a slight risk of disaster with a big risk of a small setback? We cannot simply discount each outcome by the chance it will not occur and compare those, for risk matters morally – even though two risks may compute to the same discounted value, if we get to these equal discounted figures by applying different discount rates to different possible outcomes, as we often will, we have no reason to believe that we should be morally indifferent between the two choices. Some risks are risks that morality suggests we take, and some are risks that morality suggests we eschew. And when the probabilities associated with each possible outcome are themselves disputed, we cannot even compute uncontroversial discounted expected outcomes for everything we want to compare – indeed, no single consequentialist algorithm can be applied to compare the various choices. John Broome has a proof for this,[153] which I discuss in depth elsewhere,[154] but I will not reprise that discussion here because all we need to recognize at the moment is that determining whether a change in the risk environment constitutes a gain or loss, and how much of a gain or a loss it is requires a judgment call in itself. The real work – reducing the various risks at issue to something we can compare – must take place before anything like Kaldor-Hicks can be applied.

This is why comparing states of affairs with regard to changes in a risk environment gets more complicated than people typically assume. When deciding whether something that creates new risks and increases some existing risks but also decreases or eliminates other existing or potential risks is "an improvement," we need to take a variety of factors into account. (Note that even if some change is not an improvement, it may or may not be unreasonable and therefore may or may not constitute a rights violation, but a change that is an improvement cannot constitute a rights violation.) Initially, we need apply two initial constraints or filtering devices. The purpose of these devices to eliminate extremely remote or implausible risks from consideration, for there is always some risk of almost anything happening. And this means that without such constraints, any comparison of risk environments could never get off the ground.[155]

The first of these constraints is that risks based on theoretical or empirical claims outside of what Rawls refers to as "the burdens of judgment" – that is, the reasons why people can reasonably disagree – are to be disregarded, for our comparative moral judgments must take into account only those risks that are reasonable to consider.[156] The second constraint is that risks that have only a small chance of occurring are to be disregarded because while they might indeed occur, humans have proved themselves incapable of giving remote risks of bad events the appropriate weight in their decision-making process.[157] Of course, in applying either of these constraints there is room for disagreement – it is not always clear when the arguments about a certain risk are unreasonable or when the risk is small enough to be disregarded. But the overall quality of our decision-making should be improved even so. Moral argument is only possible between those willing to search for solutions with which others cannot reasonably disagree; argument with the unreasonable is pointless. And if we consider all risks, no matter how small, we end up with either a form of decision-making paralysis, where the slight possibility of disaster no matter what we do leads us to continuously do nothing, or even worse, where the slight probability of disaster if we go in one direction is irrationally given more decision weight than the slight probability of disaster if we go in the other.[158]

After application of these filters, remaining risks are then compared using a variety of factors: the comparative degree of risk (the probability of a bad outcome), the comparative severity of the potential bad outcomes (how bad they might be), the probability and potential degree of improvement with regard

2.4 How to Determine Whether the Union Is a Basic Institution 109

to the elimination of existing risks (the probability and degree of the potential good outcome), how certain we are of the relevant probability calculations (do we know what the probability is or is even that question subject to dispute?), whether the new or additional risks created are more easily dealt with by post-institutional regulation than the risks that are currently present and therefore could be more easily reduced or eliminated, and finally and most importantly, where the burden of risk of error falls in each alternative risk environment. That is, we want to know who suffers in each case if the risk actually comes to pass. If the burden of the risk of error in the proposed new risk environment falls on a group who are better able to bear it than those on whom it falls in the existing environment, then this is a reason to treat the proposed new environment as a moral improvement. If it falls on those who are in a worse position to bear it, then the opposite is true.

Now some of these factors involve mini Kaldor-Hicks inquiries in the sense they involve a certain kind of internal balancing with regard to a single relevant factor, but some do not. What we have then is a series of inquiries, some of which involve netting and some of which do not, but in each case once the internal process used to determine that factor is concluded, each factor acts as an independent side constraint on action without being netted together themselves, so we are conducting neither a strict Pareto inquiry nor a strict Kaldor-Hicks. What we are doing is measuring what we might call "moral efficiency under conditions of uncertainty." If any measure fails, then the proposed change to the risk environment is not an improvement. In any event, it is only by performing such an analysis that we can determine whether the risks to republican liberty that arise if we do treat unions as a basic institution are morally preferable to the risks that exist if we do not.

Of course, it may be the case that only one type of liberty I have discussed – negative, economic, or republican – should matter when in deciding whether unions are a basic institution. But proving this is bound to be controversial, even if it is possible. To avoid having to resolve this controversy, we accordingly perform three types of analyses. First, we ask whether people in a hypothetical decision situation (where they are deprived of knowledge of their particular place in society and overall circumstances but know the existing facts of our society including how unions actually function) would, on balance, vote to require unionization, prohibit unionization, or something in between. This tells us whether whatever infringement of negative liberty that is caused by the option we select – and there will be an infringement of somebody's negative liberty no matter what option we select – is justified in the quasi-Rawlsian deontological sense. We then conduct a straightforward consequentialist analysis and ask whether unionization is, on balance, a boost to economic efficiency or an impediment to it. If it does contribute to economic efficiency or is at least neutral toward it, then we can conclude that our initial conclusion satisfies the concerns of those most focused on preventing unjustified infringements of negative liberty and those who (rightly or wrongly) think that economic and political liberty are related. It also ensures that whatever our conclusion with regard to unionization, we are taking a step away from and not down that slippery slope to totalitarianism. And finally, we ask whether unionization furthers or impedes the fundamental notion of self-ownership that is embodied in the idea of republican liberty, regardless of its other effects. If it does improve the risk environment for republican liberty, we have a second conformation of our initial conclusion regarding the relationship between unions and liberty, and we can be fairly certain that our initial conclusion that unionization would be a liberty-enhancing not a liberty-impeding institution of society was correct. We also can be confident that this is so even without committing to which particular interpretation of liberty is the one that matters most.

One final point: Does not my approach so far suggest I am treating the risk to republican liberty created by the firm differently than the risk to republican liberty created by unionization? Earlier, I suggested that the threat to republican liberty posed by the hierarchical structure of the firm was a key factor in determining whether we should consider the union to be a basic institution. Why is the threat to republican liberty posed by the prevalence of firms as the primary source of business organization an important justification for universal unionization, but the threat posed by universal unionization not a reason to reject the union as a basic institution? The answer is that, as I have just acknowledged, it *is* important to balance the threat to republican liberty posed by firms against the threat to all kinds of liberty (not just republican) posed by making unionization universal in deciding whether the union should be treated as a basic institution. Indeed, I shall spend a great deal of the rest of this essay doing just this in the context of performing my analysis of whether there has been an improvement in the overall risk environment. But the threat to republican liberty posed by unionization is not a reason to reject the union as a basic institution if unionization does not constitute a violation of republican liberty in itself, and as I have already argued, it does not. Otherwise, the mere fact that government represents a threat to republican liberty would be a reason to reject it as a response to that threat posed by the potential for predatory conduct among and between individuals and private associations. Only anarchists believe that, and they do so only because they ignore the threat posed by private conduct altogether. As I have already pointed out, just as the conduct of government can be regulated to reduce the risk that it does not exceed its proper role, so can unions. I am not suggesting that such regulation should not be imposed wherever it is deemed necessary or appropriate. I am merely investigating whether unions should be treated as a basic institution, subject to all the regulation that other basic institutions face today. Finally, remember that in determining whether unions are a basic institution, we are not reconstructing our world from scratch. It might be possible to design a world that has neither firms nor unions, or where firms do not pose a threat to republican liberty. But this is not the world in which we live. We are taking the world as we find it; that is, as a liberal capitalist democracy,

2.5 Unionization in Context 111

and asking whether universal unionization is necessary to ensure background justice in that world as it actually is, or perhaps feasibly could be with other less politically controversial adjustments. And this world includes firms in its baseline. We are considering whether unionization is an appropriate reaction to this, and so the two questions are not asked under similar circumstances. The first is about whether we should have firms; the second is about whether we should have unions given that firms already exist. I am not being inconsistent here in my attitude toward firms and unions. But my argument does have a long way to go. In order to determine whether universal unionization would indeed result in the requisite improvement in the risk environment, we need to examine the effects of unionization in some depth. For remember, as I noted at length in the introduction to these essays, all arguments from right consider consequences in determining what is right. This does not mean we are abandoning the argument from right for an argument for consequences. It merely means that our argument from right, which considers consequences but not only consequences in determining what is right, is tethered to reality.

2.5 UNIONIZATION IN CONTEXT

Let us begin by getting a general sense of the effects of unionization and whether there are certain overall tendencies that we can rely on, for mere anecdotal effects are not relevant to this examination except to the extent they are indicative that a certain effect is more likely than not. The current American experience provides a good laboratory for this experiment, since unionization of American society has never been more than partial and the recent decline in unionization gives us the ability to make informed judgements about the effects of lower and higher rates of unionization. The landmark study of these effects is widely recognized to be Richard Freeman and James Medoff's 1984 book *What Do Unions Do?* I will accordingly use this work as the starting point for my discussion, not only for the arguments it makes and the information it sets forth, but also for the way it organizes the relevant questions and their answers.[159] Of course, I will also rely on more recent work to the extent this contains relevant argument or information. While I am not going to be able to discuss every possible effect of unionization that has been discussed in all this literature, I will discuss the more important ones.[160] And I will begin with those that, in light of the empirical studies referred to by Freeman and Medoff and the studies conducted since, are now generally viewed as noncontroversial.

2.5.1 The Basic Effects of Unionization

2.5.1.1 *Unions Raise Wages for Both Union and Nonunion Workers*
The first part of this statement should, of course, be no surprise – if it were not true, unionization would never have provoked such opposition from

employers, and workers would not be so interested in unionization. And the wage gap between union and nonunion workers is not small. Freeman and Medoff put the gap at 20–30 percent in the 1970s.[161] Updated figures from 2001 using improved measurement techniques put the average wage gap in the private sector at 17–22 percent with unionized workers enjoying higher wages across all sectors of the economy and all demographic segments.[162] And a recent survey completed in May of 2018 put the wage premium earned by union workers today at about 20 percent and shows that this premium has actually held steady for at least 90 years, since sometime in the 1930s.[163] But the wage gap is even higher than these statistics reveal in the sense that, as the second part of this statement suggests, even nonunion wages are higher when there are high rates of unionization. One recent study, for example, estimates that nonunion wages would have been 8 percent higher in 2013 if union density were at 1979 levels.[164] Other studies show an even greater impact, 10–16 percent,[165] with those figures growing even larger when we are looking at union shop rather than right-to-work states.[166] Add these amounts back in and the wage gap remains at the 20–30 percent figure from Freeman and Medoff's study.

It also bears remarking that wages are lower for all workers when there is less unionization, but the bottom wages are lower by an even greater amount. In other words, wages are not just lower with regard to the kinds of skilled jobs that used to propel union men and women into the middle class, they are also lower for the kind of unskilled jobs that are forming an ever larger segment of the economy and are falling further and further below what is commonly referred to as the living wage.[167] Hence, the large and increasing number of protests by fast-food workers and others who remain largely nonunionized in support of raising the minimum wage.[168] Even skilled work that used to be thought of as well-paid can now generate less than a living wage in the absence of unionization.[169] And this is despite the fact that the productivity of labor has continued to increase dramatically. Between 1948 and 1973, the period in which unions were strongest, productivity gains increased at a rate that only slightly exceeded the growth in hourly compensation. But between 1973 and 2015, the period in which union strength dramatically declined, productivity has grown 6.6 times faster than hourly pay.[170]

Without unions to protect them, there have also been a growing number of incidents of wage theft from low-wage workers – that is, employers illegally paying below the minimum wage or otherwise not paying workers the wages legally due them.[171] Indeed, those not protected by a union contract are almost *twice* as likely to experience wage theft as those who are.[172] And the chances of this just went way up as a result of the Supreme Court's May 2018 decision to allow employees who feel they are the victims of wage theft to be forced to assert their claims only in prohibitively expensive individual arbitration proceedings rather than pursue their claims as class actions in court.[173] Not only is the likelihood of an individual employee being able to afford to bring such a proceeding exceedingly slim, arbitration also tends to be a much more employer-friendly forum than the courts. And even if the employee were to manage to bring such a claim and prevail, no other employee could use this victory as precedent (arbitration results, unlike court decisions, have no binding effect on future proceedings brought by different claimants and cannot even be used as argumentative precedents). Other employee-victims would accordingly have to bring their own action to recover their own losses. Employers of nonunionized employees who have the foresight to impose such arbitration provisions in their employee contracts – something that over 50 percent of nonunion employers already did before this decision came out – will now accordingly face almost no risk from committing wage theft.[174] And the amounts here are significant – one recent survey put the total amount currently being wrongfully withheld by employers at $8 billion in just the ten most populist states, reducing the earned wages of some 2.4 million workers by nearly 25 percent.[175] Because the minimum wage is by most estimates less than half of the living wage, the amounts involved and number of workers being exploited here – that is, paid less than the labor purchased actually costs to produce – are actually far greater.[176] Add to this the fact that a still significant segment of the population who would rather be working full time are only able to find part-time work,[177] or work at jobs with wildly unpredictable hours.[178] We have ended up with a situation where a quarter of the jobs that people now hold in America pay below the federal poverty line for a family of four.[179] Whatever may be the American dream, this is the American reality.

2.5.1.2 Unions Result in Increased Employee Benefits Like Pensions, Health Insurance, and Job Security

This is an unsurprising corollary to the previous statement on the effect of unionization on wages.[180] But it bears emphasis that wages are not the only thing employees care about. They also care about work-life balance – the ability to not have to work when one is not *at* work, whether the premises at which this work takes place is actual or virtual.[181] And, of course, they also care about nonwage benefits, especially in the United States where pensions and health care are generally provided through employment rather than through the government, as they are in Europe and other highly industrialized economies.[182] Indeed, in the United States, "unionized workers are 28.2 percent more likely to be covered by employer-provided health insurance and 53.9 percent more likely to have employer-provided pensions."[183] Even so, existing pensions for union workers are under serious attack.[184] And while the Obama administration had taken some steps to provide access to retirement plans for those whose employers do not provide them, these steps are being rolled back by the Trump administration,[185] so this is only going to get worse.

Not only is it important to remember that unions provide increased benefits as well as higher pay for their members. It is also important to remember that when making comparisons between union and nonunion jobs, the allocation between these two main components of total compensation can vary. This means that the more informative comparison is between total compensation, not between one of these components without regard to the other. While this does not currently lead to many problems in the private sector, when we examine public sector unionization in the next essay, we shall see that it is of critical importance, both with regard to how to make the relevant comparisons and with regard to determining whether public employees are overpaid.

2.5.1.3 Unions Reduce the Level of Wage Inequality between Workers

Unfortunately, wage inequality exists even at firms that are unionized. In other words, white men tend to be the highest paid members of any particular workforce, no matter what.[186] In 2015, for example, black men earned only 75 percent as much as white men, and Latinos earned only 69 percent.[187] Overall, 8.6 percent of white workers were paid poverty-level wages in 2017, but the figures were 19.2 percent for Hispanic workers, 14.3 percent for black workers, and 10.9 percent for Asians and Pacific Islanders, even for those that are working full-time, year-round.[188] And when we consider both race and gender, things get even worse. "Nearly *half* of all Latina workers are paid less than the 10th percentile white male worker," and "at the high end, only 1-in-20 Latina workers are paid more than white male workers in the 80th percentile."[189] Black women on average were paid only 66 cents on the dollar relative to non-Hispanic white men, even after controlling for education, years of experience, and geographic location.[190] And while wage differentials by race and ethnicity are most stark, even if we look exclusively at gender, wage differentials are substantial.[191] The overall wage gap between men and women in 2018 is 16 percent, meaning that women get paid 84 cents for every dollar earned by men.[192] And this is true not only in the United States but in the United Kingdom and in Continental Europe as well.[193]

But the level of wage inequality for all these groups is reduced by unionization.[194] This is one of the reasons why Martin Luther King Jr. was such a strong supporter of unions.[195] Indeed, black men and Latinos made substantial progress in catching up to their white counterparts until about 1980, when unionization began its dramatic decline. Since then, whatever progress had been made in reducing wage inequality has come to a screeching halt.[196] Nevertheless, unionization still makes a significant difference. In New York City's construction industry, for example, unionized black workers earn 36.2 percent more than their nonunionized black counterparts.[197] Nationally, black union workers earn on average 16.4 percent more than nonunion black workers and are also 17.4–18.3 percent more likely than nonunion black workers to have employer-provided health insurance and an employer-sponsored retirement plan.[198] Unionized Hispanic workers enjoy similar advantages over nonunionized Hispanic workers.[199] Even pure gender discrimination was reduced by unionization. One recent study showed that unionization cut the overall gender wage gap by almost

40 percent.²⁰⁰ In some cases, of course, the improvement was even greater than that. In Nevada, cocktail servers are unionized and as a result enjoy one of smallest gender pay gaps in the country.²⁰¹ And with two women now vying to be America's top union official, at least the gender wage gap among unionized workers may soon be getting smaller.²⁰² So unionization is not just about higher wages, it is about social justice and equal treatment too.

2.5.1.4 *Unions Reduce Overall Economic Inequality*
Freeman and Medoff did not really focus on the macroeconomic effects of unionization in their original work,²⁰³ but much has been done on this issue since. There are other alleged macroeffects (including unemployment and inflation), that I will discuss later, but the macroeffect I want to mention here is the effect of unionization on overall economic inequality, as opposed to inequality in wages for comparable work. There is a surprisingly strong correlation between the long but steady increase in economic inequality in the United States since the 1970s, and especially since the 1980s, and the long and steady decline in unionization over the same period.²⁰⁴ Because I have detailed this dramatic rise in economic inequality in my previous work, I will not say much about it here.²⁰⁵ But I will mention a few statistics. The share of total income enjoyed by those in the top 10 percent of the income distribution in the United States increased from about 32 percent in 1970, to 43 percent in 2002, to 50 percent in 2007. While it has not increased significantly since then because of the Great Recession, it has not dropped either, hitting 50.5 percent in 2015, "a level higher than any other year since 1917 (except for 2012) that even surpasses 1928, the peak of stock market bubble in the 'roaring' 1920s."²⁰⁶ Overall economic inequality has still increased during the post–Great Recession period, however, because the bottom has been falling, or rather the number of people at the bottom has been increasing. In 2008, the poverty rate in the United States hit 13.2 percent, the highest it had been in the United States in twelve years.²⁰⁷ But in 2010, the poverty rate hit 15.1 percent, and while it dropped to 13.5 percent in 2015, this is still greater than it was in 2006 (12.3 percent) before the Great Recession.²⁰⁸ Some 65 percent of American families lived in middle-class neighborhoods in 1970, but by 2010, that number had dropped to 44 percent with a corresponding rise in the number of neighborhoods peopled primarily by either the affluent or the poor.²⁰⁹ This trend has continued through 2014, the most recent date for which we have numbers.²¹⁰ Perhaps most importantly, while real wages for the top 1 percent, and especially for the top .01 percent, have skyrocketed since 1980,²¹¹ real wages for the vast majority of Americans have stagnated despite enormous increases in worker productivity.²¹² While real wages finally started to increase slightly, they still have miles to go before they make up for decades of lost ground,²¹³ and now they have actually begun to decline again.²¹⁴ In any event, there is not going to be a significant improvement in real wages anytime soon given how the fruits of economic growth are currently allocated.

Between the end of the Great Recession and 2010, an unprecedented 93 percent of the total real income growth for the entire country went to the top 1 percent of the income distribution.[215] The top 5 percent in the income distribution have seen their pay jump 22 percent from 2000 to July 2017, while the bottom half haven't seen their pay rise even 5 percent.[216] And while things have gotten a little less lopsided more recently, the majority of gains are still going to the very top of the income distribution.[217] Even though the unemployment rate has come down from its peak during the Great Recession, we have mostly replaced solid mid-wage jobs with precarious low-wages ones, making long-term economic inequality even greater.[218]

Of course, the decline in unionization is not singularly responsible for the current state of affairs with regard to economic inequality, but the empirical evidence shows it is not unrelated either – it is a significant contributing factor.[219] Unions reduce economic inequality because they raise wages more at the bottom and in the middle of the wage scale than at the top, and probably also serve to dampen some of the excessiveness currently running rampant at the very top.[220] Deunionization, in contrast, in addition to reducing wages at the bottom and middle of the income distribution, also results in reduced political representation for working class people, a group that is also disproportionally nonwhite, thereby reducing the legislative voice for progressive economic policies at all levels of government.[221] All in all, "deunionization can explain about a third of the entire growth of wage inequality among men and around a fifth of the growth among women from 1973 to 2007."[222] Increases in unionization rates will accordingly help put a stop to these increases and perhaps even reverse this trend not only by working to reverse some of the excesses in compensation for top management over the last thirty-plus years, but also by allowing more workers to capture their fair share of the fruits of future economic growth.

2.5.1.5 *Unions Have No Effect on Productivity*
Or, to put it more precisely, unions have neither a net negative nor a net positive effect on the productivity (meaning unionization has some negative and some positive effects on productivity, but these generally cancel each other out often within a particular firm or, at worst, in the economy as a whole). Note that this is a departure from what Freeman and Medoff originally concluded – they suggested that unionization had a net positive effect on productivity.[223] But subsequent studies called this conclusion into question, and it is now fair to say that the weight of the evidence currently suggests that the net effect of unionization on productivity is neutral.[224] At least that is the position I shall take in this essay, even though there is still evidence that unionization may indeed improve productivity. For example, other countries that have much higher rates of unionization than the United States actually have economies that are more productive than the United States.[225] This suggests that there is some consistent positive connection, and some studies of the effect of unionization on productivity in the United States do show a 7–10 percent

increase in productivity in certain industries.[226] If these studies are correct, however, this merely improves the strength of my argument, so I am content to assume that unionization does not improve productivity in my argument here.

2.5.1.6 Unions Reduce Profitability

This, of course, is widely believed because once again there would be little reason for business owners and managers to oppose unionization if they did not think that this was true. And while this effect is difficult to measure, the overwhelming majority of empirical evidence suggests that there is at least some negative effect. The question is how much and what kind of profits are reduced. There seems to be wide agreement that in the United States, unionization is associated with reductions in profitability of 10–15 percent.[227] But the amount can vary widely for any particular firm, depending on the kind of industry and the size and competitive position of that firm, with a number of studies suggesting that firms in concentrated industries with the largest market shares are the ones most affected.[228] In other words, in these firms, the profits being reduced may in large part be monopoly profits, which the firm shouldn't be earning anyway.[229] I shall say more about this (admittedly controversial claim) later, but for now, I merely want to acknowledge that there is no doubt *some* reduction even in non-monopoly profits. Although labor is becoming an ever-smaller component of the cost of production, and the effect of unionization on profits has accordingly been coming down, in a world that is obsessed with squeezing the last drop of profit out of every enterprise, this can still be enough to encourage business owners to relocate their operations to other countries where wages are lower and unions are weaker and usually both. Hence, the appeal of Donald Trump, who claims to want to stop this, to a significant segment of formerly unionized white working-class men.[230] In any event, as we shall see, this effect, whatever its extent and source, is the major consequentialist argument raised against unionization.

2.5.1.7 Unions Give Workers a Voice

Indeed, this was one of the key findings of the Freeman and Medoff's original work.[231] Of course, it is hard to imagine how unionization could not give workers a louder voice in how they are treated by both their employers and the government than they would have in the absence of unionization, at least as long as the union is not a sham. But this finding is not a mere restatement of the obvious. The term "voice" was borrowed by Freeman and Medoff from a distinction made famous by Albert O. Hirschman some fourteen years earlier in *Exit, Voice, and Loyalty: Responses to Declines in Firms*.[232] The idea was that unions provide workers with some protection within the firm with regard to certain decisions that have the potential to dramatically affect their lives. This, in turn, would provide workers with an alternative to *exit*, which is the only other option when an opportunity to voice their views effectively is lacking and mistreatment – or what is perceived as mistreatment – becomes intolerable.[233] By contrasting voice to exit, the point was that unionization would make employees less likely to quit their jobs, allowing employers to maintain an experienced workforce and avoid the transaction costs of constantly having to hire and train new workers to replace the ones they lose. This would not only have a positive effect on economic performance, it would have enough of a positive effect to overcome the supposedly anticompetitive monopolizing effect that unionization has on the price of labor.[234] And indeed, many subsequent studies have showed that unionization does indeed increase employee tenure and reduce quit rates.[235] But other studies, while conceding the effect on quit rates and employee tenure, focus on the fact that unionization decreases profitability and the more recent evidence that unionization has no net effect on productivity and use this evidence to disconnect the increase in voice to any claimed increase in economic performance.[236] And if the connection between voice and economic performance cannot be established, much of the significance of any increase in voice may simply be irrelevant, at least to those for whom economic performance is everything.

But the importance of voice need not be its effect on overall economic performance. Rather than being a way of turbocharging economic performance, the primary importance of giving workers a voice within the firm is to give workers greater control over their lives and make them less vulnerable to the arbitrary will of their managers. Some of the economic effects of this may be positive, and some may be negative; sometimes these cancel each other out, and sometimes they may lean one way or the other. It is not, however, the effect of voice on economic efficiency that matters to us here – it is the effect on whether workers are treated as free men and women while on the job, or whether they are subject to domination through subjugation to the arbitrary decisions of their managers. It is the effect of voice on workers' republican liberty that matters. Or so I shall argue in a moment.

2.5.2 Some Preliminary Points about These Effects

Before I do, however, let me make two preliminary points. First, note that the causal mechanism on which Freeman and Medoff and their subsequent defenders and critics alike rely is based on the idea that unionization, and the voice it provides, will change how workers feel and this feeling will change how workers behave and make their behavior more productive. But Freeman and Medoff acknowledged at the time that the available empirical evidence suggested that in some ways workers tended to feel *more* dissatisfied with their jobs in a unionized environment than in a nonunionized one. This finding has been largely confirmed since.[237] Workers are more satisfied with their wages and benefits, of course, but are less satisfied with their relationship with their supervisors and with management in general. Freeman and Medoff largely dismissed this finding because despite increased dissatisfaction with their jobs, workers in union firms were still less likely to leave given the voice the union provided, and therefore unionization would still increase economic efficiency overall by allowing the employer to more easily retain skilled workers.[238] These findings regarding lower quit rates among union workers and longer job tenure have also been confirmed since.[239] But unhappy workers are less efficient workers, so this "dissatisfaction effect" might help explain why unionization, despite giving workers a greater voice and thereby decreasing quit rates and increasing job tenure, does not increase productivity as much or as often as Freeman and Medoff thought it did. Why unionized workers might be less happy than nonunionized ones, in turn, is explained by the fact that in a nonunionized environment, where there are fewer channels for a worker to challenge mistreatment and more risk if the worker does, adaptive preferences may form along the lines of the "happy slave" effect – facing no prospect of an improved life, the slave decides that rather than be miserable he will accept his fate and the limited prospects this entails and be happy, whereas free men and women have the ability to overcome and therefore be dissatisfied with restrictions on their freedom.[240] In other words, in a unionized environment, workers are more likely to be willing and able to challenge mistreatment and thus adaptive preferences are less likely to form. In any event, it is not happiness we are trying to promote, but republican liberty. It is not how free the worker *feels*, but how free the worker *is*. Otherwise, liberty could be secured just by giving everyone therapy and antidepressants, or something like "soma," the fictional drug used in Aldous Huxley's *Brave New World* to make everyone feel pleasure no matter what was happening in their lives.[241] Worker satisfaction is therefore neither a reliable indicator of the degree to which unionization increases voice nor an appropriate indicator of whether voice is having the relevant (in this case liberty-enhancing) effect.

The second preliminary point I want to mention is with regard to the first four of the listed effects of unionization. As I said, these effects are essentially undisputed, and they unequivocally support unionization. Indeed, they suggest that unionization is an important force in instantiating any reasonable conception of equality. If this is true, it should not matter whether unionization decreases economic efficiency (that is, productivity), for most people who believe that decreasing economic inequality is an important element of improving background justice do not consider increasing efficiency a sufficient reason to disregard the anti-egalitarian effects of the ruthless pursuit of efficiency.[242] Otherwise, I suppose we might still have slavery, for economic efficiency was a major justification offered for maintaining slavery, although the claim that slavery is economically efficient is now recognized as highly dubious.[243] In other words, our objections to slavery did not rely only on the argument from liberty – they also (some would no doubt say primarily) relied on the argument from equality, and the argument from economic efficiency was not considered even a partial rebuttal to either argument.

What this means is that there is considerable doubt that efficiency concerns, which are not directly (and at least arguably not even indirectly) moral, could override our concern for rights derived from either equality or liberty unless the effects of this would be catastrophic. And that is certainly not the case even under the most pessimistic of studies, those that show that unionization has no net effect on productivity.[244] Now admittedly, these studies are of efficiency in the microeconomic sense, and there are some issues with regard to the effect of unionization on macroeconomic efficiency (that is, the efficiency of the economy as a whole) that need to be separately discussed, but I will get to those later. For now, I simply want to note that because the empirical evidence that unionization is an important step in combating economic inequality is very strong, the argument against recognizing unions as a basic institution that emphasizes the purported microeconomic efficiency of not having unions, a prudential not a moral argument, is comparatively weak. We therefore could begin our examination of the argument from liberty by thinking that a *prima facie* case for finding that unionization makes the background circumstances of society more just within the feasible set has already been made out. But as I have already pointed out, even if the argument from equality does support not only unionization but also treating unions as a basic institution, that would have little persuasive power for those who have traditionally been anti-union because of their reliance on the argument from liberty. We therefore begin our discussion of the argument from liberty as if we were doing so with a clean moral slate.

Which means that the primary focus of everything that follows will be on the last uncontested effect listed above, the fact that unions provide workers with a voice they would otherwise lack, and the relation of voice to liberty. For this has important and insufficiently appreciated ramifications. Workers who lack an effective voice with regard to decisions that have a significant effect on their lives are effectively disempowered and subject to the kinds of abuse and even domination we do not expect free men and women to have to put up with.[245] This lack of empowerment threatens their self-ownership, for it encourages others to see them as fungible parts of a big machine rather than as living, breathing, autonomous beings with unique talents and abilities and something importantly "individual" to contribute. It leaves them subject to the arbitrary will of another, thereby threatening their republican liberty.[246] Indeed, even highly compensated workers may not have sufficient financial resources and bargaining power to protect themselves from arbitrary treatment without the assistance of unions.[247] It is, therefore, a very significant effect of unionization that it serves to counteract this otherwise distinctly liberty-threatening attribute of the firm, regardless of whether this has any effect on economic efficiency.[248]

2.5.3 The Relationship between Voice and Republican Liberty

The effect of unionization on what we now call republican liberty was recognized long ago by the US Supreme Court in one of the most important cases in labor history:

> Employees have as clear a right to organize and select their representatives for lawful purposes as the respondent has to organize its business and select its own officers and agents. Discrimination and coercion to prevent the free exercise of the right of

2.5 Unionization in Context

employees to self-organization and representation is a proper subject for condemnation by competent government authority. Long ago we stated the reason for labor organization. We said they were organized out of the necessities of the situation; that a single employee was helpless in dealing with an employer; that he was dependent ordinarily on his daily wage for the maintenance of himself and family; that if the employer refused to pay him the wages he thought fair, he was nevertheless unable to leave the employ and resist arbitrary and unfair treatment; that union was essential to give laborers opportunity to deal on an equality with their employer.[249]

And while the Supreme Court did not speak in terms of republican liberty (this way of encapsulating that particular concept of liberty had not yet joined the lexicon at the time), it is clear that the ideas behind the republican conception of liberty are indeed what the Court had in mind. Simply put, unions are a necessary institution if employees are to resist the kind of arbitrary treatment that is within the power of the firm to impose.

A similar observation was made in 1952, again well before the modern concept of republican liberty was developed, when John Kenneth Galbraith introduced his concept of "a countervailing power." This is the term he used to describe a private economic power that arose naturally to check another private economic power and neutralize its ability to exercise arbitrary control over those who otherwise had no choice but to deal with it. Indeed, we might extend Galbraith's claim by noting that since a countervailing power can be expected to arise naturally, the universal institutionalization of unions is not an interference with the free market at all but rather a way of ensuring that free market forces that would otherwise be at work are not themselves being hampered by some defect in the market. For Galbraith, in fact, this is exactly what unionization represents:

> The operation of the countervailing power is to be seen with the greatest clarity in the labor market where it is also must fully developed. Because of his comparative immobility, the individual worker has long been highly vulnerable to private economic power. The customer of any particular steel mill, at the turn of the century, could always take himself elsewhere if he felt he was being overcharged. Or he could exercise his sovereign privilege of not buying steel at all. The worker had no comparable freedom if he felt he was being underpaid. Normally he could not move and he had to have work. Not often has the power of one man over another been used more callously than in the American labor market after the rise of the large corporation.[250]

In 1968, again before the modern concept of republican liberty had been articulated, there is a particularly eloquent but rarely cited statement about the need to protect the right to unionize from then Senator Paul Douglas:

> The individual adult workman, when standing alone, was and is no match for the average large employer. His own wages were low and his savings meagre or nonexistent. There are many unemployed all about him. It was more important for him to get a job than for the employer to hire him to fill one. Consequently he stood at a great

disadvantage when he bargained with the employers. As a result he could be forced to accept disadvantageous terms which, in turn, tended to become cumulatively self-perpetuating. And when the workers tried to form unions, they could be discharged with impunity.[251]

Most recently, the contemporary political philosopher Elizabeth Anderson characterizes the modern industrialized, nonunionized firm as an arbitrary and unaccountable private "dictatorship."[252] And similar sentiments have been expressed by many others both before and since.

Such views, moreover, are not merely those of the so-called liberal intellectual elite. Indeed, despite a relentless public relations campaign against unions being waged by the right for generations now, a majority of Americans still approve of labor unions. While there has been some ebb and flow to the level of public support, even at its lowest point, a vast majority believe that "unions are in the best interests of working people," that strong unions "are the only way for employees to get a fair shake in the average big company today," that "most working people need labor unions to protect their rights," and that "if there were no unions, most employers would quickly move to exploit their employees."[253] Even workers who are content to free ride on the protections won for all employees by unions by not contributing their fair share to the fight recognize that they have benefited from the union movement.[254] The idea that unionization is a necessary step for the protection of workers from arbitrary treatment because it acts as a check on the threat to the republican liberty of employees that is built into the very idea of the firm accordingly enjoys widespread and long-term support.

2.5.4 Voice, Liberty, and Workplace Democracy

I suppose this might be a good place to reflect on the relation between my argument for universal unionization and the growing number of people on the left clamoring for some form of workplace democracy as a solution to the problem of giving workers a voice in decisions that can have a serious impact on their lives and the lives of their families and community.[255] These arguments for workplace democracy are themselves often based on conceptions of republican liberty, and while nothing in my argument depends on rejecting this call for workplace democracy – indeed this would presumably be an issue every union would take up with management at some point – I do not see workplace democracy as a substitute for unionization. The reasons for this are several.

First, instantiating democracy in the workplace is a much more impractical and indirect way of addressing the threat to republican liberty that the hierarchical nature of the firm creates. It can easily result in tokenism rather than be a way of giving workers real influence, and even its most vigorous advocates concede that worker democracy is a viable method of having input

2.5 Unionization in Context

only for a small number of big corporate decisions.[256] The union, in contrast, can represent worker interests with regard to every corporate decision, no matter how small, and therefore would seem to be a more effective and comprehensive solution to the problem of providing a voice than the adoption of some form of workplace democracy could ever be.

Second, workplace democracy without some sort of credibly independent worker organization vetting the options available and advising workers on what is in their best interests is unlikely to produce a real and effective restraint on management's tendency to disregard the concerns of its labor force and instead spend a great deal of effort and money to support the false claim that what management is doing is in the best interests of workers. At best, workplace democracy can be a supplement and not a substitute to unionization. Even full-fledged codetermination, the approach that gives workers seats (sometimes as many as fifty percent) on the supervisory boards of major corporations in Germany and a number of other northern European countries, does not exist independent of unionization, and even so, there are rising concerns that worker board members are being co-opted by management interests.[257] Even in the unlikely event that calls to put workers on boards would begin to be successful in the United States,[258] there is reason to worry that this would be a shallow victory without greater unionization too. Simply put, workplace democracy without unionization is a grossly insufficient counterweight to the threat to republican liberty created by the firm, and with unionization, workplace democracy is simply something the firm and the union should and would be able to bargain over.

Third, for reasons that I have already discussed, I do not believe we can get a participation requirement out of a thin conception of republican liberty (one that can be appropriately promoted by a government committed to the liberal principle of neutrality). If some form of workplace democracy is required, it therefore must be required by some other principle. And if it is required by some other principle – a free-standing conception of democracy that applies to all "state-like" institutions[259] is one possibility that has been suggested – I do not see how this principle could be limited to workers providing their input to the management of the firm but not all other affected interests. Any principle that gives a right to participate in the process of making decisions to someone affected by that decision must give that right to everyone so affected or it would deny those others equal concern and respect, which is a pre-institutional principle that any liberal society must embrace. In the context of the management of the firm, this would mean that not only current employees would be entitled to an appropriate degree of input but also potential future employees, creditors, shareholders (regardless of whether voting rights attach to their stock), customers, suppliers, those who live next to the firm's production facilities or otherwise might be affected by ground, air, water, or noise pollution created by the firm, and so on. Such a principle would accordingly prove too much – it would require a radical restructuring of the institution of the firm, and while that might be worth arguing for in some contexts, it is highly unlikely to bear any fruit in the short to medium term and, in any event, is out of place when evaluating what morality requires with regard to determining whether the union is a basic institution in the context of the basic structure and institutions that currently exists in our society. Finally, even if this free-standing principle could be limited in some way, it would surely require representative democracy rather than direct democracy. If this were the case, then the representation of workers by unions would seem to more fully and indeed more effectively instantiate that principle than any other arrangement that did not involve unions.

2.5.5 Liberty and Profitability

As I have previously noted, however, unions do reduce profitability, and some people think that this is sufficient reason to disregard the liberty-enhancing aspects of unionization and its positive effect on wages, benefits, and economic equality and justify making unionization difficult or even impermissible. To the extent that any decline in profitability comes out of that portion of profits representing a return on monopoly power, however, this reduction in profitability is not a reason to oppose unions but a reason to support them, for we have independent reason to see that firms do not abuse monopoly power and redirecting such profits from the firm to its workers might discourage this. Indeed, this is the view that Freeman and Medoff express.[260] But monopoly profits are wrongful, and it does not seem that they become any less wrongful if they are used to pay higher wages rather than to increase profits for the firm itself. Besides, if redirecting what are in fact monopoly profits from company coffers to labor does discourage firms from abusing their monopoly power, then these profits will eventually disappear, so their availability as a source for higher wage payments will be only temporary. At best, then, the argument that the reduction in profits caused by unionization comes largely or at least partially out of monopoly profits and therefore creates no reason for concern is weak. In any event, a number of significant studies conducted since those referred to by Freeman and Medoff strongly suggest that the increases in wages and benefits caused by unionization come out of *non*-monopoly profits, thereby putting unionized firms at a competitive disadvantage *vis à vis* non-unionized ones, so the position taken by Freeman and Medoff looks even less sustainable today.[261]

But this is not a reason to reject unionization. On the contrary, it is a reason to reject half measures, for this problem only arises if some competitors are unionized and some are not. Therefore, the solution here is to realize that to get the full liberty-enhancing and economic benefits of unionization without the economic detriments, unionization must not merely be permitted, it must be required. In this sense, unionization presents a collective action problem, similar to the tragedy of the commons. Everyone benefits if everyone complies – that is, unionizes, but an individual firm can benefit more if it can defect and not unionize while everyone else does, thereby gaining a competitive advantage. But if too many firms think like this, an insufficient number of firms will unionize, every unionized firm will face substantial nonunion competition, and general compliance will eventually collapse, leaving everyone worse off. And unfortunately, this is exactly what game theorists tell us will inevitably happen.[262] If every significant competitor were unionized as a matter of law, however, unionization would not give one firm a competitive advantage over another and there would be no incentive to defect. The extra costs borne by each competitor from universal unionization would be equivalent. These might be offset by higher prices for firms that have some monopoly power, assuming that enforcement of the antitrust laws is not as effective as it should be, but in competitive sectors, the cost of unionization should come out of profits but still leave the sector economically viable if an efficient allocation of resources does indeed suggest the sector should exist.[263]

How could we ensure universal unionization, however, in a globalized economy? Even if we were to insist that all firms within our own nation be unionized, how would we protect them from nonunionized competition from abroad? The answer is that to the extent such protection is warranted, we already do exactly this. Of course, even unionized foreign labor may be cheaper than domestic labor. If it is, there may be reason to place tariffs on the goods produced by such labor or not, but this is a separate problem to be dealt with by separate principles of justice. To the extent foreign labor is cheaper *because* it is not unionized, however, this is unfair competition and thus something we can and should prevent, just as we can and should prevent the importation of goods made without concern for environmental, occupational health and safety, or child labor laws. And it is something we do prevent, or at least try to. For example, when negotiating the Trans Pacific Partnership (TPP), a proposed free-trade deal between various nations on the Pacific Rim that President Trump subsequently abandoned, we required Vietnam to agree to give employees the right to unionize and the right to strike in exchange for expanded free trade with us.[264] Granted, we cannot be sure that foreign unions will be independent in the same way that unions in this country are, but if they are not then this is just one more way that foreign trade may be unfair. The solution to this problem is to closely monitor what our trading partners do and impose post-institutional regulations when necessary, not to disregard the benefits of institutionalized unionization and subject our own workers to the same threats of domination that foreign workers often face from their own employers.

But isn't compulsory union membership itself an interference with liberty? It is one thing to allow unionization, it is quite another to compel it. Why should all employees have to be a member of a union? This is a far greater interference with negative liberty than we considered before, for it interferes not only with the liberty of employers but also with the liberty of their employees to refuse to join the union. But while compulsory union membership (or universal unionization, which is the more neutral way of referring to the same thing) may be an interference with negative liberty, it is not an *unjustified* interference. Not being a member of the union in a unionized workforce is "risky behavior," much like not subscribing to the dominant protective association in a libertarian utopia would be risky behavior, at least according to the right-libertarian Robert Nozick.[265] It is risky because nonmembers or "independents" put members' rights to republican liberty at risk by making it unreasonably more likely that their republican liberty will be violated. In light of this risk, it is not a violation of anyone's rights to compel membership, and the interference with negative liberty that results is justified by the protection of republican liberty this provides, at least if those who are compelled to join receive services just like every other member in return.[266]

While the argument from Nozick is truncated above, I have presented it in the first essay in this volume in great detail. Those who find the sketch of the argument set forth above insufficient may withhold their judgment on this issue until they have reviewed that argument in full. For now, it is sufficient if these doubters concede that *unless* compelling independents to join is an unjustified interference with their negative liberty, there is nothing to complain about here. For unlike republican liberty, which is a right, negative liberty is merely an interest and therefore can be and actually is widely infringed every day because there are many nonarbitrary reasons for doing so that do not violate any other actual right. Indeed, consider this: not only is any interference with negative liberty here justified by the contribution to the protection of republican liberty that universal unionization represents, it is also justified by the efficiency gains that universal unionization creates for the union itself, for remember, an interference with negative liberty can be justified by efficiency gains too. If the firm can be justified by its efficiency gains, despite not tolerating the existence of independents in its midst, the union must be justified when it does exactly the same thing, no more and no less.

There is another potential justification for universal unionization here that I also want to mention. Some of those who have heard my argument for universal unionization have wondered why I do not also rely on the argument that unions build a sense of community among members.[267] As members of a community, workers are less likely to feel isolated and disposable, like microchips in big machines, and more like part of an organism in which they each play an important part and have an important stake. They are less likely to feel alienated from society and the products of their labor, and see themselves as neither masters nor servants, but citizens. Universal unionization ensures that all workers will feel that the society in which they live is in some meaningful sense *their* society no matter where they fall on the economic ladder. Or so the argument goes, and I certainly do not deny that this is true. But I worry that this argument sounds like an argument from positive liberty – in other words, it sounds like an argument about how best to construct a society that allows its members to live a fully realized life. To the extent it is

2.5 Unionization in Context

an argument from positive liberty, it is not available in this situation because there are arguments from other conceptions of positive liberty that would contradict it and therefore make both positions controversial. So I will not rely on it here. Those who feel that such an argument could be made part of a thin theory of the good, however, are free to rely on it if they wish.

I do have one further argument that I want to make for unionization, even if it were not universal and therefore might have some negative impact on the profitability of unionized employers compared to those who were not unionized. It may indeed be true that a firm that is allowed to exploit its workers, or otherwise treat them unjustly, is often (but perhaps not always) going to be more profitable than one that is not.[268] This, in turn, could lead to a shift in investment from unionized firms to nonunionized ones.[269] Although such a shift does not appear to effect overall economic growth,[270] it is still a concern if it means that unionized firms will eventually wither and die because nonunionized firms and therefore nonunionized states are more attractive to investors. Indeed, one of the primary consequentialist arguments advanced for right-to-work laws is that they are necessary to attract new firms from out of state and encourage existing firms to remain, and thus right-to-work laws (it is argued) represent a source of economic growth and jobs. While there is in fact no evidence that this is true,[271] if it were true, it would only be true as long as right-to-work laws were not themselves universal. Once they are, any competitive advantage would be eliminated. Those who advocate right-to-work laws on the grounds that they bring investment and jobs into the state are accordingly merely advocating engaging in a race to the bottom.

Any temporary competitive advantage that might be gained by enacting right-to-work laws would also be eliminated, however, if unions were recognized as basic institutions and right-to-work laws invalidated. And this would do so without allowing right-to-work states to steal growth from other states and without allowing employers to more easily exploit their employees. Indeed, if firms were allowed to employ slave labor, this would increase their profitability too, but no one suggests we should reinstitute slavery in states that are otherwise economically disadvantaged.[272] The question, then, is not whether unions reduce profits, but whether they reduce injustice. If nonunionized firms enjoy higher profits because they are exploiting their workers or otherwise treating them unjustly, and unionized firms are not or at least not to the same extent, then competition from these nonunionized firms is unfair. Such unfair competition can and should be prohibited, just as competition from firms that flout relevant environmental laws is unfair and can and should be prohibited.[273] And there is no evidence that unions raise wages and benefits for workers to a level that would constitute exploitation or unjust treatment of their employer by eliminating profits altogether. This, of course, is not surprising. If unions were to behave so unreasonably, they would quickly put their own members of out of work, for any rational employer would soon redeploy his capital somewhere else. So the argument that unions reduce profits is not an argument that can be legitimately raised against unionization, because the amount of the reduction, if any, is not unjust.[274]

Note that this same argument can also be made with regard to externalities. Like exploiting workers, being able to impose externalities (that is, costs of production) on third parties allows producers to undercut their competition and gain market share or increase their profits or some combination of the two, at least as long as other producers cannot impose similar externalities to a similar extent. This impedes economic efficiency, not promotes it, for it means that goods may sell for less than their real cost of production and therefore will tend to be overproduced, resulting in a misallocation of economic resources. So if we are committed to creating basic institutions that are not merely designed to be just but also to be economically efficient, we want to ensure that the prices for goods and services represent their true cost of production. And without unions, this is much less likely to occur. Once again, any competitive advantage stemming from such practices would be eliminated by requiring unionization across the board, for then no one would gain an unfair advantage if we are unable to adequately police all the relevant competitors. In this case, any reduction in profitability in this environment is likely to reflect the elimination of wrongful or at least economically inefficient behavior. Which means that the argument that unions reduce profitability does not provide a reason to be against treating unions as a basic institution; it provides a reason to be for it.

2.5.6 Unions, Corruption, and the Use of Force and Violence

Another argument frequently raised to undermine the claim that unions have a positive effect on republican liberty is that they are often corrupt, amenable to infiltration by organized crime, and therefore primarily benefit union officials and the criminals who pull their strings rather than the union's general members. Freeman and Medoff, however, disagree: "The popular image of unions as boss-run, corrupt institutions is a caricature. Most unions are highly democratic and corruption problems are concentrated in only a few industries."[275] And while there have continued to be corruption problems with some unions in some industries,[276] those problems have been steadily declining and now seem to be squarely under control.[277] In any event, it is important to remember that *every* organization has the potential to be corrupted, not just unions. Indeed, even large, long-established, and economically significant firms are regularly revealed to have engaged in widespread fraud and other illegal activities.[278] At this time, corruption within firms seems to be a greater problem than corruption within unions.[279] There is at least no reason to believe that unions in general are going to be any more or less corrupt than firms in general.[280] Because no one argues that the fear of corruption is a reason to get rid of firms, it is not a reason to oppose unionization either. It is simply a reason for post-institutional vigilance. So once again, this factor does not cut against unionization, it supports it.

2.5 Unionization in Context

A related argument is that unions have a propensity to enforce their will through the threat or use of violence. This claim has receded somewhat in recent years, but at one time, it was pressed vigorously. It therefore may arise again, and should not be left unaddressed. For example, in the great tradition of the paranoid style in American politics, the right-libertarian and economic neoliberal Ludwig von Mises claimed

Labor violence is tolerated within broad limits. The labor unions are practically free to prevent by force anybody from defying their orders concerning wage rates and other labor conditions. They are free to inflict with impunity bodily evils upon strikebreakers and upon entrepreneurs who employ strikebreakers. They are free to destroy property of such employers and even to injure customers patronizing their shops. The authorities, with the approval of public opinion, condone such acts. The police do not stop such offenders, the state attorneys do not arraign them, and no opportunity is offered to the penal courts to pass judgment on their actions.[281]

Hayek also claimed something similar

[Unions] are the only privileged institution licensed to use coercion without law. The coercion on which their present power rests is the coercion of other workers who are deterred by the threat of violence from offering their labour on their own terms.[282]

And Sylvester Petro, one of the most vociferous critics of unions from the 1950s through the 1970s, was even more extreme:

Unions are battle agencies. "They are," as Henry Simons said years ago in a powerful and still frequently quoted article, "essentially occupational armies, born and reared amidst violence, led by fighters, and capable of becoming peaceful only as their power becomes irresistible."[283]

Similar claims, of course, were even more common among nonacademics and to an even greater extent still are.

In any event, prodded by such hyperbolic thoughts, there have been periodic attempts in the United States to amend the Hobbs Act,[284] which makes it a federal crime to use threats or violence to extort property from those engaged in interstate commerce. The Hobbs Act was enacted to provide a federal remedy for the extortion rackets that, at one time, were the bread and butter of organized crime. The purpose of these proposed anti-union amendments, in turn, was to reverse *United States* v. *Emmons*,[285] the 1973 Supreme Court decision that held the statute could not be used as a basis for prosecution for the threat or use of violence arising out of the pursuit of legitimate union objectives. Of course, any such acts could always and can still be prosecuted under state law, and on the rare occasions when violence has arisen in connection with a labor dispute they have been, but a reversal of *Emmons* was nevertheless seen by the right as a way of restraining legitimate union activity.[286] This is because if *Emmons* were reversed, any act of violence during a labor dispute, such as a fistfight on the picket line, would invite federal intervention, whereas an act of violence by or on behalf of management would not (management violence is not aimed at *obtaining* money, merely retaining it, and as currently interpreted, this would not be covered by the Hobbs Act). The threat of federal investigation and prosecution, in turn, could be used to intimidate union leadership, which could potentially face conspiracy charges based on the claim that their efforts on behalf of workers had somehow provoked violence.[287] Even more significantly, it is also a violation of the Hobbs Act to use "economic coercion" and not merely physical coercion to force another give up property.[288] Because property includes money, it is easy to see how without *Emmons* this statute could be used to effectively outlaw all sorts of union activity aimed at using the increased bargaining power of the collective to increase wages or other benefits for workers. Even under *Emmons,* there are still periodic cases of prosecutorial overreach with regard to legitimate union activity and tactics.[289] So, the claims of extortion that are frequently raised by employers faced with union attempts to obtain jobs, higher wages, and benefits for their members need to be treated very carefully.

Of course, the claim that violence was used as a conscious tactic by labor unions and condoned by the police was as overblown when it first appeared as the claim that illegal immigrants are unleashing a crime wave in our country is now.[290] It is true that violence does occasionally occur in connection with disputes between employers and organized labor.[291] A great deal is at stake, especially for striking workers, and some individuals will no doubt behave badly under such pressure and may even commit acts of violence. But reliable statistics on the degree of violence that can be properly claimed to have been directed or at least encouraged by union officials are hard to come by.[292] Such statistics are not maintained by any governmental or other neutral nongovernmental body, and the claims made by anti-union activists often turn out on inspection to be wildly exaggerated if not wholly fabricated.[293] Most of these acts of violence are extremely minor and always isolated, and a certain number of these incidents would be presumed to arise among any large group of people – the fact that they arise during a labor dispute may be purely coincidental and does not tell us whether they are rogue acts that are individually motivated or directed or encouraged or at least condoned from above.[294] Sometimes, those found responsible have no association with the relevant union or are in fact associated with management or strike-breaking personnel or consultants, or at least provoked by them. Remember, in the early years of the union movement, union organizers were routinely followed and beat up by company goons, and provocateurs often tried to incite violence in order to swing public opinion against striking workers.[295] Unfortunately, incidents of violence committed or sponsored by company agents continue on occasion even to this day.[296] In any event, as a historical matter, on those occasions when violence has occurred, it has usually been in connection with an

2.5 Unionization in Context

initial campaign to organize a currently nonunion firm or during strikes when nonunion strikebreakers were hired to replace union workers.[297] Because all firms would be organized as matter of law if unions were recognized as a basic institution – indeed, even replacement workers would have to be unionized, although they would of course be represented by a different union – the situations that are most likely to lead to violence around the fringes would be eliminated, so there would be less reason to expect violence to arise. Indeed, if anything, recognition that unions are a basic institution of society should *reduce* the incidence of violence.[298] It would also eliminate the incentive for relentlessly anti-union owners to try to suppress organizing efforts by retaliating against employees promoting unionization.[299] And when those organizing efforts prove successful, it would also prevent anti-union owners from end-running actual pro-union votes by closing their business down and reopening it as still nonunionized under another name,[300] a provocative act that at the very least triggers extreme resentment and may even lead some to consider responding with violence. But such punitive, bullying tactics by employers would simply be pointless once universal unionization were required, so whatever violence these might provoke would also disappear. Accordingly, regardless of the extent to which union violence may have been a problem in the past, there is no reason to believe that increased unionization would lead to an increase in violence if unionization were made universal now.

2.5.7 Unions and Unemployment

There are also some alleged macroeconomic effects of unions on efficiency that I should mention. One of these is the claim that unions make it more likely that wages will be "sticky," and sticky wages will not respond to downturns in the overall economy as quickly as they should do or perhaps even at all. This in turn puts upward pressure on unemployment and prevents the economy from restoring full employment at a lower level of demand. I won't say much about this point here because I have discussed it extensively elsewhere,[301] but I will attempt to summarize some of the most important elements of this discussion. The claim that wages are sticky is usually attributed to the legendary economist John Maynard Keynes, and he did indeed say this.[302] But it is not correct to suggest he thought that attacking the stickiness of wages was a necessary or even helpful element of any attempt to address unemployment, as many have incorrectly claimed. Nor did he ever suggest that he thought unionization made wages "stickier" than they would otherwise be or that the elimination of unions would reduce unemployment, as, for example, Hayek frequently suggested.[303] Instead, Keynes's position was that even if money wages were more flexible, this might make matters worse rather than better with regard to unemployment, for the expectation that wage rates would continue to drop in the future might encourage employers to postpone making new hires, just as a drop in prices encourages consumers to put off purchasing products today when they expect to be able to purchase these for less tomorrow.[304] And Keynes saw a variety of other reasons to worry that wage reductions might actually increase unemployment too.[305] The bottom line being that there could still be deficiencies of aggregate demand even if wages were more flexible, and it was deficiencies in aggregate demand that caused unemployment.[306]

Keynes was not the only one who thought that increasing wage flexibility was not necessarily a cure for unemployment. As the innovative Polish economist Michał Kalecki pointed out at about the same time, a decline in money or nominal wages does not necessarily lead to a decline in real wages, and even a decline in real wages does not necessarily stimulate employment.[307] The neoclassical view that unemployment is the result of the failure of wages to drop in correspondence with a drop in the demand for labor depends on the argument that if nominal wages decline, real wages will decline and therefore make labor cheaper, thereby increasing productivity and increasing employment.[308] But real wages are set in the product market, not the labor market. If nominal wages decline and therefore workers have less to spend, the prices of what they might spend their now reduced wages on will have to decrease too if output is to stay the same, and therefore real wages and unemployment will be unaffected, although the lag between these two events will mean that the standard of living for all workers will be temporarily reduced. And if prices in the product market do not decrease because producers have sufficient monopoly power to use their lower costs to increase their marginal profits rather than pass these savings on to the consumer, thereby causing an actual decline in real wages, demand and therefore output will decrease and unemployment will *increase*, and, even more disturbingly, the standard of living for all workers will be *permanently* rather than merely temporarily lowered.[309]

There is also reason to believe that wages are not as sticky as they are often thought to be, even when the employees involved are represented by unions – at least they are no stickier than product prices. Indeed, sometimes supply goes up, costs go down, and product prices to the consumer remain high. Gasoline prices, for example, seem to rise instantaneously at the slightest hint of trouble in the Middle East or any other threat to supply, yet return to their previous level much more slowly when the latest supposed reason for panic is revealed to be seriously overstated.[310] And despite significantly lower fuel costs boosting profits for airlines for some time now, fares have not gone down.[311] So stickiness is not a unique problem for wages, and reducing the stickiness of wages would not necessarily increase output, and therefore employment. It might only increase profits if product prices are also sticky. In any event, union support can often allow employers to reduce wages more quickly and more substantially and with less employee disruption and unrest than they might be able to do with unrepresented labor.[312] Therefore, the attempt to blame unions for unemployment is simply not supported by theory or the facts.[313]

2.5 Unionization in Context

I should note here, I suppose, that there is one recent study claiming that increases in the minimum wage, something that unions typically support even though it is often earned only by nonunion labor, especially since unionization has begun its long decline, has increased unemployment in Seattle.[314] The study has attracted a lot of attention from the popular press,[315] so I want to mention it briefly here in order to ensure that it is not thought to suggest something more generally about the relationship between unionization and the higher wages that unionization entails and unemployment. First, remember that even the complete elimination of unions is not likely to remove pressure on employers to increase the minimum wage. After all, the minimum wage is now 26 percent lower than it was at its high point in 1968 in today's dollars; it would be $19.33 in today's dollars instead of $7.25 if it had kept up with increases in productivity instead of merely inflation.[316] Indeed, since the elimination of unions is most likely to increase the number of minimum wage jobs at the expense of better paying jobs, that pressure is most likely to increase. In any event, the current pressure to raise the minimum wage exists and has increased despite the decimation of unions in the private sector, so at the very least we have no reason to believe that the further restriction of unionization will reduce it. Second, there is reason to be concerned that the study is fundamentally flawed. The results reported by the authors are well outside the bounds of most published research, the study finds changes in employment in areas of the labor market where the study's own theoretical assumptions predict there should be none, and the study excludes roughly 40 percent of the workforce (those who work for multi-location as opposed to single-location businesses), thereby failing to account for the fact that shifts in employment from one type of employer to another rather than the elimination of employment may be what has actually occurred.[317] There is nothing here to suggest the existence of an inverse relation between increases in the minimum wage and unemployment that calls unionization into question too. If increases in the minimum wage do lead employers to reduce the number of jobs or hours they are offering to existing employees instead of funding these increases out of available profits,[318] this merely suggest that unions are needed to put pressure on employers to not engage in such end runs and to pressure the government to simulate the economy. It does not suggest, however, that raising wages is somehow unjust given how greedy employers may possibly react or suggest that we should suppress unionization in order to ensure that one injustice (exploitation) is not replaced by another (unnecessary unemployment) or remains unabated.

Finally, and most importantly, the claim that wages would be less sticky overall and therefore unionization or at least collective bargaining should be limited is an attempt to treat workers as if they were cans of soup. But people, as many theorists concerned about the way workers are treated have been arguing for a long time, are not cans of soup.[319] Indeed, the whole point of the argument from liberty is that workers are living, breathing, autonomous beings who are entitled to be treated as free men and women with the usual panoply of rights that free men and women typically enjoy. "In survey after survey," however, "the biggest employee complaint is being treated with a lack of respect," rather than a being with rights.[320] And while the mere fact that a worker *is* a being with rights makes it clear that workers are to be treated differently than things, the right of self-ownership, the right from which all conceptions of liberty descend, does so expressly. The argument that we should do what we can to see that real wages drop in times of economic distress just like prices drop on cans of soup is accordingly antithetical to everything for which the argument from republican liberty stands, not to mention the concept of rights in general. So even if the argument connecting unionization to the stickiness of wages were correct, this would not give us reason to oppose unionization. Even if the efficiency claim for unionization were weaker than it is, any infringement of negative liberty is still more than justified by the protection of republican liberty provided.

2.5.8 Unions and Inflation

The same applies to another macroeconomic claim that is commonly asserted by those opposed to unionization. This is the argument that because unions are "always pushing for higher wages," their efforts inevitably trigger a wage-price spiral that results in ever-increasing rates of inflation. In other words, successful union demands for an increase in money wages lead employers to increase the price of their goods and services in order to cover their increased costs of production; these higher prices, in turn, erode the real value of the prior increase in money wages, leading unions to demand even higher money wages, and so on. The result of this inflationary spiral is that real wages stagnate or possibly even decline as producers try to anticipate the next wage increase and raise prices preemptively, and everyone suffers from having to cope with an inflationary environment.[321] Of course, if unions do not seek wage increases and allow gains in productivity to accrue exclusively to the accounts of employers, then real wages do not go up either. Indeed, some inflation inevitably results anyway, so real wages drop. The claim here is essentially that real wages cannot increase, no matter what, and that the only choice here is whether to allow unions to invite spiraling inflation upon us all or not.

Note that the argument here is simply a version of the "wages fund theory" posited by various classical economists. In brief, the theory was that there is only a certain amount of capital available to pay wages, and one can either pay this to more or less people – that is, pay more to some in exchange for unemployment for others, or keep wages where they are and keep more people employed. While the original wages fund theory made unemployment the dark pit ahead instead of inflation, the idea is the same. Both in its original unemployment-based version and its more recent inflation-based version,

2.5 Unionization in Context

the theory is that there is a conceptual limitation built into the economic system that prevents unions from improving real wages for workers. In either case, unions' push for higher wages must end in macroeconomic disaster. The implication being that because we cannot reasonably expect unions not to push for higher wages, it would be best if we left unions out of the equation altogether.

But the wages fund theory has long been discredited. Indeed, J. S. Mill, one of the classical economists who was originally a proponent of the theory,[322] famously recanted his support for it in 1869,[323] saying:

> The doctrine hitherto taught by all or most economists (including myself), which denied it to be possible that trade combinations can raise wages, or which limited their operations in that respect to the somewhat earlier attainment of a rise which the competition of the market would have produced without them, [has been] deprived of its scientific basis and must be thrown aside. The right and wrong of the proceedings of Trades' Unions becomes a common question of prudence and social duty, not one which is peremptorily decided by unbending necessities of political economy.[324]

Many economists naturally followed Mill in his rejection of the theory and "by the mid-1890s, it was commonplace for one to see the wage-fund theory referred to as an archaic error."[325] Indeed, more than a hundred years ago, the political economist and historian of economic thought James Bonar said "the wages fund theory is the crowning instance of an untrue abstraction ... and it has probably done more injury to the reputation of economic theory than any other generalization ever received into economics textbooks and then expunged from them."[326] What everyone eventually realized is that it was simply not true that there is anything like a fixed, rigid fund out of which wages can be paid and that cannot be used for anything else. For example, this amount includes funds that can go instead to increasing dividends to shareholders, to repurchasing stock and thereby artificially increasing earnings per share, to retiring debt to improve the appearance of the firm's balance sheet, to paying excessive compensation to top management, to funding expensive corporate acquisitions and mergers that artificially create the appearance of corporate growth, to being hoarded in the form of cash or cash equivalents, to bidding up the price of assets in environments where new investment is deemed too risky, or to a host of other unproductive places, all of which are attracting enormous amounts of money today and have been doing do so for quite some time.[327] Indeed, until very recently, the explosion in economic inequality that we have been experiencing since 1980 is mostly the result of funds that would otherwise be available to increase the real wages of rank-and-file workers going almost exclusively to top management and other highly compensated individuals.[328] Even if the wage rate were purely a distributional matter, then, there is simply no reason to believe that unions cannot raise real wages for the rank-and-file employees without causing problems in the overall economy, unemployment, inflation, or otherwise.[329]

But the amount available to be divided up between all these functions can increase or decrease fairly rapidly, meaning that the wage rate is actually not purely a distributional problem.[330] The economy can grow or shrink, and in either case, there is now ample evidence that neither unionization nor the minimum wages that unions typically support are a cause of inflation.[331] Indeed, as the past thirty years has demonstrated, the economy can experience consistent, long-term economic growth without causing wage demands to increase, for there has been virtually no upward movement to real wages until recently, even this recent movement is very slight, and we have enjoyed consistently low inflation for years.[332] Even during inflationary periods, there is reason to doubt that union demands for wage increases contribute significantly to the problem, at least according to Milton Friedman, who was no friend of the union movement.[333] More recent arguments that union demands for higher wages necessarily cause inflation have been convincingly rebutted too.[334] If management does try to protect corporate profits or its own overly generous rates of compensation in this environment by increasing prices when wages rise, it is both morally wrong and economically foolish for them to do so. Firms that do will be punished by the market, and if they are not, this means there is some form of collusion going on and the relevant market has competitive problems that need to be independently addressed. In any event, such a possible reaction certainly does not render unionization counterproductive as a conceptual macroeconomic matter.

Unfortunately, like so many other zombie-like theories in economics,[335] the wages fund theory won't stay dead, and while the various periodic attempts to revive it within the academy have all been unsuccessful,[336] it continues to have influence among those in the political class whose anti-union predispositions will not allow them to accept that it is not true.[337] Even Hayek, as late as 1980, claimed that the only way to pay for higher wages was to increase the money supply and this, in turn, would necessarily result in inflation.[338] At least most of those who currently warn of the wage-price inflationary death spiral version of the wages fund argument attempt to dress it up as something else, and to be slightly more nuanced in its presentation, claiming that a wage price death spiral is not inevitable but merely likely "in present circumstances."[339] While technically not a conceptual argument, this slightly less strident version is effectively one nonetheless because the supposedly contingent circumstances that it is said to depend on (strong unions) are deemed ever-present, despite almost forty years now of declines in union membership. Sure, union wage demands can contribute to cost-push inflation. But there are many different kinds and causes of inflation.[340] And since wages do not come from a fixed fund, there is no reason why wage increases in response to such demands must lead to inflation in the product market, or even create an unacceptable risk of this. In any event, the risk of inflation falls equally on everybody rather than exclusively on the worker, as allowing real wages to continue to stagnate does.[341] Therefore, our principles regarding the evaluation of changes in the

2.5 Unionization in Context

risk environment would still classify this as an improvement. This attempt to use the fear of inflation to erect a quasi-conceptual macroeconomic block to unionization must accordingly be deemed to fail.

2.5.9 Unions as a Check on Managerial Incompetence

Unions also act as a useful check on managerial incompetence. Remember, while a firm is a free market institution, it is not itself internally governed by free market forces. As far as its internal operations go, resources are allocated by fiat through a top-down hierarchical structure, as they would be throughout the economy in a socialist society. While this generates some savings in transaction costs for the firm and therefore potentially generates some efficiencies, at least within the capitalist context, it also allows the resources of the firm to be incompetently allocated and creates the potential for some large offsetting inefficiencies as well. If we are going to increase the likelihood of firms allocating their own resources efficiently and therefore contributing to the overall efficiency of the economy, we are accordingly going to have to take steps to counterbalance the possibility of incompetence.

The market, of course, provides one check on such behavior. Incompetent and therefore less efficient producers will be underpriced by more efficient ones and eventually driven out of business or taken over by more efficient producers.[342] But this does not prevent incompetence; it merely punishes it once it has occurred.[343] And it only punishes incompetence to the extent that the incompetence of one firm exceeds the incompetence of its competitors. In an industry in which incompetence is widespread, free market forces do nothing to improve efficiency. Even when a firm is especially incompetent and therefore subject to being disciplined by the market, punishment is often a slow and painful process, leaving unnecessary inefficiencies lingering in the system for a long time and resulting in a potentially significant loss of productivity. We should therefore not rely on the market to root out incompetence on its own. If we want to maximize efficiency and catch incompetence earlier, before it does significant damage, we are going to have put other checks in place.

Currently, the check we rely on most heavily is corporate governance. And it is true that boards of directors can replace management when management incompetence becomes apparent, and shareholders can replace directors when their incompetence becomes apparent. But such incompetence is almost never apparent enough to trigger board and/or shareholder reaction until a large amount of damage has already been done or it is otherwise too late to reverse the forces that have been put in play.[344] Because board positions are part-time, temporary, and at most a source of supplemental rather than primary income, boards are likely to tolerate management incompetence way too long even when the board is not in the pocket of management, something that is unfortunately becoming a more and more common problem in its own right.[345] Shareholders, even those who have large holdings, are much more likely to simply sell their shares and exit the scene than take an activist position when upset with management.[346] And those few who are willing to fight are now increasingly being excluded from opportunities to confront management.[347] Even when shareholders do manage to vote a director out, that does not end the matter – this director can simply be reappointed by the remaining members of the board, thereby frustrating the will of shareholders.[348] And of course, even these limited and easy-to-evade constraints do not often apply with regard to privately held corporations, some of which are large employers, because their shareholders *are* their managers or otherwise in a less than arms-length relationship with management. Certain corporations and especially foreign-based corporations whose ownership is not transparent may not even have independent boards.[349] In other words, the existing external checks on management incompetence are not enough: "In light of the limited ability of external constraints to solve the problem of managerial incompetence, the best hope for improving the ability of the corporate governance system to solve this problem lies in improving the efficiency of internal constraints."[350] To more effectively combat management incompetence, some other appropriately motivated internal watchdog is required.

Unions are indeed a watchdog that will bark when others can't or won't. A successful firm has more employees and pays its employees higher wages, or at least has the potential to do so. A firm that goes out of business, or one that shrinks or merely fails to grow as large or be as profitable as it could and should do, puts downward pressure on wages and may even put continued employment at risk. Shareholders often benefit substantially from short-term success along with management and can easily have sold out by the time the bill for whatever shortsighted measures were undertaken comes due. Employees, in contrast, are more likely to be concerned about the long term, especially given the difficulty in finding new employment the longer they have worked for one employer.[351] Hence, union willingness to sacrifice short-term salary benefits for long-term guarantees of job security.[352] But most importantly, because exit is not so easy or attractive an alternative for regular employees,[353] unions are motivated to voice objections to misguided managerial actions in ways that board members and shareholders are not.[354] In certain cases, unions can also provide a useful source of alternative financing.[355] True, unions may be incompetently run themselves, and when they are, this can impede the firm's efforts to behave efficiently. But this is not usually the case – when a union is incompetent, this most often expresses itself as a failure to effectively restrain the incompetence or wrongful behavior of management rather than as an obstructionist effort to impede enlightened management's attempt to guide the firm efficiently but also justly forward.[356] At least this is where most of the criticism of the union by its members seems to lie.[357] And if it were otherwise, one would expect to see unionized firms going out of business at a greater rate than nonunionized ones, but we do not.[358]

2.5 Unionization in Context

The one possible exception to unionization's general lack of negative impact on firm efficiency is the tendency for unions to be protectionist, for they are understandably concerned about preserving the jobs of their members and not allowing these jobs to be exported abroad even if economic efficiencies would be gained thereby.[359] In many cases, however, these economic efficiencies arise out of the firm's ability to exploit foreign workers to a greater extent than domestic workers, or from the cost savings offered by not having to abide by the same or similar environmental, occupational health and safety, child labor laws, and the like, or from the savings generated by the opportunity to pay lower taxes on their activities.[360] To the extent these efficiencies do arise of out of these practices, they are in most cases unjust,[361] and there is nothing wrong with union efforts to prevent firms from taking advantage of them.[362] Of course, unions may attempt to obstruct efforts to move jobs overseas even when there are just efficiencies to be gained by this action, and it would arguably be better for our economy (although not necessarily for the relevant workers who lose their jobs, those who would now have fewer opportunities for employment, or have to move to jobs that pay less) if these efforts were unsuccessful. We could not have lost as many manufacturing and other jobs as we have over the last fifty years, however, if union efforts to stop efficient moves to switch production overseas were usually successful. And the same can be said about union efforts to resist technological innovation that threatens jobs, even when this innovation is economically efficient.[363] So the tendency of unions to try to obstruct what in a few cases may indeed be economically efficient management decisions does not seem like something that is likely to have a widespread and significant economic effect, resulting in a net reduction in economic liberty. Indeed, whatever effect unionization has had in reducing efficiency seems very small indeed – much more objectionable activity is undertaken by management, activity that unions serve to bring to light and resist. This one small downside simply does not create a serious risk of net inefficiencies and therefore does not amount to an argument against treating unions as a basic institution, especially when we can address this one undesirable aspect of union activity even further through post-institutional regulation. In any case, if we are considering whether the interference with negative liberty that unions represent is justified, then promoting overall economic efficiency must be a sufficient reason, for this is the reason used to justify the institution of the firm in the first place. In any event, it is still true that on balance, unions are much more of a boon to economic efficiency than a burden on it.

2.5.10 Unions as a Check on the Antisocial Inclinations of Management

But let's not stop there. We also want to consider whether in addition to acting as a check on managerial incompetence and corruption, unions act as a more general check on management's inclinations to direct the firm toward antisocial behavior, and perhaps even encourage management to promote socially responsible behavior instead. Even Hayek recognizes that while "the only specific purpose which corporations ought to serve is to secure the highest long-term return on their capital, this does not mean that in the pursuit of this end they ought not to be restrained be general legal *and* moral rules. [...]. In this respect certain generally accepted rules of decency and perhaps even charitableness should probably be regarded as no less binding on corporations that the strict rules of law."[364] And while Hayek nevertheless opposed unionization for reasons that I have already mentioned, there is good reason to believe that unions do help ensure that corporate management behaves in a way that is consistent with a liberal democratic society's existing laws and moral values.

This restraining function can take two forms. First, unions may help enforce the regulations on employer activity that have a direct effect on workers, such as minimum wage, maximum hour, nondiscrimination, and occupational health and safety laws. Second, unions may help enforce a wider set of regulations designed to protect the general public from externalities. Both of these effects, if present, would support an argument that unions increase efficiency or at least ensure that the drive toward efficiency does not overrun the bounds of justice.

The first criterion speaks very strongly in favor of unionization. Unions have contributed significantly to the enactment of wage and hour laws, occupational health and safety laws, child labor laws, and other pieces of legislation that are now widely (even if not universally) regarded as essential components of a civil society.[365] These laws may represent restrictions on negative liberty, which remember is not itself a right, but we nevertheless deem these restrictions justified by the overall contribution they make to the protection of republican liberty, which *is* a right, as well as the right to be treated with equal concern and respect. But unions have not only contributed to the enactment of these laws, they have also contributed heavily to their enforcement. Compliance with the Occupational Safety and Health Act, for example, is much higher in unionized firms than in nonunionized ones.[366] This should not be surprising: government enforcement resources are limited and therefore need to be devoted to systemic firm-wide and even industry-wide violations; individual violations are much less likely to attract the attention of government enforcers or warrant the allocation of scarce government enforcement resources when they do. In other words, unions play an important institutional role is ensuring that the hard-won rights of workers exist both on the books and in practice.[367] Indeed, even minority unions, which do not enjoy collective bargaining rights, have won changes in company policies through protests and legal action and "have shown real power be getting activists who feel they were wrongfully fired their jobs back."[368] And under Trump, the threat of spotty and unenthusiastic enforcement is only going to get worse and worse,[369] making the need for unions and the enforcement pressure they can bring even more essential.[370]

Even if the relevant administrative agencies were more ready, willing, and able to do their jobs, however, there would still be reason to worry that unions are necessary if we are to ensure that enforcement of the relevant laws and regulations governing the workplace will be thorough and robust. This is because information about employer and management violations and abuses is increasingly being suppressed through the use of non-disparagement agreements.[371] Such agreements are now being routinely included in many employment contracts, and they are almost always included in any settlement agreement with employees who feel they were abused and who have threatened or brought legal action against their employer.[372] The result can be that patterns and practices of misbehavior remain in the dark. For example, managers who have allegedly engaged in sexual harassment and companies that have tolerated this can avoid being publicly outed for such misbehavior, and subsequent victims are unlikely to realize that misconduct directed at them may be coming from a repeat offender. The relevant government agencies may not even become aware of this pattern of misbehavior.[373] Unions are also important sources of protection for employees subjected to racial intimidation in the workplace, and for LGBT people too, especially in states that do not yet make discrimination on the basis of sexual orientation an actionable offense.[374] In any event, only unions have the bargaining power necessary to discourage the use of non-disparagement agreements, and only unions can provide a comprehensive source of institutional memory that can be used to highlight a pattern and practice of violations and abuses when they do occur.

What is curious here is that the criticism of the enforcement role of unions comes most often from those on the right who decry any kind of government intervention in our lives as an intolerable interference with liberty. If the existence of unions allows government to be less massive and intrusive than it would otherwise have to be in order to enforce our chosen preferences, then unionization should be viewed by these critics as a good thing. Of course, one can attack whether the preferences that current regulations reflect should have been chosen; but until these choices are changed by just democratic procedures, we undermine the liberty of everyone in our political community if we fail to enforce them, and relying on overburdened and underfunded government agencies to enforce these laws alone is simply a recipe for disaster. And it seems highly unlikely that those who oppose unionization on liberty grounds would support ramping up government enforcement resources to such an extent that internal checks on the conduct of management would no longer be necessary despite the threat to republican liberty that the firm represents, even if we were to ignore the advantages of having a system that provides internal as well as external checks. In other words, in a pairwise comparison between the world in which we actually live and one in which government enforcement resources were so massively increased that unions became unnecessary, it seems unlikely that those who are anti-union, given their anti-regulation bent, would opt for the latter. The real choice is accordingly between the world in which we actually live, and one in which unions represent a much more important and necessary part of the enforcement puzzle, and that world can realistically come into existence only through universal unionization.

The second criterion speaks in favor of unionization too, for unions can also act as a check on the wider antisocial inclinations of management – that is, efforts to evade pollution controls, commit fraud, violate consumer product safety laws, and the like.[375] True, successful evasion of these rules often adds to firm profitability and therefore has the potential to increase job security and perhaps even wages for the firm's employees, at least in the short term, so this is not something that unions are as motivated to police as violations of regulations that apply to pay, working conditions, hours, and the like. Nevertheless, despite having a less direct stake in making the firm generally law-abiding, unions have a reason to be watchful. As I have already pointed out, employees are traditionally more interested in long-term security than in short-term profits, making their investment in the long-term survival of the firm greater than management or even most shareholders, who mostly opt for exit when the firm is not being run to their satisfaction. Unions, even more so than boards of directors and shareholders, are accordingly more likely than any of these other groups to be interested in ensuring that firms are as efficient as they can be *within the limits of the law*. Firms that evade the law eventually get caught, and when they do, the resulting economic hit can be enormous, threatening the economic health of the firm and maybe even its continued viability. While much of this wrongdoing goes undetected by unions, at least unions offer a check that board members and shareholders cannot. Indeed, in heavily concentrated industries where institutional investors own a piece of each of the major participants, recent evidence suggests institutional investors may be a facilitator of management wrongdoing rather than a check on it.[376] Once again, even a world with a protective measure that is only sometimes successful is preferable to one that leaves out this potentially beneficial safety measure.

Some support for this notion comes from "Who Blows the Whistle on Corporate Fraud?" an empirical study establishing that employees are the source of revelations about fraud more than any other potential monitor. Only 6 percent of frauds are uncovered by the Securities Exchange Commission (SEC), the government agency primarily responsible for monitoring such activity, while 14 percent are uncovered by auditors, 14 percent by members of the media, 16 percent by industry regulators, and 19 percent by employees.[377] Moreover, one recent study "found a sharp and lasting drop in financial wrongdoing at companies that were subject to whistle-blower investigations,"[378] meaning that whistle blowing by employees may be an especially effective method of controlling corporate wrongdoing.[379] Since fear of retaliation against those who make such revelations is likely to be a strong motivator to keep silent, and one of the primary sources of protection against retaliation are unions, it stands to reason that a more unionized firm is less likely to engage in fraud and less likely to get away with it for a prolonged period if it does.[380] Had even some

2.5 Unionization in Context

of the thousands of Wells Fargo employees who were allegedly fired for trying to blow the whistle on the bank's fraudulent account-creation practices been unionized, for example, the problems at Wells Fargo might have come to light far earlier than they did and more of these employees would have their jobs back now or would not have been fired in the first place.[381]

The prevention and detection of antisocial behavior, however, is not limited to the role that unions play in protecting whistle-blowers – as institutional investors, unions are far more active than any other type of investor in monitoring management and rooting out corporate fraud.[382] (Note that this is also true in the public sector, where there are no institutional investors, boards of directors, or other individuals or entities with large individual incentives to engage in the monitoring of management,[383] but more on this in the next essay.) Of course, unions are no guarantee that all the antisocial inclinations of management will be successfully suppressed. Unions may even sometimes be a voice in favor of certain antisocial activities.[384] But unions are rarely, if ever, an instigator of antisocial activity on their own. When they do support antisocial activity, they are usually not doing so *over the objections* of their firms; they are simply adding their voice to those that are already encouraging the firm to misbehave.[385] Overall, unions are most likely to make serious illegal and immoral acts by management less likely to occur. Which again supports the notion that if firms are to be treated as a basic institution of society, then unions must be too. Firms and unions must come as package – firms without unions make a basic structure lopsided and unjust.

Of course, there is no doubt that on occasions unions may reach outside their core functions and take stands, even advocate policies on their own that many of their members would find contrary to their own deeply held values and perhaps even the core values of liberalism. In questioning my claim for universal unionization, for example, a number of people have raised the example of the two unions of university lecturers in the United Kingdom, the executive councils of which have each voted at one time or another to boycott academics from Israel, a move that many academics (including me) think is motivated by anti-Semitism and in any event is outside the proper scope of union activities, wrongheaded, highly objectionable, and offensive.[386] In response to these moves, many members resigned from the union or threatened to resign (as I did) if such policies were put into effect. Would my argument for universal unionization render this move by objecting members no longer possible?

Technically, it wouldn't, because universities in the United Kingdom are public employers and therefore the relevant unions are public sector unions to which my argument at this point does not on its face apply. Nevertheless, the example has moral force because a similarly objectionable position could be taken by a union in the private sector and it would be directly applicable if my argument were extended to public sector unions, so it is worth considering now how union members might be able to react to deeply offensive actions by their unions if universal unionization was in force. If unions exist, they have to represent the interests of their members – that is built into the basic idea of unions. How we are to ensure that they do this, however, is matter for post-institutional regulation. In light of these concerns, we might take various post-institutional steps to ensure that a minority does not use their union to advance their own not widely held political aims. We might, for example, prohibit union activity outside of the core areas of representing workers in disputes with management, collective bargaining for wages, benefits, better working conditions, and monitoring management for incompetence and corruption. On the other hand, we might require that union positions outside these core areas be supported by an actual majority of members, and not just the majority voting or a majority of the executive board, in which case the kind of proposals raising the most concern would almost certainly be defeated.[387] And even if such positions were supported by a majority of members, and not merely the majority voting, we might still allow objecting members to deduct from their dues any funds that go to advocacy for such positions and perhaps any sums that are used to fund activities beyond the union's core functions. In *Janus*, the majority reasoned that individual workers do not have the resources to have the calculation of such deductions independently checked and the union therefore cannot be trusted to make these calculations accurately or even in good faith.[388] But this is nonsense. Giant swaths of economic activity and cost allocation are accounted for through internal calculations, and similar objections have not been raised to this, or at least have not been held fatal to the practice. Unions can simply be required to produce audited financials, as publicly traded firms and private firms that borrow money are required do, and an independent check can be provided. Therefore, the feasibility objection to allowing union members to deduct amounts for union political activity to which they object is specious.

It is true that the option of resignation from a union whose wider political activities a particular individual member finds intolerably objectionable would no longer be available, but this is a lesser burden than it might seem. Firms certainly take political positions that are highly objectionable to many of their workers and these workers don't even get a voice in this, except of course through their union if there is one. And if objectionable positions are taken by a firm, similar positions are often taken by all firms in the entire industry, so the option of resigning from one firm and obtaining the same kind of job at another is usually not available in this case either. This is something that workers simply have to live with. The same situation arises with regard to positions taken by state, local, and national governments. So this problem is neither new nor unique. It does not mean that unions should not be a basic institution or that unionization should not be universal, for it is still more likely that society will be maximally just within the feasible set, not less, with unions than without them.[389]

2.5.11 Unions as a Check on the Authoritarian Inclinations of the Working Class

There is one more feature of unionization, however, that I want to mention before I close. Unions can also act as a check on the antidemocratic, authoritarian, and otherwise anti-liberal inclinations among elements of the working class, especially during times of economic distress. The strength of support for the authoritarian and bigoted Donald Trump among noncollege-educated white working-class men – the kind of people who used to hold jobs that at one time existed in large numbers and were heavily unionized – was repeatedly noted during the run-up to and the aftermath of the 2016 US presidential election.[390] It seems likely that at least some of this support can be connected to reduced levels of US unionization and the corresponding absence of the moderating influence these unions once provided.[391] Indeed, while Marine Le Pen also made inroads with the white working class in France using similar xenophobic and racist appeals,[392] her ultimate defeat may be partially explained by the fact that the number of workers covered by union contracts is still relatively high in France, and while not all French unions endorsed her centrist opponent, they were united in their opposition to her.[393] Some anti-immigrant "alternative" unions have begun to form in Germany, it's true, and these unions have been throwing their support behind the racist and xenophobic Alternative for Germany party (AfD). But this appears to be because German workers sometimes there see their unions as insufficiently partisan in their representation of their members – that is, too cozy with management – despite (or perhaps now because of) the enormous accomplishments these unions have achieved.[394] This, however, is a problem we are a long way from encountering most everywhere else. But even so, the ultimate rejection of the AfD in the most recent German elections was at least partly the result of the extensive lobbying against it by the established German union movement.[395] So once again, looking at the matter overall, unionization seems to be an effective antidote to the attraction of demagoguery among the working class.

For some insight into the causal process involved here, I turn to Émile Durkheim. In *The Division of Labor in Society,* Durkheim distinguishes between two types of social solidarity – mechanical solidarity and organic solidarity.[396] Organic solidarity is the higher form and is based on a sense of shared interests, objectives, and place in society, especially in the economy. Mechanical solidarity is the more primitive and is based simply on superficial resemblances; that is, likeness based on features such as race, religion, ethnic origin, and so on. Mechanical solidarity suppresses any sense of individuality, encouraging what amounts to blind allegiance to a community that is defined along the most superficial lines – to which one belongs not based upon who one is but based on features over which one has little or no control.[397] Organic solidarity, in contrast, encourages individuality by recognizing "the distinctive internal, interdependent functioning of modern, 'organized' industrial societies marked by increasing differentiation of roles, occupations, strata, and ways of living and providing the conditions under which modern individuals could come into being."[398] All modern societies need some form of solidarity to survive. Even though I am going beyond what Durkheim expressly claims here, his theory implies that in the absence of organic solidarity, which has to be positively constructed, there will be a vacuum into which the more primitive mechanical solidarity will naturally rush in to fill.[399]

While I do not want to make too much of this given that there are obviously many forces in play here, the need for cross-racial, cross-religious, and cross-cultural institutions that help us construct and maintain organic solidarity and prevent the reflexive default to mechanical solidarity when such institutions do not exist or do not do their jobs does indeed help explain what we are seeing in the current right-wing populist appeal to a large segment of the white working class. In the absence of as strong sense of social solidarity across various racial, ethnic, and religious subgroupings, a sense of organic solidarity that can only be created and maintained by social institutions, some members of society are reverting to a more primitive form of mechanical solidarity and basing their sense of who they are and what they must defend on superficial attributes of community identity instead of a recognition of the shared struggles and disabilities of individuals who occupy the same economic strata of society. The lack of unionization among the middle class may also help explain why so many whites within this group seem all too ready to accept Trump's claim that our many ills are mainly the result of too many nonwhites and non-Christians living in America. These people now see themselves as part of a white Christian nation under siege, rather than as members of a nation that is built on the idea of racial, cultural, ethnic, and religious diversity, republican liberty (freedom from arbitrary treatment), and economic mobility.[400] Obviously, the union is one institution that, when properly embedded in and supported by the larger basic structure of society, can help provide what is now an all-to-absent sense of organic solidarity to a superficially heterogeneous group of individuals, for union membership today tends to be remarkably diverse.[401] Indeed, Durkheim saw unions as a potential source for the development of organic solidarity even in his day, although the rate of unionization at that time was so limited that he saw their influence as inconsequential.[402] But when unionization eventually increased significantly from those very minimal levels, a much greater sense of organic solidarity also began to arise. Now that union membership has fallen once again, it does seem like mechanical rather than organic solidarity has once again become the primary glue holding a certain socioeconomic segment of society together.[403] In other words, using Durkheim's taxonomy does help us explain why the demise of unionization has been accompanied by a disturbing resurrection of the appeal of mechanical solidarity and a burgeoning of primitive anti-liberal ideas.[404]

Regardless of whether my application of Durkheim's insights is appropriate, however, there is quite a large body of research suggesting that in times

2.5 Unionization in Context

of economic distress, and in the presence of demagogues who provide those feeling dispossessed with easy targets to blame for their situation, unions can help keep people infused with the democratic spirit and therefore help them turn away those who would threaten the civil liberties of racial, ethnic, and religious minorities, and ultimately their own liberty as well.[405] Indeed, this was the exact point made by the sociologist Seymour Martin Lipset in a classic paper from 1959,[406] and his conclusion has been repeatedly confirmed since.[407] There is even some very recent evidence that there may be a neurochemical process involved here in some way. New research suggests that the neurotransmitters oxytocin and (to a lesser extent) vasopressin, also called neuropeptides, have an effect on our social behavior.[408] When given oxytocin, certain animals exhibit more trusting and compassionate behavior toward members of what they perceive as their own group and more hostile behavior toward members of what they perceive as outside groups.[409] There is also evidence that oxytocin has a similar effect on humans.[410] Finally, there is evidence that stress – including financial (in humans) and social (in humans and animals) stress – encourages the production of oxytocin, and not just cortisol and other hormones whose relationship to stress is well understood.[411] If this is all true, then it suggests there may be a biological predisposition for a default to mechanical solidarity under stress when the ties of organic solidarity are insufficiently established.[412]

Of course, there are a lot of uncertainties remaining here, too many still to draw any firm conclusions. And the effects of these neurotransmitters may be only marginal, simply enhancing what we are otherwise predisposed to do. Nevertheless, their operation and the tendency of humans to increase the production of these neurotransmitters under stress would help explain why right-wing populism seems to spread like a virus: the actual or perceived sense of crisis among the people of one group in one country tends to raise the stress levels of those in the same group in other countries as well, making them more susceptible to racist, xenophobic, ethnocentric, nationalistic, and otherwise intolerant behavior, which in turn raises everyone's stress levels even further, thereby increasing the production and antisocial effects of oxytocin even more and so on until the world is engulfed in the kind of rightward anti-liberal lurch it is experiencing now. This psychological effect of the release of oxytocin may also help explain the seemingly irrational levels of trust and forgiveness of those viewed as the leaders of one's "in-group."[413] And regardless of whether these psychological reactions are actually physiologically driven, many people no doubt recognize that people who perceive themselves as being in a crisis situation often react in this way, and this helps explain why those who want to encourage such behavior often try to make out that whatever is happening is even worse and more dangerous than people otherwise believe.[414] In any event, whether these effects are marginal or extreme, widespread or local, greater unionization may be one way we can combat them. Clearly, those engaged in such activities intuitively recognize unions as the enemy of such reactionary appeals to in-group/out-group distinctions. It is no coincidence that Hitler abolished trade unions as soon as he came to power, for he saw this as a necessary step in the consolidation of his power over the German government and people. "There's a lesson here for the future. American unions have a checkered history and are far from perfect. But as an institution, unions are an essential bulwark for democracy. We've allowed them to wither at our peril."[415]

2.6 HOW RECOGNIZING UNIONS AS A BASIC INSTITUTION PROTECTS LIBERTY

In light of this discussion, let us review the tripartite inquiry I described earlier in this essay and see what conclusions we might draw from it now that we have a better understanding of the empirical context within which the argument from liberty would apply. First, given that the good effects of unions vastly outweigh their bad effects, it seems highly likely that people choosing from a hypothetical decision situation behind an appropriately described veil of ignorance that deprives them of knowledge of who they are (including whether they are employers or employees) but leaves them with knowledge of everything else would support unionization among all significant competitors in a pairwise comparison between such a world and the world in which we actually live, for this would maximize their potential personal minimums.[416] This establishes that the interference with negative liberty that universal unionization represents is morally justified. The argument from negative liberty accordingly provides no impediment to universal unionization.

Second, because unions counter the inefficient inclinations of management and management corruption, even though unions may on occasion be a source of inefficiency and corruption themselves, there are powerful reasons to believe that unionization will increase productivity in some ways. While unionization may also lead to decreases in productivity in some ways, the best evidence we have available so far is that whatever productivity losses there are at one employer, these will be offset by productivity gains at another. At worst, then, the overall effect of universal unionization on the economy as a whole is neutral with regard to productivity. And if we recognize that unions are an offset to the inefficiencies generated by monopsony and oligopsony among employers, there are actually efficiency gains here to be had, albeit ones that are currently underappreciated. It is therefore clear that concerns for economic liberty, which are designed to increase productivity, do not support the argument against universal unionization.

Finally, and in my view most importantly, universal unionization clearly enhances republican liberty.[417] Unions dramatically increase the enactment and enforcement of the laws designed to protect workers from the arbitrary acts of their employers and somewhat decrease the chances of management behaving in an antisocial manner and engaging in acts of domination against

2.6 How Recognizing Union as a Basic Institution Protects Liberty   149

the general public at large. The risk that nonunionized employees face of arbitrary treatment and domination in the absence of unionization is clearly greater than the risk that employers face with regard to possible domination by the union, for unions are rarely that strong and employers almost always are. Remember also that there is profit to be gained by the employer from domination of its workers, and therefore the employer has a motive to engage in such behavior. In contrast, there is little or no profit to be gained by the union from domination of the employer because if this were successful it would eventually result in the firm going out of business, thereby making such acts of domination self-defeating. Of course, there is the danger of corruption of the union, which might lead to efforts to dominate the firm or even ordinary members of the union, but this risk and whatever other risks there are of arbitrary action by the union can be dealt with by post-institutional regulation, whereas the current sorry state of affairs for employees indicates that post-institutional regulation of the firm is not enough. And in any event, look at where the burden of the risk of error falls. In the case of universal unionization, the risks we are reducing or eliminating are risks borne by employees, whereas the risks we are creating or increasing are risks borne by employers. Because the latter are in a better position to bear these risks (and fight improper acts if they do occur using post-institutional means) than the former would be in a nonunion environment, unionization produces a moral improvement. What this means is that all three tests to be applied to determine whether universal unionization represents an enhancement of liberty or an infringement of it make clear that on balance, unions are indeed a basic institution of society, for a society in which the firm is the focus of the economy is more likely to be just with them than without them.

Other liberal capitalist nations seem to have realized this long ago. In Germany, for example, even though the rate of unionization there has been dropping as it has everywhere else, the rate is still much higher than in the United States.[418] More importantly, in addition to unions that negotiate wages largely on an industry-wide basis,[419] firms with more than five employees are encouraged to set up "works councils," which are statutorily authorized worker organizations that get seats on the supervisory board of directors and therefore a say in the management of the firm, its compliance with occupational health and safety standards, and so on.[420] While not all firms take advantage of this opportunity, 87 percent of all firms with over 500 employees have done so, and 43 percent of all employees in the West and 35 percent of employees in the East were represented by such work councils in 2013, so the use of work councils is quite widespread.[421] Under my conception of the union as a basic institution, these functions would be integrated rather than divided between unions and work councils, but this is really a detail that could go either way as long as the overall functions to which I am referring are assigned to somebody. Given that German economic performance in the post–World War II period is historically pretty impressive,[422] this should put paid to any argument that even such a limited redistribution of power from the firm to the union is antithetical to the ideas behind a capitalist economy.[423]

Unions are also effectively treated as a basic institution in the Nordic countries, with impressive economic results there as well. The unionization rate is 74 percent in Finland, 70 percent in Sweden, 67 percent in Denmark, and 52 percent in Norway.[424] These same countries also consistently outperform the global average in terms of value creation, whether we look at returns over five, ten, or fifteen year periods, and this is true across most industries.[425] Of course, this is no doubt due to many factors, and in light of this I do not want to place too much weight on these comparisons, but it seems fair to say that high rates of unionization have certainly not hampered economic performance in these countries and have probably contributed something and perhaps substantially to it. In other words, there is strong evidence that firms are not only made more just in the presence of high rates of unionization, they can also be made more economically efficient.[426]

This is not to say that no part of the approach to unionization in these countries can be subjected to economic or other forms of criticism. Remember, I am only addressing the question of whether unions are a basic institution and therefore must exist for a liberal capitalist society to be just. Even where unions are recognized as basic institutions, there are still many, many aspects of unionization and union activity that need to be regulated and, in some cases, tailored to fit the particular historical and cultural traditions of an individual society and its economic circumstances. And it may well be that certain elements of these regulations are in need of reform in some of these countries or elsewhere where unions are strong, or at least stronger than they are in the United States.[427] The details of the proper nature and scope of these regulations, however, is neither determined by recognizing that unions are a basic institution or relevant to determining whether such recognition is required by justice.

But recognizing that unions are a basic institution of society does bring out the injustice of the current US practice of letting unions form or not based on the supposed post-institutional preferences of workers. As I have already noted, while pre-institutional (hypothetical) consent is relevant to determining whether the existence of an institution is justified, post-institutional (actual) consent is not. In an appropriately described hypothetical decision situation, the postulated constraints ensure that everyone is free and equal, but this is not the kind of situation one is likely to encounter out in the real world. Indeed, out in the real world, the decision to certify a union is made only after what amounts to a political campaign with all the misinformation, undue pressure, and misleading rhetoric that such campaigns typically employ.[428] Not only are workers voting when they don't have full, accurate, and equal information,[429] they also face psychological impediments that can be exploited by a management opposed to unionization: in good times, complacency sets in and workers may not see the need for unionization; in bad times, the politics of

2.6 How Recognizing Union as a Basic Institution Protects Liberty 151

fear are likely to take hold and workers may face threats that if they unionize management will move or eliminate jobs that workers cannot afford to lose.[430] In any event, these departures from the hypothetical decision situation rob agreement out in the real world of most of its moral force. If an institution is basic, it is accountable for how it is run through the democratic process, but its existence is demanded by justice backed by the moral force of hypothetical agreement between free and equal fully informed persons. The instantiation of a such a basic institution is not subject to suppression by posthypothetical decision situation majority vote, even if the majority can be convinced that a union is not in their interests or intimidated into not voting for one. Our current practice is therefore woefully misguided because it allows for unionization to be determined by the random vagaries and inflammatory and often inaccurate rhetoric of a political campaign.[431]

As I close this section, I want to bring us briefly back to the argument from equality. One of the common complaints of those on the anti-union right is that unions are engaged in "special pleading," asking for and often receiving special privileges that other private associations do not have.[432] Unions are allowed to force nonunion workers to join using methods that no one else is allowed to use, the argument goes, and then given exemption from the antitrust laws to use their monopoly power to economically coerce employers to pay wages that are greater than competitive forces would otherwise require.[433] As if this weren't enough, they are also given both *de jure* and *de facto* exemptions from criminal laws on the use of force and violence,[434] even though as we have already seen, these claims grossly distort what is actually going on. And it is true that by arguing for the institutionalization of unions, I am suggesting that unions be given a status and protection enjoyed by some but certainly not all institutions. The claim that this amounts to seeking special privileges for unions does accordingly have some superficial plausibility.

Note that this is an odd claim for those in the anti-union camp to make given that their primary strategy is to rely on the argument from liberty and claim that any pro-union arguments from equality can be ignored because liberty trumps equality. Because I have adopted that same strategy here, albeit arguing that my version of the argument from liberty and the argument from equality each lead to the same conclusion, the same claim that liberty trumps equality would be available to me if their rather than my version of the argument from equality is correct. Nevertheless, I don't want to rely on turnabout here, for the special pleading objection is actually routinely made by those on the right to any progressive argument from equality – it is one of the responses made to the Black Lives Matter movement, to the Equal Rights Amendment, to the extension of the Voting Rights Act, to affirmative action generally, and so on. It therefore deserves a specific response. For even though it is clear that unions support equality in a myriad of ways, one cannot justify a violation of equality by pointing at other more numerous or important violations of equality that this particular violation happens to prevent. Assuming that some or even just one of the specifics of the charge of special privileges here is true, we accordingly do need to consider whether the argument presented here amounts to a violation of our notions of equality.

The answer, it should be obvious, is no. Equality does not require that everyone and everything be treated equally. It requires that persons and associations be treated equally *to the extent they are similarly situated*. The latter qualification is important. And if we keep this qualification in mind, we can see that what appear to some to be special privileges that unions are said to enjoy and that I have been trying to support are nothing of the sort – they are simply the result of recognizing that unions are a basic institution, and like other basic institutions, they are not subject to certain kinds of post-institutional regulation, the kind which would severely undermine their role in society if not wipe them out. Indeed, the whole point of establishing something as a basic institution is to show that, given its importance in creating the background circumstances most likely to secure justice, certain protections must be afforded basic institutions that need not be afforded to institutions that are not basic, or are not basic in the same way, or are basic but do not have the same vulnerabilities as other basic institutions and would therefore be hampered by the same types of regulation in less serious ways. Neither individuals nor groups that suffer from or are amenable to certain special kinds of mistreatment are being given special privileges by being expressly protected from that mistreatment, while others who are not so targeted or amenable are not. And this is all that my argument for universal unionization does.

But even if I am right that recognizing unions as a basic institution does not grant them special privileges, could my argument trespass equality in another way? Some of those to whom I have made my argument wonder whether it might not be ruled out by the difference principle on the grounds that even if universal unionization would make working people better off, it might make those who do not have jobs but are seeking them (and therefore are less advantaged) worse off. Elsewhere, I have shown that there are serious reasons to question whether the difference principle is indeed a viable principle of distributive justice.[435] But those arguments are quite lengthy, so I don't want to repeat them here. Besides, I do not need to discredit the difference principle in order to address this particular concern. In discussing the effect of unionization on unemployment, I have already shown that there is little evidence that unionization would indeed increase unemployment, or otherwise make it more difficult for the unemployed to find a job, or for the underemployed to find a job they prefer, so the empirical basis for this concern is pretty insubstantial. Moreover, even if it were true that universal unionization might lead to some marginal increase in unemployment, this would not mean that the difference principle would suggest that we not recognize the union as a basic institution. First of all, this would merely be a side effect, and there is no reason to believe that whatever upward pressure this might put on unemployment, this could not be offset by efforts to stimulate employment. As I have already noted, the fact that some post-institutional actions may be required to counteract some potential downsides of institutionalization is not a reason for rejecting institutionalization if we have reason to believe those post-institutional actions will be effective in addressing these concerns. We often cannot achieve background justice without having to ameliorate certain potential side effects of doing this; otherwise, post-institutional regulation would never be required. And I have already shown that no institution can possibly function perfectly justly in the absence of regulation – some post-institutional action will always be required. Second, even if this were not the case, the difference principle would still not militate against recognizing the union as a basic institution because again, as I have already noted, assuring liberty has lexical priority over assuring equality even under the Rawlsian system. Indeed, this is the whole reason the right tends to rely exclusively on the argument from liberty, and it is the whole reason why I have focused on the argument from liberty here. Even if we take the difference principle as expressing the appropriate attitude toward equality and justice, the difference principle is no bar to the argument I have presented here.

2.7 LIMITATIONS AND QUALIFICATIONS

2.7.1 Union Shops Are Not Closed Shops

To avoid any potential misunderstanding of my argument for universal unionization, I want to emphasize that my argument does not imply the enactment of anticompetitive exclusionary restrictions on hiring. In other words, the fact that all workers must join the relevant union upon accepting employment does not mean that employers must hire those who are already union members before hiring anyone who is not. I am arguing for union shops, not closed shops. Any worry that unions might nevertheless pressure employers to adopt a closed shop policy is simply to be treated as a post-institutional issue, to be addressed the same way other kinds of discrimination in hiring are addressed – that is, by regulation of the institution rather than by eliminating the institution in its entirety. Having relevant previous experience is not an arbitrary criterion, so existing union members may have an advantage over inexperienced new workers on this basis. But not all current nonunion workers are inexperienced, so mere union membership is not a sufficiently tight proxy for previous experience. Giving current union members priority in hiring would accordingly be an example of unjust discrimination, at least when those union members have not previously worked for this particular employer, for in this case the criterion of having gotten there "first" in terms of union membership would be arbitrary and therefore would itself be an infringement of republican liberty. My argument is therefore not one for a return to the preindustrial guild system. Unions cannot refuse membership or charge steep "initiation fees" to new hires in a union shop and thereby effectively control who the employer may hire.[436] Nor may they expel members if this would result in existing employees losing their jobs under the applicable collective bargaining agreement. Everyone has a "right to work" in this sense. My argument is simply that unionization is a basic institution. A union must accordingly exist for every workforce if the republican liberty of the employee is to have any chance of being protected from the threat of domination by the employer.

Note that this does not mean that employees get no say on which union should represent them or what policies the union will promote or actions it will pursue. These choices are up to the usual post-institutional rules that ensure an association is responsive to and reflective of the general will of its members. Unions may compete to represent a particular work force, and even after one union has been selected by the majority of the relevant employees, justice requires that there be some method to revisit this decision if enough members petition to do so. Even without such a petition, periodic contests for representation rights may be required to introduce a competitive element into the union movement and ensure that no particular union becomes complacent, corrupt, or too close to management, although such recertification proceedings should occur only after the passage of a reasonable period of time, for constant competition among unions for representation rights can be problematic for both unions and employers.[437] But that there be a union in each firm, performing the core functions I have identified, is not up for majority decision. As a basic institution of society, this is not something to which anyone has a right to object.

2.7.2 While We Are Working toward Universal Unionization: The Perfect Is Not the Enemy of the Good

I also want to say something about the claim that my argument for universal unionization is nothing more than an academic exercise because achieving this is beyond anything we could reasonably expect given the political realities of the day. Nationwide universal unionization is indeed a long way off, and global universal unionization is even further. But nothing in my argument depends on universal unionization being fully realized for it to provide ammunition for what are incremental steps toward this goal. My argument provides immediate support for various interim measures designed to stem the decline in unionization. It provides grounds to oppose right-to-work laws and other efforts to make unionization more difficult and reduce the powers of existing unions and their members. My argument also provides strong reasons to reverse right-to-work laws that have already been enacted. For even in the absence of making unionization universal, increased unionization will still have many of the liberty-enhancing effects I describe. These effects will not be as great as they could be if unionization were universal, but they will still exist and be important to workers who

2.7 Limitations and Qualifications

gain protection as a result. Because greater unionization increases the norms that all employers must follow in order to compete for workers in an environment that is only partially unionized and successfully suppress any nascent efforts to unionize their own firms, the nonunionized also benefit from increases in unionization, even if unionization is not universal. True, nonunion firms will still enjoy a competitive advantage over union firms to the extent they can get away with providing lower wages and benefits and still be able to attract and retain equally reliable and productive workers. In the short run, this will increase the profitably of nonunionized firms somewhat. In the long run too, if unionization does not spread, then unionized firms in particular industries cannot offset this disadvantage by providing a higher quality and more efficiently produced product with their more experienced workforce. But even if this advantage persists, the fact that not every new factory is built in a right-to-work state, and facilities in union states are still being expanded, shows that a nonunionized environment is not competitively decisive despite whatever *pro tanto* advantage it may provide. So even though unionization may not be immediately complete, the march toward universal unionization and the corresponding end of any competitive disadvantage for being unionized can continue. In any event, maintaining an unjust competitive advantage, no matter how large, does not provide an acceptable reason for the suppression of unionization. Even if my argument here merely helps overturn exiting right-to-work laws and leaves unionization up to employee vote, it will still have accomplished a great deal, and a great deal more than existing arguments in favor of unionization have so far proved able to do.

Pursuing universal unionization also does not require that we abandon efforts to ameliorate the unjust effects that the decline of unionization has created in our society in other ways. I have already explained why increased workplace democracy, while worth pursuing, is not an adequate alternative to unionization. And while a number of those who have heard my argument have claimed I need to show why my approach is better than any other possible (or at least feasible) alternative, I do not see why this should be the case. First, because many of the possible alternatives would address only one aspect of the problem, and thus a basket of alternatives would probably be required to accomplish what unionization could all in one go. Second, ranking unionization against some basket of alternative approaches or even some other comprehensive solution is largely a pointlessly controversial exercise, especially when pursuing one alternative does not require abandoning another. Third, while it might be the case that if we also pursue other alternatives, these may be so successful at some point that unions no longer meet the test for being a basic institution, in the unlikely event this happens, we can revisit the question then. Fourth, while there are things we could do to ameliorate some of the effects of deunionization, this is not the same as preventing these effects from arising in the first place. The advantage of universal unionization is that it will eliminate the need for a great deal of remediation, and preventing injury is always better than compensating it.[438] And finally, once again, if unions are a basic institution under current circumstances, then their existence is required by justice and the fact that the injustice of treating them as something other than a basic institution can be partially ameliorated in other ways is irrelevant. If unions are a basic institution, as I have argued that they are, the existence of post-institutional alternative approaches to reducing some of the background injustice resulting from a failure to recognize this is not a reason to treat this failure as something we should not attempt to cure.

For example, several people to whom I have made this argument have suggested that pursuing universal basic income (UBI) might be an alternative to pursuing universal unionization. The idea behind UBI is that everyone, regardless of economic circumstances, should get a guaranteed stipend to do with as they wish. The amount of the stipend should be enough to live a minimally decent life, although advocates of UBI recognize that it might have to start out as something less than this.[439] Providing a UBI, however, even in limited amounts, seems even less feasible than requiring universal unionization. After all, at least unionization covered 33 percent of the workforce in the United States at one time and still covers the overwhelming majority of the workforce in some countries, as I shall detail in a moment, whereas UBI has never caught on to any significant extent. Even if such an idea were to catch fire now after being largely ignored for decades, it would still only address the economic hardships resulting from unjustly low wages and not do anything to prevent employers from paying unjustly low wages in the first place, or from imposing unsafe working conditions, or otherwise treating employees discriminatorily or unfairly. And it would only help with unfairly low wages to the extent it was enacted as a supplement to existing social safety net provisions rather than as a substitute for them, the latter being far more likely in the current and any foreseeable political climate. And there are many other problems with the idea of UBI as well – so many, in fact, that it would be distraction to go into them all here.[440] Those who believe in UBI are free to continue to argue for it, of course – nothing in my argument for universal unionization would make that argument any harder to make than it already is. The two proposals are not inconsistent. But even in its ideal form, UBI is not an adequate remedy for all of the defects in background justice that unionization would likely be able to prevent from arising in the first place.[441]

2.7.3 Some Comments about Universal Unionization in the Public Sector

I will address the question of universal unionization in the public sector at length in the next essay, but I do want to say a few things now about this question in order to illustrate the kinds of special arguments that are often raised against unionization in the public sector and would no doubt be made against my claim that universal unionization should apply there. First, there are of course many differences between the private and public sector. Public agencies are not firms, for one, so one of the primary drivers of my argument

2.7 Limitations and Qualifications

with regard to the private sector does not apply. But public agencies are managed much like firms; that is, they employ the same hierarchical structure used in the private sector. In the absence of union representation, the relative bargaining power of the employer and the employee is dramatically unbalanced. Many of the forces in play in the public sector are accordingly the same as those in the private sector. The principle difference is that public sector unions have long been accused of being a greater impediment to the socially optimal behavior of government agencies than they are a contributor to it. Teacher unions, for example, are often accused of stifling efforts to reform education,[442] of putting the interests of their members above that of students, and even of leading to higher unemployment and lower incomes among students later in life.[443] But these claims either rely on highly suspect methodological approaches or turn out to be completely unfounded.[444] Teachers are in fact very much on the forefront of efforts to improve public education and their students' ability to learn, and not just concerned about increasing their own pay. Most school budgets have still not been restored to their prerecession levels, let alone been increased beyond that point, and in many states there are ongoing efforts to cut them further still.[445] Yet many existing facilities are falling into decrepitude and the resources available for students are already so limited that students' ability to learn has been seriously undermined.[446] A shockingly high percentage of primary and secondary school teachers currently have to use their personal funds to buy basic school supplies for the students, even though they themselves are struggling financially.[447] In higher education, unions have been at the heart of uncovering administrators' misuse of funds and other forms of abuse.[448] And not only in the United States, but in the United Kingdom too.[449] Whether unionized or not, are fighting not only for a living wage for themselves but also for sufficient resources to deliver a decent education to their students.[450] Indeed, one recent headline says it all: "Low Pay, Large Classes, Funding Cuts: Behind New Wave of US Teachers' Strikes."[451] And to the extent that teacher unions are an impediment to the removal of allegedly incompetent or otherwise ineffective teachers, this is often the result of a failure to consult the union on the standards to be applied in making these determinations, not to some alleged knee-jerk tendency for public sector unions to defend their members no matter what their transgressions.[452] Indeed, one recent survey shows that districts with strong unions actually dismiss more low-quality teachers and retain more high-quality teachers than districts with weak unions.[453]

But the accusations of antisocial behavior by public sector unions do not stop with teacher unions. Police unions have also been accused of such conduct, and especially of making it more difficult to hold officers accountable for brutal behavior. While this sometimes may be true, in many cases this is once again the result of a failure to adequately consult the union on the standards and procedures to be applied.[454] But more importantly, this criticism of unions of police officers comes almost exclusively from the otherwise pro-union left. Those on the right, in contrast, tend to see police unions as helping protect officers from attempts to micromanage their conduct after the fact in what are often incredibly difficult and dangerous situations, where split second judgments must be made under chaotic conditions. So even in these cases, it is not obvious the unions should be seen as an overall impediment to social progress rather than as an advocate for fair treatment of their members who often see themselves as under attack.

There are, however, several other claims that are raised against public unions in general that need to be addressed at greater length. First, the argument that unionization in the public sector is particularly objectionable is often tied to the argument that if we care about increasing liberty, government should be smaller not bigger, and unionization encourages movement toward the latter while impeding movement toward the former. Second, public services are often essential services, and unionization puts the provision of these services and the protection of liberty they entail at risk. Third, many public sector unions are often accused of negotiating overly generous salaries and retirement packages for their members and thereby creating an unsustainable drain on the public purse, putting the very functionality of government at risk.[455] And finally, unionization in the public sector is also accused of having various antidemocratic and otherwise liberty-suppressing effects.[456] I will embark on a detailed analysis of these more complicated claims in the next essay, but I will point out here that regardless of how one comes out on these disputed matters, the otherwise liberty-enhancing effects of unionization regarding wages, working conditions, and most importantly freedom from arbitrary dismissal and control apply in the public sector as strongly as they do in the private sector.[457] There is accordingly at least strong *prima facie* reasons and probably *pro tanto* reasons too to believe we should allow public employees to form unions that perform the core functions that unions usually perform, including collective bargaining.[458] Whether these reasons are decisive, however, is something that shall have to await discussion in the next essay.

2.7.4 Feasibility Constraints on Universal Unionization in the Private Sector

There are two ways that concerns for the infeasibility of achieving perfect background justice might impose limits on how we approach universal unionization. First, there is a question as to whether universal unionization is possible for certain occupations. Is not one of the reasons why unionization levels have dropped so precipitously that there has been a shift away from manufacturing and other jobs that are easy to unionize to more sophisticated white-collar jobs that are difficult and perhaps even impossible to unionize? Indeed, it is undeniable that unionizing jobs that are mostly white-collar presents certain obstacles

2.7 Limitations and Qualifications

that many union organizers have yet to fully overcome. Some of these obstacles are political, but those obstacles are overcome by the principle of universal unionization itself. Other obstacles, however, are practical, having to do with the nature of the work involved and the fact that this work is less standardized and therefore the workers who perform it are less amenable to being grouped together for purposes of jointly negotiating wages or setting wider standards for worker performance. Nevertheless, even these more highly educated "white-collar" workers are becoming more and more dissatisfied lately,[459] and we are beginning to see evidence that the obstacles to organizing them can be overcome. Performing artists have long had strong unions,[460] and even visual artists are now beginning to organize in ways that may lead to unionization.[461] The organization of other fields where individual work product is similarly nonstandard is also spreading. Not only graduate student teaching assistants, for example, but also other student workers have now begun to unionize, although there is still much resistance to this.[462] Many medical interns and residents have unionized in recent years, as have some dental hygienists, and a group of doctors at a medical center in Oregon formed a union of hospitalists in 2014.[463] Unionization has also begun to spread to newsroom employees at major newspapers, magazines, and digital media companies,[464] and there are growing cries for unionization among technology workers.[465] Even lawyers who are not yet partners in the firms they work for are contemplating unionization.[466] So unionization among occupations other than those traditionally viewed as providing union jobs is already spreading. Unionization rates among younger workers are beginning to exceed those among older workers too.[467] In any event, the reluctance of some white-collar workers to unionize is not the result of their failure to recognize that the stagnancy of their wages and working conditions is the result of wielding insufficient bargaining power in their negotiations with management, something that they would like to change, but rather because they fear retaliation if they try to organize, something a universal unionization requirement would eliminate. Therefore, universal unionization should indeed be feasible in this sense.

But this is not to say that in certain circumstances there are not reasons to make exceptions, which is the second way the feasibility issue comes up here. In a firm with one owner-manager and two or three employees, using the apparatus of a union to enforce good behavior by the firm seems like the imposition of an unnecessary layer of bureaucracy. When a workforce is this small, the voice of employees can be heard on its own, and if it is not heard, there is little that anyone can do about this for the same reason it is largely impossible to manage personal behavior in the family. Exactly where to draw the line here, however, is difficult to say. Any firm large enough to be publicly traded would obviously be one where compulsory unionization is required given the diffusion of ownership this creates and the corresponding reduction of the influence of ownership on management. But large privately held firms should be unionized too. Indeed, privately held firms pose an even greater threat to liberty because they do not have the oversight of largely independent shareholders and various market regulators to govern them, lame as that oversight often is, and more and more large firms are now privately owned.[468] The place to draw the line, then, seems best driven by our current practice with regard to the degree of regulation to which the firm is subject. A useful cutoff seems to be fifty or more employees, for this is the level at which a large range of government regulation becomes applicable.[469] True, this might encourage some employers to grow their firms up to that limit and then simply form another firm to avoid the added regulation that growing bigger would entail.[470] But this incentive already exists. More importantly, it is highly inefficient, for it often costs employers more than simply complying with the additional regulation that greater size would trigger.[471] And when employees number fewer than fifty, they can still opt to unionize in any event.[472] While we might expect some attempt at evasion here, the overall degree of this should be slight. The requirement could also be phased in; for example, it could initially apply only to firms with over 1,000 employees, then to firms with over 500, then 100, and finally 50.[473] At each stage, adjustments could be made to post-institutional regulations to ensure that any unintended and undesirable side effects are kept to a minimum. But eventually, it seems likely that in the current regulatory environment fifty would be a good place to stop.

There are two clarifications, however, I should make about how this cutoff should be applied. First, with the rise of the gig economy, there are a growing number of workers who are now ostensibly employed as independent contractors rather than employees.[474] Drivers for Uber, for example, are currently classified by the company as independent contractors rather than employees, even though they collectively represent a large workforce. As independent contractors, workers are ineligible for unemployment insurance or worker's compensation, denied minimum wage, overtime, and other labor law protections, and are otherwise subject to being heavily exploited.[475] Many Uber drivers, for example, currently make below the minimum wage, and even end up losing money after they pay insurance, maintenance, and other costs, one recent study has found.[476] And the supposedly independent contractors here are not the only losers either: the state is also denied needed revenue from payroll and other taxes, and firms that do classify their workers as employees and pay these taxes face tough competition given the cost savings that using independent contractors provides. The gig economy is already huge – one recent estimate put the number of people working under nontraditional arrangements in the United States at 16.5 million, with 10.6 million of these working as independent contractors, on call workers, temporary help agency workers, and the like.[477] Temps, vendors, and contract workers (TVCs) already make up 54 percent of Google's global workforce, to cite just one specific example.[478] Under the competitive financial pressure this imposes, more traditional employers may also soon attempt to switch to using independent contractors, and the labor market as we know it may further implode.[479] How would my fifty-employee cutoff apply in a world ever more populated with firms like this?

2.7 Limitations and Qualifications

The answer is that it is extremely doubtful that Uber drivers and those similarly situated really *are* independent contractors and not employees.[480] Under both the common law and the relevant statutes, the distinction is based on a number of factors, including the amount of discretion the worker has when performing his or her duties.[481] With regard to Uber as well as other cyber-employers, the only extra bit of discretion given to workers is the ability to decide how much and when they work. Otherwise, Uber drivers and these other supposed independent contractors have no more discretion about how they go about performing their jobs than workers associated with traditional employers that do classify their workers as employees. Several class actions arguing that Uber must reclassify its drivers as employees, provide the benefits these employees are entitled to by law, meet minimum wage requirements, comply with overtime rules, pay payroll taxes, and so on have already been filed, and similar actions against other firms currently employing a similar business model are sure to follow.[482] In any case, given that there are already legal standards for determining when workers may be classified as independent contractors rather than employees, it is unnecessary for our theory to articulate any further requirements here. Companies that try to end-run universal unionization by improperly classifying their workers and thereby falling under the fifty-worker cutoff already face the threat of substantial sanctions for their transgressions.

In the face of such threats, however, those on the right are now lobbying for legislative proposals that would change state law (and soon, no doubt federal law as well) to allow any firm to define its workers as independent contractors rather than employees if they are dispatched by digital platforms, no matter what other factors may be present that indicate the worker is actually an employee.[483] While few of these lobbying efforts have been successful so far, it would be foolish not to recognize that in the current environment they could easily become more so.[484] Indeed, the Trump administration's Labor Department has recently rescinded an Obama administration ruling, which stated that such workers are probably employees for purposes of federal law, and issued one suggesting that they are probably not.[485] The National Labor Relations Board (NLRB) then specifically ruled that this is the case with regard to Uber.[486] If this ruling stands, further action may be necessary to override attempts to evade years of established labor law at both the federal and state level and ensure that a uniform standard applies for determining who is a contractor and who is an employee. But for now, it should be sufficient to say that the existing well-established standards for determining this are the ones that should apply in determining who counts for purposes of the fifty-employee cutoff, since these are built on relevant criteria and not simply on a self-interested desire to make certain kinds of business models exempt from long-standing legal standards. This is not something that our recognition of unionization as a basic institution needs to address, given that this should be controlled by general well-established legal standards that would not only apply to the fifty-person cutoff but also to various other, equally important state and federal regulations too. So I will not spend any further time explicating these existing legal standards here. Of course, even if gig economy workers really are independent contractors and not employees under the current standards, they can still unionize if they want to do so, as many groups of independent contractors (including many of those in the entertainment industry and even some Uber drivers) do now.[487] Some may even strike without forming themselves into an official union,[488] although they must do so carefully, for an aggressively anti-union administration might try to attack such conduct by arguing that it is a violation of the antitrust laws, laws from which actual unions are exempt.[489]

But there is another problem here as well. Even when workers are classified as employees, there may be a question as to whether the fifty-employee cutoff is met if it is uncertain who their employer is. This comes up in the case of franchisees – if the worker is only employed by the franchisee (say, a single McDonald's restaurant), the number of workers employed by most individual franchisees might well be under fifty. On the other hand, if workers are classified as employees or joint employees of the franchisor, their numbers would vastly exceed fifty. How is this problem to be dealt with under my theory? The answer, again, is that this issue is already governed by extensive legal standards and is already working its way through the courts and the relevant administrative tribunals.[490] If these workers should indeed by classified as employees or even merely joint employees of the franchisor for any purposes, then the fifty-employee limit would be met. And the fact that many franchise agreements, especially in the fast-food industry, prohibit franchisees from hiring workers away from one another, something that would be illegal under the antitrust laws unless each franchisee was considered legally part of a single employer, strongly suggests that franchisors and franchisees do behave as joint employers at least for some purposes.[491] Indeed, in response to an investigation by the Washington State attorney general along these very lines, seven major restaurant chains have just entered into a settlement in which they have agreed to abandon these "no-poaching" clauses in their franchise agreements, apparently afraid of the collateral ramifications of pushing the "single employer" defense.[492] McDonald's attempt to settle an Obama-era federal lawsuit seeking to hold it liable for labor law violations by its franchises, have so far been unsuccessful.[493] And while the Trump administration is trying to roll back the current Labor Department rules on when franchisors and franchisees can be considered joint employers, there are substantial questions about whether these efforts will be successful and, even if they are, whether they will be upheld by the courts.[494] In any event, at the moment, at least, there seems to be no need for special rules to address when a small business is really a small business just for purposes of applying the fifty-employee trigger for unionization, for such rules already exist, and in the absence of evidence of widespread violation of these rules, it seems that there is no reason to be overly concerned that the fifty-employee trigger could be easily evaded.

2.7 Limitations and Qualifications

A more serious question is presented, however, by those who work for more traditional owner-operated restaurants. Historically, restaurant workers have been among the most exploited workers in the economy, so even if a restaurant employs less than fifty workers, as it usually does, there are real concerns if the workforce is not unionized. Of course, the workforce can always unionize voluntarily – the only issue is whether this should be made mandatory. Given the historical difficulty in doing this, however, there is reason to think the fifty-worker cutoff for this industry might be too high. But remember, we don't have to justify finding unionization a basic institution even in these cases – unionization is always required. The question is simply the proper extent of the feasibility exemption. This question will always depend on the facts and circumstances of each employment situation, so in industries with a history of worker abuse, that are difficult to organize, and where there are extensive regulations going all the way down (as is the case with food safety for restaurants and other food-handling operations) the fifty-person exemption need not apply. For restaurants, then, only where the majority of workers are related to the owner by blood or marriage and the total number of employees are under fifty would there seem to be reason to exempt the business from the universal unionization requirement. Otherwise, the fifty-employee cutoff would not apply.[495] To eliminate the need for countless numbers of bargaining sessions with numerous employers, bargaining in these industries could even be conducted on an industry-wide basis.[496] Indeed, this is how this problem is dealt with in Germany and other European nations. But this is a matter for post-institutional regulation and not something that is determined simply by recognizing the union as a basic institution.

2.7.5 Questions Remaining for Post-institutional Regulation

There are numerous other technical details, of course, as to how universal unionization would be operationalized that I have not set forth here. In addition to designing fair procedures to be used for deciding which union would initially represent a group of employees and for providing employees who become dissatisfied with the performance of their current union an avenue for acting to replace it with another, there are numerous other questions to be resolved. Could firms temporarily replace striking workers with nonunion workers as long as they did not pay these workers less than they were paying union employees, as they can do now? Could they permanently replace these workers if the replacements joined a different union that then arrived at a collective bargaining agreement with the employer? Could different unions represent employees at different levels of the firm's operations? Must employees at different levels be represented by different unions? And so on.[497] But these are all matters for post-institutional regulation. Indeed, most of this work has already been done and is contained in what are the highly detailed and extensive regulations that currently apply to labor-management relations. I am not suggesting that further refinements might not have to be enacted if we move to a system of universal unionization – there may even be controversial questions left to be decided by the usual post-institutional procedures. But this is true with regard to the instantiation of every basic institution. Nothing about the nature of unionization suggests that creating the necessary post-institutional refinements is infeasible. And the need for such further cashing out is certainly not a reason to deny something the status of a basic institution.

Another issue to be considered is that once we recognize unions a basic institution, the whole idea of "joining" a union and paying for it with "dues" becomes quaint and potentially obsolete. If unionization is universal, the decision to join or not join never arises – one just is a member of the union by reason of one's joining a particular workforce. And while union activities can continue to be financed as they have been in the past, they could also be financed through other methods. Instead of having a certain amount deducted from each employee's paycheck and paid over to the union as that individual's dues, a method that is designed to ensure that each worker experiences the financing of his union's activities as a loss from his own funds, the employer could simply be required to pay over to the union a lump sum calculated by multiplying a certain amount by the number of workers employed. This would make workers less likely to experience the financing of the union as a personal cost, to which most people are naturally averse, and more likely to see it as something that is simply part of the employer's cost of doing business, like the payroll tax, which is what it really is, or at least should be seen to be.[498] In other words, the method of financing we currently use is guaranteed to trigger the greatest possible psychological aversion to unionization, while there are other methods of financing available that would not have this effect. To reassure employers that unions will take the financial performance of the employer into account in negotiations over wages and benefits, part of the amount paid over by the employer to the union could even be calculated as a percentage of gross profits or revenues. (We would not want to give unions a share of net profits because this would create a conflict of interest, deprive them of funding when they represented employees in a failing business, and encourage firms to manipulate their balance sheets through the use of intercompany transfers to show little or no net profits; but giving them a share of gross profits or revenues would have none of these effects.) Indeed, this method of financing the union's activities could entirely replace the per head fee, distancing the cost of financing the union from each worker's personal financial contribution even further.

2.7.6 Application of the "Basic Institution" Test to Other Kinds of Institutions

Finally, I will end by speculating how my theory might apply to other potential institutions besides unions. The press, for example, is often called the fourth estate, meaning that it is typically seen as an essential institution in a liberal democracy.[499] But we have no real theoretical apparatus for testing this.

2.7 Limitations and Qualifications

My theory provides such an apparatus. While a full discussion of whether the press, expansively defined, is or is not a basic institution is well beyond the scope of what I can do here, my general sense is that it is likely to be. A vigorous, free, economically stable, and independent press provides the same kind of intuitional checks on government and private business that unions do with regard to ownership and management. The press therefore contributes significantly to republican freedom. Indeed, the press also provides a check on the behavior of unions. For a long time, it would have been reasonable to conclude that the press was in general performing this role effectively and there was accordingly no need to decide whether the press was or was not a required basic institution. But given the tremendous consolidation that has taken place in the industry, the competitive challenges imposed by the rise of the internet, the capture of major news institutions by giant conglomerates and rich individuals who have an ideological bone to pick and are not hesitant about using their media holdings to do so,[500] the proliferation of "fake news" among some elements of the media and accusations that the traditional press is itself full of "fake news,"[501] the sustained lack of independence exhibited by certain significant press outlets,[502] and the willingness of President Trump to use the power of the purse to punish businesses associated with newspapers whose coverage he does not like,[503] it may now be time to consider whether the independent voice the press has traditionally provided with regard to all sorts of abuses of republican freedom can simply be allowed to wither and die.[504] We may accordingly need to formally recognize the institutional necessity of the press and take more aggressive steps to ensure that its traditional function is not seriously undermined by our new economic and political realities.[505] How we might go about this I will leave to another time and place, but at least the theory I have proposed gives us a basis for investigating this.

Another potential basic institution that is currently under threat is the central bank, especially in the United States, where it is called the Federal Reserve, or simply "the Fed." There has always been a tension between central banks, which are supposed to either stimulate or moderate the economy depending on their own independent economic judgment, and political institutions, which often want to manipulate the economy for their own short-term political purposes no matter how much economic danger this actually presents in the middle to long term. But this tension has been particularly acute in the United States. Indeed, since its founding in 1913, the Fed "has been alternatively accused of making money too scarce and expensive or making it too plentiful and cheap."[506] The Fed has already been stripped of some of its powers by the Dodd–Frank reforms enacted in response to the Great Recession (for example, it can no longer lend quite as freely to nonbanks),[507] and the hostility toward the Fed expressed by Donald Trump during his campaign may translate into significant challenges to its independence now that he is president (if it has not already done so), and may even present it with an existential threat.[508] If such a threat does indeed materialize, the approach

I have taken here toward unionization also gives us a way of explaining why the Fed and other central banks must continue to exist and remain separate and independent institutions.

There are of course many other potentially basic institutions that I could mention here that could be evaluated using the approach laid out in this essay, but I will mention only one more: the Church, by which I mean all forms of established religion. My tentative view is that religious institutions are not a necessary institutional check on threats to republican liberty in a liberal capitalist state (indeed, they may be more likely to represent such a threat themselves), nor do they provide a necessary institutional counterweight to other institutions that are a threat to liberty like unions do. They would therefore not be considered basic institutions under the current circumstances. Under other circumstances, of course, they might, as they were in some Eastern European countries before the fall of communism. Much more would need to be said about this, of course, to come to any firm conclusions here, but in any case, the approach I have articulated at least provides a way of considering these issues that was not available before.

THIRD ESSAY

3

In Defense of Public Sector Unionization

As long as there has been a labor movement, there have been efforts to unionize the public sector. In most places in the world, however, little attention has been paid to the differences between the private and the public sector – or at least unionization is both argued for and opposed without regard to whatever differences there might be. This has not, however, been the case in the United States. For most of the history of the labor movement in the United States, while anti-union pushback focused mostly on the private sector, public sector unionization has been a target for a special set of objections.[1] But now, public sector unionization has also become the primary object of attack. In part, this is because the number of people in public employment in the United States has increased dramatically over the years, or at least many people seem to think it has (actually, public employment has increased less and often much less than the population every year since 1975, and the public sector was hemorrhaging jobs since the Great Recession until very recently – but more on this in a moment). As a result of this (mis)perception, public employment now seemed to represent a far more significant component of the employment picture than it once did. In part, this increased focus on unionization in the public sector is also the result of the dramatic decline in the rate of unionization in the private sector, making public employees far more unionized now than their private sector counterparts.[2] The number of public sector workers in a union increased tenfold between 1955 and 1975, and public sector unions have largely maintained their membership, while private sector unions have been suffering dramatic losses.[3] By 2000, in fact, "the 7.2 million public sector-union members comprised over 40 percent of the 16.7 million total union members in the U.S."[4] By 2010, only 6.7 percent of private sector workers were unionized, but 36 percent of public sector workers were unionized, which is more than the 33 percent of private sector workers who were unionized in 1953 when private sector unionization was at its peak.[5]

In any event, as a result of the perceived and actual increasing importance of public sector unionization, both relative to private sector unionization and absolutely, there was a dramatic increase in legislative and other attacks on public employee unions, especially since 2010 when the midterm elections produced a significant shift in favor of the Republican party and its ultraconservative tea party faction.[6] Some of these attempts to restrict public sector unionization were successful, such as Republican Governor Scott Walker's attention-getting push to deprive public employees of collective bargaining rights in Wisconsin.[7] Some were less so, but the pressure on public unions has remained intense ever since.[8] And this pressure has only gotten more intense now that Donald Trump is in the White House.[9] Indeed, since his election, Kentucky and Missouri have already passed right-to-work legislation[10] and an increasing number of states are considering such laws,[11] although some of the pressure behind the state-level focus of the anti-union movement has fallen off since June 2018 when the Supreme Court decided *Janus* v. *AFSCME*.[12] I will comment on that decision in some detail at the end of this essay, but for now the only point to note is that *Janus* effectively made all public employment in all states right-to-work, even those that had rejected right-to-work proposals, meaning the continued battle for right-to-work laws in these states only matters for the private sector.[13]

Nevertheless, the anti-union movement remains unsatisfied, even with regard to the public sector. The push for anti-union legislation going beyond mere right-to-work provision accordingly continues not only at the state level but at the federal level as well.[14] And what the right has so far not been able to accomplish through legislation, the Trump administration has begun to do through executive action.[15] What is most surprising, however, is that notwithstanding all the political, legislative, and judicial pressure that has been and continues to be brought to bear, public sector unionization has dropped very little. As of the end of 2016, the rate of unionization in the public sector (34.4 percent) was more than five times as great as in the private sector (6.4 percent).[16] And while many people on both the right and the left assume that one effect of *Janus* will be to dramatically reduce union membership in the public sector, this has not happened yet. So in the battle over unionization, the public sector is still where the action is.[17]

Of course, it seems obvious that the real reason behind these Republican attacks on unionization in the public sector is that public unions are seen as part of the infrastructure of the Democratic party, and anything that weakens that infrastructure weakens the Democratic party and helps ensure that Republicans obtain and maintain their dominance at the state, local, and federal level.[18] Indeed, many anti-union organizations are quite up front about this. For example:

A network of conservative thinktanks with outposts in all 50 states has [recently] embarked on a "breakthrough" campaign designed to strike a "mortal blow" against the American left. The aim is to "defund and defang" unions representing government employees as the first step towards ensuring the permanent collapse of progressive politics.[19]

For purposes of this essay, however, I shall take these attacks as based on genuinely held views about the appropriate role of public sector unions in a liberal capitalist democracy. That is, as based on concerns about "freedom" rather than simply about the allocation of political power.

Taking these concerns seriously, then, the arguments marshalled by the right against public sector unionization are several. We have the argument that the public sector is different than the private sector, and therefore whatever reasons we may have to support unionization in the private sector, these do not apply in the public sector. We have a series of arguments designed to show that suppression rather than support of unionization in the public sector is more consistent with the principles of small government that liberty supposedly entails, for government is already too big and getting bigger, and limiting unionization is an important way to counteract this trend. We have the argument that public employees provide essential services, which cannot be put at risk by strike or otherwise used to extort excessive salaries and benefits out of the government. The suppression of public employee unions is therefore essential for the common good and the protection of our lives, liberty, and property. Even if not excessive, the salaries and benefits paid to unionized public employees are still greater than they would be if public employees were not unionized, and given that the real employer here is the public and not some profit-seeking private individual or group, we have a duty to the taxpayer to try and keep the cost of public services down to its lowest possible level. Public sector unions are also accused of preventing states and localities from dealing quickly and effectively with rising fiscal constraints and of making it impossible or at least unreasonably difficult for these entities to make necessary adjustments to the way public services are delivered. Indeed, anti-union theorists claim that unionization in the public sector undermines the very essence of democracy by tying the hands of public officials to long-term contracts and giving public employees undue influence in the electoral process. In any event, regardless of whether unionization of the public sector may be good for public employees, it is bankrupting us through the overly generous pension plans that unions have negotiated, making state and local governments financially unsustainable, thereby threatening the very liberty that government is intended to ensure.[20] Finally, and most recently, we have the argument that requiring employees to pay "agency fees" (fees that cover the cost of collective bargaining and other employee services that the union performs on behalf nonunion employees) even if they choose not to join the union is a form of compelled speech that violates the free speech guarantee of the US constitution's First Amendment. These are the arguments that I intend to take on in this essay.

Let me say something first, however, about how my responses to these arguments will generalize. All of my responses are aimed at disproving claims made against public sector unionization, but that does not mean that my responses have application only to that question. Indeed, the small government argument, to which I will devote a lot of time in this essay, is raised against almost every form of government action imaginable. Indeed, one version of this argument – that we must dismantle or limit government in various ways because doing otherwise will or already has resulted in unsustainable levels of government debt – is a perennial favorite of the Republican right, at least when they are not in power. I also have no doubt that the First Amendment argument against unionization that I address at the end of this essay will soon be (and to some extent is already being) raised against a wide variety of long-standing government regulations including antidiscrimination laws, antitrust laws, public disclosure laws, health and safety laws, and so on.[21] So my discussion here, although focused on the question of unionization, has much wider application.

With regard to unionization, however, I recognize that many of these arguments I will address are raised primarily and sometimes even exclusively in the United States. This is because even anti-union activists in other countries rarely see a difference between public sector and private sector unionization, and therefore rarely raise arguments that apply to one sector but not the other. Indeed, this is itself an important reason to doubt the claim by anti-union activists in the United States that the two sectors should be treated differently. But this does not mean that the topics I take up in this essay are purely parochial. On the contrary, many of the arguments I will address in this essay, while not used to attack unionization outside the United States, are used in other countries to attack other important aspects of government activity, regulation, and design. The small government argument, to revisit that example, while being one of the central arguments driving the anti-public-sector-unionization right in the United States, is also a driving force behind Brexit and rising right-wing pressure in other countries to pull out of the European Union, which is frequently accused of being big government on steroids. In each case, the substance of the claim – that unnecessary and intrusive government regulation by distant and unaccountable bureaucrats puts national liberty at risk, is the same. Even at the national level, some of these same issues regarding the proper scope of government regulation are raised in other countries too – think, for example, of the movement to "reform" the labor laws in France.[22] The small government argument is also a significant motivator of the privatization of public assets, something that is much more common in Europe than it is in the United States, but I shall nevertheless specifically discuss privatization here as part of dissecting what the argument for smaller government could mean. And the austerity approach to dealing with government debt, which is also driving the argument for smaller government and the limitation of public sector unionization in the United States, is actually more widespread in Europe and the United Kingdom, even if it is not used there to argue against unionization.[23] So while what follows will be specifically aimed at the argumentative battlefield as it currently stands in the United States, it has relevance to the situation in other nations too.

This is especially true because the objective of what follows is not simply to refute the factual claims made by those attacking public sector unions, although

I will do this whenever necessary to show that the assumptions on which these arguments rely are false. The overriding objective of this essay is to show why these attacks on public unions are contrary to the values that those making them claim to embrace. This is an essay about the requirements of political morality, and especially about the requirements of liberty as they pertain to government organization and activity, in whatever way these questions may arise. Everything I will discuss in this essay is used as a ground for objecting to public sector unionization, but these same issues about the shape and role of government arise in a wide array of circumstances in both the United States and abroad. We begin, however, with a discussion of the differences between the private and public sector and how these differences might lead us to conclude that different attitudes toward unionization might be appropriate in the public sector.

3.1 THE DIFFERENCE BETWEEN THE PRIVATE AND THE PUBLIC SECTOR

The argument that the private and the public sector are different, of course, is not a positive argument for suppressing public sector unions – it is simply a way of trying to neutralize the arguments for unions that have had some success in the private sector.[24] It prepares the ground, so to speak, for the various arguments made by those opposed to public sector unionization by attempting to show that the existing ripostes to anti-union sentiment in the private sector have no application. And while it is true that the motivation of employees to organize remains the same whether we are in the private or the public sector, as the first essay in this volume shows, many of the background circumstances in the public sector and the private sector are different. Public agencies are not firms in the same way that private businesses are. They are generally not formed to make a profit, while most private companies are,[25] although there are some exceptions in both cases.[26] But if we stick with the central case,[27] most public agencies are not designed to generate surplus value from labor, and therefore the just distribution of such surplus value is not something we have to be concerned about. Because we do not have reason to be concerned about the just distribution of surplus value, one of the primary drivers of the need for unionization in the private sector is missing.

But it is also true that employees are subject to exploitation in the public sector just as frequently and extensively as they are in the private sector, and exploitation is an affront to both equality and liberty no matter where it happens to occur.[28] Remember, it was as because of the mistreatment of striking Memphis sanitation workers, who were public employees and who had gone on strike after two of their own had been crushed to death in a malfunctioning sanitation truck, that Martin Luther King Jr. came to Memphis and said:

You are doing many things here in this struggle. You are demanding that this city will respect the dignity of labor. So often we overlook the worth and significance of those who are not in professional jobs, or those who are not in the so-called big jobs. But let me say to you tonight, that whenever you are engaged in work that serves humanity, and is for the building of humanity, it has dignity, and it has worth. One day our society must come to see this. One day our society will come to respect the sanitation worker if it is to survive. For the person who picks up our garbage, in the final analysis, is as significant as the physician, for if he doesn't do his job, diseases are rampant. All labor has dignity.

But you are doing another thing. You are reminding, not only Memphis, but you are reminding the nation that it is a crime for people to live in this rich nation and receive starvation wages. I need not remind you that this our plight as a people all over America. [...]

Now the problem isn't only unemployment. Do you know that most of the poor people in our country are working every day? And they are making wages so low that they cannot begin to function in the main stream of the economic life of our nation. These are facts which must be seen. And it is criminal to have people working on a full time basis and a full time job getting part time income. You are here tonight to demand that Memphis do something about the conditions that our brothers face, as they work day in and day out for the well being of the total community. You are here to demand that Memphis will see the poor.[29]

On balance, then, I think the argument that the mere absence of a profit motive driving management does not suggest that the unionization of public employees is unnecessary. We still have plenty of reason to fear that public agencies will infringe the republican liberty of their employees and otherwise treat them unjustly if left to their own devices, for a variety of reasons.

First, public agencies have the same hierarchical structure as private firms and provide the same temptation to managers to impose their arbitrary will on their employees. Some public agencies are even notorious for the consistent and programmatic bullying of employees by managers (think of the US Postal Service, whose alleged mistreatment of their employees and the violent response that this mistreatment allegedly produced in some cases led to the coining of the phrase "going postal"). To the extent that unionization is a response to the threat of domination created by such a hierarchical structure – and as we have already seen, this is a major justification of the need for institutionalized protection of workers – unionization is no different in the public sector than it is in the private sector.

Second, even though public agencies are not generally designed to produce a profit, they are under constant pressure to reduce the costs of the services they provide and the taxes that are required to pay for them. Public officials who succeed in doing this are well-positioned to move up in the government bureaucracy or even run for public office. So there is still plenty of incentive for managers to attempt to increase the "productivity" of the public sector (getting more for less) by unfairly riding the backs of the public employees who toil below them.

Third, when this happens to nonunionized employees, the only avenue of relief for them is to seek protection through the courts or perhaps (when available) to pursue individual administrative remedies. Pursuing a lawsuit, however, is very expensive and time-consuming, making economic sense only for the most egregious, widespread, and financially injurious misconduct, not every day bullying and harassment. And while it is technically unnecessary for an employee to retain a lawyer to pursue an administrative remedy, the employer naturally has much greater experience handling such claims because it does so all the time, while the employee (at least we hope) does so only rarely and perhaps never before. This leaves employees justifiably worrying that they will be out of their depth if they attempt to proceed on their own. Administrative remedies also typically require the employee to first proceed internally and present their complaint to people who work for the same employer and therefore have what appears to be a significant conflict of interest. This means that employees contemplating making an administrative complaint are also likely to worry about having to go through a proceeding that is at least initially stacked against them. Taken together, these practical realties suggest that government employees, like their nonunionized private counterparts, have good reason to believe that they may be effectively left remediless when subjected to abuse if there is no union to stand up for them.

Fourth, public agencies are often monopolies, at least in specific geographic areas, so the normal restraints that flow from market competition do not apply. Indeed, public employers are not only often monopolies they are also often monopsonies, the exclusive or at least the single most dominant buyer for a particular kind of labor in a particular geographic area. This makes the need for some internal checks of management behavior even more important than in the private sector, because in the private sector, competition can be expected to exercise at least some control on the excesses of management. If one is an air traffic controller, for example, there is really only one employer for whom one can work. Accordingly, public employees who are subjected to abuse may feel they have no choice but to stand down and take it even more frequently than private employees, for if one burns one's bridges, there may be no place left to go.

Finally, while public employees are in some sense like shareholders as well as employees – in other words, they do get a vote on what management does, albeit usually quite indirectly (they get to vote for mayor, for example, but not for who is to head the city sanitation department), every other citizen served by the agency is like a shareholder too, so the votes of those who are both shareholders and employees can end up being so diluted they are unlikely to have a decisive influence on wages or conditions of employment, even for agencies that serve relatively small localities.

Take, for example, Wisconsin, where police and firefighters who tend to vote Republican were excluded from the general ban on collective bargaining by public employees promoted by the Republican governor, but were nevertheless prohibited by the same law containing that ban from having any say on their health care costs. As a result, many localities then tried to use this provision to extract retirement concessions from police and firefighters by threatening huge unilateral increases in their health care costs.³⁰ In other words, whatever political clout they may have used to get themselves exempted from the ban on collective bargaining, this was not in the end sufficient to actually protect them. I will say much more about the political power of public sector unions when I discuss the claim that the unionization of public employees undermines democracy. For now, however, the only point I want to make is that while public sector unions can deliver votes or provide money to political campaigns and candidates and therefore have political influence just like private sector unions and many other kinds of associations as well, support from any particular public sector union is rarely decisive. After all, if it were otherwise, Wisconsin's ban on collective bargaining by public employees other than police and firefighters, many of whom were also represented by strong unions, would never have gotten off the ground, nor would the subsequent effort to recall Governor Walker have been unsuccessful. And we would not be seeing such effective assaults on the employment terms of so many public employees elsewhere today, even though membership in such unions is at its height.

What all these considerations suggests is that while the background circumstances that apply to public employment are indeed somewhat different than those that apply to private employment, they are not different enough to suggest that our attitude toward unions in the private sector has no place at all in the public sector. On the contrary, some of these differences actually suggest that we may have more reason for concern in the public sector than we have in the private sector.³¹ Accordingly, if we are going to nevertheless limit union activity in the public sector in ways that we do not in the private sector, the opponents of public sector unionization are going to need to do more than point out that certain background circumstances differ between one sector and the other.

There is, however, one other difference in background circumstance that I want to mention before I close this section. The public sector employs a far higher percentage of minorities and women than the private sector.³² Indeed, the public sector is often the *only* place that many of those historically subject to discriminatory attitudes can find work.³³ While there are no doubt special obstacles for minorities and women to overcome even here, the public sector playing field is often significantly more level. When public sector employment is cut, we are accordingly removing one of the few rungs that do exist for many minorities and women to use to climb up the economic ladder. And when wages and benefits in the public sector are cut, we are helping restrain that climb even if not preventing it entirely.³⁴ This is not, moreover, an affront only to equality. Because discrimination is also a form of arbitrary treatment, it is also an affront to republican liberty. Of course, some anti-union critics no doubt see the suppression of minorities and women as a plus, and this may even form a significant motivating factor behind their anti-union views. But since the suppression of minorities and women is not a very palatable argument to present to the wider public, it is rarely expressly made, so this effect often goes unremarked. Nevertheless, I am not going to say much more about this argument here because it sounds too much like an argument that can only be made from equality, even though it is not. But I do not want to pretend this difference between the private and the public sector does not exist. For those who do want to defend unionization of the public sector by relying on the argument from equality, or to point out that the same argument can be derived from the argument from republican liberty, there are some powerful grounds to do so here. At the very least, this suggests that rather than taking a more restrictive attitude toward the unionization of the public sector, the most material difference between the two sectors actually suggests we should take a more supportive attitude. In any event, what I intend to focus on here are arguments from liberty that are not simply restatements of similar argument from equality under a different heading. And that is exactly what I shall be doing next.

3.2 PUBLIC SECTOR UNIONIZATION AND THE PROPER SIZE OF GOVERNMENT

One of the first arguments along these lines relies on a claim about the relation between public sector unions and the proper size of government. Like all organizations, associations, and private sector unions, the argument goes, public sector unions naturally want to increase their own size and influence. To do this, they need more members. And the best way to get more members is to ensure that government – and therefore the number of government employees – grows bigger. Public sector unions are therefore claimed to be unabashed supporters of the growth of government, no matter how big government has already become. And this is bad, the argument continues, because the bigger government gets, the more it does, the more intrusive it is in our lives, and the less liberty there is left for everyone else to enjoy. Restrict (or better yet eliminate) public sector unionization, and we will have taken one necessary and important step toward defeating the continued, uncontrolled growth of government and the threat to liberty that big government necessarily represents.

Note first that there are various moving parts to this argument: (1) government has been growing significantly; (2) there is a causal connection between this growth and public sector unionization; and (3) big government is a significant threat to liberty and therefore something we should do our best to avoid. The first part of this argument is empirical; the second causal, and therefore also empirical; and the third conceptual, although as we shall see, it also has a significant empirical component – the claim that bigger government necessarily results in reductions in the scope of liberty. I shall spend most of my time in this section on this last claim. But I will begin by questioning the first claim, one that that is accepted as true by almost everybody: the claim that government has grown exponentially over the years and continues to do so now.

3.2.1 Is Government Really Getting Bigger?

The idea that government has grown like a cancer and must be seriously pruned back, which is supposedly what gives the small government position its urgency and energizes its supporters, actually bears no relation to the facts. It is of course true that the public sector is now larger than it once was. Indeed, before 1960, the public sector was too small to be worthy of much interest. But between 1960 and 1975 that changed: public employment grew at an annual rate of about 5 percent, or more than twice the rate of the population. After 1975, however, the rate of growth in public sector employment slowed, actually falling behind population growth every year and eventually beginning to shrink and then shrink substantially. Between 1975 and 1983, for example, public employment rose by less than 1 percent annually, while private employment grew at an annual rate of almost 4 percent.[35] By 2004, the public sector represented only a 3 percentage-point greater share of nonfarm employment than it did in 1939.[36] This trend of very slow growth in the public sector then continued until the Great Recession of 2008. In the wake of that event, however, the austerity budgets either forced upon state and local governments and their subsidiary units or adopted voluntarily in the misguided belief that austerity was expansionary[37] caused the public sector to lose more or almost as many jobs as the post-recession private sector created.[38] During this period, in fact, federal employment in the United States fell to close to a forty-seven-year low. That's right – the same number of people (2,729,000) worked for the federal government in September 2013 (before the government shutdown) as worked for the federal government in 1966 when Lyndon Johnson was president.[39] And this is not adjusting for the relative size of the population, which had increased by over 50 percent. "Now, the federal government employs exactly 2 percent of the people with jobs in this country. In 1966, the figure was more than twice that, 4.3 percent."[40] In 1939, it was 3 percent, so one would have to go back quite some ways to find a similarly small percentage of the workforce employed by the federal government.[41] And pursuant to the federal budget recently approved by President Trump, there will be huge further reductions in the federal workforce.[42] So if we are to use federal employment as a guide to whether the federal government is too big, it is hard to see how it could be. There should accordingly be no reason for concern over public sector unionization in the federal sphere, even if there were some connection between the size of government and any form of economic, personal, or political liberty.[43]

When we turn to employment by state and local government, we do find that public employment has not shrunk quite as much. But the claim that public employment has grown exponentially in state and local government is still wildly overblown. At the state level, government employment continued to increase until it reached its height in 2008. It then dropped as a result of the Great Recession, and while it has recovered some, it is still lower than it was when the Great Recession began.[44] More significantly, excluding education (which we might reasonably do given that increasing the number of public school teachers seems to have wide bipartisan support), current state employment is now less than what it was in 1993, and only 30 percent more than it was in 1977 despite a 47 percent increase in the population.[45] At the local government level, the story is much the same. While the number of people employed by local government has increased since 1977, and more than it has increased for people employed by state government, it has still increased only about 5 percent more than the population has increased over this entire forty-year period.[46] And in some cases, it seems like local government agencies are if anything *under*staffed, requiring the agency to choose between paying large amount of expensive overtime or leaving required basic work undone.[47] In Houston, for example, pinched by a property tax cap, the police chief has said his department is short 1,500 to 2,000 officers, and there are similar dramatic shortages in Atlanta, San Jose, Hartford, and many rural locations throughout the country.[48] In North Carolina and Oklahoma, to cite just one other example, state prisons have as many as 25 percent of their positions unfilled.[49] In other states, prisoners are being guarded by teachers and secretaries.[50] Indeed, the most recent statistics put total state and local government employment as of February 2018, like federal employment, at the same level it was at in 1967.[51] Thus, the claim that the growth in public employment is out of control and therefore anything that contributes to this must be stopped at all costs is simply false. In other words, the starting premise of the small government argument against public sector unionization is simply wrong.

But it would be a mistake to end our consideration of the small government-based anti-union argument there, for two reasons. First, those who advance the small government position seem to be totally unmoved by reference to actual facts. And second (and this helps explain the first observation), even if government is not exponentially bigger than it once was, it might still be bigger than it should be. So if public sector unionization were impeding further reduction in the size of government, then the small government argument would still have some bite. I will therefore turn next to have a look at whether such a causal claim might indeed be true.

3.2.2 Is There a Relationship between Public Sector Unionization and the Size of Government?

The fact that public sector unionization has been increasing while government employment has actually been shrinking or at least not increasing very much suggests that the claimed connection between public sector unionization and the size of government is very weak, at most. But once again, it could still be true that public employment would be smaller than it currently is – and perhaps even much smaller – but for the existence of public sector unions. So the fact that public employment has not been growing exponentially does not technically resolve the matter. And this is especially true if there is a plausible causal mechanism for establishing a connection between public sector unionization and the size of government. And, in fairness, there is. The argument is that unions are no different than any other kind of organization. They want to increase their power and influence, and this means increasing their size. While this can be done simply by increasing the rate of unionization – at 33 percent there are still a lot of public employees out there who are not currently members of any union – it is perhaps easier to increase their (absolute) size by simply increasing the number of public employees. The more public employees there are, the more people there are who could be union members, even if the rate of unionization does not change. So unions have a dual incentive, it seems – not only to increase the rate of unionization but also to use their influence to increase the size of public employment and stifle efforts to reduce it, even if they have not so far been very successful at achieving this latter objective.

While there are no empirical studies that would allow us to quantify to what extent, if any, this causal mechanism is actually in operation, it is obvious, I suppose, that unions tend to oppose efforts to lay off public employees and to encourage the hiring of more personnel at the rank and file level. Of course, there is no empirical evidence that union efforts to resist the dismantling of government and to encourage a general increase in staffing do not arise from a good faith belief in how best to improve the services government provides rather than simply a self-interested concern for the size and power of their own organizations. On the contrary, a wide segment of the American people who are not public employees or members of public sector unions actually believe government is understaffed given its responsibilities. In other words, there are obviously substantive reasons that justify the anti-small-government position that unions are often perceived to take. So it remains plausible that public sector unionization does affect the size of government, at least to the extent that it is measured by the number of government employees. Which means that it is necessary to address the claim that shrinking government is an imperative of liberty, for if this is true, unionization may indeed impede efforts to ensure that our liberty is protected in this way.

3.2.3 Is Big Government a Threat to Liberty?

The argument that government should be smaller rather than larger if we are to preserve the widest amount of liberty for the governed has a surprisingly long history – as an express argument, it goes back at least to the nineteenth century, and as an implied argument, it goes back to Adam Smith, at least according to some interpreters of his work.[52] But it begins not with a claim about political liberty, it begins with a claim about economic liberty. Initially, the claim was that the free market could do everything government could do more efficiently, more effectively, and cheaper. The more government there was, the more government *regulation* there was going to be, and greater regulation meant that less real power was left in the free market to be unleashed. This, in turn, would lead to lower levels of production and therefore lower levels of wealth to be divided up between the members of society, and everyone would necessarily have a smaller share. I shall address this claim – the claim that smaller government produced greater economic liberty and therefore more national wealth – in a moment, but first I want to explain how this claim about economic liberty became a claim about political liberty.

The argument that big government is negatively correlated with economic liberty eventually (or quickly, depending on how you interpret the views of Adam Smith) moved beyond the economic realm and became politicized through what is yet another causal claim. Certain people began thinking that economic and political liberty were necessarily related; therefore, the less economic liberty available to people, the less personal and political liberty they would have available to enjoy. The causal process allegedly connecting economic to political liberty was initially unspecified, but in the wake of the Russian Revolution and the antidemocratic forces it unleashed, it began to be expressed as a slippery-slope argument. The claim was that any step toward the restriction of economic liberty would inevitably lead to totalitarianism, for the apparatus that was necessary to control an entire economy was so elaborate that it would be impossible to keep it in check and its brief would inevitably expand from interfering with our economic life to interfering with all aspects of our lives. This explanation was then popularized by Hayek after World War II and became a central tenet of neoliberalism, and it has remained the only explanation offered by those advocating small government as a political and not merely an economic proposition ever since.[53]

Note that the economic and political claims here are related in some ways but independent in others. The slippery-slope argument depends on there being interference with economic liberty, for this is what leads to infringement of personal and political liberty, but it does not depend on whether such interference is actually bad for the economy. The claim that interference with economic liberty is bad in itself because it is bad for the economy, in turn, does not depend on such interference also having wider effects. Each version of this argument accordingly relies on something different for its moral force. Nevertheless, both claims reduce to the idea that smaller government is necessarily better than bigger government, and it is better because the smaller government becomes the more liberty of both kinds there is for everyone else. But there is actually no good reason to believe that this latter claim is true.

The first problem with the use of this argument by the anti-union movement, however, is conceptual. There is an inherent contradiction in the use of these ideas to call for the suppression of union activity, public or private, for what is being called for here is not the *elimination* of government regulation – the usual small government position – but the *imposition* of government regulation designed to prevent the spread of unions the free market would otherwise produce, something the first essay in this volume showed would occur even if we lived in a libertarian utopia. Why such regulation is not a problem for those advocating for smaller government, while all other kinds of regulation should be viewed as an inappropriately intrusive interference in the workings of the free market, is unclear at best. But there does seem to be a growing tendency among some elements on the anti-union right to see government regulation as not a violation of small government principles as long as it seeks to impose policies small government advocates like on some other basis. In other words, there have been increasing calls by some of those on the right to use government power to impose specific policies on people in liberal capitalist societies, even when those policies are ones that violate rights, at least as long as these are rights that conservatives don't respect and think should never have been recognized in the first place. The fact that this smacks of authoritarianism, or exactly what the small government people are supposed to be against, seems to them to be a worry that is not worth taking seriously.[54]

But let's ignore this troubling feature of the use of the small government argument to attack public sector unions and focus simply on the merits of the claim. For it is also unclear why public sector unions should be thought of as contributing significantly to the growth of government, even if such growth is what has indeed occurred. The incentive for government units to grow and increase their own power, budgets, and importance would be in operation whether there were unions or not. If this incentive is always present, then at least unions could be counted on to help channel this growth into rank-and-file employment rather than into the growth of management, which is an even more unjustified drain on taxpayer funds (at least rank-and-file workers actually *do* something) and arguably imposes an even greater threat to overall liberty if there is any threat to liberty here at all. Bloated and overpaid management is also highly inefficient, even more inefficient than an organization that is bigger at the rank-and-file level than it should be given what it is supposed to do and would be if it did less. So there is every reason to believe that government will continue to grow and grow in an even more objectionable ways if public unionization is further limited.

Support for the claim that smaller government is positively correlated with greater overall personal and political freedom is also very weak. The two indices on which those making this claim typically rely are the Economic Freedom Index (EFI), created and maintained by the right-libertarian Fraser Institute in Canada (Fraser is heavily funded by Charles and David Koch), and the so-called Personal Freedom Index (PFI) created and maintained by the right-libertarian Cato Institute in the United States (Cato was cofounded by Charles Koch, was once heavily funded by both brothers, and is still funded by David Koch). These indices, in turn, have now been combined and are often referred to collectively as the Human Freedom Index (HFI).[55] But both of the original indices are deeply controversial.[56] Each uses a methodological

3.2 Public Sector Unionization and the Proper Size of Government 183

approach and makes various assumptions that are highly dubious and seem designed to produce the desired result.[57] For example, they each use firm figures for various attributes that are notoriously difficult to measure and assign equal weight to every factor in coming up with the individual index result, despite the fact that some measures seem intuitively more significant than others. Each index is also assigned equal weight in coming up with the combined HFI score. This not only embeds various subjective biases into each index, it also introduces a great deal of arbitrariness. Even more importantly, both indexes focus exclusively on measuring negative liberty; that is, freedom from constraint.[58] But this means that none of the indexes are actually attempting to measure whether people have the ability to take advantage of the absence of constraint to live a meaningful and productive life, a kind of positive liberty, despite the authors' acknowledgment that the effect of negative liberty on this ability is the reason why negative liberty is important.[59] Why give this as the reason for taking negative liberty so seriously and then not measure factors that reflect positive liberty more directly? This is the very problem that Charles Taylor criticized and I discussed in the first essay in this volume. In any event, because of the exclusive focus on negative liberty here, economic inequality is not included in either index, nor economic mobility, nor whether there is equal pay for equal work, nor poverty, nor racism and its effect on economic opportunity, mobility, and general well-being, nor access to medical care, nor longevity, nor infant mortality, nor the cost of housing relative to income, nor support for public education, nor the degree of exploitation in society, nor home ownership, nor are any of the many other attributes of a society that indicate whether people in a particular society really do have the opportunity to better themselves no matter what their backgrounds circumstances or the extent to which they are likely to be amenable to domination by their employer, their landlord, those with whom they do business, and so on. Homicide rates are considered but not rates of economic crime and civil fraud. Small government, besides being difficult to define and measure, is simply assumed by each index to make people more free than big government, no matter what big government does or how it does it or what small government fails to do. Higher marginal tax rates are assumed to be limits on economic freedom, instead of part of what helps provide economic freedom for the vast bulk of the population. More regulation is assumed to be more freedom infringing than less regulation, when this is in fact the question under debate. Even if we focus exclusively on negative liberty, every restriction on one person's negative liberty provides some kind of freedom from interference for someone else. No attempt is made to include the degree to which some members of society are allowed to inflict externalities such as pollution of the environment on everyone else. Government interference is assumed to be freedom restricting but not interference by private parties, even though either can be sources of such interference. Some of the measures focus on the freedom of the individual, yet others seem to focus on the freedom of the firm, effectively assigning the equal weight to each despite claiming to be attempting to measure only personal freedom.

These assumptions and omissions obviously have a significant effect on the ultimate rankings produced. According to the 2014 EFI, for example, Hong Kong, Singapore, the United Arab Emirates (UAE), and the former Soviet Republic of Georgia all offer greater economic freedom to their citizens than the United States, the United Kingdom, Canada, and Australia.[60] But it is hard to believe that anyone would seriously argue that any of the first group of countries offers all its citizens (as opposed to a select few) greater personal freedom than any of those in the second group. They certainly do not offer greater political freedom. Yet the results are claimed to show that economic freedom and personal freedom (and by implication political freedom) are indeed connected. In the 2016 EFI, the UAE dropped from 5th to 37th, a dramatic movement that is apparently the result of accounting for gender equality on this more recent survey, showing how sensitive the EFI is to just one of the factors that I have pointed to as not being previously considered. In any event, the combined 2017 HFI ranks Hong Kong as the second most free country in the world, despite its lack of a democratic government and many other attributes of a free society, a result the authors of the index recognize themselves as an "outlier."[61] Even so, the Nordic countries and most of Western Europe, all of which have wider social safety nets and similar if not stricter degrees of corporate regulation, are ranked higher on the 2017 HFI than the United States, showing that even when small government is used as a proxy for freedom, nations with larger governments and equivalent amounts of regulation are still all things considered more free. And when a somewhat less ideologically infused index is used, the result is even more dramatic: smaller government actually has a negative correlation with personal freedom, and "countries with larger government sectors tend to have more personal freedom and higher indicators of education, health, and personal safety."[62] Therefore, the attempt to make the "smaller government is better" simply a blanket causal claim clearly fails.[63] And if that claim fails, then the whole underlying moral force of the small government argument dissipates into nothing. Or at least it should do.

But it hasn't. Indeed, the empirical causal evidence supposedly supplied by these indexes smack of a post hoc justification for something for which a preexisting belief is already fixed. In other words, the claim that big government reduces both economic and political liberty is actually viewed as conceptual truth, not amenable to dispute through the presentation of contrary evidence. If the available evidence does not confirm this, it simply means that we have not found it yet, and that the apparently contrary evidence is itself erroneous or at least being misinterpreted, not that there is reason to revise our preexisting beliefs. The only way to shake those who see the small government position as a conceptual truth is to attack the conceptual argument itself: show that the conceptual justification behind the small government argument is

3.2.4 How Can We Tell How Big Government Should Be? Problems with the Functional Test

In order to defend the small government position, it must be possible to articulate a principle that tells us how big government should be. But if there is such a principle, it is hard to find. Of course, one popular answer to the question of how big government should be is that government should be small enough "that [we] can drag it into the bathroom and drown it in the bathtub."[64] While this may accurately capture the sentiment of those who see government as too big, however, it hardly constitutes a reasoned intellectual principle for anyone but an anarchist, for if consistently and continuously applied, it must eventually lead to the elimination of government altogether.[65] And it is hard to see how this could be good for economic liberty when people could not be sure that counterparties would perform their contracts (because there would be no courts to force them to do so) or that their property rights would be respected (while there might be competing private armies, there would be no police). It is hard to see why this would be good for personal or political liberty either, for while everyone would be free to do whatever they like, they would also be free to engage in predation and we would end up with the proverbial war of all against all because even those not inclined to engage in predation would nevertheless have an incentive to peremptorily attack their neighbor out of fear of being attacked themselves. Indeed, even Adam Smith, to whom the small government position is usually traced, recognized that smaller government is not necessarily better government: "Government in a civilized country is much more expensive than in a barbarous one," for "there are many expenses necessary in a civilized country for which there is no occasion in one that is barbarous."[66] In other words, the claim that President Reagan famously made in his first inaugural address that "government is not the solution to our problem, government *is* the problem,"[67] is simply not true – even in context, this depends on what it is that government means to do.

There is certainly a long tradition of arguing about what government should and should not do. The harm principle,[68] the principle of public justification,[69] the principle of neutrality,[70] both alone and in combination have all been suggested as ways of determining when government action is and is not an appropriate interference with our liberty. And while each of these principles exist in various versions and are subject to both wide and narrow interpretations, they do help us determine what government can and cannot legitimately do. Even the broadest versions of these principles, however, merely provide a basis for limiting certain kinds of government activities that could be considered examples of government excess. None of them suggest that government should be radically smaller than it now is, or even small enough that one might be justified in using "smaller is always better" as a useful proxy. If we are going to give the small government position actual substance, we are going to have to find a principle to base it on other than one of these.

Of course, if there was a principled basis for determining what was the appropriate size of government and that principle was violated by the current size of government, wouldn't it be best to simply limit the size of government using this principle and not try to accomplish that goal indirectly by limiting union activity? There could be nothing in such a principle about the size of government that could justly call for public employees to be underpaid or mistreated or otherwise exploited. Even if government size were to be properly limited, this would provide no justification for restraining public unionization, even if the latter sometimes worked to undermine the principle. The "attack unions first" approach works like an indirect blunderbuss at best. But let's put this concern aside for now and see if there is any principle that might indeed serve to operationalize the small government position.

What would such a principle look like? If "small government" was a defensible moral principle, we would not only need a way of articulating what government should and should not do but also be able to show we had unambiguously gone beyond those limits and significantly so. If we had such a principle, we would know how many people government should employ – as many as necessary to fully perform the required functions, although I suppose that even then there might be room for disagreement over what level of staffing was "necessary," and there would certainly be room for disagreement over what functions were "required." In any event, coming up with a principle that attempts to address these questions is essential. But it is also very hard to do. Remember that even the night-watchman state of a libertarian utopia is supposed to protect its citizens from fraud, theft, anticompetitive acts, and other kinds of market failures. To claim that the current degree of government regulation has gone beyond this, much less *way* beyond this as the proponents of this position typically claim, they must be able offer us some way of distinguishing regulation that is within the brief of the night-watchman state from regulation that is not, but they do not.[71] Instead, advocates of the minimal state seem to simply assume that this distinction is obvious, and do not even attempt to set forth a principle that we can use to sort what is appropriate government regulation from what is inappropriate.

The reason they don't attempt this, I think, is that the supposedly very limited functions of government of the minimal night-watchmen state actually encompass a very large amount of regulatory activity indeed. Almost every kind of regulation that government is engaged in today can be seen as a way of restricting fraud, theft, violence, and anticompetitive behavior, or correcting for market failures.[72] Indeed, when deregulated, many industries become more and more concentrated and anticompetitive, abusing their customers and charging ever higher prices.[73] Others simply glibly engage in fraud, and by the time the market

3.2 Public Sector Unionization and the Proper Size of Government

finds out, much injury has already happened and the perpetrators are as likely to escape punishment as not.[74] Even those who do not engage in outright fraud often put profits ahead of safety and place their customers' and their workers' physical well-being at substantial risk.[75] And absent government regulation, discriminatory attitudes, exploitation, and externalities abound, distorting the market and undermining the very goals the concept of the free market was meant to ensure. Discriminatory attitudes, for example, lead to the misallocation of economic resources as potentially less productive workers are hired over more productive ones. Such misallocations cannot be expected to be corrected by the market alone even in competitive sectors of the economy if discriminatory attitudes are widespread, as the election of Donald Trump proves they are.[76] Externalities (costs imposed on third parties to a transaction without their consent) such as pollution and the injuries caused by impure food, dangerous drugs, or unsafe products and methods of production mean that goods are produced below their true cost, again leading to distortions in the market and a misallocation of productive resources. Exploitation fosters and eventually institutionalizes economic inequality, and beside being a form of domination and theft, this limits the ability of an economy to unleash the demand and the growth that such demand would bring if people were given more of the funds their efforts actually generated and were therefore able to venture into the market and purchase the goods and services they could then afford.[77] And as history demonstrates, none of these market failures are likely to be corrected absent government intervention and extensive regulation. As the old institutionalists pointed out long ago, "the true ideal of society is not *laissez faire*, but economic freedom, and freedom is the child, not the enemy, of law and regulation."[78] In other words, much economic regulation enhances economic freedom rather than infringes it. Accordingly, developing a meaningful limit on the size of government using a test that simply focuses on the whether a particular regulation is within one of the supposedly limited "appropriate" functions of government seems hopeless, for aside from possibly leading to some (even then still controversial) trimming around the edges, any functional test is likely to be far too indeterminate to lead to a principled way of distinguishing between the size of the government we have now and where we supposedly should want to go.

But there is one other variant of the functional test that we need to consider. This one would not necessarily make government small in any absolute sense, but it might make it smaller than it is now. Under this test, instead of a positive principle that tells us what functions government should perform, we look for a negative principle, one that tells us which functions government should not perform. One of the functions often identified using this approach is support for the arts,[79] but a variety of more important functions are often identified as belonging to this no-go area as well, including public assistance, unemployment insurance, medical care, social security, and even public education.[80] In other words, this approach reduces to the idea whatever functions the government is supposed to perform in a free society, providing a social safety net for the young, the old, and those who have fallen on hard times, and supporting education, healthcare, and culture is not among them. But it is hard to see the connection between any of these programs and a threat to economic liberty. Indeed, Friedrich Hayek, the man who is generally thought of as the father of neoliberalism and the modern version of the small government objection, was actually in favor of such programs. For example, Hayek expressly said that "there can be no doubt that some minimum of food, shelter, and clothing, sufficient to preserve health and the capacity to work can be assured to everybody."[81] Hayek also supported public-financed education[82] and various other types of government funded assistance:

Nor is there any reason why the state should not assist the individuals in providing for those common hazards of life against, which, because of their uncertainty, few individuals can make adequate provision. Where, as in the case of sickness and accident, neither the desire to avoid such calamities nor the efforts to overcome their consequences are as a rule weakened by the provision of assistance, where, in short we deal with genuinely insurable risks, the case for the state helping to organize a comprehensive system of social insurance is very strong. There are many points of detail where those wishing to preserve the competitive system and those wishing to supersede it by something different will disagree on the details of such schemes; and it is possible under the name of social insurance to introduce measures which tend to make competition more or less ineffective. But there is no incompatibility in principle between the state providing greater security in this way and the preservation of individual freedom. To the same category belongs also the increase in security through the state rendering assistance to the victims of such "acts of God" as earthquakes and floods. Whenever communal action can mitigate disasters against which the individual can neither attempt to guard himself, nor make provision for the consequences, such communal action should undoubtedly be taken.[83]

Hayek even expressly supported government intervention in the economy to help keep the rate unemployment down:

There is, finally, the supremely important problem of combating general fluctuations of economic activity and the recurrent waves of large scale unemployment which accompany them. This is, of course, one of the gravest and most pressing problems of our time. But, though its solution will require much planning in the good sense, it does not – or at least need not – require that special kind of planning which according to its advocates is to replace the market. Many economists hope indeed that the ultimate remedy may be found in the field of monetary policy, which would involve nothing incompatible even with nineteenth-century liberalism. Others, it is true, believe that real success can be expected only from the skillful timing of public works undertaken on a very large scale. This might lead to much more serious restrictions of the competitive sphere, and in experimenting in this direction we shall have carefully to watch our step if we are to avoid making all economic activity progressively more dependent on the direction and volume of government expenditure. But this is neither the only, nor, in my opinion, the most promising way of meeting the gravest threat to economic security. In any case, the very necessary efforts to secure protection against these fluctuations do not lead to the kind of planning which constitutes such a threat to our freedom.[84]

3.2 Public Sector Unionization and the Proper Size of Government

So it seems clear that whatever justification may exist for eliminating social welfare and various other public programs that are typically the target of this version of the small government objection, protecting economic freedom is not one of them, as least according to the man who has done more than perhaps anyone else in history to popularize this objection.[85]

This, of course, also makes the slippery-slope argument that is used to get the small government folks from infringements of economic liberty to infringements of political liberty unavailable. Nevertheless, those who attack the social safety net and related programs often decry them as the first step toward socialism and all the supposed infringements of freedom that entails. Is there any plausibility to this claim? I think not. Freedom is meaningless if you have insufficient resources to do anything but beg.[86] All societies must attempt to provide a social minimum to their members, and not only because this is what basic human decency requires us to do so. This must be done because no society can consider itself free if it allows some of its members to be imprisoned by poverty in the midst of plenty. Of course, we can argue about where the social minimum should lie and what it should include, but that there be a social minimum cannot reasonably be disputed. And remember, while it might be true that excessive government coddling can sometimes sap the initiative to work, it is also true that many of those who make important contributions to the economy and to culture could not have done so without some government support. At the very least, a free market needs a continuous supply of educated, well-trained, and productive workers if it is going to be able to thrive. It is simply very difficult to believe that without governmental support for various social, cultural, and educational programs, an economy could possibly supply enough of these people if everyone were left to their own devices.

There are other practical considerations as well. History has demonstrated that a society that simply does not care about those who cannot fend for themselves, that offers no social support for economic and social mobility, and that leaves culture for advancement only by or at the direction of the wealthy, are primed for revolution and rejection of the free market system. Even in a society that provides a social safety net and other public goods, the wealthy are in a position to dominate not only the poor but everybody below them on the wealth distribution as well. Any society that does not make some attempt to give those who cannot otherwise access opportunities for personal, education, economic, and cultural improvement condemns a large proportion of its members to a life of subservience and subjugation, dependent on the charity of others. So the real threat of sliding into socialism, if there is such a threat, comes not from trying to maintain a civil society that takes reasonable steps to maintain and reproduce itself by ensuring that its members are healthy, educated, and in a position to make contributions to its economy and culture. It comes from scrapping the social minimum and support for culture and other forms of public assistance altogether and leaving in its place the law of the jungle, under which only the most ruthless predators and their progeny are likely to thrive.

Indeed, this version of the small government objection seems to have nothing to do with protecting freedom whatsoever. What it does have to do with is protecting property, for whatever social support network the government provides has to paid for, and this means taxation. Taxes are an infringement of property rights, the thinking apparently goes, and a government that respects property rights will tax the propertied less and less, and perhaps even not at all. Eliminate these "social" programs and government will not only be smaller, it will be cheaper as well. But this simply begs the questions of what functions of government are legitimate. Taxes are not an unacceptable or unjust interference with property rights to the extent they pay for legitimate functions of government, so we cannot get from the mere fact that taxes are required to pay for something to the conclusion that whatever needs to be paid for is illegitimate. In other words, this argument actually does no work. There is accordingly no version of a functional test for determining how small government should be that could make the small government objection principled, even assuming reducing the size of government is somehow made more difficult by public sector unionization.

3.2.5 Problems with the Efficiency Test

But let's see if we can come up with some other kind of principle for determining the proper size of government and consider whether this has any implications for public sector unions. If a functional principle derived from Nozick's idea of the minimal state will not work, perhaps we can derive a workable principle from the neoliberal claim that the private sector can do everything the public sector can, only cheaper. That is, perhaps we should say that government should only do those things that the free market's private sector can't or won't do at all (rural electrification, for example), won't provide in optimum amounts (like public goods), or can provide only less efficiently, that is, at higher cost. This principle is related to Nozick's functional test, and some libertarians (mistakenly) believe that it can be derived from it, but it can also be used as a free-standing principle. And not surprisingly, the idea that economic efficiency should be the relevant guideline is what many economists recommend.[87] Of course, one might still question whether economic efficiency should be used as a proxy for liberty, or at least why economic liberty should be used as a proxy for political liberty, but I shall set that question aside for now and assume the slippery-slope argument I have already described is sufficient to make the necessary connection here. Even so, there are more problems with using economic efficiency to provide a workable limit on the size of government than there were with using the functional principle we have already rejected.

First, there is the problem that even if a certain type of public service could be operated more efficiently by the private sector on an ongoing basis, privatization often involves a large transfer of wealth from the mostly poor general public to a select few already wealthy and privileged individuals. This can be the result of corruption among those in the government supervising the privatization of assets, given that the financial stakes here are often enormous. Even in the absence of corruption, however, a large transfer of wealth from the poor to the rich can still result because public assets in the form of ongoing operations are difficult to value. After all, they have not been operating with the idea of earning a profit; as a result, they have no profit history to use to attract investors. They are accordingly often sold at what amount to fire-sale prices compared to their potential to generate profit as a privately managed enterprise. Even successful privatizations can therefore entail huge transaction costs. And while on some number of occasions the subsequent profitability of these enterprises may actually be the result of the application of private management ingenuity or additional private investment, it will often be the case that there were no real efficiency gains to be had here; a small select group of individuals are simply being allowed to appropriate value that was actually created with taxpayer money.[88] One can see this, of course, throughout the former Communist Bloc where assets that were developed at great public expense have made billionaires out of a select few private individuals. But this happens in the course of privatizing assets in existing liberal capitalist democracies too. Take the sell-off of the automaker British Leyland in the United Kingdom, for example, or the privatization of British Rail.[89]

Second, once the profit motive replaces the incentive to improve the common good, it is difficult to ensure that the same criteria for measuring performance will be used with regard to the activities involved.[90] A certain quality of performance can be required by regulation of course, but if the whole idea of privatizing assets or activities is to minimize the size of government, it seems inconsistent to simultaneously advocate the enactment of more regulation to ensure that the private entities that now own and run the relevant assets and activities behave in much the same way their public operators did. Yet to achieve efficiency gains, additional regulation and supervision of the now privatized enterprise is almost always required, especially with regard to natural monopolies or activities for which the competitive environment is currently weak, as it often is with regard to industries or activities in which the government has had a substantial presence.[91] Once we move from public ownership and operation to private ownership and operation, different incentives are in play. Regulation that was unnecessary before because the primary incentive of those in charge was to act in furtherance of the public good is necessary now that the primary incentive is to maximize profits. Without such regulation, what we end up with is an activity that was once supposed to be performed in the public interest and at least sometimes was, and instead have an activity that looks superficially similar but is actually incentivized to cut as many corners as possible in order to maximize shareholder value. One can see this problem, for example, in private prisons, which are notoriously brutal and understaffed because the operators have no profit incentive to make them otherwise,[92] and in the privatization of the collection activities of the

Internal Revenue Service (IRS), which has resulted in a large increase in illegal collection practices and actually less efficient collection of revenue.[93]

Third, if the activities of government are privatized, this does not ensure that these activities will not be performed by government. This merely ensures that they will not be performed by *our own* government. Many of Britain's supposedly privatized train operating companies, for example, are now owned by companies controlled by the Dutch, French, and Chinese governments.[94] This could be prohibited by post-institutional regulation,[95] I suppose, but again this inconsistently increases rather than reduces the size of the relevant government regulatory footprint and in any event would probably run afoul of the applicable equality constraint in force in most countries absent strong national security implications for the activity in question. Which means the principle of privatization reduces to the bizarre idea that government may indeed do lots of things as long as it is *foreign* government, an idea that is hardly consistent with the preservation of liberty for the relevant country's own citizens, despite what the advocates of privatization so often contend.

Fourth, certain functions are inherently governmental and should not be performed by private parties even when they can do so cheaper.[96] Activities such as issuing definitive interpretations of the law, adjudicating guilt or innocence, depriving people of their freedom to come and go as they please, or putting them to death, to cite just some examples, are such grave interferences with liberty that only the government may do these things; they cannot be subcontracted out to private parties without adding insult to the injury to liberty involved. Simply put, there is a difference between being subjected to a body-cavity search by an employee of a private security firm and being subjected to such a search by an employee of the government, just as there is a difference between being executed by a government employee and being executed by a private contractor.[97] And the policy-making functions of government agencies and officials certainly cannot be delegated to private contractors without threatening the democratic process on which our liberty is based, even if such contractors could develop policy and enforce it on a more cost-effective basis. Accountability, transparency, and the proper alignment of incentives all become issues when certain functions are moved from government to private hands. While there can be reasonable disagreement about precisely what functions are inherently governmental, so the precise scope of this objection is controversial,[98] there is a strong argument that there are at least some things that can only be done to us (if they can be done to us at all) if they are done by the government directly, for that is the very basis of the social contract that holds society together.[99] Indeed, it is hard to imagine how anyone concerned with the protection of liberty could be unconcerned with giving certain kinds of powers to private parties merely because they will perform them cheaper. There are at least some moral constraints on what the principle of economic efficiency can do for us, and this makes it highly problematic to rely on that principle alone to determine the proper size of government.

3.2 Public Sector Unionization and the Proper Size of Government 193

Fifth, what do we do about activities that can be performed cheaper by the government but only because it does so without seeking a profit? Presumably everything – or at least a great many things – can be done cheaper by the government if it does so without having to generate a profit, including things the private sector does exclusively already, at least as long as the government goes about doing these things competently. If this principle is construed to make the delivery of goods and services at the cheapest price the criteria for determining what the government should and shouldn't do, it seems to miss a great deal of the point of the small government objection. Indeed, it would turn the principle of efficiency not into a principle recommending small government, but into a principle recommending *enormous* government. The only real limiting factor in this case becomes government incompetence, for in theory, the government should be able to do *everything* cheaper. If we were nevertheless to preclude government from doing things, this would be antithetical to the thinking behind the claim that the most efficient provider should provide the service. And while there is admittedly a long tradition of claiming that government is always incompetent no matter what it tries to do, that it therefore cannot do anything cheaper even though it does not have to earn a profit, and even that its attempts at regulation or intervention in the economy are usually ineffective and often counterproductive,[100] this is patently false.[101] Government may not be able to do everything for lower cost, but it can clearly do some things. Governments that provide medical care, for example, generally do this at a staggeringly lower cost than the United States and the privatized health care system it insists on maintaining.[102] Collection efforts by the IRS are much more efficient than collection that is contracted out.[103] While the US population has grown by 27 percent since 1992, the IRS staff has nevertheless shrunk by 34 percent, producing a significant drop in net tax revenue collected.[104] And similar stories abound.[105] Indeed, across the board, the Project on Government Oversight says, "The government actually pays service contractors at rates far exceeding the cost of employing federal employees to perform comparable functions."[106] And while Government may indeed be unlikely to build a high-quality piece of sophisticated machinery itself, history has shown that without government regulation that piece of machinery is unlikely to be as safe, effective, and as green as it should be or produced under conditions that do not subject workers to unreasonable risks.[107] In any event, if the basis of the objection here was simply incompetence, this would turn capitalism into a second-best form of socialism, and I doubt that many who take this position would be comfortable with the idea of this.

Sixth, the efficiency principle is not actually a limiting principle with regard to the size of government – it is simply an allocative principle, a principle for determining whether a function should be performed by the public or private sector once we have decided on some other basis that it should be performed. It does not help us in determining what functions should be performed. In other words, it may tell us that if we want to go to the moon this should be done by the public sector, but just because something can be done more efficiently by the public sector does not mean it should be done. Presumably there are a great many things that should not be done by the public sector even though if they were going to be done, the public sector could do them more efficiently than the private sector. And if we are to simply say that doing such things is up to the preferences of the electorate, then what we are really saying is that government can be small or enormous depending on what the voters decide. What those who advance the small government position have been telling us, however, is that there is some principle that tells us how big government should be *notwithstanding what the voters may democratically decide*. So the economic efficiency principle necessarily fails to meet the standard set by the small government advocates themselves.

A similar concern arises if we view the small government objection as not a complaint about the size of government *per se* but as a complaint about overregulation, the claim being that the regulations at issue are counterproductive because the cost of compliance exceeds the benefits the regulation provides. This is also, of course, a form of inefficiency objection. The concern here is about government taking a too fine-grained approach to assuring compliance with the requirements of justice, an approach that simply becomes counterproductive because people begin to feel that navigating the regulatory ocean is not worth the journey. This is a concern about government interference in the market in a different sense, the sense in which a referee might be said to interfere with a game by making numerous borderline calls instead of letting the players play, or a sports governing authority might be said to interfere with a game by making the rules so numerous, fine-grained, and invasive that it becomes impossible for anyone to play the game without violating some rule and therefore transforms the game from the competitive contest it was supposed to be into what better resembles a piece of litigation. The thought here is that once the rules of the game are broadly established, it undermines the nature of the game if we try to micromanage it through endlessly more fine-grained regulation and persnickety enforcement, and in the case of an economy, any such attempt is most likely to make its ultimate output less than it would otherwise be.[108]

But it is notoriously difficult to balance the prevention of certain kinds of injuries against monetary cost – just ask those who decided not to incur the fairly modest cost required to fix the Ford Pinto and lessen the danger of gas leakage and explosion following a rear-end collision.[109] Moreover, the kind of cost-benefit analysis that we are discussing here is already a widely embraced limit on government regulation. People may disagree on where to draw the line, but it seems unlikely that there is any principled basis for arguing that this test could require a vast reduction in the current number of government regulations. So it does not seem to be able to do the job that small government advocates need done if their position is to be principled and still support dramatic reductions in the size of government. Even if we were to be able to tweak the cost-benefit analysis so it became a scythe rather than a chisel, this would again simply turn the small government position into a prudential objection not a moral one, so the tenor of the objection would be all wrong given the freedom-enhancing objective the small government objection supposedly advances.

3.2.6 Can "Govern Locally" Serve as a Small Government Principle?

Another possible version of the small government position is to equate big government with centralized government and small government with localized government.[110] Of course, it may be incorrect to even treat this as a small government position – it may be more accurate to treat it is as a form of lightly bounded anarchism.[111] But this need not be the case – just because government is localized does not say anything about the extent to which it will actively insert itself into our lives. Indeed, if anything, the absence of centralized government services would seem to suggest that local government would need to become far more expansive than it is now, for there are undeniably many services that the state and federal government currently provide that people not only appreciate but affirmatively demand. The ancient city-states that those who embrace this view seem to most admire were not versions of a libertarian or neoliberal utopia. Whether government is centralized or localized, one still needs a theory about what it is that government should *do*.[112] Whatever may be the merits of this position or the proper way of characterizing it, however, there is nothing in it that suggests that hostility toward the unionization of public employees is warranted. It is far more likely that localities want the same things that unions do – it is local governments, for example, that are leading the charge for the living wage, and it is state governments, through the use of the power of preemption, that are preventing these local governments from having their way.[113] In any event, unions would seem more likely to oppose the centralization of government, just as they tend to oppose consolidation in industry.

The "govern locally" version of the small government objection also has conceptual problems. Indeed, this is one of the concerns that makes Brexit, the movement to withdraw the United Kingdom from the European Union, so mystifying. It may indeed be true that regulation by seemingly unaccountable bureaucrats in distant Brussels is objectionable, but what about Brexit ensures that bureaucrats in London will be any more accountable and reasonable? Indeed, much of the population in the United Kingdom has complained for years that London is too responsive to the concerns of those in the southeast while being largely unmoved by the concerns of those who live elsewhere. How will that change if the United Kingdom withdraws from the European Union? Is not there every reason to believe it will actually become worse? The point being that the argument for local government actually faces a kind of infinite regress – no matter how local government is, it can always be more local still. And as it becomes more local, it just puts the people who have the power to ignore and abuse others in a different physical locale – it does nothing to prevent such deafness and abuse. Indeed, are not local governments even more susceptible to corruption than state or national ones? Even the family, which is about as local as government can get, can be a form of government that is not responsive to the needs and concerns of some of its members, as each of us well knows. So the issue here is not really whether a government organization is local enough, but whether it is designed and run in such a way that those affected by its decisions not only do but also feel they do have a real voice in its affairs. And there is no reason to think that the more local the government, the moral likely they are to get this right. And when government gets this wrong, the solution is to fix this, not simply take one's ball and go home. Therefore, the "govern locally" version of the small government argument does not make much sense either.

3.2.7 Do We Simply Have More Government Than We Can Afford?

There is one other argument that could be stretched into a sort of principle for smaller government. This is the idea that whatever size government should be, it should not be bigger than we can afford. Because the federal and far too many state and local governments are far too indebted already, the argument goes (and we do seem to be experiencing an unprecedented number of government defaults and bankruptcies), government must be smaller simply because we cannot afford to maintain it at its current levels.[114] Insolvency is also a threat to liberty, for it threatens essential services just like strikes by public employees do (more on this later), and the disfunction created by over indebtedness and the sacrifices required to come out of it can put the very existence of certain communities at risk. Except for those who are really anarchists, those who advocate smaller government concede that we need *some* government in order to protect our basic liberties and especially to protect us each from predation by our neighbors, the most basic threat to liberty. Therefore, the argument from the fear of debt has both a prudential and a moral component. And while this does not really tell us anything about unionization in the public sector, if one were to believe that unions naturally support increases in the size of government and resist efforts to reduce it, and that in addition to the increased cost of bigger government, they also encourage higher wages for public employees and more expensive and allegedly overly generous retirement plans (this, after all, was a major issue in Detroit's bankruptcy), then perhaps there is some causal connection between public debt on public sector unionization. I shall discuss this argument in much further depth at the end of this essay, but for now, I want to take on the purported remedy that those decrying the amount of pubic indebtedness often offer: that reductions in the size and cost of government is in fact the best way to reduce debt in a local economy.

Unfortunately, there is a lot of popular appeal to this argument – after all, every financially responsible adult knows that once you have run out of cash

3.2 Public Sector Unionization and the Proper Size of Government

and are relying instead on ever larger amounts of debt, you have to stop spending and cut back on what you do, or else bad things will happen. But government indebtedness is not like personal, familial, or corporate indebtedness. Austerity in the public sector in all but the most unusual of circumstances will *not* decrease public debt or even help balance the budget on a going forward basis, especially during a recession or times of low economic growth. Indeed, there is a massive amount of empirical evidence available on this question, and it overwhelmingly shows that austerity with regard to government spending and employment is almost always counterproductive – it lowers economic activity to such an extent that it actually increases debt and budget deficits rather than reduces them.[115] And while most of this evidence is based on national economic performance, we now have strong evidence that the same holds true when austerity is practiced on the city or state level too. A city that has poor city services is not an attractive place for businesses that are considering moving out or moving in, as the situation in Detroit shows.[116] Of course, there are other factors at work in the Detroit case as well, but a decline in city services is clearly part of the overall problem of the City's inability to keep and to attract business and maintain its tax base.[117] And on the state level, consider the recent experience of Kansas. There, Governor Sam Brownback, backed until very recently by an ultraconservative state legislature, conducted a "real live experiment" in the effectiveness of supply-side economics and reductions in the size of government by cutting taxes heavily and reducing the number of state employees so much that the state Supreme Court ruled the government was unconstitutionally failing to adequately support public education.[118] Rather than stimulating the state's economy, bringing economic growth and job gains, and producing a balanced budget, Kansas has been one of the worst performers in the nation coming out of the recession with much lower growth and job gains than its neighbors, and it has seen is its revenue drop so precipitously that the state is now mired in an economic crisis.[119] Also Kansas is a lightly unionized longtime right-to-work state,[120] which not only illustrates that despite the claim of anti-union forces to the contrary, public sector unions are not the cause of government indebtedness – neoliberal economic policies that argue for relentlessly reducing taxes and the size of government are doing that all on their own.[121] At least greater union strength might have helped prevent such self-destructive folly. In any event, as a generalized argument against the size of government, the argument from debt is, like all the other versions of the argument for smaller government, simply not supported by a reasonable interpretation of the facts.[122]

3.2.8 If Preserving Liberty Is the Real Concern, Why Ignore the Threat to Liberty Posed by Private Parties?

The lack of any real principle for defining the proper size of government suggests that that some other agenda is really behind the small government argument. And that agenda, it seems, is that small government allows the rich and powerful to impose externalities on and exploit everybody else. Indeed, the whole basis for objecting to the size of government on the grounds it represents a threat to liberty makes no sense if we do not exhibit the same concern with regard to the potential for interference with liberty by private parties. If liberty is important, it hardly matters whether that interference is coming from the government or from a private party. Slavery, remember, was a private enterprise – the government did not own slaves, although it did employ them indirectly by hiring them through their private owners. Both government and private parties can infringe liberty, and government action is sometimes required to protect us from the latter.[123] Indeed, as I have already noted, this is something that European ordoliberals – who are just as committed to the protection of liberty as neoliberals are – realized a long time ago when they saw that private trusts were the great enablers of Hitler's rise to power.[124] It simply makes no sense to worry about liberty only when interference comes from government but not when it comes from private parties.

But government presents a *special* threat to liberty, the explanation goes; after all, government is the *Leviathan*, the vast, multitentacled organism that has intertwined itself with every aspect of our lives. That is why those interested in the defense of liberty focus on it and not on the accumulation of private wealth and power. But there is no such thing as "government" in this sense. At least in a liberal democratic capitalist society, which is the kind of society in which we live, government is nowhere near the monolithic institution that small government advocates make it out to be. Given the separation of powers in force in every advanced capitalist democracy, government power is divided into and distributed over as many differently sized, differently focused and partially if not wholly autonomous and sometimes competing bounded units as private power, and perhaps more. There is not only a federal government, multiple state or provincial governments, and a vast number of local governments; there are countless intergovernmental agencies. There are executive, legislative, judicial, and administrative branches in each, which can and often do act to check the power of their sister branches. The legislative branch is often bicameral; the judicial branch is multilayered and organized into at least two and often three levels of review with each often divided by subject matter as well; the executive branch is subject to more or less but never absolute centralized control; and the administrative branch, which is more or less part of the executive, is typically organized into many, many semiautonomous units with sometimes overlapping authority.[125] The idea that there is a nefarious army of "men in black" at the beck and call of some centrally controlled government hierarchy is the stuff only of Hollywood movies and the internet chatter of uninformed and usually paranoid government-phobes. It is not even true that government has a monopoly on the use of force, and therefore is to be feared more than any private monopolist, when we look at the reality of how a modern democratic society is actually organized. Government is not a single entity, and government units are as likely to be competitively hostile with each other as units within private corporations or as corporations are with one another. The only reason that the "fear of big government" has any visceral bite is that the word government is used collectively and equivocally, promoting a myth that there is such a thing as "government," full stop.

Nor is it true that private concentrations of wealth and power are so insignificant in comparison to government that they are not worth worrying about. We live now in another Gilded Age, where a very small group of individuals (the top hundredth of one percent) have amassed amounts of wealth that are unprecedented since the 1920s, and as we all know, that decade did not end well. Along with that wealth comes enormous political power; look at the political power wielded by the Koch Brothers, Robert and Rebecca Mercer, and other billionaires, including the one currently in the White House, in advancing the agenda of the alt-right. There has also been an unprecedented flurry of mergers and corporate acquisitions leading to huge concentrations of economic (and therefore political) power in the hands of private corporations. At the very least, those concerned with protecting liberty should be concerned with the threat to liberty posed by such individuals and corporations and not exclusively with the supposed threat to liberty by a unitary government that does not actually exist. The fact that they are not suggests that they are not in fact concerned with the preservation of liberty, but the conferral and protection of the power of the ultra-privileged few to continue to dominate the many.[126]

I could go on, but I think I have said enough to illustrate the intellectual bankruptcy of the small government position.[127] Smallness is not a defensible position – size is not a principle, nor even a helpful proxy for one.[128] Indeed, some small government advocates do not even pretend that it is – rather than attempting to provide a principled reason for limiting the size of government, they simply admit that their real motivation is simply to reduce the size and power of unions.[129] Instead of small government being a principled position that may or may not have the side effect of limiting unionization, limiting unionization is used as the reason for shrinking the size of government. Aside from the fact that this objective is not well achieved by shrinking the size of government,[130] it also needs to be independently justified, and as the various arguments I have outlined so far have demonstrated, there is no justification for this to be had, especially not one based on an argument from liberty. In other words, the small government position is essentially unprincipled. Whatever degree of public employment may be necessary for government to perform its proper functions, those who base their opposition to unionization of the public sector on this have so far utterly failed to articulate any principled way of determining how small government should be. What they have articulated is a mere slogan, and a slogan that lacks a principled basis cannot be taken seriously as a basis for a moral argument against public sector unionization.

3.3 THE ESSENTIAL SERVICES ARGUMENT

One of the obvious differences between the public and the private sector is that many workers in the public sector provide essential services; that is, services that we cannot do without, even for short periods. This makes any interruption to such services by a strike of the relevant workers a kind of threat that not only endangers the health, safety, and property of the community as a whole but also that of each of its individual members. It also represents, of course, a threat to liberty, because threats to life and property are seen as threats to the very things that liberty entails. Because of the dire consequences of a strike by those tasked with providing such essential services, in turn, public employees have a degree of bargaining power far greater than that can be brought to bear on private employers. So much bargaining power, in fact, that if public employees were ever in a position to strike, they could effectively subject the public purse to hold up and extortion.

The first thing to note about the essential services argument is that it is not really an argument against public unionization *per se*, although we will see in a moment how its advocates attempt to extend it in this way, but an argument against the right to strike. And of course, as an argument against the right to strike, it does express some valid concerns.[131] Which is why even when public employees are permitted to unionize, most public sector union members (in fact, about 80 percent) do not have a legally recognized right to strike.[132] But while this ban on strikes is ridiculously overinclusive – nothing like 80 percent of public employees provide services to which a mere temporary disruption could threaten lives and property – my argument does not claim that unionized public employees must have a right to strike. This is a matter for post-institutional regulation and is to be considered on a case-by-case basis depending on the nature of the services provided. For example, fire, police, and emergency services would be essential in the relevant sense, and therefore the employees of such services should not be given the right to strike.[133] Garbage collection and many other services would not be, or at least would not be unless a certain degree of disorder was reached, and thus unions of such employees could be permitted to strike until that degree of disorder was reached and employees ordered back to work by the declaration of the relevant executive official, a kind of authority that the executive holds now even with regard to strikes in the private sector.[134] And some public employees would not raise this specter of disruption of essential services at all, and therefore would have the right to strike and stay out as long as they saw fit subject to the usual rules about continuing to be willing to engage in good-faith negotiations.[135] Moreover, even unions of public employees that have a right to strike may and often will bargain away that right for contractual concessions from the relevant employer, and these contractual bans may then be enforced by injunction. In any event, the fact the we already have public sector unions that do not have the right to strike is proof that unionization does not have to entail this right when it puts essential services at risk.

3.3 The Essential Services Argument

But can we rely on unions in the public sector to comply with rules that deprive them of the right to strike, whether statutory or contractual? If unions of public employees were to routinely ignore such bans, then this would suggest that there is no way to ensure the continuous delivery of essential services if we allow public employees to be unionized. And there is an infamous example of just this kind of problem: the strike by the Professional Air Traffic Controllers Organization (PATCO) in 1981, which occurred despite the fact that the strike was unambiguously illegal under federal law. Remember, however, that all of the striking air traffic controllers were fired by President Reagan after they refused to return to work, replacements for these fired workers were then hired, and the union was effectively broken.[136] So anti-strike provisions can indeed be enforced. No one was physically hurt by the strike, no property was damaged or even put at risk, and normal commercial flights were not even seriously disrupted, although it did take several years and billions of dollars (much more than PATCO had gone on strike over) to return the nation's air traffic control system to its prestrike levels.[137] In any event, the lesson that public employees are unlikely to profit from an illegal strike has apparently been well learned, for there have been no significant attempts by federal workers to illegally strike in the more than thirty-five years since the PATCO incident.[138] Indeed, air traffic controllers themselves are now members of another union (the National Air Traffic Controllers Association, or NATCA), which arose out of PATCO's dust, and there have been no further strike threats there, even when controllers were forced to work without pay during the February 2019 government shutdown, although they did reasonably point out that the shutdown was imperiling air safety by encouraging its members to quit or call in sick so that they could take other employment and pay their bills as they came due, all of which suggests that the union here was trying to protect essential services, not undermine them.[139] Transportation Safety Administration (TSA) workers also did not threaten to strike, despite being unionized and also having to work by law without pay, nor did Federal Bureau of Investigation (FBI) agents or any of the other federal workers forced to work during the shutdown.[140] Strikes by state and local workers who do not have a right to strike are also rare, which is one reason why the recent West Virginia teachers' strikes were so notable.[141] Even *legal* strikes of public workers have been almost nonexistent since the PATCO debacle, despite years and years of stagnant pay.[142] In any event, given how rare unlawful strikes seem to be, the fear of unlawful strikes does not seem to be a valid reason for discouraging public sector unionization.

However, there is one final wrinkle on the essential services argument that we need to consider. This is that no matter how essential or nonessential a particular public service may be, a strike by public sector workers works differently than a strike by private sector workers. In the public sector, strikers inflict injury not on their employers by depriving them of profit, but on those third parties who look to these public service entities for services. This is especially true in areas where there are no private alternatives to the services that public workers provide (people affected by an airline strike can simply travel on a different airline, but everybody is seriously inconvenienced by a strike by a commuter rail network).[143] This is a common refrain raised by the anti-union right in response to the recent spate of teachers' strikes. For example, the State Policy Network (SPN), a right-wing organization funded largely by conservative billionaires whose current mission seems to be to advise conservatives on how to discredit striking teachers and the rise in support for increased funding for public education that the success of these strikes represents.[144] In a recent memo to interested parties, the SPN points out:

> A message that focuses on teacher hours or summer vacations will sound tone-deaf when there are dozens of videos and social media posts going viral from teachers about their second jobs, teachers having to rely on food pantries, classroom books that are falling apart, paper rationing, etc. [...] It is also not the right time to talk about school choice—that's off topic, and teachers at choice-schools are often paid less that district school teachers.[145]

Instead, the SPN memo continues, those trying to undermine public sympathy for teachers should try to shift the focus from the teachers' complaints (ignoring, apparently, the fact that these include grave concerns for the ability of their students to learn in an environment that is being starved of resources) to concerns about how kids might suffer from not being in school during the strike: "It's unfortunate that teachers are protesting low wages by punishing other low-wage parents and their children."[146] A similar messaging strategy was also apparently behind Kentucky Republican Governor Matt Bevin's claim that "I guarantee you somewhere in Kentucky today, a child was sexually assaulted that was left at home because there was nobody there to watch them."[147] Although Bevin's claim did not have the refocusing effect he intended – indeed, it provoked such a backlash of criticism he had to apologize for it – there is a sense in which the more restrained version of these indirect causal claims about the effects of strikes on third parties in the public sector is correct – the leverage exerted here is not denying the employer profit, as it is for strikes in the private sector. Indeed, strikes actually may save the relevant public entity money, for its payroll is reduced and it can simply require supervisory personnel to temporarily cover for missing workers without paying these supervisors more, for they are not entitled to overtime. What strikes by public sector workers actually do is exert leverage by subjecting public officials to criticism for their prior funding and budget decisions.[148] The causal chain here is indeed longer and less direct. But that does not amount to an argument against public sector unionization.

First, as I have already said, the recognition of public unions does not have to carry with it the right to strike. Even if there might be some occasions on which the assignment of partial or even primary causal responsibility to striking workers for any injury to third parties might have some limited validity, this does not provide a reason for denying public sector workers the right to be represented by unions and have these union bargain collectively on their behalf. Second, the claim that it is unjust to inflict suffering on third parties in order to influence the behavior of someone else is not as unassailable as these critics of public sector unionization like to pretend. Indeed, when we punish anybody, there are often collateral effects on "innocent" third parties, and sometimes quite significant effects. Imagine, for example, the effect on the family of a drug dealer or other criminal of putting him in jail. This is not a reason to hold punishment that is otherwise justly deserved unjust.[149] Even directly threatening and punishing third parties for whom the intended target cares about is sometimes used as a means of enforcement, and this is not considered necessarily morally wrong – it is, for example, what we do when we require that a family member forfeit bail when a criminal defendant fails to appear.[150] And of course, public sector workers who go on strike can also take steps to ameliorate the effects on third parties, as the West Virginia teachers did.[151] Finally, and most importantly, if the strike is for a just reason then it is the employer – that is, the public entity involved – that is primarily causally responsible for inflicting suffering on third parties, not those who are attempting to stand up against their own mistreatment. This is why there was such a negative reaction to the Kentucky governor's sexual molestation comments – the causal claim the governor made when he tried to blame striking teachers for any child abuse that happened to children who were not in school was a causal claim too far. Assigning causal responsibility requires the consideration of the causal role of many factors, and very few of the factors that make a causal contribution are properly assigned causal responsibility. Almost every major bridge ever built, for example, and almost every other major construction project ever undertaken, has resulted in someone's death or serious injury on the construction crew. But we do not blame this on the decision to undertake construction. What we are looking for when we are assigning causal responsibility is the point in the causal chain where future human intervention would be most appropriate.[152] Under that standard, the primary cause of any injury to third parties resulting from a strike is the public entity's refusal to act reasonably toward its employees. And while there may be occasions when the demands of striking workers are unreasonable, history tells us that this is relatively rare, not least because unreasonable demands are unlikely to be satisfied and therefore ultimately going to leave striking workers worse off. In any event, depriving public workers who provide nonessential services the right to unionize because if they strike and thereby interfere with their employer's power to mistreat them this might have some collateral effects on third parties, is not something that any theory of justice worth taking seriously would endorse.

3.4 THE ARGUMENT AGAINST COLLECTIVE BARGAINING

The argument against collective bargaining by public employees is potentially far more devastating than the one against the right to strike, for unlike the right to strike, the right to bargain collectively is one of the core functions of the union. Opposition to collective bargaining is simply opposition to unionization in a seemingly more indirect and therefore superficially more palatable form,[153] for unions without the right to bargain collectively are not really what we usually think of as unions at all. Of course, that said, there are still things that unions can do even without the right to bargain collectively, which is why public sector unions still exist even in states where they are denied the right to bargain collectively, albeit with far fewer members.[154] For example, public employee unions have helped pass local minimum wage laws in North Carolina, even though unions there lack collective bargaining rights.[155] Also, the recent teachers' strike in West Virginia, where unions also lack collective bargaining rights, shows us that public employees can nevertheless still engage in collective action and force wage concessions out of their employers.[156] Indeed, in the wake of the West Virginia experience, teachers in other states that lack collective bargaining rights have been pursuing similar tactics and also having some success.[157] Therefore, prohibiting collective bargaining by public employees won't necessarily kill the public-sector union movement, it will simply make organizing strikes more difficult and dangerous and bargaining over wages, hours, working conditions, and benefits more cumbersome and inefficient. Indeed, when employees lack collective bargaining rights, strikes will tend to happen only when employees have become so desperate they feel they have nothing left to lose, a state of affairs likely to produce conflicts that are going to be even uglier than they need be, and this, of course, is not good for anybody.[158]

Which is why, of course, unions have fought so hard for so long for the right to bargain collectively. And this fight, all things considered, has been pretty successful. While "only two percent of public employees had the right to bargain collectively in 1960, by 2010, that share had grown to 63 percent."[159] Of course, this is why limiting or even banning collective bargaining by public employees is a focal point of many of the attacks against public sector unionization today.[160] The strategy of attacking collective bargaining rights rather than trying to ban unionization outright also has the benefit of seeming less extreme, making it easier to sell to a potentially skeptical public, as Governor Walker's successful assault on public unions in a state with a long history of support for the union movement proves.[161] The Wisconsin ban on collective bargaining was even able to pass constitutional muster, at least in the Wisconsin Courts.[162]

While there has been no definitive ruling on this yet by the US Supreme Court, it is nevertheless important to take note of the grounds of the Wisconsin Supreme Court's ruling in order to see how this might have an impact on what I am arguing here. In *Madison Teachers, Inc. v. Walker*,[163] the Court rejected the argument that banning (most) collective bargaining by public employees (under the Wisconsin statute, public employees are still permitted to bargain collectively regarding base wages) was an impermissible infringement of union members' constitutional right to free association. There are many aspects of

3.4 The Argument against Collective Bargaining

the court's reasoning that are questionable, but rather than go into a detailed discussion of this here, I simply want to point out that my argument is not that the right to free association entails a right to bargain collectively, which was the primary argument advanced by the union in the Wisconsin case. The right of freedom of association is a derivative right entailed by the right to republican liberty, which is a fundamental moral right regardless of whether it is expressly enshrined in anyone's constitution.[164] But the right to free association is not the *only* right entailed by our commitment to republican liberty. Accordingly, even if a right to bargain collectively were not entailed by the right of free association, this would not mean that the right to bargain collectively should not be part of what universal unionization requires. Freedom of association is certainly an important aspect of the right to universal unionization – it explains why unions have a right to exist. But collective bargaining is better seen as derived from republican liberty directly, and not as a derivative right of the itself derivative right of freedom of association. Our commitment to republican liberty is what makes unionization something that the dominant protective association would be required to defend, as I argued in the first essay in this volume, and this is also what makes it a basic institution, as I argued in the second. Together this is what makes collective bargaining an irreducible core function of unionization. At least it does as long as there are no republican liberty-based arguments to suggest that the right to collectively bargain can be permissibly limited. And so this is the issue that I will be focusing on here.

Note that there are two different republican liberty-based arguments against collective bargaining. One is that collective bargaining with public unions is undemocratic; the other is that it is unfair to taxpayers because it produces excessive salaries and benefits or at least makes these greater than they need be and therefore arbitrarily increases the cost of government at a time when the public purse is already being strained to the breaking point. The Wisconsin statute banning most collective bargaining by public employees, for example, was enacted as a part of what was promoted as a "budget repair bill." The argument that austerity is required in the wake of the Great Recession and that this requires limiting the collective bargaining rights of public sector unions has otherwise proved both popular and successful.[165] Even so, in my view the argument from democracy is in many ways the stronger of the two arguments here. But it is also the more complex, so I shall deal with it in the next section. In this section, I take on the claim that the unionization of public employees ends up being unfair to taxpayers, in effect violating their republican liberty by subjecting them to arbitrary treatment, forcing them to pay what are alleged to be unjustified taxes, taxes they in fact cannot afford.

The idea behind this latter claim can itself be broken down into two parts. First, we have the claim that collective bargaining leads to excessive public salaries – eliminate collective bargaining, and public employees will no longer be paid more than they deserve.[166] The second part, rarely expressed outright, is that regardless of whether public salaries are excessive or not, they are greater than they would be if collective bargaining was not allowed (state and local government workers who are covered by a union contract earn between 10.7 and 13.6 percent more in hourly wages than their nonunion counterparts),[167] and this in turn, makes taxes arbitrarily high and unjustified. Not only is this a violation of republican liberty, it is also antithetical to the common good, for keeping taxes as low as they can be leaves more money to be spent in the private economy. Indeed, the claim goes, this is absolutely essential if we are to keep the economy humming, especially in times of financial stress.

The first claim, of course, is an empirical one, although it does depend on what one defines as excessive. But there is currently much anecdotal evidence that public sector pay is if anything woefully low, not excessive.[168] More systematized empirical evidence that public sector pay is not excessive is now accumulating at a rapid pace as well.[169] Indeed, the most recent evidence suggests that public employment, once a secure ticket to the middle class, no longer pays enough to fund even this modest lifestyle.[170] More workers employed by the federal government make less than $15 an hour than at any other employer in the United States.[171] Many public sector workers are struggling to pay rent and to meet other standard living expenses, and are just one unexpected expense away from a financial crisis.[172] Claims that public sector pay *is* excessive usually compare average private sector pay with average public sector pay. Even if that comparison were valid, it would hardly have much moral force if public sector workers cannot live on what they are being paid – if it were a fact that public sector workers are less exploited than private sector workers, that is not a compelling moral reason to level down and cut public sector worker pay, although that is effectively what those on the anti-union right are arguing.[173] Indeed, in every other context leveling down is almost universally morally condemned, especially by the (mostly anti-union) rich, for it would require lowering their income regardless of whether this increased the income of the poor.[174]

Even if it were appropriate in some circumstances, however, leveling down would not be appropriate here because it is not true that public sector workers are doing better than private sector workers. The average private sector worker is simply not the appropriate comparative. The average public sector worker has more education and more organizational responsibility than the average private sector worker. Also, given the nature of the public sector, public sector workers are more like private sector workers in large firms than in small ones, and they are also far more likely to work for a unionized employer. When the comparisons are adjusted so we are comparing like with like, public sector workers are actually at least marginally underpaid, and perhaps substantially underpaid.[175] And they are still underpaid *even when fringe benefits such as pensions are included* – in most cases, the consideration of fringe benefits merely brings them up to even with regard to total compensation.[176] Moreover,

3.4 The Argument against Collective Bargaining

because these benefits are being rapidly eroded, the comparative situation here for unionized public employees is actually getting worse.[177] Public school teachers, for example, made 1.8 percent less than their private school counterparts in 1994, but despite being heavily unionized, they made a record 17 percent less in 2015 (and still 11.1 percent less when benefits are included).[178] Indeed, teacher pay is so low in some public school districts that they are having to look for new teachers overseas.[179] At the very least, this shows that unionization of the public sector does not necessarily produce salaries or even total compensation packages that are anywhere close to being out of control.

Another indication that public salaries are not excessive is that state budget deficits are almost entirely insensitive to whether the state allows collective bargaining.[180] (I shall deal with the claim that public unions are bankrupting us later; for now, the issue is more precise: whether affording public employees the right to bargain collectively increases the size of a state's budget deficit, and it does not). So, the factual basis of the claim that collective bargaining leads to excessive wages and benefits is weak, at best. This leaves the real argument against collective bargaining by public employees as this: even if public salaries and benefits are not excessive, they are still higher than they would otherwise be – indeed, this is the whole point of unionization. And if wages and benefits were lower, taxes could be lower, and this would benefit everybody, even public employees, by leaving more work to be done in the private sector. Collective bargaining is therefore contrary to the common good, and because it makes taxes higher than they need to be, it makes those taxes arbitrary, infringing the republican liberty of everyone who is required to pay them.

But it is not even clear that the argument that lower public sector wages and benefits would permit lower taxes and/or greater services is true. When the economy is in need of stimulation, public employment is an important tool to do so, for every dollar of public spending probably contributes something like $1.30 to the economy.[181] Combined with other kinds of public spending, this "multiplier effect" can add enough to the economy to bring it out of the doldrums all by itself, or so Keynesian economists have long argued.[182] And if this does provide enough stimulation to the economy, the difference between unionized and nonunionized public salaries could effectively pay for itself. Indeed, we can find some support for this idea in the fact that the great drop-off in public employment following the Great Recession was a major reason why the recovery from that recession was so slow and, even now, is still rather unimpressive.[183]

But let's assume that the claim that lower public wages and benefits would permit lower taxes and/or greater services is true. Just because this would be an effect of banning collective bargaining by public employees does not make this an argument for doing so. Taxpayers are not entitled to obtain services for less than a just price, by which I mean the cost of production,[184] nor are they entitled to take advantage of the unequal bargaining power individuals have in dealing with any large organization even if this merely allows them to lower the amount they are then paid to the lower end of the just price range. Violating the doctrine of the just price and committing exploitation are infringements of republican liberty, and therefore not permitted even if these violations would lower taxes.[185] The principle of equality, of course, is also in operation here. Taxpayers are workers too, and if they benefit from being members of unions in the private sector that bargain collectively, equality requires that they cannot be legitimately denied those same benefits in the public sector. Indeed, if private sector unions were not permitted to bargain collectively, then the cost of goods and services in the private sector would be somewhat lower too, although not dollar for dollar lower, as some of these savings and perhaps even most or all of it would be used to increase profits. But no one worthy of being taken seriously argues that this is a reason to prohibit collective bargaining in the private sector. In any case, the mere fact that many people benefit in some sense from the exploitation of the few does not justify encouraging anyone to engage in such behavior.

The real argument here accordingly seems to be ideological – it is not the cost to taxpayers that those who attack the collective bargaining rights of public sector unions really object to, it is the fact that unions tend to encourage their members to support candidates fielded by the Democratic Party rather than the Republican Party.[186] If the collective bargaining rights of public sector unions are limited or eliminated, the thought among right-wing groups clearly goes, this will reduce the membership of such unions and thereby reduce their political influence dramatically, which cannot help but hurt the policies advanced by Democrats and help those advanced by Republicans, especially conservative Republicans.[187] But this is true of private unions too.[188] In either case, this cannot be the basis of a legitimate objection to unionization, because if we were to count this as a valid reason for government to limit the rights of unions, this would violate the limitation that liberalism places on government action, which requires the government to remain neutral between competing reasonable comprehensive conceptions of the good.[189] And as I have already shown in the first essay in this volume, this limitation would hold even in a libertarian utopia. In any event, while permitting unionization of the public sector may not be neutral in effect if such unions do tend to be more supportive of the Democratic Party than the Republican Party, such permission is neutral in justification. That is, the decision to permit unionization does not depend on the acceptance of some particular comprehensive conception of the good. As Rawls tells us, this is the relevant form of neutrality that any liberal capitalist government must respect.[190] Besides, permitting public sector workers to concentrate their economic power can only serve to offset, not overwhelm the economic power of the public monopolies for which they work, just as collective bargaining in the private sector merely serves to partially offset, not overwhelm, the economic and political power of large corporations and industry associations. If such organizations cannot be suppressed by government for their political views, organizations that allow workers to pool their economic power cannot be suppressed by the government either, even if they are in the public sector.

3.5 ARE PUBLIC SECTOR UNIONS UNDERMINING OUR DEMOCRACY?

The claim that public sector unionization, or at least collective bargaining by public employees, is undermining our democracy may strike many as particularly odd. At one time, perhaps, one of the express goals of the union movement was to undermine capitalism and the liberal democratic regimes associated with it and replace these with socialist undemocratic ones – a "dictatorship of the proletariat."[191] But this has long since ceased to be the case in Europe,[192] and never really was the case in the United States.[193] On its surface, then, the claim that public sector unionization is antithetical to democracy seems especially disingenuous, for it is designed to play on exaggerated fears that unionization was at one time a subversive force that wanted to turn capitalist societies into socialist ones and could become this once again. The argument is even more difficult to comprehend, however, if we think of it as a claim that because unions in the United States tend to support the Democratic Party and its candidates and policies,[194] this is somehow unfair to those who support opposing views because unions should be apolitical. First, it is not universally or even overwhelmingly true that unions support Democratic candidates and policies. Police and firefighter unions and unions of prison guards tend to support Republican candidates and policies, Richard Nixon had powerful support among and was actually endorsed by the Teamsters, Ronald Reagan was elected in part with the support of the white working class even when unionization was much stronger than it is today, and in the topsy-turvy world of Trumpism, members of some unions are among his biggest supporters.[195] Unions in fact do not always support Democrats and their policy initiatives, and even when they do, union support is not always decisive, even in heavily unionized states.[196] Indeed, even when unions do expressly support certain policy proposals, their funds may sometimes be used to fund the opposition as well, as was recently revealed to be the case with various rent-control propositions in California, where the investment manager Blackstone, which has ties to Donald Trump, "used money taken from real estate investments funded by California public employees" to oppose union-supported ballot measures.[197] But more importantly, the argument from democracy not only confuses neutrality in effect (what unions tend to do) with neutrality in justification (what unions are free to do), it also ignores the fact that many countries have a political party formally associated with the labor movement, such as the Labour Party in the United Kingdom, and these countries are nevertheless widely considered to be thriving democracies. How could an even looser connection between labor and a particular political party in the United States possibly put democracy at risk?[198]

3.5.1 The Historical Roots of the Claim

There is, however, a far more sophisticated version of this ideological argument that is not sufficiently addressed simply by distinguishing between neutrality in justification and neutrality in effect. And this is that it is not the particular beliefs that unions tend to advocate that makes them objectionable, it is that they advance these views in a way that is undemocratic.[199] This argument goes back to at least the 1940s,[200] but perhaps its most vociferous proponent in the United States was Sylvester Petro, who began developing and advancing it in the late 1950s.[201] Petro described public sector unionism as "irreconcilable with representative government" and claimed that if public sector collective bargaining was made compulsory, "the time will have arrived for us to take to the hills and the fields and the caves once more, as our ancestors have frequently had to do when integral – sovereign – government has broken down."[202] Essentially, Petro argued that government cannot be sovereign and yet be compelled to bargain collectively with its employees, much less be compelled to actually perform whatever agreements this collective bargaining process produces.[203] Petro said:

> In order for an institution to be a government, it needs to have undivided and unchallengeable power to perform the functions it assumes or has allocated to it by its constituents. It does not matter what the functions are, to repeat. It is all the same whether we are talking about the military, the law courts, the police or fire departments, sanitation agencies, publicly owned and operated transportation systems or other public utilities, or the public schools. In the American system, the point is peculiarly easy to grasp, because we operate on the theory that our governments should take on only supremely important tasks – those considered too vital to be left undone or even to be left to the vagaries of the market. Hence, for us, the unchallengeable, undivided nature of the authority and power appropriate to our governments within their respective spheres should go without saying. Either that or we are witless contradictory fools.[204]

And

> When the power of government to govern is challengeable from within by its own human instruments, organized civil servants, it ought in respect to the serviceableness of meaningful language no longer to be called government at all. It ought to be called pseudogovernment.[205]

Indeed, to Petro, public servants are no different than soldiers in the military, and therefore have no right to question orders or rules generated by their commanders, whether these be military generals or their counterparts in civilian service.[206]

But this is nonsense. There are all sorts of limits on government power in every democracy – indeed, the whole idea of political liberalism as a form of government is that government is not to be "unchallengeable" but limited, and those limits are generally seen as essential guarantees of liberty, not as

3.5 Are Public Sector Unions Undermining Our Democracy?

impediments to it. The small government argument that we considered earlier, in fact, takes the idea that government must be limited as its fundamental presupposition, even if fails to explain how the principle of "smallness" can be coherently cashed out. As well as there being countless external limits on government power, there are all sorts of limits that operate from within. Indeed, this is why government is not "undivided," as Petro claims it should be, but separated and compartmentalized in various ways and subject to all sorts of internal checks and balances. This ensures that no individual government unit or official becomes too powerful, something that again is generally seen as an essential guarantee of freedom. Thus, Petro's argument that public servants should be just that – servants, if not slaves – and that the preservation of democracy and the liberty that it ensures requires this, is a perversion of everything for which both democracy and liberty are otherwise thought to stand.

Moreover, Petro's argument would seem to prove too much. It not only prohibits collective bargaining, but individual bargaining as well, for in either case the government is being bound. Because government must always be free to change its mind, it cannot be subject to the normal rules that apply to contracts in either case, at least not when those contracts are with its servants, who are viewed as mere instruments of elected officials and therefore in some other class of being than members of the general public. This is the kind of government liberty (and government employee subservience) that is generally seen as essential to fascist governments, not democratic ones. Indeed, there is an uncomfortable degree of fascist thought in Petro's argument, beginning with the individual who Petro chooses to quote in the opening of his later major work. This is Oswald Spengler, who even *The American Conservative* labels a fascist, and who believed that a Caesarian dictatorship was the best form of government.[207] What this suggests is that the kind of liberty that Petro was most interested in protecting was neither negative liberty nor republican liberty nor even economic liberty, but rather the form of positive liberty embraced by the likes of Nietzsche and those fascists who drew inspiration from his work.[208] There is also reason to suspect that Petro's arguments were in part a reaction to the civil rights movement, for public employment was one of the first places that black people and other minorities could find the kind of secure employment that was then often being denied them in the private sector.[209] In any event, Petro's claims – at least in the extreme versions he expressly advanced – are clearly antithetical to liberty, not entailed by it. Which is probably why they did not really catch on at the time beyond the extreme fringes of the right.

But now that public sector unionization has become more significant, and extreme right-wing views more politically acceptable and marketable, his ideas are being resurrected.[210] Indeed, the fact that unionization rates are now so much higher in the public sector than in the private sector is held out as evidence that there has indeed been something nefarious going on in the public sector, for why wouldn't unionization rates otherwise be the same? Of course, the answer to the latter point is that the public sector has not seen the kinds of jobs that are easiest to unionize decline through the effects of globalization and the implementation of new technology that has eroded unionization in the private sector, and, until relatively recently, it has not been subject to the kind of vigorous attacks to which private sector unionization has long been subject. So the fact that unionization rates are much higher today in the public sector than in the private sector is not evidence that there has been something fishy going on in any sense in the public sector.

This, however, does not answer the claim that the unionization of public employees is undemocratic in itself, for this claim does not depend on showing that public bodies and/or officials have actually been corrupted or the democratic process undermined by the application of union power or money, but merely that it could be. Strictly speaking, it is not a consequentialist claim, but a conceptual one, even though it is often presented with many supposedly supportive examples. In any event, once stripped of the hyperbolic quality of Petro's original presentation of it, the claim is that unionization gives public employees a disproportionate voice in the democratic process, when the bedrock of our democracy is that everyone's voice should have equal weight.[211] Whether they use this advantage in a way that undermines liberty, equality, or the common good is technically beside the point.

3.5.2 The Argument from Disproportionate Influence

Of course, it is no doubt true that unions (should and sometimes do) give their members more of a voice in certain government decisions (the decisions that affect their members most directly) than certain other individuals who are not members of that particular union might have. But this is also true in a wide variety of other circumstances. For example, because the electoral college gives each state two *extra* votes regardless of population (representing one vote for each senator), it gives the residents of sparsely populated rural states a greater proportionate voice then those in densely populated mostly urbanized ones, an effect that had undeniably huge antidemocratic consequences in the last presidential election for it resulted in Donald Trump prevailing over Hillary Clinton even though Clinton received almost three million more actual votes.[212] The tortured drawing of congressional district lines has also long been criticized for intentionally and permanently disenfranchising various groups of poor, urban, and minority voters.[213] In the aftermath of the 2010 census, however, "Republican-controlled state governments in the United States engaged in a nationally coordinated effort of unprecedented scale to gerrymander election districts for state legislatures and the U.S. House of Representatives."[214] And this effort was undeniably successful. In the 2016 elections for the House, for example, Republican candidates won fewer than 50 percent of the votes, yet won more than 55 percent of the seats.²¹⁵ While many lower federal courts subsequently ruled that at least blatantly partisan gerrymandering was unconstitutional, in June 2019 the US Supreme Court upheld the practice.²¹⁶ This decision will no doubt redouble the efforts of Republican state legislatures to erode any meaningful version of proportional representation entirely and thereby capitalize on their already gerrymandered advantage. In such an environment, claiming that unionization poses a threat to democracy is simply ludicrous. If we are to respect our democratic traditions, giving union members a louder electoral voice is more necessary than ever.

This is especially true because those behind efforts to deprive parts of the population of an equal voice are still not satisfied. The enactment of voter ID laws and other voting restrictions by already gerrymandered states has also exploded, and these restrictions have had an even further disproportionate impact on poor and minority voters, depriving many of their right to vote entirely.²¹⁷ And of course, even without such restrictions, the rich have long been accused of having a greater voice than the poor.²¹⁸ So have corporations, which even though they cannot vote are often seen as having a greater voice than individual voters because corporations are richer and therefore can more easily capture politicians in desperate need of campaign contributions, especially after the *Citizens United* decision, which allowed corporations to make unlimited "independent" expenditures on political campaigns (that is, expenditures that are not coordinated with any particular campaign).²¹⁹ And of course, millions of registered voters don't actually vote, thereby affording the votes of those that do a greater influence in the overall outcome of elections than they proportionately deserve.²²⁰ Given that the overwhelming majority of those who are most vocally anti-union press no objection against any of these arguably much more significant examples of how certain people may come to have a disproportionate influence in our democratic process (presumably because they favor the viewpoints these other disproportionately empowered groups or individuals support),²²¹ we could simply dismiss the anti-union objection here as hypocritical and therefore regard it as not entitled to be taken seriously.²²²

But I shall not do that. Instead, I shall focus on whether the unionization of public employees does indeed create a conceptual threat to the democratic processes. In making that determination, however, we must keep these other distortions in mind. Not because two (or three or four) wrongs somehow make another wrong a right – to the extent that any of these imperfections in our democratic procedures lead to problematic imbalances in political influence they are unacceptable, and it would be better to correct them if we can. But no system of democracy is perfect – some distortions that give one group more power than it might have on a strict head-count basis are unavoidable, or at least impractical to address, and the only feasible way to correct for this in whole or in part may be to give the power of some unfairly disadvantaged group a boost. In considering the argument that the unionization of public employees is inconsistent with our conception of democracy, we cannot therefore pretend that the mere fact that unions increase the political power of their members is dispositive of that question. To the extent this increase merely serves to offset some otherwise difficult to address unfair imbalance in proportional political power, it is not necessarily a wrong but may simply be a remedy.

Another key point to remember here is that no government operates on the principle of direct democracy – that is, the view that everyone should have a direct and equal say in everything government does. With regard to broad questions of policy, perhaps direct democracy has a place as a way of gauging the view of the entire electorate regarding a particular issue and not just on who should hold a particular national or statewide office, as long as that issue is simple and straightforward. The problem is that this latter quality often appears as an illusion – consider the staggeringly complex and seemingly irresolvable practical difficulties raised by the momentous Brexit referendum, which at least initially seemed to many to be something that could easily be phrased as an up or down question. But when the issue to be decided is much less important and we are dealing with regulating the minutiae of our day-to-day life, as a way of devising government policy, direct democracy is often a disaster.[223] It is a prescription for paralysis or worse, an opening for irrationality, for the fine-tuning and careful balancing of competing interests required to justly regulate a modern industrialized society simply cannot take place through the popular initiative process.[224] Only with the kind of back and forth adjustment that as a practical matter is possible only between *representatives* of the larger electorate can we produce rules that are in "reflective equilibrium" with our considered judgment, which can with stand what Rawls calls the "strains of commitment" (the reasons why people may urge renegotiation or even defiance of rules that impose burdens upon them, even though such rules were enacted through impeccable democratic procedures), and that can be the focus of the kind of "overlapping consensus" that is necessary for any society to be governed effectively.[225]

Besides, even direct democracy can be heavily (and many would say improperly) influenced by those with enough money to organize effective grassroots campaigns and/or finance large and sophisticated advertising campaigns.[226] Indeed, some of the most ferocious voices on the anti-union right are actually against direct democracy because they fear that unions can too easily capture the public initiative process and therefore use the availability of such a procedure to sidestep the normal legislative process, and they cite this as one of the reasons that unions should not be allowed to exist. It is hard to take this argument seriously, however, given that those with money on the right have long used their money amplify the volume of their views and thereby disproportionately influence the democratic process and continue to do so to this day. Their long-standing and continued access to and defense of their own disproportionate voice seriously undercuts the

3.5 Are Public Sector Unions Undermining Our Democracy? 215

argument that what is improper about unions is that they allegedly have a disproportionate voice in the law-making process and that this is antithetical to our fundamental notions of democracy.[227] But the more important point to note here is that no one who believes that democracy is the best way to secure liberty could reasonably believe that direct democracy is the best way to achieve this. Indeed, the idea of *total* direct democracy – the claim that true democracy requires everyone to have an equal voice with regard to every government decision – is closer to the beliefs of fascist political philosophers, for the fascist conception of democracy is that the people and the leader are one, united in their views about everything; thus, any mediating bodies between them interfere with their liberty rather than support it.[228] Instead, the kind of democracy we embrace in a liberal society is *representative* democracy – the idea that people should pool their resources and promote their views through representatives in an ever shrinking circle of elected decision makers, which is exactly what public sector unions do. Given this approach, it is necessarily true that not every nuance in attitude present in the wider circle of the electorate will be given its true proportional weight in the decision-making process employed in an inner circle. So the amplification of power of those in each ever more concentrated inner circle, even though this results in some views in the outer circles being filtered out, is part of the nature of representative democracy, and not a defect in it. The mere fact that unions have more influence than their members would if they were not members of a union, and that the group voice of the union may dampen rather than amplify the dissenting views of some of its members, is therefore not an argument against unionization, for this is entailed by and not contrary to the nature of representative democracy itself.

This is another reason why it is not an argument against public unions that they amplify the political power of a certain group with left-leaning tendencies, for all organizations of like-minded people amplify the voices of their members. If anything, public unions simply provide some balance to what is already a system that is heavily stacked in favor of the right. The problem is not that left-leaning institutions with money threaten to exert untoward influence on our government; it is that all institutions, organizations, and individuals with large amounts of money threaten to do this and without public unions these sources of influence are far more likely to be right-leaning. And even when unions contribute heavily to election campaigns, they can easily be outspent by those with an anti-union or otherwise opposing agenda. The recent elections to the Los Angeles School Board, which runs the largest school district in the country, is an example. There, unions contributed millions to the election, but they were still outspent 2 to 1 by outside interests attempting to promote charter schools, which are not unionized. And in this case, the monetary advantage proved effective. Even though charter schools often have a dismal record of student achievement, are plagued by corruption, and employ enrollment policies that violate federal law, the union-backed candidates lost.[229] So union support is no guarantee that the candidates and issues that they favor will prevail.

Oddly enough, those on the anti-union right often deny this – that is, they deny that without unions, business owners and trade associations would have unchecked or even disproportionate lobbying power.[230] And it is true that unions are not the only organizations that can be counted on to lobby for the interests of the individual worker – there are also public-interest organizations funded largely by small individual contributions that can be counted on to lobby for the interests of those who are not individually wealthy or powerful.[231] But the interests of these organizations are naturally far wider than the interests of public employees and accordingly tend to be primarily directed elsewhere, so they cannot be counted on to always take up the defense of public employees even when the members of these organizations are sympathetic to their concerns. Some of these public interest organizations (for example, taxpayer associations and some religious organizations too) also have a decidedly anti-public employee bent, so public interest organizations are not a good substitute for unions. In any event, these public interest organizations are often outgunned monetarily by industry associations intent on undermining the effectiveness of public regulations that they cannot overturn by decimating the ranks of those charged with enforcing them. And while it is true that those with the greatest amount of money do not always win, I do not think it is accurate to suggest that money does not translate into political influence and power – indeed, if it didn't, why would anyone object to unionization, support campaign finance reform, or complain of regulatory capture? Unsurprisingly, the empirical evidence actually suggests that while government does respond to some extent to the preferences of those at every income level, it responds most often and most emphatically to the preferences of the most affluent whether they are individuals or firms or political action committees. Indeed, since unionization began its overall decline, "the results indicate that when the preferences between the well-off and the poor diverge, government policy bears absolutely no relationship to the degree of support or opposition among the poor."[232] In contrast, "responsiveness to the preferences of the 90th percentile [is] equally strong whether their preferences diverge from the poor, from the middle class, or even from the respondents at the 70th percentile of family income."[233] In other words, "under most circumstances, the preferences of the vast majority of Americans appear to have essentially no impact on which policies the government does or doesn't adopt."[234] This is hardly the sign of a healthy democracy, much less something that preserving democracy and liberty requires that we ensure continues. On the contrary, if we want to make our democracy more responsive to a wider range of economic interests, the preferences of lower- and middle-income Americans must be marshalled through organizations that both amplify the voices of their members and stimulate their participation in the electoral process. Obviously, unions are a type of organization that can play an essential role here.[235] They are not a threat

3.5 Are Public Sector Unions Undermining Our Democracy?

to democracy, but one tool in the battle to preserve it, one tool in the battle to prevent the affluent from using their economic power and the corresponding political power they can purchase with it to dominate everybody else.[236]

But the critics of public sector unions do not concede that the monetary imbalance is the correct imbalance on which to focus here. They contend that it is not money but grassroots organization that is the true source of lobbying power, and that unions have an unfair advantage over wealthy individuals, trade associations, and individual business owners because unions have a built-in grassroots organization while these other political actors do not.[237] And it is undeniable that a grassroots organization is an important (although clearly not decisive) factor in determining political success. But think about what is being argued here. The argument, essentially, is that bringing the influence of a grassroots organization to bear on the political process is somehow undemocratic because not all points of view have a similar grassroots organization at their disposal. This is equivalent to saying that it is undemocratic to allow organizations with greater popular support to lobby government. Rather than being undemocratic, however, this kind of influence is exactly the kind of influence that a democratic process strives to ensure. The claim that this allows unions to undermine the democratic process actually turns the idea of democracy on its head. Once again, under current circumstances, public sector unionization is more of a *remedy* for already existing violations of our democratic ideals than a violation of them. The fact that unions amplify the political voice of their members is accordingly a reason to support unionization of public employees, not a reason to restrict it.

Nor is there any reason to worry that because public employees are also voters, public officials and the agencies and administrative units they run are likely to be captured by the unions to the detriment of the general public.[238] Even though workers can vote and therefore can exercise some indirect influence on the decisions of their managers through the ballot box, employees are only a small portion of the electorate. Their voice at the ballot box is extremely diluted, and as a practical matter, public employees as voters often have a largely inconsequential influence on how management behaves, especially when we consider that union members only vote Democratic in slightly higher margins than the general population. Indeed, there are many firms in the private sector – including some large publicly traded firms – in which employees own stock and therefore have some voice in the direction of management too.[239] These firms, however, do not behave any differently than other firms. Although louder than in non-employee-owned firms, the voice of even employee-shareholders is rarely loud enough to cause significant changes in direction, for management is still insulated from interference by ownership in its day-to-day decisions.[240] Thus, the claim that public officials are likely to try to cement their stay in office by pandering to unions of public employees is just not very credible, especially when we consider that the same moral hazard exists with every person or entity who has the ability to deliver significant forms of political support.

If the worry here, on the other hand, is really one of corruption – that public officials will put their own private monetary gain above what they see as the public interest, that argument has even less force when it comes to the unionization of public employees. Corruption is always a possibility and we must keep a diligent eye out for it,[241] but there is nothing special about unions of public employees that make the threat of this kind of influence peddling so extraordinarily dangerous to lead us to treat such unions differently than other people or organizations who might benefit from government action. Indeed, if anything, the moral hazard created by the existence of public sector unions seems relatively slight. Kickbacks to government officials from public unions have never been the problem that kickbacks from private contractors to government managers have been, and public sector unions are often the driving force behind revealing the latter.[242] The revolving door that allows government officials to sign a valuable contract with a private firm and then leave government to work for that firm or in that industry does not operate so easily with regard to unions. Former government officials rarely become union officials, whereas they often become corporate executives or consultants. And it is rich individuals and corporations, not unions, that often look like they are buying and rewarding politicians who deliver legislation that provides them a financial benefit.[243] If it is to be taken seriously, the argument that unionization of the public sector is undemocratic has to have a more substantial basis than this.

3.5.3 The Argument from Interadministration Bindingness

But there is another way to understand this criticism from democracy that does not reduce to a simple partisan objection. Public unions lead to collective bargaining, and collective bargaining produces contracts that bind the government in certain ways, even after there is a change in administration. Indeed, one could identify this as a more tempered version of Petro's principal concern. This could frustrate the will of the people, the argument would go, for it would allow one group of elected officials to effectively bind their successors with regard to issues that should be left open to political reconsideration and adjustment.[244] And it is no doubt true that a left-leaning administration could agree to long-term contracts with certain public employees and thereby prevent a later right-leaning administration, reflecting a change in public sentiment, from taking a different approach. While this could also happen the other way around – a right-leaning administration could enter into long-term collective bargaining agreements with public employees that prevented a later left-leaning administration from taking a different approach – it is probably less likely that this sequence of events would ever arise given the political predilections of the groups of people concerned. Hence, public sector unionization seems to represent a one-way threat to democracy, favoring the left over the right. And while the argument would run even if it was a two-way threat, the fact that it is a one-way threat seems to make the threat even worse.

3.5 Are Public Sector Unions Undermining Our Democracy?

To put this argument in its strongest possible light, imagine that instead of a collective bargaining agreement, we were talking about a settlement agreement between an administrative agency and a group of aggrieved citizens or citizen groups who have brought suit against the agency alleging that the agency is not properly executing its administrative responsibilities under the law. In other words, the lawsuit alleges that the agency in question is either doing something that it should not be doing under the law or failing to do something it is required to do and possibly both. And let's assume that the claims presented in this lawsuit are reasonably contested – that is, it is not clear exactly what the agency's responsibilities are or how they should be carried out. Obviously, there is the possibility of collusion here – if the current head of the agency is worried that there might be a change in regulatory attitude or approach after the next election, he or she could agree to bind the agency to a certain interpretation of the law or even direct the agency to undertake obligations that it did not have under existing law in the name of settlement, obligations that could then be enforced as a matter of contract rather than as matter of executive discretion exercised by some subsequent head of the same agency. Indeed, this was a technique allegedly used on occasion at the end of the Carter administration to prevent the reversal of various agency approaches after the election of Ronald Reagan given fears that newly appointed agency heads would want to implement a radical change in direction.[245] The Trump administration has also begun making similar accusations against the Obama administration.[246] If true, this obviously raises some serious concerns, for it seems to turn on what are thought to be political choices about regulatory approach that were and arguably should remain open to political reconsideration by each new regulatory administration and not proscribed by long-term and potentially permanently binding contractual commitments. Even though such settlement agreements have to be approved by the relevant court as in the public interest before they can be given effect, and presumably can be reopened by a later administration by petitioning the court at a later date, as the Trump administration is now doing, to some they smack of a rather underhanded attempt by one administration to bind its successors to a particular regulatory approach despite a swing in public opinion.[247]

But it is not true that all forms of long-term contracts represent a threat to democracy in this way, even assuming these potentially more serious examples of government "self-binding" do provide reason for concern. Instead of thinking of collective bargaining agreements as judicially unsupervised settlement agreements with government agencies, why not think of them as simply another example of the kind of contract that government agencies enter into for the supply of goods and services every day? These contracts are frequently long-term or at least a long-enough term that they bind one administration to decisions made by another. Defense contracts, energy supply contracts, leases of public land, agreements not to prosecute, plea agreements and various other agreements related to regulatory enforcement, long-term leases for office space – I could go on and on – are all long-term agreements and some (like plea agreements) are even permanent. None of them (except for plea agreements) are subject to approval by a court or any other supposedly independent body to determine if they are in the public interest. Moreover, most of these kinds of agreements usually apply for a much longer term than collective bargaining agreements. They offer the same opportunity for government to bind itself as collective bargaining agreements do, except in these cases, it is usually government giving favorable treatment to large corporations and landlords, who are usually friends of the right, and thereby binding any subsequent left-leaning administration who might want to spread government business more widely. Of course, in some cases, locking in goods or services for the long term is an excellent idea, for it protects the public from unexpected spikes in the market price and assures a steady source of supply for important goods and services when supply might become uncertain. But committing to particular suppliers for a long term can also sometimes be unwise, for it may force the public to pay above market rates for long periods of time. Indeed, this has all too often been the case with regard to interest rate swaps and energy supply contracts.[248]

If wages are sticky, however, the cost of labor rarely goes down. There is accordingly less reason to be concerned about unwise commitments to pay what turns out to be an over market price when it comes to government labor, for the market price will eventually rise to meet it, and is unlikely to fall.[249] There also does not seem to be anything special about collective bargaining agreements that make them more like settlement agreements covering disputed regulatory matters that might impermissibly infringe on legislatively granted areas of administrative discretion and less like the kind of long-term supply contracts public agencies enter into every day. Collective bargaining agreements with public employees deal with the provision of services, not the exercise of executive or administrative rule-making power. They do not end up alienating the executive's authority to enforce the law; they merely interfere with the ability of government to change its mind more rapidly than it might otherwise want with regard to how much it pays its employees. If we were going to deny unions the right to bargain collectively on this basis, we would also have to object to any kind of government contract that purports to be binding on a subsequent administration. The shorter the period before the next election, the shorter all contracts would have to be. It should be obvious that the chaos resulting from this approach would render the uninterrupted provision of public services impossible. At the very least, this would raise the cost of government significantly, something that those who argue against public employee unions claim to want to reduce, making planning extremely difficult if not impossible, reducing the stability of society, and creating all sorts of inefficiencies that would overwhelm the kernel of valid concern expressed by the objection here.

3.5.4 Public Sector Unions and the "Deep State"

There is one final version of this argument that I need to mention. This is the claim that there exists something called the "deep state," a claim we are beginning to hear more and more from members of the Trump administration and its supporters as they try to find excuses for the failure of so many of the administration's policy initiatives.[250] In its more paranoid formulation, the deep state is described as a conspiracy of almost every type of organization and category of people, including both major political parties, globalists, bankers, Islamists, Jews, Marxists, the "mainstream media," academia, the federal bureaucracy, and so on, who are alleged to be combining to surreptitiously frustrate the will of the electorate to further the Trump agenda.[251] Such a list goes back at least to the French reactionary philosopher Joseph de Maistre, who called this supposedly enormous and powerful yet still secret conspiracy against the supposedly one true way *la secte*, the group of great disturbers and subverters who never sleep but are forever boring away at the foundations of society from within.[252] But there is a stripped-down version of this claim that is more rational and therefore worth taking seriously. This is the claim that wherever there is a large administrative bureaucracy, its members sometimes work against the aims and goals of political appointees or elected officials who arrive with unconventional ideas, even though the democratic process has directly or indirectly put such unconventional people in charge of the relevant administrative bodies. While the connection to public unionization is not always made explicit by those who express this concern, it sometimes is, and on occasions, public unionization is even described as its driving force.[253] In any event, it is easy to see how some people might see public sector unions as helping to create, defend, and consolidate such a bureaucratic impediment to new agency leadership when that leadership tries to implement policies and attitudes that differ substantially from those the employees of the organization tend to support. And such a concern is not at all unreasonable. Indeed, this is one way of characterizing the resistance of some police forces to efforts at reform by many left-leaning state and local administrations, the resistance of the Environmental Protection Agency (EPA) staff to efforts to gut the mission and effectiveness of the agency by the current Trump administration,[254] and the concerns expressed by employees of the Department of Homeland Security over the cruelty of the Trump administration's efforts to refuse shelter to asylum seekers.[255] The claim that we should be concerned about this even has the advantage of working in either direction as a practical and not just theoretical matter, and therefore can be seen as politically neutral. But it is nevertheless an odd claim for conservatives to embrace. It basically reflects the natural inclination of institutions to resist rapid abrupt changes in course, something that conservatives are thought to oppose anyway – indeed, this is what being a conservative was at one time thought to mean. It can also be thought of as simply another check built into the system of checks and balances that prevents changes in political leadership from completely reorienting the nature and direction of society without first establishing that this is consistent with a change in the attitude of the electorate that is durable over time. Which would make such bureaucratic resistance part of any democratic system, not antithetical to it. If a deep state exists, at least as that term might apply to a long-standing truly democratic society, it is the enemy of authoritarianism, not of democracy.[256]

3.6 ARE THEY BANKRUPTING US?

The final argument made against the unionization of public employees that I want to address is a consequentialist claim, although it does have what we might call a liberty chaser. This argument arises out of the claim that unions produce excessive salaries and benefits for public employees, but the crux of the argument is not that the salaries and benefits are excessive, or not only that the salaries and benefits are excessive, but that the financial burdens these produce are so onerous they are bankrupting us, excessive or not.[257] The idea here is that public unions are sucking up money from the public purse, more money than we have, forcing government to either raise taxes to counterproductive heights, fire currently necessary employees, or reduce services to the point they fall below minimally acceptable levels, and often all three. And by threatening the sustainability of government, that is, by threatening the existence of even the minimal state, all our liberties are put in danger. This argument is then connected to unionization of the public sector through an attack on the pensions that are owed to public employees, these obligations being expressly blamed for the financial troubles of many government units and agencies.[258] And even though only a third of public employees are unionized, unions are then identified as a significant contributor to this problem, the implication being that if unionization were more limited, this pension problem would not have arisen. Therefore, one way to prevent it from arising in the future is to roll back unionization, or at least public sector unions' right to bargain collectively.[259]

A few preliminary comments. First, note that this argument is inconsistent with the small government position, even though both arguments are often made by the same people. If government really is too big, and big government does indeed threaten our liberties, anything that causes it to shrink should be seen as a way of protecting these liberties. Indeed, in the introduction to these essays, I mentioned the "starve the beast" strategy that has been used by the right to great effect in other contexts. Using this strategy, the right claims that we cannot afford programs it detests but could not attack directly because these programs enjoy wide popular support.[260] If this strategy is acceptable in the name of liberty, I do not see how the same people can consistently attack public pensions on the grounds that the financial burdens imposed by these pensions are effectively doing the same thing as the relentless tax cuts usually advocated by the right. Of course, I do not believe the starve the beast strategy is acceptable, nor do I believe that the size of government is a helpful guide to its potential to infringe upon our liberties, so I am not suggesting that this is a reason to reject the attack on public pensions that underlies this aspect of the anti-union argument. I just want to point out that this is yet another place where the anti-union movement can be accused of hypocrisy.

Second, note that for this argument to go forward, it does not matter whether public pensions are overly generous or not – the argument from financial ruin will run either way. But the claim that public pensions are overly generous is designed to make us feel better about denying people the payments they were promised and on which they relied for what usually amounts to decades of dedicated service. The argument is therefore often dressed up with anecdotal evidence of individual cases of what seem to be the manipulation of the system to generate greater pension benefits than would be available if those receiving such benefits were not trying to take advantage of whatever favorable rules they could, as if such an approach was somehow wrongful and was not pursued with even greater intensity and at even greater cost to the public purse by just about everybody, especially and most effectively by the very rich. The strategy here is apparently to use individual cases that are not even examples of misconduct to taint an entire program that provides many with their only source of income in their later years,[261] much like the defamatory image of the exaggerated "welfare queen" was used to undermine government assistance to the poor.[262] So even though the "overly generous" argument and the "financial ruin" argument are technically separate and independent moral claims, they are generally made together. If we are to properly identify and address the moral force of each claim, however, it is best if we address them separately. I will accordingly take each up in turn.

Let us first assume that public pensions are not overly generous, and it is simply the supposed enormity of these obligations and our inability to meet them that is to be taken as the source of the argument's moral force. In this case, however, it is hard to see how the argument has any moral force at all. People are entitled to the pensions they bargained for in good faith and on which they relied in deciding to accept government employment, just as private sector employees are entitled to the retirement benefits they were promised by their employers and on which they relied in accepting and performing their duties for decades. In neither case could we reasonably expect the employees involved to have accepted or remained in employment under the other terms offered had they understood that the pension promises made to them would not be kept. By retroactively re-writing their employment contracts, we would accordingly be infringing the very notion of freedom of contract that is so often trumpeted as inviolable by those on the supposedly "liberty-defending" right. Simply put, while it may be a problem as a practical matter, the relevant government entity's inability to pay is not a moral defense to the claim that payment of these obligations is indeed due.

It is also important to remember that these types of promises – promises to provide benefits in the far-off future in exchange for services now – are especially amenable to fraud and abuse. By supporting the idea that they can be retroactively adjusted, we are accordingly creating a serious moral hazard. What unscrupulous entity or individual would not make promises of "pie in the sky when you die" if they knew that they could simply pack up operations and thereby avoid fulfilling these promises when they came due? Even if these promises were initially made in good faith, however, subsequent inability to pay does not affect the moral weight of the promisee's claim that payment is indeed due. This is why insurance companies and their promises of far-off payments, cemeteries and their supposed perpetual care agreements, pension arrangements underwritten by private companies, and other types of contracts where a significant component of one party's performance is due only after a substantial period of time and in any case well after the other party has fully performed, are so heavily regulated. If one is going to make such promises, one can only justly do so if some apparatus is first put in place to ameliorate the risk that the promisor may ultimately be financially unable to perform. This is why in all these cases there are government-mandated reinsurance schemes in place to ensure that most of the payments due will still be made if the promisor does become bankrupt and is unable to pay them itself.[263] The presence of these schemes indicates that even though we recognize that we cannot get money out of the promisor if there is no money to be had, the moral claim to that money by the party to whom it was promised remains unaffected.

But wait – surely if the promise was made in good faith, and continuing reasonable efforts were made to ensure that it could be performed, the moral weight of the promisee's claim is somewhat reduced and the now financially strapped entity has some moral claim to relief. After all, there is a long history at common law of relieving people of the burden of performing their promises when performance becomes much more burdensome than the parties could reasonably have foreseen at the time.[264] An even lesser standard applies under modern statutory provisions: under the bankruptcy laws, all the promisor has to show is that there is a general inability to pay. And when such financial circumstances are made out, we allow private companies to shed their debts and reorganize rather than simply requiring all bankrupts to liquidate and distribute whatever money they are able to raise to their creditors in proportion to their claims. In other words, in these cases, we recognize that it is in the interest of everyone for the entity to be able to shed its debts in order to create a sustainable enterprise on a going forward basis. Individuals, of course, are treated like this no matter what, for we cannot liquidate individuals, just like we cannot liquidate government entities, at least in the vast majority of cases.[265]

But there are serious differences between the plight of a creditor of such a private entity or individual and the recipients of the pension promises of the public entities at issue here. First, none of the reinsurance schemes that apply to private debtors apply in the case of those owed public pension

3.6 Are They Bankrupting Us?

payments – so if a pension debt is discharged, the pensioner will truly receive nothing. This is why public entity pension benefits in many states receive state constitutional protection.[266] Second, and most importantly, public entities do not become bankrupt or even financially strapped in the same way that private entities typically do. True, private entities sometimes become bankrupt because of fraud or mismanagement, but they often become bankrupt simply because of macroeconomic forces and changes in technology or consumer preferences over which they have no control.[267] When government entities become financially strapped, however, it is almost always in part and often in large part because they have been behaving financially irresponsibly for years. Indeed, many state and local government agencies (and even the federal government) have been using the funds that should have gone to satisfy their pension obligations as a slush fund out of which to pay for general operations and provide more services to voters without raising taxes, or at least more services than they could have provided if they did not draw on such funds. Some government entities have even been operating their pension funds like a Ponzi scheme, using current contributions to pay current obligations with no money being invested to pay future obligations to those current contributors when those obligations become due.[268] Many (if not most) of these pension funds are also being irresponsibly managed, trying to make up for their endemic underfunding by chasing unrealistically high rates of return through inappropriately risky and illiquid investment vehicles that they can access only by paying inordinately high fees to outside investment managers.[269] Now that these pension obligations have come due, the foolishness of such an approach is widely apparent, but that does not get these government entities off the moral hook. They knew what their obligations were, they ignored them for years, then panicked, and instead of addressing the underlying problem, simply took on more and more risk through ever more exotic and costly investment vehicles, and now they are asking the very people who relied on these pension promises to bear the cost of the public's own breach of promise. The cause of the financial difficulties in which many government entities now find themselves is not the size of the pensions that unions were able to negotiate, it is a combination of mismanagement and a reckless willingness to curry political support among the voters by allowing taxes to remain artificially below what it actually costs to provide the public services at issue. We would tolerate no such excuse if a private employer admitted it had raided its employees' pension fund to finance its operations and therefore should be relieved of its burden of performing its pension promises. Why should our moral attitude be different when a public agency does this? The way to prevent these failures going forward is not to get rid of unions but to strengthen them so they can highlight such abuse at the time it occurs, when it can be corrected at a more manageable cost.

But there is another important difference between public entities and private firms and individuals when they claim they have insufficient financial resources to pay their obligations as they come due. Private firms and individuals cannot simply increase their income at will, except in extremely unusual circumstances, and when they can, they are usually required to do so as a condition of emerging from bankruptcy. In contrast, public entities generally can raise substantial funds if they choose to do so. And I am not talking about borrowing, although this is often an option too. The power to tax can almost always be used to increase the income of a public entity and thereby the resources that it has available to pay its pension obligations.[270] And when it can't, this is usually because the method of taxation available to the entities that owe these obligations is too easily thwarted by those who have the ability to pay. Property taxes, for example, can go up to astronomical levels, yet can only bring diminishing returns when the rich flee to the suburbs where they are subject to far more modest rates of taxation yet still receive generous services in return.[271] In these cases, however, statewide methods of funding can be required, as they are being more and more with regard to the funding of public education.[272] The failure to employ these methods in order to satisfy existing pension obligations is a matter of choice and therefore not an excuse for any resulting inability to pay. Indeed, the overall tax burden in this country is vastly lower than in most industrialized societies, and so there is clearly much room to maneuver here.[273] The moral force of the claim that an entity has insufficient money to pay its obligations simply disappears when its lack of financial resources is self-imposed. Sure, it may be more expensive now to fund these obligations than it would have been had these entities been proceeding sensibly all along, but fund them they must, at least if the promises were not so obviously unfulfillable that no one could have reasonably relied on them, or they were outlandishly greater than those who received them could be reasonably said to deserve. Accordingly, if the elimination of public sector unions does indeed make it easier for government entities to renege on their pension promises, then this is a moral argument in favor of such unions, not against them.

This leaves us with the claim that public pensions are overly generous and undeserved, and therefore anything such as unionization that might hinder our ability to limit these pensions for future hires or require us to actually pay them to previous hires in accordance with our promises to do so has to be opposed. Part of this claim is empirical, but part of it is moral too in the sense that the idea of these promises being "overly generous" implies a moral standard. But even the empirical part of the claim is wrong. The average public pension benefit for state and local retirees in the United States is a mere $26,684. In 38 states, it is a mere $14,647 to $26,683; and in 12 states and the District of Columbia, it is between $26,685 and $36,794.[274] The average of $26,684 would put the recipient in only the 34.7 percent income percentile in 2016.[275] Even the high average of $36,794 would put someone in only the 49 percent percentile. Moreover, approximately 30 percent of employees of state and local government do not participate in Social Security, including approximately 40 percent of all public school teachers, and most if not all state and local government workers in Alaska, Colorado, Louisiana, Maine, Massachusetts, Nevada, and Ohio.[276] Which means they receive no Social Security payments to top up whatever they receive from their respective government employers. And while there are no doubt cases where a government entity might have agreed to an inappropriately generous pension scheme solely because this purchased short-term labor peace and the government officials involved knew they would be long gone when the long-term price came due, given the wider numbers on what the vast majority of public employees receive, it is hard to see public pensions as being overly generous on a systemic level.

Indeed, the claim that public pensions are overly generous on a systemic level does not rely on the kind of evidence that is most relevant to this determination, but rather on two kinds of evidence of dubious quality. First, much is made of various high-profile individual cases of abuse by nonunionized, highly compensated (and sometimes corrupt) state and local managerial officials.[277] One oft-cited example is Robert Rizzo, the city manager of Bell, California, who received a 47 percent salary increase in one year and ultimately ended up with a pension based on a salary of $800,000 for managing one of the poorest communities in California.[278] Rizzo was eventually charged with fraud, graft, and corruption and is now serving a twelve-year sentence in prison.[279] Now, I do not mean to suggest that this case is not outrageous or that similar cases of abuse need to be identified and addressed. But they are not representative. They do not establish faults within the pension system or show that unionization increases the likelihood of fraud and abuse by highly compensated individuals. They accordingly hardly serve as a basis for rolling back the collective bargaining rights of rank and file public sector workers, whose pensions as we have seen are far more modest. Indeed, if anything, members and officials of public sector unions are much more likely to point out corruption, abuse, and mismanagement by public officials than be a source of it themselves.[280]

Second, in order to attempt to show that public pensions are overly generous on a systemic level, comparisons are made between the average pension for the private and the public employee, which tend to show that public pensions are higher. But it is not clear that the average pension in each sector is what we should be comparing. First, some people get more than the average, of course; that's what focusing on the average means. But far more get less than the average, for a few high earners skew the average above the median.[281] While the average public pension benefit for state and local government workers is $26,684, the median is only $16,742.[282] Second, even if we do focus on the average, while pensions in the private sector may indeed be less generous, the average private sector job also pays more and is not as risky, so the fact that an average public pension exceeds an average private pension does not suggest that these pensions are overly generous if total compensation is similar, which it is.[283] Indeed, there is substantial reason to believe that private pensions are actually unreasonably stingy, for many private sector workers receive no pension benefits whatsoever.[284] Finally, as I have already noted in the context of attacking the argument that total compensation for public sector workers is greater than their private counterparts, the average public sector worker and the average private sector worker is not what we should be comparing. The average public sector worker is more educated and has greater amounts of job responsibility than the average private sector worker, even if we don't count first responders. Unionization rates are also much lower in the private sector than the public sector. What we should be comparing is unionized workers in each sector with similar levels of education and responsibility, not average workers, if we want the comparison to be meaningful. If we compare unionized to nonunionized workers to determine whether pension benefits are excessive, we are effectively begging the question by assuming that the pensions earned by nonunionized workers provide the appropriate baseline. And as we have already established, if we compare like public and private sector workers, while pension benefits are slightly higher in the public sector, wages are at least slightly higher and sometimes significantly higher in the private sector.[285] So on a total compensation basis, public sector workers are if anything at least slightly underpaid.[286]

Even if we take an above-average jurisdiction, it is hard to find systemically overly generous pensions there. In Los Angeles, for example, the pensions for uniformed officers are some of the highest in the country, averaging about $60,000 per annum. But these pensions were offered to keep from losing experienced officers to other agencies and other jurisdictions, not because these officers were unionized.[287] And even though Los Angeles outbid its competitors for talent, the pensions for those in law enforcement in Los Angeles are not so much higher than those in other jurisdictions that it should have been obvious to those who received these promises that they should not rely on them being paid.[288] And if we move away from first responders to other government employees – those who are members of the Los Angeles City Employees Retirement System, which covers most workers outside the police and fire departments – we find they receive an average pension of only $40,871.[289] Assuming standard deductions for federal and state income taxes, this represents annual take-home pay of about $31,000, hardly enough to be living in the lap of luxury, especially in California, where the cost of living is exceptionally high. And while some highly paid employees might be accused of gaming the system, perhaps increasing their pension beyond what was contemplated at the time the method of calculating their pensions was negotiated,[290] they would not be the first to do so – such conduct is rampant among highly compensated individuals in the private sector, and this is not a side effect of unionization. And once again, this is not typical. Marina Black, for example, worked as a city librarian in Los Angeles for 35 years. After retiring in 2002 at 74, she collects $58,935 before taxes and lives in a rent-controlled apartment. "If they took away my pension I'd be out on the street," Black says. "I need it for rent, for groceries, for everything."[291] Not much grounds to claim that her pension is overly generous, and she receives almost 50 percent more than the Los Angeles average.

3.6 Are They Bankrupting Us?

It is also important to distinguish between recent hires and those who had already been working for many years when the current panic about existing pension obligations struck.[292] If it applies to anyone at all, the claim that pension benefits are overly generous in most cases only applies to those that have already been in the system for a very long time. One recent study, for example, found that more than three-fourths of all American teachers now hired at age 25 will end up paying more into their public employee pension plan than they will get back.[293] If we look at the largest school district in each state and the District of Columbia, we find that teachers in more than half these districts must work twenty-five years or more before the retirement benefits are worth more than they put in themselves, and that in thirty-five of these fifty-one districts, three-fourths of the teachers will leave the profession before future retirement benefits will be worth more than they contributed.[294] It is also important to note that these severe limitations on pension benefits for relatively new teacher hires have taken effect despite the fact that public teacher unions – the very unions that are often the prime target of the anti-public-employee-union right – are currently relatively strong, belying the claim that unionization of the public sector necessarily leads to overly generous pensions. Nor have these reductions in pension benefits only applied to teachers. In California, which is currently one of the most heavily unionized states for public employees in the nation and has a Democratic governor and Democratic supermajorities in the legislature, pension benefits have recently been significantly reduced across the board.[295] This reduction was then upheld by the moderate to liberal California Supreme Court, despite union opposition.[296] Once again, the claim that unions are somehow making it impossible to eliminate what may now be considered overly generous pension rights is simply not supported by the facts.

Not only is it untrue that unionization is the cause of the budget crises in which many government entities find themselves, it is also untrue that union intransigence is the cause of these entities' inability to deal with their budget crises. Even though they were not the cause of these problems, unions of public employees made substantial concessions following the Great Recession to help make up the resulting shortfalls in government budgets.[297] Unions have also been instrumental in helping various cities reduce their existing pension obligations.[298] It is extremely unlikely that states and localities would have been able to obtain such concessions if they had had to negotiate these on an individual basis given the multiplicity of positions that would no doubt have arisen among those affected. So once again, unionization is not the cause of the problem, it is part of the solution to it.

Given the lack of factual support for "they are bankrupting us" argument, it seems that the only way to make sense of it is to treat it as a conceptual argument and therefore not based on facts. The idea must be that public unions will of course demand more and more for their members, and if these amounts can be paid in the future, then politicians who will not be around when the bills come due will certainly agree to these demands as a way of providing an illusion of efficient government while they are in office. The problem with this conceptual version of the claim is that it still proves too much. Politicians will often offer to reduce taxes to far below what government actually costs in order to get themselves reelected. Why does this moral hazard reflect badly on unions? Pandering to unions is not the problem here, it is pandering to a public that continues to demand more government services but also demands lower taxes even though their taxes fall below what is necessary to pay for the public services they already have. And if this is why many state and local government entities now have severely underfunded pensions, why is this a burden that unions members should bear instead of the politicians who made these false promises or the taxpayers who insisted for so long on getting something for nothing, or at least getting something for less than it actually cost? Taxpayers may indeed have to bear an increased financial burden now, but that is where the burden morally lies. To place this burden on public employees or their unions is not prohibiting them from receiving something they don't deserve, it is giving the taxpayers who should have been paying for these benefits all along something *they* don't deserve. And there is no moral argument I know of which supports the claim we should do that.

3.7 FREEDOM OF SPEECH, AGENCY FEES, AND THE COMPELLED EXTENSION OF RIGHT-TO-WORK LAWS TO THE PUBLIC SECTOR

The final challenge to public sector unionization that I will address is once again based on an argument from liberty, except this one purports to be based on freedom of speech rather than freedom of contract or some more general conception of liberty. This is the claim that states cannot require public employees who are covered by a collective bargaining agreement but nevertheless refuse to join the relevant union to pay "agency fees" to the union to cover the cost of negotiating that agreement. Despite the fact that such fees do not cover the cost of any wider expressly political and ideological union activities, the argument is that because such fees support collective bargaining, they constitute "compelled speech," and because collective bargaining is allegedly inherently political and ideological in itself, their required payment is unconstitutional under the First Amendment. If accepted, this claim would effectively relieve those who are opposed to public sector unionization from having to continue to lobby for right-to-work laws in the twenty-two states that have so far refused to adopt this particular from of anti-union legislation. With one fell swoop, all these states would become right-to-work states, at least with regard to public employees.[299]

The claim that is at the heart of this attempt has actually been around for some time.[300] Indeed, it was soundly rejected in 1977 in *Abood v. Detroit Board of Ed.*,[301] where the Court unanimously found nothing unconstitutional about this practice. Overruling *Abood* accordingly became an important objective of

3.7 Freedom of Speech, Agency Fees, and the Compelled Extension 231

the anti-union right, and as the Court became more conservative, attempts to bring this issue again before the Court became more and more frequent. One of these actually made it to the Court in 2016, when the Court was expected to overrule *Abood* and come down in favor of the "unconstitutional compelled speech" argument, only for the case to end in a 4–4 tie when the conservative Justice Antonin Scalia unexpectedly died and therefore did not get to vote in the case presenting the issue that was then before the Court.[302] The Senate then refused to consider President Obama's nomination of the moderate Merrick Garland to replace Scalia, but after Donald Trump was elected, it did consider and affirm Trump's nomination of the conservative Neil Gorsuch as Scalia's replacement. The Court then agreed to hear *Janus v. AFSCME,* another case raising the compelled speech argument,[303] and in June 2018 issued an opinion that did indeed overrule *Abood* and declare 5–4 that "public-sector agency-shop arrangements violate the First Amendment."[304] The Court said:

> States and public-sector unions may no longer extract agency fees from nonconsenting employees. [...] Neither an agency fee nor any other payment to the union may be deducted from nonmembers' wages, or may any other attempt be made to collect such a payment, unless the employee affirmatively consents to pay. By agreeing to pay nonmembers are waiving their First Amendment rights, and such a waiver cannot be presumed."[305]

As a result, numerous lawsuits have already been filed seeking to force other public employee unions not only to cease collecting agency fees in the future in light of *Janus*, but also to refund the agency fees they had collected in the past.[306] This would be an unprecedented form of retroactive relief for an activity that the Supreme Court had said was constitutional at the time, and it would likely bankrupt most public employee unions if awarded. The continued existence of public sector unions is accordingly very much currently under threat.[307] As it is, public sector unions face a potentially significant drop in funding even if the *Janus* decision is not made retroactive.[308]

I will not describe the various ways in which the majority's own arguments are seriously flawed, for such a description is already available in Justice Kagan's dissent in *Janus*. But I will make some points not made in the dissent that seem particularly pertinent here given the line of reasoning I have been advancing in this and the first two essays in this volume. Indeed, if we use the insights from the analysis of the argument from liberty that I have presented in these essays, we can see that freedom, and in particular freedom of speech, does not prohibit the imposition of agency fees in the public sector. On the contrary, it is the Court's ruling, not public sector union agency fees, which is the real threat to liberty here.

The fundamental error made by the Court was to conclude that the liberty to speak one's mind includes the right not to be compelled to subsidize someone to do or say something with which you may disagree. There is, I admit, some Supreme Court precedent that supports this conclusion,[309] and it may indeed be the case that the payment of money is a form of speech when this is done with the intention that the funds be used to put forward a particular view the payor wants to support. This, after all, is what the Court has repeatedly ruled is the course of holding various legislative restrictions imposed on campaign financing unconstitutional.[310] Regardless of whether these cases were properly decided, however, the payment of agency fees is different. Imposing limits of your ability to pay others to speak for you is not the same thing as imposing an obligation to financially contribute to an activity (in this case, collective bargaining), which, like a vast array of other kinds of activity, has discernible communicative significance. What matters, at least in the first instance, is whether your payment of money, given the circumstances under which this payment is made, has such communicative significance itself, and if it does, whether that communicative significance is something with which you disagree. In other words, the funding of speech may sometimes itself be speech and therefore protected by the First Amendment, but this does not mean that the funding of speech is *always* a form of speech, despite what some of the language in certain Supreme Court precedents decided in the run up to *Janus* suggest.[311] Properly understood, the issue in this case was not whether the activity in which the *union* was engaged in this case, and to which the plaintiff objected, had communicative significance, assuming that such a broad definition of speech is indeed appropriate, or even whether it had political and ideological communicative significance and therefore constituted a kind of speech that is of greater concern than, say, commercial speech, a point which the Court also emphasized in *Janus*. The proper way to frame the issue in this case was whether the payment of the agency fee by the *plaintiff* had communicative significance, and if it did, whether that communicative significance was something with which he disagreed. For it might indeed be the case that, like in the campaign finance cases, the expenditure of money did amount to an expression of support for the message being put forth by those to whom the money was contributed, making it a violation of freedom of speech for this expression of support to be suppressed. But remember, the plaintiff here chose not to join the union and therefore not to voluntarily pay union dues. Why should an involuntary deduction from one's paycheck in an amount calculated by others be interpreted as such an expression of support of what the union was doing and saying? Indeed, it is hard to see how such a payment would have any unambiguous communicative significance at all.

For example, it could simply mean that the plaintiff preferred to pay the agency fee rather than join the union because the agency fee was slightly cheaper than the required union dues, even though he did support what the union was doing and saying on his behalf. A lot of public workers have no doubt opted for not joining the union for exactly this reason, even in states that have not adopted right-to-work laws. The anti-union folks not only know this very well, they are *counting* on it – simply look at some of the material

3.7 Freedom of Speech, Agency Fees, and the Compelled Extension   233

that they disseminate to public sector workers in an effort to discourage them from joining the union, which prominently emphasizes that even if a worker does not join, the union must still act on their behalf.[312] Therefore, the mere payment of an agency fee does not mean that one necessarily objects to what the union is saying and doing. And if the particular nonmember did not object to what the union was doing and saying, of course, then the payment of an agency fee would not have meant the worker was being forced to say something with which he disagreed at all.

Alternatively, the fact that the plaintiff opted to pay the agency fee rather than join the union could mean that he did indeed object to what the union was doing and saying, or even that he objected to whole practice of unionization. In *Janus*, this was in fact the case.[313] But whether it was or was not, the claim that a fee payable only by those who *refused* to join the union amounted to a coerced statement of *support* for the union and its positions and activities is simply bizarre. Remember, despite being compelled to pay an agency fee, the plaintiff was not being required to say or refrain from saying anything in this case. Should he have desired to do so, he was perfectly free to express his disagreement with anything the union said or did to anyone he could get to listen, and he was free to spend money to amplify and otherwise disseminate whatever objections he wished to voice. It is simply not true that by compelling the plaintiff to pay an agency fee, words were effectively being placed within his mouth. The only way the Court avoids confronting the reality of this is by assuming that subsidization is itself always the equivalent of speech, and whether the payment at issue is coerced or not, it always amounts to an endorsement of the speech subsidized. This assumption accordingly begs the real question in this case because these are the very matters at issue, for only if they are resolved in the plaintiff's favor is the constitutionality of agency fees governed by the First Amendment instead of the usual rules governing government action, rules that are generally not so constricting.[314]

Even if the payment of the agency fee were properly treated as a compelled expression of a political and ideological view with which the plaintiff disagreed, however, this would not end the matter under existing First Amendment jurisprudence. Indeed, in *Janus* itself, the Court expressly noted that a public employer may insist that its employees deliver "any lawful message," even though the employee may personally disagree with it, when this "is part of the employee's official duties."[315] And while the Court rightly doubted that the statements made by the union in the course of its collective bargaining with the employer could be part of the employee's official duties,[316] this was not the issue. The employee himself was not engaged in collective bargaining. The issue was whether the statement made by the payment of the agency fee, whatever that statement might be, was part of his official duties and therefore could indeed be constitutionally compelled under the First Amendment. Had the plaintiff's supervisor required him to contribute to a particular political candidate or party, or even to the plaintiff's union or some other union or charity or association, that would have not been part of his official duties and would certainly run afoul of the First Amendment. But in this case, the payment at issue was made pursuant to an official contract between the employer and the union, a contract that required the employer to charge nonmember employees an agency fee. Just like wearing a uniform and carrying a gun (both of which the employee has to pay for), payment of this fee was a term of employment between the employer and the employee, and therefore performance of this obligation was the performance of an official duty. Of course, republican liberty as well as other principles also limit what public employees may be made to do or say, but I shall get to whether these limits were violated in a moment. The point to be noted here is that payment of an agency fee was not a violation of the First Amendment under the relevant line of cases, even if it amounted to a form of speech and the employee happened to object to it.

But perhaps there is a slightly more nuanced argument here to consider. Perhaps the objection raised by the plaintiff here is better stated not as a claim that the payment of agency fees is itself compelled speech, but that by being compelled to financially contribute to the union's activities, the plaintiff is being made to pay for something that he thinks is morally wrong – he is being involuntarily made causally and therefore in some sense morally responsible for the union's activities, at least in part, and one should not be forced to be responsible for activities to which one morally objects. In other words, the claim could be that it is a violation of liberty to make one an involuntary aider and abettor of an activity that one sees as a moral wrong. This is not a free speech claim, of course, but it does seem to capture the nature of the objection the Court found persuasive better than the claim the plaintiff actually presented. And this claim is also arguably rooted in the principle of liberty. The thought here being that someone who is a self-owner cannot be made to contribute money, that is, the fruits of one's labor, to something if he or she reasonably believes this will further a moral wrong. Indeed, something very much along these lines is at the heart of the cases that assert a religious liberty to refuse to aid and abet gay marriage.[317] In *Janus,* the claim was not based on religious liberty, but on what we might call "ideological" liberty, but the mechanics of the argument is the same. This extension, however, has huge ramifications. Not only will every fee that people pay under government compulsion be subject to challenge under the First Amendment, but potentially every tax they pay, every document they fill out, and every disclosure of information they would not make but for government rules that say otherwise. Under *Janus,* for example, why wouldn't the tuition fees that students are required to pay for higher education at public universities be unconstitutionally compelled speech? Obviously, such fees support the teaching of many things that could be considered political and ideological. No matter what views are taught, these are likely to be contrary to those of some student. The whole way public higher education is financed will have to revamped, or else public universities will be starved of funds and wither and die. If taxes were then used as a source of financing, with no fees charged to students, why wouldn't these also be subject to a First Amendment objection? If they weren't wouldn't this be putting form over substance? And how could the antitrust laws constitutionally prohibit agreements in restraint of trade? These, after all, are the product of express speech and not just the implied speech that the payment of a fee represents. The whole issue of whether, and if so, when and where anticompetitive conduct should be prohibited is political and ideological, not just commercial, because as we have seen throughout these essays, the antitrust laws take a view on what having a free market really means. So how could these laws stand up to the First Amendment? What about local laws that require developers to spend a certain amount of money on public art in order to get a certificate of occupancy for their new projects? Indeed, some developers have already brought legal actions alleging these requirements are "compelled speech" and therefore violations of the First Amendment.[318] And if these requirements are unconstitutionally compelled speech, why wouldn't setback regulations, set asides for low-cost housing, and various other requirements that force developers to spend money or forgo some profits be also? Of course, those with their finger on the button of a weaponized First Amendment could simply use arbitrary distinctions to erect legal barriers that prevent things from getting out of hand, but how is republican liberty protected then? The very idea of republican liberty is eviscerated if the rule of law depends on arbitrary distinctions. I could go on here, but I hope I do not need to in order to make my point that the potential breadth of the approach adopted here could be used to chisel government away until we are back to something close to what existed before the New Deal and perhaps even take us back to the proverbial state of nature.[319]

Given its popularity among some segments of the population, however, it is obvious that this argument has some intuitive appeal. But on closer inspection, it proves way too much. It would take the idea of hypothetical consent (what free and equal citizens would agree to behind the appropriate veil of ignorance that deprived them of knowledge that would allow them to act in their self-interest rather than in the general interests of everyone) on which political obligation (our obligation to obey the law) is generally thought to be based, and transform this into a requirement that there be actual consent for not only the government as a whole to be legitimate but also every individual act or omission the government performs. Such a principle could only be acceptable to anarchists, for in any collective, even a strictly libertarian one, there are a great many things done or said by representatives of the collective to which individual members might vehemently yet reasonably object. This is simply built into the idea of representative government. These objections do not give any member the right to refuse to comply; they simply provide reason for the member to seek to change the mind or the composition of the management of the collective. Because of this, it is not true that people can be justly held causally or morally responsible for things done over their objection by a collective of which they are a member. Outside of the most egregious and serious violations, which might create an obligation to disobey the law, people merely have some obligation to make one's views known, and to do what they can within the limits of the law to prevent the collective to acting immorally, but that is the extent of it.[320] Only if we believe in collective responsibility, something that political liberalism and the theories of liberty that political liberals embrace vehemently rejects, is every member of society chargeable with every moral wrong done by other members of the collective in their name.[321] Moral wrongs are simply not distributable like this.[322] And if someone does assign blame or impose punishment on this basis, that itself is a moral wrong under political liberalism. Which means that even this more general, nuanced version of the objection to the agency fees at issue in *Janus* does not work.

But the Court also makes much of the fact that fees here are being paid to a private entity, not a public one, as if being compelled to pay money to a private entity is somehow a special kind of infringement of liberty. Why this should be the case, however, is never made clear. States require individuals to pay fees to private entities in a wide variety of circumstances. Owners are required to insure their vehicles if they want to drive them on the public roads, they must pay private firms to do environmental impact studies in certain circumstances in order to get permission to build on or otherwise develop land, they must pay architects and engineers to file building plans in connection with the permitting process, they must pay lawyers in some states if they want to transfer property, and so on. If public entities have the power to tax, and it should be beyond argument at this point that they do, I see no reason why they cannot simply direct that payment be made to a private entity directly rather than to the government with the government then funding the private entity to an equivalent extent. To hold otherwise would be to put form over substance, something the Court has in many, many other contexts refused to do with regard to the payment of fees and taxes.[323] The state could simply impose a personal employment tax to cover the cost of collective bargaining and then turn these funds over the to the union, and there could be no possible objection to that. Indeed, this is exactly the reasoning used by the conservative Justice Roberts and the majority of the Court when it upheld the constitutionality of the Affordable Care Act's mandate that every individual purchase health insurance.[324] And even if we were to put form over substance here, all this would mean is that states who do not want to impose right-to-work laws on the public sector could simply enact laws that allow for indirect financing of public sector unions through taxation followed by direct subsidization by the government.

The only issue here with regard to whether there has been an improper infringement of liberty is therefore whether the requirement that payment be made, whether directly to the union or first to the government, is arbitrary, and therefore a violation of republican liberty. For remember, freedom of speech cannot provide broader protection than freedom, full stop. Indeed, the *Janus* decision is a prime example of what happens when people start relying

3.7 Freedom of Speech, Agency Fees, and the Compelled Extension 237

on derivative rights without considering the scope and intent of the more senior, general rights from which these more particularized specific rights were derived. If we return to these more senior concepts of liberty, the analysis we need to perform would be as follows. Is the requirement that agency fees be paid an interference with negative liberty? Yes, but that does not mean it is improper; it merely means this interference has to be justified. Is it a violation of republican liberty? No, it is not arbitrary to require that those who objectively benefit from an activity like collective bargaining pay their fair share of obtaining these benefits, even when they subjectively object to some of the positions that the union takes or even to unionization in its entirety, and even though it might not be arbitrary to not require them to do so. This is especially true, of course, if unions are a basic institution, as I have argued here, for it is therefore essential to the protection of everyone's republican liberty that unions not be undermined as an institution, an argument that, of course, the Court did not consider. Indeed, the whole point of finding something a basic institution is that there is a moral obligation to ensure its continued existence and financial health that does not apply with regard to institutions and associations that are not basic. The requirement that nonmembers pay an agency fee is therefore not a violation of republican liberty. It is consistent with the protection of republican liberty that it be paid. It is therefore a justified interference with negative liberty as well.

Indeed, the Court's approach in *Janus* is in direct contravention to the claim that public sector unionization is an infringement of liberty because it undermines the democratic process. The will of the people in the twenty-two states whose democratically elected legislatures have refused to enact right-to-work legislation has now been effectively overruled by what those on the right like to derogatively describe as "unelected" judges. Why aren't the anti-union folks who claim to be intent on protecting democracy outraged by this? Of course, all rights are rights precisely because they are not subject to being overridden by the majority – I am not suggesting that I disagree with this position. But as no rights have been violated here, the more general right to liberty guaranteed by the democratic process is indeed being directly undermined. Having had a voice in electing those who set policy for everyone in the state, agency fee objectors cannot be heard to complain that overriding their personal voice is an interference with liberty when to do so would undermine the whole process by which we are governed and which ensures that liberty for all, in all its various forms, exists.

What the Court has done in this case is what Justice Kagan refers to in her dissent as "weaponizing" the First Amendment.[325] Almost all antidiscrimination legislation, for example, requires certain people to say or do things that they would rather not say or do. This legislation is usually seen as instantiating our conception of equality, and it does do this, but it also does more than this. It instantiates our conception of republican liberty, for it protects people from being treating arbitrarily. But if every person who would rather treat another discriminatorily and therefore arbitrarily can argue that by forcing him to refrain from doing do so he is being forced to endorse nondiscrimination as a practice and that such a coerced endorsement is a violation of the First Amendment, then these essential protections of both equality and republican liberty would become empty and meaningless. Instead of being a shield for liberty, the First Amendment would become a sword to be used against it. And that is something that all people who love liberty should want to stand up against.

Let me bring this essay to a close by tying together the arguments I have made here to the arguments I have made in the first two essays in this volume. In essay one, I argued that unions would arise in both the private and the public sector in a libertarian utopia, and that if these unions negotiated union shop agreements, these would not conflict in any way with libertarian rights, but rather would be something that a libertarian government was required to enforce. In essay two, I argued that even if we do not live in a libertarian utopia, but in a liberal capitalist democracy, private sector unions are a basic institution, and unionization of every sizable workplace is therefore not only permissible, it is mandatory – it is a right, an aspect of the right of republican liberty, and not something that can be denied simply by majority vote or a lack of affirmative majority support. And in this essay, I have shown that there is no valid reason for treating public sector unions differently. Taken together, then, we have an argument that in the name of liberty, unionization in both the private and the public sector should be universal. The argument from liberty is not an argument against unionization, but an argument for it. It is accordingly high time that workers everywhere who are subjected to efforts by employers to exploit and abuse them be able to say, in the words of the popular song, "you don't get me I'm part of the union."[326]

Notes

INTRODUCTION

1. See Steven Greenhouse, "Union Membership in U.S. Fell Sharply in 2010," *The New York Times* (January 21, 2011) (rate of union membership at lowest level in more than 70 years); Steven Greenhouse, "Union Membership Rate Fell Again in 2011," *The New York Times* (January 27, 2012) (rate now at 11.8%); Steven Greenhouse, "Share of the Work Force in a Union Falls to a 97-Year Low," *The New York Times* (January 23, 2013); Russell Berman, "Why Can't Unions Keep Up with the Economy?" *The Atlantic* (January 23, 2015) (rate at 11.1% for 2014): Bureau of Labor Statistics, "Union Members Summary" (U.S. Department of Labor, January 26, 2017) (while rate of unionization had held steady at 11.1% in 2015, it dropped to 10.7% in 2016) (www.bls.gov/news.release/union2.nro.htm); Mike McPhate, "The Collapse of Organized Farm Labor," *The New York Times* (February 2, 2017); Lawrence Mishel, "Overall Union Membership Rises in 2017, Union Density Holds Steady," *Working Economics Blog* (Economic Policy Institute, January 19, 2018). For a state-by-state analysis of unionization, see Planet Money, "50 Years of Shrinking Union Membership in One Map" (February 23, 2015) (www.npr.org/sections/money/2015/02/23/385843576/50-years-of-shrinking-union-membership-in-one-map); James T. Bennett and Bruce E. Kaufman, "What Do Unions Do? A Twenty-Year Perspective," in *What Do Unions Do? A Twenty-Year Perspective*, eds. James T. Bennett and Bruce E. Kaufman (New Brunswick, NJ: Transaction Publishers, 2007), pp. 1–11.
2. See Department of Business Innovation & Skills, "Trade Union Membership 2014" (Statistical Bulletin, June 2015) (www.gov.uk/government/uploads/system/uploads/attachment_data/file/431564/Trade_Union_Membership_Statistics_2014.pdf); David G. Blanchflower, "Unions in the UK Public and Private Sectors" (Hanover, NH: Dartmouth College, March 16, 2005); Institute for Public Policy Research, *Prosperity and Justice: A Plan for the New Economy*

(London: Polity, 2018), p. 50 ("in the 1970s more than 70 per cent of workers [in the United Kingdom] were covered by collective bargaining agreements; today it is just 26 per cent").

3. See, e.g., Claus Schnabel and Joachim Wagner, "The Persistent Decline in Unionization in Western and Eastern Germany, 1980–2004: What Can We Learn from a Decomposition Analysis?" *Industrielle Beziehungen/The German Journal of Industrial Relations* Jahrg. 14, H. 2, Gewerkschaftsmitgliedschaft in Deutschland: Strukturen, Determinanten und Tendenzen (2007), pp. 118–132; Jean-Yves Boulin, "Trade Unions in France: How to Challenge the Trend Toward De-Unionization?" in *Trade Unions in Europe: Facing Challenges and Searching for Solutions,* eds. Jeremy Waddington and Reiner Hoffmann (Brussels: European Trade Union Institute, 2000), pp. 215–248; Bernhard Ebbinghaus, "Trade Unions' Changing Role: Membership Erosion, Organizational Reform, and Social Partnership in Europe," *Industrial Relations Journal* 33: (2002): 465–483; David Fairris and Edward Levine, "Declining Union Density in Mexico, 1984–2000," *Monthly Labor Review* (September 2004): 10–17.

4. See, e.g., Annie Lowrey, "Faces of the Minimum Wage," *The New York Times* (June 15, 2013) (while only 1.7 million workers earned the minimum wage or less in the US 2007, by 2012 this number had increased to 3.6 million, with millions of others earning just a few cents or dollars more); Catherine Rampell, "Majority of New Jobs Pay Low Wages, Study Finds," *The New York Times* (August 30, 2012); and the various articles included in the February 26, 2017, edition of *The New York Times* on "The Future of Work."

5. For an account of just some of these attacks, see, e.g., Thomas Ferguson and Joel Rogers, *Right Turn: The Decline of the Democrats and the Future of American Politics* (New York: Hill and Wang, 1986). See also Jeffrey D. Sachs, "How to Break the 40-Year Working Class Losing Streak," *The Boston Globe* (August 17, 2017); David Kotz, *The Rise and Fall of Neoliberal Capitalism* (Cambridge: Harvard University Press, 2015), pp. 26–29.

6. See generally *The Right and Labor in America,* eds. Nelson Lichtenstein and Elizabeth Tandy Shermer (Philadelphia: University of Pennsylvania Press, 2012); Tom McCarthy, "Sheldon Adelson Lost His Fight with a Union. Will It Have a Domino Effect?" *The Guardian* (February 24, 2017) ("Adelson is one of the country's most high-profile, and powerful opponents of labor unions. He spent an estimated $105m on political races in 2012, with crippling unions as his top priority, he told the Wall Street Journal at the time"). See also Patrick Healy and Monica Davey, "Behind Scott Walker, a Longstanding Conservative Alliance against Unions," *The New York Times* (June 8, 2015); Thomas B. Edsall, "Republicans Sure Love to Hate Unions," *The New York Times* (November 18, 2014). Of course, some of the most vigorous recent attacks have been directed against public sector workers. See, e.g., Editorial, "Governor Walker Resumes His War on Workers," *The New York Times* (February 20, 2016); Dan Kaufman, "The Destruction of Progressive Wisconsin," *The New York Times* (January 16, 2016); Noam Scheiber, "Supreme Court Case in Public Sector Union Fees Rouses Political Suspicions," *The New York Times* (January 10, 2016); Nelson Lichtenstein,

"Bashing Public Employees and Their Unions," in *A Contest of Ideas: Capital, Politics, and Labor* (Urbana: University of Illinois Press, 2013), pp. 197–208. But private sector workers remain under vigorous attack too. See, e.g., Editorial, "When States Fight to Overturn Good Local Labor Laws," *The New York Times* (February 19, 2016); Dan Kaufman, "Labor's Last Stand," *The New York Times* (June 14, 2015); Editorial, "Iowa's G.O.P. Statehouse Shows the Locals Who's Boss," *The New York Times* (February 21, 2017).

7. See Noam Scheiber, "Trump Takes Steps to Undo Obama Legacy on Labor," *The New York Times* (June 20, 2017); Steven Greenhouse, "Labor Movement Braces for Three-Front Battle with Trump, Congress and Courts," *The Guardian* (November 14, 2016); Steven Greenhouse, "What Unions Got Wrong about Trump," *The New York Times* (November 26, 2016); Jodi Kantor and Jennifer Medina, "Workers Say Andrew Puzder Is 'Not the One to Protect' Them, but He's Been Chosen to," *The New York Times* (January 15, 2017): Dominic Rushe and Tom Pietrasik, "'I Was Naïve': After Losing Health Care Battle, Factory Workers Fear Next Blow," *The Guardian* (February 24, 2017); Samantha Sanders and Heidi Shierholz, "How President Trump and Congressional Republicans Are Undercutting Wages and Protections for Working People," *Working Economics Blog* (Economic Policy Institute, April 19, 2017); Paul Krugman, "What Will Trump Do to American Workers?" *The New York Times* (August 21, 2017); Steven Greenhouse, "Is Trump Really Pro-Worker?" *The New York Times* (September 2, 2017); Noam Scheiber, "Trump Shifts Labor Policy Focus from Worker to Entrepreneur," *The New York Times* (September 3, 2017); Joe Davidson, "Trump Labor Adviser's Plan for Cutting Federal Compensation, Potentially Even Paid Holidays," *The Washington Post* (December 17, 2018); Noam Scheiber, "Trump Appointee Is Trying to Squelch Us, Labor Board Staff Says," *The New York Times* (January 25, 2018); Associated Press, "Trump v Trumka: President Marks Labor Day with Attack on Union Leader," *The Guardian* (September 3, 2018); Steven Greenhouse, "How Trump Betrays 'Forgotten' Americans," *The New York Times* (September 3, 2018); Editorial, "Trump's War on Worker Rights," *The New York Times* (June 3, 2019).
8. See Nelson Lichtenstein, "Obama's America: Liberalism without Unions," in *State of the Union: A Century of American Labor* (Princeton, NJ: Princeton University Press, rev. ed. 2013), pp. 276–296; Nancy MacLean, *Democracy in Chains: The Deep History of the Radical Right's Stealth Plan for America* (New York: Viking, 2017), p. xxxii; Monica Davey, "With Fewer Members, A Diminished Political Role for Wisconsin Unions," *The New York Times* (February 27, 2016); Andrew Stern and Eli Lehrer, "How to Modernize Labor Law," *National Affairs* 32 (Winter 2017) (describing "unions' shrinking influence"); Bob Hennelley, "From the Supreme Court to a Constitutional Convention, Labor Is on the Defensive," *City & State New York* (August 27, 2017); May Boeve and Michael Brune, "If US Unions Tumble, the Progressive Movement Could Go with Them," *The Guardian* (March 2, 2018); Raymond L. Hogler, *The End of American Labor Unions: The Right-to-Work Movement and the Erosion of Collective Bargaining* (Santa Barbara, CA: Praeger, 2015).

9. See, e.g., Eduardo Porter, "Shaky Jobs, Sluggish Wages: Reasons Are at Home," *The New York Times* (February 28, 2017); Laura Tyson and Ana Madgavkar, "The Great Income Stagnation," *Project Syndicate* (September 7, 2016); Richard Dobbs, et al., "Poorer than Their Parents? Flat or Falling Incomes in Advanced Economies," *McKinsey Global Institute* (July 2016) (www.mckinsey.com/global-themes/employment-and-growth/poorer-than-their-parents-a-new-perspective-on-income-inequality); Heather Long, "Half the Jobs in America Pay Less Than $18 an Hour. Can Trump Help?" *The Washington Post* (August 24, 2017); Neil Irwin, "To Understand Rising Inequality, Consider the Janitors at Two Top Companies, Then and Now," *The New York Times* (September 3, 2017) (comparing Kodak in the 1980s and Apple today).
10. See, e.g., Lawrence Summers, "America Needs Its Unions More Than Ever," *The Guardian* (September 3, 2017); Lawrence Mishel and Jessica Schieder, "As Union Membership Has Fallen, the Top 10 Percent Have Been Getting a Larger Share of Income," *Economic Snapshot* (Economic Policy Institute, May 24, 2016); Will Kimball and Lawrence Mishel, "Union's Decline and the Rise of the Top 10 Percent's Share of Income," *Economic Snapshot* (Economic Policy Institute, February 3, 2015); Benjamin Mueller, "Unionization Important to Closing Racial Wage Gap, Study Says," *The New York Times* (September 4, 2015); Ruth Milkman and Stephanie Luce, "The State of the Unions 2015: A Profile of Organized Labor in New York City, New York State, and the United States," *The Murphy Institute for Worker Education and Labor Studies* (City University of New York, September 2015) (www.gc.cuny.edu/CUNY_GC/media/CUNY-Graduate-Center/PDF/Communications/1509_Union_Density2015_RGB.pdf); Teresa Ghilarducci, "Farewell to America's Middle Class: Unions Are Basically Dead," *The Atlantic* (October 28, 2015) (as a consequence of low rates of unionization, America "leads rich nations in low-wage jobs – more than 20 percent of jobs pay less than two-thirds of the median wage," "Americans work about 1,790 hours per year on average, but workers in wealthier nations work less than 1,600"); Noam Scheiber, "A Power Broker Who Wants Labor at the Table, Not on the Menu," *The New Yorker* (July 29, 2016) (this is "probably the most perilous moment the public sector labor movement has faced since its emergence in the '60s and '70s," quoting labor historian Joseph A. McCartin); Rick Wartzman, *The End of Loyalty: The Rise and Fall of Good Jobs in America* (New York: Public Affairs, 2017).
11. See Mark R. Reiff, *Exploitation and Economic Justice in the Liberal Capitalist State* (Oxford: Oxford University Press, 2013); Mark R. Reiff, *On Unemployment, Volume I: A Micro-Theory of Economic Justice* (New York: Palgrave Macmillan, October 2015); and *On Unemployment, Volume II: Achieving Economic Justice after the Great Recession* (New York: Palgrave Macmillan, October 2015).
12. See, e.g., Daniel J. B. Mitchell and Christopher L. Erickson, "De-Unionization and Macro-Performance: What Freeman and Medoff Didn't Do," in *What Do Unions Do? A Twenty-Year Perspective*, eds. James T. Bennett and Bruce E. Kaufman (New Brunswick, NJ: Transaction Publishers, 2007), pp. 373–400, 374, 391–395.

13. See, e.g., Richard Vedder, "The Economic Effects of Right to Work Laws," *Employee Responsibilities and Rights Journal* 23 (2011): 305–310; Raymond L. Hogler, "How Right to Work Is Destroying the American Labor Movement: From the Ku Klux Klan to the Tea Party," *Employee Responsibilities and Rights Journal* 23 (2011): 295–304, 299–300.
14. For a lengthy discussion of the argument from freedom of association, see Sheldon Leader, *Freedom of Association: A Study in Labor Law and Political Theory* (New Haven, CT: Yale University Press, 1992).
15. See *Janus v. American Federation of State, County, and Municipal Employees*, 585 U.S. — (2018) (deciding that the compelled payment of agency fees is an unconstitutional form of compelled speech with regard to public sector workers); Adam Liptak, "Supreme Court Delivers a Sharp Blow to Labor Unions," *The New York Times* (June 27, 2018); Noam Scheiber, "Labor Unions Will Be Smaller after Supreme Court Decision, but Maybe Not Weaker," *The New York Times* (June 27, 2018).
16. See Robert Nozick, *Anarchy, State, and Utopia* (New York: Basic Books, 1974), pp. 28–33. Nozick did contemplate that this might not hold true if the consequences of not infringing a right would produce a "catastrophic moral horror," see Nozick, *Anarchy, State, and Utopia,* at p. 30, but no one contends that this is the case with unionization.
17. See John Rawls, *A Theory of Justice* (Cambridge: Harvard University Press, 1971, rev. ed. 1999), pp. 26–28, 266, 474–480.
18. See generally James Feigenbaum, Alexander Hertel-Fernandez, and Vanessa Williamson, "From the Bargaining Table to the Ballot Box: Political Effects of Right to Work Laws," NBER Working Paper No. 24259 (National Bureau of Economic Research, January 2018).
19. See, e.g., Steven Greenhouse, "Billionaires v Teachers: the Koch Brothers' Plan to Starve Public Education," *The Guardian* (September 7, 2018). On the starve-the-beast strategy more generally see, e.g., Bruce Bartlett, "Tax Cuts and 'Starving the Beast,'" *Forbes* (May 7, 2010); Eduardo Porter, "Tax Plan Aims to Slay a Reagan Target: The Government Beast," *The New York Times* (December 5, 2017).
20. For a recent discussion of the use of the "corral the beast" and "starve the beast" tactics to reduce the size and limit the influence of unions, see Gordon Lafer, *The One Percent Solution: How Corporations Are Remaking America One State at a Time* (Ithaca, NY: Cornell University Press, 2017).
21. For a helpful discussion of the curious absence of a more sophisticated but also non-Marxist deontological defense of unionization, see Peter Levine, "The Legitimacy of Labor Unions," *Hofstra Labor and Employment Law Journal* 18 (2001): 522–573, 528 and n. 6.
22. See generally Reiff, *Exploitation and Economic Justice*, p. 3.
23. See John Rawls, *Justice as Fairness* (Cambridge: Harvard University Press, 2001), pp. 42–43.
24. See generally Richard J. Arneson, "Luck Egalitarianism and Prioritarianism," *Ethics* 110 (2000): 339–349.
25. See Reiff, *Exploitation and Economic Justice*, pp. 47–49, Mark R. Reiff, "The Difference Principle, Rising Inequality, and Supply-Side Economics: How Rawls Got Hijacked by the Right," *Revue de Philosophie Économique/Review of Economic Philosophy* 13:2 (2012): 119–173.

26. Rawls, for example, only mentions unions three times in all his work. One of these works suggests that he thinks the difference principle does not apply to them. See John Rawls, "The Idea of Public Reason Revisited," in *Collected Papers* (Cambridge: Harvard University Press, 1999), pp. 573–615, 596. The other two merely suggest that those who benefit from the union's activities may have a duty of fair play not to be free riders; that is, they may have a duty to join the union and pay their fair share of the cost of its activities. But he says nothing to defend this proposition or place it within the larger structure of his theory of justice as fairness. See Rawls, *Collected Papers*, at pp. 61, 211.
27. See, e.g., Lafer, *The One Percent Solution*, pp. 91–92.
28. On the popularity of the argument from liberty in general among those on the right, see Paul Krugman, "Death and Tax Cuts," *The New York Times* (February 24, 2017). See also Robert O'Harrow, Jr. and Shawn Boburg, "How a 'Shadow' Universe of Charities Joined with Political Warriors to Fuel Trump's Rise," *The Washington Post* (June 3, 2017).
29. See Reiff, *Exploitation and Economic Justice*, pp. 25–26, 44–45.
30. See, e.g., Nozick, *Anarchy, State, and Utopia*. For a discussion of this tactic and an attempt to refute it, see Ronald Dworkin, "What Rights Do We Have?" in *Taking Rights Seriously* (Cambridge: Harvard University Press, 1977), pp. 266–278. See also Will Kymlicka, *Contemporary Political Philosophy* (Oxford: Oxford University Press, 2002), pp. 138–153.
31. See Rawls, *A Theory of Justice*, sec. 82, pp. 474–480.
32. See Rawls, *A Theory of Justice*, p. 266.
33. See Martin O'Neill, "Philosophy and Public Policy after Piketty," *Journal of Political Philosophy* 25 (2017): 344–375, 366.
34. Rawls, *A Theory of Justice*, p. 26. I suppose I should note that there are a few theories that purport to be able to determine rightness without considering consequences. Kant's categorical imperative would be one prominent example. But even most Kantians concede that strict adherence to the categorical imperative no matter how bad the resulting consequences is not a morally appealing approach. See also Mill's criticism of Kant in *Utilitarianism* (Oxford: Oxford University Press, 1998), pp. 51–52.
35. For further discussion and explanation of this feature of arguments from right, see Reiff, *On Unemployment, Volume I*, pp. 53–54, 159 n. 48 & 49; Reiff, "The Difference Principle, Rising Inequality, and Supply-Side Economics," pp. 143–148.
36. For an example of how consequentialist reasoning can indeed be supplemented by deontological reasoning under conditions of empirical uncertainty, see Reiff, *On Unemployment, Volume I and II*, where I construct principles of justice regarding the obligation of a just society to address unemployment under conditions of uncertainty using both methods of moral reasoning.
37. For a discussion of what other fundamental presuppositions might be on offer, see Mark R. Reiff, "The Attack on Liberalism," in *Law and Philosophy*, eds. Michael Freeman and Ross Harrison (Oxford: Oxford University Press, 2007), pp. 173–210; and Mark R. Reiff, *The Unbearable Resilience of Illiberalism* (forthcoming).
38. For further discussion of the difference between a concept and a conception, see Ronald Dworkin, *Law's Empire* (Cambridge: Harvard University Press, 1986), pp. 70–72.

39. For further discussion for the difference between "ideal" and "non-ideal" theory and citations to some of the vast amount of literature discussing this distinction, see Mark R. Reiff, "Twenty-One Statements about Political Philosophy: An Introduction and Commentary on the State of the Profession," *Teaching Philosophy* 41:1 (2018): 65–115, 85–86.
40. For a discussion of some of the regulatory options on offer here, the attitudes toward the employer-employee relationship they express, and why we might argue for one approach rather than another, see, e.g., John W. Budd and Devasheesh Bhave, "The Employment Relationship," in *The Sage Handbook of Human Resource Management*, eds. Adrian Wilkinson, Nicolas Bacon, Tom Redman, and Scott Snell (London: Sage, 2009), pp. 51–70; John W. Budd, *Employment with a Human Face* (Ithaca, NY: ILR Press, 2004); Edmund Heery, *Framing Work: Unitary, Pluralist, and Critical Perspectives in the Twenty-First Century* (Oxford: Oxford University Press, 2016).
41. See Lewis F. Powell, "Attack on American Free Enterprise System," Memorandum to Eugene B. Snyder, Jr., Chairman, Education Committee, U.S. Chamber of Commerce (August 23, 1971) (http://law2.wlu.edu/deptimages/Powell%20Archives/PowellMemorandumTypescript.pdf), pp. 32–33. Note that the Powell memo is often characterized as being anti-union, and as using coded language to encourage the kind of attacks on unionization that already had a long history and subsequently doubled in intensity. See, e.g., Peter Temin, *The Vanishing Middle Class: Prejudice and Power in a Dual Economy* (Cambridge: MIT Press, 2017), pp. 18–19. But I choose to take Powell literally. Regardless of his attacks on suggestions for overcoming other aspects political liberalism, I will accordingly take him as meaning what he said about unionization – that real, substantive unionization and collective bargaining, and not some pale version of this, is indeed an essential freedom. For a discussion of the role the Powell memo played in reactivating the radical right in the 1970s, see Jane Mayer, *Dark Money: The Hidden History Behind the Rise of the Radical Right* (New York: Doubleday, 2016), Ch. 2; Kim Phillips-Fein, *Invisible Hands: The Businessman's Crusade against the New Deal* (New York: W. W. Norton & Company, 2009), pp. 156–165.
42. See Isaiah Berlin, "Two Concepts of Liberty," in *Liberty*, ed. Henry Hardy (Oxford: Oxford University Press, 2002), pp. 166–217.
43. See generally Frank Lovett, *A General Theory of Domination and Justice* (Oxford: Oxford University Press, 2010); Philip Pettit, "Freedom: Psychological, Ethical, and Political," *Critical Review of International Social and Political Philosophy* 18 (2015): 375–389, 382–385; Philip Pettit, "The Instability of Freedom as Noninterference: The Case of Isaiah Berlin," *Ethics* 121 (2011): 693–716, 707–708; Philip Pettit, "Freedom in the Market," *Politics, Philosophy, and Economics* 5 (2006): 131–149; Philip Pettit, "Liberty as Non-Domination," in *Republicanism: A Theory of Freedom and Government* (Oxford: Oxford University Press, 1997), pp. 51–79; Quentin Skinner, *Liberty before Liberalism* (Cambridge: Cambridge University Press, 1998); Quentin Skinner, "Classical Liberty and the Coming of the English Civil War," in *Republicanism: A Shared European Heritage*, eds. Martin van Gelderen and Quentin Skinner (Cambridge: Cambridge University Press, 2002), vol. 2, pp. 9–28.

44. See Dworkin, *Law's Empire*, pp. 70–72.
45. For more on the meaning of the terms "closed shop," "union shop," "agency shop," and the difference between union dues and agency fees, see Michael Evan Gold, *An Introduction to Labor Law*, 3rd ed. (Ithaca, NY: ILR Press, 2014), pp. 31–32; John W. Budd and In-Gang Na, "The Union Membership Wage Premium for Employees Covered by Collective Bargaining Agreements," *Journal of Labor Economics* 18 (2000): 783–807, 785–787; Charles M. Rehmus and Benjamin A. Kerner, "The Agency Shop after *Abood*: No Free Ride, but What's the Fare?" *Industrial and Labor Relations Review* 34 (1980): 90–100.
46. For a very different conception of what the "right to work" should mean, see Richard Dien Winfield, "Economy and Ethical Community," in *Hegel and Capitalism* (Albany, NY: SUNY Press, 2015), pp. 133–146, 145 (discussing Hegel's views on this).
47. See *Janus v. American Federation of State, County, and Municipal Employees*, 585 U.S. — (2018); 138 S. Ct. 2448; 201 L. Ed.2d 924. For some sharp criticism of the majority's reasoning, see the dissenting opinions by Justice Kagan and Justice Sotomayor. See also Garrett Epps, "The Bogus 'Free Speech' Argument Against Unions," *The Atlantic* (February 14, 2018).
48. See, e.g., George Monbiot, "Freeing Up the Rich to Exploit the Poor – That's What Trump and Brexit Are About," *The Guardian* (April 4, 2017); Robert Barnes, "Supreme Court to Take Case on Baker Who Refused to Sell Wedding Cake to Gay Couple," *The Washington Post* (June 26, 2017); Peter Beaumont, "Israeli Airline Can't Make Women Move Seats for Religious Reasons, Court Rules," *The Guardian* (June 22, 2017); Gary Abernathy, "The Media Fundamentally Misunderstands Conservatives on Health Care," *The Washington Post* (July 7, 2017); David Taylor, "'In God We Trust' – The Bills Christian Nationalists Hope Will 'Protect Religious Freedom,'" *The Guardian* (January 14, 2019).
49. Emile Durkheim, "Preface to the Second Edition (1902)," in *The Division of Labor in Society* (New York: Free Press, 2014), pp. 9–10.
50. Ibid.

FIRST ESSAY

1. See Robert Nozick, *Anarchy, State, and Utopia* (New York: Basic Books, 1974).
2. Ibid., pp. 3–146.
3. See Mark R. Reiff, *On Unemployment, Volume I: A Micro-Theory of Economic Justice* (New York: Palgrave Macmillan, 2015). See also the section on the proper size of government in third essay in this volume, "A Defense of Public Sector Unions."
4. See Mark R. Reiff, *Exploitation and Economic Justice in the Liberal Capitalist State* (Oxford: Oxford University Press, 2013), pp. 287–288.
5. For those interested in a discussion of and attack on economic neoliberalism, see Mark R. Reiff, "Two Theories of Economic Liberalism," *Adam Smith Review* 10 (2017): 189–214.
6. See generally Peter Vallentyne and Hillel Steiner (eds.), *Left-Libertarianism and Its Critics: The Contemporary Debate* (Houndmills: Palgrave Macmillan, 2000). I consider myself a left-libertarian, although I am a left-libertarian in a

different way than most others who consider themselves left-libertarians. For example, I see the principle of self-ownership as entailing a principle of reciprocity in transfer and not merely a principle of voluntariness, while most other left-libertarians simply focus on the principle of just initial acquisition (how one comes to own things) and pay no attention to the principle of transfer at all. See generally Reiff, *Exploitation and Economic Justice*, pp. 274–295.

7. See, e.g., F. A. Hayek, "Unions, Inflation, and Profits," in *The Public Stake in Union Power*, ed. P. D. Bradley (New York: University of Virginia Press, 1959), pp. 46–62; F. A. Hayek, "Labor Unions and Employment," in *The Constitution of Liberty* (London: Routledge, 1960), pp. 233–247, esp. p. 234 ("the whole basis of a free society is gravely threatened by the powers arrogated to the unions"); F. A. Hayek, *1980s Unemployment and the Unions* (London: Institute of Economic Affairs, 1984).
8. See Bob Adelmann, "Senator Rand Paul's National Right-to-Work Act," *The New American* (February 13, 2013) (www.thenewamerican.com/economy/commentary/item/14511-senator-rand-pauls-national-right-to-work-act).
9. See S.545, "National Right-to-Work Act," 115th Congress (2017–2018) (introduced by Sen. Rand Paul on March 7, 2017) (www.congress.gov/bill/115th-congress/senate-bill/545).
10. See Daniel Schulman, *Sons of Wichita: How the Koch Brothers Became America's Most Powerful and Private Dynasty* (New York: Grand Central Publishing, 2014); Jane Mayer, *Dark Money: The Hidden History Behind the Rise of the Radical Right* (New York: Doubleday, 2016); Theda Skocpol and Alexander Hertel-Fernandez, "The Koch Effect: The Impact of a Cadre-Led Network on American Politics" (Southern Political Science Association, San Juan, Puerto Rico, January 8, 2016), pp. 47–51 (www.scholarsstrategynetwork.org/sites/default/files/the_koch_effect_for_spsa_w_apps_skocpol_and_hertel-fernandez-corrected_1-4-16_1.pdf); Ed Pilkington, "Fears Grow as Rightwing Billionaires Battle to Erode US Union Rights," *The Guardian* (February 24, 2018); Renée Feltz, "Koch-Backed Group Fights Paid Sick Leave Laws as Flu Sweeps US," *The Guardian* (February 11, 2018); Alexander Hertel-Fernandez, Caroline Tervo, Theda Skocpol, "How the Koch Brothers Built the Most Powerful Rightwing Group You've Never Heard Of," *The Guardian* (September 26, 2018).
11. See Sam Tanenhaus, "The Architect of the Radical Right," *The Atlantic* (July/August 2017).
12. See, e.g., Joseph A. McCartin and Jean-Christian Vinel, "'Compulsory Unionism': Sylvester Petro and the Career of an Anti-Union Idea, 1957–1987," in *The Right and Labor in America*, eds. Nelson Lichtenstein and Elizabeth Tandy Shermer (Philadelphia: University of Pennsylvania Press, 2012), pp. 226–251; Sylvester Petro, *The Labor Policy of the Free Society* (New York: Ronald Press, 1957); Peter Levine, "The Libertarian Critique of Labor Unions," *Philosophy & Public Policy Quarterly* 21 (2001): 17–24; Peter Levine, "The Legitimacy of Labor Unions," *Hofstra Labor and Employment Law Journal* 18 (2001): 527–573, 532–533, 545–550, 565; Walter Block, *Toward a Libertarian Society* (Auburn, AL: Mises Institute, 2014), ch. 19–23 (Block doubts there is a right to unionize, wants to bring back the "heroic" yellow dog contract, and is bitterly opposed to both closed shop and union shop agreements);

Murray N. Rothbard, *For a New Liberty: The Libertarian Manifesto* (Auburn, AL: Mises Institute, 2nd ed., 1973, 1978, 2006). See also any of the abundant anti-union material published by the libertarian Cato Institute, the Ludwig von Mises Institute, Libertarianism.org, and so on. E.g., Charles W. Baird, "Freeing Labor Markets by Reforming Union Laws," *Downsizing the Federal Government* (Cato Institute, June 1, 2011); Chris Edwards, "Public Sector Unions," *Tax & Budget Bulletin* No. 61 (Cato Institute, March 2010); George Reisman, "Labor Unions Are Anti-Labor," *Mises Daily Articles* (Mises Institute, July 28, 2014); Gary Galles, "Labor Unions and Freedom of Association," *Mises Daily Articles* (Mises Institute, March 4, 2014); Thomas J. DiLorenzo, "The Union Myth," *The Free Market* 24:10 (Mises Institute, October 1, 2004); Richard A. Epstein, "What's Wrong with Labor Unions?" *Free Thoughts Podcast*, Episode 124 (Libertaraisnism.org, March 4, 2016); Warren Meyer, "How Labor Regulation Harms Unskilled Workers," *Regulation* 41 (2018): 44–50 (Cato Institute). For further discussion of the relation between right-wing libertarianism and the anti-union movement, see Nancy MacLean, *Democracy in Chains: The Deep History of the Radical Right's Stealth Plan for America* (New York: Viking, 2017).

13. See, e.g., Noam Scheiber and Kenneth P. Vogel, "Behind a Key Anti-Labor Case, a Web of Conservative Donors," *The New York Times* (February 25, 2018) (mailing backed by biggest donors on the right encouraged workers to pay "fair-share fees" instead of union dues because "to put it simply, becoming a fair-share payer means you will have more freedom"); Maura Dolan, "California Supreme Court Rules for Farmworkers, and Upholds Binding Mediation," *Los Angeles Times* (November 27, 2017) ("we believe that coerced contracts are constitutionally at odds with free choice," says spokesman for Gerawan Farming, Inc., which had refused to negotiate with union representing its 3,000 farmworker-employees).

14. See, e.g., John Ganz, "Libertarians Have More in Common with the Alt-Right Than They Want You to Think," *The Washington Post* (September 19, 2017); Denise Cummins, "What Happens When You Believe in Ayn Rand and Modern Economic Theory," *Evonomics* (February 17, 2016).

15. See Reiff, "Two Theories of Economic Liberalism."

16. See Yves Steiner, "The Neoliberals Confront the Trade Unions," in *The Road from Mount Pèlerin*, eds. Philip Mirowski and Dieter Plehwe (Cambridge: Harvard University Press, 2009), pp. 181–203, 195. For examples of anti-union arguments that could be based on libertarian ideas or neoliberal ones or both, see George Reisman, "How Labor Unions Hurt Workers," *The Free Market* 32:6 (2014) (June 2014); Galles, "Labor Unions and Freedom of Association"; Reisman, "Labor Unions Are Anti-Labor"; George Reisman, "Labor Unions, Thugs, and Storm Troopers," *Mises Daily Articles* (January 4, 2013); DiLorenzo, "The Union Myth."

17. For a discussion and critique of Cohen's criticism, see, e.g., Andrew Williams, "Incentives, Inequality, and Publicity," *Philosophy & Public Affairs* 27 (1998): 225–247.

18. See R. H. Coase, "The Nature of the Firm," in *The Firm, the Market, and the Law* (Chicago: University of Chicago Press, 1988), pp. 33–55, 35.

19. See, e.g., Ludwig von Mises, *Economic Calculation in the Socialist Commonwealth* (Auburn, AL: Ludwig von Mises Institute, 1990 [1920]); F. A. Hayek, "The Nature and History of the Problem" and "The Present State of the Debate," in *Collectivist Economic Planning: Critical Studies on the Possibilities of Socialism*, ed. F. A. Hayek (Auburn, AL: Ludwig von Mises Institute, 2009[1935]), pp. 1–40, 201–243.
20. Economists calls this "the knowledge problem." See, e.g., F. A. Hayek, "The Use of Knowledge in Society," *American Economic Review* 35 (1945): 519–530; Israel M. Kirzner, "Economic Planning and the Knowledge Problem," *Cato Journal* 4 (1984): 407–418; Don Lavoie, *Rivalry and Central Planning: The Socialist Calculation Debate Reconsidered* (Cambridge: Cambridge University Press, 1985).
21. See Coase, "The Nature of the Firm," pp. 33–47.
22. Ibid.
23. For further discussion of the effect of the quest for monopoly power on firm size, see Frank H. Knight, "Preface to the Re-Issue," in *Risk, Uncertainty, and Profit* (Mineola, NY: Dover Publications, 1957), p. xxiii.
24. See generally Edith Tilton Penrose, *The Theory of the Growth of the Firm* (Mansfield Center, CT: Martino Publishing, 2013).
25. See, e.g., Amos Tversky and Daniel Kahneman, "Loss Aversion in Riskless Choice," *The Quarterly Journal of Economics* 106 (1991): 1039–1061.
26. For purposes of this essay, I will define surplus value as Marxists do: as the amount by which produced value exceeds variable capital, or to put it another way, the extent to which the labor time necessary to produce whatever the worker produces exceeds the labor time necessary to produce whatever he may purchase with the wages paid to him by the capitalist. For more on what Marx meant by surplus value, see G. A. Cohen, "The Labor Theory of Value and the Concept of Exploitation," *Philosophy and Public Affairs* 8 (1979): 338–360. Note, however, that my use of this Marxist term does not render the argument that follows Marxist. Surplus value is simply a handy term to use here; nothing about my argument requires adopting a Marxist view or stance.
27. See, e.g., Bryce Covert, "When Companies Supersize, Paychecks Shrink," *The New York Times* (May 13, 2018); David Streitfeld, "Amazon Delivers a Pile of Cash, but No Fireworks," *The New York Times* (July 26, 2018) (discussing how little of Amazon's success has been shared with its employees); Karen Weise, "Why Some Amazon Workers Are Fuming about Their Raise," *The New York Times* (October 9, 2018) (despite the raise, their total compensation is likely to shrink); James Bloodworth, "I worked in an Amazon Warehouse. Bernie Sanders Is Right to Target Them," *The Guardian* (September 17, 2018) (in some US states, one in three Amazon workers are on food stamps); Michael Sainato, "Whole Foods Cuts Workers' Hours after Amazon Introduces Minimum Wage," *The Guardian* (March 6, 2019).
28. James Meade, "The Meaning of 'Internal Balance,'" *The Economic Journal* 88 (1978): 423–435, 433 (address delivered upon acceptance of the Nobel Prize). See also Mancur Olson, *The Logic of Collective Action* (Cambridge: Harvard University Press, 1965), pp. 66–97.

29. See, e.g., Maite Tapia, Christian L. Ibsen, and Thomas A. Kochan, "Mapping the Frontier of Theory in Industrial Relations: The Contested Role of Worker Representation," *Socio-Economic Review* 13 (2015): 157–184 (noting that, in light of the dramatic decline in unionization, workers may be more willing to explore other forms of representation).
30. See Adam Smith, *The Wealth of Nations* (New York: Modern Library, 2000), bk. 1, ch. 8, p. 75. ("The workmen desire to get as much, the masters to give as little as possible. The former are disposed to combine in order to raise, the latter in order to lower the wages of labour.")
31. For a good summary of the popular version of these arguments, see Bill Fletcher Jr., *"They're Bankrupting Us!" And Twenty Other Myths about Unions* (Boston: Beacon Press, 2012). For a survey of the more philosophical and academic counterparts of these arguments, see Simon Larson and Bruce Nissen (eds.), *Theories of the Labor Movement* (Detroit: Wayne State University Press, 1987).
32. For more on this idea of the thin theory of the good, see Rawls, *A Theory of Justice*, pp. 347–350.
33. See Nozick's well-known footnote on this possible exception to the inviolability of rights in *Anarchy, State and Utopia* at p. 30.
34. See generally James A. Gross, "A Long Overdue Beginning," in *Workers' Rights as Human Rights* (Ithaca, NY: ILR Press, 2003), pp. 21–22. Note also that even when union membership is compulsory, some fiercely anti-union theorists believe that unionization does not violate freedom of association. See e.g., Howard Dickman, *Industrial Democracy in America* (La Salle, IL: Open Court, 1987), p. 5 ("on their face, the federal and state laws that prohibit closed shops in the name of free competition are themselves the opposite: they interfere with freedom of association and are instances of compulsion").
35. 29 U.S.C. § 103.
36. See Joel I. Seidman, "The Yellow Dog Contract," *The Quarterly Journal of Economics* 46 (1932): 348–361; Joseph E. Slater, *Public Workers: Government Employee Unions, the Law, and the State, 1900–1962* (Ithaca, NY: Cornell University Press, 2004), pp. 69–70.
37. Libertarians are split on this issue. Compare, e.g., Murray N. Rothbard, *The Ethics of Liberty* (New York: New York University Press, 1998), pp. 40–41, 135–136 and Murray N. Rothbard, *For a New Liberty*, p. 97 with Nozick, *Anarchy, State, and Utopia*, p. 331 and Peter Vallentyne, Hillel Steiner, and Michael Otsuka, "Why Left-Libertarianism Is Not Incoherent, Indeterminate, or Irrelevant: A Reply to Fried," *Philosophy and Public Affairs* 33 (2005): 201–215, 212 n. 21; J. Philmore, "The Libertarian Case for Slavery," *The Philosophical Forum* 14 (1982): 43–58; and Walter Block, "On Slavery and Libertarianism," *Journal of Economic and Social Thought* 2 (2015): 161–174.
38. See, e.g., Jan Narveson, *The Libertarian Idea* (Philadelphia: Temple University Press, 1988), pp. 27–29; Edward Helmore, "Over 400,000 People Living in 'Modern Slavery' in US, Report Finds," *The Guardian* (July 19, 2018).
39. See Kathleen Kim, "The Coercion of Trafficked Workers," *Iowa Law Review* 96 (2011): 409–474, 429–432; Alan Wertheimer, *Coercion* (Princeton: Princeton University Press, 1987).

40. See Robert Nozick, "Coercion," in *Socratic Puzzles* (Cambridge: Harvard University Press, 1997), pp. 15–44 (Nozick does not actually use the word "reasonable" in determining the sufficiency of available alternatives – if anything, Nozick view is even stricter than the reasonable alternatives test).
41. See Jose Moran, "Time for Tesla to Listen," Blog Post (February 9, 2017) (describing Tesla's reaction after some employees of its currently nonunionized Fremont plant reached out to the United Auto Workers to explore the possibility of joining the union) (https://medium.com/@moran2017j/time-for-tesla-to-listen-ab5c6259fc88).
42. For more on this method of distribution and how it might satisfy the demands of equality, see Mark R. Reiff, "Proportionality, Winner-Take-All, and Distributive Justice," *Politics, Philosophy, and Economics* 8 (2009): 5–42.
43. See generally, Robert A. Hillman, "Contract Modification under the Restatement (Second) of Contracts," *Cornell Law Review* 67 (1981–1982): 680–703; Robert A. Hillman, "Policing Contract Modifications under the UCC: Good Faith and the Doctrine of Economic Duress," *Iowa Law Review* 64 (1978–1979): 849–902, esp. 880–899; American Law Institute, *Restatement of Contracts (Second)* Sections 84 and 89 (1981); Uniform Commercial Code § 209(1).
44. For more on how to tell if the terms are unreasonable, see my *Exploitation and Economic Justice in the Liberal Capitalist State*.
45. See Reiff, "Two Theories of Economic Liberalism," p. 13.
46. See, e.g., F. A. Hayek, "The Meaning of Competition," and "'Free' Enterprise and Competitive Order," in *Individualism and Economic Order* (Chicago: University of Chicago Press, 1948), pp. 92–106 and 107–118.
47. See Jonathan Wolff, "Libertarianism, Utility, and Economic Competition," *Virginia Law Review* 92 (2006): 1605–1623.
48. See Reiff, "Two Theories of Economic Liberalism."
49. See, e.g., Ralph K. Winter, Jr., "Collective Bargaining and Competition: The Application of Antitrust Standards to Union Activities," *Yale Law Journal* 73 (1963): 14–73; Milton Handler, "Labor and Antitrust: A Bit of History," *Antitrust Law Journal* 40 (1971): 233–241; Milton Handler and William C. Zifchak, "Collective Bargaining and the Antitrust Laws: The Emasculation of the Labor Exemption," *Columbia Law Review* 81 (1981): 459–515; Richard A. Epstein, "Labor Unions: Saviors or Scourges?" *Capital University Law Review* 41 (2013): 1–33.
50. For a relatively recent description of comments to this effect, see Bruce E. Kaufman, "What Unions Do: Insights from Economic Theory," *Journal of Labor Research* 25 (2004): 351–382.
51. See Richard B. Freeman and James L. Medoff, *What Do Unions Do?* (New York: Basic Books, 1984).
52. See, e.g., Levine, "The Libertarian Critique of Labor Unions."
53. See Murray N. Rothbard, *Man, Economy, and State* (Auburn, AL: Ludwig von Mises Institute, Scholar's ed., 2nd ed., 2009), pp. 705–771 (arguing that unions are "theoretically compatible with the existence of a purely free market"); Ludwig von Mises, *Human Action: A Treatise on Economics* (Auburn, AL: Ludwig von Mises Institute, Scholar's ed., 1998), pp. 373–374.

54. See Bruce E. Kaufman, "The Impossibility of a Perfectly Competitive Labour Market," *Cambridge Journal of Economics* 31 (2007): 775–787; Bruce E. Kaufman, "An Institutional Economic Analysis of Labor Unions," *Industrial Relations* 51 (2012): 438–471.
55. See John Locke, "An Essay Concerning the True Original Extent and End of Civil Government," in *Two Treatises on Government,* ed. Peter Laslett (Cambridge: Cambridge University Press, 1960), pp. 305–307.
56. For a recent discussion of this feature of the labor market, see Alison L. Booth, "Wage Determination and Imperfect Competition," *Labour Economics* 30 (2014): 53–58.
57. See, e.g., Simon Tilford, "Why 'Brexit' Will Make Britain's Mediocre Economy Worse," *The New York Times* (May 29, 2017) (noting that in Britain, the lack of availability of affordable housing is "making it difficult for many British workers to move where the jobs are"); Derek Thompson, "Why It's So Hard for Millennials to Find a Place to Live and Work," *The Atlantic* (November 19, 2014) (noting that the same is true for the United States). And this problem is getting worse, not better. See Arthur Acolin, Scott Bernstein, and Susan Wachter, "Opportunity, Housing Access, and Infrastructure," *Housing Policy Debate* 27 (2017): 468–471; Andrew LePage, "California Million-Dollar Home Sales Climb to a Q1 Peak as Stocks Soar," *Insights Blog* (CoreLogic, May 17, 2017) (www.corelogic.com/blog/authors/andrew-lepage/2017/05/california-million-dollar-home-sales-climb-to-a-q1-peak-as-stocks-soar.aspx?WT.mc_id=crlg_170524_qhTuN#.WS3coWjysuX).
58. See Jon Nichols, "I Lost My Dream Job in a Rural Town – But Telling Me to Move Doesn't Help," *The Guardian* (June 23, 2017); Michael Sainato, "Bosses Pocket Trump Tax Windfall as Workers See Job Promises Vanish," *The New York Times* (June 16, 2019) (noting that relocating is not an option for most workers with families).
59. Barbara Ehrenreich, "Divisions of Labor," *The New York Times Magazine* (February 23, 2017).
60. See Council of Economic Advisors, "Labor Market Monopsony: Trends, Consequences, and Policy Responses," *Issue Brief* (October 2016), pp. 12–13 (https://obamawhitehouse.archives.gov/sites/default/files/page/files/20161025_labor_mrkt_monopsony_cea.pdf); Kaufman, "What Unions Do: Insights from Economic Theory," pp. 367–370. See also Henry George, "The Utility and Futility of Labor Strikes," *The Cleveland Recorder* (Sunday morning, September 5, 1897) (arguing that unionization is a just response to the monopolization of land by the idle rich, an attempt to use coercion against coercion, and to use force in resistance to force).
61. See, Kaufman, "What Unions Do: Insights from Economic Theory," in *What Do Unions Do? A Twenty-Year Perspective*, pp. 12–45, 31–32; Daniel J. B. Mitchell and Christopher L. Erickson, "De-Unionization and Macro-Performance: What Freeman and Medoff Didn't Do," in *What Do Unions Do? A Twenty-Year Perspective,* eds. James T. Bennett and Bruce E. Kaufman (New Brunswick, NJ: Transaction Publishers), pp. 373–400, 384–395. Note that the evidence typically cited for the proposition that employers do not hold monopsony power is that large employers tend to pay more than small employers. But this does not mean

that large employers have no monopsony power. They could pay more than small employers but still pay less than they would have to if labor were more mobile and had more bargaining power.

62. See, e.g., Suresh Naidu, Eric Posner, and E. Glen Weyl, "Antitrust Remedies for Labor Market Power," *Harvard Law Review* 132: (2018): 536–601: Suresh Naidu, Eric Posner, and Glen Weyl, "More and More Companies Have Monopoly Power Over Workers' Wages. That's Killing the Economy." *Vox* (April 6, 2018); Alan B. Krueger and Eric A. Posner, "Corporate America Is Suppressing Wages for Many Workers," *The New York Times* (February 28, 2018); Alan Manning, *Monopsony in Motion: Imperfect Competition in Labor Markets* (Princeton: Princeton University Press, 2003); Orley C. Ashenfelter, Henry Farber, and Michael R. Ransom, "Labor Market Monopsony," *Journal of Labor Economics* 28 (2010): 203–210; V. Bhaskar, Alan Manning, and Ted To, "Oligopsony and Monopsonistic Competition in Labor Markets," *Journal of Economic Perspectives* 16 (2002): 155–174; William M. Boal and Michael R. Ransom, "Monopsony in the Labor Market," *Journal of Economic Literature* 35 (1997): 86–112; José Azar, Iona Elena Marinescu, and Marshall Steinbaum, "Labor Market Concentration" (December 15, 2017) (available at https://papers.ssrn.com/sol3/papers.cfm?abstract_id=3088767); Efraim Benmelech, Nittai Bergman, and Hyunseob Kim, "Strong Employers and Weak Employees: How Does Employer Concentration Affect Wages?" NBER Working Paper 24307 (February 2018); Jan De Loecker and Jan Eeckhout, "The Rise of Market Power and the Macroeconomic Implications" (August 24, 2017) (www.janeeckhout.com/wp-content/uploads/RMP.pdf); Josh Bivens and Heidi Shierholz, "What Labor Market Changes Have Generated Inequality and Wage Suppression?" *Economic Policy Institute* (December 12, 2018).

63. See generally Evan P. Starr, Norman Bishara, and J. J. Prescott, "Noncompetes in the U.S. Labor Force," *Social Science Research Network* (July 28, 2017) (https://ssrn.com/abstract=2625714); Raymond Hogler, "How Noncompete Clauses Clash with US Labor Law," *The Conversation* (August 23, 2017); Matt O'Brien, "Businesses Have Hijacked Capitalism – and Left Workers Behind," *The Washington Post* (July 18, 2018).

64. Orly Lobel, "Companies Compete but Won't Let Their Workers Do the Same," *The New York Times* (May 4, 2017). See also Conor Dougherty, "Signing Away the Right to Get a New Job," *The New York Times* (May 13, 2017); Neil Irwin, "When the Guy Making Your Sandwich Has a Noncompete Clause," *The New York Times* (October 14, 2014); Alana Semuels, "Contracts, Court Rulings Give Employers Legal Upper Hand," *Los Angeles Times* (July 6, 2013); Steven Greenhouse, "Noncompete Clauses Increasingly Pop Up in Array of Jobs," *The New York Times* (June 8, 2014) (camp counselor, pesticide sprayer, yoga instructor, and so on); Matt O'Brien, "Even Janitors Have Noncompetes Now. Nobody Is Safe." *The Washington Post* (October 18, 2018).

65. See, e.g., Alan B. Krueger and Eric A. Posner, "A Proposal for Protecting Low-Income Workers from Monopsony and Collusion," *Policy Proposal, 5 2018* (The Hamilton Project, February 2018); Conor Dougherty, "Quit Your Job

for a Better One? Not if Your Live in Idaho," *The New York Times* (July 14, 2017); Conor Dougherty, "Illinois Wields New Power to Challenge Noncompete Agreements," *The New York Times* (October 25, 2018).

66. For a recent discussion of the extent to which various states currently enforce noncompete clauses, see Office of Economic Policy, United States Department of the Treasury, "Non-Compete Contracts: Economic Effects and Policy Implications" (March 2016) (www.treasury.gov/resource-center/economic-policy/Documents/UST%20Non-competes%20Report.pdf), pp. 14–17, 27–33. See also The White House, "Non-Compete Agreements: Analysis of the Usage, Potential Issues, and State Responses" (May 2016) (https://obamawhitehouse.archives.gov/sites/default/files/non-competes_report_final2.pdf).
67. See Editorial, "Agreements That Lock Up Workers, Legally," *The New York Times* (May 16, 2017); Council of Economic Advisors, "Labor Market Monopsony"; The White House, "Fact Sheet: The Obama Administration Announces New Steps to Spur Competition in the Labor Market and Accelerate Wage Growth" (Office of the Press Secretary, October 25, 2016) (https://obamawhitehouse.archives.gov/the-press-office/2016/10/25/fact-sheet-obama-administration-announces-new-steps-spur-competition); Steve Lohr, "To Compete Better, States Are Trying to Curb Noncompete Pacts," *The New York Time* (June 28, 2016).
68. See Terri Gerstein, "These Americans Are Trapped in Their Jobs: They Need to Pay $10,000 to Quit," *The Guardian* (April 8, 2018).
69. See Manning, *Monopsony in Motion*, p. 361 (listing these phenomena).
70. See, e.g., Fritz Machlup, "Monopolistic Wage Determination as a Part of the General Problem of Monopoly," in *Wage Determination and The Economics of Liberalism* (Washington, DC: Chamber of Commerce, January 11, 1947), pp. 49–82.
71. I should note that many people argue that the supposedly monopolistic nature of unions can be justified in another way: unions arise and survive only where the employer is enjoying some degree of monopoly profits in the product market. Where this is not the case, there is no surplus to be redirected to the union. Therefore, the union cannot raise wages for its members, and if it does, the employer must soon go out of business. Because unions simply redirect some portion of monopoly profits into wages, they are not anticompetitive themselves. Whether this argument is true, however, is controversial, so I choose not to rely on it here. If it is true, however, this merely makes my argument that the dominant protective association would have no reason to suppress unionization that much stronger.
72. A similar point was made long ago by John R. Commons, the American progressive institutional economist and labor historian. See John R. Commons, *Industrial Goodwill* (New York: McGraw-Hill, 1919), p. 47.
73. See, e.g., Amasa M. Eaton, "On Contracts in Restraint of Trade," *Harvard Law Review* 4 (1890): 128–137; Harry Shulman, "Labor and the Antitrust Laws," *Illinois Law Review* 34 (1939): 769–787; Robert J. Pleasure, "Collective Bargaining and the Labor-Management Antitrust Exemption," *Journal of Labor Research* 21 (2000): 557–562; Herbert Hovenkamp, *The Antitrust Enterprise* (Cambridge: Harvard University Press, 2008).

74. See, e.g., *Connell Construction Co. v. Plumbers Local 100*, 421 U.S. 616 (1975) (agreement between the union and a general contractor requiring the contractor to subcontract work only to firms that were party to a collective bargaining agreement with the union was found to constitute an illegal secondary boycott); *United Mine Workers v. Pennington*, 381 U.S. 657 (1965) (by agreeing to the demand of large coal producers that it impose identical wage and welfare fund payment requirements on all coal producers regardless of size, the union was found to have illegally conspired with large coal producers to drive small coal producers out of business).
75. This would go some way, for example, toward alleviating the concerns of those who might fear that industry-wide or even sector- or economy-wide unions would arise and become like parallel governments, threatening the very existence of the dominant protective association. See, e.g., Henry C. Simons, "Hansen on Fiscal Policy," *Journal of Political Economy* 50 (1942): 161–196, 171 (quoted with approval by Hayek in *The Constitution of Liberty*, p. 233); and Henry C. Simons, "Some Reflections on Syndicalism," *The Journal of Political Economy* 52 (1944): 1–25.
76. For a discussion of some of the history of the public sector union movement, see Richard C. Kearney and Patrice M. Mareschal, *Labor Relations in the Public Sector* (Boca Raton, FL: CRC Press, 5th ed., 2014), ch. 1.
77. See, e.g., Jeffrey H. Keefe, "A Reconsideration and Empirical Evaluation of Wellington's and Winter's, *The Unions and the Cities*," *Comparative Labor Law and Policy Journal* 34 (2013): 251–275 (criticizing Harry H. Wellington and Ralph K. Winter, *The Unions and the Cities* [Brookings Institution Press, 1971], which argued against public unions by asserting that public unions had antidemocratic effects).
78. See Jeffrey H. Keefe, "On Friedrichs v. California Teachers Association," EPI Briefing Paper #411 (Economic Policy Institute, November 2, 2015) (www.epi.org/files/pdf/94942.pdf).
79. For a historical description of how public sector unions did indeed form, even in states where public employees had no formal right to organize, see Slater, *Public Workers*.
80. See Jess Bidgood, "'I Live Paycheck to Paycheck': A West Virginia Teacher Explains Why She's on Strike" *The New York Times* (March 1, 2018); Philip Bump, "How Striking West Virginia Teachers' Salaries Compare with Teacher Pay in Other States," *The Washington Post* (March 2, 2018); Campbell Robertson and Jess Bidgood, "'All-In or Nothing': West Virginia's Teacher Strike Was Months in the Making," *The New York Times* (March 2, 2018); Michelle Goldberg, "The Teachers Revolt in West Virginia," *The New York Times* (March 5, 2018); Dana Goldstein, "West Virginia Teachers Walk Out (Again) and Score a Win in Hours," *The New York Times* (February 19, 2019). For more on the West Virginia teachers' strike and the many similar strikes that followed it, see Eric Blanc, *Red State Revolt: The Teachers' Strike Wave and Working Class Politics* (London: Verso: 2019).
81. Note, I have based my argument here on the assumption that the only way for the dominant protective association to have a right to suppress unionization in its ranks would be to have its employees sign yellow dog contracts. Some people

suggest, however, that public employment is different, and that unlike employees in the private sector, public employees have no right (meaning, in the Hohfeldian sense, no liberty) to unionize even in the absence of a yellow dog contract. If this were true, the dominant protective association might be required to attempt to suppress public unionization no matter how much economic coercion their illegally unionized employees brought to bear. I shall deal with this argument later, in "In Defense of Public Sector Unionization," the final essay of this volume. For now, readers concerned about this can simply take my argument regarding public unions here to be contingent on later showing that no such special grounds for limiting public union activity actually exists.

82. For an interesting discussion of some of the early rhetoric of the right-to-work movement, and how it compares to the rhetoric in use today, see Cedric de Leon, *The Origins of Right to Work: Antilabor Democracy in Nineteenth Century Chicago* (Ithaca, NY: ILR Press, 2015).

83. See, e.g., F. A. Hayek, *1980s Unemployment and the Unions*, p. 61. Note, however, that despite railing against compulsory unionization, Hayek seemed open to the possibility that joining a private health insurance scheme could be made compulsory without violating anyone's liberty. See F. A. Hayek, *The Constitution of Liberty* (London: Routledge, 1960), p. 259. There seems to be an inconsistency here, which I think is explained by Hayek's overpowering fear of socialism. Unions, in his view, were likely to be advocates of socialism, while private health insurance companies were not. In other words, his objection to unions was not actually based on a concern for the individualized liberty of those who might be compelled to join, but rather on his overall fear of taking even the slightest step onto what he viewed as the slippery slope toward socialism.

84. See Nozick, *Anarchy, State and Utopia*, pp. 87, 110–113.

85. Ibid., p. 95.

86. See, e.g., Eric Mack, "Robert Nozick's Political Philosophy," *Stanford Encyclopedia of Philosophy* (June 22, 2014), sec. 3.2.

87. See Nozick, *Anarchy, State and Utopia*, p. 111.

88. Ibid., pp. 110–113.

89. For the expression of a similar concern, see Robert Paul Wolff, "Robert Nozick's Derivation of the Minimal State," *Arizona Law Review* 19 (1977): 7–30, 13–14.

90. See Nozick, *Anarchy, State, and Utopia*, pp. 28–35. For a recent argument that risk imposition can indeed be a rights violation, see Maria P. Ferretti, "Risk Imposition and Freedom," *Politics, Philosophy and Economics* 15 (2015): 261–279.

91. For a review of the arguments made by various authors for the proposition that risk imposition is itself a rights violation, even if the risk does not materialize, see Ferretii, "Risk Imposition and Freedom."

92. For a similar analysis of Nozick's position, see Sheldon Leader, *Freedom of Association: A Study in Labor Law and Political Theory* (New Haven: Yale University Press, 1992), pp. 75–76.

93. Similar but not quite identical reasoning was used by the US Supreme Court in *Abood v. Detroit Board of Education*, 431 U.S. 209 (1977) to justify requiring nonmembers to pay for their fair share of collective bargaining costs in

right-to-work states, even if they are not members of the union. Attempts to bar state efforts to interfere with this practice have also been ruled unconstitutional under state constitutions. See, e.g., *International Association of Machinists v. Wisconsin,* Case No. 2015CV000628 (Dane County Circuit Court, Order Granting Summary Judgment, April 8, 2016); Monica Davey and Julie Bosman, "In Victory for Unions, Law on Dues Is Struck Down in Wisconsin," *The New York Times* (April 8, 2016). While *Abood* was recently overruled in *Janus* v. *American Federation of State, County, and Municipal Employees,* 585 U.S. — (2018), nothing in the *Janus* decision suggests that the Court now disagrees with any of the reasoning set forth in the text.

94. For a discussion of the empirical evidence suggesting that this is indeed what happens out in the real world, see William J. Moore, "The Determinants and Effects of Right-to-Work Laws: A Review of the Recent Literature," *Journal of Labor Research* 19 (1998): 450–453; Victor G. Devinatz, "The Continuing Controversy over Right-to-Work Laws in the Early Twenty-First Century," *Employee Responsibilities and Rights Journal* 23 (2011): 291–292.

95. See, e.g., Hiroko Tabuchi, "Laid-Off Walmart Workers Head to Labor Board," *The New York Times* (April 19, 2015) (Walmart accused of closing certain stores in retaliation for labor activism there); Noam Scheiber, "Amazon and Union at Odds over Firing of Staten Island Warehouse Worker," *The New York Times* (March 20, 2019) (Amazon accused of retaliating against worker for speaking out about working conditions).

96. For a similar view, see Philip Pettit, *On the People's Terms: A Republican Theory and Model of Democracy* (Cambridge: Cambridge University Press, 2012), p. 115.

97. See Ronald Dworkin, *Sovereign Virtue* (Cambridge: Harvard University Press, 2000), ch. 1–2.

98. See Joel Feinberg, "Voluntary Euthanasia and the Inalienable Right to Life," *Philosophy and Public Affairs* 7 (1978): 93–123, 102.

99. See, e.g., Jonathan Quong, "Killing in Self-Defense," *Ethics* 119 (2009): 507–537, 513–514; Jeff McMahan, *Killing in War* (Oxford: Oxford University Press, 2009), pp. 9–10 (note that while McMahan adopts this distinction, he cashes it out slightly differently than Thomson).

100. See Mark R. Reiff, "Incommensurability and Moral Value," *Politics, Philosophy, and Economics* 13 (2014): 237–268, 246–247. Other theorists reject the infringing/violating distinction as well. See, e.g., John Oberdiek, "Lost in Moral Space: On the Infringing/Violating Distinction and Its Place in the Theory of Rights," *Law and Philosophy* 23 (2003): 325–346; Hillel Steiner, "Directed Duties and Inalienable Rights," *Ethics* 123 (2013): 230–244, 235–237.

101. See Nozick, *Anarchy, State, and Utopia,* pp. 28–35 (arguing that rights are "side-constraints"); Hillel Steiner, *An Essay on Rights* (Oxford: Basil Blackwell, 1994), pp. 2–3 (arguing that rights must be "compossible;" that is, two rights cannot conflict). Of course, libertarians are not the only ones to argue that rights are absolute. See, e.g., N. E. Simmonds, "Rights at the Cutting Edge," in *A Debate over Rights* (Oxford: Oxford University Press, 1998), pp. 113–232, 205, 214–216 (discussing whether and to what extent rights have "peremptory force"); and Ronald Dworkin, "Rights as Trumps," in *Theories of Rights,* ed. Jeremy Waldron (Oxford: Oxford University Press, 1984), pp. 153–167.

102. See Reiff, "Proportionality, Winner-Take-All, and Distributive Justice."
103. For further discussion of this way of resolving supposed rights conflicts, see Reiff, "Proportionality, Winner-Take-All, and Distributive Justice."
104. See, e.g., Richard A. Epstein, *The Classical Liberal Constitution* (Cambridge: Harvard University Press, 2014), p. 440; Russ Brown, "A Deep Secret that Labor Unions Don't Want Workers to Know," *Forbes* (August 16, 2012); Block, "On Slavery and Libertarianism."
105. For a good description of the Hohfeldian system of juridical relationships, see Matthew H. Kramer, "Rights without Trimmings," in *A Debate over Rights* (Oxford: Oxford University Press, 1998), pp. 7–111, 7–60; N. E. Simmonds, *Central Issues in Jurisprudence* (London: Sweet & Maxwell, 2nd ed., 2002), pp. 275–280.
106. See, e.g., see Leader, *Freedom of Association*, pp. 12–15; N. E. Simmonds, "Rights at the Cutting Edge," pp. 169–173.
107. See Steiner, "Directed Duties and Inalienable Rights," p. 233 ("having a liberty or a power to do something does not entail a constraint (duty or disability) in anyone else").
108. My thanks to Nigel Simmonds for bringing this distinction to my attention.
109. See, e.g., Dickman, *Industrial Democracy in America*, pp. 267–269.
110. See Eric Mack, "Nozickean Arguments for a More-Than-Minimal State," in *The Cambridge Companion to Nozick's Anarchy State and Utopia*, eds. Ralf M. Bader and John Meadowcroft (Cambridge: Cambridge University Press, 2014), pp. 89–115, at p. 89.
111. The possible exception here is Murray Rothbard, who claimed that his theory of anarcho-capitalism was a form of libertarianism. See Murray N. Rothbard, *For a New Liberty*. Of course, Rothbard's claim is itself controversial, even among libertarians. More importantly, however, Rothbard's vision of a libertarian utopia would look nothing like a modern industrial state. Given that the whole purpose of the thought experiment I am undertaking in this essay is to see what the libertarian attitude should be toward unions in the modern industrialized state, interpreting our libertarian utopia as more in line with Nozick's view than with Rothbard's seems far more appropriate.
112. See Isaiah Berlin, "Two Concepts of Liberty," in *Liberty*, ed. Henry Hardy (Oxford: Oxford University Press, 2002), pp. 166–217. I recognize I have abbreviated the definition of negative liberty here, but the abbreviated definition will do for our purposes. For a robust book-length (albeit non-libertarian) explication of negative liberty, see Matthew H. Kramer, *The Quality of Freedom* (Oxford: Oxford University Press, 2003).
113. For an extended version of this argument, see Reiff, *On Unemployment, Volume I*, pp. 124–128 and Mark R. Reiff, *On Unemployment, Volume II: Achieving Economic Justice after the Great Recession* (New York: Palgrave Macmillan, 2015), pp. 75, 125–128.
114. This would be true even if, as Hillel Steiner suggests, negative liberty cannot be increased or decreased, merely redistributed. For example, if I can kill you but you cannot kill me, I have greater negative liberty than you do, but the total amount of negative liberty between us is the same as when neither of us could kill the other, or so Steiner contends. See Steiner, *An Essay on Rights*, pp 52–54; Reiff, *On Unemployment, Volume 1*, pp. 124–128. See also Hillel Steiner, "Individual Liberty," *Aristotelian Society Proceedings* 75 (1975): 35–50, reprinted in *Liberty*,

ed. David Miller (Oxford: Oxford University Press, 1991); Hillel Steiner, "On the Conflict between Liberty and Equality," in *Oxford Handbook of Freedom*, eds. David Schmidtz and Carmen Pavel (New York: Oxford University Press, 2018), pp. 76–89; Hillel Steiner, "Evaluation and the Quantification of Freedom," in *Thinking towards Humanity: Themes from Norman Geras*, eds. E. Garrard and S. de Wijze (Manchester: Manchester University Press, 2012). As Steiner points out, support for his view on what he calls "the conservation of liberty" can also be found in certain passages from Bentham, Marx, and perhaps even in Nozick and Berlin. See Steiner, "On the Conflict between Liberty and Equality." Although I agree with Steiner's view, nothing I am arguing here turns on whether Steiner's view is correct.

115. See Berlin, "Two Concepts of Liberty," pp. 172–173, 214–216. For further discussion of this point, see my *Exploitation and Economic Justice in the Liberal Capitalist State* at pp. 88–89.

116. For a similar argument, see Ronald Dworkin, "What Rights Do We Have?" in *Taking Rights Seriously* (Cambridge: Harvard University Press, 1977), pp. 266–278. For further discussion of the reasoning in use here, see Will Kymlicka, *Contemporary Political Philosophy* (Oxford: Oxford University Press, 2002), pp. 138–153.

117. See Nozick, *Anarchy, State, and Utopia*. See also Hillel Steiner, "Compensation for Liberty Lost: Left Libertarianism and Unconditional Basic Income," *Juncture* 22 (2016): 293–297 ("virtually all types of libertarianism, left and right ... regard self-ownership as a fundamental moral right").

118. See, e.g., G. A. Cohen, *Self-Ownership, Freedom, and Equality* (Cambridge: Cambridge University Press, 1995), pp. 15, 105.

119. See Reiff, *Exploitation and Economic Justice*, pp. 274–295.

120. See, e.g., Michael Otsuka, "Self-Ownership and Equality," in *Libertarianism without Inequality* (Oxford: Oxford University Press, 2003), pp. 11–40.

121. I realize much more needs to be said about my conception of republican liberty, for my conception differs substantially from that of other republican liberty theorists. In some ways, my conception is much narrower, and in some ways, it is broader. Because my conception is more fully explained in the next essay, however, and because the details of these differences are not important to any point I am making here, I will not say any more about it now. But for more on republican liberty generally, see Frank Lovett, *A General Theory of Domination and Justice* (Oxford: Oxford University Press, 2010); Philip Pettit, "Freedom: Psychological, Ethical, and Political," *Critical Review of International Social and Political Philosophy* 18 (2015): 375–389, 382–385; Philip Pettit, "The Instability of Freedom as Noninterference: The Case of Isaiah Berlin," *Ethics* 121 (2011): 693–716, 707–708; Philip Pettit, "Freedom in the Market," *Politics, Philosophy, and Economics* 5 (2006): 131–149; and Philip Pettit, "Liberty as Non-Domination," in *Republicanism: A Theory of Freedom and Government* (Oxford: Oxford University Press, 1997), pp. 51–79; Quentin Skinner, *Liberty before Liberalism* (Cambridge: Cambridge University Press, 1998); Quentin Skinner, "Classical Liberty and the Coming of the English Civil War," in *Republicanism: A Shared European Heritage,* eds. Martin van Gelderen and Quentin Skinner (Cambridge: Cambridge University Press, 2002), vol. 2, pp. 9–28.

122. See Josh Bivens et al., "How Today's Unions Help Working People," Economic Policy Institute (August 24, 2017); Lawrence Mishel and Matthew Walters, "How Unions Help All Workers," EPI Briefing Paper #143 (Economic Policy Institute, August 26, 2003); Lawrence Mishel, "Unions, Inequality, and Faltering Middle-Class Wages," EPI Briefing Paper #342 (Economic Policy Institute, August 29, 2012).
123. See Pettit, *On the People's Terms*, pp. 115–116; Kohei Saito, "Beyond Recognition in Capitalism," in *Hegel and Capitalism*, ed. Andrew Buchwalter (Albany, NY: SUNY Press, 2015), pp. 35–51, 46–48 (discussing Hegel's views on this).

SECOND ESSAY

1. John Rawls, "The Idea of Public Reason Revisited," in *Collected Papers*, ed. Samuel Freeman (Cambridge: Harvard University Press, 1999), pp. 573–615, 596.
2. By "external preferences," I mean preferences as to how goods and opportunities should be assigned to others, as opposed to "internal" or "personal" preferences, which are about how goods and opportunities should be assigned to oneself. For more on this distinction, see Ronald Dworkin, "What Rights Do We Have?" in *Taking Rights Seriously* (Cambridge: Harvard University Press, 1977), pp. 266–278, 275–276.
3. For a detailed discussion of the methods of analytic political philosophy, see my "Twenty-One Statements about Political Philosophy," *Teaching Philosophy* 41 (2018): 65–115.
4. See, e.g., Maite Tapia, Christian L. Ibsen, Thomas A. Kochan, "Mapping the Frontier of Theory in Industrial Relations: The Contested Role of Worker Representation," *Socio-Economic Review* 13 (2015): 157–184, 176 ("We would also argue that worker representation requires some kind of institutionalization to be effective").
5. For a recent statement of some of these objections, see Daniel DiSalvo, *Government against Itself: Public Union Power and Its Consequences* (Oxford: Oxford University Press, 2015).
6. See *Janus v. American Federation of State, County, and Municipal Employees*, 585 U.S. — (2018).
7. See Adam Liptak, "Supreme Court Delivers a Sharp Blow to Labor Unions," *The New York Times* (June 27, 2018); Noam Scheiber, "Labor Unions Will Be Smaller after Supreme Court Decision, but Maybe Not Weaker," *The New York Times* (June 27, 2018).
8. Rawls, *A Theory of Justice*, p. 6 (emphasis added). See also John Rawls, *Justice as Fairness* (Cambridge: Harvard University Press, 2001), sec. 4, 15–16; and John Rawls, "The Basic Structure as Subject," in *Political Liberalism* (New York: Columbia University Press, 1993, 1996), pp. 257–288.
9. Rawls, *A Theory of Justice*, p. 6.
10. Ibid., p. 8.
11. Samuel Freeman, *Rawls* (London: Routledge, 2007), p. 101.
12. Arnold Joseph Toynbee, *A Study of History, Volume I* (Oxford: Oxford University Press, 1951), p. 455.

Notes to pp. 68–70

13. See Rawls, *A Theory of Justice*, p. 47.
14. See, e.g., Liam Murphy, "Institutions and the Demands of Justice," *Philosophy and Public Affairs* 27 (1999): 251–291, 290.
15. See, e.g., Brian Berkey, "Against Rawlsian Institutionalism about Justice," *Social Theory and Practice* 42 (2016): 706–732; G. A. Cohen, *Rescuing Justice and Equality* (Cambridge: Harvard University Press, 2007), pp. 116–150. For a response to Cohen, see Samuel Scheffler, "Is the Basic Structure Basic?" in *The Egalitarian Conscience: Essays in Honour of G. A. Cohen* (Oxford: Oxford University Press, 2006), pp. 102–129.
16. Rawls makes a similar point in *A Theory of Justice* on pp. 99, 23, 398, 415.
17. Note, that while I have followed Rawls in dividing the basic structure into four elements, I have rearranged the content of these elements slightly. Instead of treating the legal and political system as one element, as Rawls does, I have treated these as separate elements. Instead of singling out a separate "system of property," I have treated the nature and enforcement of property rights as something to be dealt with by the legal system. But for purposes of the issues I am addressing in this essay, nothing important turns on this.
18. Thomas Hobbes, *On the Citizen* (Cambridge: Cambridge University Press, 1998), para. 10, p. 105. For similar remarks by Hobbes, see Hobbes, *On the Citizen*, preface, para. 14, p. 12 and ch. 1, para. 12, p. 29; Thomas Hobbes, *Leviathan* (Cambridge: Cambridge University Press, 1991, 1996), ch. 19, p. 136 and ch. 21, p. 149; Thomas Hobbes, "De Corpore Politico," in *The English Works of Thomas Hobbes of Malmsbury*, Volume 4 (London: John Bohn, 1811), pp. 77–228, ch. 8, para. 9, p. 208.
19. See H. L. A. Hart, *The Concept of Law* (Oxford University Press, 2nd ed., 1994), pp. 123, 251.
20. See, e.g., Lon L. Fuller, "Positivism and Fidelity to Law: A Reply to Professor Hart," *Harvard Law Review* 71 (1958): 630–672, 644–645. Note that while Fuller claims here that all order is good enough order, he later seems to take a step back from this view and concede that order can be good or bad. See Lon L. Fuller, "Eunomics: The Theory of Good Order and Workable Social Arrangements," in *The Principles of Social Order: Selected Essays of Lon Fuller*, ed. Kenneth I. Winston (Oxford: Hart Publishing, rev ed., 2001), pp. 59–78.
21. For a similar argument, see Matthew H. Kramer, *In Defense of Legal Positivism* (Oxford: Oxford University Press, 1999), pp. 292–295.
22. See Rawls, *A Theory of Justice*, rev. ed. p. 4: "Let us assume, to fix ideas, that a society is a more or less self-sufficient association of persons who in their relations to one another recognize certain rules of conduct as binding and who for the most part act in accordance with them." See also p. 500: "A well-ordered society is a social union of social unions," and "what binds a society's efforts into one social union is the mutual recognition and acceptance of the principles of justice." But this does not mean the basic structure is subject to principles of justice – principles of justice come in only after we have selected a basic structure and are evaluating the institutions chosen and their outputs.
23. See, e.g., John Rawls, "Marx II: His Conception of Right and Justice," in *Lectures on the History of Political Philosophy* (Cambridge: Harvard University Press, 2007), pp. 335–353, at sec. 2, pp. 337–342.

24. See John Rawls, "The Idea of a Well-Ordered Society" in *Justice as Fairness* (Cambridge: Harvard University Press, 2001), sec. 3.
25. Even Brexit is not an attempt to revise the basic structure. It is an attack on the allocation of power between the basic institutions of the European Union and the basic institutions of the United Kingdom. The details of how that relationship is expressed may change, but the United Kingdom will remain a capitalist democracy no matter what.
26. In *A Theory of Justice*, for example, Rawls notes that if his recommendations as to which principles of justice used to manage society were adopted, "many of the socialist criticisms of the market economy [would be] met." Rawls, *A Theory of Justice*, p. 248.
27. But see *Justice as Fairness: A Restatement*, p. 138, where Rawls argues that his two principles of justice as fairness could not be realized under state socialism.
28. For the clearest expression of this by Rawls himself, listen to the first 16:30 minutes of the recording of Rawls's 1984 lecture on the basic structure in Philosophy 171, his Harvard course on Modern Political Philosophy. See www.youtube.com/watch?v=tYvdmizdohE.
29. See Rawls, *Justice as Fairness*, pp. 136–138.
30. See generally Martin O'Neill and Thad Williamson (eds), *Property-Owning Democracy: Rawls and Beyond* (Oxford: Wiley-Blackwell, 2012).
31. See generally David Miller, *Market, State and Community: Theoretical Foundations of Market Socialism* (Oxford: Oxford University Press, 1989), pp. 5–11.
32. See Rawls, *Justice as Fairness*, p. 138.
33. See, e.g., Rawls, *A Theory of Justice*, p. 47, where Rawls refers to his principles of justice as fairness as "principles of justice for institutions."
34. As I have in much of my other work. See Lisa Herzog, "Capitalism, but Better?" *Res Publica* 21 (February 2015): 99–103 (review of my *Exploitation and Economic Justice in the Liberal Capitalist State* [Oxford: Oxford University Press, 2013.]).
35. For more on the ideas of the institutionalists, see Malcom Rutherford, "Institutional Economics: Then and Now," *Journal of Economic Perspectives* 15 (2001): 173–194; "Institutionalism between the Wars," *Journal of Economic Issues* (2000): 291–303; and "Understanding Institutional Economics: 1918–1929," *Journal of the History of Economic Thought* (2000): 277–308; Bruce E. Kaufman, "Labor Markets and Employment Regulation: The View of the 'Old' Institutionalists," in *Government Regulation of the Employment Relationship*, ed. Bruce E. Kaufman (Madison, WI: Industrial Relations Research Association, 1997). For an attempt to update early institutional economic analysis and apply it to labor unions, see Bruce E. Kaufman, "An Institutional Economic Analysis of Labor Unions," *Industrial Relations* 51 (2012): 438–471. For a series of essays on how certain other institutions within the liberal capitalist state should be cashed out, see Jeremy Waldron, *Political Theory: Essays on Institutions* (Cambridge: Harvard University Press, 2016).
36. See Ronald Coase, "The New Institutional Economics," *The American Economic Review* 85 (1998): 72–74, 72.

37. See, e.g., Wolfgang Streeck, "The Study of Organized Interests: Before 'The Century' and After," in *The Diversity of Democracy: Corporatism, Social Order and Political Conflict*, eds. Colin Crouch and Wolfgang Streeck (Cheltenham, UK: Edward Elgar, 2006), 3–45, 28.
38. For more on the history of corporatism, see Howard J. Wiarda, *Corporatism and Comparative Politics: The Other Great "Ism"* (London: M. E. Sharpe, 1997).
39. See Rawls, *A Theory of Justice*, p. 75.
40. Ibid., p. 74ff.
41. Ibid., p. 74.
42. Ibid.
43. The introduction of the game theoretic concept of the trembling hand and its relation to the solution of bargaining problems is usually attributed to Richard Selten. See Richard Selten, "A Reexamination of the Perfectness Concept for Equilibrium Points in Extensive Games," *International Journal of Game Theory* 4 (1975): 25–55. For an accessible discussion of how the trembling hand idea is supposed to work, see Ken Binmore, *Playing for Real: A Text on Game Theory* (Oxford University Press, 2007), pp. 411–413.
44. See my "Politics of Masochism," *Inquiry* 46 (2003): 29–63 for a full discussion of this problem.
45. Rawls, *A Theory of Justice*, p. 74.
46. Ibid.
47. Ibid., sec. 14, p. 75. See also sec. 47, p. 267–268.
48. See Rawls, *A Theory of Justice*, p. 76.
49. Ibid., p. 75.
50. My thanks to one of the anonymous referees for this manuscript for pointing this out.
51. Rawls, *A Theory of Justice*, sec. 47, pp. 273.
52. See A. C. Pigou, *The Economics of Welfare* (London: Macmillan, 4th ed., 1932).
53. See Reiff, *Exploitation and Economic Justice in the Liberal Capitalist State*, pp. 33–40.
54. See Rawls, *A Theory of Justice*, sec. 47, p. 272.
55. Ibid., p. 271.
56. Ibid., p. 243: "The idea of justice as fairness is to use the notion of pure procedural justice to handle the contingencies of particular situations. The social system is to be designed so that the resulting distribution is just no matter how things turn out."
57. Indeed, Rawls himself denies that efficiency alone could establish justice. See Rawls, *A Theory of Justice*, p. 62.
58. See Nozick, *Anarchy, State, and Utopia*, pp. 160–164.
59. See, e.g., G. A. Cohen, *Self-Ownership, Freedom, and Equality* (Cambridge: Cambridge University Press, 1995) (citing a number of ways voluntary transactions can produce injustice).
60. See Reiff, *Exploitation and Economic Justice in the Liberal Capitalist State*.
61. See generally Brad Hooker, *Ideal Code, Real World* (Oxford: Oxford University Press, 2003), pp. 93–111; Alex Rajczi, "On the Incoherence Objection to Rule Utilitarianism," *Ethical Theory and Moral Practice* 19 (2016): 857–876.
62. See Hart, *The Concept of Law*, p. 166.
63. See Rawls, *A Theory of Justice*, p. 64.

64. See Geoffrey M. Hodgson, "What Are Institutions?" *Journal of Economic Issues* 40 (2006): 1–25.
65. See Joe Hill, "The Preacher and the Slave" (1910). To see Utah Phillips perform the song and describe a bit of its history, see www.youtube.com/watch?v=PJ236CwhlPw.
66. For an extensive discussion of the nature and role of enforceability here, see my *Punishment, Compensation, and Law: A Theory of Enforceability* (Cambridge: Cambridge University Press, 2005).
67. I therefore depart here from the abstraction of the hypothetical libertarian utopia of the first essay in this volume, although I hope to show that the lessons of that abstraction are also applicable to the actual world examined here.
68. For a similar thought, see Fuller, "Eunomics," pp. 68–69: "A social institution makes of human life something that it would not otherwise have been. We cannot therefore ask of it simply, Is its end good and does it serve that end well? Instead we have to ask a question at once more vague and more complicated – something like this: Does this institution, in a context of other institutions, create a pattern of living that is satisfying and worthy of man's capacities?"
69. See, e.g., Kathleen Thelen, "Varieties of Labor Politics in the Developed Democracies," in *Varieties of Capitalism: The Institutional Foundations of Comparative Advantage,* eds. Peter A. Hall and David Soskice (Oxford: Oxford University Press, 2001), pp. 71–103.
70. But perhaps not for long. As of this moment, the British Labour Party looks destined for oblivion, see Matthew J. Goodwin, "Old Labour, New Labour, No Labour," *The New York Times* (January 11, 2017), no doubt in part (but of course only in part) because of the decline in unionization in the United Kingdom.
71. For further discussion of the difference between general rights to liberty and equality and more particularized rights like freedom of association or freedom of speech, see Dworkin, "What Rights Do We Have?"
72. See John Locke, "Second Treatise on Government," in *Two Treatises on Government,* ed. Pater Laslett (Cambridge: Cambridge University Press, 1988 [1698]), sec. 7, 8, and 10.
73. See generally Vittorio Bufacchi, "Theoretical Foundations for Human Rights," *Political Studies* 66 (2018): 601–617.
74. See Jeremy Bentham, *Rights, Representation, and Reform: Nonsense on Stilts and Other Writings on the French Revolution,* ed. Philip Schofield, Catherine Pease-Watkin, and Cyprian Blamires (Oxford: Oxford University Press, 2002).
75. See generally Michael Freeman, *Human Rights* (Oxford: Polity, 2002); Margaret MacDonald, "Natural Rights," in *Theories of Rights,* ed. Jeremy Waldron (Oxford: Oxford University Press, 1984), pp. 21–40; Leo Strauss, *Natural Right and History* (Chicago: University of Chicago Press, 1953).
76. See, e.g., James A. Gross, *A Shameful Business: The Case for Human Rights in the American Workplace* (Ithaca, NY: ILR Press, 2010); James A. Gross (ed.), *Workers' Rights as Human Rights* (Ithaca, NY: ILR Press, 2003).
77. See, e.g., H. L. A. Hart, "Are There Any Natural Rights?" *The Philosophical Review* 64 (1955): 175–191.

78. The one exception here is that the pre-institutional and post-institutional distinction also comes up in the context of discussing whether desert can function as a theory of justice, for many theorists question whether desert claims can make sense before the institutions that generate the outputs that people claim to deserve exist. See, e.g., Serena Olsaretti, "Introduction," in *Desert and Justice* (Oxford: Oxford University Press, 2003), pp. 1–24, 9–11.
79. Note however, that it would still be possible to use consequentialist and perhaps even other forms of moral standards to make choices regarding basic institutions even if there were no such rights, so acceptance of the idea of there being both pre-institutional and post-institutional rights is not essential to my project. In context, however, this choice should be relatively uncontroversial.
80. For further discussion of the difference between a concept and a conception, see Ronald Dworkin, *Law's Empire* (Cambridge: Harvard University Press, 1986), pp. 70–72.
81. See Reiff, *Exploitation and Economic Justice in the Liberal Capitalist State*.
82. See Sara Diamond, *Roads to Dominion: Right-Wing Movements and Political Power in the United States* (New York: Guildford Press, 1995), pp. 22–23; Melvin Dubofsky, *The State and Labor in Modern America* (University of North Carolina Press, 1994), p. 132; Frederick Rudolph, "The American Liberty League, 1934-1940," *The American Historical Review* 56 (1950): 19–33; George Wolfskill, *The Revolt of the Conservatives: A History of the American Liberty League, 1934-1940* (New York: Houghton-Mifflin, 1962).
83. See Isaiah Berlin, "Two Concepts of Liberty," in *Liberty*, ed. Henry Hardy (Oxford: Oxford University Press, 2002), pp. 168–217; Matthew Kramer, *The Quality of Freedom* (Oxford: Oxford University Press, 2003).
84. See Charles Taylor, "What's Wrong with Negative Liberty?" in *Philosophy and the Human Sciences: Philosophical Papers* 2 (Cambridge: Cambridge University Press, 1985), pp. 211–229.
85. I also talk about these various concepts of liberty in the first essay in this volume and in some of my other works. See, e.g., Mark R. Reiff, *On Unemployment, Volume II: Achieving Economic Justice after the Great Recession* (New York: Palgrave Macmillan, 2015), pp. 75, 124–129; Reiff, *Exploitation and Economic Justice in the Liberal Capitalist State*, pp. 288–289.
86. In other words, as Ronald Dworkin contends, there is no *general* right to negative liberty. See Dworkin, "What Rights Do We Have?"
87. See Taylor, "What's Wrong with Negative Liberty?"
88. Indeed, according to Dworkin, rights to specific liberties like freedom of speech and freedom of association are actually derived from a general right to equality, not liberty. See Dworkin, "What Rights Do We Have?"
89. See Taylor, "What's Wrong with Negative Liberty?" pp. 213–217.
90. See, e.g., Berlin, "Two Concepts of Liberty"; Nozick, *Anarchy, State and Utopia*, pp. 33, 297, 351 n. 1. Note, however, that what we are looking for here is neutrality in justification not effect.
91. For more on this argument, albeit in a different context, see Mark R. Reiff, "A Philosopher Argues Why No One Has the Right to Refuse Service to LGBT People," *The Conversation* (July 25, 2017) (https://theconversation.com/a-philosopher-argues-why-no-one-has-the-right-to-refuse-services-to-lgbt-people-80365).

92. For more on republican liberty generally, see Frank Lovett, *A General Theory of Domination and Justice* (Oxford: Oxford University Press, 2010); Philip Pettit, "Freedom: Psychological, Ethical, and Political," *Critical Review of International Social and Political Philosophy* 18 (2015): 375–389, 382–385; Philip Pettit, "Freedom as Non-Domination," in *On the People's Terms*, pp. 26–74; Philip Pettit, "The Instability of Freedom as Noninterference: The Case of Isaiah Berlin," *Ethics* 121 (2011): 693–716, 707–708; Philip Pettit, "Freedom in the Market," *Politics, Philosophy, and Economics* 5 (2006): 131–149; Philip Pettit, "Liberty as Non-Domination," in *Republicanism: A Theory of Freedom and Government* (Oxford: Oxford University Press, 1997), pp. 51–79; Quentin Skinner, *Liberty before Liberalism* (Cambridge: Cambridge University Press, 1998); Quentin Skinner, "Classical Liberty and the Coming of the English Civil War," in *Republicanism: A Shared European Heritage*, eds. Martin van Gelderen and Quentin Skinner (Cambridge: Cambridge University Press, 2002), vol. 2, pp. 9–28.
93. See, e.g., Pettit, *On the People's Terms*.
94. See, e.g., Robert S. Taylor, *Exit Left: Markets and Mobility in Republican Thought* (Oxford: Oxford University Press, 2017); Alan Thomas, *Republic of Equals: Predistribution and Property-Owning Democracy* (Oxford: Oxford University Press (2017).
95. See Rawls, *A Theory of Justice*, sec. 60, pp. 347–350; sec. 66, pp. 380–386.
96. For a similar example of arbitrariness in connection with the imposition of harsher punishment on certain groups but not others, see Erica L. Green, "Why Are Black Students Punished So Often? Minnesota Confronts a National Quandary," *The New York Times* (March 18, 2018).
97. See John Rawls, *Political Liberalism* (New York: Columbia University Press, 1993, 1996), pp. 54ff.
98. See, e.g., *Motor Vehicle Manufacturers Association v. State Farm Mutual Insurance Co.*, 463 US 29 (1983) (reaffirming what has become known as "the hard look doctrine"). According to the Court, a decision of an administrative agency would count as arbitrary if "the agency has relied on factors which Congress has not intended it to consider, entirely failed to consider an important aspect of the problem, offered an explanation for its decision that runs counter to the evidence before the agency, or is so implausible that it could not be ascribed to a difference in view or the product of agency expertise." Ibid. at 43. The same idea, in my view, is captured in the idea of republican liberty, which can be applied to any decision maker.
99. Contrast this with the view of Philip Pettit, who does include an intent requirement in his conception of what constitutes a violation of republican liberty. See, e.g., Pettit, *Republicanism*, pp. 26, 52–53, 79, 83–84, 272.
100. For criticism of those republican liberty theorists who do include an intent requirement, see Kramer, *The Quality of Freedom*, pp. 133–134.
101. See Phillip Pettit, "Liberty as Non-Domination," pp. 51–80, esp. pp. 55–58 (an act or omission is arbitrary when it is chosen or rejected without reference to the interests or the opinions of those affected); Quentin Skinner, "A Third Concept of Liberty," *Proceedings of the British Academy* 117 (2002): 237–268, 248 (an arbitrary power is one that is capable of interfering without activities without having to consider our interests).

102. I have borrowed this example from John Broome. See John Broome, "Fairness," in *Ethics Out of Economics* (Cambridge: Cambridge University Press, 1999), pp. 113–120.
103. See Ben Hubbard, "Saudi Women Rise Up, Quietly, and Slide into the Driver's Seat," *The New York Times* (October 26, 2013).
104. For a discussion of "adaptive preferences," see Jon Elster, *Sour Grapes: Studies in the Subversion of Rationality* (Cambridge: Cambridge University Press, 1983), pp. 109–140; Ben Colburn, "Autonomy and Adaptive Preferences," *Utilitas* 23 (2011): 52–71.
105. See generally Erwin Chemerinsky, "Substantive Due Process," *Touro Law Review* 15 (1999): 1501–1534.
106. See, e.g., Philip Pettit, "Keeping Republican Freedom Simple: On a Difference with Quentin Skinner," *Political Theory* 30 (2002): 339–356, 340.
107. See Matthew H. Kramer, "Liberty and Domination," in *Republicanism and Political Theory*, eds. Cecile Laborde and John Maynor (Oxford: Blackwell, 2008), pp. 31–57.
108. See, e.g., Skinner, *Liberty before Liberalism*, pp. 74–75.
109. For further discussion of and argument for my view on this, see Reiff, *Exploitation and Economic Justice in the Liberal Capitalist State*, p. 88. See also Dworkin, "What Rights Do We Have?"
110. Called the "Porter Hypothesis" after a series of academic articles by the economist Michael Porter in the 1990s, this has been shown to hold true in several studies across a wide range of industries. See Farhad Manjoo, "Trump Says Regulations Impede. Perhaps Not in the Electric Car Business," *The New York Times* (March 22, 2017); Luke Stewart, "The Impact of Regulation on Innovation in the United States: A Cross-Industry Literature Review," *Information Technology & Innovation Foundation* (June 2010) (www.itif.org/files/2011-impact-regulation-innovation.pdf); Celine McNicholas, Heidi Shierholz, and Marni von Wilpert, "Workers Health, Safety, and Pay Are Among the Casualties of Trump's War on Regulations," *Report* (Economic Policy Institute, January 29, 2018), p. 2 (noting that federal regulations currently provide new benefits to society of over $1,000 billion per year); Jag Bhalla, "The American Healthcare System Shows Why We Can't Trust Free Market Ideologues," *Evonomics* (April 6, 2018) (interviewing economist Robert H. Frank); Diane Coyle, "Three Cheers for Regulation," *Project Syndicate* (July 17, 2018) (discussing how regulation made the market for cell phone hardware and services possible through the enforcement of universal technical standards).
111. See, e.g., F. A. Hayek, *The Road to Serfdom* (London: Routledge, 1944), esp. ch. 7; F. A. Hayek, *The Constitution of Liberty* (London: Routledge, 1960), ch. 18; Milton Friedman, *Capitalism and Freedom* (Chicago: University of Chicago Press, 1962), esp. ch. 1; Milton Friedman and Rose Friedman, *Free to Choose* (Orlando, FL: Harcourt, Inc, 1980). The argument made by Hayek and Friedman and those similarly minded actually goes back to J. S. Mill, although Mill rejected the idea that the protection of liberty alone provided a sufficient reason to prohibit government interference in the market in all circumstances. See J. S. Mill, *Principles of Political Economy* (London: John W. Parker, 1849), bk. 5, ch. 11, sec. 3.

112. See Mark R. Reiff, "Two Theories of Economic Liberalism," *The Adam Smith Review* 10 (2017): 189–214; David M. Kotz, *The Rise and Fall of Neoliberal Capitalism* (Cambridge: Harvard University Press, 2015), pp. 8–84.
113. See Reiff, "Two Theories of Economic Liberalism"; Reiff, *Exploitation and Economic Justice in the Liberal Capitalist State*, pp. 287–291, Mark R. Reiff, *On Unemployment, Volume I: A Micro-Theory of Economic Justice* (New York: Palgrave Macmillan, 2015), pp. 128–130.
114. For an extensive discussion of the problems with using voluntariness as a pre-institutional guide to anything, see my *Exploitation and Economic Justice in the Liberal Capitalist State*, pp. 84–93.
115. Coase was the first to draw attention to this paradox. See R. H. Coase, "The Nature of the Firm," in *The Firm, the Market, and the Law* (Chicago: University of Chicago Press, 1988), pp. 33–55. See also Alfred D. Chandler, Jr., *The Visible Hand: The Managerial Revolution in American Business* (Cambridge: Harvard University Press, 1977), p. 1: "The theme propounded here is that the modern business enterprise took the place of market mechanisms in coordinating the activities of the economy. In many sectors of the economy the visible hand of management replaced what Adam Smith referred to as the invisible hand of market forces. The market remained the generator of demand for goods and services, but modern business enterprise took over the functions of coordinating flows of goods through exiting processes of production and distribution. As modern business enterprise acquired functions hitherto carried out by the market, it became the most powerful institution in the American economy and its managers the most influential group of economic decision makers."
116. For more on my particular conception of republican liberty, see the first essay in this volume, as well as Reiff, *On Unemployment, Volume II*, pp. 75, 124–129; and Reiff, *Exploitation and Economic Justice in the Liberal Capitalist State*, pp. 288–289.
117. Adam Smith, *Lectures on Jurisprudence* (Oxford: Oxford University Press, 1978), iii, 130, p. 192. For a discussion of the concern for what we now call republican liberty in various places in Smith's work, see Lisa Herzog, "The Normative Stakes of Economic Growth; Or, Why Adam Smith Does Not Rely on 'Trickle Down'," *Journal of Politics* 78 (2016): 50–62, 56.
118. See, e.g., Paul Marginson, "Power and Efficiency in the Firm: Understanding the Employment Relationship," in *Transaction Costs, Markets and Hierarchies*, ed. Christos Pitelis (Oxford: Blackwell, 1993), pp. 133–165.
119. Pettit, *Republicanism*, p. 61.
120. See Rawls, *Justice as Fairness*, pp. 14–16. Marx, of course, made a similar point. See Karl Marx, *Capital Volume 1: A Critique of Political Economy* (London: Penguin, 1992). See also Robert Hale, "Coercion and Distribution in a Supposedly Non-Coercive State," *Political Science Quarterly* 38 (1923): 470–494.
121. Rawls envisions the original position as involving a four-stage sequence of decisions during which the constraints imposed by the veil of ignorance are gradually lifted. See Rawls, *A Theory of Justice*, sec. 31. Exactly where to place the decision I am referring to here within Rawls's schema is a matter solely of Rawlsian exegesis and therefore not relevant to what I am discussing here, so I will not take a position on this. Suffice it to say, the decision to which I refer takes place in a hypothetical world where everything but the outcome of this

Notes to pp. 97–100

particular decision is as it actually is. Whether such a decision can be placed within the Rawlsian four-stage sequence or whether it takes place at some later stage is entirely beside the point.

122. See Coase, "The Nature of the Firm," pp. 33–47; Oliver E. Williamson, *The Economic Institutions of Capitalism* (New York: Free Press, 1985), p. 1 (economic institutions such as the firm "have the main purpose and effect of economizing on transaction costs").

123. For further discussions of firm size, see Coase, "The Nature of the Firm," pp. 33–47; Armen Alchian and Harold Demsetz, "Production, Information Costs, and Economic Organization," *American Economic Review* 62 (1975): 777–795; Williamson, *The Economic Institutions of Capitalism*, esp. ch. 6. For a discussion of the pressure to grow even among the already humongous, see, Om Malik, "Apple, Google, Amazon, and the Advantages of Bigness," *The New Yorker* (August 9, 2016).

124. Indeed, this is one way to read the Brexit vote. The majority of UK voters were willing to sacrifice some degree of economic efficiency and well-being to protect themselves from what they saw as the arbitrary domination of Brussels. See Neil Irwin, "How a Quest by Elites Is Driving 'Brexit' and Trump," *The New York Times* (July 1, 2016).

125. See generally Michael Beer and Russell A. Eisenstat, "The Silent Killers of Strategy Implementation and Learning," *Sloan Management Review* 41 (2000): 29–40.

126. See generally Werner Bonefeld, "Freedom and the Strong State: On German Ordo-Liberalism," *New Political Economy* 17 (2012): 633–656; Werner Bonefeld, "On the Strong Liberal State: Beyond Berghahn and Young" *New Political Economy* 18 (2013): 779–783.

127. See Reiff, "Two Theories of Economic Liberalism."

128. See A. James Gregor, *The Ideology of Fascism* (New York: The Free Press, 1969), p. 301.

129. See Masha Gessen, *The Man without a Face: The Unlikely Rise of Vladimir Putin* (New York: Riverhead Books, 2012).

130. Pontifical Council for Justice and Peace, *Compendium of the Social Doctrine of the Church* (Washington, DC: United States Conference of Catholic Bishops, 2004), p. 151 (*quoting* John Paul II, Encyclical Letter *Centesimus Annus* 40: *AAS* 93 (1991), 843).

131. See Tim Wu, "Be Afraid of Economic 'Bigness.' Be Very Afraid," *The New York Times* (November 10, 2018); Tim Wu, *The Curse of Bigness: Antitrust in the New Gilded Age* (New York: Columbia Global Reports, 2018).

132. See Henry Scott Wallace, "American Fascism, in 1944 and Today," *The New York Times* (May 12, 2017); Paul Waldman, "Welcome to the Trump Kleptocracy," *The Washington Post* (November 16, 2016).

133. Or an anti-liberal, someone who believed that morality was a trick employed by the weak to dominate the strong. See, e.g., Friedrich Nietzsche, *On the Genealogy of Morality* (Cambridge: Cambridge University Press, 1994), pp. 11–37.

134. F. A. Hayek, "Labor Unions and Employment," in *The Constitution of Liberty* (London: Routledge, 1960), pp. 233–247, p. 234.

135. See Yves Steiner, "The Neoliberals Confront the Trade Unions," in *The Road from Mount Pèlerin*, eds. Philip Mirowski and Dieter Plehwe (Cambridge: Harvard University Press, 2009), pp. 181–203, esp. 195; Benjamin Jackson, "Hayek, Hutt and the Trade Unions," in *Hayek: A Collective Biography: Part V Hayek's Great Society of Free Men*, ed. Robert Leeson (London: Palgrave Macmillan, 2015), pp. 159–175.
136. See Reiff, "Two Theories of Economic Liberalism."
137. For an extended discussion of this point, see Reiff, *On Unemployment, Volume I*, pp. 38–43, 47–52.
138. Ibid. at p. 84.
139. See, e.g., Michael Sainato, "Accidents at Amazon: Workers Left to Suffer after Warehouse Injuries," *The Guardian* (July 30, 2018).
140. Note that those who proffer efficiency as the guide for all action seem perfectly happy to disregard the inefficiency that arises from the failure to account for social costs, presumably because they believe there is no moral obligation to do so, effectively conceding that efficiency is subject to moral requirements.
141. For further discussion of this phenomenon, see Mark R. Reiff, "No Such Thing as Accident: Rethinking the Relation between Causal and Moral Responsibility," *Canadian Journal of Law and Jurisprudence* 28 (2015): 371–397.
142. See Rawls, *A Theory of Justice*, sec. 21, esp. pp. 106–108.
143. See generally James Gleick, *Chaos: Making a New Science* (New York: Penguin Books, 1987), pp. 9–32; Edward N. Lorenz, *The Essence of Chaos* (University of Washington Press, 1993), esp. app. 1.
144. On "right-to-work" laws generally, see William J. Moore, "The Determinants and Effects of Right-to-Work Laws: A Review of the Recent Literature," *Journal of Labor Research* 19 (1998): 445–469, and Victor G. Devinatz, "The Continuing Controversy over Right-to-Work Laws in the Early Twenty-First Century," *Employee Responsibilities and Rights Journal* 23 (2011): 287–293.
145. Backwards induction is a form of reasoning that determines what state of affairs must have held in the beginning by taking the end result as fixed and then reasoning backwards to try to determine what series of choices must have produced these fixed points.
146. And this is notwithstanding the right-wing version of the argument from equality – the claim that complaining about inequality amounts to "special pleading" and doing something about it means giving certain people "special rights," rights the rest of us supposedly don't have.
147. For the strong version of Steiner's view, see Hillel Steiner, *An Essay on Rights* (Oxford: Blackwell, 1994), pp. 52–54. See also Hillel Steiner, "Slavery, Socialism, and Private Property," in *Property*, eds. J. Roland Pennock and John W. Chapman (New York: New York University Press, 1980), pp. 244–265, 245–246; Hillel Steiner, "Individual Liberty," *Aristotelian Society Proceedings* 75 (1975): 35–50, reprinted in *Liberty*, ed. David Miller (Oxford: Oxford University Press, 1991); Hillel Steiner, "On the Conflict between Liberty and Equality," in *Oxford Handbook of Freedom*, eds. David Schmidtz and Carmen Pavel (New York: Oxford University Press, 2018), pp. 76–89; Hillel Steiner, "Evaluation and the Quantification of Freedom," in *Thinking towards Humanity: Themes from Norman Geras*, eds. E. Garrard and S. de Wijze

(Manchester: Manchester University Press, 2012). Support for Steiner's view can also be found in Bentham, Marx, and perhaps even in Nozick and Berlin. See Steiner, "On the Conflict between Liberty and Equality."

148. For criticism of Steiner's view, see Kramer, *The Quality of Freedom*, pp. 209–222; Ian Carter, *A Measure of Freedom* (Oxford: Oxford University Press, 1999), pp. 247–248, 258–267. While I am not relying on Steiner's view here, I nevertheless do find Steiner's view appealing and defend it in Reiff, *On Unemployment, Volume I*, pp. 125–127.

149. See Steiner, "On the Conflict between Liberty and Equality." The strong version, in contrast, states that there can be no gains without *equal* offsetting losses – that is, it claims that negative liberty is a zero-sum concept. If the strong version is true, of course, there could never be grounds for objecting to anything on the grounds it decreased negative liberty.

150. See, e.g., Geoffrey Mohan, "Farmworkers Union Underpaid Its Own Organizers, Judge Rules," *Los Angeles Times* (March 29, 2017).

151. See Reiff, *On Unemployment, Volume II*, pp. 120, 207 n. 44 and 45.

152. This answers the objection to the concept of republican liberty raised in Thomas W. Simpson, "The Impossibility of Republican Freedom," *Philosophy & Public Affairs* 45 (2017): 27–53. See also Frank Lovett and Philip Pettit, "Preserving Republican Freedom: A Reply to Simpson," *Philosophy and Public Affairs* (2019): 1–21.

153. See John Broome, *Weighing Goods* (Oxford: Basil Blackwell, 1991), pp. 121–159.

154. See Reiff, *On Unemployment, Volume I*, pp. 53–54, 159 n. 48; Mark R. Reiff, "The Difference Principle, Rising Inequality, and Supply-Side Economics: How Rawls Got Hijacked by the Right," *Revue de Philosophie Économique/Review of Economic Philosophy* 13:2 (2012): 119–173.

155. See Reiff, *On Unemployment, Volume I*, pp. 54–56.

156. For a discussion of the burdens of judgment, see Rawls, *Political Liberalism*, pp. 54ff.

157. See generally Daniel Kahneman, *Thinking, Fast and Slow* (New York: Farrar, Strauss and Giroux, 2011), pp. 322–341.

158. Think of this latter constraint, then, as an *anti*-precautionary principle of the sort advocated in Cass Sunstein, *Laws of Fear: Beyond the Precautionary Principle* (Cambridge: Cambridge University Press, 2005).

159. See Richard B. Freeman and James L. Medoff, *What Do Unions Do?* (New York: Basic Books, 1984).

160. For a full list of all the claims made in Freeman and Medoff's original book, see James T. Bennett and Bruce E. Kaufman, "What Do Unions Do? A Twenty-Year Perspective," in *What Do Unions Do? A Twenty-Year Perspective*, eds. James T. Bennett and Bruce E. Kaufman (New Brunswick, NJ: Transaction Publishers, 2007), pp. 1–11, 5–6.

161. See Freeman and Medoff, *What Do Unions Do?* p. 46.

162. See David G. Blanchflower and Alex Bryson, "What Effect Do Unions Have on Wages Now and Would Freeman and Medoff Be Surprised?" in *What Do Unions Do? A Twenty-Year Perspective*, eds. James T. Bennett and Bruce E. Kaufman (New Brunswick, NJ: Transaction Publishers, 2007), pp. 79–113, 83, 90; Meyer, "Union Membership Trends in the United States," Congressional Research

Service (Washington, DC, 2004) (http://digitalcommons.ilr.cornell.edu/cgi/viewcontent.cgi?article=1176&context=key_workplace), p. 6 (putting wage gap at 10–30 percent).
163. See Susan Dynarski, "Fresh Proof that Strong Unions Help Reduce Income Inequality," *The New York Times* (July 6, 2018).
164. See Jake Rosenfeld, Patrick Denice, and Jennifer Laird, "Union Decline Lowers Wages of Nonunion Workers: The Overlooked Reason Why Wages Are Stuck and Inequality is Growing" (Economic Policy Institute, August 30, 2016) (file:///C:/Users/mreif/Documents/Unionization/EPI%20Report%20on%20Non%20union%20workers.pdf). See also Economic Policy Institute, "Drop in Union Membership Has Taken $14 to $52 Out of Nonunion Workers' Weekly Wages," in *The Top Charts of 2016* (December 22, 2016) (www.epi.org/publication/the-top-charts-of-2016-13-charts-that-show-the-difference-between-the-economy-we-have-now-and-the-economy-we-could-have/?mc_cid=f022fe6a6f&mc_eid=494a829c5c#chart6).
165. See, e.g., Jeffrey H. Keefe, "Eliminating Fair Share Fees and Making Public Employment 'Right-to-Work' Would Increase the Pay Penalty for Working in State and Local Government," EPI Briefing Paper #408 (October 13, 2015) (www.epi.org/files/pdf/93216.pdf) (public sector unions boost wages for all public sector employees 5–8 percent, and private sector unions boost wages for all private sector employees by twice that amount); Richard C. Kearney and Patrice M. Mareschal, *Labor Relations in the Public Sector* (Boca Raton, FL: CRC Press, 5th ed., 2014), pp. 171–172 (reporting similar figures).
166. See Elise Gould and Will Kimball, "'Right-to-Work' States Still Have Lower Wages," EPI Briefing Paper #395 (Economic Policy Institute, April 22, 2015) (finding that wages are 3.1 percent lower in RTW states than in non-RTW states) (http://s1.epi.org/files/pdf/82934.pdf); Russell Wilson, "Anti-Union Push Begins Again in Maine Legislature," *Maine Beacon* (February 6, 2017) (noting that the Bureau of Labor Statistics study shows that employees in right-to-work states earn wages that are 12.2 percent lower than in other states). On other effects of right-to-work laws, see Moore, "The Determinants and Effects of Right-to-Work Laws," and Devinatz, "The Continuing Controversy over Right-to-Work Laws in the Early Twenty-First Century."
167. See Steven Greenhouse, "Low-Wage Workers Finding It's Easier to Fall into Poverty, and Harder to Get Out," *The New York Times* (March 16, 2014); Kashana Cauley, "Why Millennials Should Lead the Next Labor Movement," *The New York Times* (July 13, 2017) ("The lack of unionization has sent the bottom flying out of the Middle Class"); Dominic Rushe, "Fran Works Six Days a Week in Fast Food, and Yet She's Homeless: 'It's Economic Slavery,'" *The Guardian* (August 21, 2017). Workers who have *not* experienced these problems, in contrast, tend to be those represented by unions. See The Working Life, "Some Retail Workers Find Better Deals with Unions," *The New York Times* (September 7, 2014).
168. See Daniel Gross, "McDonald's and Visa Conjure Fantasy Budget for Low-Wage Employees," *The Daily Beast* (July 16, 2013) (describing recent guide given out to its employees by McDonald's on how to survive on low wages as suggesting that workers get a second job and stop squandering their funds on luxury items like heat and health care); Peter S. Goodman, "McDonald's

Budget Plan Leaves Out Critical Line: Corporate Welfare," *The Huffington Post* (July 17, 2013); Steven Greenhouse, "Movement to Increase McDonald's Minimum Wage Broadens Its Tactics," *The New York Times* (March 30, 2015); Noam Scheiber, "In Test for Unions and Politicians, a Nationwide Protest on Pay," *The New York Times* (April 15, 2015); Kari Lydersen, "Thousands of Protesters Brand McDonald's the 'Trump of Corporations,'" *The Guardian* (May 24, 2017); Abi Wilkinson, "McDonald's Workers to Coordinate Strike with Allies Around the World," *The Guardian* (August 21, 2017); Steven Greenhouse, "Fast-Food Workers Claim Victory in a New York Labor Effort," *The New York Times* (January 9, 2018); Taylor Telford, "Thousands of Service Industry Workers Will Strike Next Week to Demand Unions," *The Washington Post* (September 27, 2018); Mary Kay Henry, "How Workers Are Winning $15 an Hour: By Acting Like a Union," *The Guardian* (January 17, 2019).

169. See, e.g., Lizette Alvarez, "He Stars in a Spanish-Language Soap. Why Is He Driving for Uber?" *The New York Times* (October 20, 2016).

170. See Economic Policy Institute, "The Productivity-Pay Gap" (updated August 2016) (www.epi.org/productivity-pay-gap/?utm_source=Economic+Policy+Institute&utm_campaign=54f5cc5f0a-EMAIL_CAMPAIGN_2017_05_15&utm_medium=email&utm_term=0_e7c5826c50-54f5cc5f0a-58070685&mc_cid=54f5cc5f0a&mc_eid=494a829c5c).

171. See Steven Greenhouse, "Study Finds Violations of Wage Law in New York and California," *The New York Times* (December 3, 2014) (according to a new study by the US Labor Department, 3.5–6.5 percent of all wage and salary workers in New York and California are being illegally paid less than the applicable minimum wage); Steven Greenhouse, "McDonald's Is Charged with Punishing Workers," *The New York Times* (December 19, 2014); Steven Greenhouse, "More Workers Are Claiming 'Wage Theft'," *The New York Times* (August 31, 2014); Brady Meixell and Ross Eisenbrey, "An Epidemic of Wage Theft is Costing Workers Hundreds of Millions of Dollars a Year," EPI Issue Brief #385 (Economic Policy Institute, September 11, 2014), p. 2 (noting that $933 million had been recovered for the victims of wage theft by private attorneys and government agencies in 2012 alone) (http://s3.epi.org/files/2014/wage-theft.pdf); Associated Press, "NBCUniversal to Settle Suit Over Unpaid Interns," *The New York Times* (October 24, 2014) ($6.4 million settlement agreed between NBCUniversal and "interns" who were not but allegedly should have been paid under the relevant labor laws); Patrick McGeehan, "Millions Due in Back Pay to Dancers at Manhattan Strip Club," *The New York Times* (November 14, 2014) (trail court ruled that strip club treated dancers as employees and therefore owed them at least $10.8 million for hourly work performed between 2005 and 2012). See also Greenhouse, "McDonald's Is Charged with Punishing Workers"; Tim Judson and Cristina Francisco-McGuire, "Where Theft is Legal: Mapping Wage Theft Laws in the 50 States," *Progressive States Network* (June 2012) (www.leg.state.co.us/CLICS/CLICS2013A/commsumm.nsf/b4a3962433b52fa787256e5f00670a71/e9b1f269d522a83b87257b3a006a03c8/$FILE/130326%20AttachE.pdf); Noam Scheiber, "Uber to Repay Millions to Drivers, Who Could be Owed Far More," *The New York Times* (May 23, 2017); Noam Scheiber, "Uber Says It Just Noticed

Error on Pay, but It Was No Secret," *The New York Times* (June 1, 2017); Noam Scheiber, "How Uber's Tax Calculations May Have Cost Drivers Hundreds of Millions," *The New York Times* (July 6, 2017); Mike Elk, "Christmas Tree Cutters' Labor Fight Shines Light on Holiday Season's Forgotten Workers," *The Guardian* (December 18, 2017) (describing how low-wage Latinos who harvest Christmas Tress won a $350,000 settlement for wage theft by their employers); Andrew Khouri, "More Workers Are saying Their Bosses Are Threatening to Have Them Deported," *Los Angeles Times* (January 2, 2018) (if they complain about wage theft): James C, McKinley Jr., "Laborers on a 'Billionaires' Row' Tower Cheated of Wages, D.A. Says," *The New York Times* (May 16, 2018); Fenit Nirappil and Tim Carman, "Tipping the Pay Scales: Initiative 77 Could Dramatically Alter D.C. Restaurant Culture," *The Washington Post* (June 16, 2018) (5 percent of tipped workers at nearly 600 restaurants audited since 2006 were paid below the minimum wage even with tips, and employer failed to make up the difference despite being required to do so by law); Julie Carrie Wong, "'A White-Collar Sweatshop': Google Assistant Contractors Allege Wage Theft," *The Guardian* (May 29, 2019).

172. See David Cooper and Teresa Kroeger, "Employers Steal Billions from Workers' Paychecks Each Year" (Economic Policy Institute, May 10, 2017) (www.epi.org/files/pdf/125116.pdf), pp. 26–27; Tracy Tullis, "A Multimillion Dollar Payday, at the Carwash," *The New York Times* (February 22, 2019) (noting that wage theft cases are notoriously hard to prove).

173. See *Epic Systems Corp. v. Lewis,* United States Supreme Court (May 21, 2018) (www.supremecourt.gov/opinions/17pdf/16-285_q8l1.pdf); Kate Hamaji, Rachel Deutsch, and Elizabeth Nicolas (for the Center for Popular Democracy), and Celine McNicholas, Heidi Shierholz, and Margaret Poydock (for the Economic Policy Institute), "Unchecked Corporate Power: Forced Arbitration, the Enforcement Crisis, and How Workers Are Fighting Back" (May 2019). See also, Catherine Ho, "Uber Sees Legal Win in Appeal of Case over Driver Status," *San Francisco Chronicle* (September 25, 2018).

174. See Alexander J. S. Colvin, "The Growing Use of Mandatory Arbitration," Economic Policy Institute (September 27, 2017); Editorial, "The Supreme Court Sticks It to Workers, Again," *The New York Times* (May 24, 2018); David G. Savage, "Supreme Court Upholds Arbitration that Bans Workers from Joining Forces over Lost Wages," *Los Angeles Times* (May 21, 2018); Adam Liptak, "Supreme Court Upholds Workplace Arbitration Contracts Barring Class Actions," *The New York Times* (May 21, 2017).

175. Cooper and Kroeger, "Employers Steal Billions from Workers' Paychecks Each Year," p. 1. See also Celine McNicholas, Zane Mokhiber, and Adam Chaikof, "Two Billion Dollars in Stolen Wages Were Recovered for Workers in 2015 and 2016 – And That's Just a Drop in the Bucket," *Report* (Economic Policy Institute, December 13, 2017) (noting that the amount recovered is only a fraction of the amount stolen).

176. For a non-Marxist book-length discussion of how to calculate the cost of production of labor and how that calculation is relevant to determining whether a worker is being exploited or not, see my *Exploitation and Economic Justice in the Liberal Capitalist State.*

177. See Bureau of Labor Statistics, Table A-15, "Alternative Measures of Labor Underutilization," Measure U-6 (May 5, 2017) (www.bls.gov/news.release/empsit.t15.htm) (showing that total unemployed plus total employed only part time for economic reasons as of April 2017 is still 8.6 percent, which is much higher than at this point in past economic recoveries).
178. See Patricia Cohen, "Steady Jobs, with Pay and Hours That Are Anything But," *The New York Times* (May 31, 2017).
179. See Erin Hatton, "The Rise of the Permanent Temp Economy," *The New York Times* (January 26, 2013). And there is good reason to think that this line is currently set unrealistically low. See Reiff, *Exploitation and Economic Justice*, p. 5, n. 14.
180. See Josh Bivens, et al., "How Today's Unions Help Working People" (Economic Policy Institute, August 24, 2017) (www.epi.org/files/pdf/133275.pdf); Lawrence Mishel with Matthew Walters, "How Unions Help All Workers," EPI Briefing Paper #143 (Economic Policy Institute, August 26, 2003) (www.epi.org/publication/briefingpapers_bp143/); John W. Budd, "The Effect of Unions on Employee Benefits and Non-Wage Compensation: Monopoly Power, Collective Voice, and Facilitation," in *What Do Unions Do? A Twenty-Year Perspective*, eds. James T. Bennett and Bruce E. Kaufman (New Brunswick, NJ: Transaction Publishers, 2007), pp. 160–192, 166–169;
181. See Guy Chazan, "German Union Wins Right to 28-hour Working Week and 4.3% Pay Rise," *Financial Times* (February 6, 2018).
182. See, e.g., Natalie Kitroeff, "Californians Compete for a Rare Prize: A Blue-Collar Union Job Paying up to $200,000," *Los Angeles Times* (January 27, 2017) (and full benefits your entire life).
183. Lawrence Mishel, "Unions, Inequality, and Faltering Middle-Class Wages," Issue Brief #342 (Economic Policy Institute, August 29, 2012) (www.epi.org/publication/ib342-unions-inequality-faltering-middle-class/).
184. See, e.g., Damian Paletta, "Trouble in Candy Land," *The Washington Post* (March 29, 2018).
185. See Noah Weiland, "Senate Narrowly Passes Rollback of Obama-Era 'Auto-I.R.A.' Rule," *The New York Times* (March 30, 2017).
186. They also are often claimed to receive cushier work assignments than black employees. See, e.g., Noam Scheiber, "Racially Charged Nissan Vote Is a Test for U.A.W. in the South," *The New York Times* (August 2, 2017); AFSCME Local 3299, "Race, Gender, and Income Disparities at the University of California" (April 2018) (www.dropbox.com/s/39pjpl3gf26b93t/A3299_PioneeringInequality_WhitePaperNEW_Web_lo-res.pdf?dl=0).
187. See Eileen Patten, "Racial, Gender Wage Gaps Persist in U.S. Despite Some Progress," *Pew Research Center* (July 1, 2016) (www.pewresearch.org/fact-tank/2016/07/01/racial-gender-wage-gaps-persist-in-u-s-despite-some-progress/). See also Elise Gould and Celine McNicholas, "Unions Help Narrow the Gender Wage Gap," *Working Economics Blog* (Economic Policy Institute, April 3, 2017).
188. See David Cooper, "Workers of Color Are Far More Likely to be Paid Poverty-Level Wages than White Workers," *Working Economic Blog* (Economic Policy Institute, June 21, 2018).

189. Elise Gould and Adriana Krugler, "Latina Workers Have to Work 10 Months into 2017 to be Paid the Same as White Non-Hispanic Men in 2016," *Working Economic Blog* (Economic Policy Institute, November 1, 2017) (emphasis adjusted).
190. See Madison Matthews and Valerie Wilson, "Separate Is Still Unequal: How Patterns of Occupational Segregation Impact Pay for Black Women," *Working Economics Blog* (Economic Policy Institute, August 6, 2018).
191. See, e.g., Mona Chalabi and Amanda Holpuch, "What that Google Memo Didn't Tell You About Pay Inequality in America," *The Guardian* (August 11, 2017); Daisuke Wakabayashi, "At Google, Employee-Led Effort Finds Men Are Paid More Than Women," *The New York Times* (September 8, 2017); Mona Chalabi, "The History of 2017 in Seven Charts," *The Guardian* (December 29, 2017) (charting gender gap); Amie Tsang, "BBC Managers Face Barrage of Criticism in Gender Pay Dispute," *The New York Times* (January 31, 2018); Stacy Cowley, "Nike Will Raise Wages for Thousands after Outcry over Inequality," *The New York Times* (July 22, 2018).
192. See Elise Gould, "State of Working America Wages 2018," Economic Policy Institute (February 22, 2019).
193. See Amie Tsang, "Pay Gap for Men and Women Grew at Many British Employers, Report Shows," *The New York Times* (April 5, 2019).
194. See Bivens, et al., "How Today's Unions Help Working People"; Mishel and Walters, "How Unions Help All Workers"; David Card, "The Effect of Unions on Wage Inequality in the US Labor Market," *Industrial and Labor Relations Review* 54 (2001): 354–367; Valerie Wilson and Julia Wolfe, "A Missouri 'Right-to-Work' Law Is More Likely to Harm Black Workers, Who are More Likely to be Covered by a Union Contract than Other Workers," Economic Policy Institute (May 15, 2018).
195. See generally Peter Cole, "Martin Luther King Jr., Union Man," *The Conversation* (January 18, 2019).
196. See, e.g., Valerie Wilson and William M. Rodgers III, "Black and White Wages Gaps Expand with Rising Wage Inequality," Economic Policy Institute (September 16, 2016) (www.epi.org/files/pdf/101972.pdf); Elise Gould, "Racial Gaps in Wages, Wealth, and More: A Quick Recap," Economic Policy Institute (January 26, 2017) (www.epi.org/blog/racial-gaps-in-wages-wealth-and-more-a-quick-recap/); Tatiana Walk-Morris, "Anti-Black Hiring Discrimination Hasn't Improved in 25 Years. What Can We Do?" *The Guardian* (September 21, 2017); Marie T. Mora and Alberto Dávilla, "The Hispanic–White Wage Gap Has Remained Wide and Relatively Steady," Economic Policy Institute (July 2, 2018). And this is not because black people are not working as hard as their white counterparts. See Valerie Wilson and Janelle Jones, "Low-Wage African American Workers Have Increased Annual Work Hours Most Since 1979" (Economic Policy Institute, March 27, 2017) (www.epi.org/blog/low-wage-african-american-workers-have-increased-annual-work-hours-most-since-1979/?utm_source=Economic+Policy+Institute&utm_campaign=20d6e60719-EMAIL_CAMPAIGN_2017_03_30&utm_medium=email&utm_term=0_e7c5826c50-20d6e60719-58070685&mc_cid=20d6e60719&mc_eid=494a829c5c).
197. See Lawrence Mishel, "Diversity in the New York City Union and Nonunion Construction Sectors," Economic Policy Institute Report (March 2, 2017) (www.epi.org/files/pdf/119517.pdf). See also Gerry Hudson, "The Labor

Movement Fought for Civil Rights Before. We Will Do It Again," *The Guardian* (September 4, 2017) (black men in unions earn 35 percent more than their nonunion counterparts; black women 37 percent more); Cherrie Bucknor, "Black Workers, Unions, and Inequality," *Center for Economic and Policy Research* (August 2016) (http://cepr.net/images/stories/reports/black-workers-unions-2016-08.pdf?v=2).

198. See Cherrie Bucknor, "Black Workers, Unions, and Inequality"; Mike Elk, "Justice in the Factory: How Black Lives Matter Breathed New Life into Unions," *The Guardian* (February 10, 2018).
199. Mishel, "Diversity in the New York City Union and Nonunion Construction Services."
200. See Elise Gould, Jessica Schieder, and Kathleen Geier, *What Is the Gender Pay Gap and Is It Real?* (Economic Policy Institute, October 20, 2016), pp. 4, 23–24 (www.epi.org/files/pdf/112962.pdf). See also Graham Ruddick and Jamie Grierson, "BBC Gender Pay Gap: Male Staff Earn 9% More Than Female Colleagues," *The Guardian* (October 4, 2017); Xaquín G.V., "Can We Talk About the Gender Pay Gap?" *The Washington Post* (October 26, 2017).
201. Brittany Bronson, "How Unions Help Cocktail Servers," *The New York Times* (August 17, 2016).
202. See Steven Greenhouse, "AFL-CIO Leadership: The Two Women Vying to be America's Top Labor Official," *The Guardian* (July 8, 2019). See also Kim Kelly, "Sara Nelson's Art of War," *New Republic* (May 13, 2019).
203. See Daniel J. B. Mitchell and Christopher L. Erickson, "De-Unionization and Macro-Performance: What Freeman and Medoff Didn't Do," in *What Do Unions Do? A Twenty-Year Perspective,* eds. James T. Bennett and Bruce E. Kaufman (New Brunswick, NJ: Transaction Publishers, 2007), pp. 373–400.
204. See generally Council of Economic Advisers, Annual Report (February 2016), pp. 39–40 (https://obamawhitehouse.archives.gov/sites/default/files/docs/ERP_2016_Book_Complete%20JA.pdf).
205. For this extensive discussion, see Reiff, *Exploitation and Economic Justice,* pp. 3–12. See also Thomas Piketty and Emanuel Saez, "Income and Wage Inequality in the United States, 1913–2002," in *Top Incomes over the Twentieth Century,* eds. A. B. Atkinson and T. Piketty (Oxford: Oxford University Press, 2006), pp. 141–225; Emmanuel Saez, "Striking it Richer: The Evolution of Top Incomes in the United States" (Updated with 2015 preliminary estimates) (June 30, 2016) (https://eml.berkeley.edu/~saez/saez-UStopincomes-2015.pdf); Estelle Sommeiller and Mark Price, "The New Gilded Age," Economic Policy Institute (July 19, 2018) (www.epi.org/files/pdf/147963.pdf).
206. Emmanuel Saez, "Striking it Richer." (Updated with 2015 preliminary estimates) See also Piketty and Saez, "Income and Wage Inequality in the United States, 1913–2002," p. 147.
207. See Erik Eckholm, "Last Year's Poverty Rate Was Highest in Twelve Years: Median Family Income Fell," *The New York Times* (September 11, 2009). See also Carmen DeNevas-Walt, Bernadette D. Proctor, and Jessica C. Smith, U.S. Census Bureau, Current Population Reports, P60-238, *Income, Poverty, and Health Insurance Coverage in the United States: 2009* (Washington: U.S. Government Printing Office, September 2010).

208. See United States Census Bureau, "Income, Poverty, and Health Insurance Coverage in the United States: 2015," Release Number CB16-158 (September 13, 2016) (www.census.gov/newsroom/press-releases/2016/cb16-158.html); Mark Gongloff, "45 Million Americans Still Stuck below Poverty Line: Census," *The Huffington Post* (September 16, 2014). See also United States Census Bureau, "The Supplemental Poverty Measure: 2015," Report Number P60-258 (September 13, 2016) (www.census.gov/library/publications/2016/demo/p60-258.html).
209. See Sean F. Reardon and Kendra Bischoff, "Growth in the Residential Segregation of Families by Income, 1970–2009," *US2010 Project* (Russell Sage Foundation/Brown University, November 2011).
210. See Pew Research Center, "America's Shrinking Middle Class: A Close Look at Changes Within Metropolitan Areas" (May 11, 2016) (middle class lost ground in nearly nine in ten US metropolitan areas examined); Richard Florida, "The Geography of Middle Class Decline," *CityLab* (November 15, 2016).
211. See, e.g., David Cay Johnston, "Scary New Wage Data," *Tax Notes* 129 (October 25, 2010): 481–484, at 481–482; Gretchen Morgenson, "Paychecks as Big as Tajikistan," *The New York Times* (June 18, 2011). The figures here come from Jack T. Ciesielski, "S&P 500 Executive Pay: Bigger Than ... Whatever You Think It Is," *The Analyst's Accounting Observer* 20:7 (May 23, 2011); Natasha Singer, "In Executive Pay, a Rich Game of Thrones," *The New York Times* (April 7, 2012).
212. See Thomas Piketty, Emmanuel Saez, and Gabriel Zucman, "Distributional National Accounts: Methods and Estimates for the United States," NBER Working Paper 22945 (National Bureau of Economic Research, December 2016), p. 3; Elise Gould, "2014 Continues a 35-Year Trend of Broad-Based Wage Stagnation," Issue Brief #393 (Economic Policy Institute, February 19, 2015) (www.epi.org/publication/stagnant-wages-in-2014/); Lawrence Mishel, Elise Gould, and Josh Bivens, "Wage Stagnation in Nine Charts," Economic Policy Institute (January 6, 2015) (www.epi.org/publication/charting-wage-stagnation/?utm_source=Economic+Policy+Institute&utm_campaign=27719c052c-EPI_News&utm_medium=email&utm_term=0_e7c5826c50-27719c052c-55957733); Lawrence H. Summers and Ed Balls, Report of the Commission on Inclusive Prosperity (Center for American Progress, January 2015) (https://cdn.americanprogress.org/wp-content/uploads/2015/01/IPC-PDF-full.pdf); Dionne Searcey, "Job Growth Fails to Help Paycheck of Workers," *The New York Times* (January 9, 2015); Neil Irwin, "Job Growth Looks Great; Wage Growth, Less So," *The New York Times* (January 9, 2015); Patricia Cohen, "'Superstar Firms' May Have Shrunk Workers' Share of Income," *The New York Times* (March 8, 2017); Gabriel Winant, "How the American Economy Conspires to Keep Wages Down," *The Guardian* (April 13, 2018); Natalie Kitroeff, "Jobless Rate Looks Like Old Times, but the Economy Doesn't," *The New York Times* (May 4, 2018); Paul Krugman, "Is the Recession Still Holding Down Wages? (Wonkish)," *The New York Times* (May 4, 2018).
213. See Elise Gould, "The State of American Wages 2016" (Economic Policy Institute, March 9, 2017) (www.epi.org/files/pdf/122078.pdf), p. 4; Elise Gould, "First Half 2017 Data Reveal Broadly Based Wage Growth, but Inequality

Persists" (Economic Policy Institute, August 1, 2017) (www.epi.org/blog/first-half-2017-data-reveal-broadly-based-wage-growth-but-inequality-persists/); Neil Irwin, "The Question Isn't Why Wage Growth Is So Low, It's Why It's So High," *The New York Times* (May 26, 2017) (noting that 84 percent of time since 1966, average real wages have grown more slowly than we would expect given increases in productivity, and that trend has only reversed slightly in the last few years); Heather Long, "Half the Jobs in America Pay Less Than $18 an Hour. Can Trump Help?" *The Washington Post* (August 24, 2017) (and 40 percent pay less $15.50); Ben Casselman, "Feel That Post-Recession Bounce? The Rich Feel It the Most," *The New York Times* (September 27, 2017).

214. See Jeff Stein and Andrew Van Dam, "For the Biggest Group of American Workers, Wages Aren't Just Flat. They're Falling." *The Washington Post* (June 15, 2018); David Leonhardt, "For Wages, a Trump Slump," *The New York Times* (August 5, 2018).

215. See Saez, "Striking it Richer" (Updated with 2009 and 2010 Estimates); Justin Wolfers, "The Gains from the Economic Recovery Are Still Limited to the Top One Percent," *The New York Times* (January 27, 2015).

216. See Long, "Half the Jobs in America Pay Less Than $18 an Hour."

217. See Emmanuel Saez, "Striking it Richer" (Updated with 2015 preliminary estimates).

218. For a series of helpful graphs showing this dramatic change in the job market, see Alicia Parlapiano, Shaila Dewan, and Nelson D. Schwartz, "The Nation's Economy, This Side of the Recession," *The New York Times* (June 14, 2014). See also Nelson D. Schwartz and Patricia Cowen, "Falling Wages at Factories Squeeze the Middle Class," *The New York Times* (December 15, 2014); Laura D'Andrea Tyson, "The Quality of Jobs: The New Normal and the Old Normal," *The New York Times* (September 20, 2013); Steven Greenhouse, "The Changing Face of Temporary Employment," *The New York Times* (August 31, 2014): Patricia Cohen, "If Workers Are Scarce, Is It the Work or the Wages?" *The New York Times* (July 13, 2017); Ed Pilkington, "What Happened When Walmart Left," *The Guardian* (July 9, 2017) (describing what happens when nonunionized corporate giants open up in an area, overpower the existing local competition, force the closure of mom-and-pop stores for up to 20 miles around, and then close down itself, leaving behind a trial of lost jobs and broken promises).

219. See Economic Policy Institute, "When Workers Have More Leverage, Income Growth Is More Equal: Union Membership and Share of Income Going to the Top 10 Percent in the U.S., 1917–2015," in Top Charts of 2017 (December 21, 2017); Joseph Stiglitz, "Joseph Stiglitz Says Standard Economics Is Wrong. Inequality and Unearned Income Kills the Economy," *Evonomics* (September 9, 2016) (noting that the recent decline in unionization is partly responsible for the dramatic rise in inequality); Joseph Stiglitz, *The Price of Inequality* (New York: Norton, 2012), esp. pp. 64–67, 79–80, and 281–282; Will Kimball and Lawrence Mishel, "Union's Decline and the Rise of the Top 10 Percent's Share of Income," *Economic Snapshot* (Economic Policy Institute, February 3, 2015); Mishel, "Unions, Inequality, and Faltering Middle-Class Wages"; Bruce Western and Jake Rosenfeld, "Unions, Norms, and the Rise of U.S. Wage Inequality," *American Sociological Review* 76 (2011): 513–537; David Card, Thomas Lemieux, and W. Craig Riddell, "Unionization and Wage Inequality:

A Comparative Study of the U.S., the U.K., and Canada," NBER Working Paper No. 9473 (National Bureau of Economic Research, 2003); Andrew Van Dam, "Is It Great To Be a Worker in the U.S.? Not Compared to the Rest of the Developed World," *The Washington Post* (July 4, 2018); Henry Farber, Daniel Herbst, Ilyana Kuziemko, Suresh Naidu, "Unions and Inequality over the Twentieth Century: New Evidence from Survey Data" (May 1, 2018) (http://tuvalu.santafe.edu/~snaidu/papers/union_sub3.pdf); Josh Bivens and Heidi Shierholz, "What Labor Market Changes Have Generated Inequality and Wage Suppression?" Economic Policy Institute (December 12, 2018).

220. See Lawrence Mishel, Josh Bivens, Elise Gould, Heidi Shierholz, *The State of Working America* (Economic Policy Institute, Cornell University Press, 12th ed., 2012), p. 275.

221. See James Feigenbaum, Alexander Hertel-Fernandez, and Vanessa Williamson, "Right-to-Work Laws Have Devasted Unions – and Democrats," *The New York Times* (March 8, 2018).

222. Mishel, "Unions, Inequality, and Faltering Middle-Class Wages." See also Ben Bernanke, "The Level and Distribution of Well-Being," *Board of Governors of the Federal Reserve System* (speech before the greater Omaha Chamber of Commerce, February 6, 2007); Noam Scheiber, "6 Reasons that Pay Has Lagged Behind U.S. Job Growth," *The New York Times* (February 1, 2018) (declining unionization being one of them).

223. See Freeman and Medoff, *What Do Unions Do?* pp. 162–180.

224. See Barry T. Hirsch, "What Do Unions Do for Economic Performance?" in *What Do Unions Do? A Twenty-Year Perspective*, eds. James T. Bennett and Bruce E. Kaufman (New Brunswick, NJ: Transaction Publishers, 2007), pp. 193–237, 205–211; Christos Doucouliagos and Patrice Laroche, "What Do Unions Do to Productivity? A Meta-Analysis," *Industrial Relations* 42 (2003): 650–691, 654, 667, 682.

225. See Ross Eisenbrey, "Strong Unions, Strong Productivity," Economic Snapshot (Economic Policy Institute, June 20, 2007) (www.epi.org/publication/webfeatures_snapshots_20070620/) (noting that other advanced countries throughout the world with much higher rates of unionization actually have economies that are as or more productive than the United States); See also Eduardo Porter, "How Waning Competition Deepens Labor's Plight," *The New York Times* (November 1, 2016) (reporting that unions can be a force against merger mania and other forms of anticompetitive behavior that reduce productivity).

226. See, e.g., Kim B. Clark, "Unionization and Firm Performance: The Impact on Profits, Growth, and Productivity," *American Economic Review* 74 (1984): 893–919.

227. See John T. Addison and Barry T. Hirsch, "Union Effects on Productivity, Profits, and Growth: Has the Long Run Arrived?" *Journal of Labor Economics* 7 (1989): 72–105; John T. Addison and Clive R. Belfield, "Union Voice," in *What Do Unions Do? A Twenty-Year Perspective*, pp. 238–274, 247–248.

228. See Freeman and Medoff, *What Do Unions Do?* pp. 181–190; Christos Doucouliagos and Patrice Laroche, "Unions and Profits: A Meta-Regression Analysis," *Industrial Relations* 48 (2009): 146–180; Hirsch, "What Do Unions Do for Economic Performance?" pp. 211–214; Clark, "Unionization and Firm Performance."

229. See, e.g., Toke Aidt and Zafiris Tzannatos, *Unions and Collective Bargaining: Economic Effects in a Global Environment* (Washington, DC: World Bank, 2002), pp. 67–68.
230. For more on this, see Mark R. Reiff, "Trump and the End of Liberalism," *The Critique* (January 15, 2017) (http://www.markreiff.org/categories/2-publications.htm#categories-4); Sabrina Tavernise, "With His Job Gone, an Autoworker Wonders, 'What Am I as a Man?'" *The New York Times* (May 27, 2019).
231. See Freeman and Medoff, *What Do Unions Do?* ch. 6.
232. See Albert O. Hirschman, *Exit, Voice, and Loyalty: Responses to Declines in Firms* (Harvard University Press, New ed., 1970).
233. For a recent example of this, see Brian Lyman, "Over Bentley's Objections, Golden Dragon Plant Votes for Union," *Montgomery Advertiser* (November 16, 2014) (workers who voted to unionize Alabama plant "just want a say in their working conditions").
234. See Freeman and Medoff, *What Do Unions Do?* esp. ch. 6. For the reasons discussed in the first essay in this volume, however, I deny that unions have the monopolistic effects that Freeman and Medoff assumed.
235. See, e.g., Addison and Belfield, "Union Voice," pp. 238–274, esp. p. 258; Gerald Meyer, "Union Membership Trends in the United States."
236. See, e.g., David Lewin, "Unionism and Employment Conflict Resolution: Rethinking Collective Voice and Its Consequences," in *What Do Unions Do? A Twenty-Year Perspective*, eds. James T. Bennett and Bruce E. Kaufman (New Brunswick, NJ: Transaction Publishers, 2007), pp. 313–345.
237. See Addison and Belfield, "Union Voice," pp. 238–274, 249–258; Tove Helland Hammer and Ariel Avgar, "The Impact of Unions on Job Satisfaction, Organizational Commitment, and Turnover," in *What Do Unions Do? A Twenty-Year Perspective*, eds. James T. Bennett and Bruce E. Kaufman (New Brunswick, NJ: Transaction Publishers, 2007), pp. 346–372.
238. See Freeman and Medoff, *What Do Unions Do?* ch. 9.
239. See Addison and Belfield, "Union Voice"; Hammer and Avgar, "The Impact of Unions on Job Satisfaction, Organizational Commitment, and Turnover."
240. See Elster, *Sour Grapes*, pp. 109–111; Jon Elster and John E. Roemer, "Introduction," in *Interpersonal Comparisons of Well-Being* (Cambridge: Cambridge University Press, 1991), pp. 1–11, 6.
241. Aldous Huxley, *Brave New World* (London: Chatto & Windus, 1932).
242. See Arthur M. Okun, *Equality and Efficiency: The Big Tradeoff* (Washington, D.C.: Brookings, 1975).
243. See C. W. and A. J. K. D, "Did Slavery Make Economic Sense?" *The Economist* (September 27, 2013); Gordon Tullock, "The Economics of Slavery," *Left and Right* 3 (1967): 5–16; Robert William Fogel, *Without Consent or Contract: The Rise and Fall of American Slavery* (New York: Norton, 1989), esp. ch. 3.
244. Even those studies which suggest that unionization leads to an underinvestment in research and development, new plant and equipment, and so on (see, e.g., Hirsch, "What Do Unions Do for Economic Performance?" pp. 214–216) do not raise the economic costs of unionization anywhere near the catastrophic level, and thereby do not constitute an argument against unionization's

liberty-enhancing features. And it is important to remember that in the current climate, very little investment is going into these areas anyway, even at the low rates of unionization we are currently experiencing. So there are clearly other factors that affect new investment much more dramatically than unionization. It is therefore these factors that we need to address, not unionization, for unionization is not a significant cause of the problem here, assuming it is a contributing factor at all.

245. For an example of how poorly even highly educated and skilled workers can be treated in an environment without unions, see Dan Lyons, "Congratulations! You've Been Fired," *The New York Times* (April 9, 2016). See also Brett Murphy, "Rigged: Forced into Debt. Worked Past Exhaustion. Left with Nothing," *USA Today* (June 16, 2017) (describing how nonunionized port truckers are treated like indentured servants).

246. See Keith Breen, "Freedom, Republicanism, and Workplace Democracy," *Critical Review of International Social and Political Philosophy* (2015): 470–485, 475. Alex Gourevitch, "Quitting Work but Not the Job: Liberty and the Right to Strike," *Perspectives on Politics* 14 (2016): 307–323. For a recent example, see Sarah Maslin Nir, "A Manhattan Diner's New Management Has Servers Singing a Defiant Tune," *The New York Times* (August 26, 2016) (describing employees' unionization efforts as a response to new management's "campaign of arbitrary discipline," which has resulted in "mass firing of longtime servers, many for small offenses or ones seemingly beyond their control"); Noam Scheiber and Christopher Drew, "Union Vote at Boeing Plant Tests Labor's Sway under Trump," *The New York Times* (February 13, 2017) (noting that one of the reasons driving the effort by employees to unionize South Carolina Boeing plant was that "workers felt their [performance] evaluations were frequently arbitrary"); Noam Scheiber, "Chinese-Owned Factory in Ohio Fights Off Unionization Plan," *The New York Times* (November 9, 2017) ("Many workers said they had been frustrated by what they considered a harsh and arbitrary management style. They said some colleagues had been fired for minor infractions or disciplined for making earnest suggestions to improve production while favored workers have received a pass when breaking rules"); Moshe Z. Marvit and Shaun Richman, "American Workers Need Better Job Protections," *The New York Times* (December 28, 2017).

247. See, e.g., Victor Mather, "Union Files Grievance against N.F.L. Supporting Eric Reid," *The New York Times* (May 7, 2018).

248. While I think it is fair to say that this view is now almost universally held, there is the occasional dissenting voice. Iñigo González-Ricoy, for example, argues that unionism is insufficient to give workers the required voice because "the influence of unions depends on their de facto and variable power." Iñigo González-Ricoy, "The Republican Case for Workplace Democracy," *Social Theory and Practice* 40 (2014): 232–254, 250. The institutionalization of unions, however, would seem to solve this problem. Nevertheless, nothing in my argument precludes anyone from arguing that workplace democratization is also required if they fear that institutionalized unionization is not enough.

249. See *NLRB v. Jones & Laughlin Steel Corp.*, 301 U.S. 1, 33 (1937) (citing *American Steel Foundries v. Tri-City Central Trades Council*, 257 U.S. 184, 190 (1921)).

250. John Kenneth Galbraith, *American Capitalism: The Concept of the Countervailing Power* (New Brunswick, NJ: Transaction Publishers, 1993), p. 114. For a similar argument, see James S. Coleman, *The Power and the Structure of Society* (New York: Norton, 1974), p. 73; Pettit, *On the People's Terms,* pp. 115–116.
251. See Paul H. Douglass, *First Lecture,* in Paul H. Douglas and J. Enoch Powell, *How Big Should Government Be?* (Washington, DC: American Enterprise Institute, 1968), pp. 1–37, 29–30.
252. See Elizabeth Anderson, *Private Government: How Employers Rule Our Lives (and Why We Don't Talk about it)* (Princeton: Princeton University Press, 2017).
253. Seymour Martin Lipset, "Labor Unions in the Public Mind," in *Unions in Transition: Entering the Second Century,* ed. Seymour Martin Lipset (San Francisco: Institute for Contemporary Studies, 1986), pp. 287–321, 299–301 (for an update of some of the key figures given here see www.gallup.com/poll/12751/labor-unions.aspx). See also Thomas Kochan, Duanyi Yang, Erin L. Kelly, and Will Kimball, "Who Wants to Join a Union? A Growing Number of Americans," *The Conversation* (August 30, 2018) (noting that interest in joining a union today is at a four-decade high).
254. See www.gallup.com/poll/12751/labor-unions.aspx.
255. See generally Daniel Jacob and Christian Neuhäuser, "Workplace Democracy, Market Competition and Republican Self-Respect," *Ethical Theory and Moral Practice* 21 (2018): 927–944; Isabelle Ferreras, *Firms as Political Entities* (Cambridge: Cambridge University Press, 2017), esp. pp. 155–168; Keith Breen, "Freedom, Republicanism, and Workplace Democracy"; Nien-Hê Hsieh, "Justice in Production," *The Journal of Political Philosophy* 16 (2008): 72–100; Nien-Hê Hsieh, "Rawlsian Justice and Workplace Republicanism," *Social Theory and Practice* 31 (2005): 115–142; Nien-Hê Hsieh, "Workplace Democracy, Workplace Republicanism, and Economic Democracy," *Revue de Philosophie Économique* 8 (2008): 57–78; Robert A. Dahl, *Democracy and Its Critics* (New Haven: Yale University Press, 1989), pp. 328–332.
256. See, e.g., Hsieh, "Justice in Production," p. 92.
257. See generally Gregory Jackson, "Contested Boundaries: Ambiguity and Creativity in the Evolution of German Codetermination," in *Beyond Continuity: Institutional Change in Advanced Political Economies* (Oxford: Oxford University Press, 2005), pp. 229–254, 236–249; Andrei S. Markovits, *The Politics of West German Trade Unions* (Cambridge: Cambridge University Press, 1986), pp. 53–60; David F. Heathfield (ed.), *The Economics of Co-Determination* (London: Macmillan, 1977); Jack Ewing, "Prosecutors Investigate Payments to Volkswagen Labor Leader," *The New York Times* (May 12, 2017); Susan R. Holmberg, "Workers on Corporate Boards? Germany's Had Them for Decades," *The New York Times* (January 6, 2019).
258. See, e.g., Sheelah Kolhatkar, "Walmart and the Push to Put Workers on Company Boards," *The New Yorker* (March 26, 2019).
259. See, e.g., Hélène Landemore and Isabelle Ferreras, "In Defense of Workplace Democracy: Towards Justification of the Firm-State Analogy," *Political Theory* 44 (2016): 53–81; Robert A. Dahl, *A Preface to Economic Democracy* (Berkeley: University of California Press, 1985); Iris Young, "Self-Determination as Principle of Justice," *The Philosophical Forum* (1979): 30–46.

260. See *What Do Unions Do?* ch.12. Others have expressed this view too. See, e.g. Dale Belman, "Unions, The Quality of Labor Relations, and Firm Performance," in *Unions and Economic Competitiveness,* eds. Lawrence Mishel and Paula B. Voos (Armonk, NY: M.E. Sharpe, 1992), pp. 41–107, 60–63.
261. See Hirsch, "What Do Unions Do for Economic Performance?" pp. 211–214.
262. For an extended discussion of the tragedy of the commons and the various impediments to successful collective action presented by such a situation, see Reiff, *Punishment, Compensation, and Law,* pp. 58–61.
263. See, e.g., Sarah Betancourt, "Stop & Shop Hit by Strike as 31,000 Workers Walk off Job," *The Guardian* (April 15, 2019) (workers striking to restrain rise in health care costs against corporate employers that had profits last year of $2 billion and received substantial tax cut this year).
264. See Jackie Calmes, "In Pacific Trade Deal, Vietnam Agrees to U.S. Terms on Labor Rights," *The New York Times* (November 5, 2015). Note that now that President Trump has backed out of the TPP, workers in Vietnam fear increased suppression of the independent labor movement there. See Neil Gough, "The Workers Who Regret Trump's Scrapping of a Trade Deal," *The New York Times* (March 1, 2017). Unionized workers in the United States also face job losses because goods that could have been built here and freely exported to Asian markets under the TPP will now have to be built in factories overseas. See, e.g., Neil Gough, "Even Harley-Davidson Can't Resist the Tug of Overseas Factories," *The New York Times* (May 23, 2017); Alan Rappeport, "Harley-Davidson, Blaming E.U. Tariffs, Will Move Some Production Out of U.S.," *The New York Times* (June 25, 2018).
265. See Nozick, *Anarchy, State, and Utopia,* esp. pp. 88–118.
266. Note that I have not tried to justify the compelled unionization of independents by arguing that they would otherwise be allowed to be free riders, benefiting from the existence of the union and the dues paid by others but not bearing any of the costs of membership themselves. As Nozick argues, the mere receipt of benefits that one did not ask for does not obligate one to pay for those benefits. See Nozick, *Anarchy, State and Utopia,* p. 95. Indeed, those who work for other firms or do not work at all also benefit from the existence of unions and their activities and thus are in some sense free riders too, but no one suggests that these people are somehow obligated to pay for these benefits.
267. See generally, Dorothee Schneider, *Trade Unions and Community* (Urbana, IL: University of Illinois Press, 1994).
268. See Warren Meyer, "How Labor Regulation Harms Unskilled Workers," *Regulation* 41 (2018): 44–50 (Cato Institute).
269. See Freeman and Medoff, *What do Unions Do?*, p. 12.
270. Ibid. at 13.
271. See Gordon Lafer, *The One Percent Solution: How Corporations Are Remaking America One State at a Time* (Ithaca, NY: Cornell University Press), pp. 84–90.
272. They do, however, sometimes suggest that increasing wages makes the goods produced more expensive, as if making prices cheaper for third parties is an excuse for exploiting workers. See Angela Hart, "Labor Got Higher Wages in California's Housing Deal. Will Affordable Homes Still be Built?" *Sacramento Bee* (October 6, 2017).
273. See Reiff, *Exploitation and Economic Justice in the Liberal Capitalist State.*

274. Note that under my theory of exploitation, not all violations of the just price doctrine constitute exploitation – only *intolerable* violations do. How we determine when these violations are intolerable, however, is a complicated matter that I will not be able to adequately summarize here. Those interested in a further explanation of this, and an explanation of how the just price itself is to be calculated under my theory, should see *Exploitation and Economic Justice in the Liberal Capitalist State*.
275. Bennett and Kaufman, "What Do Unions Do? A Twenty-Year Perspective," pp. 1–11, 6.
276. See, e.g., Editorial, "Violence and Corruption in a Prison Union," *The New York Times* (June 8, 2016); Joseph Goldstein, "Along New York Harbor, 'On the Waterfront' Endures," *The New York Times* (January 7, 2017); Neal E. Boudette, "Ex-Fiat Chrysler Executive Accused of Siphoning Millions with Union Leader," *The New York Times* (July 26, 2017); Michael McGowan, "Fake Black Lives Matter Facebook Page Run by Australian Union Official – Report," *The Guardian* (April 9, 2018); Zoe Greenberg, "Norman Seabrook, Ex-Leader of Jail Officers, Guilty of Bribery in Trial that Cast Shadow over de Blasio," *The New York Times* (August 15, 2018).
277. See A. J. Thieblot, "Perspectives on Union Corruption: Lessons from the Databases," *Journal of Labor Research* 28 (2006): 513–534 (setting forth recent cases of corruption in great detail); James Rufus Koren, "L.A. Longshoremen Sentenced to 41 Months for Bilking Union Healthcare Plan," *Los Angeles Times* (January 16, 2017); Reuters, "Former U.A.W. Official Charged in Fiat Chrysler Payoff Case," *The New York Times* (August 18, 2017).
278. See, e.g., Volkswagen, Mitsubishi, Peabody Coal, Enron, Wells Fargo and many other firms in the financial industry, and so on.
279. For a similar point, see Nicholas Kristof, "The Cost of a Decline in Unions," *The New York Times* (February 19, 2015).
280. Take, for example, covering up sexual harassment. Although some unions do seem to have a problem with this, see Mike Elk, "Unions Leader Faces Members' Protest over Sexual Misconduct Claims," *The Guardian* (April 22, 2018), this is obviously a widespread problem within many firms as well, and there is no evidence that this is any greater problem for unions than it is for firms in general.
281. Ludwig von Mises, *Human Action: A Treatise on Economics* (Auburn, AL: Ludwig von Mises Institute, scholar's ed., 1988), p. 772.
282. F. A. Hayek, *1980s Unemployment and the Unions* (London: Institute of Economic Affairs, 2nd ed., 1984), p. 61.
283. Sylvester Petro, "Sovereignty and Compulsory Public Sector Bargaining," *Wake Forest Law Review* 10 (1974–1975): 25–166, 77 (quoting Henry C. Simmons, *Economic Policy for a Free Society* [Chicago: University of Chicago Press, 1948], p. 152). See also Sylvester Petro, *The Labor Policy of the Free Society* (New York: The Ronald Press, 1957), p. 109 (claiming that unions tend to use "violence and coercive methods at every stage of their operations").
284. 18 U.S.C § 1951.
285. 410 U.S. 396 (1973).
286. See, e.g., United States Congress, Senate Committee on the Judiciary, Subcommittee on Criminal Law, *S. 613, a bill to amend the Hobbs Act: Hearings before the Subcommittee on Criminal Law of the Committee on the Judiciary, United States*

Senate, 97th Cong. first and second sessions, on S. 613 (December 10, 1981 and March 11, 1982) Washington, DC: U.S. G.P.O. (note that S. 613 was introduced by Senator Strom Thurmond, the ultraconservative Republican senator from South Carolina).

287. Indeed, just prior to the *Emmons* case itself, the Justice Department had attempted to bring a Hobbs Act prosecution against a picketer who had struck a strikebreaker and against an organizer who had vandalized a basket of dirty laundry being collected by a laundry company against which there was a strike. See United States Congress, Senate Committee on the Judiciary, Subcommittee on Criminal Law, *S. 613, a bill to amend the Hobbs Act.*

288. For the current prosecutorial guidelines for an action under the Hobbs Act, see United States Attorneys' Office, *Criminal Resources Manual* § 2403 (www.justice.gov/usam/criminal-resource-manual-2403-hobbs-act-extortion-force-violence-or-fear).

289. See Maria Cramer, "Released from Prison, Ex-Teamsters Lash Out at 'Evil' Prosecutors Who Put Them There," *Boston Globe* (April 10, 2018).

290. See Richard Pérez-Peña, "Contrary to Trump's Claims, Immigrants Are Less Likely to Commit Crimes," *The New York Times* (January 26, 2017).

291. See Liz Alderman, "Labor Tactic Raises Fear for France," *The New York Times* (January 7, 2013) (recounting how desperate workers about to lose their jobs at a Goodyear tire factory in northern France "kidnapped" two senior executives as an act of "guerilla theater" that was then suppressed by police).

292. See James A. Craft, "Union Violence: A Review and Critical Discussion," *Journal of Labor Research* 22 (2001): 679–688 (noting that claims of labor violence are most often based on statistics provided by the National Right to Work Legal Defence Foundation, a notorious anti-union organization).

293. See, e.g., United States Congress, Senate Committee on the Judiciary, Subcommittee on Criminal Law, *S. 613, a bill to amend the Hobbs Act.*

294. See, e.g., Kim Willsher, "French Unions Accused of 'Passive Complicity' in Protest Violence," *The Guardian* (May 27, 2018).

295. See generally Robert Michael Smith, *From Blackjacks to Briefcases: A History of Commercialized Strikebreaking and Unionbusting in the United States* (Athens, OH: Ohio University Press, 2003); Stephen H. Norwood, *Strikebreaking and Intimidation: Mercenaries and Masculinity in Twentieth-Century America* (Chapel Hill, NC: University of North Carolina Press, 2002); Louis Adamic, *Dynamite: The Story of Class Violence in America* (New York: Viking, 1931); Kotz, *The Rise and Fall of Neoliberalism,* p. 58 (describing a famous incident when United Auto Workers leader Walter Reuther was severely beaten by security guards in the employ of the Ford Motor Company, while he was leafletting near a Ford plant gate).

296. See, e.g., Jack Ewing, "Amazon's Labor Relations Under Scrutiny in Germany," *The New York Times* (March 3, 2013) (discussing German documentary that implies Amazon used neo-Nazi thugs at its German Distribution center to keep temporary workers bused in from neighboring countries in line); David Streitfeld, "Amazon Workers in Germany Strike Again," *The New York Times* (December 16, 2013); Cathie Anderson, "Major Labor Union Alleges UC Is Intimidating Members, Sabotaging Strike," *Sacramento Bee* (March 29, 2019).

Notes to pp. 131–132

297. See Daniel Bell, *The End of Ideology* (Glencoe, Ill: Free Press, 1960), pp. 195–197.
298. While some union workers might no doubt still cross picket lines, it seems unlikely that they would be seen as enough of a threat to lead anyone to commit violent acts against them.
299. While unlawful, such retaliation still happens and often goes unpunished today. See, e.g., Michael Sainato, "Tesla Workers Speak Out: 'Anything Pro-Union Is Shut Down Really Fast,'" *The Guardian* (September 10, 2018); Michael Sainato, "'It's Because We Were Union Members': Boeing Fires Workers Who Organized," *The Guardian* (May 3, 2019); Julia Carrie, "'I've Paid a Huge Personal Cost': Google Walkout Organizer Resigns over Alleged Retaliation," *The Guardian* (June 7, 2019); Michael Sainato, "Miami Airport Workers Fighting for Better Conditions Face Retaliation," *The Guardian* (May 17, 2019).
300. See Andy Newman and John Leland, "DNAinfo and Gothamist Are Shut Down After Vote to Unionize," *The New York Times* (November 2, 2017); Hamilton Nolan, "A Billionaire Destroyed His Newsrooms Out of Spite," *The New York Times* (November 3, 2017); Edward Helmore, "News Workers Unionized. Days Later, They Were Jobless. Was It Payback?" *The Guardian* (November 4, 2018).
301. See Reiff *On Unemployment, Volume I*, pp. 74–81.
302. See John Maynard Keynes, *The General Theory of Employment, Interest, and Money* (San Diego: Harvest/Harcourt edition), ch. 17, pp. 232–238.
303. See, e.g., Hayek, *The Constitution of Liberty*, ch. 18 ("Labor Unions and Employment").
304. See Keynes, *The General Theory*, p. 232.
305. For a good discussion of Keynes's thoughts on this subject, see Alvin H. Hansen, *A Guide to Keynes* (New York: McGraw-Hill, 1953), pp. 175–178.
306. See James Tobin, "The Future of Keynesian Economics," in *Policies for Prosperity* (Cambridge: MIT Press, 1987), pp. 14–23, 16.
307. See Michał Kalecki, "Money and Real Wages" (1939), in *Collected Works of Michał Kalecki: Volume II* (Oxford: Oxford University Press, 1991), pp. 21–50.
308. See, e.g., A. C. Pigou, *Employment and Equilibrium* (London: Macmillan, 1941), pp. 82–87.
309. See Michał Kalecki, "Reduction of Wages During Crisis" (1932), in *Collected Works of Michał Kalecki: Volume I* (Oxford: Oxford University Press, 1990), pp. 41–44; Kalecki, "Money and Real Wages" (1939); Malcolm C. Sawyer, *The Economics of Michał Kalecki* (London: Macmillan, 1985), pp. 15, 110–118. Keynes also made similar arguments, although he presented them a little more tentatively. See Sawyer, *The Economics of Michał Kalecki*, pp. 110–118; Keynes, *The General Theory*, ch. 19.
310. For example, even though gasoline prices have been dropping recently, this is the result of increases in supply that have been going on for quite some time. See Clifford Krauss and Stanley Reed, "Oil Prices: What's Behind the Drop? Simple Economics," *The New York Times* (January 12, 2015); Clifford Krauss, "After Steadily Falling, Price for Gas Notches an Increase," *The New York Times* (January 27, 2015). When there are threats to supply, however, the resulting increases in prices are often immediate. Indeed, when prices started going up again recently after falling slowly but steadily for some time, they shot up astonishingly fast, see Mark Glover, "Gas Prices in Sacramento, throughout

California Are in Full Flight," *The Sacramento Bee* (March 2, 2015) (local averages spike 40 cents in one week), proving once again that prices tend to go up much quicker than they come down.

311. See Jad Mouawad and Nicola Clark, "Slide in Fuel Costs Lifts Profits for Airlines, but Fares Won't Fall," *The New York Times* (December 10, 2014); Editorial, "No Relief for Air Travelers," *The New York Times* (December 15, 2014).

312. See Reiff, *On Unemployment, Volume I*, p. 76. See also Graham Ruddick, "Steelworkers to Vote on Port Talbot Rescue Plan," *The Guardian* (January 29, 2017) (unions supporting a proposed 10 percent reduction in pension benefits); Richard B. Freeman and Eunice Han, "The War against Public Sector Collective Bargaining in the US," *Journal of Industrial Relations* 54 (2012): 386–408, 398–399 (noting a wide range of evidence that unions made substantial wage and benefit concessions to save jobs and preserve public services after the Great Recession).

313. For further argument on this see Reiff, *Exploitation and Economic Justice*, pp. 197–203; Reiff, *On Unemployment, Volume I*, pp. 74–81 (discussing how deunionization does not make wages less "sticky" and more responsive to changes in demand, thereby leading to a quicker restoration of the employment equilibrium following a downturn in the economy).

314. See Ekaterina Jardim, et al., "Minimum Wage Increases, Wages, and Low-Employment: Evidence from Seattle," NBER Working Paper No. 23532 (National Bureau of Economic Research, June 2017); Arindrajit Dube, "Minimum Wage and Job Loss: One Alarming Seattle Study Is Not the Last Word," *The New York Times* (July 20, 2017).

315. See, e.g., Noam Scheiber, "How Raising Minimum Wage Affects Jobs in Seattle," *The New York Times* (June 26, 2017).

316. See David Cooper, "Another Year of Federal Inaction Has Further Eroded the Federal Minimum Wage," *Economic Snapshot* (Economic Policy Institute, July 24, 2017).

317. Ben Zipperer and John Schmitt, "The 'High Road' Seattle Labor Market and the Effects of the Minimum Wage Increase" (Economic Policy Institute, June 26, 2017). See also Julie Weed, "Hotel Boom in SeaTac Is Unfettered by $15 Minimum Wage," *The New York Times* (July 31, 2017).

318. See Karen Weise, "Why Some Amazon Workers Are Fuming about Their Raise," *The New York Times* (October 9, 2018) (despite the raise, their total compensation is likely to shrink); Michael Sainato, "Whole Foods Cuts Workers' Hours after Amazon Introduces Minimum Wage," *The Guardian* (March 6, 2019).

319. For further discussion of this point, see Reiff, *On Unemployment, Volume I*, pp. 74–81; Neil Irwin, "To Understand Rising Inequality, Consider the Janitors at Two Top Companies, Then and Now," *The New York Times* (September 3, 2017) ("what has changed in the last generation is that companies today view more and more of the labor it takes to produce their goods and services as akin to staplers"); John W. Budd, Raphael Gomez, Noah M. Meltz, "Why Balance is Best: The Pluralist Industrial Relations Paradigm of Balancing Competing Interests," in *Theoretical Perspectives on Work and the Employment Relationship*, ed. Bruce Kaufman (Champaign, IL: Industrial Relations Association Press, 2004), pp. 195–227, esp. 197 ("workers are human being with aspirations, feelings, emotions, needs, and rights").

320. Edward Luce, *The Retreat of Western Liberalism* (New York: Atlantic Monthly Press, 2017).
321. See, e.g., F. A. Hayek, "Unions, Inflation, and Profits," in *The Public Stake in Union Power*, ed. P. D. Bradley (New York: University of Virginia Press, 1959), pp. 46–62; Gottfried Haberler, "Wage Policy and Inflation," in *The Public Stake in Union Power*, pp. 63–85, 84 (advocating the prohibition of mass picketing, closed and union shop agreements, protection of those who are willing to work, prevention of violence and coercion, and application of the Sherman [Antitrust] Act to labor unions); Oliver J. Blanchard, "The Wage Price Spiral," *The Quarterly Journal of Economics* 101 (1986): 543–566.
322. See Mill, *Principles of Political Economy*, bk. 2, ch. 11, sec. 1.
323. J. S. Mill, "Thornton on Labour and Its Claims," *Fortnightly Review*, Part I (May, 1869), pp. 505–518, Part II (June, 1869), pp. 680–700.
324. Ibid. at part I, p. 518.
325. Scott Gordon, "The Wage-Fund Controversy: The Second Round," *History of Political Economy* 5 (1973): 14–35, 28.
326. James Bonar, *Disturbing Elements in the Study and Teaching of Political Economy* (Baltimore: Johns Hopkins Press, 1911), p. 75.
327. For an extensive discussion and examples of each of these phenomena, see my *Exploitation and Economic Justice in the Liberal Capitalist State* and my *On Unemployment, Volume I* and *Volume II*. For some even more recent examples, see David Leonhardt, "The Charts that Show How Big Business Is Winning," *The New York Times* (June 17, 2018).
328. See Thomas Piketty, Emmanuel Saez, and Gabriel Zucman, "Distributional National Accounts," p. 4 ("There is a widespread view that rising income inequality mostly owes to booming wages at the top end, i.e., a rise of the 'working rich.' Our results confirm that this view is correct from the 1970s to the 1990s. But in contrast to earlier decades, the increase in income concentration over the last fifteen years owes to a boom in the income from equity and bonds at the top. The working rich are either turning into or being replaced by rentiers. Top earners became younger in the 1980s and 1990s but have been growing older since then").
329. See my extensive discussion of this issue in *On Unemployment, Volume II*, pp. 41–60.
330. See A. C. Pigou, "Mill and the Wages Fund," *The Economic Journal* 59 (1949): 171–180.
331. See generally Reiff, *Exploitation and Economic Justice*, pp. 216–226; Reiff, *On Unemployment, Volume II*, pp. 41–61.
332. See David Leonhardt, "The Great Wage Slowdown of the 21st Century," *The New York Times* (October 7, 2014); Elise Gould, "2014 Continues a 35-Year Trend of Broad-Based Wage Stagnation."
333. See Milton Friedman, "Some Comments on the Significance of Labor Unions for Economic Policy," in *The Impact of the Union*, ed. David McCord Wright (New York, 1951), pp. 204–234; Lloyd Ullman, "Marshall and Friedman on Union Strength," *The Review of Economics and Statistics* 37 (1955): 384–401; Milton Friedman, "Marshall and Friedman on Union Strength: Comment," *The Review of Economics and Statistics* 37 (1955): 401–406. I should note, I suppose, that Friedman based his view on the fact that unionization was too

limited for union wage demands to have any significant macroeconomic inflationary effect. But if unionization was universal, as I argue that it should be, this would obviously no longer be the case. Nevertheless, there is reason to believe that Friedman would still see unionization as having only a minor influence on inflation. According to Friedman, inflation is primarily a self-fulfilling prophecy created by people's expectations. If people believe that inflation will be 2 percent, they will act accordingly with regard to their wage demands and pricing decisions, and as a result of this behavior, inflation will be 2 percent. If they expect it to be more, it will be more, and if they expect it to be less, it will be less. See, e.g., Milton Friedman, "The Role of Monetary Policy," *American Economic Review* 58 (1968): 1–17; Milton Friedman "Inflation and Unemployment," *Journal of Political Economy* 85 (1977): 451–472, 458. While there are many things wrong with this theory, nothing in it suggests that it in any way depends on the rate of unionization. Expectations are expectations whether unionization is high or low. Indeed, if we wanted to control expectations, it would be far better to have unions around to help us do so rather than having to depend on a diffuse collection of sources of information and misinformation that were difficult to tell apart. In any event, for an extensive discussion and critique of Friedman's view of the causes of inflation, see Reiff, *On Unemployment, Volume II*, pp. 52–61; Reiff, *Exploitation and Economic Justice in the Liberal Capitalist State*, pp. 221–224.

334. For an extensive discussion and rebuttal to the claim that unionization causes inflation, see Barry T. Hirsch and John T. Addison, *The Economic Analysis of Unions: New Approaches and Evidence* (Boston: Allen & Unwin, 1984), pp. 218–267, 286–293.

335. See generally John Quiggin, *Zombie Economics: How Dead Ideas Still Walk among Us* (Princeton: Princeton University Press, 2010).

336. See, e.g., E. G. West and R. W. Hafer, "J. S. Mill, and the Wages Fund Recantation: A Reinterpretation – Reply," *The Quarterly Journal of Economics* 96 (1981): 543–549; E. G. West and R. W. Hafer, "J. S. Mill, and the Wages Fund Recantation: A Reinterpretation," *The Quarterly Journal of Economics* 92 (1978): 603–619; William Breit, "The Wages Fund Controversy Revisited," *The Canadian Journal of Economics and Political Science/Revue Canadienne d'Economique et de Science Politique* 33 (1967): 509–528.

337. See Daniel J. B. Mitchell and Christopher L. Erickson, "De-Unionization and Macro-Performance," 392–395.

338. See F. A. Hayek, "A Testing Time for Monetarism," Letter to the Editor, *The Times* (June 13, 1980).

339. See, e.g., Hayek, "Unions, Inflation, and Profits," pp. 46–62, 47–48.

340. For a general discussion of these, see Reiff, *On Unemployment, Volume II*, pp. 41–61.

341. For further discussion of this point, albeit in terms of unemployment, see Reiff, *On Unemployment, Volume II*, pp. 45–47.

342. For a discussion of the tender offer as a form of punishment for the target's management's incompetence, see Frank H. Easterbrook and Daniel R. Fischel, "The Proper Role of a Target's Management in Responding to a Tender Offer," *Harvard Law Review* 94 (1981): 1161–1205, 1169–1174.

343. Of course, *ex post* punishment can act as an *ex ante* deterrent in many circumstances, see Reiff, *Punishment, Compensation, and Law,* but the threat of market punishment is unlikely to deter incompetence. After all, if the incompetent could see that they were behaving foolishly, they wouldn't be behaving that way in the first place.
344. See Martin Lipton and Jay W. Lorsch, "A Modest Proposal for Improved Corporate Governance," *The Business Lawyer* 48 (1992): 59–77 (bemoaning the failure of too many boards of directors to exercise the requisite oversight of management failure in a timely fashion). See also William D. Cohan, "Documents Open Curtain on Boardroom Drama at Valeant," *The New York Times* (December 29, 2016); Gretchen Morgenson, "The Fed Wants to Make Life Easier for Big-Bank Directors," *The New York Times* (August 11, 2017) (noting that the Fed has recently proposed *reducing* directors' oversight of banking institutions).
345. For a discussion of some of the reasons boards often fail to act, see David Rhodes, Colin Carter, and Stephen Sutherland, "Looking for Smoke under the Door: The Case for an Actively Engaged Board" (Boston Consulting Group, August 2016) (www.bcgperspectives.com/Images/BCG-Looking-for-Smoke-Under-the-Door-Aug-2016_tcm80-213612.pdf).
346. See Gretchen Morgenson, "In Whole Foods Backlash, a Chance to Air Out Stagnant Boardrooms," *The New York Times* (February 21, 2015) ("large, institutional investors in the United States are generally a passive lot"); Gretchen Morgenson, "Daring to Knock on the Boardroom Door," *The New York Times* (April 20, 2013).
347. See Gretchen Morgenson, "Management, to the Barricades!" *The New York Times* (May 4, 2013); Steven Davidoff Solomon, "The Boardroom Strikes Back," *The New York Times* (April 21, 2015); Gretchen Morgenson, "Meet the Shareholders? Not at These Shareholder Meetings," *The New York Times* (March 31, 2017); Gretchen Morgenson, "Dubious Corporate Practices Get a Rubber Stamp from Big Investors," *The New York Times* (May 19, 2017); Gretchen Morgenson, "Meet the Legislation Designed to Stifle Shareholders," *The New York Times* (June 16, 2017).
348. See Gretchen Morgenson, "Shareholders?" Fuhgeddaboudit!" *The New York Times* (May 25, 2013).
349. See, e.g., Sui-Lee Wee, "Who Owns Anbang of China? A U.S. Labor Union Wants to Know." *The New York Times* (August 11, 2017); David Barboza, "Mounting Questions about Who Controls HNA, a Top Chinese Conglomerate," *The New York Times* (August 24, 2017).
350. D. Gordon Smith, "Corporate Governance and Managerial Incompetence: Lessons from Kmart," *North Carolina Law Review* 74 (1996): 1037–1139, at 1112 (footnote in original omitted).
351. For more on this, see Mark R. Reiff, *On Unemployment, Volume I,* p. 84.
352. See ibid. at p. 76; Associated Press, "California Court Decision Keeps Teacher Tenure Protections," *The New York Times* (August 22, 2016) ("Teachers [and their unions] have long argued that tenure protects them from being fired on a whim, preserves academic freedom and helps attract talented people to a profession that doesn't pay well").
353. See Hirschman, *Exit, Voice, and Loyalty.*

354. See, e.g., Wee, "Who Owns Anbang of China?" (union is concerned that company may be taking on excessive debt).
355. See Marick Masters, "How Union Stakes in Ailing Papers Like the Chicago Sun-Times May Keep Them Alive," *The Conversation* (August 16, 2017).
356. See, e.g., David Macaray, "Union Contracts," *Huffington Post* (July 28, 2016).
357. See, e.g., Anonymous, "The Secret Life of a Trade Union Employee: I Do Little but the Benefits Are Incredible," *The Guardian* (August 8, 2016).
358. See John DiNardo and David S. Lee, "Do Unions Cause Business Failures?" NBER (March 2003) (www.princeton.edu/~davidlee/wp/unionbf.pdf).
359. See Louis Uchitelle, "How the Loss of Union Power Has Hurt American Manufacturing," *The New York Times* (April 20, 2018) ("when organized labor dug in its heels – as it did regularly until late in the 20th century – manufacturing companies thought twice about shutting a factory and transferring production to another country"); Noam Scheiber, "AT&T Agrees to Contract, and Union Backs Time Warner Deal," *The New York Times* (December 13, 2017) (new union contract includes AT&T commitment to bring work back from overseas). Note, however, that while often protectionist, unions are no longer anti-immigrant. See Esther Yu Hsi Lee, "Labor Unions Move to Protect Immigrants, Regardless of Legal Status," *ThinkProgress* (May 26, 2018); Michael Kazin, "How Labor Learned to Love Immigration," *The New Republic* (May 13, 2013); Editorial, "Immigration and the Unions," *New York Times* (April 20, 2009).
360. See, e.g., Gethin Chamberlain, "Underpaid and Exhausted: The Human Cost of Your Kindle," *The Guardian* (June 9, 2018).
361. See Reiff, *On Unemployment, Volume II*, ch. 4.12 and 4.15. For further discussion of tax competition and when it is unjust, see Peter Dietsch, *Catching Capital: The Ethics of Tax Competition* (Oxford: Oxford University Press, 2015).
362. See Eduardo Porter, "Labor Wants to Make NAFTA Its Friend. Here's the Problem," *The New York Times* (August 22, 2017) (AFL-CIO asks that renegotiated North American Free Trade Agreement guarantee workers the right to a living wage in the society in which they live); Ian Austen, "G.M. Workers Strike in Canada as Mexico Jobs Raise Tension," *The New York Times* (September 18, 2017); Reuters, "Canada Union Calls for Boycott of GM Mexico-Made Vehicles" (January 25, 2019).
363. Note, however, that not all technological innovation *is* economically efficient. See Reiff, *On Unemployment, Volume I*, pp. 65–66. There are nevertheless reasons why management might be interested in pursuing such innovation – reducing the power and influence of unions being one of them. These are cases where union opposition to innovation might be both just and efficient.
364. F. A. Hayek, "The Corporation in a Democratic Society: In Whose Interest Ought It to and Will It be Run?" in *Studies in Philosophy, Politics and Economics* (London: Routledge & Kegan Paul, 1967), pp. 300–312, 301 (emphasis in original).
365. See, e.g., Bivens, et al., "How Today's Unions Help Working People," esp. pp. 6–7; Mishel and Walters, "How Unions Help All Workers"; Steven Greenhouse, "How the $15 Minimum Wage Went from Laughable to Viable," *The New York Times* (April 1, 2016); Alejandro Donado and Klaus Wälde, "How Trade Unions Increase Welfare," *The Economic Journal* 122 (2012): 990–1009; Michael Hiltzik, "Are Unions Necessary?" *Los Angeles Times* (February 27, 2014).

366. See David Weil, "Enforcing OSHA: The Role of Labor Unions," *Industrial Relations* 30 (1991): 20–36. For an example of the kinds of abuses that occur in nonunionized firms and where attempts at unionization have been successfully repulsed, see Michael Grabell, "Exploitation and Abuse at the Chicken Plant," *The New Yorker* (May 8, 2017); Rachel Abrams, "Walmart Is Accused of Punishing Workers for Sick Days," *The New York Times* (June 1, 2017); Noam Scheiber and Keith Bradsher, "Culture Clash at a Chinses-Owned Plant in Ohio," *The New York Times* (June 10, 2017).

367. See, e.g., Franz L. Neumann, "Labor Law in Modern Society," in *The Rule of Law under Siege: Selected Essays of Franz L. Neumann and Otto Kirchheimer*, ed. William E. Scheurerman (Berkeley: University of California Press, 1996), pp. 231–242, 236: "The protection of individual rights for the worker does not merely depend on the quality of the court system and its procedural guarantees. Equally important, perhaps even more important, is whether the social organizations that aspire to protect the rights of the worker have the power and will to do so. The best statute for labor courts can never succeed without effective labor unions." For examples of this idea at work, see Gwyn Topham, "Monarch Collapse: Union Launches Legal Action over Redundancies," *The Guardian* (October 4, 2017); Dominic Rushe, "Unions Reach $2.3m Settlement in Bangladesh Textile Factory Safety," *The Guardian* (January 22, 2018); Noam Scheiber, "Senate Bill to Curtail Labor Rights on Tribal Land Falls Short," *The New York Times* (April 16, 2018); Stacy Cowley, "Teachers Sue Navient, Claiming Student Loan Forgiveness Failures," *The New York Times* (October 3, 2018) (and lawsuit underwritten by union).

368. Mike Elk, "Can Unions Rebuild the Labor Movement in the US South?" *The Guardian* (April 28, 2017).

369. See, e.g., Barry Meier and Danielle Ivory, "Under Trump, Worker Protections Are Viewed with New Skepticism," *The New York Times* (June 5, 2017); Martin Pengelly, "Company Town: 'Quiet Tragedy' of an Arkansas Community vs the Kochs," *The Guardian* (September 10, 2017).

370. See Noam Scheiber and Bill Vlasic, "U.A.W. Says Nissan Workers Seek a Union Vote in Mississippi," *The New York Times* (July 11, 2017).

371. See Katie Benner, "Abuses Hide in the Silence of Nondisparagement Agreements," *The New York Times* (July 21, 2017).

372. See Noah C. Davis, "The Yelper and the Negative Review: The Developing Battle Over Nondisparagement Clauses," *American Bar Association GPSolo eReport* 3:10 (May 24, 2014).

373. See Benner, "Abuses Hide in the Silence of Nondisparagement Agreements."

374. See Jared Odessky and Miriam Frank, "Janus Is this Term's Worst L.G.B.T. Ruling," *The New York Times* (June 27, 2018); Human Rights Campaign, et al., "Brief as Amici Curiae in Support of Respondents in *Janus*, v. *AFSCME*," No, 16-1466, Supreme Court of the United States (January 19, 2018) (www.lambdalegal.org/sites/default/files/legal-docs/downloads/janus_v_american_federation_amicus_final_to_be_filed.pdf); Joe Davidson, "Racist Incidents on the Rise, Union for Government Workers Warns," *The Washington Post* (November 20, 2018).

375. See, e.g., Naomi Klein, "Labor Leaders' Cheap Deal with Trump," *The New York Times* (February 7, 2017) (discussing how many, even if not all, unions have opposed Trump's anti-environment and anti-immigrant initiatives); Owen

Jones, "Why Britain's Trains Don't Run on Time: Capitalism," *The New York Times* (April 4, 2017) (detailing long-running battle between Britain's rail unions and train operating companies over fares, lack of maintenance, eliminating guards from trains, the failure to upgrade rolling stock, and so on); Aditya Chakrabortty, "Boots Staff Under Pressure to Milk the NHS for Cash, Says Pharmacists' Union," *The Guardian* (April 13, 2016).

376. See Steven Davidoff Solomon, "Rise of Institutional Investors Raises Questions of Collusion," *The New York Times* (April 12, 2016); José Azar, Martin C. Schmalz, and Isabel Tecu, "Anti-Competitive Effects of Common Ownership," *Journal of Finance* 73 (2018): 1513–1565.

377. Alexander Dyck, Adair Morse, and Luigi Zingales, "Who Blows the Whistle on Corporate Fraud," Working Paper 12882 (National Bureau of Economic Research, February 2007) (http://faculty.chicagobooth.edu/finance/papers/who%20blows%20the%20whistle.pdf).

378. Gretchen Morgenson, "Whistle-Blowers Spur Companies to Change Their Ways," *The New York Times* (December 16, 2016).

379. See Jaron H. Wilde, "The Deterrent Effect of Employee Whistleblowing on Firms' Financial Misreporting and Tax Aggressiveness" (November 2016); James Rufus Koren, "Feds Order Wells Fargo to Rehire Whistleblower and Pay Him $5.4 Million," *Los Angeles Times* (April 3, 2017) (detailing the extent of retaliation by managers against nonunion employees who reported fears of fraud).

380. See Dyck, Morse, and Zingales, at p. 31 ("the surprising part ... is not that most employees do not talk; it is that some talk at all ... In 45% of the cases, the costs of blowing the whistle are eliminated by keeping the identity of the whistleblower concealed. This is often the case when the company is unionized. The union seems to be in a good position to protect the whistle blowing employee from the potential retaliation.") (footnote omitted from quote). Interestingly, in a later version of this paper, the reference to the role of unions is removed. No reason is given for this modification. See "Who Blows the Whistle on Corporate Fraud?" *Journal of Finance* 65 (2010): 2213–2253, 2245. See also Gretchen Morgenson, "A Whistle Was Blown, but Who Was Listening?" *The New York Times* (April 28, 2017) (detailing failure of the SEC to act on a retaliation complaint); Jeyup S. Kwaak, "Hyundai Whistle-Blower, in Rarity for South Korea, Prompts Recall," *The New York Times* (May 16, 2017) (according to one survey in South Korea, 60 percent of whistle-blowers were fired and experienced financial hardship and ostracism from colleagues).

381. See James B. Stewart, "Wells Fargo Whistle-Blowers' Fate becomes Just a Footnote," *The New York Times* (May 4, 2017) (detailing the continuing difficulty of those who were allegedly fired for blowing the whistle on Wells Fargo's fraudulent account-creation practices); Keith Ellison, "John Stumpf's Wells Fargo Racket Shows Why Bank Workers Need a Union," *The Daily Beast* (September 28, 2016).

382. See Stewart J. Schwab and Randall S. Thomas, "Realigning Corporate Governance: Shareholder Activism by Labor Unions," *Michigan Law Review* 96 (1997–1998): 1018–1094.

383. See, e.g., Sawsan Morrar, "California State University Stashed $1.5 Billion in Reserves While Hiking Tuition, Audit Says," *Sacramento Bee* (June 20, 2019) (audit was conducted at the request of the CSU Employees Union).

384. See, e.g., Eduardo Porter, "The Challenge of Cutting Coal Dependence," *The New York Times* (August 30, 2016) (noting that the German federal government's attempt to cut dependence on coal in light of environmental concerns was rolled back in response to opposition from companies, unions, and regional governments); David Weber, "The Real Reason the Investor Class Hates Pensions," *The New York Times* (March 5, 2018) (arguing that the movement to convert public-employee pension plans into individual retirement accounts is motivated in part by a desire to protect company managers from the scrutiny they currently receive from large centrally managed public-employee pension funds).
385. See, e.g., Meissa Hampton, "Hollywood's Biggest Union Turned a Blind Eye to Sexual Abuse," *The Guardian* (January 18, 2018).
386. See James Meikle, "Lecturers Vote for Boycott of Israeli Universities," *The Guardian* (May 31, 2007); Benjamin Joffe-Walt, "Lecturers Back Boycott of Israeli Academics," *The Guardian* (May 29, 2006). For the text of the boycott proposal as put before the University and College Union (UCU), which was formed through a merger of the two previous unions of university lecturers, the AUT and NATFHE, see www.ucu.org.uk/circ/html/ucu31.html.
387. Indeed, both these constraints have ultimately stopped proposals for a union supported boycott from going forward. See James Meikle, "Lecturers Drop Israeli Universities Boycott Call after Legal Advice," *The Guardian* (September 28, 2007).
388. See *Janus* v. *ASCME*, 585 U.S. — (2018), slip op. at pp. 38–41.
389. I want to mention here the work of William H. Hutt, an Englishmen who spent most of his career in South Africa and was rabidly anti-union. See W. H. Hutt, *The Theory of Collective Bargaining, 1930–1975* (San Francisco: Cato Institute, 1980 [1930]). Supposedly, it was his South African experience and his view that white trade unions seeking to protect what they saw as white jobs were at least partially responsible for apartheid there, which he is claimed to have opposed, that was behind his anti-unionism. See Benjamin Jackson, "Hayek, Hutt and the Trade Unions," in *Hayek: A Collaborative Biography, Part V*, ed. Robert Leeson (London: Palgrave Macmillan, 2015), pp. 159–175; W. H. Hutt, *The Economics of the Colour Bar* (London: Andre Deutsch, 1964). I have my doubts about this explanation of his views, which seem to be driven far more by his (in my view highly dubious) analysis of the economics of unionization than his concern that unions were anti-social institutions. Be that as it may, however, even if his characterization of the role of certain unions in the pre-apartheid South African context is correct, this does not establish that unions can be a threat to republican liberty in contemporary liberal capitalist democracies where forming whites-only unions would be barred by appropriate post-institutional regulation, just as forming whites-only firms would be.
390. See, e.g., Associated Press, "Angst over the Economy Helps Trump Flip Great Lake States," *The New York Times* (November 9, 2016); Scott Clement, "Donald Trump Is Splitting the White Vote in Ways We've Never Seen Before," *The Washington Post* (May 31, 2016); Thomas B. Edsall, "Is Trump Wrecking Both Parties?" *The New York Times* (August 11, 2016); Jeremey W. Peters, "Donald Trump's Crucial Pillar of Support, White Men, Shows Weakness," *The New York Times* (August 18, 2016); Matthew C. MacWilliams, "Donald Trump Is Attracting Authoritarian Primary Voters, and It May Help Him Gain the Nomination," *LSE US Centre Blog* (January 27, 2016) (http://bit.ly/1KFzeCo).

391. See, e.g., Trip Gabriel, "My Union or My President? Dueling Loyalties Mark Pennsylvania Race," *The New York Times* (March 11, 2018).
392. Anne-Sylvaine Chassany, "How France's National Front is Winning Working Class Voters," *Financial Times* (October 21, 2016).
393. See Aurelien Breeden, "As Le Pen and Macron Fight for Presidency in France, Unions are Split," *The New York Times* (May 1, 2017).
394. See Katrin Bennhold, "Workers of Germany, Unite: The New Siren Call of the Far Right," *The New York Times* (February 5, 2018).
395. See Vauhini Vara, "Can Unions Stop the Far Right?" *The Atlantic* (December 2017).
396. See Émile Durkheim, *The Division of Labor in Society* (New York: Free Press, 2014).
397. See Durkheim, p. 101: At which point "our individuality is zero." In other words, mechanical solidarity embraces a perfectionist conception of community. Under the perfectionist conception, the community is prior to the individual, individuals form their identity by drawing on their conception of the community, and therefore a community may exist even if it has no current members. See Reiff, "The Attack on Liberalism."
398. Steven Lukes, "Introduction to This Edition," in Durkheim, p. xxviii. Organic solidarity therefore also has a conception of community, but it is a liberal conception: under this conception, the individual is prior to the community and the community draws its identity from the individuals that make it up, not the other way around. Under the liberal conception, accordingly, a community cannot exist if it has no members. See Reiff, "The Attack on Liberalism."
399. My thanks to Lisa Herzog for sharing with me an early version of her "Durkheim on Social Justice: The Argument from Organic Solidarity," *American Political Science Review* 112 (2017): 112–124, which inspired this extension of Durkheim's work on solidarity.
400. See Reiff, "Trump and the End of Liberalism"; Robert F. Jones, "The Collapse of American Identity," *The New York Times* (May 2, 2017); The Associated Press-NORC Center for Public Affairs Research, "The American Identity: Points of Pride, Conflicting Views, and a Distinct Culture" (2017) (http://apnorc.org/projects/Pages/HTML%20Reports/points-of-pride-conflicting-views-and-a-distinct-culture.aspx); David Taylor, "'In God We Trust' – The Bills Christian Nationalists Hope Will 'Protect Religious Freedom'," *The Guardian* (January 14, 2019).
401. See Kayla Blado, Dan Escrow, and Lawrence Mishel, "Who Are Today's Union Members?" *Economic Snapshot* (Economic Policy Institute, August 31, 2017).
402. See Durkheim, pp. 12, 26, 236.
403. See, e.g., Douglass Williams, "This Is What Emboldened White Supremacists Look Like," *The Guardian* (May 15, 2017) (citing the labor movement as "that magnificent engine that builds equality through solidarity and shared struggle").
404. See also Mary Parker Follett, *The New State* (London: Longmans, Greens and Co., 1923), esp. p. 341 n.1.
405. See Richard Trumka, "Don't Let Trump Speak for Workers," *The New York Times* (December 27, 2016); Mike Elk, "Undocumented Workers Find New Ally as Unions Act to Halt Deportations," *The Guardian* (March 22, 2018).

406. See Seymour Martin Lipset, "Democracy and Working Class Authoritarianism," *American Sociological Review* 24 (1959): 482–501.
407. See, e.g., Timothy J. Minchin, "A Pivotal Role? The AFL-CIO and the 2008 Presidential Election," *Labor History* 57 (2016): 299–322 (white men who didn't belong to unions voted overwhelmingly for John McCain, but unionized white men overcame their racial distrust and supported Barack Obama); Christine Arndt and Line Rennwald, "Union Members at the Polls in Diverse Trade Union Landscapes," *European Journal of Political Research* (July 21, 2016) (http://onlinelibrary.wiley.com/doi/10.1111/1475-6765.12157/full) (union membership helps inoculate workers against the far right's message); Rory Carroll, "The Mysterious Lynching of Frank Little: Activist Who Fought Inequality and Lost," *The Guardian* (September 21, 2016) (noting that "in the absence of powerful unions, or a shared identity with the working poor of other races, blue collar white men are Trump's strongest supporters").
408. See generally Robert M. Sapolsky, *Behave: The Biology of Humans at Our Best and Worst* (New York: Penguin, 2017), pp. 107–117.
409. See, e.g., Adam S. Smith, et al., "Manipulation of the Oxytocin System Alters Social Behavior and Attraction in Pair-Bonding Primates, *Callithrix Penicillata*," *Hormones and Behavior* 57 (2010): 255–262; Zoe R. Donaldson and Larry J. Young, "Oxytocin, Vasopressin, and the Neurogenetics of Sociality," *Science* 322 (2008): 900–904.
410. See Carsten K. W. De Dreu, "Oxytocin Modulates Cooperation with and Competition between Groups: An Integrative Review and Research Agenda," *Hormones and Behavior* 61 (2012): 419–428; Carsten K. W. De Dreu, et al., "Oxytocin Promotes Human Ethnocentrism," *PNAS* 108 (2011): 1262–1266; Carsten K. W. De Dreu, et al., "The Neuropeptide Oxytocin Regulates Parochial Altruism in Intergroup Conflict among Humans," *Science* 328 (2010): 1408–1411; Carolyn H. Declerck, Christophe Boone, and Toko Kiyonari, "Oxytocin and Cooperation under Conditions of Uncertainty: The Modulating Role of Incentives and Social Information," *Hormones and Behavior* 57 (2010): 368–374; Simone G. Shamay-Tsoory, et al., "Intranasal Administration of Oxytocin Increases Envy and Schadenfreude (Gloating)," *Biological Psychiatry* 66 (2009): 864–870; Thomas Baumgartner, et al., "Oxytocin Shapes the Neural Circuitry of Trust and Trust Adaptation in Humans," *Neuron* 58 (2008): 639–650.
411. See, "Stress Increases Oxytocin Release within the Hypothalamic Paraventricular Nucleus," *Brain Research* 781 (1998): 57–61.
412. See Robert Sapolsky, "This Is Your Brain on Nationalism: The Biology of Us and Them," *Foreign Affairs* (March/April 2019).
413. See Michael Kosfeld, et al., "Oxytocin Increases Trust in Humans," *Nature* 435 (2005): 673–676; Moïra Mikolajczak, et al., "Oxytocin Not Only Increases Trust When Money Is at Sake, but also When Confidential Information Is in the Balance," *Biological Psychology* 85 (2010): 182–184; Salomon Israel, et al., "The Oxytocin Receptor (OXTR) Contributes to Prosocial Fund Allocations in the Dictator Game and the Social Value Orientations Task," *PLOS One* 4 (2009): 5535; James K. Billing, et al., "Effects of Oxytocin and Vasopressin on Cooperative Behavior and Associated Brain Activity in Men," *Psychoneuroendocrinology* 37 (2012): 447–461.

414. For the tendency of those most opposed to the toleration of outsiders to maintain that liberal society is in crisis, see Reiff, "The Attack on Liberalism." See also, Mark R. Reiff, *The Unbearable Resilience of Illiberalism* (forthcoming).
415. Neil Gross, "The Decline of Unions and the Rise of Trump," *The New York Times* (August 12, 2016).
416. See, e.g., Peter Waldman, "Inside Alabama's Auto Jobs Boom: Cheap Wages, Little Training, Crushed Limbs," *Bloomberg Businessweek* (March 23, 2017) (detailing the low wages, long hours, intense pressure, and lack of safety concern and execution in nonunionized plants compared to unionized ones).
417. For a similar claim, albeit is a somewhat different context, see Anderson, *Private Government*, p. 47.
418. See Lowell Turner, "Institutions and Activism: Crisis and Opportunity for a German Labor Movement in Decline," *Industrial and Labor Relations Review* 62 (2009): 294–312. For more current figures, see Peter Ellguth and Susanne Kohaut, "Tarifbindung und betriebliche Interessenvertretung: Ergebnisse aus dem IAB-Betriebspanel 2014," *WSI-Mitteilungen* 4/2015: 290–229 (www.boeckler.de/wsi-mitteilungen_54287_54297.htm) (showing that 55 percent of employees in private industry in the West and 48 percent of employees in private industry in the East are covered by a union-negotiated collective agreement, although not all of the employees covered by those agreements are officially members of the union. This is because in Germany, one can enjoy the benefits of the agreement negotiated by the union without joining it or paying dues. For a good discussion of the history of unionization in postwar Germany through the end of the twentieth century, see Richard Hyman, *Understanding European Trade Unionism: Between Market, Class and Society* (London: Sage, 2001), pp. 115–142. For a discussion of some of the current problems with the union movement in Germany, see Oliver Nachtwey, "It Doesn't Matter Who Replaces Merkel. Germany Is Broken." *The New York Times* (December 7, 2018).
419. See, e.g., http://en.dgb.de/our-functions-and-principles.
420. See generally Martin Behrens, "Still Married after All These Years? Union Organizing and the Role of Works Councils in German Industrial Relations," *Industrial and Labor Relations Review* 62 (2009): 275–293. A similar idea was proposed in the United Kingdom for firms with more than 2,000 employees in the Report of the Committee of Inquiry on Industrial Democracy (London: HMSO 1977), p. 129, known as "the Bullock Report" after the Chairman of the Committee, but was never enacted. It was apparently revived for a time, however, by Theresa May, when she became Leader of the Conservative Party and Prime Minister of the United Kingdom. See Nils Pratley, "Theresa May's Plan to Put Workers in Boardrooms Is Extraordinary," *The Guardian* (July 11, 2016).
421. See L. Fulton, "Worker Representation in Europe" (European Trade Union Institute, 2015) (www.worker-participation.eu/National-Industrial-Relations/Countries/Germany/Workplace-Representation). Some 28 percent of employees in the West and 15 percent of employees in the East were represented by *both* works councils and unions.
422. See Martin Behrens, Michael Fichter, and Carola M. Frege, "Unions in Germany: Regaining the Initiative?" *European Journal of Industrial Relations* 9 (2003): 25–42.

423. See Jonathan Rauch, "The Conservative Case for Unions: How a New Kind of Labor Organization Could Address the Grievances Underlying Populist Anger," *The Atlantic* (July/August 2017).
424. See L. Fulton, "Worker Representation in Europe" (European Trade Union Institute, 2015) (www.worker-participation.eu/National-Industrial-Relations/Across-Europe/Trade-Unions2).
425. See Lars Faeste, et al., *How Nordic Boards Create Exceptional Value* (Boston Consulting Group, June 2016).
426. See also James A. Piazza, *Going Global: Unions and Globalization in the United States, Sweden and Germany* (Lanham, MD: Lexington Books, 2002), esp. pp. 99–109; Peter Swenson, *Fair Shares: Unions, Pay, and Politics in Sweden and West Germany* (Ithaca, NY: Cornell University Press, 1989).
427. See, e.g., Liz Alderman, "Unions Back Revisions of Labor Law in France," *The New York Times* (January 11, 2013); Adam Nossiter, "Marcon Takes on France's Labor Code, 100 Years in the Making," *The New York Times* (August 4, 2017); Aurelien Breeden, "France Unveils Contentious Labor Overhaul in Big Test for Macron," *The New York Times* (August 31, 2017); Peter S. Goodman, "Nordic-Style Designs Sit at Heart of French Labor Plan," *The New York Times* (October 26, 2017); Liz Alderman, "French Companies Have Newfound Freedom ... to Fire," *The New York Times* (January 23, 2018); Liz Alderman, "Air France Dispute Threatens to Escalate Macron's Battle with Labor," *The New York Times* (May 7, 2018); Alissa J. Rubin, "Can Strikes in France Still Make a Difference?" *The New York Times* (June 12, 2018).
428. See, e.g., Steven Greenhouse, *The Big Squeeze: Tough Times for the American Worker* (New York: Random House, 2008), pp. 247–254: "75 percent of companies facing organizing drives hired anti-union consultants. Ninety-two percent forced employees to attend meetings to hear anti-union propaganda, while 78 percent required workers to attend one-on-one meetings in which managers force-fed them the company's anti-union message ... 51 percent of companies threatened to close plants if the union won, while just 1 percent actually closed operations after a union victory." Ibid. at 247. The statistics here come from Kate Bronfenbrenner, "Uneasy Terrain: The Impact of Capital Mobility on Workers, Wages, and Union Organizing," *Report Submitted to the U.S. Trade Deficit Review Commission* (September 6, 2000) (http://digitalcommons.ilr.cornell.edu/cgi/viewcontent.cgi?article=1002&context=reports). See also Mike Elk, "Pro-Union Rally in Mississippi Unites Workers with Community: 'We Are Ready,'" *The Guardian* (March 5, 2017) (detailing various recent campaigns mounted against unionization at large plants in various states, and what unions have done to attempt to counter this); Mike Elk, "Nissan Attacked for One of 'Nastiest Anti-Union Campaigns' in Modern History," *The Guardian* (August 1, 2017); Bernie Sanders, "Nissan Dispute Could Go Down as Most Vicious Anti-Union Crusade on Decades," *The Guardian* (August 3, 2017); Michael Sainato, "Amazon Training Videos Coach Whole Foods Staff on How to Discourage Unions," *The Guardian* (September 27, 2018); Michael Sainato, "'It's Union Busting 101': Documents Reveal Verizon Attacks on Organized Labor," *The Guardian* (January 16, 2019); Steven Greenhouse, "Dear Delta Air Lines: Video Games and Beer Cannot Compete with Joining a Union," *The Guardian* (May 11, 2019) (detailing efforts by Delta to defeat unionization, and past history of other companies firing union activists

after unsuccessful campaigns); Noam Scheiber, "Volkswagen Factory Workers in Tennessee Reject Union," *The New York Times* (June 14, 2019) (noting that supervisors made anti-union comments in meetings and chief executive publicly blamed unionization for the demise of a Volkswagen plant in Philadelphia).

429. The Trump administration has even rescinded a rule that had required the disclosure of the source of the anti-union messages employees receive during union drives. See Marni von Wilpert, "By Rescinding the Persuader Rule, Trump Is Once Again Siding with Corporate Interests over Working People," *Working Economic Blog* (Economic Policy Institute, June 13, 2017).

430. See, e.g., Editorial, "Union's Loss Is the South's Loss, Too," *The New York Times* (August 12, 2017); Noam Scheiber, "U.A.W. Accuses Nissan of 'Scare Tactics' as Workers Reject Union Bid," *The New York Times* (August 5, 2017); Noam Scheiber, "Boeing Workers Reject a Union in South Carolina," *The New York Times* (February 15, 2017) (describing widespread misinformation circulated by management and unrelenting anti-union pressure from local politicians); Nick Wingfield, "Amazon Proves Infertile Soil for Unions, So Far," *The New York Times* (May 16, 2016) (describing how a recent campaign to unionize one of Amazon's warehouse facilities was influenced by one worker's impassioned story of how his union had abandoned him that seems now to have been completely false – indeed, it is doubtful that the fellow was even a worker and may have instead been an anti-union management plant); Steven Greenhouse, "In a Bid for Revote, Union Claims Tennessee Officials Frightened Workers," *The New York Times* (April 4, 2014) (government officials accused of telling workers that a VW plant would not get necessary government subsidies if workers voted to form a union). For an extensive discussion of the tactics used by management and its agents to influence unionization votes, see Kate Bronfenbrenner, "No Holds Barred: The Intensification of Employer Opposition to Organizing," EPI Briefing Paper #235 (Economic Policy Institute, May 20, 2009) (www.epi.org/files/page/-/pdf/bp235.pdf); Marty Jay Levitt, *Confessions of a Union Buster* (New York: Crown Publishers, 1993) ("a campaign against a union is an assault on individuals and a war on the truth"); Michael Sainato, "Exploited Amazon Workers Need a Union. When Will They Get One?" *The Guardian* (July 8, 2018).

431. For an example of one recent attempt to put pressure on a corporate employer to recognize this, see Mike Elk, "Danny Glover and Bernie Sanders Seek France's Help after Nissan Union Vote," *The Guardian* (August 12, 2017) (the French government owns 20 percent of Renault, which is unionized, and Renault owns a significant share of Nissan).

432. See, e.g., Morgan O. Reynolds, *Power and Privilege: Labor Unions in America* (New York: Manhattan Institute for Policy Research, 1984), esp. p. 285 (listing 13 alleged "special privileges" granted to unions); J. Enoch Powell in Paul H. Douglas and J. Enoch Powell, *How Big Should Government Be?* p. 72: "In talking about unions, we are not talking about voluntary associations, men availing themselves of the basic human freedom of free association. We are talking about groups endowed by legislation with immunity from civil and criminal responsibility which would otherwise attach to the actions which they contemplate." For a recent example of this argument in the popular press, see Trey Kovacs, "Time to Pare Back Union Legal Privileges," *Newsday* (September 2, 2016): Hayek, "A Testing Time for Monetarism"

("As I see it, within the time available what is required can be achieved only if the Government, in the near future, obtains through a referendum popular instruction at once to rescind all the special privileges which have been granted to the trade unions by law").

433. See, e.g., Henry C. Simons, "Hansen on Fiscal Policy," *Journal of Political Economy* 50 (1942): 161–196, 171; Henry C. Simons, "Some Reflections on Syndicalism," *The Journal of Political Economy* 52 (1944): 1–25; Charles W. Baird, "Unions and Antitrust," *Journal of Labor Research* 21 (2000): 585–600.

434. See, e.g., von Mises, *Human Action*, p. 772; Hayek, *The Constitution of Liberty*, pp. 233–242; Hayek, *1980s Unemployment and the Unions*, esp. p. 61 ("[unions] are the only privileged institution licensed to use coercion without law"). Hayek's views on what he sees as union exceptionalism are neatly summarized in Charles W. Baird, "Hayek on Labor Unions: Coercion and the Rules of Law," *Journal of Private Enterprise* 23 (2007): 30–51.

435. See Reiff, "The Difference Principle, Rising Inequality, and Supply-Side Economics"; Reiff, "The Politics of Masochism."

436. This would go some way toward undermining the objections to closed and union shops raised by, *inter alia*, Sylvester Petro. See Petro, *The Labor Policy of the Free Society*, pp. 110–112.

437. See Shaun Richman, "If the Supreme Court Rules against Unions, Conservatives Won't Like What Happens Next," *The Washington Post* (March 1, 2018) (arguing that constant competition for representation rights could vitiate no-strike clauses and lead to continuous labor unrest).

438. See generally Reiff, *Punishment, Compensation, and Law*.

439. See Philippe Van Parijs, "Why Surfers Should be Fed: The Liberal Case for an Unconditional Basic Income," *Philosophy & Public Affairs* 20 (1991): 101–131; Philippe Van Parijs, *Real Freedom for All* (Oxford: Oxford University Press, 1995); Philippe van Parijs and Yannick Vanderborght, *Basic Income: A Radical Proposal for a Free Society and a Sane Economy* (Cambridge: Harvard University Press, 2017).

440. Those looking to get a sense of the variety of criticisms that have been raised against UBI, however, should consult Antti Jauhiainen and Joona-Hermanni Mäkinen, "Why Finland's Basic Income Experiment Isn't Working," *The New York Times* (July 20, 2017); Douglass Ruchkoff, "Silicon Valley's Push for Universal Basic Income Is – Surprise! – Totally Self-Serving," *The Guardian* (July 21, 2017); Sonia Sodha, "Mark Zuckerberg's Got Some Cheek, Advocating a Universal Basic Income," *The Guardian* (July 10, 2017); Alex Gourevitch and Lucas Stanczyk, "The Basic Income Illusion," *Catalyst* 1 (Winter 2018); Anna Coote, "Universal Basic Income Doesn't Work. Let's Boost the Public Realm Instead," *The Guardian* (May 6, 2019).

441. See Anna Coote and Edenur Yazicic, "Universal Basic Income: A Union Perspective," *New Economics Foundation* (April 2019).

442. See, e.g., Steven Brill, "The Teachers' Unions Last Stand," *The New York Times Magazine* (May 17, 2010); Michael Lovenheim and Alexander Willén, "The Long-Run Effects of Teacher Collective Bargaining," CESifo Working Paper, No 5977 (June 30, 2016) (http://hdl.handle.net/10419/145012). For a particularly aggressive attack on a teachers' union comprised of public university professors, see Liz Robbins, "L.I.U.-Brooklyn Locks Out Professors Amid

Contract Dispute," *The New York Times* (September 6, 2016); Scot Lehigh, "Teachers Union Tries to Torpedo Ed Reform," *The Boston Globe* (March 23, 2017).

443. See, e.g., Michael F. Lovenheim and Alexander Willén, "The Long-Run Effects of Teacher Collective Bargaining" (October 2017) (presented at the American Economic Association annual conference, panel on New Evidence on the Effects of Teachers' Unions on Student Outcomes, Teacher Labor Markets, and the Allocation of School Resources, January 6, 2018) (see www.aeaweb.org/conference/2018/preliminary/1282?q=eNoIjEsKgDAQQ 69cIlm7UMGN5_ACRQcZ6A-nKqXo7o6ou_eSkAIhEQ5-zpEwlV8xoU-cLOslcJ-UBtYURCYuK5ol2p-RNoq2xjQ1-43SsrKL1avK3YocvnUzX87_ HqMHYodYb3LpcJxo).

444. See, e.g., Emma Garcia and Lawrence Mishel, "Unions and the Allocation of Teacher Quality in Public Schools," *EPI Report* (Economic Policy Institute, April 7, 2016) (finding that the strength or weakness of teachers' unions has no apparent connection to the allocation of teaching resources between high-poverty and other public schools) (www.epi.org/publication/unions-and-the-allocation-of-teacher-quality-in-public-schools/?utm_source=Economic+Policy+Insti tute&utm_campaign=5f58bb3994-EPI_News_04_08_164_8_2016&utm_ medium=email&utm_term=0_e7c5826c50-5f58bb3994-58070685). See also *Vergara v. California*, 246 Cal.App.4th 619 (2016) (finding that union-supported teacher tenure rules have no such connection either); Emma Garcia and John Schmitt, "Teacher Unions and Students' Long-Term Economic Prospects," *Working Economics Blog* (Economic Policy Institute, April 19, 2018).

445. See Robert Gebeloff, "The Numbers that Explain Why Teachers Are in Revolt," *The New York Times* (June 4, 2018); Sylvia Allegretto and Lawrence Mishel, "The Teacher Weekly Wage Penalty Hit 21.4 Percent in 2018, a Record High," Economic Policy Institute (April 24, 2019).

446. See Debbie Truong, "'Borderline Criminal': Many Public Schools Teeter on the Edge of Decrepitude," *The Guardian* (May 25, 2019).

447. See Niraj Chokshi, "94 Percent of U.S. Teachers Spend Their Own Money on School Supplies, Survey Finds," *The New York Times* (May 16, 2018).

448. See Sawsan Morrar, "California State University Stashed $1.5 Billion in Reserves While Hiking Tuition, Audit Says," *Sacramento Bee* (June 20, 2019) (audit was conducted at the request of the CSU Employees Union).

449. See Sally Weale, "Fifth of Teachers Plan to Leave Profession within Two Years," *The Guardian* (April 16, 2019) (and a fifth more within five years).

450. See, e.g., Melissa Smith, "I Work at One of America's Underfunded Schools. It's Falling Apart," *The Guardian* (May 26, 2018) ("while some of [the recent teacher walkout in Oklahoma] was about teacher salaries, it was more about the conditions in our schools – conditions that resulted from years of underfunding education"); Benjamin Wallace-Wells, "The New Politics of the West Virginia Teachers' Strike," *The New Yorker* (March 2, 2018) (given that West Virginia teachers were so severely underpaid relative to neighboring states, many West Virginia schools were having trouble filling open positions); E. J. Dionne Jr., "What Striking Teachers Teach Us," *The Washington Post* (April 4, 2018) (noting that teachers strikes are in part "a revolt against decades of policies that gutted public institutions"); Leah Varjacques, Taige Jensen, and

Japhet Weeks, "We Are Republican Teachers Striking in Arizona. It's Time to Raise Taxes," *The New York Times* (April 26, 2018); Simon Romero and Julie Turkewitz, "Teachers in Arizona and Colorado Walk Out for Funding and Pay Raises," *The New York Times* (April 26, 2018); Michelle Goldberg, "The Teachers' Revolt Spreads to Arizona," *The New York Times* (April 27, 2018); Dana Goldstein, "Arizona Teachers End Walkout as Governor Signs Bill Approving Raises," *The New York Times* (May 3, 2018) (Governor signs budget bill that provides teachers with 20 percent raise and new funds for classrooms); Jennifer Medina, Tim Arango, Dana Goldstein, and Louis Keene, "Los Angeles Teachers Strike, Disrupting Classes for 500,00 Students," *The New York Times* (January 14, 2019) (demands include not only higher pay but also smaller class sizes and more support staff in schools): Michael Sainato, "Denver Teachers Set to Strike Over Better Pay and Working Conditions," *The Guardian* (February 10, 2019); Vivian Ho, "Oakland Teachers Strike for Better Pay as Tech Wealth Transforms City," *The Guardian* (February 21, 2019) (teachers seeking better pay, smaller class sizes, and more resources for their students); E. Tammy Kim, "The Striking Demands of LA Teachers," *The New York Review of Books* (January 23, 2019); Jennifer Medina and Dana Goldstein, "Los Angeles Teachers' Strike to End as Deal Is Reached," *The New York Times* (January 22, 2019) (detailing numerous gains unrelated to pay and benefits obtained through the strike).

451. Michael Sainato, "Low Pay, Large Classes, Funding Cuts: Behind New Wave of US Teachers' Strikes," *The Guardian* (February 27, 2019).
452. See Martin Malin, "Does Public Employee Collective Bargaining Distort Democracy? A Perspective from the United States," *Comparative Labor Law & Policy Journal* 34 (2013): 277–306, 284–285; Martin H. Malin, "The Paradox of Public Sector Labor Law," *Indiana Law Journal* 84 (2009): 1369–1400; Martin H. Malin and Charles Taylor Kerchner, "Charter Schools and Collective Bargaining: Compatible Marriage or Illegitimate Relationship?" *Harvard Journal of Law and Public Policy* 30 (2007): 885–937.
453. See Valerie Strauss, "Think Teachers Can't Be Fired Because of Unions? Surprising Results from a New Study," *The Washington Post* (July 21, 2016); Eunice S. Han, "The Myth of Unions' Overprotection of Bad Teachers: Evidence from the District-Teacher Matched Panel Data on Teacher Turnover," Wesley College (February 27, 2016) (http://haveyouheardblog.com/wp-content/uploads/2016/07/Han_Teacher_dismissal_Feb_16.pdf).
454. See, e.g., Editorial, "When Police Unions Impede Justice," *The New York Times* (September 3, 2016) (arguing that "municipal governments have signed contracts with police unions including provisions that shield officers from punishment for brutal behaviour as well as from legitimate complaints by the citizens they are supposed to serve"); Editorial, "Shining a Light on Police Misconduct," *The Baltimore Sun* (July 14, 2016) (police union resisting opening up its disciplinary procedures to public scrutiny); Richard Pérez-Peña and Sheryl Gay Stolberg, "Police Unions Hail Trump's Easing of Scrutiny. Local Officials Worry." *The New York Times* (April 4, 2017); Alan Feuer, "Police Unions Complains of 'Blue Racism,' Then Regrets Word Choice," *The New York Times* (August 22, 2017); Ashley Southall, "New York Police Union Sues to Stop Release of Body Camera Videos," *The New York Times* (January 9,

2018); Tim Arango, "California Has a High Rate of Police Shootings. Could a New Open-Records Law Change That?" *The New York Times* (February 12, 2019) (noting opposition of police unions); Ashley Southall, "Police Union Criticized for Comparing Arrested N.F.L. Player to 'Wild Animal'," *The New York Times* (January 27, 2019).

455. See, e.g., Gretchen Morgenson, "Playing Pension Games," *The New York Times* (December 7, 2013); Rick Lyman and Mary Williams Walsh, "Police Salaries and Pensions Push California City to the Brink," *The New York Times* (December 27, 2013); Monica Davey, "Chicago Mayor Seeks Alterations to Repair Badly Underfunded Pension Plan," *The New York Time* (April 1, 2014); David W. Chen and Mary Williams Walsh, "New York City Pension System Is Strained by Costs and Politics," *The New York Times* (August 3, 2014); Noam Scheiber, "Public Pension Cuts Exempt Police and Firefighters," *The New York Times* (March 19, 2015); David Zahniser, "L.A. Plans to Undo 2012 Pension Cuts in New Union Pay Deal," *Los Angeles Times* (September 5, 2015); Mary Williams Walsh, "Study Finds Public Pension Promises Exceed Ability to Pay," *The New York Times* (March 17, 2016). But there is also evidence that many of these claims are overblown. See Tara Siegel Bernard, "Think Your Retirement Plan Is Bad? Talk to a Teacher," *The New York Times* (October 21, 2016); *In re City of Detroit*, – B.R. –, (2013 WL 6331931) (Bkrtcy. E.D. Mich., Dec. 5, 2013), p. 6 (despite claims that Detroit granted overly generous pensions to its municipal employees, the average annual benefit received by pensioners from the Detroit system was actually only $18,000 per annum with regard to its nonuniformed personnel and only $30,000 for its uniformed personnel).

456. See Harry H. Wellington and Ralph K. Winter, *The Unions and the Cities* (Brookings Institution Press, 1971) and Jeffrey H. Keefe, "A Reconsideration and Empirical Evaluation of Wellington's and Winter's, '*The Unions and the Cities*'," *Comparative Labor Law and Policy Journal* 34 (2013): 251–275 (criticizing Wellington and Winter's claim that public unions have antidemocratic effects).

457. Keefe, "Eliminating Fair Share Fees and Making Public Employment 'Right-to-Work' Would Increase the Pay Penalty for Working in State and Local Government"; Kearney and Mareschal, *Labor Relations in the Public Sector*; Jeffrey H. Keefe, "On Friedrichs v. California Teachers Association," EPI Briefing Paper #411 (Economic Policy Institute, November 2, 2015) (www.epi.org/files/pdf/94942.pdf) (when public employees are unionized, public and private earn equivalent amounts of total compensation [wages plus benefits]; when they are not unionized, public employees earn 10 percent less on average than their private sector counterparts).

458. See Reiff, "The Libertarian Argument for Unions."

459. See Gabriel Winant, "Why Are So Many White Collar Professionals in Revolt?" *The Guardian* (May 27, 2018).

460. See, e.g., Michael Cooper, "Labor Unrest Hits Ballet Theater, and Dancers Consider a Strike," *The New York Times* (January 10, 2018).

461. See Sarah Cowan, "Can Artists Organize? The Story of WAGE," *The New Yorker* (December 14, 2018).

462. Editorial, "Unions in the Ivory Tower," *The New York Times* (August 24, 2016) (35,000 graduate research and teaching assistants are currently in unions); Teresa Tritch, "Unions Knocking on the Academy's Doors," *The New York Times*

(September 12, 2016); Erin McCann and Richard Pérez-Peña, "Faculty Members at 14 State Universities in Pennsylvania Go on Strike," *The New York Times* (October 19, 2016); Elizabeth A. Harris, "Columbia Challenges Vote by Graduate Students to Unionize," *The New York Times* (December 19, 2016); Thomas Frank, "Are Elite Universities 'Safe Spaces'? Not If You're Starting a Union," *The Guardian* (September 9, 2017); Elizabeth Harris, "Columbia University Says It Won't Bargain with Graduate Student Union," *The New York Times* (January 30, 2018); Teresa Kroeger, Celine McNicholas, Marnia von Wilpert, and Julia Wolfe, "The State of Graduate Student Employee Unions," Report (Economic Policy Institute, January 11, 2018); Lauren Aratani, "'Blatant Scare Tactics': Iowa University Leads Crackdown on Student Unions," *The Guardian* (December 11, 2018).

463. See Noam Scheiber, "Grad Students Win Right to Unionize in an Ivy League Case," *The New York Times* (August 23, 2016); Cary Hester Seckman, "The Unions: How Organized Labor Is Landing a Helping Hand to Dental Hygiene," *RDH Magazine* (April 2004); Cathie Anderson, "A Week After Worker Strike, UC Davis Hospital Residents and Interns Seek to Join Union," *Sacramento Bee* (March 26, 2019); Cathie Anderson, "Resident Doctors Say UC Davis Health Has Agreed to Bargain with Their Union," *Sacramento Bee* (May 30, 2019).

464. See Sydney Ember, "Journalists at Gawker Media's Websites Are Planning to Unionize," *The New York Times* (April 16, 2015); Sydney Ember, "Los Angeles Times Newsroom, Challenging Tronc, Goes Public with Union Push," *The New York Times* (October 4, 2017); Eli Rosenberg, "Journalists at Gothamist and DNAinfo Agree to Join Labor Union," *The New York Times* (April 12, 2017); Sydney Ember, "Union Is Formed at Los Angeles Times and Publisher Put on Leave," *The New York Times* (January 19, 2018); Matthew Sedacca, "Unions Are Gaining a Foothold at Digital Media Companies," *The New York Times* (December 26, 2017); Daniel Victor, "The New Yorker Joins a Growing List of Media Companies to Unionize," *The New York Times* (June 6, 2018); Jaclyn Peiser, "'Not All Fun and Memes': BuzzFeed News Employees Plan to Form a Union," *The New York Times* (February 12, 2019).

465. See Chi Onwurah, "All Workers Need Unions – Including Those in Silicon Valley," *The Guardian* (January 31, 2018); Kevin Roose, "Workers of Silicon Valley, It's Time to Organize," *The New York Times* (April 26, 2018); Noam Scheiber, "Google Workers Reject Silicon Valley Individualism in Walkout," *The New York Times* (November 6, 2018).

466. See ibid. Indeed, unionization may be exactly what it takes to bring some gender equity into the profession. See, e.g., Elizabeth Olson, "'A Bleak Picture' for Women Trying to Rise at Law Firms," *The New York Times* (July 24, 2017) (while women make up over 50 percent of law school graduates and 35 percent of lawyers at private law firm, they still represent only 20 percent of equity partners, and this number has not improved in years).

467. See Michelle Chen, "Millennials Are Keeping Unions Alive," *The Nation* (February 2, 2018).

468. "In 1996, there were 8,025 public listed companies in the United States; by 2012, the number of companies was about half: 4,101, according to the National Bureau of Economic Research." Andrew Ross Sorkin, "C.E.O.s Meet in Secret Over the Sorry State of Public Companies," *The New York Times* (July 21, 2016).

469. See www.sba.gov/managing-business/small-business-health-care/employers-50-or-more-employees. The same is true in the United Kingdom. See www.gov.uk/annual-accounts/microentities-small-and-dormant-companies.
470. This is indeed what often happens in France, although not in the United States. See Reiff, *On Unemployment, Volume II*, pp. 114–115.
471. See Reiff, *On Unemployment, Volume II*, pp. 114–115.
472. See, e.g., Rachel Abrams, "Sex Shop Workers Welcome the Protections of a Retail Union," *The New York Times* (May 23, 2016) (noting that the 25 employees of Babeland, an adult toy store with three locations in New York City, have just voted to join the Retail, Wholesale and Department Store Union).
473. All of these cutoffs have been used at one time or another by some liberal capitalist democracy. See The Bullock Report, p. 128; Reiff, *On Unemployment, Volume II*, pp. 114–115.
474. See Jesus College Cambridge, "The Future of Work," Rustat Conference Report (November 22, 2016) (file:///C:/Users/mreif/Downloads/Rustat%20Conference%20Future%20Of%20Work%20report_0.pdf), p. 19 (estimating that 20–30 percent of the working-age population in the United States is now part of the gig economy to some degree).
475. See, e.g., Carla Green and Sam Levin, "Homeless, Assaulted, Broke: Drivers Left Behind as Uber Promises Change at the Top," *The Guardian* (June 17, 2017); Sarah Butler and Gwyn Topham, "Uber Should Lose Its Licence If It Doesn't Improve Workers' Rights, Say Drivers," *The Guardian* (May 9, 2017); Editorial, "The Gig Economy's False Promise," *The New York Times* (April 10, 2017); Noam Scheiber, "How Uber Uses Psychological Tricks to Push Its Drivers' Buttons," *The New York Times* (April 2, 2017); Sarah Butler, "Uber Driver Tells MPs: I Work 90 Hours but Still Need to Claim Benefits," *The Guardian* (February 6, 2017); Robert Booth, Tara Evans, and Hilary Osborne, "Revealed: Delivery Giant Hermes Pays Some Couriers Less Than Living Wage," *The Guardian* (July 18, 2016); John McDermott, "Uber Is about to Kill a Lot More Jobs," *MEL Magazine* (January 11, 2017) (https://melmagazine.com/uber-is-about-to-kill-a-lot-more-jobs-f4497f5538d); Robert Booth, "UK Mail Driver Who Was Unable to Work after Car Accident Charged £800," *The Guardian* (March 19, 2017); Annalee Newitz, "The Secret Lives of Google Raters," *Ars Technica* (April 27, 2017) (https://arstechnica.com/features/2017/04/the-secret-lives-of-google-raters/) (describing how Google raters just had their hours drastically cut); Jia Tolentino, "The Gig Economy Celebrates Working Yourself to Death," *The New Yorker* (March 22, 2017): Nathan Heller, "Is the Gig Economy Working?" *The New Yorker* (May 15, 2017); National Employment Law Project, "Independent Contractor Misclassification Imposes Huge Costs on Workers and Federal and State Treasuries," *Fact Sheet* (July 2015) (www.nelp.org/content/uploads/Independent-Contractor-Costs.pdf).
476. See Lawrence Mishel, "Uber and the Labor Market," Economic Policy Institute (May 15, 2018) ("the W-2 equivalent hourly wage falls below the mandated minimum hourly wage in the majority of major Uber urban markets"); Sam Levin, "Uber Drivers Often Make Below Minimum Wage, Report Finds," *The Guardian* (March 5, 2018). The latter study's initial claims are being revisited after the study's methodology was criticized by Uber, but even when recalculated according to Uber's favored approach, the study still shows that 41 percent of drivers earn below the minimum wage and 4 percent actually lose money.

See Stephen Zoepf, "The Economics of Ride Hailing, Revisited" (March 5, 2018) (http://ceepr.mit.edu/files/papers/2018-005%20Authors%20Statement.pdf). See also Tracy Lien, "Most Uber and Lyft Drivers in L.A. Work Full Time and Still Struggle to Make Ends Meet, Study Says," *Los Angeles Times* (May 30, 2018); James A. Parrott and Michael Reich, "An Earnings Standard for New York City's App-based Drivers: Economic Analysis and Policy Assessment," Report for the New York City Taxi and Limousine Commission (Center for New York City Affairs/Center on Wage and Employment Dynamics, July 2018) (showing that 40 percent of NYC app-based drivers have income so low they qualify for Medicaid, and another 18 percent qualify for food stamps); Sarah Mason, "High Score, Low Pay: Why the Gig Economy Loves Gamification," *The Guardian* (November 20, 2018); Kari Paul, "The Uber Drivers Forced to Sleep in Parking Lots to Make a Decent Living," *The Guardian* (May 8, 2019).

477. See Caleb Gayle, "US Gig Economy: Data Shows 16m People in 'Contingent or Alternative' Work," *The Guardian* (June 7, 2018).

478. See Julie Carrie Wong, "Google Staff Call Out Treatment of Temp Workers in 'Historic' Show of Solidarity," *The Guardian* (April 2, 2019); Daisuke Wakabayashi, "Google's Shadow Work Force: Temps Who Outnumber Full-Time Employees," *The New York Times* (May 28, 2019).

479. See, e.g., Jack Flemming, "L.A. and Long Beach Port Workers Begin Striking," *Los Angeles Times* (June 19, 2018) (arguing that truck drivers have been misclassified as independent contractors).

480. See Noam Scheiber, "Uber Drivers Ruled Eligible for Jobless Payments by New York State," *The New York Times* (October 12, 2016); Chris Roberts, "Another Uber Driver Awarded Unemployment Benefits," *SF Weekly* (March 4, 2016); Aditya Chakrabortty, "Uber Ruling Is a Massive Boost for a Fairer Jobs Market," *The Guardian* (October 28, 2016); Sean Farrell, "Uber is Misleading Drivers about Its Legal Defeat, Claims Union," *The Guardian* (October 30, 2016); Robert Booth, "Uber Granted Right to Appeal against Ruling on UK Drivers' Rights," *The Guardian* (April 19, 2017); Prashant S. Rao, "Uber Hit with New Blow in London as Panel Says Drivers Aren't Self-Employed," *The New York Times* (November 10, 2017). See also Sarah Butler and Hilary Osborne, "Courier Wins Holiday Pay in Key Tribunal Ruling on Gig Economy," *The Guardian* (January 6, 2017).

481. See generally Internal Revenue Service, "Publication 15-A" (Department of the Treasury, January 5, 2017), pp. 7–10; *Dynamex Operations West, Inc. v. Superior Court of Los Angeles*, No. S222732 (Cal. Sup. Ct. Apr. 30, 2018); Kari Paul, "Gig Economy: California Bill Granting Employee Status Passes Assembly," *The Guardian* (May 29, 2019).

482. See, e.g., Noam Scheiber, "Gig Economy Business Model Dealt a Blow in California Ruling," *The New York Times* (April 30, 2018); *Dynamex Operations West, Inc. v. Superior Court,* Supreme Court of California (April 30, 2018); Amie Tsang, "Uber Is Dealt a Fresh Blow in European Legal Case," *The New York Times* (July 4, 2017); "Order Denying Plaintiff's Motion for Preliminary Approval," in *O'Connor v. Uber Technologies,* Civ. Action No. 13-CV-03826-EMC (N.D. Cal.) and *Yucesoy v. Uber Technologies,* Civ. Action No. 15-CV-00262-EMC (N.D. Cal.) (http://uberlawsuit.com/Uber%20order%20re%20preliminary%20approval.pdf) (August 18, 2016).

Similar actions are also pending in Europe. See Mark Scott, "In Europe, Is Uber a Transportation Service or a Digital Platform?" *The New York Times* (November 27, 2016); Jamie Grierson and Rob Davies, "Pimlico Plumbers Loses Appeal against Self-Employed Status," *The Guardian* (February 10, 2017); Robert Booth, "Hermes Facing Legal Challenge from Its Self-Employed Workers," *The Guardian* (January 26, 2017); Robert Booth, "Tax Barrister Plans to Take Uber to Court Over Alleged £20m Black Hole," *The Guardian* (February 21, 2017); Sarah Butler, "Ikea Enters Gig Economy By Buying Freelance Labour Firm TaskRabbit," *The Guardian* (September 28, 2017); Liz Alderman, "Uber Dealt Setback after European Court Rules It Is a Taxi Service," *The New York Times* (December 20, 2017); Amie Tsang, "U.K. Court Rules against Plumbing Contractor in 'Gig Economy' Case," *The New York Times* (June 13, 2018).

483. See Noam Scheiber, "Is Gig Work a Job? Uber and Others Are Maneuvering to Shape the Answer," *The New York Times* (March 26, 2019).

484. See Ross Barkan, "Trump's Labor Department Is Giving the Gig Economy Carte Blanche," *The Guardian* (May 6, 2019).

485. See Noam Scheiber, "Labor Dept. Says Workers at a Gig Company Are Contractors," *The New York Times* (April 29, 2019).

486. See Noam Scheiber, "Uber Drivers Are Contractors, Not Employees, Labor Board Says," *The New York Times* (May 14, 2019).

487. See, e.g., Noam Scheiber, "Uber Has a Union of Sorts, but Faces Doubts on Its Autonomy," *The New York Times* (May 12, 2017); Julia Carrie Wong, "Uber's Seattle Woes: Union Battle Could See Company Leave Another Major City," *The Guardian* (April 5, 2017); Brooks Barnes, "Hollywood Writers Kept the Heat on Studios to Win Their Contract," *The New York Times* (May 2, 2017); Samantha Masunaga, "L.A. and Long Beach Port Truckers and Warehouse Workers Begin Strike," *Los Angeles Times* (October 1, 2018) (strike was over classification of port workers as independent contractors); Noam Scheiber, "Debate Over Uber and Lyft Drivers' Rights in California Has Split Labor," *The New York Times* (June 29, 2019).

488. See, e.g., Faiz Siddiqui, "Uber and Lyft Drivers Strike for Pay Transparency – after Algorithms Made It Harder to Understand," *The Guardian* (May 8, 2019).

489. See Sandeep Naheesan, "America's Most Insidious Union-Buster? Its Own Government," *The Guardian* (June 29, 2018).

490. See, e.g., Celine McNicholas and Marni von Wilpert, "The Joint Employer Standard and the National Labor Relations Board," Report (Economic Policy Institute, May 31, 2017) (www.epi.org/files/pdf/129265.pdf); Noam Scheiber and Stephanie Strom, "Labor Board Ruling Eases Way for Fast-Food Unions' Efforts," *The New York Times* (August 27, 2015); Browning-Ferris Industries and Sanitary Truck Drivers and Helpers, Case No. 32-RC-109684, 362 NLRB No. 186 (August 27, 2015) (finding franchisors "joint employers" in certain circumstances); Stacy Cowley, "Labor Board Ruling on Joint Employers Leaves Some Companies Scratching Their Heads," *The New York Times* (August 28, 2015); Noam Scheiber, "Labor Board's Do-Over Leaves an Obama-Era Rule Intact," *The New York Times* (February 26, 2018); Noam Scheiber, "Push to Settle McDonald's Case, a Threat to Franchise Model," *The New York Times* (March 19, 2018).

Notes to pp. 162–165

491. Rachel Abrams, "Why Aren't Paychecks Growing? A Burger-Joint Clause Offers a Clue," *The New York Times* (September 27, 2017): Rachel Abrams, "'No Poach' Deals for Fast-Food Workers Face Scrutiny by States," *The New York Times* (July 9, 2018); Alan B. Krueger and Orley Ashenfelter, "Theory and Evidence on Employer Collusion in the Franchise Sector," NBER Working Paper No. 24831 (July 2018). See also Julia Carrie Wong, "Revealed: Google's 'Two-Tier' Workforce Training Document," *The Guardian* (December 12, 2018) (designed to minimize chances of Google being found to be a joint employer of temps, vendors, and contractors).
492. See Rachel Abrams, "7 Fast-Food Chains to End 'No-Poach' Deals that Lock Down Low-Wage Workers," *The New York Times* (July 12, 2018); Rachel Abrams, "8 Fast-Food Chains Will End 'No-Poach' Policies," *The New York Times* (August 20, 2018).
493. See Noam Scheiber, "Judge Rejects Settlement Over McDonald's Labor Practices," *The New York Times* (July 17, 2018).
494. See Noam Scheiber, "U.S. Moves to Limit Wage Claims Against Chains Like McDonald's," *The New York Times* (April 1, 2019); Moshe Z. Marvit, "The Joint Employer Standard in Limbo," *The Regulatory Review* (April 2, 2019).
495. Home care workers and farm workers are other occupations where abuse has long been rampant and therefore no threshold to number-of-employees requirement should apply. See Sarah Jaffe, "Home Care Workers Have Our Lives in Their Hands. They're Paid Only $10 an Hour," *The Guardian* (July 13, 2017); Jessica Glenza, "Tobacco: A Deadly Business: Big Tobacco Still Sees Big Business in America's Poor," *The Guardian* (July 13, 2017).
496. For a similar suggestion, see William E. Forbath and Brishen Rogers, "A New Type of Labor Law for a New Type of Worker," *The New York Times* (September 4, 2017).
497. See, e.g., John W. Budd, "Canadian Strike Replacement Legislation and Collective Bargaining: Lessons for the United States," *Industrial Relations* 35 (1996): 245–260.
498. For a further discussion of how framing can affect how people view a particular expense, see Amos Tversky and Daniel Kahneman, "The Framing of Decisions and the Psychology of Choice," *Science* 211 (1981): 453–458; Amos Tversky and Daniel Kahneman, "Loss Aversion in Riskless Choice," *Quarterly Journal of Economics* 106 (1991): 1039–1061; Daniel Kahneman, Jack L. Knetsch, and Richard Thaler, "The Endowment Effect, Loss Aversion, and the Status Quo Bias," *Journal of Economic Perspectives* 5 (1991): 193–206; Richard H. Thaler, "Mental Accounting Matters," *Journal of Behavioral Decision Making* 12 (1999): 183–206.
499. See generally Julianne Schultz, *Reviving the Fourth Estate: Democracy, Accountability, and the Media* (Cambridge: Cambridge University Press, 1998).
500. See, e.g., Sheelah Kolhatkar, "The Growth of Sinclair's Conservative Media Empire," *The New Yorker* (October 22, 2018); Jon Swaine, "Sinclair TV Chairman to Trump: 'We Are Here to Deliver Your Message,'" *The Guardian* (April 10, 2018); Jack Healy, "Denver Post Editor Who Criticized Paper's Ownership Resigns," *The New York Times* (May 3, 2018); Michael M. Grynbaum, "Fox News Once Gave Trump a Perch. Now It's His Bullhorn." *The New York Times* (July 1, 2018);

Zach Schonbrun, "When a Local Paper Gets New Owners, Partisan Strife Hits Its Doorstep," *The New York Times* (August 5, 2018); Jane Mayer, "Can Time Inc. Survive the Kochs?" *The New Yorker* (November 28, 2017).

501. See, e.g., Scott Shane, "From Headline to Photograph, a Fake News Masterpiece," *The New York Times* (January 18, 2017); Jeremy W. Peters, "Wielding Claims of 'Fake News,' Conservatives Take Aim at Mainstream Media," *The New York Times* (December 25, 2016).

502. See Jane Mayer, "The Making of the Fox News White House," *The New Yorker* (March 11, 2019).

503. See, e.g., Damian Paletta and Josh Dawsey, "Trump Personally Pushed Postmaster General to Double Rates on Amazon, Other Firms," *The Washington Post* (May 18, 2018); Catie Edmondson and Jaclyn Peiser, "Trump's Tariffs on Canadian Newsprint Hasten Local Newspapers' Demise," *The New York Times* (August 9, 2018); David Remnick, "Trump and the Enemies of the People," *The New Yorker* (August 15, 2018).

504. See Lawrence Douglass, "Why Trump Wants to Disempower Institutions that Protect the Truth," *The Guardian* (February 2, 2017); Jim Rutenberg, "News Outlets to Seek Bargaining Rights against Google and Facebook," *The New York Times* (July 9, 2017); Katherine Rosman and Jaclyn Peiser, "Denver Post Journalists Go to New York to Protest Their Owner," *The New York Times* (May 8, 2018); Mara Gay, "New York without the Daily New Will Be Less Alive, and Less Democratic," *The New York Times* (July 24, 2018); Barry Lynn, "Google and Facebook Are Strangling the Free Press to Death. Democracy is the Loser," *The Guardian* (July 26, 2018); Erin Durkin, "Almost 350 News Outlets to Publish Editorials Denouncing Trump's 'Dirty War' on the Press," *The Guardian* (August 15, 2018).

505. See, e.g., Michael Casey, "Loss of Local News Hinders Ability to Watchdog Government," *Sacramento Bee* (March 10, 2019).

506. Eduardo Porter, "Fed's Challenge, after Raising Rates, May Be Existential," *The New York Times* (March 14, 2017).

507. See generally Alexander Mehra, "Legal Authority in Unusual and Exigent Circumstances: The Federal Reserve and the Financial Crisis," *University of Pennsylvania Journal of Business Law* 13 (2010): 223–273; Eric Posner, "What Legal Authority Does the Fed Need During a Financial Crisis?" (Coase-Sandor Working Paper Series in Law and Economics No. 741, 2016).

508. See Kate Davidson, "Donald Trump's Comments on the Fed, Interest Rate Policy and Janet Yellen," *The Wall Street Journal* (November 9, 2016).

THIRD ESSAY

1. See generally criticizing Harry H. Wellington and Ralph K. Winter, *The Unions and the Cities* (Brookings Institution Press, 1971); Nelson Lichtenstein, "Bashing Public Employees and Their Unions," in *A Contest of Ideas: Capital, Politics, and Labor* (Chicago: University of Illinois Press, 2013), pp. 197–206.

2. See Étienne Cantin, "The Politics of Austerity and the Conservative Offensive against US Public Sector Unions, 2008–2012," *Relations Industrielles* 67 (2012): 612–632, 616.

3. See Joseph A. McCartin, "Approaching Extinction: The Decline of Strikes in the United States, 1960–2005," in *Strikes around the World, 1968–2005*, eds. Sjaak van der Velden, Heiner Dribbusch, Dave Lyddon, and Kurt Vandaele (Amsterdam;

Aksant, 2007), pp. 133–154, 138; Henry S. Farber, "Union Membership in the United States: The Divergence between the Public and Private Sectors," *Working Paper #503* (Princeton University, Industrial Relations Section: September 2005) (https://core.ac.uk/download/pdf/6894934.pdf).
4. McCartin, "Approaching Extinction," p. 138.
5. See Richard B. Freeman and Eunice Han, "The War against Public Sector Collective Bargaining in the US," *Journal of Industrial Relations* 54 (2012): 386–408.
6. Following the Republican triumph at the polls, there was a huge outpouring of public sector collective bargaining and labor union bills in 2011–2012. There were 733 bills in 42 states relating to public employee unions, 140 bills relating to union dues/agency fees, 53 bills on political activities and contributions, 171 bills for public safety employees, and additional bills in other categories making a total of 1707 bills in 50 states, the majority of which were designed to weaken public unions, limit their activities, and undermine their financing. See Freeman and Han, "The War Against Public Sector Bargaining in the U.S.," at 393; Lichtenstein, "Bashing Public Employees and Their Unions." Some of these attempts to restrict public sector unionization were successful, some were not, but the sponsors of those that were not have remained undaunted. For descriptions of each of these legislative initiatives by year and their current status, see The National Conference of State Legislatures, "Collective Bargaining and Labor Union Database" (www.ncsl.org/research/labor-and-employment/collective-bargaining-legislation-database.aspx) (last updated July 1, 2016).
7. For a lengthy discussion of what happened in Wisconsin, see Robert Hebdon, Joseph E. Slater, and Marick F., Masters, "Public Sector Collective Bargaining: Tumultuous Times," in *Collective Bargaining under Stress: Case Studies of Major U.S. Industries,* eds. Howard R. Stanger, Ann C. Frost, and Paul F. Clark (Champaign, IL: Labor and Employment Relations Association, 2013), pp. 251–292, 276–280.
8. For descriptions of each of these legislative initiatives by year and their current status, see The National Conference of State Legislatures, "Collective Bargaining and Labor Union Database."
9. See, e.g., Noam Scheiber, Maggie Haberman, and Glenn Thrush, "Trump's Inroads in Union Ranks Have Labor Leaders Scrambling," *The New York Times* (February 17, 2017); Noam Scheiber, "Trump Nominee Is Behind Anti-Union Legal Campaign," *The New York Times* (July 16, 2018); Noam Scheiber, "Federal Workers Brace for New Push on Trump Anti-Labor Goals," *The New York Times* (September 2, 2018).
10. See Dave Jamieson, "Missouri Governor Signs Right-to-Work Bill Passed by GOP Legislature," *The Huffington Post* (February 6, 2017); Reid Wilson, "Kentucky Governor Signs Right to Work Law," *The Hill* (January 8, 2017). Note, however, that the Missouri law has now been overturned by a union-sponsored ballot referendum. See Jeff Stein, "Missouri Voters Defeat GOP-Backed 'Right to Work' Law, in Victory for Unions, Associated Press Projects," *The Washington Post* (August 7, 2018).
11. See Russell Wilson, "Anti-Union Push Begins Again in Maine Legislature," *Maine Beacon* (February 6, 2017); Ed Sealover, "Colorado Senate Passes Bill to Become 'Right-to-Work State," *Denver Business Journal* (February 14, 2017).
12. 585 U.S. — (2018).

13. See Editorial, "After Janus, Unions Must Save Themselves," *The New York Times* (June 27, 2018).
14. See, e.g., Michael Paarlberg, "With All Eyes on Trump, Republicans Are Planning to Break Unions for Good," *The Guardian* (February 2, 2017) (discussing national right-to-work bill now working its way through Congress); Russ Buettner and Noam Scheiber, "For Andrew Puzder, Labor Nominee, Fighting for Owners' Interests Began Early," *The New York Times* (February 3, 2017); Emily Peck, "If Trump Really Cared about the Working Class, Puzder Never Would've Been Nominated," *The Huffington Post* (February 15, 2017).
15. See Lisa Rein, "Trump Takes Aim at Federal Bureaucracy with New Executive Orders Rolling Back Civil Service Protections," *The Washington Post* (May 25, 2018); Noam Scheiber, "Trump Moves to Ease the Firing of Federal Workers," *The New York Times* (May 25, 2018); Lisa Rein, "Trump's Fight with Federal Employee Unions Gets Real on Monday," *The Washington Post* (July 8, 2018); Michael Sainato, "Social Security Workers Call New Trump Administration Contract 'Union-Busting,'" *The Guardian* (July 3, 2019).
16. Bureau of Labor Statistics, "Union Members Summary" (U.S. Department of Labor, January 26, 2017) (www.bls.gov/news.release/union2.nr0.htm).
17. See, e.g., Noam Scheiber, "Service Union Plans Big Push to Turn Midwest Political Tide," *The New York Times* (August 24, 2017).
18. See Noam Scheiber and Kenneth P. Vogel, "Behind a Key Anti-Labor Case, a Web of Conservative Donors," *The New York Times* (February 25, 2018); Anne Marie Lofaso, "In Defense of Public Sector Unions," *Hofstra Labor and Employment Law Journal* 28 (2011): 301–334, 305–306; Daniel DiSalvo, "Janus Decision Reins in Unions' Political Power," *The New York Times* (June 27, 2018) (complaining that "nearly all union political spending supports the Democratic Party or liberal causes"); Noam Scheiber, "Supreme Court Labor Decision Wasn't Just a Loss for Unions," *The New York Times* (July 1, 2018) (noting that conservatives have acknowledged that drive to deprive public sector unions of funding is intended to undermine their support of progressive agenda).
19. Ed Pilkington, "Rightwing Alliance Plots Assault to 'Defund and Defang' American Unions," *The Guardian* (August 30, 2017) (referring to an April 22, 2016 ten-page fundraising letter sent out by the State Policy Network, an alliance of 66 state-based conservative think tanks). See also Adam Liptak, "Supreme Court Delivers a Sharp Blow to Labor Unions," *The New York Times* (June 27, 2018) (noting that President Trump characterized the *Janus* decision as a "big loss for the coffers of the Democrats!"),
20. For a recent example of most of these arguments in motion, see Daniel DiSalvo, "The Trouble with Public Sector Unions," *National Affairs* 5 (Fall 2010): 3–19. See also Michael Hicks, "Ruling against Public-Sector Unions Makes Us Freer," *IndyStar* (July 1, 2018).
21. See, e.g., Robert Pear, "Trump Rule Would Compel Drug Makers to Disclose Prices in TV Commercials," *The New York Times* (October 15, 2018).
22. See, e.g., Liz Alderman, "French Labor Overhaul Led by Unusual Figure: A Business Executive," *The New York Times* (August 14, 2018).

23. For a general discussion of the impact of austerity policies in Europe, see Mark R. Reiff, *On Unemployment, Volume I*, pp. 113–134; Mark R. Reiff, *On Unemployment, Volume II*, pp. 1–40. For some more recent examples, see, e.g., Benjamin Mueller, "Fewer Officers, More Calls: U.K. Police Are Stretched by Austerity," *The New York Times* (February 1, 2019).
24. See, e.g., Jonah Goldberg, "Public Unions Must Go," *Los Angeles Times* (February 22, 2011).
25. See M. S., "What the Difference Exactly: The Distinction between Private- and Public-Sector Unions," *The Economist* (February 9, 2011).
26. Some private companies, for example, are expressly designated as "not-for-profit," and some public agencies, the most significant example being the US Postal Service, are at least supposed to pay for themselves. See generally The Postal Accountability and Enhancement Act of 2006; Angie Drobnic Holan, "Ad from Save America's Postal Service Claims Rule from Congress Is Causing USPS's Financial Problems," *Politifact* (September 29, 2011). See also Anonymous Academic, "I Thought US Universities Were Driven by Profit – Until I Moved to the UK," *The Guardian* (April 27, 2018).
27. On the appropriateness of central case analysis, see H. L. A. Hart, *The Concept of Law* (Oxford: Oxford University Press, 2nd ed. 1994) p. 81.
28. See Mark R. Reiff, *Exploitation and Economic Justice in the Liberal Capitalist State* (Oxford: Oxford University Press, 2013).
29. See Martin Luther King, Jr., "Address to Striking Sanitation Workers in Memphis, Tennessee" (March 18, 1968). For more on Martin Luther King, Jr.'s speeches on labor rights and economic justice, see Martin Luther King, Jr. *All Labor Has Dignity,* ed. Michael K. Honey (Boston: Beacon Press, 1963, 1986, 2011).
30. See Pioneer Press, "Wisconsin Police, Firefighter Unions Allege Blackmail over Benefits," *Twin Cites Pioneer Press* (January 5, 2012).
31. See Marni von Wilpert, "Fighting for Public Sector Union Rights 50 Years after MLK's Assassination," *Working Economic Blog* (Economic Policy Institute, January 12, 2018).
32. See, e.g., David Cooper, Mary Gable, and Algernon Austin, "The Public sector Job Crisis: Women and African Americans Hit Hardest by Job Losses in State and Local Governments," EPI Briefing Paper #339 (Washington, DC: Economic Policy Institute, May 2, 2012); Celine McNicholas and Janelle Jones, "Black Women Will Be Most Affected by *Janus*," *Economic Snapshot* (Economic Policy Institute, February 13, 2018); Julia Wolfe and John Schmitt, "A Profile of Workers in State and Local Government," *Economic Policy Institute* (June 7, 2018).
33. See, e.g., Tiffany Hsu, "Trucks Built by a Woman Are Still Rare in America Even as Worker Shortages Loom," *The New York Times* (September 27, 2018).
34. See, e.g., Timothy Williams, "As Public Sector Sheds Jobs, Blacks are Hit Hardest," *The New York Times* (November 28, 2011); Catherine Rampell, "Employed Women, Dropping Out of Labor Force," *The New York Times* (December 6, 2011); Patrick McGeehan, "Blacks Miss Out as Jobs Rebound in New York City," *The New York Times* (June 20, 2012); Caleb Gayle, "Unions Brought Black Americans into the Middle Class. They're Now Being

Decimated," *The Guardian* (August 14, 2018); Jamiles Lartey, "'Barely above Water': US Shutdown Hits Black Federal Workers Hardest," *The Guardian* (January 11, 2019).
35. See David Lewin, "Public Employee Unionism in the 1980s: An Analysis of Transformation," in *Unions in Transition: Entering the Second Century,* ed. Seymour Martin Lipset (San Francisco: Institute for Contemporary Studies, 1986), pp. 241–264, 243; Farber, "Union Membership in the United States: The Divergence between the Public and Private Sectors," p. 6. For a more general discussion of the rise of public sector unionism, see Richard B. Freeman, "Unionism Comes to the Public Sector," *NBER Working Paper* No. 1452 (National Bureau of Economic Research, September 1984).
36. Julia Hatch, "Employment in the Public Sector: Two Recessions' Impact on Jobs," *Monthly Labor Review* (October 2004): 38–47.
37. For extended criticism of the view that austerity is expansionary, see Reiff, *On Unemployment, Volume I*, pp. 113–134.
38. See Heidi Shierholz, "At a Time of Persistent Economic Weakness, Today's Jobs Report Represents an Ongoing Disaster," *Press Release* (Economic Policy Institute, May 3, 2013) (noting that since the recovery began in June 2009, the public sector has lost 741,000 jobs); Floyd Norris, "The Lagging Public Sector," *The New York Times* (July 5, 2013); Floyd Norris, "Four Years Later, 28,000 More Jobs," *The New York Times* (January 4, 2013); Paul Krugman, "We Don't Need No Education," *The New York Times* (June 14, 2012); Shaila Dewan and Motoko Rich, "Public Workers Face Continued Layoffs, Hurting the Recovery," *The New York Times* (June 10, 2012); Michael Greenstone and Adam Looney, "A Record Decline in Government Jobs: Implications for the Economy and America's Workforce," *The Hamilton Project* (August 3, 2012) (www.hamiltonproject.org/files/downloads_and_links/0803_jobs_government_employment.pdf); Matthew O'Brien, "Our Historic Austerity – In 1 Crazy Chart," *The Atlantic* (December 2013) (showing that public employment after the Great Recession has fallen more than 600,000 *during the recovery alone,* while public employment actually *increased* after the previous recession by 400,000).
39. To see this, go to the Bureau of Labor Statistics, United States Department of Labor, "Databases, Tables & Calculators by Subject" (http://data.bls.gov/pdq/SurveyOutputServlet), click on federal government employment, and enter the relevant years.
40. Floyd Norris, "Bloated Government? Federal Employment at 47-Year Low," *The New York Times* (October 22, 2013).
41. Compare Bureau of Labor Statistics, United States Department of Labor, "Databases, Tables & Calculators by Subject," total nonfarm employment with federal government employment using the calculator at http://data.bls.gov/pdq/SurveyOutputServlet. Unfortunately, the figures in this database only go back to 1939.
42. See Damian Paletta, "Trump Budget Expected to Seek Historic Reduction in Federal Workforce," *The Washington Post* (March 12, 2017); Ben Jacobs, "Small Hand of Government: Trump's Aim to Shrink the State Pleases Conservatives," *The Guardian* (April 1, 2017); Lisa Rein and Andrew Ba Tran, "How the Trump

Era Is Changing the Federal Bureaucracy," *The Washington Post* (December 30, 2017); Aaron Gregg, "While Federal Employment Shrinks in D.C., Government Contractors Are on a Hiring Spree," *The Washington Post* (July 22, 2018).

43. The same is true if we measure the size of government by the ratio of federal net outlays to GDP, as some advocates of small government like to do, although it is not clear why this should be thought to be a measure of the influence of public sector unions. In any event, federal net outlays as a percentage of GDP have remained remarkably constant since about 1953. At the time, they represented about 19.5 percent of GDP; today they represent 20.75 percent, which is less than they were through most of the 1980s and 1990s, and this is despite the fact that for much of the last 15 years we have been fighting two of the longest and most expensive wars in our history (next to World War II) and are still struggling to fully emerge from the aftereffects of the Great Recession. See Federal Reserve Bank of St. Louis and U.S. Office of Management and Budget, "Federal Net Outlays as Percent of Gross Domestic Product," Federal Reserve Bank of St. Louis (updated March 31, 2017) (https://fred.stlouisfed.org/series/FYONGDA188S).
44. See Bureau of Labor Statistics, "Databases, Tables & Calculations by Subject" (http://data.bls.gov/pdq/SurveyOutputServlet) to retrieve the relevant data. See also Drew DeSilver, "Job Shifts under Obama: Fewer Government Workers, More Caregivers, Servers and Temps," *Pew Research Center* (January 14, 2015) (www.pewresearch.org/fact-tank/2015/01/14/job-shifts-under-obama-fewer-government-workers-more-caregivers-servers-and-temps/).
45. In 1977, the US population was 220.2 million. On January 1, 2016 it was 322.8 million, or approximately 47 percent greater than it was in 1977.
46. See Bureau of Labor Statistics, "Databases, Tables & Calculations by Subject" to retrieve the relevant data.
47. See Thomas Peele, "Three BART Janitors Swept Up $365,000 in OT Last Year," *East Bay Times* (June 1, 2017); Teri Sforza, "Southern California Firefighters Pull in a Quarter-Million Dollars in Overtime, and Then Some," *Orange County Register* (June 21, 2017).
48. See Kate Rogers, "Where the Jobs Are: Houston's Police Shortage," *CNBC* (February 2, 2018).
49. See Patricia Cohen and Robert Gebeloff, "Public Servants Are Losing Their Foothold in the Middle Class," *The New York Times* (April 22, 2018).
50. See Danielle Ivory and Caitlin Dickerson, "Safety Concerns Grow as Inmates Are Guarded by Teachers and Secretaries," *The New York Times* (June 17, 2018).
51. See U.S. Bureau of Labor Statistics, All Employees: Government: Local Government [CES9093000001], retrieved from FRED, Federal Reserve Bank of St. Louis; https://fred.stlouisfed.org/series/CES9093000001, April 23, 2018.
52. See Eric MacGilvray, *The Invention of Market Freedom* (Cambridge: Cambridge University Press, 2011), pp. 166–173; Mark Reiff, "Two Theories of Economic Liberalism," *The Adam Smith Review* 10: 189–214.
53. See MacGilvray, *The Invention of Market Freedom*, pp. 166–173; Reiff "Two Theories of Economic Liberalism"; David Sloan Wilson and Daron Acemoglu, "Stop Crying about the Size of Government: Start Caring about Who Controls It." *Evonomics* (March 25, 2016).

54. See, e.g., Ross Douthat, "The Era of Limited Government Is Over," *The New York Times* (February 26, 2019).
55. See Ian Vásquez and Tanja Porčnik, "The Human Freedom Index 2017" (a Cato Institute, Fraser Institute, and Friedrich Naumann Foundation for Freedom copublication, 2017) (https://object.cato.org/sites/cato.org/files/human-freedom-index-files/2017-human-freedom-index.pdf).
56. See Jenny Uechi, "U.S. Republican Koch Oil Billionaires Help Fund the Fraser Institute. Why the Fraser Institute?" *Vancouver Observer* (April 28, 2012); David Weigel, "Who the Hell Is Going to Take a Think Tank Seriously If It's Controlled by Billionaire Oil Guys?' Cato's President Speaks." *Slate* (March 22, 2012); Kenneth P. Vogel, "Cato, Kochs Settle Ownership Fight," *Politico* (June 5, 2012).
57. See Ed Dolan, "Quality of Government, Not Size, Is the Key to Freedom and Prosperity," *Evonomics* (May 6, 2017); Ed Dolan, "Freedom, Prosperity, and Big Government," *The First Principle* (Niskanen Center, April 20, 2017) (https://niskanencenter.org/blog/freedom-government-part-one/). Note that the Niskanen Center is itself a right-libertarian organization named after a former chairman of the Cato Institute and run by Jerry Taylor, who spent 23 years at the Cato Institute and who is also associated with the American Legislative Exchange Council (ALEC), the ultraconservative organization in the business for drafting model legislation for far-right elected officials to promote and introduce. See Nancy Scola, "Exposing ALEC: How Conservative-Backed State Laws Are All Connected," *The Atlantic* (April 14, 2012).
58. See HFI Index at pp. 11–13.
59. See HFI Index at p. 12. In other words, the authors claim to care only about the liberty of Herbert Spencer but do so only because they say this facilitates the liberty of his contemporary T. H. Green. For a helpful discussion of why such a claim is internally contradictory, see MacGilvray, *The Invention of Market Freedom*, pp. 166–173.
60. See Fraser Institute, "Economic Freedom Ranking 2014" (2017) (www.fraserinstitute.org/economic-freedom/map?page=map&year=2014). For more information on how the EFI is calculated, see James Gwartney, Robert Lawson, and Joseph Hall, "Economic Freedom in the World: 2016 Annual Report" (Fraser Institute, 2016) (www.fraserinstitute.org/sites/default/files/economic-freedom-of-the-world-2016.pdf), pp. 273–285. Note that in the 2016 EFI, the United States has moved up to 6th, while Mauritius and Georgia are now 7th and 8th, and the UAE dropped from 5th to 37th, a dramatic movement that is apparently the result of accounting for gender equality on this more recent survey, showing how sensitive the index is to factors that have not been previously considered. See Fraser Institute, "Economic Freedom of the World: 2018 Annual Report" (www.cato.org/economic-freedom-world).
61. See HFI at p. 6. In the newest version of the HFI, Hong Kong is ranked third. See Ian Vásquez and Tanja Porčnik, "The Human Freedom Index 2018" (a Cato Institute, Fraser Institute, and Friedrich Naumann Foundation for Freedom copublication, 2018) (www.fraserinstitute.org/sites/default/files/human-freedom-index-2018.pdf).
62. Dolan, "Freedom, Prosperity, and Big Government."

63. For a debunking of various other consequentialist arguments for why smaller government is supposedly always better, see Lane Kenworthy, "Is Big Government Bad for Freedom, Civil Society, and Happiness?" *Evonomics* (May 2017) (http://evonomics.com/big-government-bad-freedom-civil-society-happiness/).
64. This quip was made by Grover Norquist, president of Americans for tax reform, during an interview on National Public Radio's *Morning Edition* on May 25, 2001.
65. See, e.g., Kirk Johnson, "Where Anti-Tax Fervor Means 'All Services Will Cease,'" *The New York Times* (May 13, 2017) (southwest Oregon local government has gotten so small in can no longer even conduct elections or provide round-the-clock police services).
66. Adam Smith, *Lectures on Jurisprudence* (Oxford: Oxford University Press, 1978 [1766]), pp. 530–531. See Jon Bakija, Lane Kenworthy, Peter Lindert, and Jeff Madrick, *How Big Should Our Government Be?* (Oakland, CA: University of California Press, 2016).
67. Ronald Reagan, "Inaugural Address," (January 20, 1981) (www.presidency.ucsb.edu/ws/?pid=43130). In this, Reagan appears to have been channeling Albert Jay Nock, who railed against the New Deal policies of FDR in the 1930s. See Albert Jay Nock, *Our Enemy, the State* (New York: CreateSpace Independent Publishing, 2014).
68. See J. S. Mill, *On Liberty* (Cambridge: Cambridge University Press, 1989), p. 13.
69. See, e.g., Gerald F. Gaus, *Justificatory Liberalism* (Oxford: Oxford University Press, 1996). For a good summary of Gaus's view, see Steven Wall, "On Justificatory Liberalism," *Politics, Philosophy, and Economics* 9 (2010): 123–149, 124–128. See also Gerald Gaus, "On Two Critics of Justificatory Liberalism: A Response to Wall and Lister," *Politics, Philosophy, and Economics* 9 (2010): 177–212.
70. See, e.g., John Rawls, "Priority of the Right and Ideas of the Good," in *Political Liberalism* (New York: Columbia University Press, 1993, 1996), pp. 173–211, 191–195; Ronald Dworkin, "Liberalism," in *A Matter of Principle* (Cambridge: Harvard University Press, 1985), pp. 181–204, 191ff; Joseph Raz, *The Morality of Freedom* (Oxford: Oxford University Press, 1986), pp. 114ff; Will Kymlicka, "Liberal Individualism and Liberal Neutrality," *Ethics* 99 (1989):883–905.
71. See Eric Beerbohm, "Must Rawlsians be Hamiltonians? Small Government and Political Illiberalism," *The American Journal of Jurisprudence* 62 (2017): 21–28, 21 (noting that "the question of the size of government hasn't been taken up directly and in a systematic way by analytic political philosophy").
72. See, e.g., Binyamin Appelbaum, "Yellen Warns against Erasing Regulations Made after the Financial Crisis," *The New York Times* (August 25, 2017).
73. See, e.g., Robert Kuttner, "How the Airlines Became Abusive Cartels," *The New York Times* (April 17, 2017); Nelson D. Schwartz, "Route to Air Travel Discomfort Starts on Wall Street," *The New York Times* (May 28, 2017).
74. See Edward J. Ballereisen, *Fraud: An American History from Barnum to Madoff* (Princeton: Princeton University Press, 2017), esp. ch. 12; Carina Chicano, "From Wells Fargo to Frye Festival, the Scam Economy Is Entering Its Baroque Phase," *The New York Times Magazine* (May 16, 2017); Mark R. Reiff, "Punishment in the Executive Suite: Moral Responsibility, Causal Responsibility, and Financial Crime," in *Just Financial Markets? Finance in*

a Just Society, ed. Lisa Herzog (Oxford: Oxford University Press, 2017), pp. 125–153; Jesse Eisinger, *The Chickenshit Club: Why the Justice Department Fails to Prosecute Executives* (New York: Simon & Schuster, 2017).

75. See, e.g., Steven Erlanger, "After Grenfell Tower Fire, U.K. Asks: Has Deregulation Gone Too Far?" *The New York Times* (June 28, 2017).
76. See Mark R. Reiff, "Trump and the End of Liberalism: Some Hard Truths about the Degradation of American Democracy," *The Critique* (January 15, 2017) (http://www.markreiff.org/categories/2-publications.htm#categories-4).
77. See Reiff, *Exploitation and Economic Justice in the Liberal Capitalist State*.
78. Thomas Sewall Adams and Helen Laura Sumner, *Labor Problems* (New York: Macmillan, 1905), p. 15.
79. See, e.g., Graham Bowley, "What If Trump Really Does End Money for the Arts?" *The New York Times* (January 30, 2017); Josephine Livingstone, "Why Are Americans So Hostile to State-Funded Art?" *The New Republic* (May 26, 2017).
80. See, e.g., Glenn Thrush and Erica L. Green, "Behind Trump's Plan to Overhaul the Government: Scaling Back the Safety Net," *The New York Times* (June 21, 2018). See also Jamiles Lartey, "Will the 35-Day Shutdown Lead to Privatizing Government Functions? *The Guardian* (January 27, 2019) (air traffic control and airport security).
81. F. A. Hayek, *The Road to Serfdom* (London: Routledge, 1944), pp. 124–125.
82. F. A. Hayek, *The Constitution of Liberty* (London: Routledge, 1960), pp. 325–329.
83. Hayek, *The Road to Serfdom*, pp. 125. See also Hayek, *The Constitution of Liberty*, ch. 19.
84. Hayek, *The Road to Serfdom*, pp. 125–126. See also F. A. Hayek, "Economic Freedom and Representative Government," in *New Studies in Philosophy, Politics, Economics and the History of Ideas* (London: Routledge & Kegan Paul, 1978), pp. 105–118, 111.
85. For a recent argument to the same effect, see Aris Trantidis and Nick Cowen, "Hayek versus Trump: The Radical Right's Road to Serfdom," *Polity* (2019).
86. See G. A. Cohen, "Are Freedom and Equality Compatible?" in *Self-Ownership, Freedom, and Equality* (Cambridge: Cambridge University Press, 1995), pp. 92–115, 99–100 (criticizing Nozick's conception of the self-ownership of the impoverished as merely formal and empty).
87. See, e.g., Martin Feldstein, "How Big Should Government Be?" *National Tax Journal* 50 (1997): 197–213, for a similar (albeit not identical) proposal.
88. See, e.g., William L. Megginson and Jeffrey M. Netter, "From State to Market: A Survey of Empirical Studies on Privatization," *Journal of Economic Literature* 39 (2002): 321–389, 351 (noting that investors who purchase shares of newly privatized entities at the offering price and then sell them at the first post-issue trading prices earn significant excess market-adjusted returns).
89. See generally David Parker, *The Official History of Privatisation, Volume II, Popular Capitalism, 1987–1997* (London: Routledge, 2012). See also Owen Jones, "Why Britain's Trains Don't Run on Time: Capitalism," *The New York Times* (April 4, 2017); Patrick Collinson, "The Train Companies Pocket Millions in Compensation for Delays," *The Guardian* (December 31, 2016); Neil Clark, "Angry about Fares? Get on Board the Renationalisation Express," *The Guardian* (August 13, 2013).

90. See, e.g., Mike McPhate, "California Today: Battle over a Bill Reaches the State Senate," *The New York Times* (August 24, 2017); Bob Schoonover, "SEIU Defends AB 1250," Letters to Editor, *Sacramento Bee* (July 22, 2017).
91. See George Yarrow, et al., "Privatization in Theory and Practice," *Economic Policy* 1 (1986): 323–377, 364; J. A. Kay and D. J. Thompson, "Privatisation: A Policy in Search of a Rationale," *The Economic Journal* 96 (1986): 18–32, 31; John Vickers and George Yarrow, "Economic Perspectives on Privatization," *Journal of Economic Perspectives* 5 (1991): 111–132.
92. See James Surowicki, "Trump Sets Private Prisons Free," *The New Yorker* (December 5, 2016); Eduardo Porter, "Prisons Run by C.E.O.s? Privatization under Trump Could Carry a Heavy Price," *The New York Times* (January 10, 2017); Timothy Williams, "Inside a Private Prison: Blood, Suicide and Poorly Paid Guards," *The New York Times* (April 3, 2018); Timothy Williams and Richard A. Oppel, Jr., "Escapes Riots and Beatings: But States Can't Seem to Ditch Private Prisons," *The New York Times* (April 10, 2018); Azadeh Shahshahani, "Why Are For-Profit US Prisons Subjecting Detainees to Forced Labor?" *The Guardian* (May 17, 2018); Shane Bauer, *American Prison: A Reporter's Undercover Journey into the Business of Punishment* (New York: Penguin, 2018).
93. See Stacy Cowley and Jessica Silver-Greenberg, "Outside Collectors for I.R.S. Are Accused of Illegal Practices," *The New York Times* (June 23, 2017); Patricia Cohen, "I.R.S. Paid $20 Million to Collect $6.7 Million in Tax Debts," *The New York Times* (January 10, 2018).
94. See Gwyn Topham, "British Rail is Nationalised All Over Again – By Foreign States," *The Guardian* (April 1, 2017).
95. See, e.g., U.S. Department of Transportation, Air Fitness Division, "How to Become a Certified Air Carrier" (Washington, D.C.: September 2012), pp. 10–15 (www.transportation.gov/sites/dot.gov/files/docs/Certificated_Packet_2012_final.pdf) (explaining statutory requirement of Title 49 United States Code that air carriers who operate within the United States not be foreign owned).
96. See generally Paul R. Verkuil, "Public Law Limitations on Privatization of Government Functions," *North Carolina Law Review* (2006): 397–469; Alon Harel, "Why Privatization Matters: The Democratic Case against Privatization," in *Privatization: Nomos LX*, eds. Jack L. Knight and Melissa Schwartzberg (New York: New York University Press, 2019), pp. 52–78.
97. One of the hottest areas of current debate over what functions should be treated as inherently governmental has to do with what can be done to foreigners and by whom; in other words, the permissible scope of the role of private military contractors. For a discussion of how this issue has been addressed over the years, see Elke Krahmann, *States, Citizens and the Privatization of Security* (Cambridge: Cambridge University Press, 2010), pp. 125–139.
98. See, e.g., L. Elaine Halchin, Kate M. Manuel, Shawn Reese, and Moshe Schwartz, Inherently Governmental Functions and Other Work Reserved for Performance by Federal Government Employees: The Obama Administration's Proposed Policy Letter (Washington, D.C.: Congressional Research Service, October 1, 2010) (http://digitalcommons.ilr.cornell.edu/key_workplace/761/).

99. In the United States, this idea goes all the way back to *The Federalist Papers*. See General Accountability Office, "Government Contractors: Are Service Contractors Performing Inherently Governmental Functions?" GGD-92-11 (November 18, 1991), p. 2.
100. See, e.g., Herbert Spencer, "Over-Legislation," in *Essays: Scientific, Political, & Speculative, Volume III* (London: Williams and Norgate, 1891 [1853]), pp. 229–282.
101. See, e.g., E. J. Dionne Jr., "Don't Buy the Spin. Government Works." *The Washington Post* (January 21, 2018) (pointing, among other things, to the highly successful bailout of the US auto industry in the wake of the Great Recession).
102. See, e.g., Kirsten Korosec, "Why U.S. Health Care Costs Are Twice as High as Other High-Income Countries," *Forbes* (March 14, 2018); Diane Archer, "Medicare Is More Efficient Than Private Insurance," *Forbes* (September 20, 2011).
103. See Cohen, "I.R.S. Paid $20 Million to Collect $6.7 Million in Tax Debts" ; Adam Chodorow, "The IRS Is Using Private Debt Collectors Again," *Forbes* (April 14, 2017); Dennis J. Varney Jr., "Why Steve Mnuchin Wants a Stronger I.R.S.," *The New York Times* (March 27, 2018) (IRS recovers about $10 for every $1 dollar spent internally on collection efforts).
104. See David Cay Johnston, "We Need Tax Police – and They Should Go After the Likes of Donald Trump," *The Guardian* (October 13, 2018); Editorial, "A Gutted I.R.S. Makes the Rich Richer," *The New York Times* (December 25, 2018).
105. See Walter M. Shaub Jr., "Five Myths about the Federal Workforce," *The Washington Post* (February 14, 2019).
106. Project on Government Oversight, "Bad Business: Billions of Taxpayer Dollars Wasted on Hiring Contractors" (September 13, 2011) (https://docs.pogo.org/report/2011/bad-business-report-only-2011.pdf?mtime=20180803144205&_ga=2.84350105.1054705783.1551121378-1188413719.1551121378).
107. Even Spencer recognized this. See Herbert Spencer, "Representative Government – What Is It Good For?" in *Essays: Scientific, Political, & Speculative, Volume III* (London: Williams and Norgate, 1891 [1853]), pp. 283–325, 320 ("it is clear, both *a priori* and *a posteriori*, that representative government is especially adapted for the maintenance and establishment of just laws"); Herbert Spencer, "The Proper Sphere of Government," in *Political Writings*, ed. John Offer (Cambridge: Cambridge University Press, 1994), pp. 3–57, p. 7 (the role of government is "to defend the natural rights of man – to protect person and property – to prevent the aggressions of the powerful against the weak – in a word, to administer justice. It was not intended to do less: it ought not be allowed to do more.").
108. See, e.g., Ludwig von Mises, *Human Action: A Treatise on Economics* (London: William Hodge, 1949), pp. 854–857.
109. See *Grimshaw v. Ford Motor Company*, 174 Cal.Rptr. 348 (Ct. App. 1981). In that 1978 case, Ford's failure to take sufficient precautions to prevent post-collision fires in the Ford Pinto resulted in a jury verdict of $2.5 million in compensatory damages and $125 million in punitive damages (later reduced to $3.5 million by the trial judge) and eventually a "voluntary"

recall. According to evidence adduced at trial, Ford decided it would be cheaper to pay damages to the few people who ended up burned to death than recall the car and fix the problem. Ford made its cost-benefit decision after assigning a value of $200,000 to human life, a figure the jury in these cases obviously found unreasonably low. For a discussion of this and similar cases, see Gary T. Schwartz, "The Myth of the Ford Pinto Case." *Rutgers University Law Review* 43 (2001): 1013–1068; and Mark Geistfeld, "Reconciling Cost-Benefit Analysis with the Principle that Safety Matters More Than Money," *New York University Law Review* 76 (2001): 114–189. For a discussion of problems with the cost-benefit analysis as a principle of decision-making more generally, see Reiff, *Punishment, Compensation, and Law: A Theory of Enforceability* (Cambridge: Cambridge University Press), p. 220 & n. 8 and 9.

110. See, e.g., Peter L. P. Simpson, *Political Illiberalism: A Defense of Freedom* (New Brunswick, NJ: Transaction Publishers, 2017); David Brooks, "The Localist Revolution," *The New York Times* (July 19, 2018); James Buchannan and Gordon Tullock, *The Calculus of Consent* (Ann Arbor, MI: University of Michigan Press, 1962), pp. 114–115.

111. See Beerbohm, "Must Rawlsians be Hamiltonians? Small Government and *Political Illiberalism*," 21–28, 22.

112. See Masha Gessen, "Barcelona's Experiment in Radical Democracy," *The New Yorker* (August 6, 2018) (discussing the rise of "municipalism").

113. See, e.g., Marni von Wilpert, "City Governments Are Raising Standards for Working People – and State Legislators Are Lowering Them Back Down," Economic Policy Institute (August 26, 2017) (www.epi.org/files/pdf/133463.pdf).

114. Cities and counties recently experiencing bankruptcy or bankruptcy-like conditions include: the City of Detroit (2013) $19 Billion in debt; the City of Stockton, California (2013), $1.03 billion in debt; Jefferson County, Alabama (2011), $4.2 billion in debt; Orange County, California (1994), $1.7 billion in debt; the City of San Bernardino, California (2013), $492 million in debt; and the City of Vallejo, California (2008), $175 million in debt. See Monica Davey and Mary Williams Walsh, "Billions in Debt, Detroit Tumbles into Insolvency," *The New York Times* (July 18, 2013); Peter Hecht, "Lambasting Wall Street, Federal Judge Allows Stockton to Seek Bankruptcy Protection," *Sacramento Bee* (April 2, 2013). And then there is of course Puerto Rico, which declared a form of bankruptcy in 2017 with debts of approximately $123 billion. See Mary Williams Walsh, "Puerto Rico Declares a Form of Bankruptcy," *The New York Times* (May 3, 2017).

115. For citations to some of the recent studies on this, see Reiff, *On Unemployment, Volume II*, pp. 13, 137–138.

116. See Peter Applebome, "In Detroit's 2-Speed Recovery, Downtown Roars and Neighborhoods Sputter," *The New York Times* (August 12, 2016).

117. See generally Amy Padani, "Anatomy of Detroit's Decline," *The New York Times* (December 8, 2013).

118. See Russell Berman, "Kansas Republicans Sour on Their Tax-Cut Experiment," *The Atlantic* (February 24, 2017); Mitch Smith and Julie Bosman, "Kansas Supreme Court Says State Education Spending Is Too Low," *The New York*

Times (March 2, 2017); Peter Hancock, "Public Employee Unions Fear Loss of Numbers under New Kansas Law," *Lawrence Journal-World* (July 6, 2015) (noting that the number of state employees and membership in state employee union is down 30 percent from 2007 and 2008).

119. See Michael Mazerov, "Kansas' Tax Cut Experience Refutes Economic Growth Predictions of Trump Tax Advisors," *Center for Budget and Policy Priorities* (August 12, 2016); Editorial, "Kansas' Trickle-Down Flood of Red Ink," *The New York Times* (February 27, 2017); Paul Krugman, "Zombies of Voodoo Economics," *The New York Times* (April 24, 2017); Monica Davey, "Brownback Tax Cuts Set Off a Revolt by Kansas Republicans," *The New York Times* (June 7, 2017); Scott Lehigh, "Consider Kansas: Tax Cuts Don't Pay for Themselves," *Boston Globe* (June 15, 2017).

120. See Bureau of Labor Statistics, "Union Affiliation of Employed Wage and Salary Workers by Occupation and Industry," and "Union Affiliation of Employed Wage and Salary Workers by State," Table 3 and Table 5 (January 26, 2017).

121. See Dominic Rushe, "'We Are a Cautionary Tale': Kansas Feels the Pain of Massive Trump-Style Tax Cuts," *The Guardian* (May 15, 2017); David Cooper, "As Wisconsin's and Minnesota's Lawmakers Took Divergent Paths, So Did Their Economies," Economic Policy Institute (May 8, 2018) (since 2010, Minnesota's economy, spurred by a slate of progressive economic policies, has outperformed Wisconsin's with its slate of conservative ones).

122. For extensive discussion of this issue and the empirical evidence that relates to it, see Reiff, *On Unemployment, Volume I*, sec. 4.6.1–4.6.2; *On Unemployment, Volume II*, sec. 4.6.3–4.6.6.

123. See, e.g., Francis Fukuyama, "Big Government Skeptic," *The New York Times* (May 8, 2011); Arthur Schlesinger, Jr., "Should Conservatives Embrace Big Government? *The New York Times* (February 3, 1983); Ben Tarnoff, "How Privatization Could Spell the End of Democracy," *The Guardian* (June 21, 2017).

124. See generally Reiff, "Two Theories of Economic Liberalism."

125. Oddly enough, it is those who advocate shrinking the size of government in the name of liberty that also tend to advance the most extreme form of the "unitary executive" position – the idea that every element of the executive branch is subject to the absolute control of the president, and thus subsidiary administrative or other executive officials cannot even give their opinions to Congress when asked to do as part of a congressional investigation, but must simply channel the President's views. See generally John Harrison, "The Unitary Executive and the Scope of Executive Power," *The Yale Law Journal Forum* 125 (January 24, 2017): 374–380; Jeffry Rosen, "The Roberts Court and Executive Power," *Pepperdine Law Review* 35 (2008): 503–508. While the two positions are not directly contradictory, a strongly unitary executive is a much greater threat to liberty than a weakly unitary one, for it could effectively stymie Congress's oversight responsibilities, which is supposed to be one of the primary checks on executive power.

126. See Celine McNicholas, Zane Mokhiber, and Marni von Wilpert, "*Janus* and Fair Share Fees," Economic Policy Institute (February 21, 2018) ("challenging fair share fees in the courts appears to be part of a broader billionaire-financed agenda to weaken unions and shift power away from ordinary workers").

127. For more on this point, however, see Reiff, *On Unemployment, Volume I*, pp. 116–122.
128. See Ronald Dworkin, *Justice for Hedgehogs* (Cambridge: Harvard University Press, 2011), p. 423.
129. See, e.g., Yarrow, "Privatization in Theory and Practice," p. 355; Peter Temin, *The Vanishing Middle Class: Prejudice and Power in a Dual Economy* (Cambridge: MIT Press, 2017), p. 19 ("limited government was first expressed in the deregulation of finance and airlines in the 1970s, and 'individual freedom' was code for the destruction of unions"). See also Temin, pp. 21, 80–81.
130. See Yarrow.
131. See L. J. Macfarlane, *The Right to Strike* (Harmondsworth, Middlesex, UK: Penguin, 1981), pp. 136–140.
132. See Jeffrey H. Keefe, "Laws Enabling Public Sector Collective Bargaining Have Not Led to Excessive Public Sector Pay," *EPI Briefing Paper* (Economic Policy Institute, October 16, 2015).
133. But see Kim Willsher, "French Prison Blockades Spread as Minister Meets Union Leaders," *The Guardian* (January 22, 2018), showing that even supposedly essential corrections officers are not as essential as we might initially believe, for strikes by such officers do not necessarily result in a disruption of essential services.
134. See generally Michael H. LeRoy and John H. Johnson IV, "Death by Lethal Injunction: National Emergency Strikes Under the Taft–Hartley Act and the Moribund Right to Strike," *Arizona Law Review* (2001): 63-134; Jared S. Gross, "Yet Another Reappraisal of the Taft–Hartley Act Emergency Injunctions," *University of Pennsylvania Journal of Labor and Employment Law* 7 (2005): 305–339.
135. See, e.g., Teresa Watanabe, "More Then 50,000 UC Workers Set to Strike This Week but Campuses Will Remain Open," *Los Angeles Times* (May 6, 2018).
136. For a detailed history of the events that led up to the strike and Reagan's reaction to it, see Joseph A. McCartin, *Collision Course: Ronald Reagan, the Air Traffic Controllers, and the Strike* (Oxford: Oxford University Press, 2011).
137. Ibid.
138. See Joseph A. McCartin, "The Strike That Busted Unions," *The New York Times* (August 2, 2011).
139. See Matt Stevens, "Aviation Professionals Warn of Dire Risk Amid Shutdown," *The New York Times* (January 23, 2019); Kim Kelly, "Sara Nelson's Art of War," *The New Republic* (May 13, 2019).
140. See Anonymous, "Forced to Work, and Unable to Strike: US Federal Workers Need Solidarity," *The Guardian* (January 24, 2019); Lauren Gambino, "Senate to Vote on Pair of Bills that Could End Government Shutdown," *The Guardian* (January 22, 2019) (discussing concerns of FBI agents).
141. See Michelle Goldberg, "The Teachers Revolt in West Virginia," *The New York Times* (March 5, 2018); Dana Goldstein, "West Virginia Teachers Walk Out (Again) and Score a Win in Hours," *The New York Times* (February 19, 2019).
142. See McCartin, *Collision Course*, at 254–255. The same is true in the private sector. See Associated Press, "Law Vegas Casino Workers Vote for First Mass Strike in More Than 30 Years," *The Guardian* (May 23, 2018).

143. Compare, for example, Amie Tsang, "Ryanair Hit with Its First Pilot Strike, in Germany," *The New York Times* (December 22, 2017) ("it was a win-win situation; we hit the company without hitting the passengers," said a union spokesman) with Adam Rossiter, "Stranded French Commuters Could Test Macron's Reform Agenda," *The New York Times* (April 4, 2018) (strike on France's heavily used rail network "has the potential to either make the president buckle by crippling France's economy or infuriate its citizens and turn them against the unions").
144. See Ed Pilkington, "Revealed: Secret Rightwing Strategy to Discredit Teacher Strikes," *The Guardian* (April 12, 2018).
145. State Policy Network, "Messaging Guide: How to Talk about Teacher Strikes," reprinted in Pilkington, "Revealed: Secret Rightwing Strategy to Discredit Teacher Strikes."
146. Ibid.
147. See Alex Horton, "Kentucky Governor Apologizes for Comments Suggesting Kids Were Sexually Assaulted While Teachers Protested," *The Washington Post* (April 15, 2015).
148. See Sally Weale, "University Strikes Could Hit Exams and Graduation Ceremonies," *The Guardian* (February 19, 2018).
149. I should note here that the point I am making in the text should not be construed as a defense of the "zero-tolerance" policy of the Trump administration that entailed separating parents who had illegally crossed the southern border from their children for extended periods of time. First, the punishment here is way out of proportion with the alleged offense, which is a misdemeanor that is generally treated as justifying only a day or two in jail. Second, the policy was implemented in such a cruel and careless way that it made eventual reunification of these children with their parents difficult if not impossible without the assistance of lawyers and other kinds of trained advocates to which the parents did not have easy access. Third, the policy was actually enacted as a deterrent to further illegal crossings, not as a deserved punishment, and therefore is unjustified because it uses both the children and their parents as mere means, and not as ends in themselves, and therefore violates Kant's famous categorical imperative. And there are many other grounds for objection too. See generally Jonathan Blitzer, "How the Trump Administration Got Comfortable Separating Immigrant Kids from Their Parents," *The New Yorker* (May 30, 2018); Julie Hirschfeld Davis and Michael D. Shear, "How Trump Came to Enforce a Practice of Separating Migrant Families," *The New York Times* (June 16, 2018); Salvador Rizzo, "The Facts about Trump's Policy of Separating Families at the Border," *The Washington Post* (June 19, 2018). The point I am making in the text is simply that there are almost always collateral effects on innocents when anyone is punished, and that this mere fact alone is not enough to render the punishment wrong. Whether it is or not depends on many other factors.
150. See Reiff, *Punishment, Compensation, and Law*, pp. 21–22, 79–80.
151. See, e.g., Meghan Holohan, "Striking Teachers Go Out of Their Way to Make Sure Students Have Food," *Today* (March 5, 2018).
152. See generally Mark R. Reiff, "No Such Thing as Accident: Rethinking the Relation between Causal and Moral Responsibility," *Canadian Journal of Law and Jurisprudence* 28 (2015): 371–397.

153. See Roy J. Adams, "Collective Bargaining as a Minimum Employment Standard," *Economic and Labor Relations Review* 22 (2011): 153–164, 158.
154. "States with collective bargaining laws for all public sector workers had a public sector union density of 33%. States with collective bargaining laws for some groups of public sector workers but not others had a public sector union density of 21%. States that outlawed public sector collective bargaining had a public sector union density of 12.5%." Freeman and Han, "The War against Public Sector Collective Bargaining in the US," p. 388. See also Steven Greenhouse, "Wisconsin's Legacy for Unions," *The New York Times* (February 22, 2014) (following enactment of Wisconsin's ban on collective bargaining, membership in the Wisconsin State Employees Unions has dropped 60 percent and its annual budget has plunged from $6 million to $2 million).
155. See Mike Elk, "North Carolina Activists Pick Next Battle after $15 Minimum Wage Win," *The Guardian* (May 31, 2018).
156. See Editorial, "West Virginia Teachers Give a Lesson in Union Power," *The New York Times* (March 2, 2018); Goldberg, "The Teachers Revolt in West Virginia"; Jess Bidgood, "West Virginia Raises Teachers' Pay to End Statewide Strike," *The New York Times* (March 6, 2018); Jess Bidgood and Campbell Robertson, "West Virginia Walkouts a Lesson in the Power of a Crowd-Sourced Strike," *The New York Times* (March 8, 2018).
157. See Dana Goldstein, "Their Pay Has Stood Still: Now Oklahoma Teachers Could be the Next to Walk," *The New York Times* (March 20, 2018); Elizabeth A. Harris, "Jersey City Teachers Go on Strike Over Health Insurance," *The New York Times* (March 16, 2018); Mike Elk, "Wave of Teachers' Wildcat Strikes Spreads to Oklahoma and Kentucky," *The Guardian* (April 2, 2018); Dana Goldstein, "Teachers in Oklahoma and Kentucky Walk Out: 'It Really Is a Wildfire,'" *The New York Times* (April 2, 2018); Mike Elk, "'Arab Spring for Teachers': Educators in Oklahoma Join Wave of Strikes," *The Guardian* (April 4, 2018); Andrea DenHoed, "Striking Oklahoma Teachers Win Historic School-Funding Increase and Keep on Marching," *The New Yorker* (April 4, 2018); Dana Goldstein and Alexander Burns, "Teacher Walkouts Threaten Republican Grip on Conservative States," *The New York Times* (April 12, 2018); Dana Goldstein and Elizabeth Dias, "Oklahoma Teachers End Walkout after Winning Raises and Additional Funding," *The New York Times* (April 12, 2018).Leah Varjacques, Taige Jensen, and Japhet Weeks, "We Are Republican Teachers Striking in Arizona: It's Time to Raise Taxes." *The New York Times* (April 26, 2018); Simon Romero, Jack Healy, and Julie Turkewitz, "Teachers in Arizona and Colorado Walk Out over Education Funding," *The New York Times* (April 26, 2018); Dana Goldstein, "Arizona Teachers End Walkout as Governor Signs Bill Approving Raises," *The New York Times* (May 3, 2018); Mike Elk, "North Carolina Teachers Join Wave of Strikes with One-Day Walkout," *The Guardian* (May 16, 2018) ("it's a bold move for North Carolina as teachers in the state lack collective bargaining rights"). See, however, Dana Goldstein, "Why the Teacher Walkout Movement Won't Reach Every State," *The New York Times* (May 16, 2018) (statewide walkouts are only likely to be effective where state rather than locality provides majority of funding); Caleb Gayle, "Oklahoma Teachers' Salary Raise in Limbo Following Historic Win," *The Guardian* (June 16, 2018).

158. See Noam Scheiber, "Can Weak Unions Get Teachers More Money?" *The New York Times* (May 5, 2018) (noting how unions that remained intact after Wisconsin limited their collective bargaining rights became much more aggressive).
159. Keefe, "Laws Enabling Public Sector Collective Bargaining Have Not Led to Excessive Public Sector Pay."
160. See generally, Melvyn Dubofsky and Joseph A. McCartin, *Labor in America: A History* (Malden, MA: Wiley Blackwell, 9th ed., 2017), pp. 404–406.
161. Including Wisconsin, six states now explicitly prohibit collective bargaining with public employee unions. And the list will no doubt be growing. See David Morris, "When Unions Are Strong, Americans Enjoy the Fruits of Their Labor," Institute for Local Self-Reliance (March 31, 2011) (https://ilsr.org/when-unions-are-strong-americans-enjoy-the-fruits-of-their-labor/) (listing five states that prohibited most collective bargaining at the time, to which I have added Wisconsin, which was not included in that count, and noting that eighteen additional states have proposed legislation that would remove some or all collective bargaining powers from public employee unions). For a more detailed discussion of how certain states currently limit collective bargaining by public employees, see Martin Malin, "Does Public Employee Collective Bargaining Distort Democracy? A Perspective from the United States," *Comparative Labor Law & Policy Journal* 34 (2013): 277–306.
162. Ed Treleven, "In 5–2 Ruling, Supreme Court Issues Final Word on Act 10," *Wisconsin State Journal* (July 31, 2014).
163. Wisconsin Supreme Court, No. 2012AP2067, 2014 WI 99 (July 31, 2014).
164. As it is, according to the Supreme Court of Canada, in the Canadian Charter of Rights and Freedoms. See *Health Services and Support Facilities Subsector Bargaining Assn. v. British Columbia*, [2007] 2 S.C.R. 391, 2007 SCC 27.
165. See Cantin, "The Politics of Austerity and the Conservative Offensive against US Public Sector Unions, 2008–2012," 612–632.
166. See, e.g., Steven Greenhut, "Salary Info Shows Fruits of Union Muscle," *The San Diego Union-Tribune* (December 26, 2014).
167. See Celine McNicholas and Heidi Shierholz, "Supreme Court Decision in *Janus* Threatens the Quality of Public-Sector Jobs and Public Services," Economic Policy Institute (June 13, 2018).
168. See, e.g., Mike Elk, "America's Teachers on Strike: 'We Are Done Being the Frog that Is Being Boiled,'" *The Guardian* (May 5, 2018).
169. See Jeffrey Keefe, "State and Local Public Employees: Are They Overcompensated?" *ABA Journal of Labor and Employment Law* 27 (2012): 239–255; Keefe, "Law Enabling Public Sector Collective Bargaining Have Not Led to Excessive Public Sector Pay"; David Lewin, Jeffrey Keefe, and Thomas A. Kochan, "The New Great Debate about Unionism and Collective Bargaining in U.S. State and Local Governments," *ILR Review* (2012): 749–778, 753–760; Keith Bender and John Heywood, "Trends in the Relative Compensation of State and Local Employees," in *Public Jobs and Political Agendas: The Public Sector in an Era of Economic Stress*, ed. Daniel Mitchell (Champaign, IL: Labor and Employment Relations Association, 2012), pp. 133–166, 144–146 (showing state workers are paid 6.6 percent less than their otherwise equal private sector counterparts, and local government workers are paid 3.3 percent less than their private sector counterparts).

170. See Cohen and Gebeloff, "Public Servants Are Losing Their Foothold in the Middle Class"; Paul Krugman, "We Don't Need No Education," *The New York Times* (April 23, 2018); E. Timothy Kim, "Can Arizona's Teachers Still Consider Themselves Middle Class?" *The New Yorker* (May 2, 2018).
171. See Mike Elk, "US Government Failing Millions by Paying Below $15 an Hour, Study Finds," *The Guardian* (August 10, 2018); George Faraday, "Trump's Government is America's Top Low Wage Job Creator," *Good Jobs Nation* (August 2018) (http://goodjobsnation.org/content/uploads/2018/08/Broken-Promises1.pdf).
172. See, e.g., Rick Hurd, "Oakland Workers Strike, Bringing City Services to a Halt, with No End in Sight," *East Bay Times* (December 5, 2017); Zoe Williams, "Overpaid Public Sector? Philip Hammond's Divisive Talk Is No Longer Working," *The Guardian* (July 16, 2017) (noting that public sector nurses in the United Kingdom have to resort to food banks to make ends meet).
173. See Lichtenstein, "Bashing Public Employees and Their Unions," pp. 204–205.
174. See, e.g., Campbell Brown, "Giving Up Levelling Down." *Economics and Philosophy* 19 (2003): 111–134, 112; Larry Temkin. "Equality, Priority, and the Levelling Down Objection," in *The Ideal of Equality,* eds. Matthew Clayton and Andrew Williams (New York: Palgrave, 2000), pp. 126–161, 130–132; Elizabeth Anderson, "What Is the Point of Equality?" *Ethics* 109 (1999): 287–337, 291.
175. See Eric Yoder, "Federal Employees Lag Behind Private Sector Workers in Salaries by 32 Percent on Average, Report Says," *The Washington Post* (April 11, 2018); Moriah Balingit, "'It Just Hurts My Heart': Low Pay, Big Classes Are the Plight of Oklahoma Teachers," *The Washington Post* (March 30, 2018); Moriah Balingit, "'They Are So Underpaid': School Support Staff Scrape by on Meager Earnings," *The Washington Post* (April 25, 2018).
176. See Bender and Heywood, "Trends in the Relative Compensation of State and Local Employees," pp. 161–162.
177. See, e.g., Jessica Glenza, "'Double Whammy': Teachers Strike as Healthcare Costs Cut into Earnings," *The Guardian* (April 2, 2018).
178. See Sylvia A. Allegretto and Lawrence Mishel, "The Teacher Pay Gap Is Wider Than Ever," Economic Policy Institute Report (August 9, 2016) (www.epi.org/files/pdf/110964.pdf); Sylvia A. Allegretto and Lawrence Mishel, "The Teacher Pay Penalty Has Hit a New High," Economic Policy Institute (September 5, 2018) (www.epi.org/files/pdf/153196.pdf) (noting that public sector teachers made a staggering 18.7 percent less in 2017 than comparably educated and experienced workers).
179. See Dana Goldstein, "Teacher Pay Is So Low in Some U.S. School Districts That They're Recruiting Overseas," *The New York Times* (May 2, 2018).
180. See Freeman and Han, "The War against Public Sector Collective Bargaining in the US," pp. 393–394.
181. For more on the multiplier effect in general, see Reiff, *On Unemployment, Volume I,* pp. 109–133, 182 n. 72.
182. Of course, the literature on the Keynesian position is massive. For an introduction to and summary of its major claims, however, see chapter 4 in Reiff, *On Unemployment, Volumes I and II.*
183. See Reiff, *On Unemployment, Volume II,* p. 13.

184. See my *Exploitation and Economic Justice in the Liberal Capitalist State* for an extensive discussion of and justification for this metric and how it applies to labor.
185. See Reiff, *Exploitation and Economic Justice in the Liberal Capitalist State.*
186. See, e.g., Scheiber and Vogel, "Behind a Key Anti-Labor Case, a Web of Conservative Donors"; DiSalvo, "Janus Decision Reins in Unions' Political Power."
187. See Freeman and Han, "The War against Public Sector Collective Bargaining in the US," p. 389; Ed Pilkington, "How Rightwing Groups Wield Secret 'Toolkit' to Plot against US Unions," *The Guardian* (May 15, 2018) (describing the antiunion marketing drive currently under way in all 50 states to "defund and defang" public sector unions as a means of attacking on reversing the policies initiated and supported by "the American left").
188. Note, however, that some leaders of unions of private sector employees have even come out in favor of President Trump. See, e.g., Naomi Klein, "Labor Leaders' Cheap Deal with Trump," *The New York Times* (February 7, 2017).
189. See generally, Mark R. Reiff, "The Attack on Liberalism," in *Law and Philosophy,* eds. Michael Freeman and Ross Harrison (Oxford: Oxford University Press, 2007), pp. 173–210, 178–179.
190. For an extended discussion of this argument from Rawls, see Kymlicka, "Liberal Individualism and Liberal Neutrality," 883–905. For a discussion of this distinction by Rawls himself, see John Rawls, "The Priority of Right and Ideas of the Good," in *Collected Papers* (Cambridge: Harvard University Press, 1999), pp. 449–472, 458–460.
191. See generally Kenneth Lapidus (ed.), *Marx and Engels on the Trade Unions* (New York: International Publishers, 1987).
192. See, e.g., Peter Gourevitch, et al. (eds.), *Unions and Economic Crisis: Britain, West Germany, and Sweden* (London: George Allen & Unwin, 1984), pp. 116–119 (discussing the change in the approach of the West German union movement by the Dusseldorf Program of 1963).
193. See, e.g., Edward R. Chamberlain, "Labour Union Power and the Public Interest," in *The Public Stake in Union Power,* ed. Philip D. Bradley (Charlottesville, VA: University of Virginia Press, 1959), pp. 3–20, 6 (discussing the rejection of radical unionism in the United States); D. Quinn Mills, "Flawed Victory in Labor Law Reform," *Harvard Business Review* 57 (1979): 92–102, 101; Hiba Hafiz, "The Red-Scare Relic that Holds Back Smart Labor Policy," *The New York Times* (May 1, 2018).
194. See, e.g., Mike Elk, "Alabama Unions See Doug Jones's Win as a Victory for Organized Labor," *The Guardian* (December 16, 2017); Adam Gabbatt, "Seven Months Long, 1,800 out...epic strike mirrors US Unions' Fight to Survive," *The Guardian* (November 3, 2017) (noting how decline in unionization has weakened the Democratic Party and other associated progressive organizations).
195. See Lichtenstein, "Bashing Public Employee and Their Unions," p. 201; James R. Dickerson, "Teamsters, GOP Forged Increasingly Close Links," *The Washington Post* (July 25, 1985); Steven Greenhouse, "The Unions That Like

Trump," *The New York Times* (April 8, 2017); Richard Pérez-Peña and Sheryl Gay Stolberg, "Police Unions Hail Trump's Easing of Scrutiny: Local Officials Worry." *The New York Times* (April 4, 2017).

196. See, e.g., Shane Goldmacher, "Police Union Is Sending Officers to Iowa to Protest de Blasio,'" *The New York Times* (December 18, 2017); Jeffrey C. Mays, "De Blasio, a Pro-Labor Mayor, Is Sued Over Bargaining Tactics," *The New York Times* (January 31, 2018); Wes Venteicher, "California Public Employees' Pension Perks Can Be Taken Away, Court Rules," *Sacramento Bee* (March 4, 2019).

197. David Sirota, "How California Public Employees Fund Anti-Rent Control Fight Unwittingly," *The Guardian* (October 23, 2018).

198. See also Joshua Cohen and Joel Rogers, "Secondary Associations and Democratic Governance," in *Associations and Democracy,* ed. Erik Olin Wright (London: Verso, 1995), pp. 7–98, 79–82 (arguing that greater unionization will increase satisfaction of democratic norms, not undermine them).

199. See, e.g., Daniel DiSalvo, *Government against Itself: Public Union Power and Its Consequences* (Oxford: Oxford University Press, 2015), pp. 21–22, 28–30, 57–92; Malin, "Does Public Employee Collective Bargaining Distort Democracy?"

200. See Lichtenstein, "Bashing Public Employees and Their Unions," p. 199.

201. See, e.g., Sylvester Petro, *The Labor Policy of a Free Society* (Auburn, AL: The Ludwig von Mises Institute, 2007) (originally published 1957).

202. Sylvester Petro, "Sovereignty and Compulsory Public Sector Bargaining," *Wake Forest Law Review* 10 (1974–1975): 25–166, 25, 28.

203. See Petro, "Sovereignty and Compulsory Public Sector Bargaining," pp. 48, 64–112.

204. Ibid. at 66.

205. Ibid. at 79.

206. Ibid. at 79–80. For the expression of a similar view of unions in the United Kingdom, see David M. Walker, "Trade Unions," in *The Oxford Companion to Law* (Oxford: Oxford University Press, 1980), pp. 1128–30, 1229: "The modern situation is that trade unions and their members have a legal position relative to the State very like that of the mediaeval Church and its clergy, having legal privileges and immunities from contractual and tortious liability, easily the most privileged in the community ... they represent the gravest threat yet known to democracy, liberty, economic progress and prosperity yet known and constantly call for law to be kept out of industrial relations to enable anarchy to be promoted." Note that this book was a basic reference work on law in the United Kingdom and was not updated and replaced until 2008.

207. See B. R. Meyers, "Oswald Spengler: Pessimism's Prophet," *The American Conservative* (December 23, 2016).

208. For a general discussion of this, see Reiff, "The Attack on Liberalism."

209. For further discussion and critique of Petro's views, see Joseph A. McCartin and Jean-Christian Vinel, "'Compulsory Unionism': Sylvester Petro and the Career of an Anti-Union Idea, 1957–1987," in *The Right and Labor in America*, eds. Nelson Lichtenstein and Elizabeth Tandy Shermer (Philadelphia: University of Pennsylvania Press, 2012), pp. 226–251.

210. See, e.g., Robert S. Summers, *Collective Bargaining and Public Benefit Conferral: A Jurisprudential Critique* (Ithaca, NY: Institute of Public Employment, Cornell University Press, 1976); Robert S. Summers, "Public Sector Collective Bargaining Substantially Diminishes Democracy," *Government Union Review* 1 (1980): 5–22.
211. See, e.g., Wellington and Winter, *The Unions and the Cities*, esp. pp. 29–30; Summers, "Public Sector Collective Bargaining Substantially Diminishes Democracy," pp. 5–22; *Commonwealth v. Country board of Arlington County*, 232 S.E.2d 30, 39 (Va. 1977).
212. See, e.g., Steven Johnson, "Why Blue States Are the Real 'Tea Party'," *The New York Times* (December 3, 2017); Emily Badger "As American as Apple Pie? The Rural Vote's Disproportionate Slice of Power," *The New York Times* (November 20, 2016); Philip Bump, "In about 20 Years, Half the Population Will Live in Eight States," *The Washington Post* (July 12, 2018).
213. See Anthony J. McGann, Charles Anthony Smith, Michael Latner, and Alex Keena, *Gerrymandering in America* (Cambridge: Cambridge University Press, 2016); Dana Millbank, "Republican Gerrymandering Makes the Difference in the House," *The Washington Post* (January 4, 2013); Sam Wang, "Let Math Save Our Democracy," *The New York Times* (December 5, 2015); Lee Drutman, "The Divided States of America," *The New York Times* (September 22, 2016); Charles Fried, "It's Unfair and Unjust. So Why Has Gerrymandering Lasted This Long? *The Boston Globe* (July 10, 2017); David Denby, "Eric Holder's Battle against Gerrymandering," *The New Yorker* (November 14, 2017); Linda Greenhouse, "Two Ways of Looking at Gerrymandering," *The New York Times* (January 4, 2018); Alan Blinder and Michael Wines, "North Carolina Is Ordered to Redraw Its Congressional Map," *The New York Times* (January 9, 2018); Quoctrung Bui and Nate Cohn, "Adventures in Extreme Gerrymandering," *The New York Times* (January 17, 2018); Jeffrey Tobin, "The Courts Take Aim at Partisan Gerrymandering," *The New Yorker* (January 23, 2018); Trip Gabriel, "In a Comically Drawn Pennsylvania District, the Voters Are Not Amused," *The New York Times* (January 26, 2018); Alexander Burns, "Eric Holder's Group Targets All-G.O.P. States to Attack Gerrymandering," *The New York Times* (February 6, 2018); Michael Tomasky, "Ratfucked Again," *The New York Review of Books* (June 7, 2018); Michael Wines, "Kennedy's Retirement Could Threaten Efforts to End Partisan Gerrymandering," *The New York Times* (June 30, 2018); Michael Wines, "Drive against Gerrymandering Finds New Life in Ballot Initiatives," *The New York Times* (July 23, 2018).
214. Charles R. Beitz, "How Is Partisan Gerrymandering Unfair?" *Philosophy and Public Affairs* 46 (2019): 323–358, 323.
215. Ibid. See also Christopher Ingraham, "One State Fixed Its Gerrymandered Districts, the Other Didn't: Here's How the Election Played Out in Both." *The Washington Post* (November 9, 2018); Ian Samuel, "Rigging the Vote: How the American Right Is on the Way to Permanent Minority Rule," *The Guardian* (November 4, 2018).
216. See *Rucho v. Common Cause*, US Supreme Court, No. 18-422 (June 27, 2019).
217. See, e.g., Zoltan Hajnal, Nazita Lajevardi, and Lindsay Nielson, "Do Voter Identification Laws Suppress Minority Voting? Yes. We Did the Research," *Washington Post* (February 15, 2017); Kathleen Ronayne and Christina A. Cassidy,

"Republican State Lawmakers Push for Restrictions on Voting," *The Washington Post* (February 9, 2017). See also Zoltan Hajnal, Nazita Lajevardi, and Lindsay Nielson, "Voter Identification Laws and the Suppression of Minority Votes," *The Journal of Politics* 79:2 (2017): 363–379; Associated Press, "Supreme Court Ohio Voter Ruling Is 'Green Light' to Purge Rolls, Say Critics," *The Guardian* (June 11, 2018); Maggie Astor, "Seven Ways Alabama Has Made It Harder to Vote," *The New York Times* (June 23, 2018); Ed Pilkington, "Thousands at Risk from Rightwing Push to Purge Eligible Voters from US Rolls," *The Guardian* (September 23, 2018); Michelle Goldberg, "Democracy in Danger in Georgia," *The New York Times* (October 12, 2018); Julian Brave NoiseCat, "Republicans Wanted to Suppress the Native American Vote. It's Working," *The Guardian* (October 26, 2018); Vivian Wang, "Why Deep Blue New York Is 'Voter Suppression Land,'" *The New York Times* (December 19, 2018) (because of refusal by Republican-controlled state senate to back electoral reforms).

218. Michael Luo and Stephanie Strom, "Donor Names Remain Secret as Rules Shift," *The New York Times* (September 20, 2010); Noam Scheiber, "Betsy DeVos, Trump's Education Pick, Plays Hardball with Her Wealth," *The New York Times* (January 9, 2017); Philip Elliott, "The Koch Brothers Plan to Spend a Record-Setting $400 Million," *Time* (January 28, 2018).

219. See Eduardo Porter, "How the Big Money Finds a Way In," *The New York Times* (September 17, 2011).

220. See Marcos Breton, "Upset with Trump? Well, Maybe You Should Have Voted," *Sacramento Bee* (February 8, 2017).

221. See, e.g., Carol Anderson, "The Real Theft of American Democracy," *The New York Times* (March 14, 2019) ("and Republicans are the thieves").

222. Is hypocrisy also a moral wrong? If it is wrong to X, then it is wrong to say it is not and wrong to do it. If I say it is wrong and I nevertheless do it, I am guilty of weakness of will and I have also provided evidence that I do not believe X *is* wrong, or I do not believe I should not do wrong things, and this subjects me to moral criticism beyond that due for simply doing something wrong and having a mere weakness of will. If I do it and then say it is wrong, I have come to my senses, so there no real basis for moral criticism here beyond that due for doing something wrong, which is perhaps lessened by my subsequent admission. If it is not wrong to do X and I say it is wrong and then do it, I have provided evidence that I do not believe it is wrong and that I do not believe what I say. If it is not wrong to X and I do it and then say it is wrong, this is evidence that I do not believe what I say or do not do what I believe, and I am subject to moral criticism for this even though it is not wrong to X. For a slightly different view about the wrongness of hypocrisy, see Gerald Laing, "What's Wrong with Hypocrisy?" (unpublished).

223. See generally Max Fisher and Amanda Taub, "When More Democracy Isn't More Democratic," *The New York Times* (January 21, 2019).

224. See C. B. McPherson, *The Life and Times of Liberal Democracy* (Oxford: Oxford University Press, 1977), pp. 94–98.

225. All of the quoted phrases here are Rawlsian terms. For more on the concept of reflective equilibrium, see John Rawls, *Justice as Fairness* (Cambridge: Harvard University Press, 2001), pp. 42–43, sec. 10 and sec. 37; John Rawls,

A Theory of Justice (Cambridge: Harvard University Press, 1971, rev. ed. 1999), sec. 4, pp. 18–19. For more on the strains of commitment, see Rawls, *Justice as Fairness*, sec. 29.3 and sec. 37; Rawls, *A Theory of Justice*, sec. 25, pp. 125–26, and sec. 29, at p. 153. And for more on the idea of an overlapping consensus, see Rawls, *Justice as Fairness*, sec. 11; Rawls, *A Theory of Justice*, sec. 59, p. 340.

226. See, e.g., Editorial, "The Sad State of California's Direct Democracy," *Sacramento Bee* (October 15, 2016); George Monbiot, "Lies, Fearmongering and Fables: That's Our Democracy," *The Guardian* (October 4, 2016) (and direct democracy is even worse!); Leader, "Lessons from California: The Perils of Extreme Democracy," *The Economist* (April 20, 2011); Joe Matthews, "Amending California's Direct Democracy," *Los Angeles Times* (October 19, 2009); John Diaz, "A Long Way from the Grassroots," *San Francisco Chronicle* (October 12, 2008).

227. See DiSalvo, "The Distortion of Direct Democracy," in *Government against Itself*, pp. 92–110.

228. See, e.g., Giovanni Gentile, *Origins and Doctrine of Fascism*, ed. A. James Gregor (New Brunswick, NJ: Transaction Publishers, 2002), pp. xii, 28, 30. See also A. James Gregor, *The Ideology of Fascism* (New York: Macmillan, 1969), pp. 211–214.

229. See Howard Blume and Anna M. Phillips, "Charter Backers Win Their First L.A. School Board Majority," *Los Angeles Times* (May 16, 2017); Valerie Strauss, "How Messed Up Is California's Charter School Sector? You Won't Believe How Much." *The Washington Post* (September 9, 2016); Valerie Strauss, "In California's Charter World, a Tangled Web of For-Profit Companies and Nonprofit Schools," *The Washington Post* (October 14, 2016); Valerie Strauss, "Charter Schools in California Are Operating Where They Aren't Needed, Study Says," *The Washington Post* (April 14, 2017); Gordon Lafer, "Spending Blind: The Failure of Policy Planning in California Charter School Funding," *In the Public Interest* (April 2017) (www.inthepublicinterest.org/wp-content/uploads/FINAL_ITPI_SpendingBlind_April2017.pdf).

230. See, e.g., DiSalvo, at p. 140: "The Argument Public Sector Unions Will Act As a Counterweight to 'Big Business' in Some Generalized Sense Does Not Withstand Scrutiny."

231. See, e.g., Paul Schwartzman and Fenit Nirappil, "D.C. Voters Approve Initiative to Raise Minimum Wage for Tipped Workers to $15," *The Washington Post* (June 19, 2018) (the initiative was backed by a New York-based advocacy group).

232. Martin Gilens, *"Affluence and Influence: Economic Inequality and Political Influence in America"* (Princeton: Princeton University Press, 2012), p. 81.

233. Gilens, *Affluence and Influence*, p. 82. Note that these statistics are based on a data set covering the period 1981 to 2002. See Gilens, p. 83.

234. Gilens, *Affluence and Influence*, p. 1. See also Martin Gilens and Benjamin I. Page, "Testing Theories of American Politics: Elites, Interest Groups, and Average Citizens," *Perspectives on Politics* 12 (2014): 564–581, prompting the BBC to declare that "study finds US is an oligarchy, not a democracy." BBC, "Study: US Is an Oligarchy, Not a Democracy," *BBC News* (April 17, 2014).

235. See, e.g., Jim Miller, "Union Power on Display in California's Just Completed Legislative Session," *Sacramento Bee* (September 1, 2017); Martin O'Neill and Stuart White, "Trade Unions and Political Equality," in *Philosophical Foundations of Labour Law*, eds. Hugh Collins, Gillian Lester, and Virginia Mantouvalou (Oxford: Oxford University Press, 2018), pp. 252–270.

236. See Gordon Lafer, *The One Percent Solution: How Corporations Are Remaking America One State at a Time* (Ithaca, NY: Cornell University Press, 2017), pp. 157–158; Institute for Public Policy Research, "Prosperity and Justice: A Plan for the New Economy" (London: Polity, 2018).
237. See DiSalvo, pp. 125–140.
238. This is the argument, for example, of Charles Murray, the right-libertarian political scientist and author of the controversial book *The Bell Curve*. See Natalie Goodnow, "'By the People': A Q&A with Charles Murray," *American Enterprise Institute* (May 11, 2015), in which Murray claims: "The public employees' unions are so powerful that the mayor and city council owe their elections to the unions. The key to better government functioning at every level is prohibition of unions of public employees."
239. For a current list of such firms, see National Center for Employee Ownership, "The Employee Ownership 100: America's Largest Majority Employee-Owned Companies" (www.nceo.org/articles/employee-ownership-100).
240. See Corey Rosen, "Observations on Employee Ownership: United Airlines, ESOPs, and Employee Ownership" (National Center for Employee Ownership, November 2002) (www.nceo.org/observations-employee-ownership/c/united-airlines-esops-employee-ownership/printable).
241. See, e.g., Vivian Wang, "Focus of Corruption Trial Returns to Actions of Jail Officers' Union Chief," *The New York Times* (November 7, 2018).
242. See, e.g., Jim Dwyer and Emma G. Fitzsimmons, "$462,646 in Pay for One Worker: M.T.A. Overtime Scrutinized by Prosecutors," *The New York Times* (May 17, 2019) (noting that the union had been criticizing the M.T.A.'s incestuous and allegedly corrupt relationships with outside consultants, which are often filled with former transit management officials).
243. See, e.g., Alex Kotch, "After Scoring Huge Tax Cuts, Charles Koch Floods Ryan with Cash," *International Business Times* (January 19, 2018).
244. For an expression of similar concerns regarding government-to-government trade agreements, see George Monbiot, "Donald Trump Was Right: The Rest of the G7 Were Wrong," *The Guardian* (June 13, 2018).
245. See, e.g., *Environmental Defense Fund v. Costle*, 636 F.2d 1229 (D.C. Cir. 1980); Robert V. Percival, "The Bounds of Consent: Consent Decrees, Settlement and Federal Environmental Policy Making," *University of Chicago Legal Forum* 1 (1987): 327–351.
246. See Sheryl Gay Stolberg and Eric Lichtblau, "Sweeping Federal Review Could Affect Consent Decrees Nationwide," *The New York Times* (April 3, 2017); Katie Benner, "Sessions, in Last-Minute Act, Sharpley Limits Use of Consent Decrees to Curb Police Abuses," *The New York Times* (November 8, 2018).
247. See Daniel Victor, "Judge Approves Consent Decree to Overhaul Baltimore Police Department," *The New York Times* (April 7, 2017) (quoting Trump Attorney General Jeff Sessions as complaining that the decree "was negotiated during a rushed process by the previous administration and signed only days before they left office"); Hiroko Tabuchi, "U.S. Reopens Harley Settlement, Cutting Funds for Pollution Reduction Plan," *The New York Times* (July 20, 2017).
248. See, e.g., Refund Transit Coalition, "Riding the Gravy Train: How Wall Street is Bankrupting Our Public Transit Agencies by Profiteering Off of Toxic Swap Deals" (June 2012); *In re City of Detroit*, — B.R. —, (2013 WL 6331931

(Bkrtcy. E.D. Mich., December 5, 2013), p. 8; Nancy Rivera Brooks, Thomas S. Mulligan, and Tim Reiterman, "Memo Shows Enron Role in Hiking Prices," *Los Angeles Times* (May 7, 2002) (noting that price manipulation by Enron led California to enter into costly long-term contracts with electricity sellers during the worst of California's energy crisis in early 2001).

249. On the stickiness of wages in general, see Reiff, *On Unemployment, Volume I*, pp. 74–80. The observation that wages are sticky comes originally from Keynes. See John Maynard Keynes, *The General Theory of Employment, Interest, and Money* (San Diego: Harvest/Harcourt edition, 1964 [1936]), ch. 17, pp. 232–238.

250. See, e.g., Julie Hirschfeld Davis, "Rumblings of a 'Deep State' Undermining Trump? It was Once a Foreign Concept," *The New York Times* (March 6, 2017); Evan Osnos, "Trump vs. the 'Deep State,'" *The New Yorker* (May 21, 2018).

251. See Jana Winter and Elias Groll, "Here's the Memo That Blew Up the NSC," *Foreign Policy* (August 10, 2017); David Smith, "How Trump's Paranoid White House Sees 'Deep State' Enemies on All Sides," *The Guardian* (August 13, 2017); Rich Higgins, "POTUS and Political Warfare" (May 2017) (https://assets.documentcloud.org/documents/3922874/Political-Warfare.pdf).

252. See Isaiah Berlin, "Joseph de Maistre and the Origins of Fascism," in *The Crooked Timber of Humanity* (Princeton: Princeton University Press, 1990), p. 119.

253. See, e.g., Ed Ring, "California's Public Sector Union 'Deep State,'" *California Policy Center* (February 28, 2017) (http://californiapolicycenter.org/californias-public sector-union-deep-state/); Editorial, "Can Trump Win His Battle with the Unionized, Bureaucratic 'Deep State'?" *Investor's Business Daily* (January 24, 2017). See also Ed Rogers, "The 'Deep State' Is Real: The 'Alt Right' Is Fake," *The Washington Post* (February 21, 2017).

254. See Coral Davenport and Eric Lipton, "Scott Pruitt Is Carrying Out His E.P.A. Agenda in Secret, Critics Say," *The New York Times* (August 11, 2017) (noting staff member union's objections to the secretive nature of the new EPA administrator's efforts to radically alter the role and policies of the EPA).

255. See Mihir Zaveri, "Asylum Officers' Union Says Trump Migration Policy 'Abandon's' American Tradition," *The New York Times* (June 26, 2019).

256. See Eugene Robinson, "God Bless the 'Deep State,'" *The Washington Post* (July 19, 2018).

257. See, e.g., Little Hoover Commission, "Public Pensions for Retirement Security" (February 2011)(https://lhc.ca.gov/sites/lhc.ca.gov/files/Reports/204/Report204.pdf), p. 53 (characterizing pension formulas for current and future workers in California as both "overly generous and unsustainable"); Mark Janus, "Why I Took My Case over Forced Union Dues to the Supreme Court," *The Washington Post* (July 1, 2018) (claiming that his "union's demands for higher salaries and benefits...were bankrupting the state").

258. See George Skelton, "Democrats Running for California Governor Need to Stop Talking about Trump and Start Talking about Public Pensions," *Los Angeles Times* (January 18, 2018); Rick Rojas and Mary Williams Walsh, "Hartford, with Its Finances in Disarray, Veers toward Bankruptcy," *The New York Times* (August 15, 2017); Mary Williams Walsh, "After Puerto Rico's Debt Crisis, Worries Shift to Virgin Islands," *The New York Times* (June 25, 2017); Judy Lin, "Cutting Jobs,

Street Repairs, Library Books to Keep up with Pension Costs," *Los Angeles Times* (February 6, 2017); Dan Walters, "Realty Penetrates California's Public Employee Pension System, but Not Far Enough," *Sacramento Bee* (January 2, 2017); Mary Williams Walsh, "Calpers Cuts Investment Targets, Increasing Strain on Municipalities," *The New York Times* (December 21, 2016); Mary Williams Walsh, "Dallas Stares Down a Texas-Size Threat of Bankruptcy," *The New York Times* (November 20, 2016) (without an immense bailout, city pension fund for police officers and firefighters may collapse); Mary Williams Walsh, "Study Finds Public Pension Promises Exceed Ability to Pay," *The New York Times* (March 17, 2016); Farooq Hanif, et al., "The Coming Pension Crisis: Recommendations for Keeping the Global Pensions System Afloat," *Citi GPS: Global Perspectives & Solutions* (March 2016) (https://ir.citi.com/A44lKhe6CVSitfkypsON6kDXypHYjJ%2BENxq8FLMoTBde6kse9Kt9KQ%3D%3D); Mary Williams Walsh, "$1.6 Million Bill Tests Tiny Town and 'Bulletproof' Public Pensions," *The New York Times* (October 9, 2016) (California Public Employees' Retirement System ("Calpers") claims that Loyalton, California has 30 days to turn over $1.6 million, more than its entire budget, to fund pensions of four retirees); Mary Williams Walsh, "A Sour Surprise for Public Pensions: Two Sets of Books," *The New York Times* (September 17, 2016) (Calpers claims that the pension obligations of Citrus Pest Control District No. 2, serving just six people in California, is underfunded by half a million dollars); Patrick McGeehan, "Pensions for Lifeguards? Officials Say Atlantic City Can't Afford Them Anymore," *The New York Times* (May 6, 2016); Noam Scheiber, "Pension Benefit Cuts Planned at T.V.A., Breaking a Federal Firewall," *The New York Times* (March 3, 2016); Susanne Craig, "New York City's Pension System in Danger of 'Operational Failure,' Report Says," *The New York Times* (January 26, 2016); Funston Advisory Services, "Setting a Course for the Future: Management and Operations Study and Best Practice Review for the New York City Office of the Comptroller's Asset Management Function," *Final Report* (December 15, 2015) (www.nytimes.com/interactive/2016/01/26/nyregion/new-york-city-pension-system-report.html); Mary Williams Walsh, "Major Changes under Rhode Island Pension Overhaul," *The New York Times* (September 23, 2015; David Zahniser, "L.A. Plans to Undo 2012 Pension Cuts in New Union Pay Deal," *Los Angeles Times* (September 5, 2015) (City Council votes to undo 2012 pension deal and revert back to older, more lucrative retirement benefits that have been in place for decades and are widely viewed as unsustainable); Mary Williams Walsh, "Bad Math and a Coming Public Pension Crisis," *The New York Times* (July 8, 2015); Alexi Koseff, "Rising Retirement Costs Help Drive UC Plan to Raise Tuition," *The Sacramento Bee* (November 16, 2014; Peter Jamison, "Paying for Public Retirees Has Never Cost L.A. Taxpayers More. And That's after Pension Reform," *Los Angeles Times* (November 18, 2016) (reporting retirement benefits now eat up 20 percent of L.A.'s operating revenue, and L.A is not unique – retirement benefits eat up at least 15 percent of the operating revenue of San Francisco, San Diego, San Jose, Sacramento, Oakland, and Bakersfield; San Jose was the largest at 28 percent); Robert Novy-Marx and Joshua Rauh, "The Crisis in Local Government Pensions in the United States," in *Growing Old: Paying for Retirement And Institutional Money Management after the Financial Crisis*, eds. Yasuyuki Fuchita, Richard J. Herring, and Robert E. Litan (Washington, DC: Brookings Institution Press, 2011), pp. 47–74; John O. McGinnis and Max Schanzenbach, "The Case against

Public Sector Unions," *Policy Review* (Hoover Institution, August 1, 2010) (www.hoover.org/research/case-against-public sector-unions); Robert J. Samuelson, "The Deeper Cause Behind the School Strikes: Teachers Are Competing against the Elderly," *The Washington Post* (April 8, 2018); Niraj Chokshi, "Kentucky Governor Compares State Workers to Drowning Victims: 'You Just Need to Knock Them Out,'" *The New York Times* (August 14, 2018); and so on.

259. See, e.g., Little Hoover Commission, "Public Pensions for Retirement Security," pp. iv, 6, 14, 33, 36, 39, 45–46, 50, 52.

260. See Bruce Bartlett, "Tax Cuts and 'Starving the Beast,'" *Forbes* (May 7, 2010); Ross Barkan, "Republicans' Lack of Alarm overt the Shutdown Reveals a Disturbing Truth," *The Guardian* (January 18, 2019). See also Paul H. Douglass, *First Lecture*, in Paul H. Douglas and J. Enoch Powell, *How Big Should Government Be?* (Washington, DC: American Enterprise Institute, 1968), pp. 1–37, 19–23 (cataloging how the right attacks government spending only when it is on programs that help the poor and the weak).

261. See Jack M. Beermann, "The Public Pension Crisis," *Washington & Lee Law Review* 70 (2013): 3–94, 16–26.

262. See Editorial, "California Deposes Its 'Welfare Queen,'" *The New York Times* (July 23, 2016); New York Times, "'Welfare Queen' Becomes Issue in Reagan Campaign," *The New York Times* (February 15, 1976).

263. See, e.g., Peter Whoriskey, "As a Grocery Chain Is Dismantled, Investors Recover Their Money. Worker Pensions Are Short Millions." *The Washington Post* (December 28, 2018); Spencer L. Kimball and Noreen J. Parrett, "Creation of the Guarantee Association System," *Journal of Insurance Regulation* 19 (2000): 259–272; The Pension Benefit Guaranty Corporation, a US government agency established by 29 U.S. Code § 1302 (www.pbgc.gov/about/who-we-are.html); Code of Virginia, Title 54.1, Ch. 23.1, § 54.1-2316, "Certain Representations Unlawful; Perpetual Care Trust Fund Required" (2004).

264. See generally Sheldon W. Halpern, "Application of the Doctrine of Commercial Impracticability: Searching for 'The Wisdom of Solomon,'" *University of Pennsylvania Law Review* 135 (1987): 1123–1178.

265. Note, however, that many individuals feel the moral pull of their debts even after these have been discharged in bankruptcy and are therefore no longer legally collectable. For example, both Sir Walter Scott and Mark Twain worked for years to repay their debts even though these were discharged in bankruptcy. See Reiff, *Punishment, Compensation, and Law*, p. 215 n. 1.

266. See Maura Dolan, "California Promised Public Employees Generous Retirements. Will the Courts Give Government a Way Out?" *Los Angeles Times* (October 20, 2016) (pensions receive constitutional protection in California and twelve other states, although the degree of constitutional protection varies).

267. See, e.g., David Zahniser, "A City Pension Board Vote Could Add to Los Angeles' Budget Woes," *The Los Angeles Times* (July 10, 2017).

268. See Mary Williams Walsh, "In Puerto Rico, Teachers' Pension Fund Works Like a Ponzi Scheme," *The New York Times* (March 8, 2017); Editorial, "MBTA Pension System Operates Like a Ponizi Scheme," *Boston Globe* (February 25, 2019).

269. See Gretchen Morgenson, "Strapped Pension Funds, and the Hefty Investment Fees They Pay," *The New York Times* (May 12, 2017).
270. Even financially strapped Puerto Rico, for example, still has room to raise funds through additional taxation. See Mary Williams Walsh, "Puerto Rico, Mired in Debt, Has a New Rescue Plan," *The New York Times* (March 13, 2017).
271. See, e.g., Rojas and Walsh, "Hartford, with Its Finances in Disarray, Veers toward Bankruptcy."
272. See, e.g., Elizabeth A. Harris, "Judge, Citing Inequality, Orders Connecticut to Overhaul Its School System," *The New York Times* (September 7, 2016).
273. See Derek Thompson, "How Low Are U.S. Taxes Compared to Other Countries?" *The Atlantic* (January 14, 2013); Drew Desilver, "Among Developed Nations, Americans' Tax Bills Are Below Average," *Pew Research Center* (April 11, 2016); Eduardo Porter, "Considering the Cost of Lower Taxes," *The New York Times* (November 14, 2017).
274. See Phillip Vidal, "Annual Survey of Public Pensions: State and Locally-Administered Defined Benefit Data Summary Brief: 2015," U.S. Census Bureau (June 2016) (www.census.gov/content/dam/Census/library/publications/2016/econ/g15-aspp-sl.pdf). The states with the higher average are California, Oregon, Nevada, Colorado, Illinois, Ohio, New York, Massachusetts, New Jersey, Connecticut, Rhode Island, and Georgia.
275. See DQYDJ (Don't Quit Your Day Job), "Income Percentile Calculator for 2016 US Data" (https://dqydj.com/household-income-percentile-calculator-2016/).
276. See National Association of State Retirement Administrators, "Public Fund Survey" (March 2016) (www.nasra.org/publicfundsurvey).
277. For some recent examples, see Howard Blume, "L.A. School Board Salaries More Than Double to $125.000 a Year," *The Los Angeles Times* (July 10, 2017); and Mary Williams Walsh, "A $76,000 Monthly Pension: Why States and Cities Are Short of Cash," *The New York Times* (April 14, 2018); Mitch Daniels, "Connecticut Is Drowning in Debt. Should the Rest of Us Have to Pay?" *The Washington Post* (July 23, 2018); Jack Dolan, "Before Becoming LAPD Chief, Moore Retired, Collected a $1.27-Million Payout, then Was Rehired," *Los Angeles Times* (August 11, 2018).
278. See, e.g., Little Hoover Commission, "Public Pensions for Retirement Security," p. 37.
279. See Corina Knoll and Jeff Gottlieb, "Rizzo Gets 12 Years in Prison, Marking End to Scandal that Rocked Bell," *Los Angeles Times* (April 16, 2014). For another similar example, see Larry Altman and Megan Barnes, "Former Centinela Valley Superintendent Jose Fernandez Arrested on Public Corruption Charges," *Daily Breeze* (August 30, 2017).
280. See, e.g., Preston Jackson, "Sac City Unified School District Needs More Sunshine," *Sacramento Bee* (March 6, 2019).
281. See, e.g., Thomas Peele, "San Jose City Manager, Police Chief Highest Paid in Salary Survey of 200 Cities," *The Mercury News* (May 1, 2017). See also Transparent California, Salary and Pension Survey (2017) (http://transparentcalifornia.com/).
282. See Pension Rights Center, "Income from Pensions" (March 15, 2017) (www.pensionrights.org/publications/statistic/income-pensions).
283. See Freeman and Han, "The War against Public Sector Collective Bargaining in the US," p. 396.

284. See, e.g., Tara Siegel Bernard, "New York Envisions a State-Run Retirement Plan for Private Workers," *The New York Times* (April 2, 2018).
285. See Yoder, "Federal Employees Lag Behind Private Sector Workers in Salaries by 32 Percent on Average, Report Says."
286. See Keefe, "Laws Enabling Public Sector Collective Bargaining Have Not Led to Excessive Public Sector Pay."
287. See Jamison, "Paying for Public Retirees Never Cost L.A. Taxpayers More."
288. Ibid.
289. Ibid.
290. See Little Hoover Commission, "Public Pensions for Retirement Security," pp. 35–36.
291. Ibid.
292. See, e.g., Richard W. Johnson and Benjamin G. Southgate, "Evaluating Retirement Income Security for Illinois Public School Teachers," Public Pension Project Report (Urban Institute, July 2014) (www.urban.org/sites/default/files/publication/22821/413196-Evaluating-Retirement-Income-Security-for-Illinois-Public-School-Teachers.PDF).
293. See Walsh, "In Puerto Rico, Teachers' Pension Fund Works Like a Ponzi Scheme."
294. See Thomas Fordham Institute, "(No) Money in the Bank: Which Retirement Systems Penalize New Teachers" (January 26, 2017) (https://edexcellence.net/publications/no-money-in-the-bank).
295. See Adam Ashton and Phillip Reese, "With Pension Reform Looming, These California Departments Went on a Hiring Spree," *Sacramento Bee* (February 12, 2017).
296. See Venteicher, "California Public Employees' Pension Perks Can Be Taken Away, Court Rules."
297. See Freeman and Han, "The War against Public Sector Collective Bargaining in the US," p. 399.
298. See, e.g., Mary Williams Walsh, "In Texas, Some Rare Good News about Cities with Pension Woes," *The New York Times* (June 1, 2017) (discussing how Dallas and Houston's future pension obligations were reduced by $1.3 billion with the assistance of the relevant unions of public employees and retirees); Monica Davey, "Detroit's Retirees Vote to Lower Pensions, in Support of Bankruptcy Plan," *The New York Times* (July 22, 2014) (describing how unions called on members to support proposed concessions); Ryan Hagen, "San Bernardino Officially Out of Bankruptcy," *San Bernardino County Sun* (June 19, 2017).
299. See, e.g., Dana Goldstein and Erica L. Green, "What the Janus Decision Means for Teacher Unions," *The New York Times* (June 27, 2018).
300. See generally John Cassidy, "As Kennedy Retires, the Supreme Court's Attack on Labor Unions Is a Sign of Things to Come," *The New Yorker* (June 27, 2018).
301. 431 U.S. 209 (1977).
302. See *Friedrichs v. California Teachers Association*, 578 U.S. — (2016) (per curiam); Adam Liptak, "Victory for Unions as Supreme Court, Scalia Gone, Ties 4–4," *The New York Times* (March 29, 2016).

303. See Steven Greenhouse, "Labor Movement Braces for the Three-Front Battle with Trump, Congress and Courts," *The Guardian* (November 14, 2016); Adam Liptak, "Supreme Court Will Hear Case on Mandatory Fees to Unions," *The New York Times* (September 26, 2017).
304. Slip op. at 33.
305. Slip op. at 48.
306. See, e.g., Adam Ashton and Web Venteicher, "Want Out of Your Union? Conservative Groups Are Recruiting Public Workers for Lawsuits," *Sacramento Bee* (March 26, 2019).
307. See Scheiber, "Trump Nominee Is Behind Anti-Union Legal Campaign."
308. See, e.g., Erica L. Green, "Teachers Unions Scramble to Save Themselves after Supreme Court's Blow," *The New York Times* (July 14, 2018). There is some evidence, however, that the drop-off in fee income may not be as great as many people on both sides expect. See Adam Ashton, "New Contracts, Fees, Rules Helping Unions See Members Bump," *Sacramento Bee* (October 24, 2018); Katherine Barrett and Richard Greene, "Defying Predictions, Union Membership Isn't Dropping Post-Janus," *Governing* (December 10, 2018) (noting it may take some time before *Janus* ruling has the expected effect).
309. See slip op. at 9–11.
310. See *Buckley v. Valeo*, 424 U.S. 1 (1976) and its progeny, especially *Citizens United v. FEC*, 558 U.S. 310 (2010).
311. See, e.g., *Knox v. Service Employees*, 567 U.S. 298, 310–311 (2012).
312. See, e.g., National Right to Work Legal Defense Foundation, "Your Right to Work Rights – in Three Minutes" (www.nrtw.org/your-right-to-work-rights-in-three-minutes/). In response to *Janus*, unions are stepping up their efforts to combat the free-riding that conservative groups encourage. See Mike Elk, "'Vilified Too Long': Teachers' Unions Fight Back after Supreme Court Ruling," *The Guardian* (July 1, 2018).
313. See Janus, "Why I Took My Case over Forced Union Dues to the Supreme Court."
314. See slip op. at 9–10.
315. Slip op. at 25. See also *Garcetti v. Ceballos*, 547 U.S. 410 (2006); *Connick v. Myers*, 461 U.S. 138 (1983); *Pickering v. Board of Ed. of Township High School Dist. 205, Will City*, 391 U.S. 563 (1968).
316. Slip op. at 26–27.
317. See generally Mark R Reiff, "A Philosopher Argues Why No One Has the Right to Refuse Service to LGBT People," *The Conversation* (July 25, 2017).
318. See Daniel Grant, "Developers Fight Efforts to Make Them Pay for Public Art," *The New York Times* (July 10, 2018).
319. See Eric Posner, "The Far-Reaching Threats of a Conservative Court," *The New York Times* (October 23, 2018); Jeffrey Toobin, "The Supreme Court Is Quietly Changing the Status of Religion in American Life," *The New Yorker* (March 6, 2019).
320. For a more detailed discussion of the scope and limits of our duty to obey the law, see Matthew H. Kramer, *In Defense of Legal Positivism: Law Without Trimmings* (Oxford: Oxford University Press, 1999), ch. 9.
321. See generally, Mark R. Reiff, "Terrorism, Retribution, and Collective Responsibility," *Social Theory and Practice* 34 (2008): 209–242.

322. See Mark R. Reiff, "Collective Responsibility," *Encyclopedia of Political Theory*, ed. Mark Bevir (London: Sage, 2010).
323. See *Gregory v. Helvering*, 295 U.S. 465 (1935).
324. See *National Federation of Independent Business v. Sibelius*, 576 U.S. 519 (2012); David Cole, "Obamacare Upheld: How and Why Did Justice Roberts Do It? *The Nation* (June 28, 2012).
325. See Adam Liptak, "How Conservatives Weaponized the First Amendment," *The New York Times* (June 30, 2018).
326. Strawbs, "Part of the Union," on Bursting at the Seams (Remastered), A & M Records, 1973 (1998 reissue) (album).

Bibliography

Abernathy, Gary. 2017. "The Media Fundamentally Misunderstands Conservatives on Health Care." *The Washington Post* (July 7).
Abrams, Rachel. 2016. "Sex Shop Workers Welcome the Protections of a Retail Union." *The New York Times* (May 23).
  2017. "Walmart Is Accused of Punishing Workers for Sick Days." *The New York Times* (June 1).
  2017. "Why Aren't Paychecks Growing? A Burger-Joint Clause Offers a Clue." *The New York Times* (September 27).
  2018. "'No Poach' Deals for Fast-Food Workers Face Scrutiny by States." *The New York Times* (July 9).
  2018. "7 Fast-Food Chains to End 'No-Poach' Deals That Lock Down Low-Wage Workers." *The New York Times* (July 12).
  2018. "8 Fast-Food Chains Will End 'No-Poach' Policies." *The New York Times* (August 20).
Acolin, Arthur, Scott Bernstein, and Susan Wachter. 2017. "Opportunity, Housing Access, and Infrastructure." *Housing Policy Debate* 27: 468–471.
Adamic, Louis. 1931. *Dynamite: The Story of Class Violence in America*. New York: Viking.
Adams, Roy J. 2011. "Collective Bargaining as a Minimum Employment Standard." *Economic and Labor Relations Review* 22: 153–164.
Adams, Thomas Sewall and Helen Laura Sumner. 1905. *Labor Problems*. New York: Macmillan.
Addison, John T. and Clive R. Belfield. 2007. "Union Voice." In *What Do Unions Do? A Twenty-Year Perspective,* eds. James T. Bennett and Bruce E. Kaufman (New Brunswick, NJ: Transaction Publishers), pp. 238–274.
Addison, John T. and Barry T. Hirsch. 1989. "Union Effects on Productivity, Profits, and Growth: Has the Long Run Arrived?" *Journal of Labor Economics* 7: 72–105.
AFSCME Local 3299. 2018. "Race, Gender, and Income Disparities at the University of California" (April) (https://afscme3299.org/documents/reports/Pioneering-Inequality_WhitePaper.pdf).

Aidt, Toke and Zafiris Tzannatos. 2002. *Unions and Collective Bargaining: Economic Effects in a Global Environment*. Washington, DC: World Bank.
Alchian, Armen and Harold Demsetz. 1975. "Production, Information Costs, and Economic Organization." *American Economic Review* 62: 777–795.
Alderman, Liz. 2013. "Labor Tactic Raises Fear for France." *The New York Times* (January 7).
  2013. "Unions Back Revisions of Labor Law in France." *The New York Times* (January 11).
  2017. "Uber Dealt Setback after European Court Rules It Is a Taxi Service." *The New York Times* (December 20).
  2018. "French Companies Have Newfound Freedom...to Fire." *The New York Times* (January 23).
  2018. "Air France Dispute Threatens to Escalate Macron's Battle with Labor." *The New York Times* (May 7).
  2018. "French Labor Overhaul Led by Unusual Figure: A Business Executive." *The New York Times* (August 14).
Allegretto, Sylvia A. and Lawrence Mishel. 2016. "The Teacher Pay Gap Is Wider Than Ever." Economic Policy Institute (August 9) (www.epi.org/files/pdf/110964.pdf).
  2018. "The Teacher Pay Penalty Has Hit a New High." Economic Policy Institute (September 5) (www.epi.org/files/pdf/153196.pdf).
  2019. "The Teacher Weekly Wage Penalty Hit 21.4 Percent in 2018, a Record High." Economic Policy Institute (April 24).
Altman, Larry and Megan Barnes. 2017. "Former Centinela Valley Superintendent Jose Fernandez Arrested on Public Corruption Charges." *Daily Breeze* (August 30).
Alvarez, Lizette. 2016. "He Stars in a Spanish-Language Soap. Why Is He Driving for Uber?" *The New York Times* (October 20).
American Law Institute. 1981. *Restatement of Contracts (Second)*.
Anderson, Carol. 2019. "The Real Theft of American Democracy." *The New York Times* (March 14).
Anderson, Cathie. 2019. "A Week after Worker Strike, UC Davis Hospital Residents and Interns Seek to Join Union." *Sacramento Bee* (March 26).
  2019. "Major Labor Union Alleges UC Is Intimidating Members, Sabotaging Strike." *Sacramento Bee* (March 29).
  2019. "Resident Doctors Say UC Davis Health Has Agreed to Bargain with Their Union." *Sacramento Bee* (May 30).
Anderson, Elizabeth. 1999. "What Is the Point of Equality?" *Ethics* 109: 287–337.
  2017. *Private Government: How Employers Rule Our Lives (and Why We Don't Talk about It)*. Princeton: Princeton University Press.
Anonymous. 2016. "The Secret Life of a Trade Union Employee: I Do Little but the Benefits Are Incredible." *The Guardian* (August 8).
Anonymous. 2019. "Forced to Work, and Unable to Strike: US Federal Workers Need Solidarity." *The Guardian* (January 24).
Anonymous Academic. 2018. "I Thought US Universities Were Driven by Profit—Until I Moved to the UK." *The Guardian* (April 27).
Appelbaum, Binyamin. 2017. "Yellen Warns against Erasing Regulations Made after the Financial Crisis." *The New York Times* (August 25).
Applebome, Peter. 2016. "In Detroit's 2-Speed Recovery, Downtown Roars and Neighborhoods Sputter." *The New York Times* (August 12).

Arango, Tim. 2019. "California Has a High Rate of Police Shootings. Could a New Open-Records Law Change That?" *The New York Times* (February 12).
Aratani, Lauren. 2018. "'Blatant Scare Tactics': Iowa University Leads Crackdown on Student Unions." *The Guardian* (December 11).
Archer, Diane. 2011. "Medicare Is More Efficient Than Private Insurance." *Forbes* (September 20).
Arndt, Christine and Line Rennwald. 2016. "Union Members at the Polls in Diverse Trade Union Landscapes." *European Journal of Political Research* (July 21) (http://onlinelibrary.wiley.com/doi/10.1111/1475-6765.12157/full).
Arneson, Richard J. 2000. "Luck Egalitarianism and Prioritarianism." *Ethics* 110: 339–349.
Ashenfelter, Orley C., Henry Farber, and Michael R. Ransom. 2010. "Labor Market Monopsony." *Journal of Labor Economics* 28: 203–210.
Ashton, Adam. 2018. "New Contracts, Fees, Rules Helping Unions See Members Bump." *Sacramento Bee* (October 24).
Ashton, Adam and Phillip Reese. 2017. "With Pension Reform Looming, These California Departments Went on a Hiring Spree." *Sacramento Bee* (February 12).
Ashton, Adam and Web Venteicher. 2019. "Want Out of Your Union? Conservative Groups Are Recruiting Public Workers for Lawsuits." *Sacramento Bee* (March 26).
Associated Press. 2014. "NBCUniversal to Settle Suit over Unpaid Interns." *The New York Times* (October 24).
  2016. "California Court Decision Keeps Teacher Tenure Protections." *The New York Times* (August 22).
  2016. "Angst over the Economy Helps Trump Flip Great Lake States." *The New York Times* (November 9).
  2018. "Law Vegas Casino Workers Vote for First Mass Strike in More than 30 Years." *The Guardian* (May 23).
  2018. "Supreme Court Ohio Voter Ruling Is 'Green Light' to Purge Rolls, Say Critics." *The Guardian* (June 11).
  2018. "Trump v Trumka: President Marks Labor Day with Attack on Union Leader." *The Guardian* (September 3).
Astor, Maggie. 2018. "Seven Ways Alabama Has Made It Harder to Vote." *The New York Times* (June 23).
Austen, Ian. 2017. "G.M. Workers Strike in Canada as Mexico Jobs Raise Tension." *The New York Times* (September 18).
Azar, José, Iona Elena Marinescu, and Marshall Steinbaum. 2017. "Labor Market Concentration." (December 15) (https://papers.ssrn.com/sol3/papers.cfm?abstract_id=3088767).
Azar, José, Martin C. Schmalz, and Isabel Tecu. 2018. "Anti-competitive Effects of Common Ownership." *Journal of Finance* 73: 1513–1565.
Badger, Emily. 2016. "As American as Apple Pie? The Rural Vote's Disproportionate Slice of Power." *The New York Times* (November 20).
Baird, Charles W. 2000. "Unions and Antitrust." *Journal of Labor Research* 21: 585–600.
  2007. "Hayek on Labor Unions: Coercion and the Rules of Law." *Journal of Private Enterprise* 23: 30–51.

2011. "Freeing Labor Markets by Reforming Union Laws." *Downsizing the Federal Government* (Cato Institute, June 1).
Bakija, Jon, Lane Kenworthy, Peter Lindert, and Jeff Madrick. *How Big Should Our Government Be?* Oakland: University of California Press.
Balingit, Moriah. 2018. "'It Just Hurts My Heart': Low Pay, Big Classes Are the Plight of Oklahoma Teachers." *The Washington Post* (March 30).
2018. "'They Are So Underpaid': School Support Staff Scrape by on Meager Earnings." *The Washington Post* (April 25).
Ballereisen, Edward J. 2017. *Fraud: An American History from Barnum to Madoff.* Princeton, NJ: Princeton University Press.
Barboza, David. 2017. "Mounting Questions about Who Controls HNA, a Top Chinese Conglomerate." *The New York Times* (August 24).
Barkan, Ross. 2019. "Republicans' Lack of Alarm over the Shutdown Reveals a Disturbing Truth." *The Guardian* (January 18).
2019. "Trump's Labor Department Is Giving the Gig Economy Carte Blanche." *The Guardian* (May 6, 2019).
Barnes, Brooks. 2017. "Hollywood Writers Kept the Heat on Studios to Win Their Contract." *The New York Times* (May 2).
Barnes, Robert. 2017. "Supreme Court to Take Case on Baker Who Refused to Sell Wedding Cake to Gay Couple." *The Washington Post* (June 26).
Barrett, Katherine and Richard Greene. 2018. "Defying Predictions, Union Membership Isn't Dropping Post-Janus." *Governing* (December 10).
Bartlett, Bruce. 2010. "Tax Cuts and 'Starving the Beast.'" *Forbes* (May 7).
Bauer, Shane. 2018. *American Prison: A Reporter's Undercover Journey into the Business of Punishment.* New York: Penguin.
Baumgartner, Thomas, et al. 2008. "Oxytocin Shapes the Neural Circuitry of Trust and Trust Adaptation in Humans." *Neuron* 58: 639–650.
BBC. 2014. "Study: US Is an Oligarchy, Not a Democracy." *BBC News* (April 17).
Beaumont, Peter. 2017. "Israeli Airline Can't Make Women Move Seats for Religious Reasons, Court Rules." *The Guardian* (June 22).
Beer, Michael and Russell A. Eisenstat. 2000. "The Silent Killers of Strategy Implementation and Learning." *Sloan Management Review* 41: 29–40.
Beerbohm, Eric. 2017. "Must Rawlsians Be Hamiltonians? Small Government and Political Illiberalism." *The American Journal of Jurisprudence* 62: 21–28.
Beermann, Jack M. 2013. "The Public Pension Crisis." *Washington & Lee Law Review* 70: 3–94.
Behrens, Martin. 2009. "Still Married after All These Years? Union Organizing and the Role of Works Councils in German Industrial Relations." *Industrial and Labor Relations Review* 62: 275–293.
Behrens, Martin, Michael Fichter, and Carola M. Frege. 2003. "Unions in Germany: Regaining the Initiative?" *European Journal of Industrial Relations* 9: 25–42.
Beitz, Charles R. 2019. "How Is Partisan Gerrymandering Unfair?" *Philosophy and Public Affairs* 46: 323–358.
Bell, Daniel. 1960. *The End of Ideology.* Glencoe, IL: Free Press.
Belman, Dale. 1992. "Unions, The Quality of Labor Relations, and Firm Performance." In *Unions and Economic Competitiveness*, eds. Lawrence Mishel and Paula B. Voos (Armonk, NY: M.E. Sharpe), pp. 41–107.

Bender, Keith and John Heywood. 2012. "Trends in the Relative Compensation of State and Local Employees." In *Public Jobs and Political Agendas: The Public Sector in an Era of Economic Stress*, ed. Daniel Mitchell (Champaign, IL: Labor and Employment Relations Association), pp. 133–166.

Benmelech, Efraim, Nittai Bergman, and Hyunseob Kim. 2018. "Strong Employers and Weak Employees: How Does Employer Concentration Affect Wages?" NBER Working Paper 24307 (February).

Benner, Katie. 2017. "Abuses Hide in the Silence of Nondisparagement Agreements." *The New York Times* (July 21).

2018. "Sessions, in Last-Minute Act, Sharpley Limits Use of Consent Decrees to Curb Police Abuses." *The New York Times* (November 8).

Bennett James T. and Bruce E. Kaufman. 2007. "What Do Unions Do? A Twenty-Year Perspective." In *What Do Unions Do? A Twenty-Year Perspective*, eds. James T. Bennett and Bruce E. Kaufman (New Brunswick, NJ: Transaction Publishers, 2007), pp. 1–11.

Bennhold, Katrin. 2018. "Workers of Germany, Unite: The New Siren Call of the Far Right." *The New York Times* (February 5).

Bentham, Jeremy. 2002. *Rights, Representation, and Reform: Nonsense on Stilts and Other Writings on the French Revolution*, eds. Philip Schofield, Catherine Pease-Watkin, and Cyprian Blamires. Oxford: Oxford University Press.

Berkey, Brian. 2016. "Against Rawlsian Institutionalism about Justice." *Social Theory and Practice* 42: 706–732.

Berlin, Isaiah. 1990. "Joseph de Maistre and the Origins of Fascism." In *The Crooked Timber of Humanity*, ed. Henry Hardy (Princeton, NJ: Princeton University Press).

2002. "Two Concepts of Liberty." In *Liberty*, ed. Henry Hardy (Oxford: Oxford University Press), pp. 166–217.

Berman, Russell. 2014. "Why Can't Unions Keep Up with the Economy?" *The Atlantic* (January 23).

2017. "Kansas Republicans Sour on Their Tax-Cut Experiment." *The Atlantic* (February 24).

Bernanke, Ben. 2007. "The Level and Distribution of Well-Being." *Board of Governors of the Federal Reserve System* (Speech before the greater Omaha Chamber of Commerce, February 6).

Bernard, Tara Siegel. 2016. "Think Your Retirement Plan Is Bad? Talk to a Teacher." *The New York Times* (October 21).

2018. "New York Envisions a State-Run Retirement Plan for Private Workers." *The New York Times* (April 2).

Betancourt, Sarah. 2019. "Stop & Shop Hit by Strike as 31,000 Workers Walk Off Job." *The Guardian* (April 15).

Bhalla, Jag. 2018. "The American Healthcare System Shows Why We Can't Trust Free Market Ideologues." *Evonomics* (April 6).

Bhaskar, V., Alan Manning, and Ted To. 2002. "Oligopsony and Monopsonistic Competition in Labor Markets." *Journal of Economic Perspectives* 16: 155–174.

Bidgood, Jess. 2018. "West Virginia Raises Teachers' Pay to End Statewide Strike." *The New York Times* (March 6).

Bidgood, Jess and Campbell Robertson. 2018. "West Virginia Walkouts a Lesson in the Power of a Crowd-Sourced Strike." *The New York Times* (March 8).

Billing, James K., et al. 2012. "Effects of Oxytocin and Vasopressin on Cooperative Behavior and Associated Brain Activity in Men." *Psychoneuroendocrinology* 37: 447–461.

Binmore, Ken. 2007. *Playing for Real: A Text on Game Theory*. New York: Oxford University Press.

Bivens, Josh and Heidi Shierholz. 2018. "What Labor Market Changes Have Generated Inequality and Wage Suppression?" Economic Policy Institute (December 12).

Bivens, Josh, et al. 2017. "How Today's Unions Help Working People." Economic Policy Institute (August 24) (www.epi.org/files/pdf/133275.pdf).

Blado, Kayla, Dan Escrow, and Lawrence Mishel. 2017. "Who Are Today's Union Members?" *Economic Snapshot*. Economic Policy Institute (August 31).

Blanc, Eric. 2019. *Red State Revolt: The Teachers' Strike Wave and Working Class Politics*. London: Verso.

Blanchard, Oliver J. 1986. "The Wage Price Spiral." *The Quarterly Journal of Economics* 101: 543–566.

Blanchflower, David G. 2005. "Unions in the UK Public and Private Sectors" (Hanover, NH: Dartmouth College, March 16).

Blanchflower, David G. and Alex Bryson. 2007. "What Effect Do Unions Have on Wages Now and Would Freeman and Medoff Be Surprised?" In *What Do Unions Do? A Twenty-Year Perspective*, eds. James T. Bennett and Bruce E. Kaufman (New Brunswick, NJ: Transaction Publishers), pp. 79–113.

Blinder, Alan and Michael Wines. 2018. "North Carolina Is Ordered to Redraw Its Congressional Map." *The New York Times* (January 9).

Blitzer, Jonathan. 2018. "How the Trump Administration Got Comfortable Separating Immigrant Kids from Their Parents." *The New Yorker* (May 30).

Block, Walter. 2014. *Toward a Libertarian Society*. Auburn, AL: Mises Institute.

2015. "On Slavery and Libertarianism." *Journal of Economic and Social Thought* 2: 161–174.

Bloodworth, James. 2018. "I Worked in an Amazon Warehouse. Bernie Sanders Is Right to Target Them." *The Guardian* (September 17).

Blume, Howard. 2017. "L.A. School Board Salaries More Than Double to $125.000 a Year." *The Los Angeles Times* (July 10).

Blume, Howard and Anna M. Phillips. 2017. "Charter Backers Win Their First L.A. School Board Majority." *Los Angeles Times* (May 16).

Boal, William M. and Michael R. Ransom. 1997. "Monopsony in the Labor Market." *Journal of Economic Literature* 35: 86–112.

Boeve, May and Michael Brune. 2018. "If US Unions Tumble, the Progressive Movement Could Go with Them." *The Guardian* (March 2).

Bonar, James. 1911. *Disturbing Elements in the Study and Teaching of Political Economy*. Baltimore, MD: Johns Hopkins Press.

Bonefeld, Werner. 2012. "Freedom and the Strong State: On German Ordo-Liberalism." *New Political Economy* 17: 633–656.

2013. "On the Strong Liberal State: Beyond Berghahn and Young." *New Political Economy* 18: 779–783.

Booth, Alison L. 2014. "Wage Determination and Imperfect Competition." *Labour Economics* 30: 53–58.

Booth, Robert. 2017. "Hermes Facing Legal Challenge from Its Self-Employed Workers." *The Guardian* (January 26).
   2017. "Tax Barrister Plans to Take Uber to Court Over Alleged £20m Black Hole." *The Guardian* (February 21, 2017).
   2017. "UK Mail Driver Who Was Unable to Work after Car Accident Charged £800." *The Guardian* (March 19).
   2017. "Uber Granted Right to Appeal against Ruling on UK Drivers' Rights." *The Guardian* (April 19).
Booth, Robert, Tara Evans, and Hilary Osborne. 2016. "Revealed: Delivery Giant Hermes Pays Some Couriers Less Than Living Wage." *The Guardian* (July 18).
Boudette, Neal E. 2017. "Ex-Fiat Chrysler Executive Accused of Siphoning Millions with Union Leader." *The New York Times* (July 26).
Boulin, Jean-Yves. 2000. "Trade Unions in France: How to Challenge the Trend Toward De-Unionization?" In *Trade Unions in Europe: Facing Challenges and Searching for Solutions*, eds. Jeremy Waddington and Reiner Hoffmann (Brussels: European Trade Union Institute), pp. 215–248.
Bowley, Graham. 2017. "What If Trump Really Does End Money for the Arts?" *The New York Times* (January 30).
Breeden, Aurelien. 2017. "As Le Pen and Macron Fight for Presidency in France, Unions Are Split." *The New York Times* (May 1).
   2017. "France Unveils Contentious Labor Overhaul in Big Test for Macron." *The New York Times* (August 31).
Breen, Keith. 2015. "Freedom, Republicanism, and Workplace Democracy." *Critical Review of International Social and Political Philosophy* 2015: 470–485.
Breit, William. 1967. "The Wages Fund Controversy Revisited." *The Canadian Journal of Economics and Political Science/Revue Canadienne d'Economique et de Science Politique* 33: 509–528.
Breton, Marcos. 2017. "Upset with Trump? Well, Maybe You Should Have Voted." *Sacramento Bee* (February 8).
Brill, Steven. 2010. "The Teachers' Unions Last Stand." *The New York Times* (May 17).
Bronfenbrenner, Kate. 2000. "Uneasy Terrain: The Impact of Capital Mobility on Workers, Wages, and Union Organizing." Report Submitted to the U.S. Trade Deficit Review Commission (September 6) (http://digitalcommons.ilr.cornell.edu/cgi/viewcontent.cgi?article=1002&context=reports).
   2009. "No Holds Barred: The Intensification of Employer Opposition to Organizing." EPI Briefing Paper #235, Economic Policy Institute (May 20) (www.epi.org/files/page/-/pdf/bp235.pdf).
Bronson, Brittany. 2016. "How Unions Help Cocktail Servers." *The New York Times* (August 17).
Brooks, David. 2018. "The Localist Revolution." *The New York Times* (July 19).
Brooks, Nancy Rivera, Thomas S. Mulligan, and Tim Reiterman. 2002. "Memo Shows Enron Role in Hiking Prices." *Los Angeles Times* (May 7).
Broome, John. 1991. *Weighing Goods*. Oxford: Basil Blackwell.
   1999. "Fairness." In *Ethics Out of Economics* (Cambridge: Cambridge University Press), pp. 113–120.
Brown, Campbell. 2003. "Giving Up Levelling Down." *Economics and Philosophy* 19: 111–134.

Brown, Russ. 2012. "A Deep Secret that Labor Unions Don't Want Workers to Know." *Forbes* (August 16).
Browning-Ferris Industries and Sanitary Truck Drivers and Helpers, Case No. 32-RC-109684, 362 NLRB No. 186 (August 27, 2015).
Buchannan, James, and Gordon Tullock. 1962. *The Calculus of Consent*. Ann Arbor: University of Michigan Press.
Bucknor, Cherrie. 2016. "Black Workers, Unions, and Inequality." Center for Economic and Policy Research (August) (http://cepr.net/images/stories/reports/black-workers-unions-2016-08.pdf?v=2).
Budd, John W. 1996. "Canadian Strike Replacement Legislation and Collective Bargaining: Lessons for the United States." *Industrial Relations* 35: 245–260.
   2004. *Employment with a Human Face*. Ithaca, NY: ILR Press.
   2007. "The Effect of Unions on Employee Benefits and Non-Wage Compensation: Monopoly Power, Collective Voice, and Facilitation." In *What Do Unions Do? A Twenty-Year Perspective*, eds. James T. Bennett and Bruce E. Kaufman (New Brunswick, NJ: Transaction Publishers), pp. 160–192.
Budd, John W. and Devasheesh Bhave. 2009. "The Employment Relationship." In *The Sage Handbook of Human Resource Management*, eds. Adrian Wilkinson, Nicolas Bacon, Tom Redman, and Scott Snell (London: Sage), pp. 51–70.
Budd, John W. and In-Gang Na. 2000. "The Union Membership Wage Premium for Employees Covered by Collective Bargaining Agreements." *Journal of Labor Economics* 18: 783–807.
Budd, John W., Raphael Gomez, Noah M. Meltz. 2004. "Why Balance Is Best: The Pluralist Industrial Relations Paradigm of Balancing Competing Interests." In *Theoretical Perspectives on Work and the Employment Relationship*, ed. Bruce Kaufman (Champaign, IL: Industrial Relations Association Press), pp. 195–227.
Buettner, Russ and Noam Scheiber. 2017. "For Andrew Puzder, Labor Nominee, Fighting for Owners' Interests Began Early." *The New York Times* (February 3).
Bufacchi, Vittorio. 2018. "Theoretical Foundations for Human Rights." *Political Studies* 66 (2018): 601–617.
Bui, Quoctrung and Nate Cohn. 2018. "Adventures in Extreme Gerrymandering." *The New York Times* (January 17).
Bump, Philip. 2018. "In about 20 Years, Half the Population Will Live in Eight States." *The Washington Post* (July 12).
Bureau of Labor Statistics. 2017. "Union Affiliation of Employed Wage and Salary Workers by Occupation and Industry," and "Union Affiliation of Employed Wage and Salary Workers by State," Table 3 and Table 5 (January 26).
   2017. "Union Members Summary" (U.S. Department of Labor, January 26) (www.bls.gov/news.release/union2.nr0.htm).
   2017. "Alternative Measures of Labor Underutilization." Table A-15, Measure U-6 (May 5, 2017) (www.bls.gov/news.release/empsit.t15.htm).
Bureau of Labor Statistics, United States Department of Labor. "Databases, Tables & Calculators by Subject" (www.bls.gov/data/) (accessed November 8, 2019).
Burns, Alexander. 2018. "Eric Holder's Group Targets All-G.O.P. States to Attack Gerrymandering." *The New York Times* (February 6).
Butler, Sarah. 2017. "Ikea Enters Gig Economy by Buying Freelance Labour Firm TaskRabbit." *The Guardian* (September 28).

2017. "Uber Driver Tells MPs: I Work 90 Hours but Still Need to Claim Benefits." *The Guardian* (February 6).
Butler, Sarah and Hilary Osborne. 2017. "Courier Wins Holiday Pay in Key Tribunal Ruling on Gig Economy." *The Guardian* (January 6).
Butler, Sarah and Gwyn Topham. 2017. "Uber Should Lose Its Licence If It Doesn't Improve Workers' Rights, Say Drivers." *The Guardian* (May 9).
Calmes, Jackie. 2015. "In Pacific Trade Deal, Vietnam Agrees to U.S. Terms on Labor Rights." *The New York Times* (November 5).
Cantin, Étienne. 2012. "The Politics of Austerity and the Conservative Offensive against US Public Sector Unions, 2008–2012." *Relations Industrielles* 67: 612–632.
Card, David. 2001. "The Effect of Unions on Wage Inequality in the US Labor Market." *Industrial and Labor Relations Review* 54: 354–367.
Card, David, Thomas Lemieux, and W. Craig Riddell. 2003. "Unionization and Wage Inequality: A Comparative Study of the U.S., the U.K., and Canada." NBER Working Paper No. 9473, National Bureau of Economic Research (January).
Carroll, Rory. 2016. "The Mysterious Lynching of Frank Little: Activist Who Fought Inequality and Lost." *The Guardian* (September 21).
Carter, Ian. 1999. *A Measure of Freedom*. Oxford: Oxford University Press.
Carrie, Julia. 2019. "'I've Paid a Huge Personal Cost': Google Walkout Organizer Resigns over Alleged Retaliation." *The Guardian* (June 7).
Casey, Michael. 2019. "Loss of Local News Hinders Ability to Watchdog Government." *Sacramento Bee* (March 10).
Casselman, Ben. 2017. "Feel That Post-Recession Bounce? The Rich Feel It the Most." *The New York Times* (September 27).
Cassidy, John. 2018. "As Kennedy Retires, the Supreme Court's Attack on Labor Unions Is a Sign of Things to Come." *The New Yorker* (June 27).
Cauley, Kashana. 2017. "Why Millennials Should Lead the Next Labor Movement." *The New York Times* (July 13).
Chakrabortty, Aditya. 2016. "Boots Staff Under Pressure to Milk the NHS for Cash, Says Pharmacists' Union." *The Guardian* (April 13).
  2016. "Uber Ruling Is a Massive Boost for a Fairer Jobs Market." *The Guardian* (October 28).
Chalabi, Mona. 2017. "The History of 2017 in Seven Charts." *The Guardian* (December 29).
Chalabi, Mona and Amanda Holpuch. 2017. "What That Google Memo Didn't Tell You about Pay Inequality in America." *The Guardian* (August 11).
Chamberlain, Edward R. 1959. "Labour Union Power and the Public Interest." In *The Public Stake in Union Power*, ed. Philip D. Bradley (Charlottesville: University of Virginia Press), pp. 3–20.
Chamberlain, Gethin. 2018. "Underpaid and Exhausted: The Human Cost of Your Kindle." *The Guardian* (June 9).
Chandler, Alfred D. Jr. 1977. *The Visible Hand: The Managerial Revolution in American Business*. Cambridge: Harvard University Press.
Chassany, Anne-Sylvaine. 2016. "How France's National Front Is Winning Working Class Voters." *Financial Times* (October 21).
Chazan, Guy. 2018. "German Union Wins Right to 28-Hour Working Week and 4.3% Pay Rise." *Financial Times* (February 6).

Chemerinsky, Erwin. 1999. "Substantive Due Process." *Touro Law Review* 15: 1501–1534.
Chen, David W. and Mary Williams Walsh. 2014. "New York City Pension System Is Strained by Costs and Politics." *The New York Times* (August 3).
Chen, Michelle. 2018. "Millennials Are Keeping Unions Alive." *The Nation* (February 2).
Chicano, Carina. 2017. "From Wells Fargo to Frye Festival, the Scam Economy Is Entering Its Baroque Phase." *The New York Times* (May 16).
Chodorow, Adam. 2017. "The IRS Is Using Private Debt Collectors Again." *Forbes* (April 14).
Chokshi, Niraj. 2018. "94 Percent of U.S. Teachers Spend Their Own Money on School Supplies, Survey Finds." *The New York Times* (May 16).
 2018. "Kentucky Governor Compares State Workers to Drowning Victims: 'You Just Need to Knock Them Out.'" *The New York Times* (August 14).
Ciesielski, Jack T. 2011. "S&P 500 Executive Pay: Bigger Than…Whatever You Think It Is." *The Analyst's Accounting Observer* 20:7 (May 23).
Clark, Kim B. 1984. "Unionization and Firm Performance: The Impact on Profits, Growth, and Productivity." *American Economic Review* 74: 893–919.
Clark, Neil. 2013. "Angry about Fares? Get on Board the Renationalisation Express." *The Guardian* (August 13).
Clement, Scott. 2016. "Donald Trump Is Splitting the White Vote in Ways We've Never Seen Before." *The Washington Post* (May 31).
Coase, Ronald H. 1988. "The Nature of the Firm." In *The Firm, the Market, and the Law* (Chicago, IL: University of Chicago Press), pp. 33–55.
 1998. "The New Institutional Economics." *The American Economic Review* 85: 72–74.
Cohan, William D. 2016. "Documents Open Curtain on Boardroom Drama at Valeant." *The New York Times* (December 29).
Cohen, Gerald A. 1979. "The Labor Theory of Value and the Concept of Exploitation." *Philosophy and Public Affairs* 8: 338–360.
 1995. "Are Freedom and Equality Compatible?" In *Self-Ownership, Freedom, and Equality* (Cambridge: Cambridge University Press), pp. 92–115.
 1995. *Self-Ownership, Freedom, and Equality*. Cambridge: Cambridge University Press.
 2007. *Rescuing Justice and Equality*. Cambridge: Harvard University Press.
Cohen, Joshua and Joel Rogers. 1995. "Secondary Associations and Democratic Governance." In *Associations and Democracy*, ed. Erik Olin Wright (London: Verso), pp. 7–98.
Cohen, Patricia. 2017. "'Superstar Firms' May Have Shrunk Workers' Share of Income." *The New York Times* (March 8).
 2017. "Steady Jobs, with Pay and Hours That Are Anything But." *The New York Times* (May 31).
 2017. "If Workers Are Scarce, Is It the Work or the Wages?" *The New York Times* (July 13).
 2018. "I.R.S. Paid $20 Million to Collect $6.7 Million in Tax Debts." *The New York Times* (January 10).
Cohen, Patricia and Robert Gebeloff. 2018. "Public Servants Are Losing Their Foothold in the Middle Class." *The New York Times* (April 22).
Colburn, Ben. 2011. "Autonomy and Adaptive Preferences." *Utilitas* 23: 52–71.

Cole, David. 2012. "Obamacare Upheld: How and Why Did Justice Roberts Do It?" *The Nation* (June 28).
Cole, Peter. 2019. "Martin Luther King Jr., Union Man." *The Conversation* (January 18).
Coleman, James S. 1974. *The Power and the Structure of Society*. New York: Norton.
Collinson, Patrick. 2016. "The Train Companies Pocket Millions in Compensation for Delays." *The Guardian* (December 31).
Cooper, David. 2018. "As Wisconsin's and Minnesota's Lawmakers Took Divergent Paths, So Did Their Economies." Economic Policy Institute (May 8).
  2018. "Workers of Color Are Far More Likely to Be Paid Poverty-Level Wages than White Workers." *Working Economic Blog*, Economic Policy Institute (June 21).
Colvin, Alexander J. S. 2017. "The Growing Use of Mandatory Arbitration." Economic Policy Institute (September 27).
Commons, John R. 1919. *Industrial Goodwill*. New York: McGraw-Hill.
Cooper, David. 2017. "Another Year of Federal Inaction Has Further Eroded the Federal Minimum Wage." *Economic Snapshot*. Economic Policy Institute (July 24).
Cooper, David and Teresa Kroeger. 2017. "Employers Steal Billions from Workers' Paychecks Each Year." Economic Policy Institute (May 10) (www.epi.org/files/pdf/125116.pdf).
Cooper, David, Mary Gable, and Algernon Austin. 2012. "The Public sector Job Crisis: Women and African Americans Hit Hardest by Job Losses in State and Local Governments." EPI Briefing Paper #339 (Washington, DC: Economic Policy Institute, May 2).
Cooper, Michael. 2018. "Labor Unrest Hits Ballet Theater, and Dancers Consider a Strike." *The New York Times* (January 10).
Coote, Anna. 2019. "Universal Basic Income Doesn't Work. Let's Boost the Public Realm Instead." *The Guardian* (May 6).
Coote, Anna and Edenur Yazicic. 2019. "Universal Basic Income: A Union Perspective." *New Economics Foundation* (April).
Council of Economic Advisers. 2016. Annual Report (February) (https://obamawhitehouse.archives.gov/sites/default/files/docs/ERP_2016_Book_Complete%20JA.pdf).
  2016. "Labor Market Monopsony: Trends, Consequences, and Policy Responses." *Issue Brief* (October) (https://obamawhitehouse.archives.gov/sites/default/files/page/files/20161025_labor_mrkt_monopsony_cea.pdf).
Covert, Bryce. 2018. "When Companies Supersize, Paychecks Shrink." *The New York Times* (May 13).
Cowan, Sarah. 2018. "Can Artists Organize? The Story of WAGE." *The New Yorker* (December 14).
Cowley, Stacy. 2015. "Labor Board Ruling on Joint Employers Leaves Some Companies Scratching Their Heads." *The New York Times* (August 28).
  2018. "Nike Will Raise Wages for Thousands after Outcry over Inequality." *The New York Times* (July 22).
  2018. "Teachers Sue Navient, Claiming Student Loan Forgiveness Failures." *The New York Times* (October 3).
Cowley, Stacy and Jessica Silver-Greenberg. 2017. "Outside Collectors for I.R.S. Are Accused of Illegal Practices." *The New York Times* (June 23).
Coyle, Diane. 2018. "Three Cheers for Regulation." *Project Syndicate* (July 17).
Craft, James A. 2001. "Union Violence: A Review and Critical Discussion." *Journal of Labor Research* 22: 679–688.

Craig, Susanne. 2016. "New York City's Pension System in Danger of 'Operational Failure,' Report Says." *The New York Times* (January 26).
Cramer, Maria. 2018. "Released from Prison, Ex-Teamsters Lash Out at 'Evil' Prosecutors Who Put Them There." *Boston Globe* (April 10).
Cummins, Denise. 2016. "What Happens When You Believe in Ayn Rand and Modern Economic Theory." *Evonomics* (February 17).
Dahl, Robert A. 1985. *A Preface to Economic Democracy*. Berkeley: University of California Press.
  1989. *Democracy and Its Critics*. New Haven, CT: Yale University Press.
Dam, Andrew Van. 2018. "Is It Great to Be a Worker in the U.S.? Not Compared to the Rest of the Developed World." *The Washington Post* (July 4).
Daniels, Mitch. 2018. "Connecticut Is Drowning in Debt. Should the Rest of Us Have to Pay?" *The Washington Post* (July 23).
Davenport, Coral and Eric Lipton. 2017. "Scott Pruitt Is Carrying Out His E.P.A. Agenda in Secret, Critics Say." *The New York Times* (August 11).
Davey, Monica. 2014. "Chicago Mayor Seeks Alterations to Repair Badly Underfunded Pension Plan." *The New York Times* (April 1).
  2014. "Detroit's Retirees Vote to Lower Pensions, in Support of Bankruptcy Plan." *The New York Times* (July 22).
  2017. "Brownback Tax Cuts Set Off a Revolt by Kansas Republicans." *The New York Times* (June 7).
Davey, Monica and Julie Bosman. 2016. "In Victory for Unions, Law on Dues Is Struck Down in Wisconsin." *The New York Times* (April 8).
Davey, Monica and Mary Williams Walsh. 2013. "Billions in Debt, Detroit Tumbles into Insolvency." *The New York Times* (July 18).
Davidson, Joe. 2018. "Racist Incidents on the Rise, Union for Government Workers Warns." *The Washington Post* (November 20).
  2018. "Trump Labor Adviser's Plan for Cutting Federal Compensation, Potentially even Paid Holidays." *The Washington Post* (December 17).
Davidson, Kate. "Donald Trump's Comments on the Fed, Interest Rate Policy and Janet Yellen." *The Wall Street Journal* (November 9).
Davis, Julie Hirschfeld. 2017. "Rumblings of a 'Deep State' Undermining Trump? It Was Once a Foreign Concept." *The New York Times* (March 6).
Davis, Julie Hirschfeld and Michael D. Shear. 2018. "How Trump Came to Enforce a Practice of Separating Migrant Families." *The New York Times* (June 16).
Davis, Noah C. 2014. "The Yelper and the Negative Review: The Developing Battle Over Nondisparagement Clauses." *American Bar Association GPSolo eReport* 3:10 (May 24).
Declerck, Carolyn H., Christophe Boone, and Toko Kiyonari. 2010. "Oxytocin and Cooperation under Conditions of Uncertainty: The Modulating Role of Incentives and Social Information." *Hormones and Behavior* 57: 368–374.
Denby, David. 2017. "Eric Holder's Battle against Gerrymandering." *The New Yorker* (November 14).
DeNevas-Walt, Carmen, Bernadette D. Proctor, and Jessica C. Smith. 2010. U.S. Census Bureau, Current Population Reports, P60-238, *Income, Poverty, and Health Insurance Coverage in the United States: 2009* (Washington, DC: U.S. Government Printing Office, September).

DenHoed, Andrea. 2018. "Striking Oklahoma Teachers Win Historic School-Funding Increase and Keep on Marching." *The New Yorker* (April 4).
Department of Business Innovation & Skills. 2015. "Trade Union Membership 2014." *Statistical Bulletin* (June) (www.gov.uk/government/uploads/system/uploads/attachment_data/file/431564/Trade_Union_Membership_Statistics_2014.pdf).
Desilver, Drew. 2015. "Job Shifts under Obama: Fewer Government Workers, More Caregivers, Servers and Temps." Pew Research Center (January 14) (www.pewresearch.org/fact-tank/2015/01/14/job-shifts-under-obama-fewer-government-workers-more-caregivers-servers-and-temps/).
    2016. "Among Developed Nations, Americans' Tax Bills Are Below Average." Pew Research Center (April 11).
Devinatz, Victor G. 2011. "The Continuing Controversy over Right-to-Work Laws in the Early Twenty-First Century." *Employee Responsibilities and Rights Journal* 23: 287–293.
Dewan, Shaila and Motoko Rich. 2012. "Public Workers Face Continued Layoffs, Hurting the Recovery." *The New York Times* (June 10).
Diamond, Sara. 1995. *Roads to Dominion: Right-Wing Movements and Political Power in the United States*. New York: Guildford Press.
Diaz, John. 2008. "A Long Way from the Grassroots." *San Francisco Chronicle* (October 12).
Dickerson, James R. 1985. "Teamsters, GOP Forged Increasingly Close Links." *The Washington Post* (July 25).
Dickman, Howard. 1987. *Industrial Democracy in America*. La Salle, IL: Open Court.
Dietsch, Peter. 2015. *Catching Capital: The Ethics of Tax Competition*. Oxford: Oxford University Press.
DiLorenzo, Thomas J. 2004. "The Union Myth." *The Free Market* 24:10 (Mises Institute, October 1).
DiNardo, John and David S. Lee. 2003. "Do Unions Cause Business Failures?" *NBER* (March) (www.princeton.edu/~davidlee/wp/unionbf.pdf).
Dionne Eugene Joseph Jr. 2018. "Don't Buy the Spin. Government Works." *The Washington Post* (January 21).
    2018. "What Striking Teachers Teach Us." *The Washington Post* (April 4).
DiSalvo, Daniel. 2010. "The Trouble with Public Sector Unions." *National Affairs* 5: 3–19.
    2015. *Government against Itself: Public Union Power and Its Consequences*. Oxford: Oxford University Press.
    2018. "Janus Decision Reins in Unions' Political Power." *The New York Times* (June 27).
Dobbs, Richard, et al. 2016. "Poorer than Their Parents? Flat or Falling Incomes in Advanced Economies." McKinsey Global Institute (July) (www.mckinsey.com/~/media/mckinsey/featured%20insights/Employment%20and%20Growth/Poorer%20than%20their%20parents%20A%20new%20perspective%20on%20income%20inequality/MGI-Income%20-Inequality-Executive-summary-July-2016.ashx).
Dolan, Ed. 2017. "Freedom, Prosperity, and Big Government." *The First Principle* (Niskanen Center, April 20) (https://niskanencenter.org/blog/freedom-government-part-one/).
    2017. "Quality of Government, Not Size, Is the Key to Freedom and Prosperity." *Evonomics* (May 6).

Dolan, Jack. 2018. "Before Becoming LAPD Chief, Moore Retired, Collected a $1.27-Million Payout, then Was Rehired." *Los Angeles Times* (August 11).

Dolan, Maura. 2016. "California Promised Public Employees Generous Retirements. Will the Courts Give Government a Way Out?" *Los Angeles Times* (October 20).

2017. "California Supreme Court Rules for Farmworkers, and Upholds Binding Mediation." *Los Angeles Times* (November 27).

Donado, Alejandro and Klaus Wälde. 2012. "How Trade Unions Increase Welfare." *The Economic Journal* 122: 990–1009.

Donaldson, Zoe R. and Larry J. Young. 2008. "Oxytocin, Vasopressin, and the Neurogenetics of Sociality." *Science* 322: 900–904.

Doucouliagos, Christos and Patrice Laroche. 2003. "What Do Unions Do to Productivity? A Meta-Analysis." *Industrial Relations* 42: 650–691.

2009. "Unions and Profits: A Meta-Regression Analysis." *Industrial Relations* 48: 146–180.

Dougherty, Conor. 2017. "Signing Away the Right to Get a New Job." *The New York Times* (May 13).

2017. "Quit Your Job for a Better One? Not if Your Live in Idaho." *The New York Times* (July 14).

2018. "Illinois Wields New Power to Challenge Noncompete Agreements." *The New York Times* (October 25).

Douglas, Paul H. and J. Enoch Powell. *How Big Should Government Be?* Washington, DC: American Enterprise Institute.

Douglass, Lawrence. 2017. "Why Trump Wants to Disempower Institutions That Protect the Truth." *The Guardian* (February 2).

Douthat, Ross. 2019. "The Era of Limited Government Is Over." *The New York Times* (February 26).

DQYDJ (Don't Quit Your Day Job). "Income Percentile Calculator for 2016 US Data" (https://dqydj.com/household-income-percentile-calculator-2016/).

Dreu, Carsten K. W. De, et al. 2010. "The Neuropeptide Oxytocin Regulates Parochial Altruism in Intergroup Conflict among Humans." *Science* 328: 1408–1411.

2011. "Oxytocin Promotes Human Ethnocentrism." *PNAS* 108: 1262–1266.

Dreu, Carsten K. W. De. 2012. "Oxytocin Modulates Cooperation with and Competition between Groups: An Integrative Review and Research Agenda." *Hormones and Behavior* 61: 419–428.

Drutman, Lee. 2015. "The Divided States of America." *The New York Times* (September 22).

Dube, Arindrajit. 2017. "Minimum Wage and Job Loss: One Alarming Seattle Study Is Not the Last Word." *The New York Times* (July 20).

Dubofsky, Melvyn. 1994. *The State and Labor in Modern America*. Chapel Hill: University of North Carolina Press.

Dubofsky, Melvyn and Joseph A. McCartin. 2017. *Labor in America: A History*, 9th ed. Malden, MA: Wiley Blackwell.

Durkheim, Émile. 2014. "Preface to the Second Edition (1902)." In *The Division of Labor in Society*. New York: Free Press.

2014. *The Division of Labor in Society*. New York: Free Press.

Durkin, Erin. 2018. "Almost 350 News Outlets to Publish Editorials Denouncing Trump's 'Dirty War' on the Press." *The Guardian* (August 15).

Dworkin, Ronald. 1977. "What Rights Do We Have?" In *Taking Rights Seriously* (Cambridge: Harvard University Press), pp. 266–278.
  1984. "Rights as Trumps." In *Theories of Rights*, ed. Jeremy Waldron (Oxford: Oxford University Press), pp. 153–167.
  1985. "Liberalism." In *A Matter of Principle* (Cambridge: Harvard University Press), pp. 181–204.
  1986. *Law's Empire*. Cambridge: Harvard University Press.
  2000. *Sovereign Virtue*. Cambridge: Harvard University Press.
  2011. *Justice for Hedgehogs*. Cambridge: Harvard University Press.
Dwyer, Jim and Emma G. Fitzsimmons. 2019. "$462,646 in Pay for One Worker: M.T.A. Overtime Scrutinized by Prosecutors." *The New York Times* (May 17).
Dyck, Alexander, Adair Morse, and Luigi Zingales. 2007. "Who Blows the Whistle on Corporate Fraud." Working Paper 12882, National Bureau of Economic Research (February) (www.nber.org/papers/w12882.pdf).
  2010. "Who Blows the Whistle on Corporate Fraud?" *Journal of Finance* 65: 2213–2253.
Dynarski, Susan. 2018. "Fresh Proof That Strong Unions Help Reduce Income Inequality." *The New York Tines* (July 6).
Easterbrook, Frank H. and Daniel R. Fischel. 1981. "The Proper Role of a Target's Management in Responding to a Tender Offer." *Harvard Law Review* 94: 1161–1205.
Eaton, Amasa M. 1890. "On Contracts in Restraint of Trade." *Harvard Law Review* 4: 128–137.
Ebbinghaus, Bernhard. 2002. "Trade Unions' Changing Role: Membership Erosion, Organizational Reform, and Social Partnership in Europe." *Industrial Relations Journal* 2002: 465–483.
Eckholm, Erik. 2009. "Last Year's Poverty Rate Was Highest in Twelve Years: Median Family Income Fell." *The New York Times* (September 11).
Economic Policy Institute. 2016. "Drop in Union Membership Has Taken $14 to $52 Out of Nonunion Workers' Weekly Wages." In *The Top Charts of 2016* (December 22) (www.epi.org/publication/the-top-charts-of-2016-13-charts-that-show-the-difference-between-the-economy-we-have-now-and-the-economy-we-could-have/?mc_cid=f022fe6a6f&mc_eid=494a829c5c#chart6).
  2016. "The Productivity-Pay Gap" (updated August) (www.epi.org/productivity-pay-gap/?utm_source=Economic+Policy+Institute&utm_campaign=54f5cc5f0a-EMAIL_CAMPAIGN_2017_05_15&utm_medium=email&utm_term=0_e7c5826c50-54f5cc5f0a-58070685&mc_cid=54f5cc5f0a&mc_eid=494a829c5c).
  2017. "When Workers Have More Leverage, Income Growth Is More Equal: Union Membership and Share of Income Going to the Top 10 Percent in the U.S., 1917–2015." In Top Charts of 2017 (December 21).
Editorial. 2009. "Immigration and the Unions." *New York Times* (April 20).
  2014. "No Relief for Air Travelers." *The New York Times* (December 15).
  2016. "When States Fight to Overturn Good Local Labor Laws." *The New York Times* (February 19).
  2016. "Governor Walker Resumes His War on Workers." *The New York Times* (February 20).
  2016. "Violence and Corruption in a Prison Union." *The New York Times* (June 8).
  2016. "Shining a Light on Police Misconduct." *The Baltimore Sun* (July 14).

2016. "California Deposes Its 'Welfare Queen.'" *The New York Times* (July 23).
2016. "Unions in the Ivory Tower." *The New York Times* (August 24).
2016. "When Police Unions Impede Justice." *The New York Times* (September 3).
2016. "The Sad State of California's Direct Democracy." *Sacramento Bee* (October 15).
2017. "Can Trump Win His Battle with the Unionized, Bureaucratic 'Deep State'?" *Investor's Business Daily* (January 24).
2017. "Iowa's G.O.P. Statehouse Shows the Locals Who's Boss." *The New York Times* (February 21).
2017. "Kansas' Trickle-Down Flood of Red Ink." *The New York Times* (February 27).
2017. "The Gig Economy's False Promise." *The New York Times* (April 10).
2017. "Agreements That Lock Up Workers, Legally." *The New York Times* (May 16).
2017. "Union's Loss Is the South's Loss, Too." *The New York Times* (August 12).
2018. "West Virginia Teachers Give a Lesson in Union Power." *The New York Times* (March 2).
2018. "The Supreme Court Sticks It to Workers, Again." *The New York Times* (May 24).
2018. "After Janus, Unions Must Save Themselves." *The New York Times* (June 27).
2018. "A Gutted I.R.S. Makes the Rich Richer." *The New York Times* (December 25).
2019. "MBTA Pension System Operates Like a Ponzi Scheme." *Boston Globe* (February 25).
2019. "Trump's War on Worker Rights." *The New York Times* (June 3).
Edmondson, Catie and Jaclyn Peiser. 2018. "Trump's Tariffs on Canadian Newsprint Hasten Local Newspapers' Demise." *The New York Times* (August 9).
Edsall, Thomas B. 2014. "Republicans Sure Love to Hate Unions." *The New York Times* (November 18).
2016. "Is Trump Wrecking Both Parties?" *The New York Times* (August 11).
Edwards, Chris. 2010. "Public Sector Unions." *Tax & Budget Bulletin* No. 61 (Cato Institute, March).
Ehrenreich, Barbara. 2017. "Divisions of Labor." *The New York Times* (February 23).
Eisenbrey, Ross. 2007. "Strong Unions, Strong Productivity." *Economic Snapshot*. Economic Policy Institute (June 20) (www.epi.org/publication/webfeatures_snapshots_20070620/).
Eisinger, Jesse. 2017. *The Chickenshit Club: Why the Justice Department Fails to Prosecute Executives*. New York: Simon & Schuster.
Elk, Mike. 2017. "Pro-Union Rally in Mississippi Unites Workers with Community: 'We Are Ready.'" *The Guardian* (March 5).
2017. "Can Unions Rebuild the Labor Movement in the US South?" *The Guardian* (April 28).
2017. "Nissan Attacked for One of 'Nastiest Anti-Union Campaigns' in Modern History." *The Guardian* (August 1).
2017. "Danny Glover and Bernie Sanders Seek France's Help after Nissan Union Vote." *The Guardian* (August 12).
2017. "Alabama Unions See Doug Jones's Win as a Victory for Organized Labor." *The Guardian* (December 16).
2017. "Christmas Tree Cutters' Labor Fight Shines Light on Holiday Season's Forgotten Workers." *The Guardian* (December 18).

2018. "Justice in the Factory: How Black Lives Matter Breathed New Life into Unions." *The Guardian* (February 10).
2018. "Undocumented Workers Find New Ally as Unions Act to Halt Deportations." *The Guardian* (March 22).
2018. "Wave of Teachers' Wildcat Strikes Spreads to Oklahoma and Kentucky." *The Guardian* (April 2).
2018. "'Arab Spring for Teachers': Educators in Oklahoma Join Wave of Strikes." *The Guardian* (April 4).
2018. "Unions Leader Faces Members' Protest over Sexual Misconduct Claims." *The Guardian* (April 22).
2018. "America's Teachers on Strike: 'We Are Done Being the Frog That Is Being Boiled.'" *The Guardian* (May 5).
2018. "North Carolina Teachers Join Wave of Strikes with One-Day Walkout." *The Guardian* (May 16).
2018. "North Carolina Activists Pick Next Battle after $15 Minimum Wage Win." *The Guardian* (May 31).
2018. "'Vilified Too Long': Teachers' Unions Fight Back after Supreme Court Ruling." *The Guardian* (July 1).
2018. "US Government Failing Millions by Paying below $15 an Hour, Study Finds." *The Guardian* (August 10).
Ellguth, Peter and Susanne Kohaut. 2015. "Tarifbindung und betriebliche Interessenvertretung: Ergebnisse aus dem IAB-Betriebspanel 2014." *WSI-Mitteilungen* 4/2015: 290-29 (www.boeckler.de/wsi-mitteilungen_54287_54297.htm).
Elliott, Philip. 2018. "The Koch Brothers Plan to Spend a Record-Setting $400 Million." *Time* (January 28).
Ellison, Keith. 2016. "John Stumpf's Wells Fargo Racket Shows Why Bank Workers Need a Union." *The Daily Beast* (September 28).
Elster, Jon. 1983. *Sour Grapes: Studies in the Subversion of Rationality.* Cambridge: Cambridge University Press.
Elster, Jon and John E. Roemer. 1991. "Introduction." In *Interpersonal Comparisons of Well-Being* (Cambridge: Cambridge University Press), pp. 1–11.
Ember, Sydney. 2015. "Journalists at Gawker Media's Websites Are Planning to Unionize." *The New York Times* (April 16).
2017. "Los Angeles Times Newsroom, Challenging Tronc, Goes Public with Union Push." *The New York Times* (October 4).
2018. "Union Is Formed at Los Angeles Times and Publisher Put on Leave." *The New York Times* (January 19).
Epps, Garrett. 2018. "The Bogus 'Free Speech' Argument Against Unions." *The Atlantic* (February 14).
Epstein, Richard A. 2013. "Labor Unions: Saviors or Scourges?" *Capital University Law Review* 41: 1–33.
2014. *The Classical Liberal Constitution.* Cambridge: Harvard University Press.
2016. "What's Wrong with Labor Unions?" *Free Thoughts Podcast,* Episode 124 (Libertaraisnism.org., March 4) (www.libertarianism.org/media/free-thoughts/whats-wrong-labor-unions).
Erlanger, Steven. 2017. "After Grenfell Tower Fire, U.K. Asks: Has Deregulation Gone Too Far?" *The New York Times* (June 28).

Ewing, Jack. 2013. "Amazon's Labor Relations Under Scrutiny in Germany." *The New York Times* (March 3).
  2017. "Prosecutors Investigate Payments to Volkswagen Labor Leader." *The New York Times* (May 12).
Faeste, Lars, et al. 2016. "How Nordic Boards Create Exceptional Value." Boston Consulting Group (June).
Fairris, David and Edward Levine. 2004. "Declining Union Density in Mexico, 1984–2000." *Monthly Labor Review* 127: 10–17.
Faraday, George. 2018. "Trump's Government Is America's Top Low Wage Job Creator." *Good Jobs Nation* (August 2018) (http://goodjobsnation.org/content/uploads/2018/08/Broken-Promises1.pdf).
Farber, Henry S. 2005. "Union Membership in the United States: The Divergence between the Public and Private Sectors." Working Paper #503, Princeton University, Industrial Relations Section (September) (https://core.ac.uk/download/pdf/6894934.pdf).
Farber, Henry S., Daniel Herbst, Ilyana Kuziemko, and Suresh Naidu. 2018. "Unions and Inequality over the Twentieth Century: New Evidence from Survey Data." (May 1) (http://tuvalu.santafe.edu/~snaidu/papers/union_sub3.pdf).
Farrell, Sean. 2016. "Uber Is Misleading Drivers about Its Legal Defeat, Claims Union." *The Guardian* (October 30).
Federal Reserve Bank of St. Louis and U.S. Office of Management and Budget. 2017. "Federal Net Outlays as Percent of Gross Domestic Product." Federal Reserve Bank of St. Louis (updated March 31, 2017) (https://fred.stlouisfed.org/series/FYONGDA188S).
Feigenbaum, James, Alexander Hertel-Fernandez, and Vanessa Williamson. 2018. "From the Bargaining Table to the Ballot Box: Political Effects of Right to Work Laws." *NBER Working Paper No. 24259*, National Bureau of Economic Research (January).
  2018. "Right-to-Work Laws Have Devasted Unions – and Democrats." *The New York Times* (March 8).
Feinberg, Joel. 1978. "Voluntary Euthanasia and the Inalienable Right to Life." *Philosophy and Public Affairs* 7: 93–123.
Feldstein, Martin. 1997. "How Big Should Government Be?" *National Tax Journal* 50: 197–213.
Ferguson, Thomas and Joel Rogers. 1986. *Right Turn: The Decline of the Democrats and the Future of American Politics*. New York: Hill and Wang.
Ferreras, Isabelle. 2017. *Firms as Political Entities*. Cambridge: Cambridge University Press.
Ferretii, Maria P. 2016. "Risk Imposition and Freedom." *Politics, Philosophy, and Economics* 15: 261–279.
Feuer, Alan. 2017. "Police Unions Complains of 'Blue Racism,' Then Regrets Word Choice." *The New York Times* (August 22).
Fisher, Max, and Amanda Taub. 2019. "When More Democracy Isn't More Democratic." *The New York Times* (January 21).
Fletcher, Bill Jr., 2012. *"They're Bankrupting Us!" And Twenty Other Myths about Unions*. Boston, MA: Beacon Press.
Flemming, Jack. 2018. "L.A. and Long Beach Port Workers Begin Striking." *Los Angeles Times* (June 19).

Florida, Richard. 2016. "The Geography of Middle Class Decline." *CityLab* (November 15).
Fogel, Robert William. 1989. *Without Consent or Contract: The Rise and Fall of American Slavery*. New York: Norton.
Follett, Mary Parker. 1923. *The New State*. London: Longmans, Greens and Co.
Forbath, William E. and Brishen Rogers. 2017. "A New Type of Labor Law for a New Type of Worker." *The New York Times* (September 4).
Frank, Thomas. 2017. "Are Elite Universities 'Safe Spaces'? Not If You're Starting a Union." *The Guardian* (September 9).
Fraser Institute. 2017. "Economic Freedom Ranking 2014" (www.fraserinstitute.org/economic-freedom/map?page=map&year=2014) (last accessed November 8, 2019).
  2018. "Economic Freedom of the World: 2018 Annual Report" (www.cato.org/economic-freedom-world).
Freeman, Michael. 2002. *Human Rights*. Oxford: Polity.
Freeman, Richard B. 1984. "Unionism Comes to the Public Sector." *NBER Working Paper No. 1452*, National Bureau of Economic Research (September).
Freeman, Richard B. and Eunice Han. 2012. "The War against Public Sector Collective Bargaining in the US." *Journal of Industrial Relations* 54: 386–408.
Freeman, Richard B. and James L. Medoff. 1984. *What Do Unions Do?* New York: Basic Books.
Freeman, Samuel. 2007. *Rawls*. London: Routledge.
Fried, Charles. 2017. "It's Unfair and Unjust. So Why Has Gerrymandering Lasted This Long? *The Boston Globe* (July 10).
Friedman, Milton. 1951. "Some Comments on the Significance of Labor Unions for Economic Policy." In *The Impact of the Union*, ed. David McCord Wright (New York: Harcourt, Brace), pp. 204–234.
  1955. "Marshall and Friedman on Union Strength: Comment." *The Review of Economics and Statistics* 37: 401–406.
  1962. *Capitalism and Freedom*. Chicago, IL: University of Chicago Press.
  1968. "The Role of Monetary Policy." *American Economic Review* 58: 1–17.
  1977. "Inflation and Unemployment." *Journal of Political Economy* 85: 451–472.
Friedman, Milton and Rose Friedman. 1980. *Free to Choose*. Orlando, FL: Harcourt, Inc.
Fukuyama, Francis. 2011. "Big Government Skeptic." *The New York Times* (May 8).
Fuller, Lon L. 1958. "Positivism and Fidelity to Law: A Reply to Professor Hart." *Harvard Law Review* 71: 630–672.
  2001. "Eunomics: The Theory of Good Order and Workable Social Arrangements." In *The Principles of Social Order: Selected Essays of Lon Fuller*, ed. Kenneth I. Winston (Oxford: Hart Publishing, rev ed.), pp. 59–78.
Fulton, L. 2015. "Worker Representation in Europe." European Trade Union Institute (www.worker-participation.eu/National-Industrial-Relations/Across-Europe/Trade-Unions2) (last accessed November 8, 2019).
Funston Advisory Services. 2015. "Setting a Course for the Future: Management and Operations Study and Best Practice Review for the New York City Office of the Comptroller's Asset Management Function." *Final Report* (December 15) (www.nytimes.com/interactive/2016/01/26/nyregion/new-york-city-pension-system-report.html).

Gabbatt, Adam. 2017. "Seven Months Long, 1,800 Out...Epic Strike Mirrors US Unions' Fight to Survive." *The Guardian* (November 3).
Gabriel, Trip. 2018. "In a Comically Drawn Pennsylvania District, the Voters Are Not Amused." *The New York Times* (January 26).
  2018. "My Union or My President? Dueling Loyalties Mark Pennsylvania Race." *The New York Times* (March 11).
Galbraith, John Kenneth. 1993. *American Capitalism: The Concept of the Countervailing Power*. New Brunswick, NJ: Transaction Publishers.
Galles, Gary. 2014. "Labor Unions and Freedom of Association." *Mises Daily Articles* (Mises Institute, March 4).
Gambino, Lauren. 2019. "Senate to Vote on Pair of Bills that Could End Government Shutdown." *The Guardian* (January 22).
Ganz, John. 2017. "Libertarians Have More in Common with the Alt-Right than They Want You to Think." *The Washington Post* (September 19).
Garcia, Emma and Lawrence Mishel. 2016. "Unions and the Allocation of Teacher Quality in Public Schools." *EPI Report*. Economic Policy Institute. (April 7) (www.epi.org/publication/unions-and-the-allocation-of-teacher-quality-in-public-schools/?utm_source=Economic+Policy+Institute&utm_campaign=5f58bb3994-EPI_News_04_08_164_8_2016&utm_medium=email&utm_term=0_e7c5826c50-5f58bb3994-58070685).
Garcia, Emma and John Schmitt. 2018. "Teacher Unions and Students' Long-Term Economic Prospects." *Working Economics Blog*, Economic Policy Institute. (April 19).
Gaus, Gerald F. 1996. *Justificatory Liberalism*. Oxford: Oxford University Press.
  2010. "On Two Critics of Justificatory Liberalism: A Response to Wall and Lister." *Politics, Philosophy, and Economics* 9: 177–212.
Gay, Mara. 2018. "New York without the Daily New Will Be Less Alive, and Less Democratic." *The New York Times* (July 24).
Gayle, Caleb. 2018. "US Gig Economy: Data Shows 16m People in 'Contingent or Alternative' Work." *The Guardian* (June 7).
  2018. "Oklahoma Teachers' Salary Raise in Limbo Following Historic Win." *The Guardian* (June 16).
  2018. "Unions Brought Black Americans into the Middle Class. They're Now Being Decimated." *The Guardian* (August 14, 2018).
Gebeloff, Robert. 2018. "The Numbers That Explain Why Teachers Are in Revolt." *The New York Times* (June 4).
Geistfeld, Mark. 2001. "Reconciling Cost-Benefit Analysis with the Principle That Safety Matters More Than Money." *New York University Law Review* 76: 114–189.
General Accountability Office. 1991. "Government Contractors: Are Service Contractors Performing Inherently Governmental Functions?" GGD-92-11 (November 18).
Gentile, Giovanni. 2002. *Origins and Doctrine of Fascism*, ed. A. James Gregor. New Brunswick, NJ: Transaction Publishers.
George, Henry. 1897. "The Utility and Futility of Labor Strikes." *The Cleveland Recorder* (Sunday morning, September 5).
Gerstein, Terri. 2018. "These Americans Are Trapped in Their Jobs: They Need to Pay $10,000 to Quit." *The Guardian* (April 8).

Bibliography

Gessen, Masha. 2012. *The Man without a Face: The Unlikely Rise of Vladimir Putin.* New York: Riverhead Books.
  2018. "Barcelona's Experiment in Radical Democracy." *The New Yorker* (August 6).
Ghilarducci, Teresa. 2015. "Farewell to America's Middle Class: Unions Are Basically Dead." *The Atlantic* (October 28).
Gilens, Martin. 2012. *Affluence and Influence: Economic Inequality and Political Influence in America.* Princeton, NJ: Princeton University Press.
Gilens, Martin and Benjamin I. Page. 2014. "Testing Theories of American Politics: Elites, Interest Groups, and Average Citizens." *Perspectives on Politics* 12: 564–581.
Gleick, James. 1987. *Chaos: Making a New Science.* New York: Penguin Books.
Glenza, Jessica. 2017. "Tobacco: A Deadly Business: Big Tobacco Still Sees Big Business in America's Poor." *The Guardian* (July 13).
  2018. "'Double Whammy': Teachers Strike as Healthcare Costs Cut into Earnings." *The Guardian* (April 2).
Glover, Mark. 2015. "Gas Prices in Sacramento, throughout California Are in Full Flight." *The Sacramento Bee* (March 2).
Gold, Michael Evan. 2014. *An Introduction to Labor Law*, 3rd ed. Ithaca, NY: ILR Press.
Goldberg, Jonah. 2011. "Public Unions Must Go." *Los Angeles Times* (February 22).
Goldberg, Michelle. 2018. "The Teachers Revolt in West Virginia." *The New York Times* (March 5).
  2018. "The Teachers' Revolt Spreads to Arizona." *The New York Times* (April 27).
  2018. "Democracy in Danger in Georgia." *The New York Times* (October 12).
Goldmacher, Shane. 2017. "Police Union Is Sending Officers to Iowa to Protest de Blasio.' *The New York Times* (December 18).
Goldstein, Dana. 2018. "Their Pay Has Stood Still. Now Oklahoma Teachers Could Be the Next to Walk." *The New York Times* (March 20).
  2018. "Teachers in Oklahoma and Kentucky Walk Out: 'It Really Is a Wildfire.'" *The New York Times* (April 2).
  2018. "Teacher Pay Is So Low in Some U.S. School Districts That They're Recruiting Overseas." *The New York Times* (May 2).
  2018. "Arizona Teachers End Walkout as Governor Signs Bill Approving Raises." *The New York Times* (May 3).
  2018. "Why the Teacher Walkout Movement Won't Reach Every State." *The New York Times* (May 16).
Goldstein, Dana and Alexander Burns. 2018. "Teacher Walkouts Threaten Republican Grip on Conservative States." *The New York Times* (April 12).
Goldstein, Dana and Elizabeth Dias. 2018. "Oklahoma Teachers End Walkout after Winning Raises and Additional Funding." *The New York Times* (April 12).
Goldstein, Dana and Erica L. Green. 2018. "What the Janus Decision Means for Teacher Unions." *The New York Times* (June 27).
Goldstein, Joseph. 2017. "Along New York Harbor, 'On the Waterfront' Endures." *The New York Times* (January 7).
Gongloff, Mark. 2014. "45 Million Americans Still Stuck below Poverty Line: Census." *The Huffington Post* (September 16).
González-Ricoy, Iñigo. 2014. "The Republican Case for Workplace Democracy." *Social Theory and Practice* 40: 232–254.
Goodman, Peter S. 2013. "McDonald's Budget Plan Leaves Out Critical Line: Corporate Welfare." *The Huffington Post* (July 17).

2017. "Nordic-Style Designs Sit at Heart of French Labor Plan." *The New York Times* (October 26).
Goodnow, Natalie. 2015. "'By the People': A Q&A with Charles Murray." American Enterprise Institute (May 11).
Goodwin, Matthew J. 2017. "Old Labour, New Labour, No Labour." *The New York Times* (January 11).
Gordon, Scott. 1973. "The Wage-Fund Controversy: The Second Round." *History of Political Economy* 5: 14–35.
Gough, Neil. 2017. "The Workers Who Regret Trump's Scrapping of a Trade Deal." *The New York Times* (March 1).
2017. "Even Harley-Davidson Can't Resist the Tug of Overseas Factories." *The New York Times* (May 23).
Gould, Elise. 2015. "2014 Continues a 35-Year Trend of Broad-Based Wage Stagnation." *Issue Brief #393*. Economic Policy Institute (February 19) (www.epi.org/publication/stagnant-wages-in-2014/).
2017. "Racial Gaps in Wages, Wealth, and More: A Quick Recap." Economic Policy Institute (January 26) (www.epi.org/blog/racial-gaps-in-wages-wealth-and-more-a-quick-recap/).
2017. "The State of American Wages 2016." Economic Policy Institute (March 9) (www.epi.org/files/pdf/122078.pdf).
2017. "First Half 2017 Data Reveal Broadly Based Wage Growth, but Inequality Persists." Economic Policy Institute (August 1) (www.epi.org/blog/first-half-2017-data-reveal-broadly-based-wage-growth-but-inequality-persists/).
2019. "State of Working America Wages 2018." Economic Policy Institute (February 22).
Gould, Elise and Will Kimball. 2015. "'Right-to-Work' States Still Have Lower Wages." EPI Briefing Paper #395, Economic Policy Institute (April 22) (http://s1.epi.org/files/pdf/82934.pdf).
Gould, Elise and Adriana Krugler. 2017. "Latina Workers Have to Work 10 Months into 2017 to Be Paid the Same as White Non-Hispanic Men in 2016." *Working Economic Blog*, Economic Policy Institute (November 1).
Gould, Elise and Celine McNicholas. 2017. "Unions Help Narrow the Gender Wage Gap." *Working Economics Blog*, Economic Policy Institute (April 3).
Gould, Elise, Jessica Schieder, and Kathleen Geier. 2016. "What Is the Gender Pay Gap and Is It Real?" Economic Policy Institute (October 20) (www.epi.org/files/pdf/112962.pdf).
Gourevitch, Alex. 2016. "Quitting Work but Not the Job: Liberty and the Right to Strike." *Perspectives on Politics* 14: 307–323.
Gourevitch, Alex and Lucas Stanczyk. 2018. "The Basic Income Illusion." *Catalyst* 1(Winter): 151–177.
Gourevitch, Peter et al., eds. 1984. *Unions and Economic Crisis: Britain, West Germany, and Sweden*. London: George Allen & Unwin.
Grabell, Michael. 2017. "Exploitation and Abuse at the Chicken Plant." *The New Yorker* (May 8).
Grant, Daniel. 2018. "Developers Fight Efforts to Make Them Pay for Public Art." *The New York Times* (July 10).
Green, Carla and Sam Levin. 2017. "Homeless, Assaulted, Broke: Drivers Left Behind as Uber Promises Change at the Top." *The Guardian* (June 17).

Green, Erica L. 2018. "Teachers Unions Scramble to Save Themselves after Supreme Court's Blow." *The New York Times* (July 14).
Greenberg, Zoe. 2018. "Norman Seabrook, Ex-Leader of Jail Officers, Guilty of Bribery in Trial That Cast Shadow over de Blasio." *The New York Times* (August 15).
Greenhouse, Linda. 2018. "Two Ways of Looking at Gerrymandering." *The New York Times* (January 4).
Greenhouse, Steven. 2004. *The Big Squeeze: Tough Times for the American Worker*. New York: Random House.
  2011. "Union Membership in U.S. Fell Sharply in 2010." *The New York Times* (January 1).
  2012. "Union Membership Rate Fell Again in 2011." *The New York Times* (January 27, 2012).
  2013. "Share of the Work Force in a Union Falls to a 97-Year Low." *The New York Times* (January 23).
  2014. "Wisconsin's Legacy for Unions." *The New York Times* (February 22).
  2014. "Low-Wage Workers Finding It's Easier to Fall into Poverty, and Harder to Get Out." *The New York Times* (March 16).
  2014. "In a Bid for Revote, Union Claims Tennessee Officials Frightened Workers." *The New York Times* (April 4).
  2014. "Noncompete Clauses Increasingly Pop Up in Array of Jobs." *The New York Times* (June 8).
  2014. "The Changing Face of Temporary Employment." *The New York Times* (August 31).
  2014. "More Workers Are Claiming 'Wage Theft'." *The New York Times* (August 31).
  2014. "Study Finds Violations of Wage Law in New York and California." *The New York Times* (December 3).
  2014. "McDonald's Is Charged with Punishing Workers." *The New York Times* (December 19).
  2015. "Movement to Increase McDonald's Minimum Wage Broadens Its Tactics." *The New York Times* (March 30).
  2016. "How the $15 Minimum Wage Went from Laughable to Viable." *The New York Times* (April 1).
  2016. "Labor Movement Braces for Three-Front Battle with Trump, Congress and Courts." *The Guardian* (November 14).
  2016. "What Unions Got Wrong about Trump." *The New York Times* (November 26).
  2017. "The Unions That Like Trump." *The New York Times* (April 8).
  2017. "Is Trump Really Pro-Worker?" *The New York Times* (September 2).
  2018. "Fast-Food Workers Claim Victory in a New York Labor Effort." *The New York Times* (January 9).
  2018. "How Trump Betrays 'Forgotten' Americans." *The New York Times* (September 3).
  2018. "Billionaires v Teachers: The Koch Brothers' Plan to Starve Public Education." *The Guardian* (September 7).
  2019. "Dear Delta Air Lines: Video Games and Beer Cannot Compete with Joining a Union." *The Guardian* (May 11).
  2019. "AFL-CIO Leadership: The Two Women Vying to Be America's Top Labor Official." *The Guardian* (July 8).

Greenhut, Steven. 2014. "Salary Info Shows Fruits of Union Muscle." *The San Diego Union-Tribune* (December 26).

Greenstone, Michael and Adam Looney. 2012. "A Record Decline in Government Jobs: Implications for the Economy and America's Workforce." *The Hamilton Project* (August 3) (www.hamiltonproject.org/files/downloads_and_links/0803_jobs_government_employment.pdf)

Gregg, Aaron. 2018. "While Federal Employment Shrinks in D.C., Government Contractors Are on a Hiring Spree." *The Washington Post* (July 22).

Gregor, A. James. 1969. *The Ideology of Fascism*. New York: The Free Press.

Grierson, Jamie and Rob Davies. 2017. "Pimlico Plumbers Loses Appeal against Self-Employed Status." *The Guardian* (February 10).

Gross, Daniel. 2013. "McDonald's and Visa Conjure Fantasy Budget for Low-Wage Employees." *The Daily Beast* (July 16).

Gross, James A., ed. 2003. *Workers' Rights as Human Rights*. Ithaca, NY: ILR Press.

Gross, James A. 2003. "A Long Overdue Beginning." In *Workers' Rights as Human Rights* (Ithaca, NY: ILR Press), pp. 21–22.

   2010. *A Shameful Business: The Case for Human Rights in the American Workplace*. Ithaca, NY: ILR Press.

Gross, Jared S. 2005. "Yet Another Reappraisal of the Taft-Hartley Act Emergency Injunctions." *University of Pennsylvania Journal of Labor and Employment Law* 7: 305–339.

Gross, Neil. 2016. "The Decline of Unions and the Rise of Trump." *The New York Times* (August 12).

Grynbaum, Michael M. 2018. "Fox News Once Gave Trump a Perch. Now It's His Bullhorn." *The New York Times* (July 1).

Gwartney, James, Robert Lawson, and Joseph Hall. 2016. "Economic Freedom in the World: 2016 Annual Report." Fraser Institute (www.fraserinstitute.org/sites/default/files/economic-freedom-of-the-world-2016.pdf) (last accessed November 8, 2019).

Haberler, Gottfried. 1959. "Wage Policy and Inflation." In *The Public Stake in Union Power*, ed. Philip D. Bradley (New York: University of Virginia Press), pp. 63–85.

Hafiz, Hiba. 2018. "The Red-Scare Relic That Holds Back Smart Labor Policy." *The New York Times* (May 1).

Hagen, Ryan. 2017. "San Bernardino Officially Out of Bankruptcy." *San Bernardino County Sun* (June 19).

Hajnal, Zoltan, Nazita Lajevardi, and Lindsay Nielson. 2017. "Do Voter Identification Laws Suppress Minority Voting? Yes. We Did the Research." *Washington Post* (February 15).

   2017. "Voter Identification Laws and the Suppression of Minority Votes." *The Journal of Politics* 79: 363–379.

Halchin, L. Elaine, Kate M. Manuel, Shawn Reese, and Moshe Schwartz. 2010. "Inherently Governmental Functions and Other Work Reserved for Performance by Federal Government Employees: The Obama Administration's Proposed Policy Letter." Washington, DC: Congressional Research Service (October 1) (http://digitalcommons.ilr.cornell.edu/key_workplace/761/).

Hale, Robert. 1923. "Coercion and Distribution in a Supposedly Non-Coercive State." *Political Science Quarterly* 38: 470–494.

Halpern, Sheldon W. 1987. "Application of the Doctrine of Commercial Impracticability: Searching for 'the Wisdom of Solomon.'" *University of Pennsylvania Law Review* 135: 1123–1178.
Hamaji, Kate, Rachel Deutsch, and Elizabeth Nicolas (for the Center for Popular Democracy), and Celine McNicholas, Heidi Shierholz, and Margaret Poydock (for the Economic Policy Institute), "Unchecked Corporate Power: Forced Arbitration, the Enforcement Crisis, and How Workers Are Fighting Back" (May 2019).
Hammer, Tove Helland and Ariel Avgar. 2007. "The Impact of Unions on Job Satisfaction, Organizational Commitment, and Turnover." In *What Do Unions Do? A Twenty-Year Perspective*, eds. James T. Bennett and Bruce E. Kaufman (New Brunswick, NJ: Transaction Publishers), pp. 346–372.
Hampton, Meissa. 2018. "Hollywood's Biggest Union Turned a Blind Eye to Sexual Abuse." *The Guardian* (January 18).
Han, Eunice S. 2016. "The Myth of Unions' Overprotection of Bad Teachers: Evidence from the District-Teacher Matched Panel Data on Teacher Turnover." Wellesley College (February 27) (http://haveyouheardblog.com/wp-content/uploads/2016/07/Han_Teacher_dismissal_Feb_16.pdf).
Hancock, Peter. 2015. "Public Employee Unions Fear Loss of Numbers under New Kansas Law." *Lawrence Journal-World* (July 6).
Handler, Milton. 1971. "Labor and Antitrust: A Bit of History." *Antitrust Law Journal* 40: 233–241.
Handler, Milton and William C. Zifchak. 1981. "Collective Bargaining and the Antitrust Laws: The Emasculation of the Labor Exemption." *Columbia Law Review* 81: 459–515.
Hanif, Farooq, et al. 2016. "The Coming Pension Crisis: Recommendations for Keeping the Global Pensions System Afloat." *Citi GPS: Global Perspectives & Solutions* (March) (https://ir.citi.com/A44lKhe6CVSitfkypsON6kDXypHYjJ%2BENxq8FLMoTBde6kse9Kt9KQ%3D%3D).
Hansen, Alvin H. 1953. *A Guide to Keynes*. New York: McGraw-Hill.
Harel, Alon. 2019. "Why Privatization Matters: The Democratic Case against Privatization." In *Privatization: Nomos LX*, eds. Jack L. Knight and Melissa Schwartzberg (New York: New York University Press), pp. 52–78.
Harris, Elizabeth A. 2016. "Judge, Citing Inequality, Orders Connecticut to Overhaul Its School System." *The New York Times* (September 7).
  2016. "Columbia Challenges Vote by Graduate Students to Unionize." *The New York Times* (December 19).
  2018. "Columbia University Says It Won't Bargain with Graduate Student Union." *The New York Times* (January 30).
  2018. "Jersey City Teachers Go on Strike Over Health Insurance." *The New York Times* (March 16).
Harrison, John. 2017. "The Unitary Executive and the Scope of Executive Power." *The Yale Law Journal Forum* 125 (January 24): 374–380.
Hart, Angela. 2017. "Labor Got Higher Wages in California's Housing Deal. Will Affordable Homes Still Be Built?" *Sacramento Bee* (October 6).
Hart, Herbert Lionel Adolphus. 1955. "Are There Any Natural Rights?" *The Philosophical Review* 64: 175–191.
  1994. *The Concept of Law*, 2nd ed. Oxford: Oxford University Press.

Hatch, Julia. 2004. "Employment in the Public Sector: Two Recessions' Impact on Jobs." *Monthly Labor Review* 127(October): 38–47.
Hatton, Erin. 2013. "The Rise of the Permanent Temp Economy." *The New York Times* (January 26).
Hayek, Friedrich A. 2009 [1935]. "The Nature and History of the Problem." In *Collectivist Economic Planning: Critical Studies on the Possibilities of Socialism*, ed. Friedrich A. Hayek (Auburn, AL: Ludwig von Mises Institute), pp. 1–40.
  2009 [1935]. "The Present State of the Debate." In *Collectivist Economic Planning: Critical Studies on the Possibilities of Socialism*, ed. Friedrich A. Hayek (Auburn, AL: Ludwig von Mises Institute), pp. 201–243.
  1944. *The Road to Serfdom*. London: Routledge.
  1945. "The Use of Knowledge in Society." *American Economic Review* 35:519–530.
  1948. "'Free' Enterprise and Competitive Order." In *Individualism and Economic Order* (Chicago, IL: University of Chicago Press), pp. 107–118.
  1948. "The Meaning of Competition." In *Individualism and Economic Order* (Chicago, IL: University of Chicago Press), pp. 92–106.
  1959. "Unions, Inflation, and Profits." In *The Public Stake in Union Power*, ed. Philip D. Bradley (New York: University of Virginia Press), pp. 46–62.
  1960. "Labor Unions and Employment." In *The Constitution of Liberty* (London: Routledge), pp. 233–247.
  1960. *The Constitution of Liberty*. London: Routledge.
  1967. "The Corporation in a Democratic Society: In Whose Interest Ought It to and Will It Be Run?" In *Studies in Philosophy, Politics and Economics* (London: Routledge & Kegan Paul), pp. 300–312.
  1978. "Economic Freedom and Representative Government." In *New Studies in Philosophy, Politics, Economics and the History of Ideas* (London: Routledge & Kegan Paul), pp. 105–118.
  1980. "A Testing Time for Monetarism." Letter to the Editor, *The Times* (June 13).
  1984. *1980s Unemployment and the Unions*, 2nd ed. London: Institute of Economic Affairs.
Healy, Jack. 2018. "Denver Post Editor Who Criticized Paper's Ownership Resigns." *The New York Times* (May 3).
Healy, Patrick and Monica Davey. 2015. "Behind Scott Walker, a Longstanding Conservative Alliance against Unions." *The New York Times* (June 8).
Heathfield, David F., ed. 1977. *The Economics of Co-Determination*. London: Macmillan.
Hebdon, Robert, Joseph E. Slater, and Marick F. Masters. 2013. "Public Sector Collective Bargaining: Tumultuous Times." In *Collective Bargaining under Stress: Case Studies of Major U.S. Industries*, eds. Howard R. Stanger, Ann C. Frost, and Paul F. Clark (Champaign, IL: Labor and Employment Relations Association), pp. 251–292.
Hecht, Peter. 2013. "Lambasting Wall Street, Federal Judge Allows Stockton to Seek Bankruptcy Protection." *Sacramento Bee* (April 2).
Heery, Edmund. 2016. *Framing Work: Unitary, Pluralist, and Critical Perspectives in the Twentieth-First Century*. Oxford: Oxford University Press.
Heller, Nathan. 2017. "Is the Gig Economy Working?" *The New Yorker* (May 15).
Helmore, Edward. 2018. "Over 400,000 People Living in 'Modern Slavery' in US, Report Finds." *The Guardian* (July 19).
  2018. "News Workers Unionized. Days Later, They Were Jobless. Was It Payback?" *The Guardian* (November 4).

Hennelley, Bob. 2017. "From the Supreme Court to a Constitutional Convention, Labor Is on the Defensive." City & State New York (August 27).
Henry, Mary Kay. 2019. "How Workers Are Winning $15 an Hour: By Acting Like a Union." *The Guardian* (January 17).
Hertel-Fernandez, Alexander, Caroline Tervo, and Theda Skocpol. 2018. "How the Koch Brothers Built the Most Powerful Rightwing Group You've Never Heard Of." *The Guardian* (September 26).
Herzog, Lisa. 2015. "Capitalism, but Better?" *Res Publica* 21: 99–103.
  2016. "The Normative Stakes of Economic Growth; Or, Why Adam Smith Does Not Rely on 'Trickle Down.'" *Journal of Politics* 78: 50–62.
  2017. "Durkheim on Social Justice: The Argument from Organic Solidarity." *American Political Science Review* 112: 112–124.
Hicks, Michael. 2018. "Ruling against Public-Sector Unions Makes Us Freer." *IndyStar* (July 1).
Higgins, Rich. 2017. "POTUS and Political Warfare." (May) (https://assets.documentcloud.org/documents/3922874/Political-Warfare.pdf).
Hill, Joe. 1910. "The Preacher and the Slave" (www.youtube.com/watch?v=PJ236CwhlPw) (as performed by Utah Phillips, January 9, 2011) (last accessed November 8, 2019).
Hillman, Robert A. 1978–1979. "Policing Contract Modifications under the UCC: Good Faith and the Doctrine of Economic Duress." *Iowa Law Review* 64 (1978–1979): 849–902.
  1981–1982. "Contract Modification under the Restatement (Second) of Contracts." *Cornell Law Review* 67: 680–703.
Hiltzik, Michael. 2014. "Are Unions Necessary?" *Los Angeles Times* (February 27).
Hirsch, Barry T. 2007. "What Do Unions Do for Economic Performance?" In *What Do Unions Do? A Twenty-Year Perspective*, eds. James T. Bennett and Bruce E. Kaufman (New Brunswick, NJ: Transaction Publishers), pp. 193–237.
Hirsch, Barry T. and John T. Addison. 1984. *The Economic Analysis of Unions: New Approaches and Evidence*. Boston, MA: Allen & Unwin.
Hirschman, Albert O. 1970. *Exit, Voice, and Loyalty: Responses to Declines in Firms*, New ed. Cambridge: Harvard University Press.
Ho, Catherine. 2018. "Uber Sees Legal Win in Appeal of Case over Driver Status." *San Francisco Chronicle* (September 25).
Ho, Vivian. 2019. "Oakland Teachers Strike for Better Pay as Tech Wealth Transforms City." *The Guardian* (February 21).
Hobbes, Thomas. 1811. "De Corpore Politico." In *The English Works of Thomas Hobbes of Malmsbury*, Volume 4 (London: John Bohn), pp. 77–228.
  1991, 1996. *Leviathan*. Cambridge: Cambridge University Press.
  1998. *On the Citizen*. Cambridge: Cambridge University Press.
Hodgson, Geoffrey M. 2006. "What Are Institutions?" *Journal of Economic Issues* 40: 1–25.
Hogler, Raymond L. 2011. "How Right to Work Is Destroying the American Labor Movement: From the Ku Klux Klan to the Tea Party." *Employee Responsibilities and Rights Journal* 23: 295–304.
  2015. *The End of American Labor Unions: The Right-to-Work Movement and the Erosion of Collective Bargaining*. Santa Barbara, CA: Praeger.
  2017. "How Noncompete Clauses Clash with US Labor Law." *The Conversation* (August 23).

Holan, Angie Drobnic. 2011. "Ad from Save America's Postal Service Claims Rule from Congress Is Causing USPS's Financial Problems." *Politifact* (September 29).
Holmberg, Susan R. 2019. "Workers on Corporate Boards? Germany's Had Them, for Decades." *The New York Times* (January 6).
Holohan, Meghan. 2018. "Striking Teachers Go Out of Their Way to Make Sure Students Have Food." *Today* (March 5).
Hooker, Brad. 2003. *Ideal Code, Real World*. Oxford: Oxford University Press.
Horton, Alex. 2015. "Kentucky Governor Apologizes for Comments Suggesting Kids Were Sexually Assaulted While Teachers Protested." *The Washington Post* (April 15).
Hovenkamp, Herbert. 2008. *The Antitrust Enterprise*. Cambridge: Harvard University Press.
Hsieh, Nien-Hê. 2005. "Rawlsian Justice and Workplace Republicanism." *Social Theory and Practice* 31: 115–142.
  2008. "Justice in Production." *The Journal of Political Philosophy* 16: 72–100.
  2008. "Workplace Democracy, Workplace Republicanism, and Economic Democracy." *Revue de Philosophie Économique/Review of Economic Philosophy* 8: 57–78.
Hsu, Tiffany. 2018. "Trucks Built by a Woman Are Still Rare in America Even as Worker Shortages Loom." *The New York Times* (September 27, 2018).
Hubbard, Ben. 2013. "Saudi Women Rise Up, Quietly, and Slide into the Driver's Seat." *The New York Times* (October 26).
Hudson, Gerry. 2017. "The Labor Movement Fought for Civil Rights Before. We Will Do It Again." *The Guardian* (September 4).
Human Rights Campaign, et al. 2018. "Brief as Amici Curiae in Support of Respondents in Janus v. AFSCME," No, 16-1466, Supreme Court of the United States (January 19) (www.lambdalegal.org/sites/default/files/legal-docs/downloads/janus_v_american_federation_amicus_final_to_be_filed.pdf).
Hurd, Rick. 2017. "Oakland Workers Strike, Bringing City Services to a Halt, with No End in Sight." *East Bay Times* (December 5).
Hutt, William H. 1964. *The Economics of the Colour Bar*. London: Andre Deutsch.
  1980. *The Theory of Collective Bargaining, 1930–1975*. San Francisco, CA: Cato Institute, [1930].
Huxley, Aldous. 1932. *Brave New World*. London: Chatto & Windus.
Hyman, Richard. 2001. *Understanding European Trade Unionism: Between Market, Class and Society*. London: Sage.
Ingraham, Christopher. 2018. "One State Fixed Its Gerrymandered Districts, the Other Didn't. Here's How the Election Played Out in Both." *The Washington Post* (November 9).
Institute for Public Policy Research. 2018. *Prosperity and Justice: A Plan for the New Economy*. London: Polity.
Internal Revenue Service. 2017. "Publication 15-A." Department of the Treasury (January 5).
Irwin, Neil. 2014. "When the Guy Making Your Sandwich Has a Noncompete Clause." *The New York Times* (October 14).
  2015. "Job Growth Looks Great; Wage Growth, Less So." *The New York Times* (January 9).
  2016. "How a Quest by Elites Is Driving 'Brexit' and Trump." *The New York Times* (July 1).

2017. "The Question Isn't Why Wage Growth Is So Low, It's Why It's So High." *The New York Times* (May 26).
2017. "To Understand Rising Inequality, Consider the Janitors at Two Top Companies, Then and Now." *The New York Times* (September 3).
Israel, Salomon, et al. 2009. "The Oxytocin Receptor (OXTR) Contributes to Prosocial Fund Allocations in the Dictator Game and the Social Value Orientations Task." *PLOS One* 4: e5535.
Ivory, Danielle and Caitlin Dickerson. 2018. "Safety Concerns Grow as Inmates Are Guarded by Teachers and Secretaries." *The New York Times* (June 17).
Jackson, Benjamin. 2015. "Hayek, Hutt and the Trade Unions." In *Hayek: A Collaborative Biography: Part V Hayek's Great Society of Free Men*, ed. Robert Leeson (London: Palgrave Macmillan), pp. 159–175.
Jackson, Gregory. 2005. "Contested Boundaries: Ambiguity and Creativity in the Evolution of German Codetermination." In *Beyond Continuity: Institutional Change in Advanced Political Economies* (Oxford: Oxford University Press), pp. 229–254.
Jackson, Preston. 2019. "Sac City Unified School District Needs More Sunshine." *Sacramento Bee* (March 6).
Jacob, Daniel and Christian Neuhäuser. 2018. "Workplace Democracy, Market Competition and Republican Self-Respect." *Ethical Theory and Moral Practice* 21: 927–944.
Jacobs, Ben. 2017. "Small Hand of Government: Trump's Aim to Shrink the State Pleases Conservatives." *The Guardian* (April 1).
Jaffe, Sarah. 2017. "Home Care Workers Have Our Lives in Their Hands. They're Paid Only $10 an Hour." *The Guardian* (July 13).
Jamieson, Dave. 2017. "Missouri Governor Signs Right-to-Work Bill Passed by GOP Legislature." *The Huffington Post* (February 6).
Jamison, Peter. 2016. "Paying for Public Retirees Has Never Cost L.A. Taxpayers More. And That's after Pension Reform." *Los Angeles Times* (November 18).
Janus, Mark. 2018. "Why I Took My Case over Forced Union Dues to the Supreme Court." *The Washington Post* (July 1).
Jardim, Ekaterina, et al. 2017. "Minimum Wage Increases, Wages, and Low-Employment: Evidence from Seattle." *NBER Working Paper No. 23532*, National Bureau of Economic Research (June).
Jauhiainen, Antti and Joona-Hermanni Mäkinen. 2017. "Why Finland's Basic Income Experiment Isn't Working." *The New York Times* (July 20).
Jesus College Cambridge. 2016. "The Future of Work." Rustat Conference Report (November 22) (www.jesus.cam.ac.uk/sites/default/files/inline/files/Rustat%20Conference%20Future%20Of%20Work%20report_0_0.pdf).
Joffe-Walt, Benjamin. 2006. "Lecturers Back Boycott of Israeli Academics." *The Guardian* (May 29).
John Paul II. 1991. Encyclical Letter. Centesimus Annus 40: AAS 93, 843.
Johnson, Kirk. 2017. "Where Anti-Tax Fervor Means 'All Services Will Cease.'" *The New York Times* (May 13).
Johnson, Richard W. and Benjamin G. Southgate. 2014. "Evaluating Retirement Income Security for Illinois Public School Teachers." Public Pension Project Report (Urban Institute, July) (www.urban.org/sites/default/files/publication/22821/413196-Evaluating-Retirement-Income-Security-for-Illinois-Public-School-Teachers.PDF).

Johnson, Steven. 2017. "Why Blue States Are the Real 'Tea Party.'" *The New York Times* (December 3).
Johnston, David Cay. 2010. "Scary New Wage Data." *Tax Notes* 129: 481–484.
  2018. "We Need Tax Police – and They Should Go after the Likes of Donald Trump." *The Guardian* (October 13).
Jones, Owen. 2017. "Why Britain's Trains Don't Run on Time: Capitalism." *The New York Times* (April 4).
Jones, Robert F. 2017. "The Collapse of American Identity." *The New York Times* (May 2).
Judson, Tim and Cristina Francisco-McGuire. 2012. "Where Theft Is Legal: Mapping Wage Theft Laws in the 50 States." *Progressive States Network* (June) (www.leg.state.co.us/CLICS/CLICS2013A/commsumm.nsf/b4a3962433b52fa787256e5f00670a71/e9b1f269d522a83b87257b3a006a03c8/$FILE/130326%20AttachE.pdf).
Kahneman, Daniel. 2011. *Thinking, Fast and Slow*. New York: Farrar, Strauss and Giroux.
Kahneman, Daniel, Jack L. Knetsch, and Richard Thaler. 1991. "The Endowment Effect, Loss Aversion, and the Status Quo Bias." *Journal of Economic Perspectives* 5: 193–206.
Kalecki, Michał. 1990. "Reduction of Wages during Crisis" (1932). In *Collected Works of Michał Kalecki: Volume I*, ed. Jerzy Osiatyński (Oxford: Oxford University Press), pp. 41–44.
  1991. "Money and Real Wages" (1939). In *Collected Works of Michał Kalecki: Volume II*, ed. Jerzy Osiatyński (Oxford: Oxford University Press), pp. 21–50.
Kantor, Jodi and Jennifer Medina. 2017. "Workers Say Andrew Puzder Is 'Not the One to Protect' Them, but He's Been Chosen To." *The New York Times* (January 15).
Kaufman, Bruce E. 1997. "Labor Markets and Employment Regulation: The View of the 'Old' Institutionalists." In *Government Regulation of the Employment Relationship*, ed. Bruce E. Kaufman (Madison, WI: Industrial Relations Research Association).
  2004. "What Unions Do: Insights from Economic Theory." *Journal of Labor Research* 25: 351–382.
  2007. "The Impossibility of a Perfectly Competitive Labour Market." *Cambridge Journal of Economics* 31: 775–787.
  2012. "An Institutional Economic Analysis of Labor Unions." *Industrial Relations* 51: 438–471.
Kaufman, Dan. 2015. "Labor's Last Stand." *The New York Times* (June 14).
  2016. "The Destruction of Progressive Wisconsin." *The New York Times* (January 16).
Kay, John Alexander and David J. Thompson. 1986. "Privatisation: A Policy in Search of a Rationale." *The Economic Journal* 96: 18–32.
Kazin, Michael. 2013. "How Labor Learned to Love Immigration." *The New Republic* (May 13).
Kearney, Richard C. and Patrice M. Mareschal. 2014. *Labor Relations in the Public Sector*, 5th ed. Boca Raton, LA: CRC Press.
Keefe, Jeffrey H. 2012. "State and Local Public Employees: Are They Overcompensated?" *ABA Journal of Labor and Employment Law* 27: 239–255.
  2013. "A Reconsideration and Empirical Evaluation of Wellington's and Winter's, 'The Unions and the Cities.'" *Comparative Labor Law and Policy Journal* 34: 251–275.

2015. "Eliminating Fair Share Fees and Making Public Employment 'Right-to-Work' Would Increase the Pay Penalty for Working in State and Local Government." EPI Briefing Paper #408 (October 13) (www.epi.org/files/pdf/93216.pdf).

2015. "Laws Enabling Public Sector Collective Bargaining Have Not Led to Excessive Public Sector Pay." EPI Briefing Paper, Economic Policy Institute (October 16).

2015. "On Friedrichs v. California Teachers Association." EPI Briefing Paper #411, Economic Policy Institute (November 2) (www.epi.org/files/pdf/94942.pdf).

Kelly, Kim. 2019. "Sara Nelson's Art of War." *The New Republic* (May 13).

Kenworthy, Lane. 2017. "Is Big Government Bad for Freedom, Civil Society, and Happiness?" *Evonomics* (May) (http://evonomics.com/big-government-bad-freedom-civil-society-happiness/).

Keynes, John Maynard. 1964 [1936]. *The General Theory of Employment, Interest, and Money*. San Diego, CA: Harvest/Harcourt edition.

Khouri, Andrew. 2018. "More Workers Are Saying Their Bosses Are Threatening to Have Them Deported." *Los Angeles Times* (January 2).

Kim, Kathleen. 2011. "The Coercion of Trafficked Workers." *Iowa Law Review* 96: 409–474.

Kim, E. Timothy. 2018. "Can Arizona's Teachers Still Consider Themselves Middle Class?" *The New Yorker* (May 2).

Kim, E. Tammy. 2019. "The Striking Demands of LA Teachers." *The New York Review of Books* (January 23).

Kimball, Will and Lawrence Mishel. 2015. "Union's Decline and the Rise of the Top 10 Percent's Share of Income." *Economic Snapshot*. Economic Policy Institute (February 3).

Kimball, Spencer L. and Noreen J. Parrett. 2000. "Creation of the Guarantee Association System." *Journal of Insurance Regulation* 19: 259–272.

King, Martin Luther Jr. 1968. "Address to Striking Sanitation Workers in Memphis, Tennessee." (March 18).

2011. *All Labor Has Dignity*, ed. Michael K. Honey (Boston, MA: Beacon Press).

Kirzner, Israel M. 1984. "Economic Planning and the Knowledge Problem." *Cato Journal* 4: 407–418.

Kitroeff, Natalie. 2017. "Californians Compete for a Rare Prize: A Blue-Collar Union Job Paying up to $200,000." *Los Angeles Times* (January 27).

2018. "Jobless Rate Looks Like Old Times, but the Economy Doesn't." *The New York Times* (May 4).

Klein, Naomi. 2017. "Labor Leaders' Cheap Deal with Trump." *The New York Times* (February 7).

Knight, Frank H. 1957. "Preface to the Re-Issue." In *Risk, Uncertainty, and Profit* (Mineola, NY: Dover Publications).

Knoll, Corina and Jeff Gottlieb. 2014. "Rizzo Gets 12 Years in Prison, Marking End to Scandal That Rocked Bell." *Los Angeles Times* (April 16).

Kochan, Thomas, Duanyi Yang, Erin L. Kelly, and Will Kimball. 2018. "Who Wants to Join a Union? A Growing Number of Americans." *The Conversation* (August 30).

Kolhatkar, Sheelah. 2018. "The Growth of Sinclair's Conservative Media Empire." *The New Yorker* (October 22).

2019. "Walmart and the Push to Put Workers on Company Boards." *The New Yorker* (March 26).

Koren, James Rufus. 2017. "L.A. Longshoremen Sentenced to 41 Months for Bilking Union Healthcare Plan." *Los Angeles Times* (January 16).
  2017. "Feds Order Wells Fargo to Rehire Whistleblower and Pay Him $5.4 Million." *Los Angeles Times* (April 3).
Korosec, Kirsten. 2018. "Why U.S. Health Care Costs Are Twice as High as Other High-Income Countries." *Forbes* (March 14).
Koseff, Alexi. 2014. "Rising Retirement Costs Help Drive UC Plan to Raise Tuition." *The Sacramento Bee* (November 16).
Kosfeld, Michael, et al. 2005. "Oxytocin Increases Trust in Humans." *Nature* 435: 673–676.
Kotch, Alex. 2018. "After Scoring Huge Tax Cuts, Charles Koch Floods Ryan with Cash." *International Business Times* (January 19).
Kotz, David M. 2015. *The Rise and Fall of Neoliberal Capitalism*. Cambridge: Harvard University Press.
Kovacs, Trey. 2016. "Time to Pare Back Union Legal Privileges." *Newsday* (September 2).
Krahmann, Elke. 2010. *States, Citizens and the Privatization of Security*. Cambridge: Cambridge University Press.
Kramer, Matthew H. 1998. "Rights without Trimmings." In *A Debate over Rights* (Oxford: Oxford University Press), pp. 7–111.
  1999. *In Defense of Legal Positivism: Law Without Trimmings*. Oxford: Oxford University Press.
  2003. *The Quality of Freedom*. Oxford: Oxford University Press.
  2008. "Liberty and Domination." In *Republicanism and Political Theory*, eds. Cecile Laborde and John Maynor (Oxford: Blackwell), pp. 31–57.
Krauss, Clifford. 2015. "After Steadily Falling, Price for Gas Notches an Increase." *The New York Times* (January 27).
Krauss, Clifford and Stanley Reed. 2015. "Oil Prices: What's behind the Drop? Simple Economics." *The New York Times* (January 12).
Kristof, Nicholas. 2015. "The Cost of a Decline in Unions." *The New York Times* (February 19).
Kroeger, Teresa, Celine McNicholas, Marnia von Wilpert, and Julia Wolfe. 2018. "The State of Graduate Student Employee Unions." Report. Economic Policy Institute (January 11).
Krueger, Alan B. and Orley Ashenfelter. 2018. "Theory and Evidence on Employer Collusion in the Franchise Sector." *NBER Working Paper No. 24831*, National Bureau of Economic Research (July).
Krueger, Alan B. and Eric A. Posner. 2018. "Corporate America Is Suppressing Wages for Many Workers." *The New York Times* (February 28).
  2018. "A Proposal for Protecting Low-Income Workers from Monopsony and Collusion." Policy Proposal 2018-5 (The Hamilton Project, February).
Krugman, Paul. 2012. "We Don't Need No Education." *The New York Times* (June 14).
  2017. "Death and Tax Cuts." *The New York Times* (February 24).
  2017. "Zombies of Voodoo Economics." *The New York Times* (April 24).
  2017. "What Will Trump Do to American Workers?" *The New York Times* (August 21).
  2018. "Is the Recession Still Holding Down Wages? (Wonkish)." *The New York Times* (May 4).

Kuttner, Robert. 2017. "How the Airlines Became Abusive Cartels." *The New York Times* (April 17).
Kwaak, Jeyup S. 2017. "Hyundai Whistle-Blower, in Rarity for South Korea, Prompts Recall." *The New York Times* (May 16).
Kymlicka, Will. 1989. "Liberal Individualism and Liberal Neutrality." *Ethics* 99: 883–905.
  2002. *Contemporary Political Philosophy*. Oxford: Oxford University Press, second edition.
Lafer, Gordon. 2017. "Spending Blind: The Failure of Policy Planning in California Charter School Funding." *In the Public Interest* (April) (www.inthepublicinterest.org/wp-content/uploads/FINAL_ITPI_SpendingBlind_April2017.pdf).
  2017. *The One Percent Solution: How Corporations Are Remaking America One State at a Time*. Ithaca, NY: Cornell University Press.
Laing, Gerald. Unpublished. "What's Wrong with Hypocrisy?"
Landemore, Hélène and Isabelle Ferreras. "In Defense of Workplace Democracy: Towards Justification of the Firm-State Analogy." *Political Theory* 44: 53–81.
Lapidus, Kenneth, ed. 1987. *Marx and Engels on the Trade Unions*. New York: International Publishers.
Larson, Simon and Bruce Nissen, eds. 1987. *Theories of the Labor Movement*. Detroit, MI: Wayne State University Press.
Lartey, Jamiles. 2019. "'Barely above Water': US Shutdown Hits Black Federal Workers Hardest." *The Guardian* (January 11).
  2019. "Will the 35-Day Shutdown Lead to Privatizing Government Functions?" *The Guardian* (January 27).
Lavoie, Don. 1985. *Rivalry and Central Planning: The Socialist Calculation Debate Reconsidered*. Cambridge: Cambridge University Press.
Leader, Sheldon. 1992. *Freedom of Association: A Study in Labor Law and Political Theory*. New Haven, CT: Yale University Press.
Leader. 2011. "Lessons from California: The Perils of Extreme Democracy." *The Economist* (April 20).
Lee, Esther Yu Hsi. 2018. "Labor Unions Move to Protect Immigrants, Regardless of Legal Status." *ThinkProgress* (May 26).
Lehigh, Scot. 2017. "Teachers Union Tries to Torpedo Ed Reform." *The Boston Globe* (March 23).
  2017. "Consider Kansas: Tax Cuts Don't Pay for Themselves." *Boston Globe* (June 15).
Leonhardt, David. 2014. "The Great Wage Slowdown of the 21st Century." *The New York Times* (October 7).
  2018. "The Charts that Show How Big Business Is Winning." *The New York Times* (June 17).
  2018. "For Wages, a Trump Slump." *The New York Times* (August 5).
LePage, Andrew. 2017. "California Million-Dollar Home Sales Climb to a Q1 Peak as Stocks Soar." *Insights Blog* (CoreLogic, May 17) (www.corelogic.com/blog/2017/05/california-million-dollar-home-sales-climb-to-a-q1-peak-as-stocks-soar.aspx).
LeRoy, Michael H. and John H. Johnson IV. 2001. "Death by Lethal Injunction: National Emergency Strikes under the Taft-Hartley Act and the Moribund Right to Strike." *Arizona Law Review* 2001: 63–134.

Levin, Sam. 2018. "Uber Drivers Often Make Below Minimum Wage, Report Finds." *The Guardian* (March 5).
Levine, Peter. 2001. "The Legitimacy of Labor Unions." *Hofstra Labor and Employment Law Journal* 18: 522–573.
  2001. "The Libertarian Critique of Labor Unions." *Philosophy and Public Policy Quarterly* 21: 17–24.
Levitt, Marty Jay. 1993. *Confessions of a Union Buster*. New York: Crown Publishers.
Lewin, David. 1986. "Public Employee Unionism in the 1980s: An Analysis of Transformation." In *Unions in Transition: Entering the Second Century*, ed. Seymour Martin Lipset (San Francisco, CA: Institute for Contemporary Studies), pp. 241–264.
  2007. "Unionism and Employment Conflict Resolution: Rethinking Collective Voice and Its Consequences." In *What Do Unions Do? A Twenty-Year Perspective*, eds. James T. Bennett and Bruce E. Kaufman (New Brunswick, NJ: Transaction Publishers), pp. 313–345.
Lewin, David, Jeffrey Keefe, and Thomas A. Kochan. 2012. "The New Great Debate about Unionism and Collective Bargaining in U.S. State and Local Governments." *ILR Review* 2012: 749–778.
Lichtenstein, Nelson. 2013. "Bashing Public Employees and Their Unions." In *A Contest of Ideas: Capital, Politics, and Labor*. Urbana: University of Illinois Press, pp. 197–208.
  2013. "Obama's America: Liberalism without Unions." In *State of the Union: A Century of American Labor*, rev. ed. (Princeton, NJ: Princeton University Press), pp. 276–296.
Lichtenstein, Nelson and Elizabeth Tandy Shermer, eds. 2012. *The Right and Labor in America*. Philadelphia: University of Pennsylvania Press.
Lien, Tracy. 2018. "Most Uber and Lyft Drives in L.A. Work Full Time and Still Struggle to Make Ends Meet, Study Says." *Los Angeles Times* (May 30).
Lin, Judy. 2017. "Cutting Jobs, Street Repairs, Library Books to Keep Up with Pension Costs." *Los Angeles Times* (February 6).
Lipset, Seymour Martin. 1959. "Democracy and Working Class Authoritarianism." *American Sociological Review* 24: 482–501.
  1986. "Labor Unions in the Public Mind." In *Unions in Transition: Entering the Second Century*, ed. Seymour Martin Lipset (San Francisco, CA: Institute for Contemporary Studies), pp. 287–321.
Liptak, Adam. 2016. "Victory for Unions as Supreme Court, Scalia Gone, Ties 4-4." *The New York Times* (March 29).
  2017. "Supreme Court Upholds Workplace Arbitration Contracts Barring Class Actions." *The New York Times* (May 21).
  2017. "Supreme Court Will Hear Case on Mandatory Fees to Unions." *The New York Times* (September 26).
  2018. "Supreme Court Delivers a Sharp Blow to Labor Unions." *The New York Times* (June 27).
  2018. "How Conservatives Weaponized the First Amendment." *The New York Times* (June 30).
Lipton, Martin and Jay W. Lorsch. 1992. "A Modest Proposal for Improved Corporate Governance." *The Business Lawyer* 48: 59–77.
Little Hoover Commission. 2011. "Public Pensions for Retirement Security" (February) (https://lhc.ca.gov/sites/lhc.ca.gov/files/Reports/204/Report204.pdf).

Livingstone, Josephine. 2017. "Why Are Americans So Hostile to State-Funded Art?" *The New Republic* (May 26, 2017).
Lobel, Orly. 2017. "Companies Compete but Won't Let Their Workers Do the Same." *The New York Times* (May 4).
Locke, John. 1960. "An Essay Concerning the True Original Extent and End of Civil Government." In *Two Treatises on Government*, ed. Peter Laslett (Cambridge: Cambridge University Press), pp. 305–307.
　1988. "Second Treatise on Government" [1698]. In *Two Treatises on Government*, ed. Pater Laslett (Cambridge: Cambridge University Press).
Loecker, Jan De and Jan Eeckhout. 2017. "The Rise of Market Power and the Macroeconomic Implications" (August 24) (www.janeeckhout.com/wp-content/uploads/RMP.pdf).
Lofaso, Anne Marie. 2011. "In Defense of Public Sector Unions." *Hofstra Labor and Employment Law Journal* 28: 301–334.
Lohr, Steve. 2016. "To Compete Better, States Are Trying to Curb Noncompete Pacts." *The New York Time* (June 28).
Long, Heather. 2017. "Half the Jobs in America Pay Less Than $18 an Hour. Can Trump Help?" *The Washington Post* (August 24).
Lorenz, Edward N. 1993. *The Essence of Chaos*. Seattle: University of Washington Press.
Lovenheim, Michael F. and Alexander Willén. 2016. "The Long-Run Effects of Teacher Collective Bargaining." *CESifo Working Paper, No 5977* (June 30) (http://hdl.handle.net/10419/145012).
　2018. "The Long-Run Effects of Teacher Collective Bargaining." Presented at the American Economic Association annual conference, panel on New Evidence on the Effects of Teachers' Unions on Student Outcomes, Teacher Labor Markets, and the Allocation of School Resources, January 6, 2018 (see www.aeaweb.org/conference/2018/preliminary/1282?q=eNo1jEsKgDAQQ69cIlm7UMGN5_ACRQcZ6A-nKqXo7o6ou_eSkAIhEQ5-zpEwlV8xoUcLOslcJ-UBtYURCYuK5ol2p-RNoq2xjQ1-43SsrKL1avK3YocvnUzX87_HqMHYodYb3LpcJxo).
Lovett, Frank. 2010. *A General Theory of Domination and Justice*. Oxford: Oxford University Press.
Lovett, Frank, and Philip Pettit. 2019. "Preserving Republican Freedom: A Reply to Simpson." *Philosophy and Public Affairs* 2019: 1–21.
Lowrey, Annie. 2013. "Faces of the Minimum Wage." *The New York Times* (June 15, 2013).
Luce, Edward. 2017. *The Retreat of Western Liberalism*. New York: Atlantic Monthly Press.
Luo, Michael and Stephanie Strom. 2010. "Donor Names Remain Secret as Rules Shift." *The New York Times* (September 20).
Lydersen, Kari. 2017. "Thousands of Protesters Brand McDonald's the 'Trump of Corporations.'" *The Guardian* (May 24).
Lyman, Brian. 2014. "Over Bentley's Objections, Golden Dragon Plant Votes for Union." *Montgomery Advertiser* (November 16).
Lyman, Rick and Mary Williams Walsh. 2013. "Police Salaries and Pensions Push California City to the Brink." *The New York Times* (December 27).
Lynn, Barry. 2018. "Google and Facebook Are Strangling the Free Press to Death. Democracy Is the Loser." *The Guardian* (July 26).
Lyons, Dan. 2016. "Congratulations! You've Been Fired." *The New York Times* (April 9).

Macaray, David. 2016. "Union Contracts." *Huffington Post* (July 28).
MacDonald, Margaret. 1984. "Natural Rights." In *Theories of Rights*, ed. JeremyWaldron (Oxford: Oxford University Press), pp. 21–40.
Macfarlane, Leslie John. 1981. *The Right to Strike*. Harmondsworth, Middlesex: Penguin.
MacGilvray, Eric. 2011. *The Invention of Market Freedom*. Cambridge: Cambridge University Press.
Machlup, Fritz. 1947. "Monopolistic Wage Determination as a Part of the General Problem of Monopoly." In *Wage Determination and the Economics of Liberalism*, eds. E. Wright Bakke, John T. Dunlop, and Fritz Machlup et al. (Washington, DC: Chamber of Commerce, January 11), pp. 49–82.
Mack, Eric. 2014. "Robert Nozick's Political Philosophy." *Stanford Encyclopedia of Philosophy* (June 22).
MacLean, Nancy. 2017. *Democracy in Chains: The Deep History of the Radical Right's Stealth Plan for America*. New York: Viking.
MacWilliams, Matthew C. 2016. "Donald Trump Is Attracting Authoritarian Primary Voters, and It May Help Him Gain the Nomination." *LSE US Centre Blog*, London School of Economics and Political Science–US Centre? (January 27) (http://bit.ly/1KFzeC0).
Malik, Om. 2016. "Apple, Google, Amazon, and the Advantages of Bigness." *The New Yorker* (August 9).
Malin, Martin H. 2009. "The Paradox of Public Sector Labor Law." *Indiana Law Journal* 84: 1369–1400.
  2013. "Does Public Employee Collective Bargaining Distort Democracy? A Perspective from the United States." *Comparative Labor Law & Policy Journal* 34: 277–306.
Malin, Martin H. and Charles Taylor Kerchner. 2007. "Charter Schools and Collective Bargaining: Compatible Marriage or Illegitimate Relationship?" *Harvard Journal of Law and Public Policy* 30: 885–937.
Manjoo, Farhad. 2017. "Trump Says Regulations Impede. Perhaps Not in the Electric Car Business." *The New York Times* (March 22).
Manning, Alan. 2003. *Monopsony in Motion: Imperfect Competition in Labor Markets*. Princeton: Princeton University Press.
Marginson, Paul. 1993. "Power and Efficiency in the Firm: Understanding the Employment Relationship." In *Transaction Costs, Markets and Hierarchies*, ed. Christos Pitelis (Oxford: Blackwell), pp. 133–165.
Markovits, Andrei S. 1986. *The Politics of West German Trade Unions*. Cambridge: Cambridge University Press.
Marvit, Moshe Z. 2019. "The Joint Employer Standard in Limbo." *The Regulatory Review* (April 2).
Marvit, Moshe Z. and Shaun Richman. 2017. "American Workers Need Better Job Protections." *The New York Times* (December 28).
Marx, Karl. 1992. *Capital Volume 1: A Critique of Political Economy*. London: Penguin.
Mason, Sarah. 2018. "High Score, Low Pay: Why the Gig Economy Loves Gamification." *The Guardian* (November 20).
Masters, Marick. 2017. "How Union Stakes in Ailing Papers Like the Chicago Sun-Times May Keep Them Alive." *The Conversation* (August 16).

Masunaga, Samantha. 2018. "L.A. and Long Beach Port Truckers and Warehouse Workers Begin Strike." *Los Angeles Times* (October 1).

Mather, Victor. 2018. "Union Files Grievance against N.F.L. Supporting Eric Reid." *The New York Times* (May 7).

Matthews, Joe. 2009. "Amending California's Direct Democracy." *Los Angeles Times* (October 19).

Matthews, Madison and Valerie Wilson. 2018. "Separate Is Still Unequal: How Patterns of Occupational Segregation Impact Pay for Black Women." *Working Economics Blog*, Economic Policy Institute (August 6).

Mayer, Jane. 2016. *Dark Money: The Hidden History Behind the Rise of the Radical Right*. New York: Doubleday.

  2017. "Can Time Inc. Survive the Kochs?" *The New Yorker* (November 28).

  2019. "The Making of the Fox News White House." *The New Yorker* (March 11).

Mays, Jeffrey C. 2018. "De Blasio, a Pro-Labor Mayor, Is Sued Over Bargaining Tactics." *The New York Times* (January 31).

Mazerov, Michael. 2016. "Kansas' Tax Cut Experience Refutes Economic Growth Predictions of Trump Tax Advisors." *Center for Budget and Policy Priorities* (August 12).

McCann, Erin and Richard Pérez-Peña. 2016. "Faculty Members at 14 State Universities in Pennsylvania Go on Strike." *The New York Times* (October 19).

McCarthy, Tom. 2017. "Sheldon Adelson Lost His Fight with a Union. Will It Have a Domino Effect?" *The Guardian* (February 24).

McCartin, Joseph A. 2007. "Approaching Extinction: The Decline of Strikes in the United States, 1960–2005." In *Strikes around the World, 1968–2005*, eds. Sjaak van der Velden, Heiner Dribbusch, Dave Lyddon, and Kurt Vandaele (Amsterdam, The Netherlands: Aksant), pp. 133–154.

  2011. *Collision Course: Ronald Reagan, the Air Traffic Controllers, and the Strike*. Oxford: Oxford University Press.

  2011. "The Strike That Busted Unions." *The New York Times* (August 2).

McCartin, Joseph A. and Jean-Christian Vinel. 2012. "'Compulsory Unionism': Sylvester Petro and the Career of an Anti-Union Idea, 1957–1987." In *The Right and Labor in America*, eds. Nelson Lichtenstein and Elizabeth Tandy Shermer (Philadelphia: University of Pennsylvania Press), pp. 226–251.

McDermott, John. 2017. "Uber Is about to Kill a Lot More Jobs." *MEL Magazine* (January 11) (https://melmagazine.com/uber-is-about-to-kill-a-lot-more-jobs-f4497f5538d).

McGann, Anthony J., Charles Anthony Smith, Michael Latner, and Alex Keena. 2016. *Gerrymandering in America*. Cambridge: Cambridge University Press.

McGeehan, Patrick. 2012. "Blacks Miss Out as Jobs Rebound in New York City." *The New York Times* (June 20).

  2014. "Millions Due in Back Pay to Dancers at Manhattan Strip Club." *The New York Times* (November 14).

  2016. "Pensions for Lifeguards? Officials Say Atlantic City Can't Afford Them Anymore." *The New York Times* (May 6).

McGinnis, John O. and Max Schanzenbach. 2010. "The Case against Public Sector Unions." *Policy Review*. Hoover Institution (August 1) (www.hoover.org/research/case-against-public-sector-unions).

McGowan, Michael. 2018. "Fake Black Lives Matter Facebook Page Run by Australian Union Official – Report." *The Guardian* (April 9).

McKinley, James C, Jr. 2018. "Laborers on a 'Billionaires' Row' Tower Cheated of Wages, D.A. Says." *The New York Times* (May 16).
McMahan, Jeff. 2009. *Killing in War*. Oxford: Oxford University Press.
McNicholas, Celine and Janelle Jones. 2018. "Black Women Will Be Most Affected by Janus." *Economic Snapshot*. Economic Policy Institute (February 13).
McNicholas, Celine and Marni von Wilpert. 2017. "The Joint Employer Standard and the National Labor Relations Board." Report. Economic Policy Institute (May 31) (www.epi.org/files/pdf/129265.pdf).
McNicholas, Celine and Heidi Shierholz. 2018. "Supreme Court Decision in Janus Threatens the Quality of Public-Sector Jobs and Public Services." Economic Policy Institute (June 13).
McNicholas, Celine, Heidi Shierholz, and Marni von Wilpert. 2018. "Workers Health, Safety, and Pay Are among the Casualties of Trump's War on Regulations." Report. Economic Policy Institute (January 29).
McNicholas, Celine, Zane Mokhiber, and Adam Chaikof. 2017. "Two Billion Dollars in Stolen Wages Were Recovered for Workers in 2015 and 2016 – And That's Just a Drop in the Bucket." Report. Economic Policy Institute (December 13).
McNicholas, Celine, Zane Mokhiber, and Marni von Wilpert. 2018. "Janus and Fair Share Fees." Economic Policy Institute (February 21).
McPhate, Mike. 2017. "The Collapse of Organized Farm Labor." *The New York Times* (February 2).
  2017. "California Today: Battle over a Bill Reaches the State Senate." *The New York Times* (August 24).
McPherson, Crawford Brough. 1977. *The Life and Times of Liberal Democracy*. Oxford: Oxford University Press.
Meade, James. 1978. "The Meaning of 'Internal Balance.'" *The Economic Journal* 88: 423–435.
Medina, Jennifer and Dana Goldstein. 2019. "Los Angeles Teachers' Strike to End as Deal Is Reached." *The New York Times* (January 22).
Medina, Jennifer, Tim Arango, Dana Goldstein, and Louis Keene. 2019. "Los Angeles Teachers Strike, Disrupting Classes for 500,00 Students." *The New York Times* (January 14).
Megginson, William L. and Jeffrey M. Netter. 2002. "From State to Market: A Survey of Empirical Studies on Privatization." *Journal of Economic Literature* 39: 321–389.
Mehra, Alexander. 2010. "Legal Authority in Unusual and Exigent Circumstances: The Federal Reserve and the Financial Crisis." *University of Pennsylvania Journal of Business Law* 13: 223–273.
Meier, Barry and Danielle Ivory. 2017. "Under Trump, Worker Protections Are Viewed with New Skepticism." *The New York Times* (June 5).
Meikle, James. 2007. "Lecturers Vote for Boycott of Israeli Universities." *The Guardian* (May 31).
  2007. "Lecturers Drop Israeli Universities Boycott Call after Legal Advice." *The Guardian* (September 28).
Meixell, Brady and Ross Eisenbrey. 2014. "An Epidemic of Wage Theft Is Costing Workers Hundreds of Millions of Dollars a Year." EPI Issue Brief #385. Economic Policy Institute (September 11) (http://s3.epi.org/files/2014/wage-theft.pdf).

Meyer, Gerald. 2004. "Union Membership Trends in the United States." *Congressional Research Service* (Washington, DC) (http://digitalcommons.ilr.cornell.edu/cgi/viewcontent.cgi?article=1176&context=key_workplace).

Meyer, Warren. 2018. "How Labor Regulation Harms Unskilled Workers." *Regulation* 41: 44-50 (Cato Institute).

Meyers, B. R. 2016. "Oswald Spengler: Pessimism's Prophet." *The American Conservative* (December 23).

Mikolajczak, Moïra, et al. 2010. "Oxytocin Not Only Increases Trust When Money Is at Sake, but also When Confidential Information Is in the Balance." *Biological Psychology* 85: 182–184.

Milkman, Ruth and Stephanie Luce. 2015. "The State of the Unions 2015: A Profile of Organized Labor in New York City, New York State, and the United States." The Joseph S. Murphy Institute for Worker Education and Labor Studies (City University of New York, September) (www.gc.cuny.edu/CUNY_GC/media/CUNY-Graduate-Center/PDF/Communications/1509_Union_Density2015_RGB.pdf).

Mill, John Stuart. 1849. *Principles of Political Economy*. London: John W. Parker.

  1869. "Thornton on Labour and Its Claims." *Fortnightly Review, Part I* (May), pp. 505–518, Part II (June), pp. 680–700.

  1989. *On Liberty*. Cambridge: Cambridge University Press.

Millbank, Dana. 2013. "Republican Gerrymandering Makes the Difference in the House." *The Washington Post* (January 4).

Miller, David. 1989. *Market, State and Community: Theoretical Foundations of Market Socialism*. Oxford: Oxford University Press.

Miller, Jim. 2017. "Union Power on Display in California's Just Completed Legislative Session." *Sacramento Bee* (September 1).

Mills, D. Quinn. 1979. "Flawed Victory in Labor Law Reform." *Harvard Business Review* 57: 92–102.

Minchin, Timothy J. 2016. "A Pivotal Role? The AFL-CIO and the 2008 Presidential Election." *Labor History* 57: 299–322.

Mises, Ludwig von. 1990 [1920]. *Economic Calculation in the Socialist Commonwealth*. Auburn, AL: Ludwig von Mises Institute.

  1998. *Human Action: A Treatise on Economics*, Scholar's ed. Auburn, AL: Ludwig von Mises Institute.

  2012. "Unions, Inequality, and Faltering Middle-Class Wages." Issue Brief #342. Economic Policy Institute (August 29) (www.epi.org/publication/ib342-unions-inequality-faltering-middle-class/).

  2017. "Diversity in the New York City Union and Nonunion Construction Sectors." Economic Policy Institute Report (March 2) (www.epi.org/files/pdf/119517.pdf).

  2018. "Overall Union Membership Rises in 2017, Union Density Holds Steady." *Working Economics Blog*, Economic Policy Institute (January 19).

  2018. "Uber and the Labor Market." Economic Policy Institute (May 15).

Mishel, Lawrence and Jessica Schieder. 2016. "As Union Membership Has Fallen, the Top 10 Percent Have Been Getting a Larger Share of Income." *Economic Snapshot*. Economic Policy Institute (May 24).

Mishel, Lawrence with Matthew Walters. 2003. "How Unions Help All Workers." EPI Briefing Paper #143, Economic Policy Institute (August 26) (www.epi.org/publication/briefingpapers_bp143/).

Mishel, Lawrence, Elise Gould, and Josh Bivens. 2015. "Wage Stagnation in Nine Charts." Economic Policy Institute (January 6) (www.epi.org/publication/charting-wage-stagnation/?utm_source=Economic+Policy+Institute&utm_campaign=27719c052c-EPI_News&utm_medium=email&utm_term=0_e7c5826c50-27719c052c-55957733).

Mishel, Lawrence, Josh Bivens, Elise Gould, and Heidi Shierholz. 2012. *The State of Working America*, 12th ed. Ithaca, NY: Economic Policy Institute Cornell University Press.

Mitchell, Daniel J. B. and Christopher L. Erickson. 2007. "De-Unionization and Macro-Performance: What Freeman and Medoff Didn't Do." In *What Do Unions Do? A Twenty-Year Perspective*, eds. James T. Bennett and Bruce E. Kaufman (New Brunswick, NJ: Transaction Publishers), pp. 373–400.

Mohan, Geoffrey. 2017. "Farmworkers Union Underpaid Its Own Organizers, Judge Rules." *Los Angeles Times* (March 29).

Monbiot, George. 2016. "Lies, Fearmongering and Fables: That's Our Democracy." *The Guardian* (October 4).

2017. "Freeing Up the Rich to Exploit the Poor – That's What Trump and Brexit Are About." *The Guardian* (April 4).

2018. "Donald Trump Was Right. The Rest of the G7 Were Wrong." *The Guardian* (June 13).

Monica, Davey, "With Fewer Members, A Diminished Political Role for Wisconsin Unions." *The New York Times* (February 27, 2016).

Moore, William J. 1998. "The Determinants and Effects of Right-to-Work Laws: A Review of the Recent Literature." *Journal of Labor Research* 19: 445–469.

Mora, Marie T. and Alberto Dávila. 2018. "The Hispanic–White Wage Gap Has Remained Wide and Relatively Steady." Economic Policy Institute (July 2).

Moran, Jose. 2017. "Time for Tesla to Listen." Blog Post (February 9) (https://medium.com/@moran2017j/time-for-tesla-to-listen-ab5c6259fc88).

Morgenson, Gretchen. 2011. "Paychecks as Big as Tajikistan." *The New York Times* (June 18).

2013. "Daring to Knock on the Boardroom Door." *The New York Times* (April 20).

2013. "Management, to the Barricades!" *The New York Times* (May 4).

2013. "Shareholders? Fuhgeddaboudit!" *The New York Times* (May 25).

2013. "Playing Pension Games." *The New York Times* (December 7).

2015. "In Whole Foods Backlash, a Chance to Air Out Stagnant Boardrooms." *The New York Times* (February 21).

2016. "Whistle-Blowers Spur Companies to Change Their Ways." *The New York Times* (December 16).

2017. "Meet the Shareholders? Not at These Shareholder Meetings." *The New York Times* (March 31).

2017. "A Whistle Was Blown, but Who Was Listening?" *The New York Times* (April 28).

2017. "Strapped Pension Funds, and the Hefty Investment Fees They Pay." *The New York Times* (May 12).

2017. "Dubious Corporate Practices Get a Rubber Stamp from Big Investors." *The New York Times* (May 19).

2017. "Meet the Legislation Designed to Stifle Shareholders." *The New York Times* (June 16).

2017. "The Fed Wants to Make Life Easier for Big-Bank Directors." *The New York Times* (August 11).
Morrar, Sawsan. 2019. "California State University Stashed $1.5 Billion in Reserves While Hiking Tuition, Audit Says." *Sacramento Bee* (June 20).
Morris, David. 2011. "When Unions Are Strong, Americans Enjoy the Fruits of Their Labor." Institute for Local Self-Reliance (March 31) (https://ilsr.org/when-unions-are-strong-americans-enjoy-the-fruits-of-their-labor/).
Mouawad, Jad and Nicola Clark. 2014. "Slide in Fuel Costs Lifts Profits for Airlines, but Fares Won't Fall." *The New York Times* (December 10).
Mueller, Benjamin. 2015. "Unionization Important to Closing Racial Wage Gap, Study Says." *The New York Times* (September 4).
2019. "Fewer Officers, More Calls: U.K. Police Are Stretched by Austerity." *The New York Times* (February 1).
Murphy, Brett. 2017. "Rigged: Forced into Debt. Worked Past Exhaustion. Left with Nothing." *USA Today* (June 16).
Murphy, Liam. 1999. "Institutions and the Demands of Justice." *Philosophy and Public Affairs* 27: 251–291.
Nachtwey, Oliver. 2018. "It Doesn't Matter Who Replaces Merkel. Germany Is Broken." *The New York Times* (December 7).
Naheesan, Sandeep. 2018. "America's Most Insidious Union-Buster? Its Own Government." *The Guardian* (June 29).
Naidu, Suresh, Eric Posner, and E. Glen Wayl. 2018. "Antitrust Remedies for Labor Market Power." *Harvard Law Review* 132 (2018): 536-601.
2018. "More and More Companies Have Monopoly Power Over Workers' Wages. That's Killing the Economy." *Vox* (April 6).
Narveson, Jan. 1988. *The Libertarian Idea*. Philadelphia, PA: Temple University Press.
National Association of State Retirement Administrators. 2016. "Public Fund Survey" (March) (www.nasra.org/publicfundsurvey).
National Center for Employee Ownership, "The Employee Ownership 100: America's Largest Majority Employee-Owned Companies" (www.nceo.org/articles/employee-ownership-100).
National Employment Law Project. 2015. "Independent Contractor Misclassification Imposes Huge Costs on Workers and Federal and State Treasuries." *Fact Sheet* (July) (https://s27147.pcdn.co/wp-content/uploads/Independent-Contractor-Costs.pdf).
National Right to Work Legal Defense Foundation. "Your Right to Work Rights – in Three Minutes" (www.nrtw.org/your-right-to-work-rights-in-three-minutes/).
Neumann, Franz L. 1996. "Labor Law in Modern Society." In *The Rule of Law under Siege: Selected Essays of Franz L. Neumann and Otto Kirchheimer*, ed. William E. Scheurerman (Berkeley: University of California Press), pp. 231–242.
New York Times. 1976. "'Welfare Queen' Becomes Issue in Reagan Campaign." *The New York Times* (February 15).
Newitz, Annalee. 2017. "The Secret Lives of Google Raters." *Ars Technica* (April 27) (https://arstechnica.com/features/2017/04/the-secret-lives-of-google-raters/).
Newman, Andy and John Leland. 2017. "DNAinfo and Gothamist Are Shut Down After Vote to Unionize." *The New York Times* (November 2).

Nichols, Jon. 2017. "I Lost My Dream Job in a Rural Town – But Telling Me to Move Doesn't Help." *The Guardian* (June 23).
Nietzsche, Friedrich. 1994. *On the Genealogy of Morality*. Cambridge: Cambridge University Press.
Nir, Sarah Maslin. 2016. "A Manhattan Diner's New Management Has Servers Singing a Defiant Tune." *The New York Times* (August 26).
Nirappil, Fenit and Tim Carman. 2018. "Tipping the Pay Scales: Initiative 77 Could Dramatically Alter D.C. Restaurant Culture." *The Washington Post* (June 16).
Nishioka, Tatsuya, et al. 1998. "Stress Increases Oxytocin Release within the Hypothalamic Paraventricular Nucleus." *Brain Research* 781: 57–61.
Nock, Albert Jay. 2014. *Our Enemy, the State*. New York: CreateSpace Independent Publishing.
NoiseCat, Julian Brave. 2018. "Republicans Wanted to Suppress the Native American Vote. It's Working." *The Guardian* (October 26).
Nolan, Hamilton. 2017. "A Billionaire Destroyed His Newsrooms Out of Spite." *The New York Times* (November 3).
Norquist, Grover. 2001. Interview with President of Americans for Tax Reform, National Public Radio, Morning Edition (May 25).
Norris, Floyd. 2013. "Four Years Later, 28,000 More Jobs." *The New York Times* (January 4).
  2013. "The Lagging Public Sector." *The New York Times* (July 5).
  2013. "Bloated Government? Federal Employment at 47-Year Low." *The New York Times* (October 22).
Norwood, Stephen H. 2002. *Strikebreaking and Intimidation: Mercenaries and Masculinity in Twentieth-Century America*. Chapel Hill: University of North Carolina Press.
Nossiter, Adam. 2017. "Marcon Takes on France's Labor Code, 100 Years in the Making." *The New York Times* (August 4).
Novy-Marx, Robert and Joshua Rauh. 2011. "The Crisis in Local Government Pensions in the United States." In *Growing Old: Paying for Retirement And Institutional Money Management after the Financial Crisis*, eds. Yasuyuki Fuchita, Richard J. Herring, and Robert E. Litan (Washington, DC: Brookings Institution Press), pp. 47–74.
Nozick, Robert. 1974. *Anarchy, State, and Utopia*. New York: Basic Books.
  1997. "Coercion." In *Socratic Puzzles* (Cambridge: Harvard University Press), pp. 15–44.
O'Brien, Matt. 2018. "Businesses Have Hijacked Capitalism – and Left Workers Behind." *The Washington Post* (July 18).
  2018. "Even Janitors Have Noncompetes Now. Nobody Is Safe." *The Washington Post* (October 18).
O'Harrow, Robert Jr. and Shawn Boburg. 2017. "How a 'Shadow' Universe of Charities Joined with Political Warriors to Fuel Trump's Rise." *The Washington Post* (June 3).
O'Neill, Martin. 2017. "Philosophy and Public Policy after Piketty." *Journal of Political Philosophy* 25: 344–375.
O'Neill, Martin and Stuart White. 2018. "Trade Unions and Political Equality." In *Philosophical Foundations of Labour Law*, eds. Hugh Collins, Gillian Lester, and Virginia Mantouvalou (Oxford: Oxford University Press), pp. 252–270.

O'Neill, Martin and Thad Williamson, eds. 2012. *Property-Owning Democracy: Rawls and Beyond*. Oxford: Wiley-Blackwell.
Oberdiek, John. 2003. "Lost in Moral Space: On the Infringing/Violating Distinction and Its Place in the Theory of Rights." *Law and Philosophy* 23: 325–346.
O'Brien, Matthew. 2013. "Our Historic Austerity – In 1 Crazy Chart." *The Atlantic* (December).
Odessky, Jared and Miriam Frank. 2018. "Janus Is this Term's Worst L.G.B.T. Ruling." *The New York Times* (June 27).
Office of Economic Policy, United States Department of the Treasury. 2016. "Non-Compete Contracts: Economic Effects and Policy Implications" (March) (www.treasury.gov/resource-center/economic-policy/Documents/UST%20Non-competes%20Report.pdf).
Okun, Arthur M. 1975. *Equality and Efficiency: The Big Tradeoff*. Washington, DC: Brookings.
Olsaretti, Serena. 2003. "Introduction." In *Desert and Justice* (Oxford: Oxford University Press), pp. 1–24.
Olson, Elizabeth. 2017. "'A Bleak Picture' for Women Trying to Rise at Law Firms." *The New York Times* (July 24).
Olson, Mancur. 1965. *The Logic of Collective Action*. Cambridge: Harvard University Press.
Onwurah, Chi. 2018. "All Workers Need Unions – Including Those in Silicon Valley." *The Guardian* (January 31).
"Order Denying Plaintiff's Motion for Preliminary Approval," in O'Connor v. Uber Technologies, Civ. Action No. 13-CV-03826-EMC (N.D. Cal.) and Yucesoy v. Uber Technologies, Civ. Action No. 15-CV-00262-EMC (N.D. Cal.) (August 18, 2016) (http://uberlawsuit.com/Uber%20order%20re%20preliminary%20approval.pdf).
Osnos, Evan. 2018. "Trump vs. the 'Deep State.'" *The New Yorker* (May 21).
Paarlberg, Michael. 2017. "With All Eyes on Trump, Republicans Are Planning to Break Unions for Good." *The Guardian* (February 2).
Padani, Amy. 2013. "Anatomy of Detroit's Decline." *The New York Times* (December 8).
Paletta, Damian. 2017. "Trump Budget Expected to Seek Historic Reduction in Federal Workforce." *The Washington Post* (March 12).
  2018. "Trouble in Candy Land." *The Washington Post* (March 29).
Paletta, Damian and Josh Dawsey. 2018. "Trump Personally Pushed Postmaster General to Double Rates on Amazon, Other Firms." *The Washington Post* (May 18).
Parker, David. 2012. *The Official History of Privatisation, Volume II, Popular Capitalism, 1987–1997*. London: Routledge.
Parlapiano, Alicia, Shaila Dewan, and Nelson D. Schwartz. 2014. "The Nation's Economy, This Side of the Recession. *The New York Times* (June 14).
Parrott, James A. and Michael Reich. 2018. "An Earnings Standard for New York City's App-based Drivers: Economic Analysis and Policy Assessment." Report for the New York City Taxi and Limousine Commission (Center for New York City Affairs/Center on Wage and Employment Dynamics, July).
Pear, Robert. 2018. "Trump Rule Would Compel Drug Makers to Disclose Prices in TV Commercials." *The New York Times* (October 15).
Patten, Eileen. 2016. "Racial, Gender Wage Gaps Persist in U.S. Despite Some Progress." Pew Research Center (July 1) (www.pewresearch.org/fact-tank/2016/07/01/racial-gender-wage-gaps-persist-in-u-s-despite-some-progress/).

Paul, Kari. 2019. "The Uber Drivers Forced to Sleep in Parking Lots to Make a Decent Living." *The Guardian* (May 8).
   2019. "Gig Economy: California Bill Granting Employee Status Passes Assembly." *The Guardian* (May 29).
Peck, Emily. 2017. "If Trump Really Cared about the Working Class, Puzder Never Would've Been Nominated." *The Huffington Post* (February 15).
Peele, Thomas. 2017. "San Jose City Manager, Police Chief Highest Paid in Salary Survey of 200 Cities." *The Mercury News* (May 1).
   2017. "Three BART Janitors Swept Up $365,000 in OT Last Year." *East Bay Times* (June 1).
Peiser, Jaclyn. 2019. "'Not All Fun and Memes': BuzzFeed News Employees Plan to Form a Union." *The New York Times* (February 12).
Pengelly, Martin. 2017. "Company Town: 'Quiet Tragedy' of an Arkansas Community vs the Kochs." *The Guardian* (September 10).
Penrose, Edith Tilton. 2013. *The Theory of the Growth of the Firm*. Mansfield Center, CT: Martino Publishing.
Pension Rights Center. 2017. "Income from Pensions" (March 15) (www.pensionrights.org/publications/statistic/income-pensions).
Percival, Robert V. 1987. "The Bounds of Consent: Consent Decrees, Settlement and Federal Environmental Policy Making." *University of Chicago Legal Forum* 1: 327–351.
Pérez-Peña, Richard. 2017. "Contrary to Trump's Claims, Immigrants Are Less Likely to Commit Crimes." *The New York Times* (January 26).
Pérez-Peña, Richard and Sheryl Gay Stolberg. 2017. "Police Unions Hail Trump's Easing of Scrutiny. Local Officials Worry." *The New York Times* (April 4).
Peters, Jeremey W. 2016. "Donald Trump's Crucial Pillar of Support, White Men, Shows Weakness." *The New York Times* (August 18).
   2016. "Wielding Claims of 'Fake News,' Conservatives Take Aim at Mainstream Media." *The New York Times* (December 25).
Petro, Sylvester. 1957. *The Labor Policy of a Free Society*. New York: The Ronald Press.
   1974. "Sovereignty and Compulsory Public Sector Bargaining." *Wake Forest Law Review* 10 (1974-1975): 25–166.
Pettit, Philip. 1997. "Liberty as Non-Domination." In *Republicanism: A Theory of Freedom and Government* (Oxford: Oxford University Press), pp. 51–79.
   1997. *Republicanism: A Theory of Freedom and Government*. Oxford: Oxford University Press.
   2002. "Keeping Republican Freedom Simple: On a Difference with Quentin Skinner." *Political Theory* 30: 339–356.
   2006. "Freedom in the Market." *Politics, Philosophy, and Economics* 5: 131–149.
   2011. "The Instability of Freedom as Noninterference: The Case of Isaiah Berlin." *Ethics* 121: 693–716.
   2012. *On the People's Terms: A Republican Theory and Model of Democracy*. Cambridge: Cambridge University Press.
   2015. "Freedom: Psychological, Ethical, and Political." *Critical Review of International Social and Political Philosophy* 18: 375–389.
Pew Research Center. 2016. "America's Shrinking Middle Class: A Close Look at Changes within Metropolitan Areas." (May 11).

Phillips-Fein, Kim. 2009. *Invisible Hands: The Businessman's Crusade against the New Deal*. New York: W. W. Norton & Company.
Philmore, J. 1982. "The Libertarian Case for Slavery." *The Philosophical Forum* 14: 43–58.
Piazza, James A. 2002. *Going Global: Unions and Globalization in the United States, Sweden and Germany*. Lanham, MD: Lexington Books.
Pigou, Arthur Cecil. 1932. *The Economics of Welfare*, 4th ed. London: Macmillan.
　1941. *Employment and Equilibrium*. London: Macmillan.
　1949. "Mill and the Wages Fund." *The Economic Journal* 59: 171–180.
Piketty, Thomas and Emanuel Saez. 2006. "Income and Wage Inequality in the United States, 1913–2002." In *Top Incomes over the Twentieth Century*, eds. Anthony Barnes Atkinson and Thomas Piketty (Oxford: Oxford University Press), pp. 141–225.
Piketty, Thomas, Emmanuel Saez, and Gabriel Zucman. 2016. "Distributional National Accounts: Methods and Estimates for the United States." *NBER Working Paper* 22945, National Bureau of Economic Research (December).
Pilkington, Ed. 2017. "What Happened When Walmart Left." *The Guardian* (July 9).
　2017. "Rightwing Alliance Plots Assault to 'Defund and Defang' American Unions." *The Guardian* (August 30).
　2018. "Revealed: Secret Rightwing Strategy to Discredit Teacher Strikes." *The Guardian* (April 12).
　2018. "How Rightwing Groups Wield Secret 'Toolkit' to Plot against US Unions." *The Guardian* (May 15).
　2018. "Thousands at Risk from Rightwing Push to Purge Eligible Voters from US Rolls." *The Guardian* (September 23).
Pioneer Press. 2012. "Wisconsin Police, Firefighter Unions Allege Blackmail over Benefits." *Twin Cites Pioneer Press* (January 5).
Planet Money. 2015. "50 Years of Shrinking Union Membership in One Map" (February 23) (www.npr.org/sections/money/2015/02/23/385843576/50-years-of-shrinking-union-membership-in-one-map).
Pleasure, Robert J. 2000. "Collective Bargaining and the Labor-Management Antitrust Exemption." *Journal of Labor Research* 21:557–562.
Pontifical Council for Justice and Peace. 2004. *Compendium of the Social Doctrine of the Church*. Washington, DC: United States Conference of Catholic Bishops.
Porter, Eduardo. 2011. "How the Big Money Finds a Way In." *The New York Times* (September 17).
　2016. "The Challenge of Cutting Coal Dependence." *The New York Times* (August 30).
　2016. "How Waning Competition Deepens Labor's Plight." *The New York Times* (November 1).
　2017. "Prisons Run by C.E.O.s? Privatization under Trump Could Carry a Heavy Price." *The New York Times* (January 10).
　2017. "Shaky Jobs, Sluggish Wages: Reasons Are at Home." *The New York Times* (February 28).
　2017. "Fed's Challenge, after Raising Rates, May Be Existential." *The New York Times* (March 14).
　2017. "Labor Wants to Make NAFTA Its Friend. Here's the Problem." *The New York Times* (August 22).

2017. "Considering the Cost of Lower Taxes." *The New York Times* (November 14).

2017. "Tax Plan Aims to Slay a Reagan Target: The Government Beast." *The New York Times* (December 5).

Posner, Eric. 2016. "What Legal Authority Does the Fed Need During a Financial Crisis?" Coase-Sandor Working Paper Series in Law and Economics No. 741.

2018. "The Far-Reaching Threats of a Conservative Court." *The New York Times* (October 23).

Powell, Lewis F. 1971. "Attack on American Free Enterprise System." Memorandum to Eugene B. Snyder, Jr., Chairman, Education Committee, U.S. Chamber of Commerce (August 23, 1971) (http://law2.wlu.edu/deptimages/Powell%20Archives/PowellMemorandumTypescript.pdf).

Pratley, Nils. 2016. "Theresa May's Plan to Put Workers in Boardrooms Is Extraordinary." *The Guardian* (July 11).

Project on Government Oversight. 2011. "Bad Business: Billions of Taxpayer Dollars Wasted on Hiring Contractors." (September 13) (https://docs.pogo.org/report/2011/bad-business-report-only-2011.pdf?mtime=20180803144205&_ga=2.84350105.1054705783.1551121378-1188413719.1551121378).

Quiggin, John. 2010. *Zombie Economics: How Dead Ideas Still Walk among Us*. Princeton, NJ: Princeton University Press.

Quong, Jonathan. 2009. "Killing in Self-Defense." *Ethics* 119: 507–537.

Rajczi, Alex. 2016. "On the Incoherence Objection to Rule Utilitarianism." *Ethical Theory and Moral Practice* 19: 857–876.

Rampell, Catherine. 2011. "Employed Women, Dropping Out of Labor Force." *The New York Times* (December 6).

2012. "Majority of New Jobs Pay Low Wages, Study Finds." *The New York Times* (August 30).

Rao, Prashant S. 2017. "Uber Hit with New Blow in London as Panel Says Drivers Aren't Self-Employed." *The New York Times* (November 10).

Rappeport, Alan. 2018. "Harley-Davidson, Blaming E.U. Tariffs, Will Move Some Production Out of U.S." *The New York Times* (June 25).

Rauch, Jonathan. 2017. "The Conservative Case for Unions: How a New Kind of Labor Organization Could Address the Grievances Underlying Populist Anger." *The Atlantic* (July/August).

Rawls, John. 1996. "The Basic Structure as Subject." In *Political Liberalism* (New York: Columbia University Press), pp. 257–288.

1984. Lecture on the Basic Structure in Philosophy 171, Modern Political Philosophy, Harvard University (www.youtube.com/watch?v=tYvdmizdohE).

1996. *Political Liberalism*. New York: Columbia University Press.

1996. "Priority of the Right and Ideas of the Good." In *Political Liberalism* (New York: Columbia University Press), pp. 173–211.

1999. *A Theory of Justice*, rev. ed. Cambridge: Harvard University Press, 1971.

1999. "The Idea of Public Reason Revisited." In *Collected Papers*, ed. Samuel Freeman (Cambridge: Harvard University Press), pp. 573–615.

1999. "The Priority of Right and Ideas of the Good." In *Collected Papers* (Cambridge: Harvard University Press), pp. 449–472.

2001. *Justice as Fairness*. Cambridge: Harvard University Press.

2001. "The Idea of a Well-Ordered Society." In *Justice as Fairness* (Cambridge: Harvard University Press).
2007. "Marx II: His Conception of Right and Justice." In *Lectures on the History of Political Philosophy* (Cambridge: Harvard University Press), pp. 335–353.
Raz, Joseph. 1986. *The Morality of Freedom*. Oxford: Oxford University Press.
Reagan, Ronald. 1981. "Inaugural Address" (January 20). (www.presidency.ucsb.edu/documents/inaugural-address-11).
Reardon, Sean F. and Kendra Bischoff. 2011. "Growth in the Residential Segregation of Families by Income, 1970–2009." US2010 Project. Russell Sage Foundation/Brown University (November).
Refund Transit Coalition. 2012. "Riding the Gravy Train: How Wall Street Is Bankrupting Our Public Transit Agencies by Profiteering Off of Toxic Swap Deals" (June).
Rehmus, Charles M. and Benjamin A. Kerner. 1980. "The Agency Shop after Abood: No Free Ride, but What's the Fare?" *Industrial and Labor Relations Review* 34: 90–100.
Reiff, Mark R. 2003. "Politics of Masochism." *Inquiry* 46: 29–63.
2005. *Punishment, Compensation, and Law: A Theory of Enforceability*. Cambridge: Cambridge University Press.
2007. "The Attack on Liberalism." In *Law and Philosophy*, eds. Michael Freeman and Ross Harrison (Oxford: Oxford University Press), pp. 173–210.
2008. "Terrorism, Retribution, and Collective Responsibility." *Social Theory and Practice* 34: 209–242.
2009. "Proportionality, Winner-Take-All, and Distributive Justice." *Politics, Philosophy, and Economics* 8: 5–42.
2010. "Collective Responsibility." *Encyclopedia of Political Theory*, ed. Mark Bevir (London: Sage).
2012. "The Difference Principle, Rising Inequality, and Supply-Side Economics: How Rawls Got Hijacked by the Right." *Revue de Philosophie Économique/Review of Economic Philosophy* 13(2): 119–173.
2013. *Exploitation and Economic Justice in the Liberal Capitalist State*. Oxford: Oxford University Press.
2014. "Incommensurability and Moral Value." *Politics, Philosophy, and Economics* 13: 237–268.
2015. "No Such Thing as Accident: Rethinking the Relation between Causal and Moral Responsibility." *Canadian Journal of Law and Jurisprudence* 28: 371–397.
2015. *On Unemployment, Volume I: A Micro-Theory of Economic Justice*. New York: Palgrave Macmillan.
2015. *On Unemployment, Volume II: Achieving Economic Justice after the Great Recession*. New York: Palgrave Macmillan.
2017. "A Philosopher Argues Why No One Has the Right to Refuse Service to LGBT People." *The Conversation* (July 25).
2017. "Punishment in the Executive Suite: Moral Responsibility, Causal Responsibility, and Financial Crime." In *Just Financial Markets? Finance in a Just Society*, ed. Lisa Herzog (Oxford: Oxford University Press), pp. 125–153.

2017. "Trump and the End of Liberalism." *The Critique* (January 15, 2017).

2017. "Two Theories of Economic Liberalism." *The Adam Smith Review* 10: 189–214.

2018. "Twenty-One Statements about Political Philosophy: An Introduction and Commentary on the State of the Profession." *Teaching Philosophy* 41:65–115.

Manuscript. *The Unbearable Resilience of Illiberalism*.

Rein, Lisa. 2018. "Trump Takes Aim at Federal Bureaucracy with New Executive Orders Rolling Back Civil Service Protections." *The Washington Post* (May 25).

2018. "Trump's Fight with Federal Employee Unions Gets Real on Monday." *The Washington Post* (July 8).

Rein, Lisa and Andrew Ba Tran. 2017. "How the Trump Era Is Changing the Federal Bureaucracy." *The Washington Post* (December 30).

Reisman, George. 2014. "Labor Unions Are Anti-Labor." *Mises Daily Articles* (Mises Institute, July 28).

2013. "Labor Unions, Thugs, and Storm Troopers." *Mises Daily Articles* (January 4).

2014. "How Labor Unions Hurt Workers." *The Free Market* 32:6 (June).

Remnick, David. 2018. "Trump and the Enemies of the People." *The New Yorker* (August 15).

Report of the Committee of Inquiry on Industrial Democracy ("The Bullock Report"). 1977 (London: HMSO).

Reuters. 2017. "Former U.A.W. Official Charged in Fiat Chrysler Payoff Case." *The New York Times* (August 18).

2019. "Canada Union Calls for Boycott of GM Mexico-Made Vehicles" (January 25).

Reynolds, Morgan O. 1984. *Power and Privilege: Labor Unions in America*. New York: Manhattan Institute for Policy Research.

Rhodes, David, Colin Carter, and Stephen Sutherland. 2016. "Looking for Smoke under the Door: The Case for an Actively Engaged Board." Boston Consulting Group (August) (www.bcgperspectives.com/Images/BCG-Looking-for-Smoke-Under-the-Door-Aug-2016_tcm80-213612.pdf).

Richman, Shaun. 2018. "If the Supreme Court Rules against Unions, Conservatives Won't Like What Happens Next." *The Washington Post* (March 1).

Ring, Ed. 2017. "California's Public Sector Union 'Deep State.'" California Policy Center (February 28) (https://californiapolicycenter.org/californias-public-sector-union-deep-state/).

Rizzo, Salvador. 2018. "The Facts about Trump's Policy of Separating Families at the Border." *The Washington Post* (June 19).

Robbins, Liz. 2016. "L.I.U.-Brooklyn Locks Out Professors Amid Contract Dispute." *The New York Times* (September 6).

Roberts, Chris. 2016. "Another Uber Driver Awarded Unemployment Benefits." *SF Weekly* (March 4).

Robinson, Eugene. 2018. "God Bless the 'Deep State.'" *The Washington Post* (July 19).

Rogers, Ed. 2017. "The 'Deep State' Is Real. The 'Alt Right' Is Fake." *The Washington Post* (February 21).

Rogers, Kate. 2018. "Where the Jobs: Houston's Police Shortage." *CNBC* (February 2).

Rojas, Rick and Mary Williams Walsh. 2017. "Hartford, with Its Finances in Disarray, Veers toward Bankruptcy." *The New York Times* (August 15).

Romero, Simon and Julie Turkewitz. 2018. "Teachers in Arizona and Colorado Walk Out for Funding and Pay Raises." *The New York Times* (April 26).
Romero, Simon, Jack Healy, and Julie Turkewitz. 2018. "Teachers in Arizona and Colorado Walk Out over Education Funding." *The New York Times* (April 26).
Ronayne, Kathleen and Christina A. Cassidy. 2017. "Republican State Lawmakers Push for Restrictions on Voting." *The Washington Post* (February 9).
Roose, Kevin. 2018. "Workers of Silicon Valley, It's Time to Organize." *The New York Times* (April 26).
Rosen, Corey. 2002. "Observations on Employee Ownership: United Airlines, ESOPs, and Employee Ownership." *National Center for Employee Ownership* (November) (www.nceo.org/observations-employee-ownership/c/united-airlines-esops-employee-ownership).
Rosen, Jeffry. 2008. "The Roberts Court and Executive Power." *Pepperdine Law Review* 35: 503–508.
Rosenberg, Eli. 2017. "Journalists at Gothamist and DNAinfo Agree to Join Labor Union." *The New York Times* (April 12).
Rosenfeld, Jake, Patrick Denice, and Jennifer Laird. 2016. "Union Decline Lowers Wages of Nonunion Workers: The Overlooked Reason Why Wages Are Stuck and Inequality Is Growing." Economic Policy Institute (August 30) (www.epi.org/files/pdf/112811.pdf).
Rosman, Katherine and Jaclyn Peiser. 2018. "Denver Post Journalists Go to New York to Protest Their Owner." *The New York Times* (May 8).
Rossiter, Adam. 2018. "Stranded French Commuters Could Test Macron's Reform Agenda." *The New York Times* (April 4).
Rothbard, Murray N. 1998. *The Ethics of Liberty*. New York: New York University Press.
  2006. *For a New Liberty: The Libertarian Manifesto*, 2nd ed. Auburn, AL: Ludwig von Mises Institute.
  2009. *Man, Economy, and State*, Scholar's ed., 2nd ed. Auburn, AL: Ludwig von Mises Institute.
Rubin, Alissa J. 2018. "Can Strikes in France Still Make a Difference?" *The New York Times* (June 12).
Ruchkoff, Douglass. 2017. "Silicon Valley's Push for Universal Basic Income Is – Surprise! – Totally Self-Serving." *The Guardian* (July 21).
Ruddick, Graham. 2017. "Steelworkers to Vote on Port Talbot Rescue Plan." *The Guardian* (January 29).
Ruddick, Graham and Jamie Grierson. 2017. "BBC Gender Pay Gap: Male Staff Earn 9% More Than Female Colleagues." *The Guardian* (October 4).
Rudolph, Frederick. 1950. "The American Liberty League, 1934–1940." *The American Historical Review* 56: 19–33.
Rushe, Dominic. 2017. "'We Are a Cautionary Tale': Kansas Feels the Pain of Massive Trump-Style Tax Cuts." *The Guardian* (May 15).
  2017. "Fran Works Six Days a Week in Fast Food, and Yet She's Homeless: 'It's Economic Slavery.'" *The Guardian* (August 21).
  2018. "Unions Reach $2.3m Settlement in Bangladesh Textile Factory Safety." *The Guardian* (January 22).

Rushe, Dominic and Tom Pietrasik. 2017. "'I Was Naïve': After Losing Health Care Battle, Factory Workers Fear Next Blow." *The Guardian* (February 24).

Rutenberg, Jim. 2017. "News Outlets to Seek Bargaining Rights against Google and Facebook." *The New York Times* (July 9).

Rutherford, Malcom. 2000. "Institutionalism between the Wars." *Journal of Economic Issues* 34: 291–303.

2000. "Understanding Institutional Economics: 1918–1929." *Journal of the History of Economic Thought* 22: 277–308.

2001. "Institutional Economics: Then and Now." *Journal of Economic Perspectives* 15: 173–194.

S., M. 2011. "What the Difference Exactly: The Distinction between Private- and Public-Sector Unions." *The Economist* (February 9).

Sachs, Jeffrey D. 2017. "How to Break the 40-Year Working Class Losing Streak." *The Boston Globe* (August 17).

Saez, Emmanuel. 2016. "Striking It Richer: The Evolution of Top Incomes in the United States" (Updated with 2015 preliminary estimates) (June 30) (https://eml.berkeley.edu/~saez/saez-UStopincomes-2015.pdf).

Sainato, Michael. 2018. "Exploited Amazon Workers Need a Union. When Will They Get One?" *The Guardian* (July 8).

2018. "Accidents at Amazon: Workers Left to Suffer after Warehouse Injuries." *The Guardian* (July 30).

2018. "Tesla Workers Speak Out: 'Anything Pro-Union Is Shut Down Really Fast.'" *The Guardian* (September 10).

2018. "Amazon Training Videos Coach Whole Foods Staff on How to Discourage Unions." *The Guardian* (September 27).

2019. "'It's Union Busting 101': Documents Reveal Verizon Attacks on Organized Labor." *The Guardian* (January 16).

2019. "Denver Teachers Set to Strike Over Better Pay and Working Conditions." *The Guardian* (February 10).

2019. "Low Pay, Large Classes, Funding Cuts: Behind New Wave of US Teachers' Strikes." *The Guardian* (February 27).

2019. "Whole Foods Cuts Workers' Hours after Amazon Introduces Minimum Wage." *The Guardian* (March 6).

2019. "Miami Airport Workers Fighting for Better Conditions Face Retaliation." *The Guardian* (May 17).

2019. "Bosses Pocket Trump Tax Windfall as Workers See Job Promises Vanish." *The New York Times* (June 16).

2019. "Social Security Workers Call New Trump Administration Contract 'Union-Busting.'" *The Guardian* (July 3).

Samuel, Ian. 2018. "Rigging the Vote: How the American Right Is on the Way to Permanent Minority Rule." *The Guardian* (November 4).

Samuelson, Robert J. 2018. "The Deeper Cause behind the School Strikes: Teachers Are Competing against the Elderly." *The Washington Post* (April 8).

Sanders, Bernie. 2017. "Nissan Dispute Could Go Down as Most Vicious Anti-Union Crusade on Decades." *The Guardian* (August 3).

Sanders, Samantha and Heidi Shierholz. 2017. "How President Trump and Congressional Republicans Are Undercutting Wages and Protections for Working People." *Working Economics Blog*, Economic Policy Institute (April 19).

Sapolsky, Robert M. 2017. *Behave: The Biology of Humans at Our Best and Worst*. New York: Penguin.
   2019. "This Is Your Brain on Nationalism: The Biology of Us and Them." *Foreign Affairs* (March/April).
Savage, David G. 2018. "Supreme Court Upholds Arbitration That Bans Workers from Joining Forces over Lost Wages." *Los Angeles Times* (May 21).
Sawyer, Malcolm C. 1985. *The Economics of Michal Kalecki*. London: Macmillan.
Scheffler, Samuel. 2006. "Is the Basic Structure Basic?" In *The Egalitarian Conscience: Essays in Honour of G. A. Cohen* (Oxford: Oxford University Press), pp. 102–129.
Scheiber, Noam. 2015. "Public Pension Cuts Exempt Police and Firefighters." *The New York Times* (March 19).
   2015. "In Test for Unions and Politicians, a Nationwide Protest on Pay." *The New York Times* (April 15).
   2016. "Supreme Court Case in Public Sector Union Fees Rouses Political Suspicions." *The New York Times* (January 10).
   2016. "Pension Benefit Cuts Planned at T.V.A., Breaking a Federal Firewall." *The New York Times* (March 3).
   2016. "A Power Broker Who Wants Labor at the Table, Not on the Menu." *The New Yorker* (July 29).
   2016. "Grad Students Win Right to Unionize in an Ivy League Case." *The New York Times* (August 23).
   2016. "Uber Drivers Ruled Eligible for Jobless Payments by New York State." *The New York Times* (October 12).
   2017. "Betsy DeVos, Trump's Education Pick, Plays Hardball with Her Wealth." *The New York Times* (January 9).
   2017. "Boeing Workers Reject a Union in South Carolina." *The New York Times* (February 15).
   2017. "How Uber Uses Psychological Tricks to Push Its Drivers' Buttons." *The New York Times* (April 2).
   2017. "Uber Has a Union of Sorts, but Faces Doubts on Its Autonomy." *The New York Times* (May 12).
   2017. "Uber to Repay Millions to Drivers, Who Could Be Owed Far More." *The New York Times* (May 23).
   2017. "Uber Says It Just Noticed Error on Pay, but It Was No Secret." *The New York Times* (June 1).
   2017. "Trump Takes Steps to Undo Obama Legacy on Labor." *The New York Times* (June 20).
   2017. "How Raising Minimum Wage Affects Jobs in Seattle." *The New York Times* (June 26).
   2017. "How Uber's Tax Calculations May Have Cost Drivers Hundreds of Millions." *The New York Times* (July 6).
   2017. "Racially Charged Nissan Vote Is a Test for U.A.W. in the South." *The New York Times* (August 2).
   2017. "U.A.W. Accuses Nissan of 'Scare Tactics' as Workers Reject Union Bid." *The New York Times* (August 5).
   2017. "Service Union Plans Big Push to Turn Midwest Political Tide." *The New York Times* (August 24).

2017. "Trump Shifts Labor Policy Focus from Worker to Entrepreneur." *The New York Times* (September 3).
2017. "Chinese-Owned Factory in Ohio Fights Off Unionization Plan." *The New York Times* (November 9).
2017. "AT&T Agrees to Contract, and Union Backs Time Warner Deal." *The New York Times* (December 13).
2018. "Trump Appointee Is Trying to Squelch Us, Labor Board Staff Says." *The New York Times* (January 25).
2018. "6 Reasons that Pay Has Lagged Behind U.S. Job Growth." *The New York Times* (February 1).
2018. "Labor Board's Do-Over Leaves an Obama-Era Rule Intact." *The New York Times* (February 26).
2018. "Push to Settle McDonald's Case, a Threat to Franchise Model." *The New York Times* (March 19).
2018. "Senate Bill to Curtail Labor Rights on Tribal Land Falls Short." *The New York Times* (April 16).
2018. "Gig Economy Business Model Dealt a Blow in California Ruling." *The New York Times* (April 30).
2018. "Can Weak Unions Get Teachers More Money?" *The New York Times* (May 5).
2018. "Trump Moves to Ease the Firing of Federal Workers." *The New York Times* (May 25).
2018. "Labor Unions Will Be Smaller after Supreme Court Decision, but Maybe Not Weaker." *The New York Times* (June 27).
2018. "Supreme Court Labor Decision Wasn't Just a Loss for Unions." *The New York Times* (July 1).
2018. "Trump Nominee Is Behind Anti-Union Legal Campaign." *The New York Times* (July 16).
2018. "Judge Rejects Settlement over McDonald's Labor Practices." *The New York Times* (July 17).
2018. "Federal Workers Brace for New Push on Trump Anti-Labor Goals." *The New York Times* (September 2).
2018. "Google Workers Reject Silicon Valley Individualism in Walkout." *The New York Times* (November 6).
2019. "Amazon and Union at Odds over Firing of Staten Island Warehouse Worker." *The New York Times* (March 20).
2019. "Is Gig Work a Job? Uber and Others Are Maneuvering to Shape the Answer." *The New York Times* (March 26).
2019. "U.S. Moves to Limit Wage Claims against Chains Like McDonald's." *The New York Times* (April 1).
2019. "Labor Dept. Says Workers at a Gig Company Are Contractors." *The New York Times* (April 29).
2019. "Uber Drivers Are Contractors, Not Employees, Labor Board Says." *The New York Times* (May 14).
2019. "Volkswagen Factory Workers in Tennessee Reject Union." *The New York Times* (June 14).
2019. "Debate over Uber and Lyft Drivers' Rights in California Has Split Labor." *The New York Times* (June 29).

Scheiber, Noam and Bill Vlasic. 2017. "U.A.W. Says Nissan Workers Seek a Union Vote in Mississippi." *The New York Times* (July 11).

Scheiber, Noam and Keith Bradsher. 2017. "Culture Clash at a Chinses-Owned Plant in Ohio." *The New York Times* (June 10).

Scheiber, Noam and Christopher Drew. 2017. "Union Vote at Boeing Plant Tests Labor's Sway under Trump." *The New York Times* (February 13).

Scheiber, Noam and Stephanie Strom. 2015. "Labor Board Ruling Eases Way for Fast-Food Unions' Efforts." *The New York Times* (August 27).

Scheiber, Noam and Kenneth P. Vogel. 2018. "Behind a Key Anti-Labor Case, a Web of Conservative Donors." *The New York Times* (February 25).

Scheiber, Noam, Maggie Haberman, and Glenn Thrush. 2017. "Trump's Inroads in Union Ranks Have Labor Leaders Scrambling." *The New York Times* (February 17).

Schlesinger, Arthur Jr. 1983. "Should Conservatives Embrace Big Government? *The New York Times* (February 3).

Schnabel, Claus and Joachim Wagner, 2007. "The Persistent Decline in Unionization in Western and Eastern Germany, 1980–2004: What Can We Learn from a Decomposition Analysis?" *Industrielle Beziehungen/The German Journal of Industrial Relations* Jahrg. 14, H. 2, Gewerkschaftsmitgliedschaft in Deutschland: Strukturen, Determinanten und Tendenzen (2007), pp. 118–132.

Schneider, Dorothee. 1994. *Trade Unions and Community*. Urbana, IL: University of Illinois Press.

Schonbrun, Zach. 2018. "When a Local Paper Gets New Owners, Partisan Strife Hits Its Doorstep." *The New York Times* (August 5).

Schoonover, Bob. 2017. "SEIU Defends AB 1250." Letters to Editor, *Sacramento Bee* (July 22).

Schultz, Julianne. 1998. *Reviving the Fourth Estate: Democracy, Accountability, and the Media*. Cambridge: Cambridge University Press.

Schwab, Stewart J. and Randall S. Thomas. 1997–1998. "Realigning Corporate Governance: Shareholder Activism by Labor Unions." *Michigan Law Review* 96: 1018–1094.

Schwartz, Gary T. 2001. "The Myth of the Ford Pinto Case." *Rutgers University Law Review* 43: 1013–1068.

Schwartz, Nelson D. 2017. "Route to Air Travel Discomfort Starts on Wall Street." *The New York Times* (May 28).

Schwartz, Nelson D. and Patricia Cowen. 2014. "Falling Wages at Factories Squeeze the Middle Class." *The New York Times* (December 15).

Schwartzman, Paul and Fenit Nirappil. 2018. "D.C. Voters Approve Initiative to Raise Minimum Wage for Tipped Workers to $15." *The Washington Post* (June 19).

Scola, Nancy. 2012. "Exposing ALEC: How Conservative-Backed State Laws Are All Connected." *The Atlantic* (April 14).

Scott, Mark. 2016. "In Europe, Is Uber a Transportation Service or a Digital Platform?" *The New York Times* (November 27).

Sealover, Ed. 2017. "Colorado Senate Passes Bill to Become 'Right-to-Work State." *Denver Business Journal* (February 14).

Searcey, Dionne. 2015. "Job Growth Fails to Help Paycheck of Workers." *The New York Times* (January 9).

Seckman, Cary Hester. 2004. "The Unions: How Organized Labor Is Landing a Helping Hand to Dental Hygiene." *RDH Magazine* (April).

Sedacca, Matthew. 2017. "Unions Are Gaining a Foothold at Digital Media Companies." *The New York Times* (December 26).
Seidman, Joel I. 1932. "The Yellow Dog Contract." *The Quarterly Journal of Economics* 46: 348–361.
Selten, Richard. 1975. "A Reexamination of the Perfectness Concept for Equilibrium Points in Extensive Games." *International Journal of Game Theory* 4: 25–55.
Semuels, Alana. 2013. "Contracts, Court Rulings Give Employers Legal Upper Hand." *Los Angeles Times* (July 6).
Sforza, Teri. 2017. "Southern California Firefighters Pull in a Quarter-Million Dollars in Overtime, and Then Some." *Orange County Register* (June 21).
Shahshahani, Azadeh. 2018. "Why Are For-Profit US Prisons Subjecting Detainees to Forced Labor?" *The Guardian* (May 17).
Shamay-Tsoory, Simone G., et al. 2009. "Intranasal Administration of Oxytocin Increases Envy and Schadenfreude (Gloating)." *Biological Psychiatry* 66: 864–870.
Shane, Scott. 2017. "From Headline to Photograph, a Fake News Masterpiece." *The New York Times* (January 18).
Shaub, Walter M. Jr. 2019. "Five Myths about the Federal Workforce." *The Washington Post* (February 14).
Shierholz, Heidi. 2013. "At a Time of Persistent Economic Weakness, Today's Jobs Report Represents an Ongoing Disaster." *Press Release*. Economic Policy Institute (May 3).
Shulman, Harry. 1939. "Labor and the Antitrust Laws." *Illinois Law Review* 34: 769–787.
Siddiqui, Faiz. 2019. "Uber and Lyft Drivers Strike for Pay Transparency – after Algorithms Made It Harder to Understand." *The Washington Post* (May 8).
Simmonds, Nigel E. 1998. "Rights at the Cutting Edge." In *A Debate over Rights* (Oxford: Oxford University Press), pp. 113–232.
  2002. *Central Issues in Jurisprudence*, 2nd ed. London: Sweet & Maxwell.
Simmons, Henry C. 1942. "Hansen on Fiscal Policy." *Journal of Political Economy* 50: 161–196.
  1944. "Some Reflections on Syndicalism." *The Journal of Political Economy* 52: 1–25.
  1948. *Economic Policy for a Free Society*. Chicago, IL: University of Chicago Press.
Simpson, Peter L. P. 2018. *Political Illiberalism: A Defense of Freedom*. New Brunswick, NJ: Transaction Publishers.
Simpson, Thomas W. 2017. "The Impossibility of Republican Freedom." *Philosophy & Public Affairs* 45: 27–53.
Singer, Natasha. 2012. "In Executive Pay, a Rich Game of Thrones." *The New York Times* (April 7).
Sirota, David. 2018. "How California Public Employees Fund Anti-Rent Control Fight Unwittingly." *The Guardian* (October 23).
Skelton, George. 2018. "Democrats Running for California Governor Need to Stop Talking about Trump and Start Talking about Public Pensions." *Los Angeles Times* (January 18).
Skinner, Quentin. 1998. *Liberty before Liberalism*. Cambridge: Cambridge University Press.

2002. "A Third Concept of Liberty." *Proceedings of the British Academy* 117: 237–268.

2002. "Classical Liberty and the Coming of the English Civil War." In *Republicanism: A Shared European Heritage*, eds. Martinvan Gelderen and Quentin Skinner (Cambridge: Cambridge University Press), vol. 2, pp. 9–28.

Slater, Joseph E. 2004. *Public Workers: Government Employee Unions, the Law, and the State, 1900–1962*. Ithaca, NY: Cornell University Press.

Smith, Adam. 1978. *Lectures on Jurisprudence*. Oxford: Oxford University Press [1766].

2000. *The Wealth of Nations*. New York: Modern Library.

Smith, Adam S., et al. 2010. "Manipulation of the Oxytocin System Alters Social Behavior and Attraction in Pair-Bonding Primates, Callithrix Penicillata." *Hormones and Behavior* 57: 255–262.

Smith, D. Gordon. 1996. "Corporate Governance and Managerial Incompetence: Lessons from Kmart." *North Carolina Law Review* 74: 1037–1139.

Smith, David. 2017. "How Trump's Paranoid White House Sees 'Deep State' Enemies on All Sides." *The Guardian* (August 13).

Smith, Melissa. 2018. "I Work at One of America's Underfunded Schools. It's Falling Apart." *The Guardian* (May 26).

Smith, Mitch and Julie Bosman. 2017. "Kansas Supreme Court Says State Education Spending Is Too Low." *The New York Times* (March 2).

Smith, Robert Michael. 2003. *From Blackjacks to Briefcases: A History of Commercialized Strikebreaking and Unionbusting in the United States*. Athens, OH: Ohio University Press.

Sodha, Sonia. 2017. "Mark Zuckerberg's Got Some Cheek, Advocating a Universal Basic Income." *The Guardian* (July 10).

Solomon, Steven Davidoff. 2015. "The Boardroom Strikes Back." *The New York Times* (April 21).

2016. "Rise of Institutional Investors Raises Questions of Collusion." *The New York Times* (April 12).

Sommeiller, Estelle and Mark Price. 2018. "The New Gilded Age." *Economic Policy Institute* (July 19) (www.epi.org/files/pdf/147963.pdf).

Sorkin, Andrew Ross. 2016. "C.E.O.s Meet in Secret over the Sorry State of Public Companies." *The New York Times* (July 21).

Southall, Ashley. 2018. "New York Police Union Sues to Stop Release of Body Camera Videos." *The New York Times* (January 9).

2019. "Police Union Criticized for Comparing Arrested N.F.L. Player to 'Wild Animal.'" *The New York Times* (January 27).

Spencer, Herbert. 1891 [1853]. "Over-Legislation." In *Essays: Scientific, Political, & Speculative, Volume III* (London: Williams and Norgate), pp. 229–282.

1891 [1853]. "Representative Government – What Is It Good For?" In *Essays: Scientific, Political, & Speculative, Volume III* (London: Williams and Norgate), pp. 283–325.

1994. "The Proper Sphere of Government." In *Political Writings*, ed. John Offer (Cambridge: Cambridge University Press), pp. 3–57.

Starr, Evan P., Norman Bishara, and J. J. Prescott. 2017. "Noncompetes in the U.S. Labor Force." *Social Science Research Network* (July 28) (https://ssrn.com/abstract=2625714).

State Policy Network. 2018. "Messaging Guide: How to Talk about Teacher Strikes." Reprinted in Ed Pilkington, "Revealed: Secret Rightwing Strategy to Discredit Teacher Strikes." *The Guardian* (April 12).

Stein, Jeff. 2018. "Missouri Voters Defeat GOP-Backed 'Right to Work' Law, in Victory for Unions, Associated Press Projects." *The Washington Post* (August 7).

Stein, Jeff and Andrew Van Dam. 2018. "For the Biggest Group of American Workers, Wages Aren't Just Flat. They're Falling." *The Washington Post* (June 15).

Steiner, Hillel. 1975. "Individual Liberty." *Aristotelian Society Proceedings* 75: 35–50, reprinted in *Liberty*, ed. David Miller (Oxford: Oxford University Press, 1991).

  1980. "Slavery, Socialism, and Private Property." In *Property*, eds. J. Roland Pennock and John W. Chapman (New York: New York University Press), pp. 244–265.

  1994. *An Essay on Rights*. Oxford: Basil Blackwell.

  2012. "Evaluation and the Quantification of Freedom." In *Thinking towards Humanity: Themes from Norman Geras*, eds. Eve Garrard and Stephen de Wijze (Manchester: Manchester University Press).

  2013. "Directed Duties and Inalienable Rights." *Ethics* 123: 230–244.

  2018. "On the Conflict between Liberty and Equality." In *Oxford Handbook of Freedom*, eds. David Schmidtz and Carmen Pavel (New York: Oxford University Press), pp. 76–89.

Steiner, Yves. 2009. "The Neoliberals Confront the Trade Unions." In *The Road from Mount Pèlerin*, eds. Philip Mirowski and Dieter Plehwe (Cambridge: Harvard University Press), pp. 181–203.

Stern, Andrew and Eli Lehrer. 2017. "How to Modernize Labor Law." *National Affairs* 32 (Winter).

Stevens, Matt. 2019. "Aviation Professionals Warn of Dire Risk Amid Shutdown." *The New York Times* (January 23).

Stewart, James B. 2017. "Wells Fargo Whistle-Blowers' Fate Becomes Just a Footnote." *The New York Times* (May 4).

Stewart, Luke. 2010. "The Impact of Regulation on Innovation in the United States: A Cross-Industry Literature Review." *Information Technology & Innovation Foundation* (June) (www.itif.org/files/2011-impact-regulation-innovation.pdf).

Stiglitz, Joseph. 2012. *The Price of Inequality*. New York: Norton.

  2016. "Joseph Stiglitz Says Standard Economics Is Wrong. Inequality and Unearned Income Kills the Economy." *Evonomics* (September 9).

Stolberg, Sheryl Gay and Eric Lichtblau. 2017. "Sweeping Federal Review Could Affect Consent Decrees Nationwide." *The New York Times* (April 3).

Strauss, Leo. 1953. *Natural Right and History*. Chicago, IL: University of Chicago Press.

Strauss, Valerie. 2016. "Think Teachers Can't Be Fired Because of Unions? Surprising Results from a New Study." *The Washington Post* (July 21).

  2016. "How Messed Up Is California's Charter School Sector? You Won't Believe How Much." *The Washington Post* (September 9).

  2016. "In California's Charter World, a Tangled Web of For-Profit Companies and Nonprofit Schools." *The Washington Post* (October 14).

  2017. "Charter Schools in California Are Operating Where They Aren't Needed, Study Says." *The Washington Post* (April 14).

Strawbs, 1973. "Part of the Union," on Bursting at the Seams (Remastered), A & M Records (1998 reissue) (album).
Streeck, Wolfgang. 2006. "The Study of Organized Interests: Before 'The Century' and After." In *The Diversity of Democracy: Corporatism, Social Order and Political Conflict*, eds. Colin Crouch and Wolfgang Streeck (Cheltenham: Edward Elgar), pp. 3–45.
Streitfeld, David. 2013. "Amazon Workers in Germany Strike Again." *The New York Times* (December 16).
  2018. "Amazon Delivers a Pile of Cash, but No Fireworks." *The New York Times* (July 26).
Summers, Lawrence. 2017. "America Needs Its Unions More Than Ever." *The Guardian* (September 3).
Summers, Lawrence H. and Ed Balls. 2015. Report of the Commission on Inclusive Prosperity. Center for American Progress (January) (https://cdn.americanprogress.org/wp-content/uploads/2015/01/IPC-PDF-full.pdf).
Summers, Robert S. 1976. *Collective Bargaining and Public Benefit Conferral: A Jurisprudential Critique*. Ithaca, NY: Institute of Public Employment, Cornell University Press.
  1980. "Public Sector Collective Bargaining Substantially Diminishes Democracy." *Government Union Review* 1: 5–22.
Sunstein, Cass. 2005. *Laws of Fear: Beyond the Precautionary Principle*. Cambridge: Cambridge University Press.
Surowicki, James. 2016. "Trump Sets Private Prisons Free." *The New Yorker* (December 5).
Swaine, Jon. 2018. "Sinclair TV Chairman to Trump: 'We Are Here to Deliver Your Message.'" *The Guardian* (April 10).
Swenson, Peter. 1989. *Fair Shares: Unions, Pay, and Politics in Sweden and West Germany*. Ithaca, NY: Cornell University Press.
Tabuchi, Hiroko. 2015. "Laid-Off Walmart Workers Head to Labor Board." *The New York Times* (April 19).
  2017. "U.S. Reopens Harley Settlement, Cutting Funds for Pollution Reduction Plan." *The New York Times* (July 20).
Tapia, Maite, Christian L. Ibsen, and Thomas A. Kochan. 2015. "Mapping the Frontier of Theory in Industrial Relations: The Contested Role of Worker Representation." *Socio-Economic Review* 13: 157–184.
Tarnoff, Ben. 2017. "How Privatization Could Spell the End of Democracy." *The Guardian* (June 21).
Tavernise, Sabrina. 2019. "With His Job Gone, an Autoworker Wonders, 'What Am I as a Man?'" *The New York Times* (May 27).
Taylor, Charles. 1985. "What's Wrong with Negative Liberty?" In *Philosophy and the Human Sciences: Philosophical Papers 2*. (Cambridge: Cambridge University Press), pp. 211–229.
Taylor, David. 2019. "'In God We Trust'- The Bills Christian Nationalists Hope Will 'Protect Religious Freedom.'" *The Guardian* (January 14).
Taylor, Robert S. 2017. *Exit Left: Markets and Mobility in Republican Thought*. Oxford: Oxford University Press.

Telford, Taylor. 2018. "Thousands of Service Industry Workers Will Strike Next Week to Demand Unions." *The Washington Post* (September 27).
Temin, Peter. 2017. *The Vanishing Middle Class: Prejudice and Power in a Dual Economy*. Cambridge, MA: MIT Press.
Temkin, Larry. 2000. "Equality, Priority, and the Levelling Down Objection." In *The Ideal of Equality*, eds. Matthew Clayton and Andrew Williams (New York: Palgrave), pp. 126–161.
Thaler, Richard H. 1999. "Mental Accounting Matters." *Journal of Behavioral Decision Making* 12: 183–206.
The Associated Press–NORC Center for Public Affairs Research. 2017. "The American Identity: Points of Pride, Conflicting Views, and a Distinct Culture" (http://apnorc.org/projects/Pages/HTML%20Reports/points-of-pride-conflicting-views-and-a-distinct-culture.aspx).
"The Future of Work." 2017. *The New York Times* (February 26).
The National Conference of State Legislatures. 2016. "Collective Bargaining and Labor Union Database" (www.ncsl.org/research/labor-and-employment/collective-bargaining-legislation-database.aspx) (last updated July 1).
The White House. 2016. "Non-Compete Agreements: Analysis of the Usage, Potential Issues, and State Responses" (May) (https://obamawhitehouse.archives.gov/sites/default/files/non-competes_report_final2.pdf).
  2016. "Fact Sheet: The Obama Administration Announces New Steps to Spur Competition in the Labor Market and Accelerate Wage Growth." Office of the Press Secretary (October 25) (https://obamawhitehouse.archives.gov/the-press-office/2016/10/25/fact-sheet-obama-administration-announces-new-steps-spur-competition).
The Working Life. 2014. "Some Retail Workers Find Better Deals with Unions." *The New York Times* (September 7).
Thelen, Kathleen. 2001. "Varieties of Labor Politics in the Developed Democracies." In *Varieties of Capitalism: The Institutional Foundations of Comparative Advantage*, eds. Peter A. Hall and David Soskice (Oxford: Oxford University Press), pp. 71–103.
Thieblot, Armand J. 2006. "Perspectives on Union Corruption: Lessons from the Databases." *Journal of Labor Research* 28: 513–534.
Thomas Fordham Institute. 2017. "(No) Money in the Bank: Which Retirement Systems Penalize New Teachers." (January 26) (https://edexcellence.net/publications/no-money-in-the-bank).
Thompson, Derek. 2013. "How Low Are U.S. Taxes Compared to Other Countries?" *The Atlantic* (January 14).
  2014. "Why It's So Hard for Millennials to Find a Place to Live and Work." *The Atlantic* (November 19).
Thrush, Glenn and Erica L. Green. 2018. "Behind Trump's Plan to Overhaul the Government: Scaling Back the Safety Net." *The New York Times* (June 21).
Tilford, Simon. 2017. "Why 'Brexit' Will Make Britain's Mediocre Economy Worse." *The New York Times* (May 29).
Tobin, James. 1987. "The Future of Keynesian Economics." In *Policies for Prosperity* (Cambridge, MA: MIT Press), pp. 14–23.
Tobin, Jeffrey. 2018. "The Courts Take Aim at Partisan Gerrymandering." *The New Yorker* (January 23).

Tolentino, Jia. 2017. "The Gig Economy Celebrates Working Yourself to Death." *The New Yorker* (March 22).
Tomasky, Michael. 2018. "Ratfucked Again." *The New York Review of Books* (June 7).
Toobin, Jeffrey. 2019. "The Supreme Court Is Quietly Changing the Status of Religion in American Life." *The New Yorker* (March 6).
Topham, Gwyn. 2017. "British Rail Is Nationalised All over Again – By Foreign States." *The Guardian* (April 1).
  2017. "Monarch Collapse: Union Launches Legal Action over Redundancies." *The Guardian* (October 4).
Toynbee, Arnold Joseph. 1951. *A Study of History, Volume I.* Oxford: Oxford University Press.
Transparent California. 2017. "Salary and Pension Survey." (http://transparentcalifornia.com/) (last accessed November 8, 2019).
Trantidis, Aris and Nick Cowen. 2019. "Hayek versus Trump: The Radical Right's Road to Serfdom." Polity.
Treleven, Ed. 2014. "In 5-2 Ruling, Supreme Court Issues Final Word on Act 10." *Wisconsin State Journal* (July 31).
Tritch, Teresa. 2016. "Unions Knocking on the Academy's Doors." *The New York Times* (September 12).
Trumka, Richard. 2018. "Don't Let Trump Speak for Workers." *The New York Times* (December 27).
Truong, Debbie. 2019. "'Borderline Criminal': Many Public Schools Teeter on the Edge of Decrepitude." *The Guardian* (May 25).
Tsang, Amie. 2017. "Uber Is Dealt a Fresh Blow in European Legal Case." *The New York Times* (July 4).
  2017. "Ryanair Hit with Its First Pilot Strike, in Germany." *The New York Times* (December 22).
  2018. "BBC Managers Face Barrage of Criticism in Gender Pay Dispute." *The New York Times* (January 31).
  2018. "U.K. Court Rules against Plumbing Contractor in 'Gig Economy' Case." *The New York Times* (June 13).
  2019. "Pay Gap for Men and Women Grew at Many British Employers, Report Shows." *The New York Times* (April 5).
Tullis, Tracy. 2019. "A Multimillion Dollar Payday, at the Carwash." *The New York Times* (February 22).
Tullock, Gordon. 1967. "The Economics of Slavery." *Left and Right* 3: 5–16.
Turner, Lowell. 2009. "Institutions and Activism: Crisis and Opportunity for a German Labor Movement in Decline." *Industrial and Labor Relations Review* 62: 294–312.
Tversky, Amos and Daniel Kahneman. 1981. "The Framing of Decisions and the Psychology of Choice." *Science* 211: 453–458.
  1991. "Loss Aversion in Riskless Choice." *Quarterly Journal of Economics* 106: 1039–1061.
Tyson, Laura D'Andrea. 2013. "The Quality of Jobs: The New Normal and the Old Normal." *The New York Times* (September 20).
Tyson, Laura and Ana Madgavkar. 2016. "The Great Income Stagnation." *Project Syndicate* (September 7).

United States Congress, Senate Committee on the Judiciary, Subcommittee on Criminal Law. (1982). *S. 613, a bill to amend the Hobbs Act: Hearings before the Subcommittee on Criminal Law of the Committee on the Judiciary, United States Senate,* 97th Cong. first and second sessions, on S. 613 (December 10, 1981 and March 11, 1982) Washington, DC: U.S. G.P.O.

U.S. Bureau of Labor Statistics. All Employees: Government: Local Government [CES9093000001], retrieved from FRED, Federal Reserve Bank of St. Louis (April 23, 2018) (https://fred.stlouisfed.org/series/CES9093000001).

U.S. Department of Transportation, Air Fitness Division. 2012. "How to Become a Certified Air Carrier." Washington, DC (September). (www.transportation.gov/sites/dot.gov/files/docs/Certificated_Packet_2012_final.pdf).

Uchitelle, Louis. 2018. "How the Loss of Union Power Has Hurt American Manufacturing." *The New York Times* (April 20).

Uechi, Jenny. 2012. "U.S. Republican Koch Oil Billionaires Help Fund the Fraser Institute. Why the Fraser Institute?" *Vancouver Observer* (April 28).

Ullman, Lloyd. 1955. "Marshall and Friedman on Union Strength." *The Review of Economics and Statistics* 37: 384–401.

United States Attorney's Office. *Criminal Resources Manual* (www.justice.gov/usam/criminal-resource-manual-2403-hobbs-act-extortion-force-violence-or-fear) (last accessed November 8, 2019).

United States Census Bureau. 2016. "Income, Poverty, and Health Insurance Coverage in the United States: 2015." Release Number CB16-158 (September 13) (www.census.gov/newsroom/press-releases/2016/cb16-158.html).

2016. "The Supplemental Poverty Measure: 2015." Report Number P60-258 (September 13) (www.census.gov/library/publications/2016/demo/p60-258.html).

Vallentyne, Peter, Hillel Steiner, and Michael Otsuka. 2005. "Why Left-Libertarianism Is Not Incoherent, Indeterminate, or Irrelevant: A Reply to Fried." *Philosophy and Public Affairs* 33: 201–215.

Van Parijs, Philippe. 1991. "Why Surfers Should Be Fed: The Liberal Case for an Unconditional Basic Income." *Philosophy & Public Affairs* 20: 101–131.

1995. *Real Freedom for All.* Oxford: Oxford University Press.

Van Parijs, Philippe and Yannick Vanderborght. 2017. *Basic Income: A Radical Proposal for a Free Society and a Sane Economy.* Cambridge: Harvard University Press.

Vara, Vauhini. 2017. "Can Unions Stop the Far Right?" *The Atlantic* (December).

Varjacques, Leah, Taige Jensen, and Japhet Weeks. 2018. "We Are Republican Teachers Striking in Arizona. It's Time to Raise Taxes." *The New York Times* (April 26).

Varney, Dennis J. Jr. 2018. "Why Steve Mnuchin Wants a Stronger I.R.S." *The New York Times* (March 27).

Vásquez, Ian and Tanja Porčnik. 2017. "The Human Freedom Index 2017." A Cato Institute, Fraser Institute, and Friedrich Naumann Foundation for Freedom co-publication (https://object.cato.org/sites/cato.org/files/human-freedom-index-files/2017-human-freedom-index.pdf) (last accessed November 8, 2019).

2018. "The Human Freedom Index 2018." A Cato Institute, Fraser Institute, and Friedrich Naumann Foundation for Freedom co-publication (www.fraserinstitute.org/sites/default/files/human-freedom-index-2018.pdf).

Vedder, Richard. 2011. "The Economic Effects of Right to Work Laws." *Employee Responsibilities and Rights Journal* 23: 305–310.
Venteicher, Wes. 2019. "California Public Employees' Pension Perks Can Be Taken Away, Court Rules." *Sacramento Bee* (March 4).
Verkuil, Paul R. 2006. "Public Law Limitations on Privatization of Government Functions." *North Carolina Law Review* 84: 397–469.
Vickers, John and George Yarrow. 1991. "Economic Perspectives on Privatization." *Journal of Economic Perspectives* 5: 111–132.
Victor, Daniel. 2016. "The New Yorker Joins a Growing List of Media Companies to Unionize." *The New York Times* (June 6).
  2017. "Judge Approves Consent Decree to Overhaul Baltimore Police Department." *The New York Times* (April 7).
Vidal, Phillip. 2016. "Annual Survey of Public Pensions: State and Locally-Administered Defined Benefit Data Summary Brief: 2015." U.A. Census Bureau (June) (www.census.gov/content/dam/Census/library/publications/2016/econ/g15-aspp-sl.pdf).
Vogel, Kenneth P. 2012. "Cato, Kochs Settle Ownership Fight." *Politico* (June 5).
W., C. and A. J. K. D. 2013. "Did Slavery Make Economic Sense?" *The Economist* (September 27).
Wakabayashi, Daisuke. 2017. "At Google, Employee-Led Effort Finds Men Are Paid More Than Women." *The New York Times* (September 8).
  2019. "Google's Shadow Work Force: Temps Who Outnumber Full-Time Employees." *The New York Times* (May 28).
Waldman, Paul. 2016. "Welcome to the Trump Kleptocracy." *The Washington Post* (November 16).
Waldman, Peter. 2017. "Inside Alabama's Auto Jobs Boom: Cheap Wages, Little Training, Crushed Limbs." *Bloomberg Businessweek* (March 23).
Waldron, Jeremy. 2016. *Political Theory: Essays on Institutions*. Cambridge: Harvard University Press.
Walker, David M. 1980. "Trade Unions." In *The Oxford Companion to Law* (Oxford: Oxford University Press), pp. 1128–1130.
Walk-Morris, Tatiana. 2017. "Anti-Black Hiring Discrimination Hasn't Improved in 25 Years. What Can We Do?" *The Guardian* (September 21).
Wall, Steven. 2010. "On Justificatory Liberalism." *Politics, Philosophy, and Economics* 9: 123–149.
Wallace, Henry Scott. 2017. "American Fascism, in 1944 and Today." *The New York Times* (May 12).
Wallace-Wells, Benjamin. 2018. "The New Politics of the West Virginia Teachers' Strike." *The New Yorker* (March 2).
Walsh, Mary Williams. 2015. "Bad Math and a Coming Public Pension Crisis." *The New York Times* (July 8).
  2015. "Major Changes under Rhode Island Pension Overhaul." *The New York Times* (September 23).
  2016. "Study Finds Public Pension Promises Exceed Ability to Pay." *The New York Times* (March 17).
  2016. "A Sour Surprise for Public Pensions: Two Sets of Books." *The New York Times* (September 17).

2016. "$1.6 Million Bill Tests Tiny Town and 'Bulletproof' Public Pensions." *The New York Times* (October 9).
2016. "Dallas Stares Down a Texas-Size Threat of Bankruptcy." *The New York Times* (November 20).
2016. "Calpers Cuts Investment Targets, Increasing Strain on Municipalities." *The New York Times* (December 21).
2017. "In Puerto Rico, Teachers' Pension Fund Works Like a Ponzi Scheme." *The New York Times* (March 8).
2017. "Puerto Rico, Mired in Debt, Has a New Rescue Plan." *The New York Times* (March 13).
2017. "Puerto Rico Declares a Form of Bankruptcy." *The New York Times* (May 3).
2017. "In Texas, Some Rare Good News about Cities with Pension Woes." *The New York Times* (June 1).
2017. "After Puerto Rico's Debt Crisis, Worries Shift to Virgin Islands." *The New York Times* (June 25).
2018. "A $76,000 Monthly Pension: Why States and Cities Are Short of Cash." *The New York Times* (April 14).
Walters, Dan. 2017. "Realty Penetrates California's Public Employee Pension System, but Not Far Enough." *Sacramento Bee* (January 2).
Wang, Sam. 2015. "Let Math Save Our Democracy." *The New York Times* (December 5).
Wang, Vivian. 2018. "Focus of Corruption Trial Returns to Actions of Jail Officers' Union Chief." *The New York Times* (November 7).
2018. "Why Deep Blue New York Is 'Voter Suppression Land.'" *The New York Times* (December 19).
Wartzman, Rick. 2017. *The End of Loyalty: The Rise and Fall of Good Jobs in America*. New York: Public Affairs.
Watanabe, Teresa. 2018. "More Than 50,000 UC Workers Set to Strike This Week but Campuses Will Remain Open." *Los Angeles Times* (May 6).
Weale, Sally. 2018. "University Strikes Could Hit Exams and Graduation Ceremonies." *The Guardian* (February 19).
2019. "Fifth of Teachers Plan to Leave Profession within Two Years." *The Guardian* (April 16).
Weber, David. 2018. "The Real Reason the Investor Class Hates Pensions." *The New York Times* (March 5).
Wee, Sui-Lee. 2017. "Who Owns Anbang of China? A U.S. Labor Union Wants to Know." *The New York Times* (August 11).
Weed, Julie. 2017. "Hotel Boom in SeaTac Is Unfettered by $15 Minimum Wage." *The New York Times* (July 31).
Weigel, David. 2012. "Who the Hell Is Going to Take a Think Tank Seriously If It's Controlled by Billionaire Oil Guys?' Cato's President Speaks." *Slate* (March 22).
Weil, David. 1991. "Enforcing OSHA: The Role of Labor Unions." *Industrial Relations* 30: 20–36.
Weiland, Noah. 2017. "Senate Narrowly Passes Rollback of Obama-Era 'Auto-I.R.A. Rule.'" *The New York Times* (March 30).
Weise, Karen. 2018. "Why Some Amazon Workers Are Fuming about Their Raise." *The New York Times* (October 9).

Wellington, Harry H. and Ralph K. Winter. 1971. *The Unions and the Cities.* Brookings Institution Press.
Wertheimer, Alan. 1987. *Coercion.* Princeton: Princeton University Press.
West, Edwin G. and Rik W. Hafer. 1978. "J. S. Mill, and the Wages Fund Recantation: A Reinterpretation." *The Quarterly Journal of Economics* 92: 603–619.
  1981. "J. S. Mill, and the Wages Fund Recantation: A Reinterpretation – Reply." *The Quarterly Journal of Economics* 96: 543–549.
Western, Bruce and Jake Rosenfeld. 2011. "Unions, Norms, and the Rise of U.S. Wage Inequality." *American Sociological Review* 76: 513–537.
Whoriskey, Peter. 2018. "As a Grocery Chain Is Dismantled, Investors Recover Their Money. Worker Pensions Are Short Millions." *The Washington Post* (December 28).
Wiarda, Howard J. 1997. *Corporatism and Comparative Politics: The Other Great "Ism."* London: M. E. Sharpe.
Wilde, Jaron H. 2016. "The Deterrent Effect of Employee Whistleblowing on Firms' Financial Misreporting and Tax Aggressiveness" (November).
Wilkinson, Abi. 2017. "McDonald's Workers to Coordinate Strike with Allies Around the World." *The Guardian* (August 21).
Williams, Andrew. 1998. "Incentives, Inequality, and Publicity." *Philosophy & Public Affairs* 27: 225–247.
Williams, Douglass. 2017. "This Is What Emboldened White Supremacists Look Like." *The Guardian* (May 15).
Williams, Timothy. 2011. "As Public Sector Sheds Jobs, Blacks Are Hit Hardest." *The New York Times* (November 28).
  2018. "Inside a Private Prison: Blood, Suicide and Poorly Paid Guards." *The New York Times* (April 3).
Williams, Timothy and Richard A. Oppel, Jr. 2018. "Escapes Riots and Beatings. But States Can't Seem to Ditch Private Prisons." *The New York Times* (April 10).
Williams, Zoe. 2017. "Overpaid Public Sector? Philip Hammond's Divisive Talk Is No Longer Working." *The Guardian* (July 16).
Williamson, Oliver E. 1985. *The Economic Institutions of Capitalism.* New York: Free Press.
Willsher, Kim. 2018. "French Prison Blockades Spread as Minister Meets Union Leaders." *The Guardian* (January 22).
  2018. "French Unions Accused of 'Passive Complicity' in Protest Violence." *The Guardian* (May 27).
Wilpert, Marni von. 2017. "By Rescinding the Persuader Rule, Trump Is Once Again Siding with Corporate Interests over Working People." *Working Economic Blog*, Economic Policy Institute (June 13).
  2017. "City Governments Are Raising Standards for Working People – and State Legislators Are Lowering Them Back Down." Economic Policy Institute (August 26) (www.epi.org/files/pdf/133463.pdf).
  2018. "Fighting for Public Sector Union Rights 50 Years after MLK's Assassination." *Working Economic Blog*, Economic Policy Institute (January 12).
Wilson, David Sloan and Daron Acemoglu. 2016. "Stop Crying about the Size of Government. Start Caring about Who Controls It." *Evonomics* (March 25).
Wilson, Reid. 2017. "Kentucky Governor Signs Right to Work Law." *The Hill* (January 8).

Wilson, Russell. 2017. "Anti-Union Push Begins Again in Maine Legislature." *Maine Beacon* (February 6).

Wilson, Valerie and Janelle Jones. 2017. "Low-Wage African American Workers Have Increased Annual Work Hours Most Since 1979." Economic Policy Institute (March 27) (www.epi.org/blog/low-wage-african-american-workers-have-increased-annual-work-hours-most-since-1979/?utm_source=Economic+Policy+Institute&utm_campaign=20d6e60719-EMAIL_CAMPAIGN_2017_03_30&utm_medium=email&utm_term=0_e7c5826c50-20d6e60719-58070685&mc_cid=20d6e60719&mc_eid=494a829c5c).

Wilson, Valerie and Julia Wolfe. 2018. "A Missouri 'Right-to-Work' Law Is More Likely to Harm Black Workers, Who Are More Likely to Be Covered by a Union Contract than Other Workers." Economic Policy Institute (May 15).

Wilson, Valerie and William M. Rodgers III. 2016. "Black and White Wages Gaps Expand with Rising Wage Inequality." Economic Policy Institute (September 16) (www.epi.org/files/pdf/101972.pdf).

Winant, Gabriel. 2018. "How the American Economy Conspires to Keep Wages Down." *The Guardian* (April 13).

2018. "Why Are So Many White Collar Professionals in Revolt?" *The Guardian* (May 27).

Wines, Michael. 2018. "Drive against Gerrymandering Finds New Life in Ballot Initiatives." *The New York Times* (July 23).

2018. "Kennedy's Retirement Could Threaten Efforts to End Partisan Gerrymandering." *The New York Times* (June 30).

Winfield, Richard Dien. 2015. "Economy and Ethical Community." In *Hegel and Capitalism* (Albany, NY: SUNY Press), pp. 133–146.

Wingfield, Nick. 2016. "Amazon Proves Infertile Soil for Unions, So Far." *The New York Times* (May 16).

Winter, Jana and Elias Groll. 2017. "Here's the Memo That Blew Up the NSC." *Foreign Policy* (August 10).

Winter, Ralph K. Jr. 1963. "Collective Bargaining and Competition: The Application of Antitrust Standards to Union Activities." *Yale Law Journal* 73: 14–73.

Wolfe, Julia and John Schmitt. 2018. "A Profile of Workers in State and Local Government." Economic Policy Institute (June 7).

Wolfers, Justin. 2015. "The Gains from the Economic Recovery Are Still Limited to the Top One Percent." *The New York Times* (January 27).

Wolff, Jonathan. 2006. "Libertarianism, Utility, and Economic Competition." *Virginia Law Review* 92: 1605–1623.

Wolff, Robert Paul. 1977. "Robert Nozick's Derivation of the Minimal State." *Arizona Law Review* 19: 7–30.

Wolfskill, George. 1962. *The Revolt of the Conservatives: A History of the American Liberty League, 1934–1940*. New York: Houghton-Mifflin.

Wong, Julia Carrie. 2017. "Uber's Seattle Woes: Union Battle Could See Company Leave Another Major City." *The Guardian* (April 5).

2018. "Revealed: Google's 'Two-Tier' Workforce Training Document." *The Guardian* (December 12).

2019. "Google Staff Call Out Treatment of Temp Workers in 'Historic' Show of Solidarity." *The Guardian* (April 2).

2019. "'A White-Collar Sweatshop': Google Assistant Contractors Allege Wage Theft." *The Guardian* (May 29).
Wu, Tim. 2018. "Be Afraid of Economic 'Bigness.' Be Very Afraid." *The New York Times* (November 10).
2018. *The Curse of Bigness: Antitrust in the New Gilded Age*. New York: Columbia Global Reports.
Xaquín, G. V. 2017. "Can We Talk about the Gender Pay Gap?" *The Washington Post* (October 26).
Yarrow, George, et al. 1986. "Privatization in Theory and Practice." *Economic Policy* 1: 323–377.
Yoder, Eric. 2018. "Federal Employees Lag Behind Private Sector Workers in Salaries by 32 Percent on Average, Report Says." *The Washington Post* (April 11).
Young, Iris. 1979. "Self-Determination as Principle of Justice." *The Philosophical Forum* 11:30–46.
Zahniser, David. 2015. "L.A. Plans to Undo 2012 Pension Cuts in New Union Pay Deal." *Los Angeles Times* (September 5).
2017. "A City Pension Board Vote Could Add to Los Angeles' Budget Woes." *The Los Angeles Times* (July 10).
Zaveri, Mihir. 2019. "Asylum Officers' Union Says Trump Migration Policy 'Abandon's' American Tradition." *The New York Times* (June 26).
Zipperer, Ben and John Schmitt. 2017. "The 'High Road' Seattle Labor Market and the Effects of the Minimum Wage Increase." Economic Policy Institute (June 26).
Zoepf, Stephen. 2018. "The Economics of Ride Hailing, Revisited." (March 5) (http://ceepr.mit.edu/files/papers/2018-005%20Authors%20Statement.pdf).

Index

Abood v. Detroit Board of Ed., 230, 231, 257
actual consent
  in general, 96, 150, 235
  moral force of, 96
adaptive preferences and measurement of liberty, 92, 119
adding up problem, 75
adjudicative services, defined, 21
affirmative action, 151
Affordable Care Act, 236
agency fees, 15, 16, 24, 171, 230, 231, 232, 233, 234, 236, 237, 257
Alternative for Germany party (AfD), 145
American dream, 113
anarchism
  and libertarianism distinguished, 54
  and small government argument, 195
anarchists, 55, 110, 196, 235
anarcho-capitalism, 258
Anarchy, State, and Utopia, 21
Anderson, Elizabeth, 122
anticompetitive behavior
  in general, 36, 37, 38, 39, 41, 101, 186, 235
  in minimal state, 21, 28, 35, 36, 40, 41, 186
  monopolization, 36, 37, 132
  price-fixing, 36
  secondary boycotts, 41
  unionization as, 35, 36, 37, 39, 40, 41, 42, 118, 153, 254
anti-liberalism, 270
anti-Semitism, 143
antisocial behavior
  by management, 142, 143

  and unionization, 67, 101, 102, 140, 143, 157
  by unions, 143
antitrust laws, 36, 41, 125, 151, 162, 172, 235
anti-union legislation, 5, 170, 230
arbitrariness
  defined, 89, 266
  and failure to take interests or opinions into account, 91
  in general, 14, 57, 58, 64, 78, 86, 88, 89, 90, 91, 92, 93, 95, 101, 106, 118, 120, 121, 122, 126, 146, 148, 149, 153, 158, 174, 176, 205, 207, 235, 236, 237
  and intent, 91
  and republican liberty, 88, 89, 90, 91, 92, 93, 183
arbitration, 112, 113
austerity, 172, 178, 197, 205
automation. *See* technological innovation

background justice, 11, 64, 75, 78, 82, 84, 111, 119, 153, 156
bankruptcy, 3, 13, 171, 207, 224, 226, 229, 231
  as allegedly caused by excessive salaries and pensions, 222
  of Detroit, 196
  of public entities, 225, 321
  individuals who pay even after discharge, 337
basic institutions
  and basic structure, 67, 68, 72, 83
  central banks as, 165

basic institutions (cont.)
  definition of, 13, 63, 64, 65, 66, 68, 78, 79, 80, 82, 90, 152, 164
  firms as, 143
  free press as, 165
  moral evaluation of, 67, 68, 71, 73, 76, 78, 79, 80, 83, 85, 90, 95, 102, 104, 151, 205, 237
  and post-institutional rights, 103
  Rawls on, 67, 72, 74, 76, 84
  religious institutions as, 166
  slavery as, 80
  unions as, 11, 12, 13, 63, 64, 66, 67, 82, 83, 84, 86, 87, 102, 103, 104, 109, 110, 120, 124, 127, 128, 131, 139, 144, 149, 150, 152, 153, 154, 155, 156, 161, 163, 164, 237, 238
basic structure, 63, 66, 67, 69, 72, 73, 74, 76, 79, 80, 83, 105, 106, 124, 143, 146
  and basic institutions compared, 72, 73
  functionality of, 73
  moral evaluation of, 69, 70, 71
  Rawls on, 63, 67, 68, 71, 74, 75, 76, 84, 97, 261
  and well-ordered society, 71
Bentham, Jeremy, 84
Berlin, Isaiah, 14, 55
Bevin, Matt, 202
Black, Marina, 228
Black Lives Matter, 151
boards of directors and supervision of management, 137, 138
Bonar, James, 135
Brave New World, 70
Brexit, 172, 195, 214, 262, 269
Brownback, Sam, 197
Buchanan, James, 23
burden of the risk of error, 109, 149
burdens of judgment, 90, 108

capitalism
  in general, 70, 71, 72, 79, 81, 82, 83, 95, 102, 193, 209
  laissez faire, 71, 187
  welfare state, 71, 72
Carter, Jimmy, 219
categorical imperative, 81
Catholic Church on economic freedom, 99
Cato Institute, 182
causation, 2, 8, 51, 85, 103, 118, 136, 145, 177, 179, 180, 181, 184, 196, 202, 203, 222
central banks as basic institutions, 165, 166

charter schools, 215
Citizens United, 213
Clark, John Bates, 75
Clark, John M., 72
Clinton, Hillary, 212
closed shop agreements, 15, 16, 153
Coase, Ronald, 27, 28
codetermination, 123
Cohen, G. A., 24
collective action problems, 21
collective bargaining
  arguments against, 13, 22, 41, 203, 204, 205, 208, 211, 219
  as core function of unions, 13, 66, 158, 203, 205
  cost of, 15, 24, 57, 171, 232, 236, 237
  and free association, 205
  and free speech, 233
  in general, 7, 12, 34, 40, 46, 66, 133, 140, 154, 163, 207, 208, 210
  Nixon on, 11
  by public employees, 204, 207, 209, 210, 218, 230, 325, 326
  right to, 3, 4, 11, 144, 170, 175, 204, 205, 207, 208, 220, 222, 227
  and strikes, 204
  as undemocratic, 205, 219, 220
collective responsibility, 236
common good, 2, 3, 4, 6, 7, 9, 11, 42, 64, 65, 97, 171, 191, 206, 207, 212
Commons, John R., 72
communism, 86, 100, 166
commutative justice, 5, 6
compelled speech, 16, 171, 230, 231, 234, 235
compulsory unionization. *See* universal unionization
conceptions of the good, 30, 43, 58, 105, 208
concepts and conceptions, distinction between, 14
consequentialist arguments, 4, 8
  and arguments from right distinguished, 8, 9, 65
  and unionization, 3, 6, 8, 30, 42, 43, 127
corporate governance as check on management incompetence, 137, 138
corporatism, 72
corral the beast, 4
corruption, 64, 66, 101, 102, 128, 139, 144, 148, 149, 191, 196, 215, 218, 227
  within unions, 128

Index

cost-benefit analysis, difficulty of, 194, 195
counterfactual comparisons, nature of, 103

deep state, 221
demagogues, 146
democracy, 17, 59, 70, 71, 72, 122, 123, 165, 198, 210, 213, 214, 216, 219, 222, 237
   direct, 215
   representative, 215
Democratic Party and unionization, 170, 175, 208, 209, 217
democratic socialism, as distinguished from capitalism, 71
desert as theory of justice, 265
Detroit, 197, 230
   bankruptcy, 196
de-unionization, effects of, 155
difference principle, 4, 24, 64, 68, 85, 152
dissatisfaction effect, 119
distinctness of persons, 81
distributive justice, 3, 5, 56, 74, 152
division of labor, 26, 41, 48
dominant protective association, 21, 26, 29, 30, 31, 33, 34, 35, 36, 41, 42, 43, 44, 45, 46, 48, 49, 50, 51, 52, 54, 58, 107, 126, 205
   membership in, 47
   unionization of, 45
domination
   and negative liberty, 106
   and republican liberty, 14, 57, 58, 86, 95, 96, 99, 106, 118, 120, 125, 148, 149, 154, 183, 187
Douglas, Paul, 121
due process, 92
   substantive *versus* procedural, 92
Durkheim, Emile, 17, 145
   and distinction between mechanical solidarity and organic solidarity, 145
   on unions as source of organic solidarity, 146

Economic Freedom Index (EFI), 182, 184
economic growth and unionization, 94, 115, 116, 127, 136, 197
economic inequality
   and exploitation, 6, 187
   in general, 2, 4, 5, 6, 85, 115, 116, 119, 135, 183
   and unionization, 1–2, 4, 5, 67, 85, 115, 116, 120
   as violation of right, 5

economic liberty, 24, 66, 94, 100, 101, 104, 139, 148, 181, 185, 188, 211
   connection with political liberty, 94, 109–10, 181, 184, 189, 190
   connection with positive liberty, 181
   not a right, 94
efficiency. *See also* Kaldor-Hicks efficiency; Pareto efficiency
   and anticompetitive behavior, 101
   and externalities, 128
   and firm, 29, 97, 98, 137, 138
   Kaldor Hicks *versus* Pareto, 104
   and liberty, 94, 98
   macroeconomic, 137
   microeconomic, 120
   and morality, 30, 75, 76, 98, 109, 119, 190
   and privatization, 191
   and proper size of government, 192, 193, 194
   and social costs, 270
   and unions, 102, 109, 118–19, 120, 126, 131, 134, 139, 140, 148
employee tenure, 118
Enlightenment, 7, 13
Equal Rights Amendment, 151
equality
   argument from, 4, 5, 6, 7, 17, 18, 86, 87, 104, 119, 120, 151, 177
   and exploitation, 173
   in general, 3, 5, 6, 7, 34, 56, 64, 66, 83, 84–85, 86, 87, 103, 104, 119, 121, 124, 151, 152, 176, 184, 192, 208, 212, 237
   meaning of, 152
   right to, 4, 7
essential services, 13, 171, 196, 200, 201, 203, 323
Exit, Voice, and Loyalty: Responses to Declines in Firms, 117
exploitation, 6, 64, 85, 101, 113, 127, 128, 133, 163, 173, 183, 186, 187, 197–98, 206, 208, 285
   and economic inequality, 187
   of foreign workers, 139
   of independent contractors, 160
   and monopsony, 39
   by non-unionized firms, 1, 49
   and profitability, 127
   and unionization, 122, 127, 238
   and voluntariness, 78
Exploitation and Economic Justice in the Liberal Capitalist State, 75, 77
external preferences, 64, 260
externalities, 102, 128, 140, 183, 187, 198

fair share fees. *See* agency fees
farm workers, 309
fascism, 99, 182, 211, 215
fast-food workers, 40, 112, 162
feasibility constraint, 10, 25, 29, 75, 80, 82, 98, 102, 103–4, 120, 144, 155, 156, 159, 213
Feinberg, Joel, 51
financial crisis of 2008, 101. *See also* Great Recession
firm size, 27, 28, 98
  and economies of scale, 28
  limits on, 29
firms
  anticompetitive behavior of, 36
  and appropriation of surplus value, 32
  as basic form of business organization, 12–13
  bargaining power of, 29
  Coase on, 268
  and divison of labor, 26
  external checks on behavior of, 101
  hierarchical structure of, 96, 97, 122
  justification for, 27, 96, 97, 102, 126, 139
  in libertarian utopia, 23
  regulation of, 22
  relationship with independent contractors, 50, 57
  remedies against, 58
  and suppression of price mechanism, 27, 95
  as threat to liberty, 66, 97, 98, 99, 101, 102, 110, 120, 123, 141
  unionization of, 22, 54, 137, 138, 149, 150, 163
First Amendment, 16, 171, 172, 230, 231, 232, 233, 234, 238. *See also* free speech
  weaponizing of, 237
foreign workers, 125, 139
France, 83, 145, 172
franchise agreements, no poaching clauses, 162
Fraser Institute, 182
fraud, 21, 36, 55, 101, 128, 142, 143, 183, 186, 224, 225, 227
  uncovering of, 142
free market, 12, 22, 36, 37, 38, 79, 82, 94, 95, 97, 102, 121, 137, 180, 181–82, 187, 189, 190, 235, 268
free press as basic institution, 164–65
free riding, 16, 45, 284
free speech, 3, 13, 64, 234
  as based on equality, 265

and communicative significance, 232
money as form of, 231–32
freedom. *See* liberty
freedom of association, 3, 4, 6, 26, 31, 33, 34, 35, 43, 46, 52–53, 54, 64, 83, 84, 204, 205
  as based on equality, 265
  does not include right to not associate, 53
freedom of contract, 26, 31, 35, 64, 94, 223, 230
freedom of religion, 53
Freeman, Richard B., 111, 112, 115, 116, 117, 118, 119, 124, 128
Freeman, Samuel, 67
friction, defined, 28
Friedman, Milton, 136, 290
Fuller, Lon
  on basic institutions, 264
fundamental moral presuppositions, 9, 38, 211

Galbraith, John Kenneth, 121
  and concept of countervailing power, 121
game theory, 8, 125, 263
gay marriage, 234
Germany, 72, 83, 99, 123, 145, 148, 149, 163, 298
  and use of works councils, 149
gerrymandering, 213
gig economy, 160, 162
Gilded Age, 199
globalization and unionization, 125
government shutdown of February 2019, 178, 201
Great Depression, 85
Great Recession, 115–16, 165, 169, 178–79, 205, 207, 229. *See also* financial crisis of 2008

Hamilton, Walter, 72
Hart, H. L. A., 69, 78
Hayek, Friedrich, 23, 100, 129, 131, 136, 140, 181, 188
  fear of socialism, 256
  on public education, 188
  on unemployment, 188
health care, 113, 175
health insurance and unionization, 17, 113, 114, 236
heavy manufacturing, shift of jobs overseas, 1
Hill, Joe, 81
Hitchman Coal & Coke Company v. Mitchell, 31
Hitler, Adolph, 99, 148, 198

Index

Hobbes, Thomas, 69
Hobbs Act, 129, 286
home-care workers, 309
human capital, 95
Human Freedom Index (HFI), 182, 183, 184
human nature, 8, 10, 25, 69, 84
human rights, 84
Hutt, William H., 100, 295
Huxley, Aldous, 70, 119
hypocrisy, 223, 331
hypothetical consent, 150, 151
   moral force of, 97, 235

ideal theory, 10, 25
   and non-ideal theory contrasted, 10
immigration policy, 324–25
incompetence of management, 64, 66, 67, 101, 102, 137, 138, 139–40, 144, 193
independent contractors
   as employees, 25, 160, 161, 162
   and employees compared, 57
independents
   as free riders, 45, 46, 284
   in minimal state, 21, 46–47, 48–49, 50, 52, 54, 107, 126
   within firm, 51
   within union, 45, 46, 49, 50, 52, 54, 126
individual right, 5, 9, 54, 64, 83, 84, 85
   argument from, 5
industrial relations, 7, 65
inflation
   Friedman on, 136, 290
   and unionization, 67, 115, 133, 134, 135, 136, 137
   and wages fund theory, 134–35
inherently governmental functions, 192, 320
institutionalism, 72, 187, 262
Internal Revenue Service (IRS), 191–92, 193
invisible hand, 268

James, Lebron, 96
Janus v. AFSCME, 65, 144, 170, 231, 232, 233, 234, 236–37
job security, 2, 138, 142
joint employees, classifciation as, 162
just price, doctrine of, 207, 285
justice as fairness, principles of, 24, 63, 64, 76, 85, 263

Kaldor-Hicks efficiency, 104, 105, 106, 107, 109
   and measuring improvements in risk environment, 107, 108, 109

Kalecki, Michal, 132
Kansas, 197
   supply-side tax experiment, 197
Keynes, John Maynard, 131, 132, 207
King, Martin Luther Jr.
   on sanitation workers strike, 173
   on unions, 114
kleptocrats, 99
knowledge problem, 249
Koch, Charles, 23, 182
Koch, David, 23, 182
Koch Brothers, 199

la secte, 221
labor economics, 7, 65
labor market
   defined, 37, 38, 39, 40, 121, 132, 133, 160
   and perfect competition, 37
laissez faire, 71, 187
law of conservation of liberty, 104, 105, 259
Le Pen, Marine, 145
left-libertarianism. *See under* libertarianism
leveling down, 206
LGBT people, 17, 141
liberal capitalist democracy, 11, 12, 16, 59, 100, 110–11, 171, 238
liberal egalitarianism, 3, 4, 13, 64, 82
liberal political theory and neglect of unionization, 8
libertarian utopia
   arguments available in, 30–31, 51–52, 208
   firm size in, 28
   free-riding in, 47
   government regulation in, 182, 186, 195
   membership in dominant protective association, 47, 107, 126
   and negative liberty, 57
   and republican liberty, 58
   rise of firms in, 29
   role of dominant protective association in, 21, 26
   union shop agreements in, 51, 238
   unionization in, 32, 35, 42, 45, 46, 48, 54, 57, 58, 59, 238
   unionization of dominant protective association in, 42, 43, 44, 45
   yellow dog contracts in, 31, 32, 33, 34, 54
libertarianism
   among general public, 23, 55
   and anarchism distinguished, 54, 235
   and arguments for common good, 42

libertarianism (cont.)
  attitude toward anticompetitive behavior, 28, 35, 36, 40, 41
  and Charles and David Koch, 23
  faux, 23
  and free association, 34, 52, 54
  hybird, consequentilaist, and deontological libertarianism compared, 36
  and James Buchanan, 23
  left, 13, 22, 246, 247
  in libertarian utopia, 21, 22, 23, 24, 25, 26, 27, 28, 29
  and market regulation, 22
  and minimal state, 42
  and negative liberty, 55, 56
  and neoliberalism distinguished, 24
  and noncompete agreements, 40
  not plea for return to agrarian form of life, 25–26
  Nozick on, 21
  and Rand Paul, 23
  and redistribution of wealth, 22
  and republican liberty, 57, 58
  right, 13, 22, 23, 126, 129, 182
  and right to equal treatment, 33
  and rights as side-constraints, 3
  and slavery, 32
  and union shop agreements, 54, 57, 58
  and unionization, 12, 22, 23, 34, 42, 59, 82, 238
liberty. *See also* economic liberty; negative liberty; political liberty; positive liberty
  anti-union argument from, 2, 3, 6, 13, 23, 24, 25, 86, 100, 125, 141, 151, 178
  and argument against slavery, 119
  as argument from right, 5, 6
  and collective responsibility, 236
  conflict with equality, 6, 153
  and democracy, 215, 216, 237
  Durkheim on, 17
  and efficiency, 190
  and exploitation, 173
  and firm, 96
  forms of, 109
  and free speech, 230, 231, 236
  and freedom of association, 53
  in general, 2, 7, 9, 13, 14, 38, 66, 83, 84, 85, 87, 88, 89, 90, 92, 94, 95, 104, 105, 119, 147, 212
  general right to, 2, 8, 10, 56
  Hohfeld on, 53
  and LGBT rights, 234
  in libertarian utopia, 12, 31, 36, 55, 56, 57, 58, 59
  pre-institutional concept of, 64, 103
  pro-union argument from, 7, 17, 95, 98, 99, 100, 101, 102, 124, 133, 148, 154, 158, 159
  and small government argument, 171, 172, 173, 177, 180, 182, 184, 185, 192, 196, 198, 199, 210, 222, 223
  strikes to essential services as threat to, 200
  threats by private parties to, 199, 236
  and union shop agreements, 57
  and voice, 120
Liberty League, 85
Lipset, Seymour Martin, 147
living wage, 112, 113, 157, 195
long-term agreements and inter-adminsitration bindingness, 220
Los Angeles School Board, 215
luck egalitarianism, 4, 5, 64, 85

Machlup, Fritz, 100
macroeconomic effects of unionization, 115, 120, 131, 134, 135, 136, 137
Madison Teachers, Inc. v. Walker, 204
Maistre, Joseph de, 221
marginal net productivity of labor, 75
market failures, 186, 187
market socialism. *See* democratic socialism as distinguished from capitalism
Marshall, Alfred, 27, 75
Medoff, James, 111, 112, 115, 116, 117, 118, 119, 124, 128
Memphis, 173, 174
Mercer, Rebecca, 199
Mercer, Robert, 199
microeconomic economic effects of unionization, 120
middle class, 112, 115, 146, 206, 216
Mill, J. S., 134, 135
minimal state, 21, 35, 36, 43, 47, 54, 186, 190, 222
  and modern capitalist state compared, 22
minimum wage, 112, 113, 133, 136, 140, 160, 161, 204
minorities and women, and unionization, 176
Mises, Ludwig von, 37, 100, 129
Mitchell, Wesley, 72
monopoly profits and wages, 28, 117, 124
monopsony, 38, 39, 40, 148
mountain cabin hypothetical, 51
multiplier effect, 207

Index

Murray, Charles, 333
Mussolini, Benito, 99

National Labor Relations Board, 161
Nazis, 99
negative liberty
   Berlin on, 14, 55
   definition of, 55, 86
   and economic liberty, 94, 104
   and efficiency, 97, 98
   equality of, 56, 87
   and firm, 98, 99, 102
   justification for interference with, 88, 105, 109, 134, 237
   measurement of, 104, 105, 183
   minimum required, 56, 57
   as moral notion, 86, 98
   no general right to, 56, 126, 140
   and other forms of liberty, 66, 87
   Petro on, 211
   and republican liberty, 94, 95, 97, 106, 107
   and unionization, 125, 126, 139, 148, 237
   and voluntariness, 95
neoliberalism, 12, 22, 24, 94, 99, 100, 129, 181, 188, 190, 195, 197, 198
neutrality, 66, 89, 104, 123, 185, 208, 209, 210
Nietzsche, Friedrich, 211
Nixon, Richard, 11, 209
no friend, 136
noncompete agreements, 39, 40
non-disparagement agreements, 141
non-ideal theory and ideal theory contrasted, 10
Norris–LaGuardia Act, 31
Nozick, Robert, 3, 21, 33, 35, 46, 47, 48, 49, 52, 54, 56, 76, 126, 190

Obama, Barack, 113, 161, 162, 219, 231
oligopoly, 38, 39
oligopsony, 39, 148
ordoliberalism, 99, 100, 198
original position, 97, 269
overlapping consensus, 214

Pareto efficiency, 104, 105, 106, 107
   and measuring improvements in risk environment, 107, 109
Paul, Rand, 23
pensions, 206, 222, 223, 225, 226, 227, 228, 229, 230
   as allegedly excessive, 223, 228, 229
   average for public employees, 226, 227
   constitutional protection of, 225, 229
   for Los Angeles city employees, 228
   public and private compared, 228
   for public school teachers, 229
   when irresponsibly managed, 225
perfect competition, defined, 37
perfectionism, 82, 296
Petro, Sylvester, 100, 129, 210, 211, 212, 218
Pettit, Philip, 88, 89, 96
Pigou, A. C., 75
plutocrats, 99
police unions, behavior of, 157
political liberalism, 72, 82, 101, 210, 236
political liberty, 24, 94, 100, 101, 110, 178, 180, 181, 184, 185, 189, 190
Ponzi scheme and pension funds, 225
Porter hypothesis, 267
positive liberty, 14, 66, 86, 87, 88, 89, 93, 104, 126, 127, 183
   and fascism, 211
post-institutional regulation, 11, 13, 63, 66, 85, 98, 103, 109, 139, 144, 149, 152, 153, 163, 192, 200
poverty line, 113
Powell Memo, 11, 245
pre-institutional rights, 83, 84, 104, 265
price mechanism, 27, 41, 82, 95
prioritarianism, 13
prisons, understaffing and brutality of, 179, 191
private sector unionization
   and antisocial behavior by unions, 143
   and background justice, 12
   and back-to-work orders, 200
   as basic institution, 12, 13, 65, 238
   and distribution of surplus value, 173
   effect of globalization and automation, 212
   effect of strikes, 202
   effect on wages, 112, 114
   and employee-owned firms, 217
   and expenditure on research and development, 281
   and exploitation, 173, 206
   and hierarchical structure of firm, 157
   history of, 169
   in libertarian utopia, 42, 43, 44, 58
   and minorities and women, 176
   outside of US, 172
   and political influence, 176
   rates of, 133, 169, 170, 211
   and retirement benefits, 223, 227
   and right to bargain collectively, 208

private sector unionization (*cont.*)
  and right-to-work laws, 170
  and taxpayers, 208
  and yellow dog contracts, 31, 43, 44
privately held corporations and supervision of management, 138
privatization, 172, 190, 191, 192, 193
procedural justice, 73, 75, 76, 78
  imperfect, 76
  perfect, 73, 74, 76, 77
  pure, 74, 75, 76, 77, 263
  and substantive justice distinguished, 73, 79
product market, defined, 37, 38, 39, 132, 136
product prices, stickiness of, 132, 288
productivity and unionization, 26, 67, 75, 112, 115, 116, 117, 118, 119, 120, 132, 133, 134, 137, 148, 174, 189
Professional Air Traffic Controllers Organization (PATCO) 1981 strike, 201
profitability and unionization, 67, 117, 118, 124, 127, 128, 142, 191
property-owning democracy, defined, 71
protective services, provision of, 21, 46, 47, 48, 49
public agencies, hierarchical structure of, 174
public education, 183, 187, 197, 202, 226
public employment, rate of growth, 178, 180
public sector unionization
  and allegedly excessive public salaries and benefits, 44, 114, 158, 171, 196, 206, 207, 228, 229
  as allegedly undemocratic, 13, 145, 158, 170, 171, 176, 181, 208, 209, 211, 212, 215, 217, 218, 221, 226
  and antisocial behavior by management, 143
  and antisocial behavior by unions, 143, 157
  and argument from equality, 177
  and argument from liberty, 3, 7, 13, 59, 171, 231, 237, 238
  as check on management behavior, 175
  and consequentialist arguments, 4, 42
  and corruption, 218, 227
  differences with private sector, 13, 65, 157, 158, 169, 171, 173, 174, 176, 177, 190, 212, 228, 238
  effect of *Janus* decision on, 170, 231, 236
  and essential services, 200
  and exploitation, 173, 206
  and free speech, 3, 16, 230, 231, 233
  history of, 169
  increased importance of, 170
  in libertarian utopia, 12, 42, 44, 45, 58, 238
  and minorities and women, 176, 177, 211
  outside of US, 172
  Petro on, 210
  and public debt, 172, 196, 197, 222
  public employees like shareholders, 175
  rates of, 4, 169, 170, 211, 212, 228
  and right to bargain collectively, 3, 204, 205, 208, 222, 227
  and right to strike, 200, 201, 202, 203
  and right to work, 16, 65, 230
  and size of public workforce, 169, 177, 178, 180
  and small government argument, 3, 171, 177, 179, 180, 182, 190, 194, 199
  special arguments against, 65, 169, 170, 171, 173
  and teacher strikes, 202
  and yellow dog contracts, 31, 43
Putin, Vladimir, 99

quit rates, 118, 119

Rawls, John, 3, 4, 6, 7, 8, 24, 63, 67, 68, 69, 71, 72, 73, 74, 75, 76, 77, 78, 79, 84, 85, 89, 90, 96, 97, 102, 108, 109, 153, 208, 214
  on unions, 63, 244
Reagan, Ronald, 185, 201
reciprocity as moral doctrine, 77
religious institutions as basic institutions, 166
religious liberty, 234
rent-control, 209
replacement workers, use of, 131, 163, 201
republican liberty. *See also* arbitrariness; domination
  and agency fees, 236, 237
  and arbitrariness, 58, 88, 91, 120
  and collective bargaining in public sector, 205
  and concentrations of economic power, 99
  as countervailing power, 121
  definition of, 14, 57, 86, 92
  and discrimination, 176, 177, 237, 238
  and domination, 57
  and efficiency, 97, 98
  and exploitation, 208
  and firm, 96, 97, 98, 110, 141
  and free speech, 234, 235
  and happiness, 119
  and libertarianism, 58
  measurement of, 106

Index

and negative liberty, 88, 96
no dependence requirement, 93
no intent requirement, 90
no participation requirement, 93, 123
and other forms of liberty, 66
Petro on, 211
and public agencies, 174
and religious institutions, 166
as right, 58, 126, 140, 205
Senator Paul Douglass on, 121
and taxpayers, 205, 206, 207
thin conception of, 14, 89, 93, 259
and unionization, 59, 94, 102, 104, 106, 109, 110, 122, 126, 128, 134, 146, 148, 153, 154, 238
US Supreme Court on, 120, 121
and voice, 118
and workplace democracy, 122, 123
Republican party, 14, 23, 87, 88, 100, 170, 172, 175, 202, 208, 209, 212, 213
restaurant workers, special rules for, 163
right libertarianism. *See under* libertarianism
right-to-work, 12, 15, 16, 23, 24, 46, 54, 65, 103, 112, 127, 154, 170, 171, 197, 230, 232, 236, 237
rights
as distinguished from liberties, 53
infringing *versus* violating, 51
pre-institutional *versus* post-institutional, 83
as side-constraints, 52
risk
and burden of risk of error, 109
measuring improvements in risk environment, 107, 108, 109
and morality, 107
treatement of implausible risk, 108
trivial risks to be disregarded, 108
risk aversion and firm size, 29
risky behavior as rights violation, 46, 47, 48, 49, 50, 107, 126
Rizzo, Robert, 227
Robinson, Joan, 75
Rothbard, Murray, 37, 258

sanitation workers, 173
Saudi Arabia, 91
Seattle study on effect of raising minimum wage, 133
Securities Exchange Commission (SEC), 142

self-ownership, 56, 57, 58, 86, 110, 120, 134
and ownership of one's labor, 38
sexual harassment, 285
shareholders
and supervision of directors, 137
and supervision of management, 137, 138
Skinner, Quentin, 88, 89
slavery, 14, 31, 32, 80, 81, 96, 119, 127, 198
and argument from liberty, 119
slaves, 81, 198, 211
slippery slope arguments, 94, 110, 181, 189, 190
small government argument, 3, 13, 171, 172, 177, 179, 180, 181, 182, 183, 184, 185, 186, 188, 189, 190, 193, 194, 195, 196, 197, 198, 199, 210, 222, 315
Smith, Adam, 96, 180, 181, 185
social cooperation, 63, 67, 69, 81, 84, 98
social solidarity
effect of oxytocin on, 147
unions as source of, 145, 146, 296
socialism, 27, 70, 71, 79, 95, 100, 170, 189, 193
socialist society, heirarchical structure of, 137
Spengler, Oswald, 211
starve the beast, 4, 222
State Policy Network (SPN), 202
Steiner, Hillel, 104, 258
Stewart, Walter, 72
strains of commitment, 214
strict egalitarianism, 4
strict liability for violations of republican liberty, 90
strike, right to, 4, 44, 49, 125, 130, 162, 170, 171, 173, 200, 201, 202, 203, 204, 209
substantive justice, 73, 76, 93
sufficientarianism, 13
supply-side economics, 197
Supreme Court, United States, 11, 16, 31, 65, 112, 120, 129, 170, 197, 204, 213, 229, 231, 232
surplus value, 29, 32, 173, 249

Taylor, Charles, 86, 183
teacher unions, 157, 229
technological innovation, 1, 41, 94, 139
theft, 21, 36, 55, 101, 186
A Theory of Justice, 71
thin theory of the good, concept of, 30, 44, 58, 89, 93, 127
thin *versus* thick conceptions, 15

Thomson, Judith, 51
    on difference between violating and infringing a right, 51
traditional conservativism, 13
Trans Pacific Partnership (TPP), 125
transaction costs, 27, 37, 39, 118, 137, 191
Trump, Donald, 1, 100, 113, 117, 125, 140, 145, 146, 161, 162, 165, 170, 178, 187, 209, 212, 219, 221, 231, 324, 328

Uber, 160, 161
underemployment, 50, 101
unemployment, 2, 132, 160, 174, 187
    and deficiencies in aggregate demand, 132
    Hayek on, 188
    and minimum wage, 133
    neoclassical view, 132
    and real wages, 131, 132
    since Great Recession, 2, 100, 116
    and unionization, 1, 2, 67, 114, 131, 132, 133, 135, 152, 157
    and wages fund theory, 134
union certification as political campaign, 150, 151
union dues, 3, 4, 6, 11, 12, 15, 22, 44, 45, 46, 47, 48, 49, 50, 52, 57, 63, 103, 144, 164, 232. *See also* agency fees
union shop, 11, 12, 13, 15, 16, 24, 34, 46, 50, 54, 55, 57, 58, 112, 154, 238
union shop agreements, 24, 49, 50, 51, 54, 153
unionization rates
    in Denmark, 150
    in Finland, 150
    in general, 1, 146, 159, 180
    in Germany, 149
    and inequality, 116
    and non-union wages, 112
    in Norway, 150
    in private sector, 133, 169, 170, 211, 228
    and productivity, 150
    in public sector, 169, 170, 211, 222
    in Sweden, 150
    in United Kingdom, 1
    in US, 1, 4, 111, 170, 211
unions. *See also* private sector unionization; public sector unionization; union dues; universal unionization
    and alleged special privileges, 151, 152, 301
    as check on antisocial inclinations of boards and management, 142
    as check on authoritarian inclinations of working class, 145
    as check on management incompetence, 138
    core functions of, 11, 66, 143, 144, 154, 158, 203, 205
    and democracy, 3, 12, 148, 171, 176, 205, 209, 212, 213, 217, 218, 237
    and economic efficiency, 139
    and enforcement of labor regulations, 140, 141
    Friedman on, 290
    and movement of jobs overseas, 1, 139
    support for Trump, 328
    tendency to be protectionist, 139
    use of rhetoric by and against, 15
    and white-collar workers, 158, 159
unitary executive, 323
United Kingdom, 1, 17, 83, 114, 143, 157, 172, 184, 191, 195, 209
United States v. Emmons, 129
universal basic income, 156
universal unionization, 3, 11, 12, 13, 15, 16, 18, 103, 125, 142, 152, 153
    and antisocial behavior by unions, 143
    and argument from equality, 104
    and argument from liberty, 2, 3, 8, 22, 23, 58, 59, 110, 125, 126, 148
    and background justice, 11, 64
    as basic institution, 103
    as building sense of community, 126
    and difference principle, 152
    effect on productivity, 148
    effect on violence, 131
    and elimination of competitive advantage for non-union firms, 125, 155
    exception for firms with less than 50 employees, 160
    feasibility constraints on, 10, 154, 155, 158, 159, 163
    and globalization, 125
    and independent contractors, 161
    in libertarian utopia, 102
    in other liberal capitalist democracies, 13
    in private sector, 65
    and replacement workers, 163
    right to, 7, 13
    and right to bargain collectively, 205
    and UBI, 156
    and workplace democracy, 122
unreasonable restraints on trade, 41
utilitarianism, 3, 77

Index

Veblen, Thorstein, 72
veil of ignorance, 97, 148, 235
violence
  and economic coercion distinguished, 35
  and factory closures, 131
  and Hobbs Act, 129
  by management, 130
  and minimal state, 186
  protection of free market from, 36
  by unions, 129, 130, 151, 287
  and universal unionization, 131
voice and unionization, 66, 67, 93, 116, 117, 118, 119, 120, 122, 138, 143, 144, 159, 165, 196, 212, 213, 215, 217, 233, 237
voluntariness, 66, 77, 78, 95
Voting Rights Act, 151

wage inequality in general, 114, 116
wage theft, 112, 113
wages
  effect of noncompete agreements on, 40
  effect of right-to-work laws on, 57
  effect of unionization on, 2, 30, 37, 40, 67, 112, 113, 116, 118, 124, 127, 133, 158, 175, 196
  and externalities, 142
  as marginal net product of labor, 75
  for minorities and women, 176
  money, 131, 134
  and monopoly profits, 124
  poverty level, 114
  and profitability, 138
  public and private compared, 44
  real, 1, 115, 132, 134, 135, 136
  set in product market, 132
  stagnancy of, 159
  stickiness of, 131, 132, 134, 220, 334
  for teachers, 202
  and UBI, 156
  union and non-union compared, 112, 155, 206, 228
wages fund theory, 134, 135, 136
  Mill on, 135
  revival of, 136
Walker, Scott, 170
well-ordered society, 71, 261
West Virginia teachers strike, 45, 201, 203, 204
  and similar strikes in other states, 325–26
What Do Unions Do?, 111
whistle blowers, 142, 143
  retaliation against, 142
Wilt Chamberlain example, 76
Wisconsin ban on collective bargaining by public employees, 170, 175, 204, 205
working conditions, 2, 30, 33, 39, 42, 57, 66, 101, 142, 144, 156, 158, 159, 204
work-life balance, 113
workplace democracy, 122, 123, 155, 282

yellow dog contracts, 24, 31, 32, 33, 34, 35, 43, 44, 54, 256
  confidentiality agreements, 33

For EU product safety concerns, contact us at Calle de José Abascal, 56–1°, 28003 Madrid, Spain or eugpsr@cambridge.org.

www.ingramcontent.com/pod-product-compliance
Lightning Source LLC
LaVergne TN
LVHW041617060526
838200LV00040B/1317